Where Did My Country Go?

Where Did My Country Go?

Volume 1 of 2 Volumes

*How the Liberal Left throughout history has
stolen the true American and Christian heritage . . .
by lies, deception, hoaxes, threats, violence, revisionism,
and south Chicago politics — all "treason from within"
. . . and what we must do to take our country back.*

R. Dean Chrisco

Total Fusion Press
Strasburg, Ohio

Where Did My Country Go?
Published by Total Fusion Press
PO Box 123, Strasburg, OH 44680
www.totalfusionpress.com

Copyright © 2014 by Vineyard Way, LLC

All rights reserved. No part of this book may be reproduced or transmitted in any form or by any means, electronic or mechanical, including photocopying and recording, or by any information storage and retrieval system, without permission in writing from the publisher.

ISBN (paperback): 978-0-9903100-6-8
ISBN (hardcover): 978-0-9903100-4-4

Library of Congress Control Number: 2014956401

Cover Design by Sarah Kuehn
Interior Design by Kara Starcher
Edited by Linnette Hayden

Published in Association with Total Fusion Ministries, Strasburg, OH.
www.totalfusionministries.org

24 23 22 21 20 19 18 17 16   2 3 4 5

Dedication

For Kristi

For Beth

Praise for this book – Volume 1

In these scholarly and informative books, Dean presents a thought-provoking recipe for reclaiming America's heritage of liberty and self-governance. I may not agree with all the solutions proposed here, but our author definitely nails the problems he identifies from our history as well as our Framer's dreams for America. This is a must read for any Conservative.

Senator Brian D. Nieves

*26th District Missouri State Senator, 2010 – Present;
Former Majority Whip in the Missouri House of Representatives, 2002 – 2010*

Praise ...

FINALLY! A writer who writes the true history of America! If you have read any other book, on the history and degradation of this nation's civilization, you wasted your time. You should have read this one first. The treatise contained in this book, volumes 1 & 2, should be in every classroom in America. Our author serves as a guide, to help move the American people away from the precipice where we now stand. If we follow Dean's roadmap, we can still find that America can be saved, with our best days ahead.

Nicholas Watts

Entrepreneur, business owner, and community leader

Praise ...

I love biographies, in particular biographies of famous people in history. Ancient biographies from Job, Daniel, Moses and Esther to George Washington, Benjamin Franklin, Admiral Byrd, Patton, Ronald Reagan, Lee Iacocca and Norman Schwarzkopf to name a few. I love history; biographies are a way to absorb history on a personal, relatable scale.

Like a biography, as you wander the pages of this book, your heart will feel like you are getting reacquainted with an old friend whom you haven't seen for many years — a friend who will reveal to you stories you never heard, secrets of lineage, struggles of birth, searching of youth, indiscretions of adolescence, the rise to a beacon on a hill. This tome is the biography of America, the biography of us. Come; sit with your old friend for a while. This old friend needs you now more than ever.

Paul Lambi

American, Nuclear Submarine Veteran, Four-Term Mayor of Wentzville Missouri, Co-Founder: Graduate America Priority One.

Praise ...

National problems that will rob America's children of their future are identified. The root of each issue is exposed. The gang that is trying to make God insignificant is uncovered.

Instead of rearranging the deck chairs on the Titanic, Dean offers alternatives to right the Ship of State. Without the Bible, or Constitution, the Flagship is listing in the wind. To avoid the inevitable death spiral, the author argues for a course correction. With historical perspective as a map, the needle of the Moral Compass is pointed to God.

This is a must read for anyone overwhelmed by the contents of the daily news cycle, or disgusted by the distortion and omissions of rewritten history. God is not dead, and neither is America. This book offers life support to a nation in critical condition.

Fred Zimmermann
Retired school administrator with 34 years' experience in education

Praise ...

A Medical Book for deathly ill America is needed. This is it! Within these pages, our author provides insight for the healing of America. In today's America, freedom seems cheap and is taken for granted; the gift of liberty granted by our Framers is traded for bobbles and empty promises. People in American don't even know what being American really means anymore. Trading self-reliance for reliance on government, we have people who rely on the same government for cradle to grave provisions. Kennedy's quote of "Ask not what the country can do for you but what you can do for the country" has fallen on deaf ears. It is time that we give of ourselves to save our country. It is time to give until it hurts or if we continue down our path we will hurt until we give in. And it is time to read this must read provided by an author for any citizen who loves freedom. And it's in language you will understand.

Representative Bryan E. Spencer

63rd District, Missouri House of Representatives, 2012 – Present;
Public School Teacher, Grades 7 – 12, Certified in
Social Science, Behavior Disorder, Learning Disabilities,
Taught Government and U. S. History 1990 – Present

Praise ...

In his seminal work, Dean charts the way to the beginning of a turnaround in the direction our country is headed. *"Where Did My Country Go?"* provides a comprehensive, articulate and thoughtful account of our country's history and the events and influences that have impacted its evolution. Against this backdrop, Dean analyzes how we arrived at our current state, addresses the fundamental issues facing our country today and points the way to positive change for our nation and our way of life. This is essential reading for anyone concerned about the future of our country.

Charles "Chuck" MacNab

Past Vice President and President, American Airline Pilots Association (All airlines); Vice Chairman of the International Council of Airline Pilots Association (All airlines); Past Member of the New York City Aviation Development Council; Editor and Publisher, Riteon.org

Table of Contents

Foreword		xv
Author's Note		xvii
Introduction	How Did We Get Here?	xxi
Chapter 1	Lost in the Land of the Lost!	1
Chapter 2	America's Secret War	29
Chapter 3	The Deception of Liberalism That Led to This Darkness	41
Chapter 4	The Illusion of Government That's Captivated America	67
Chapter 5	The 50s: They Were Something Special!	85
Chapter 6	Decades That Changed America	99
	The 50s	100
	The 60s	107
	The 70s	118
	The 80s	125
	The 90s	152
	The 00s	164
Chapter 7	Where's the Beef?	169
Chapter 8	History Schmistory, Who Needs It?	181
Chapter 9	Definitions in a New, Progressive Society	211
Chapter 10	Those Robbin' Hoods of 'Rotting'ham Forest	225
Chapter 11	"No Gods Allowed in Here!"	255
Chapter 12	Honey, I Shrunk the Morals	289
Chapter 13	Who Moved the Hedge?	319
Chapter 14	There's Nothing Legal about Illegals	351
Chapter 15	The Trouble with Islamists	363
Chapter 16	Having the Right to Own and Bear Arms	381
Chapter 17	An Invitation to Sit Down and Shut Up	401
Appendices		419
Notes		424

Foreword

THERE ARE TWO MAJOR AND OPPOSING battle cries heard in America today. One says democracy and capitalism have failed the world; that cry comes from a group seeking more Marxism, Collectivism as the answer to the young generation's needs. The other battle cry is ancient like the first, but conversely calls for more unfettered democracy and free enterprise. It beckons more freedom, more liberty, more true justice, and less government intrusion. This latter cry as it is heard grows louder and louder each day as the patient lies in intensive care, near death. The cry is heard down the streets and alleyways, and through the countryside, the mountains, and the plains, and there is a growing response to it. The patient that is dying needs immediate help. She is America. She is in trouble and on life support because she has been lied to, beaten, and assaulted by an enemy within her own gates.

A similar cry for freedom was heard in 1773 while the American colonies braced for more egregious government assaults under King George III. Today the characters have changed, the scenery is modern, but the setting is hauntingly the same. Washington, D. C. has sought to colonize America again, not with a free people but with subjects once again being enslaved by a central government. Ronald Reagan said it best, "Government is not the solution to the problem; government is the problem." We live in very perilous times.

Just in time, along comes a book from my friend Dean that provides a roadmap of where we started, where we are, and where we need to go. Dean rescues us from the inevitable destruction of the future if we heed the warning signs and follow the solution he offers. We are destroying ourselves from within, not because of an abundance of freedom as Liberals say, but because our freedoms are wasted on frivolous bobbles, and is being restricted and regulated in many of the same ways that America was restricted when Britain had control of the colonies. The current path will take us not only into destruction but into a dark hell of 1,000 years if we do not wake up quickly. This book presents us with three very distinct steps. It helps us to see the experience of America from its beginning to our current situation; it helps us to see the strength of the idea of individual freedom, and then gives us the hope that we can reclaim the country that we experienced.

Like an old town crier, our author is attempting to awaken America and give them the news. We have been asleep far too long. And while we were asleep at the switch, our nation has been stolen away. What you are about to read in my opinion is one of the most important books on the story of our country that you will read in a long, long time. Its importance cannot be underestimated. If we don't get a grasp on which we are as a country, we are doomed to fail just like every other representative republic that was ever created.

I for one want my country back. I am looking for a group of faithful people to follow the plan laid out in this treatise. There is no reason for us to continue to go down the current path of self-destruction. America was and is the greatest country the world has ever known. But on this slippery slide, we have lost ground and are now faced with having to take our country back. We must stand together now as never before, before it is too late. Be aware, there is a price to pay for standing up and doing what needs to be done in the face of today's Liberal Progressive watchers. The elements of this evil scour the land now to find those who will not bow the knee to the secular humanist god.

I have known this author since 1977 when we attended graduate school together at UCLA. In every word and deed, I have known him to be a man of honor and firm character, one who loves his God, his family, and his country. He has been a business leader in Corporate America for over thirty years, often winning awards for performance; a trend-setter for professional peers. His writing of years past has thrilled my soul at times when I felt all was lost; he has served me as a pathfinder in times of trouble. I predict that Dean will become one of the major voices in America helping to restore faith in our nation. When you read just the first few pages of this book, I guarantee you will not be able to put it down and you will understand the power of conviction that is in his heart. He knows what a mountain top experience is, and he knows the heartache of the valley of the shadow of death — Dean lost a daughter to a terrible accident a few years ago. Though his life has experienced tragedy of unspeakable pain it also has been filled with the joy of knowing the depths of faith, hope and love. And now he has turned his love and hope toward us and his country.

This book is a call to action. It is a guide to waking up and to start migrating down the path of reconciliation. It is about how to prepare yourself and your loved ones for coming tragedies; the eroding culture, the disintegrating moral framework, and vanishing ethics. Most of all, it is a guide to digging down through the Liberal rubble and touching the bedrock of truth about who we are, and taking America back; to reclaim it, redeem it and restore it. Here it is . . .

Joseph R. Finnell,

Retired business owner and pastor;
Past President, Southern California Ministerial Association.

Author's Note

NO SINGLE PERSON IS SELF-MADE; that is especially true of me. The 17th Century poet and cleric, John Donne, knew that too and the connection we all have with others. He wrote, "No man is an island, entire of itself; everyman is a piece of the Continent..." which he wrote in Meditation 17 of his Devotions upon Emergent Occasions published in 1624. While he wrote within the context of his extreme illness, I write from a framework of the great debt of gratitude I owe to more than a few. Each has been an incredible encouragement to me along my pathway and in the penning of the book I privately refer to as "Country."

From the days of contemplation, preparation, and its eventual writing, I became only more aware of my unworthiness, how little I know, and my need for the One Who sustains me — Jesus of Nazareth. To Him, this work is dedicated.

My conscience and teacher through life has been my Mom. Though illness took her from this life over four decades ago, her loving, and at times, very stern words have lasted a lifetime in my ears and mind; they still help me remember where my "out-of-bounds" lines are, as I call them. To each who knew her in life, their independent narrative seemed always phrased with the same, identical words; "My, she was an angel." That description falls short, but does come close.

Second, a great encourager to me was a friend nicknamed "Doc", who prodded and pushed me for years to write again. I am thankful for his importunity. A myriad of others, both friends and family, have encouraged me . . . Neighbors Nancy, Joel, and Rob as well as Jim, Charlie, Derek, Gary, Gary Dean, Paul, Patty, Gloria, Dave, and Etcyl . . . they have provided support in unique ways encouraging me to stay the course.

A mammoth encourager has been Nick. He deserves more than honorable mention, as early on he became so excited when reading an early draft of the treatise. In many ways, he has become the son that I never had. A many-talented business leader, he is best known for what many call his "Midnight Gun Emporium."

My high school English teacher's lessons on grammar and syntax haunted me during this writing. Editors, Fred and Elaine, worked hard to alleviate my nightmares that this book would exit its printing looking similar to Lord Timothy Dexter's work of the 19th Century. First of all, this self-appointed Lord wrote a book containing only 8,847 words; many of them misspelled, and there were no punctuation marks of any kind. In spite of the fact he was forced to give away his book for free at first because of its bad grammar, it still became so popular that eight editions were printed and all were sold out. He did print a separate edition having a page containing 13 lines of nothing but punctuation marks with the instruction, "Distribute them as you please."

My hope is this writing will help in restoring the America I remember. My family, and friends should inherit a nation that is freer, healthier, and more responsible than the one my generation is leaving behind. Here's hoping for the restoration and safeguarding of this magnificent gift, America, which they will receive.

- Dean

And indeed there is a serious criticism here, to anyone who knows history; since the things that grow are not always the things that remain; and pumpkins of that expansiveness have a tendency to burst. I was always told that Americans were harsh, hustling, rather rude and perhaps vulgar; but they were very practical and the future belonged to them. I confess I felt a fine shade of difference; I liked the Americans; I thought they were sympathetic, imaginative, and full of fine enthusiasms; the one thing I could not always feel clear about was their future. I believe they were happier in the frame-houses than most people in most houses; having democracy, good education, and a hobby of work; the one doubt that did float across me was something like, "Will all this be here at all in two hundred years?"

A visitor from England, G. K. Chesterton,
In What I Saw in America, 1922

Introduction

ARMY SERGEANT HEARL C. SMITH arose just after midnight preparing to lead the soldiers of his company into what history would record as one of the bloodiest; most vicious fights of the European theatre, the "Battle of the Argonne Forest" — this against a burrowed-in and well-armed German enemy that autumn morning of September 26, 1918 just outside Cheppy, France. Just 8 days earlier, Hearl had been promoted from Corporal machine gunner to Sergeant, taking command of half the men of Company F in the 35th Division within the 140th Infantry Regiment, A.E.F. Company F was home for all the men and boys from the Willow Springs unit of the Missouri National Guard.[1] Ironically two of Hearl's younger brothers, Mack and Irvin, were in the same company. The next day was going to be a personal day of valor for Hearl as he single-handedly rescued over a dozen of his fellow troops, many of them wounded, and he killed over two dozen of the German enemy. The German attack had been incessant and unrelenting, pinning down some of the troops. Then Hearl decided to rush a German machine gun nest in order to help rescue those Allied Forces who were pinned down. There he was mortally wounded, yet continued to direct his men in the attack upon the enemy while his life bled out on the French soil — in the late afternoon of September 27, 1918. That was just 44 full days before the end of "the war to end all wars." For those selfless acts, he was one of the first recipients of the "Distinguished Service Cross" from World War I.[2] "The Cross" is the second highest military award given, and "is awarded to a person who, while serving in any capacity with the Army, distinguishes himself or herself by extraordinary heroism ... so notable and have involved risk of life so extraordinary as to set the individual apart from his comrades."[3] Hearl was my great uncle, my maternal grandfather's brother. Over 40 years ago I learned these details of his remarkable war record, as well as other facts of the life of this intriguing twenty-five year-old who grew up in my hometown in Missouri. He certainly earned his "Cross" that day, which was awarded in 1919 — meaning he was decorated posthumously. Today just outside Cheppy, France, stands a monument given by the State of Missouri — a thank-you to members of the Missouri National Guard, and I like to think also to Hearl, who gave their lives liberating the town's people in Meuse Lorraine from the German assault nearly 100 years ago.

This discovery of Hearl's remarkable sacrifice and service was a welcome note of pride for my family and especially me. Mostly, it was the beginning of what I refer to as "my wakeup call" regarding freedom and its extreme high cost. Every few years, the area papers from West Plains and Springfield, Missouri will run a full page story of Hearl's war record and life. His service, coupled with that of my dad in WW II, as well as other veterans' noteworthy service in subsequent wars with which I am aware, has helped to redirect my thinking about America, my subsequent historical studies, and the awesome wonder of those who've protected our homeland through the decades.

It was all an opening as I said; Hearl's story started cracking open other doors, to reveal deeper, even more significant events and facts reaching well beyond the nobility of a family member, or my hometown history, reaching to the soul of our nation and its history, our other wars, including the American Revolution, dating back to when General George Washington led the continental army at our nation's founding. Many of these facts and true stories were unknown to me until then. Significant and documented information was the facilitator which led to more learning and subsequent changes in my life — how I view and appreciate the courage of those who blazed trails before me. For one, simply my activities on Memorial Day and July 4th annually have reformed and matured over the years, remembering many of the sacrifices our men and women in uniform have made throughout our history for each of us.

In the decades that followed, there have been exponentially numerous more "eureka" moments — times of historical discovery which have been both enlightening, and some rather disquieting. These discoveries came from my continued study and exploration of our nation's pilgrimage, our revolution, founding, our exceptional colonial, state and national constitutions, and as the underpinnings of all these, our Christian heritage, our factual history.

Allow me to set the table for you with some important and intriguing accounts of this history you probably were never taught in public school.

Initially, consider the Plymouth settlers who came to the New World in the early 17th century; they learned the hard way that the pride in ownership of private property was responsible for their very survival, and ultimately the creation of this nation we call America. School children are taught nowadays that in Plymouth, the Indians saved the Pilgrims, who allegedly did not know enough to even tie their own shoes. The truth is, the collectivist or communist experiment they were thrust into that first year, almost killed the whole bunch. In The Noblest Triumph: Property and Prosperity Through the Ages, Tom Bethell explains that the American settlers originally adopted communal ownership of land and property [as directed by Tom Weston who ran the Mayflower Company which financed the Plymouth Colony] and as a result most of them starved to death or died of disease — a problem endured in later centuries by virtually every communist country that adopted collectivized agriculture.[4]

Today, our school children are taught that socialism or collectivism is foundational for a utopia to exist and solving all the world's problems because it theoretically levels the playing field. While it may level the playing field in some liberal's mind, in truth, it's a lie that has killed and still kills large segments of the population wherever it's attempted — whether they be Pilgrims in America, subjects of the Red Chinese government, the proletariat of the former U.S.S.R., or any others throughout human history.

Prior to Pilgrims landing at Plymouth, the Jamestown settlement, my second reference of untaught history, was a tragic microcosm of socialism's results in the New World. The [very] first American settlers arrived in Jamestown in May of 1607. There, in the Virginia Tidewater region, they found incredibly fertile soil and a cornucopia of seafood, wild game such as deer and turkey, and fruits of all kind. Nevertheless, within six months, all but 38 of the original 104 Jamestown settlers were dead, most having succumbed to famine.[5] Two years later, the Virginia Company sent 500 more "recruits" to settle Virginia, and within six months a staggering 440 of them were dead by starvation and disease. One particular eyewitness's account is described as follows in old English: *"So great was our famine, that a Savage we slew and buried, the poorer sort took him up againe and eat him; and so did divers one another boyled and stewed with roots and herbs."*[6] This man understood the crux of the problem when he remarked on the irony of such massive starvation occurring amidst such plenty — game, fish, fruits, nuts, and so forth. The cause of starvation, he said, was *"want of providence, industrie....and not the barennesse and defect of the Countrie, as is generally supposed."*[7] The true problem was that members in Jamestown were indentured servants who had "no skin in the game" — they could not even make a profit from their own work. For seven years, everything they made was to go into a common pool to be used to support the colony and generate profits for the Virginia Company. To work harder, longer, or smarter in this socialized system, was of no absolute benefit to them, and so they responded as anyone does even today, they just shirked their duties. "Good enough for government work," as one might say, and everything basically failed.

In 1611, the British government sent Sir Thomas Dale to serve as the "high marshal" of the Virginia Colony. Dale noted that although most of the settlers had starved to death, the remaining ones were spending much of their time playing games in the streets and he immediately identified the problem: the system of communal ownership.[8] Dale awarded each man three acres, which they were required to work for profit, with the equivalent of only one month's wages going to taxes per year. No more free rides — everyone bore full responsibility and consequence for the output of their land and labor, receiving full reward for what they produced and accomplished. And when he put the property ownership into place, the colony immediately began to prosper. There was incentive to increase both their effort and products. Or as one author states, "As soon as the settlers were thrown upon their own resources, and each freeman had acquired the right of owning property, the colonists quickly developed what became the distinguishing characteristic of Americans — an aptitude for all kinds of craftsmanship coupled with an innate genius for experimentation and invention."[9]

Thomas Dale's decision to give three-acre plots of land to the Jamestown settlers worked so well, that when Thomas Weston became familiar with it, in light of the failure at Plymouth — due to similar communal or socialistic approaches to the local government that retarded progress — he pushed for a similar land ownership model. So Plymouth, under Governor Bradford quickly went to the private property approach, tossing away the earlier communistic or socialistic model. Quickly Bradford noted that lazy and indolent individuals quickly became "very industrious" so much so that women who had previously pleaded frailty now worked long and hard — once they saw how they and their families could benefit from such hard work. Bradford went on to blame the disastrous policy of collectivism on "that conceit of Plato's" — the Greek philosopher's advocacy of collective ownership of land, an idea that Aristotle had refuted. Those who mistakenly believed that communal property could make people "happy and flourishing," wrote Bradford, deluded themselves into thinking they were "wiser than God."[10] The same self-promoted, misguided, and irrational "wisdom" is a common trait of Socialists, Marxists, Liberals, and Progressives today.

A third and prime example of history that's not taught comes from the 18th Century. My research shows this: Despite what most of us were taught in the public school system about the Colonists all uniting in harmony to fight the British in our American Revolution — that is wrong. Historians estimate at the height for support of independence, 40-45 percent supported the rebellion against the crown.[11] Those participating in the rebellion made up about 15 percent. Regarding the loyalists who remained faithful to the Crown, historian Robert Calhoon writes, "Historians' best estimates put the proportion of loyalists and Tories, supporting the Crown, at between 15-20 percent . . . half the colonists of European ancestry tried to avoid involvement in the struggle — some of them deliberate pacifists, others recent immigrants, and many more simple apolitical folk."[12] The largest number of loyalists were in the middle colonies; many tenant farmers of New York supported the King, as did many of the Dutch of the colony and in New Jersey . . . Highland Scots in the Carolinas, a fair number of Anglican clergy and their parishioners in Connecticut and New York, a few Presbyterians in southern colonies, and a large number of Iroquois Indians stayed loyal to the King.[13] Historians estimate of the 2.5 million whites in the colonies, Loyalists and Tories made up approximately 500,000 men, women and children.[14]

Take the early Constitutions, another sample of untaught history. Many of the constitutions of those original colonies and other states stated the requirement for anyone to hold public office to make two public confessions: One, that Jesus Christ is the Son of God and Savior of the world, and; Two, that the Bible is the inspired Word of God.[15] Added to that, are the multiple dozens of Biblical references and Scripture verses engraved in and upon our government buildings in Washington, D.C. Each is a bold declaration of our founders and earlier citizens of how the Christian faith was front and center in building our government. When secular humanists argue that religion had no part in our country or our government, my simple question goes unanswered: "If you are correct, what are all those engravings of Bible verses and statues of Biblical characters doing yet today on and in our government buildings?" Some divert attention saying, "We are a post-Christian nation!" My reply: "Why in your Gnostic thought do you think yourself wiser than nations of history that claimed the same and failed miserably?"

<u>A critical fact regarding the 4th of July from early in our national history is another microcosm of what is not taught in public schools today</u>. It regards the seriousness of that holiday. The founders regarded this date to be so important and sacred that it stood as the people's most reverent holiday, second only to Christmas! It becomes obvious after reading the speech given by President John Quincy Adams, our 6th president at the 61st anniversary of our Declaration of Independence on July 4, 1837, during the town gathering of Newburyport, Mass. His oration pointed out that the celebration was holy and not one of drunkenness, BBQs, and debauchery as is done today, but a day of deep soul-searching as he said, "Are you then assembled here. . . . In gratitude for blessings enjoyed. . . . In exultation at the energies of your fathers . . . You are not here to unite in echoes of mutual gratulation for the separation of your forefathers from their kindred of the British Islands. You are not here even to commemorate in the annual revolution of the earth in her orbit round the sun, this was the birthday of the Nation. You are here, to pause a moment and take breath, in the ceaseless and rapid race of time — to look back and forward — to take your point of departure from the ever memorable transactions of the day of which this is the anniversary, and while offering your tribute of thanks- giving to the Creator of all worlds, for the bounties of his Providence lavished upon your fathers and upon you, . . . appealing to the Supreme Judge of the world for the rectitude of his intentions, covenanting with all the rest that they would for life and death be faithful members of that community, and bear true allegiance to that Sovereign, upon the principles set forth in that paper. The lives, the fortunes, and the honour, of every free human being forming a part of those Colonies, were pledged, in the face of God and man, to the principles therein promulgated. [D]evoted to the worship of almighty God, I would repeat the question with which this discourse was introduced: — Why are you assembled in this place? It is that the first words uttered by the Genius of our country, in announcing his existence to the world of mankind, was, — Freedom to the slave! Liberty to the captives! Redemption! Redemption forever to the race of man, from the yoke of oppression! It is not the work of a day; it is not the labor of an age; it is not the consummation of a century that we are assembled to commemorate. It is the emancipation of our race."[16]

One more event I'll reference which you and I were never taught in school. That fact regards the first legal owner of a "chattel" (permanent slave) in America. He was Anthony Johnson, none other than a black man, or African American, from Virginia. He won a case in the highest Virginia court, Northampton Court in 1655 dealing with John Casor. Casor was an indentured servant who had served his time for Johnson and was due to be released. Johnson had other thoughts, informing Casor he was extending the time. Casor fled to the neighboring farm of Robert Parker, just down the road. Johnson sued and the court awarded him Casor as "property," to hold as long as he wanted. The court gave judicial sanction for blacks to own slaves of their own race. Thus Casor became the first permanent slave, or chattel, in America making Johnson the first slave owner. This fact is kept under wraps today for obvious politically correct reasons.[17] The liberal powers that be, including the media, continue to bandy about a totally different picture regarding slavery in America; that Blacks were always the only victim. True history speaks differently.

Just granules pulled from the annals of history — each one is important to properly view the mosaic of America. But they and thousands of other truths are all conveniently left out of our education because they do not support the liberal progressive agenda today. Discovering each restricted subject or absence of actual events in the teaching of historical truths leads down a path eventually exposing the complete agenda of the Progressive camp. That is to hide most true facts of our heritage, the true value of free-enterprise, and Christianity's role in western civilization. Liberals hunger to uncouple students from the truth of our robust past — a time and place where people through faith placed confidence in God, in their own initiative, and in spiritual absolutes. The Liberals work hard, attempting to destroy our foundations of facts, crafting an injudicious vision of America. It is a devilish scheme, all based not in the authenticity of our history, but rather their corrosive lies. The following reasons for their actions are critical points to remember:

- They do this because they despise moral absolutes, individualism, capitalism, and its resulting free-enterprise;
- They want to manipulate people; shift them away from firm moral foundations, and away from self-reliance;
- They want people to be totally reliant on the state authority and their statist views, giving themselves final power and control over the people.

Never mind that the true reason why our nation advanced as it did during its first 200 years and why we have enjoyed the level of life that existed in America for decades. No, liberals do not want to hear that. They want to quash any mention of "special heritage" or "spiritual roots," calling those notions pure foolishness. Arrogantly, they say the foundation of their belief is "science" and "reason." In reality all the science in the world without an appropriate foundation of beliefs and morality always result in the suspension of civilization.

In contrast to those beliefs, following the establishment of this country came the gallant declarations of our founders and framers. Theirs were declarations about God, Christian beliefs, Biblical liberty, and the idea of freedom to pursue your own dreams in a capitalistic manner. America became the greatest nation the world has ever seen because its beginning was different from any other nation in history. It was made exceptional and magnificent, not due to socialism, not due to some leveling of the playing field, not by taking money from those who work and giving it to those who won't. Conversely, we became great due to the unique foundation of the framers:

- The faith principles from Judeo-Christianity formed the main underpinnings and corner stone;
- The opportunity to dream and work hard to accomplish those dreams formed a part of the foundation;
- The freedom, the pursuit of individual liberty and private property ownership forming a solid foundation for business and personal success.

Simply view how Christian beliefs was integral and a "no brainer" to pilgrims, colonists, founders and early American Citizens in their daily activities, businesses, governing laws and written declarations. Based on all these evidences, coupled with current experience, provides alarming witness to how this truth is absent when our history is reported. Over the past 50 years I have noticed on TV shows, history specials, the news, in periodicals, and even in our schools today, the steady erosion of these important facts; how they are totally left out. Not only are the facts omitted, but it is obvious the truth is replaced by outright lies told by the Liberal left, and the Progressives. These lies have become prevalent, repetitious — growing exponentially each year, becoming cemented legends in our kid's ears.

The result today is a remanufactured, politically correct, phony, and deceptive history that has been inscribed. In addition, calls come from the Left for America to be just like other nations, where godless governments have instituted untold misery. The Left teaches relativism, thus misleading people not only about the nation's founding, but also our original spiritual and moral pillars of society as well. At a minimum, progressives have brought about a diluting of details, on occasion a whitewash of, and in most cases a total eradication of our Christian heritage. More to the point, Liberal progressives have moved from simply lying about our heritage, freedom-loving and Christian as it is, to attacking the pillars of morality, and now to open and violent attacks on Christians. Their end game starts with an assault on our governing document — the Constitution. We know for example that without the Ten Commandments there would be no U.S. Constitution or Bill of Rights. And the Left hates the Constitution. However, they hate the Christian and Jewish faiths more. Progressives hate the ideals that spring from these faiths — that of having dreams and working hard to achieve them, in a free-enterprise system — they want this social equality in all outcomes. Tragically, that plan of social justice spells misery for all, just like it did in Jamestown and Plymouth, not an opportunity or utopia as they teach. As with our Constitution, they attack the Judeo-Christian heritage and the Bible. They despise all these principles, aiming to deteriorate the strength of the Constitution, moral absolutes, and civil rights of our society, hoping to create a collapse of our current way of life. That as we all fall, we'll be equal at the bottom of a heap of rubble. That is an accurate picture of their illogical brand of social justice.

Over time, the clearly socialistic media, entrenched in the "Progressive" liberal way, has promoted their plan suckering many Americans into believing their propaganda — hearing the repetition of manufactured lies from network news. The lies are believed due to poor education, or no education, which is all the wrong education.

What has followed seems sinister standing on its own, but I suppose a natural step for today's Liberal Progressive. They are rewriting our history to eventually change the story of our true heritage as if it never happened. This has been a deliberate act since they have changed the elementary and high school curriculum, including other basic history books. With wave after wave of changes, they pledge to discount, dilute, edit the content of, or totally erase the true facts of our Christian heritage and its' associated values which were practiced by pilgrims, colonists and founders. If you think this would be the end of their work, or as some say the "icing on their fake cake," it is not.

Today, their work continues behind their leadership that has been indoctrinated by South Side Chicago politics. What comes forth is a rapid mix and rapidly increasing plethora of political decisions — legislation and executive orders to push Marxist, anti-Christian, pro-Muslim, and radically liberal ideologies down our throats. They consist of a blend of class envy, free handouts, and tribal tactics whose leaders emulate African dictators. Whether here or abroad, the Left hates that for which America has stood. To see what is happening now in America is to remember how African tribal leaders learned to control the lives of their people through the art of distraction. Political power tends to corrupt, and absolute power corrupts absolutely. Many hailed as great people today are often irredeemable. With this current backdrop, is there a more corrupt portion of this country than what lies within "the Beltway" of Washington, D.C.? All has produced a culture and laws taking us light years from the goodness of our original national practices. Every early American document screams out as a conscience from the past to tell us how adrift we are, with treason from within.

We are adrift and in danger. Like a ship at sea with no sail, no engine and no rudder, cultural tides pull us farther from the safety of land. Progressivism has taken a toll. We are becoming like an evil foreign country — I do not even recognize America any more. National attributes are indecent and criminal. Many politicians prey on God-fearing people like a pack of rabid dogs. Personal freedoms are eroding fast. It is front page news; assaults on free speech, being armed for self-defense, and the right to assemble peaceably are all personal rights protected by early amendments in our Constitution — but they are all under attack. Attacks on Christians creating an onslaught of tribulation have shadowed these proceedings, as reported through reliable and responsible media. The picture is not pleasant. Peaceful God-fearing folks are labeled, "terrorists," "extremists," "homophobes," or "radicals," while the real terrorists are given carte blanche to spin their wickedness within our land. Screaming from another spot are these queer, gay leftists — calling for special rights on marriage. Public threats are made to any businesses that won't use their resources to support their "protected way of life." In truth, all citizens should be protected from "the protected classes" mantras and their politicians.

From another corner, young "text" generation individuals threaten society if they do not receive abortion rights, on demand, and at no cost. They salute their leader with vocal calls of "Hail Satan!" (It is ironic how his name comes up at such rallies; the one whom I identify as the old adversary behind an elongated war against us. Apparently liberal "reason" and "science" allows for the belief in Satan but not God.) New tax onuses come out of Washington looking for prey, like bats flying out of a cave — Obamacare anyone? Follows is the brazen yell of "who cares what the people want" spoken by plutocrats, voiced in particular by the now former speaker of the house. An eerie carnival atmosphere permeates the nation's capital celebrating the never ending prizes; the spending for giveaways in our capitol; the presidential vacations, and political junkets. The picture which comes to mind of our president and other Washingtonians is a person I identify as "a man made of money" from an insurance ad that is overblown on TV. You have seen him. He is driving his motorcycle or steering a boat, with money covering his face and entire body as part of his skin, hair and clothing, while money is flying off his body because of the waste he practices. Our founder's words from the past cry out as a conscience, denouncing these practices, as assaults on our future, our lives, our personal liberty.

Add to this madness, the threat of attack, nuclear or otherwise, from Muslim radicals and other anti-Christian entities. All these ingredients make what I call an "apocalyptic stew," and we have not even added what is happening in the Middle East which threatens to erupt into worldwide chaos all driven from America's horrible foreign policy and the Muslim Brotherhood. Go to any café, book store, restaurant, or small town coffee shop, where just moderately conservative people gather, and you will hear these "end of days" talk at their "tables of knowledge" every morning.

These scenes and rhetoric speak of a war that is raging against America. News is, it has been for a long time. This is a unique war different from any military battle. However, make no mistake; the war has very observable threats and casualties to our moral fiber and existence. What is the answer? It starts by recalling our history and the price paid to establish and over time keep our freedom. You will find that the Leftists despise the pillars of our history.

In retracing my steps, I am ever more thankful to fellow Americans who have served this country within the military in one or more of our branches, and possibly in one of our nation's wars, dating back to the American Revolution. So many heroes have traversed our streets and to them every American owes a huge debt of gratitude. Men and women from across this land fought for our freedom. In many instances they watched their closest friends fall by their side. They have suffered broken hearts while shouldering the burden of being wounded in war, sacrificing their warrior body receiving physical wounds. Some came home on crutches, on canes, and in wheelchairs. Some did not come home at all. They paid the price for us, whom they did not even know. Some made the ultimate sacrifice, usually in a far off land, so you and I could have tomorrow to enjoy. Collectively, all their work, all their blood, all their heroism, all their sacrifices hang in the balance at a serious crossroads in the US. On our watch, our generation stands to lose it all! That's right! All our heroes' sacrifices and victories through the last 240 years — they could all be gone in the blink of an eye. Meaning every sacrifice and death would have been given for naught, as if they never happened — they would simply vanish. With them will go our freedom and liberty if we don't awaken, address problems, and return to the heritage that made us a once great nation.

We were the "bright and shining city on a hill" as Ronald Reagan put it. It may be too late, we may have passed the event horizon of our country's destruction, but we have no chance for survival if we do not attempt to regain a grip on principles our Founders understood. A grip on those principles could be the ignition this nation needs to become great again. The same tyrannical enemy which our heroes fought over the past two centuries on foreign soil is now entrenched here. They are in our schools and universities, government, businesses and even our churches and synagogues. We are now in a fight for our borders, our language, our culture, and our family values. My generation has been too silent too long in telling the real story of us: our real history.

Whether you're single or married, young or old, a father, mother, grandparent, a child, a teacher, professor, student, doctor, nurse practitioner, attorney, sales person, executive, factory worker, union member, housewife, restaurant worker, member of the armed forces, or law enforcement officer — you have skin in this game. You hold a key to bring change, "win the future" to restore the dream of America and to stop the secular-socialist machine.

My favorite graduate school professor, Dr. Myron Taylor, often said, "A word spoken is a deed done." So, in this time of extreme national crisis, I feel an urgency to tell a national truth. In doing so, hopefully I will perform a good deed and blaze a trail. Likely I will follow in the footsteps of others who have blazed trails, or who are currently blazing one. This truth remains:

1. We have a "Stage 4" national health crisis — Our nation is dying. We must identify the causes;

2. There is a solution that is a cure;

3. There are critical steps in implementing the solution. We must act soon. Time is of the essence. There is no one but us to "carry this torch" and share the truth.

Our need for truth is immediate. It must be told unashamedly, boldly, thoroughly, with critical logical thought. Telling the truth of our overlooked national heritage and God's protective hedge that made America a great, magnificent country, the envy of the world, is just the beginning of a journey to take our country back. Truth will not hurt us; truth is an ally. By it we arm ourselves for battle. My goal in writing is simple: To show you the historical data, the unmistakable trail of evidence, combined with my personal experience; to tell you truth as I see it. I hope you will see it too.

The Missouri First World War Monument at Cheppy, France. Dedicated to the men of Missouri who gave their lives during the World War. Located at the road junction, south of the town of Cheppy (Meuse). Consists of a stone shaft surmounted by bronze figure. Erected: 1922 by the State of Missouri.

"It is the duty of all nations to acknowledge the providence of Almighty God, to obey His will, to be grateful for His benefits, and humbly to implore His protection and favor."

~ George Washington

*General, Revolutionary Army;
Signer, Declaration of Independence;
1st President of the United States*

Chapter One

Lost in the Land of the Lost!

INVESTIGATING SOME OF OUR PROBLEMS IS first on the agenda.

More than two thousand years ago, the great orator and statesman Marcus Tullius Cicero is said to have foretold the decline and fall of the Roman Empire with these words; they exquisitely tell the ravages of lying politicians:

> "A nation can survive its fools, and even the ambitious. But it cannot survive treason from within. An enemy at the gates is less formidable, for he is known and carries his banner openly. But the traitor moves amongst those within the gate freely, his sly whispers rustling through all the alleys, heard in the very halls of government itself. For the traitor appears not a traitor; he speaks in accents familiar to his victims, and he wears their face and their arguments, he appeals to the baseness that lies deep in the hearts of all men. He rots the soul of a nation, he works secretly and unknown in the night to undermine the pillars of the city, he infects the body politic so that it can no longer resist. A murderer is less to fear."

Elevated nearly to the level of a prophet, Cicero's words seem most descriptive of the political landscape in America today, especially that of Liberal Progressive politicians, who over the past 100 years have led to our nation becoming what it is today: the land of the lost.

Step with me into this world of the civil, philosophical, and economic madness which has been delivered by the shovelfuls that regrettably are the scene of "the new America." The passage to this point is the result of a political storm which gathered generations ago. The craft of Socialist Ideologue windbags and Marxist Progressives — all evil partisan architects, who for a century have used their words and rhetoric like hammers and chisels against the longstanding educational, cultural, financial, and philosophical institutions in our society. Wave after wave of their evil ideological storms over time supported by an army of evil and liberal academia have served to be a devourer, a spoiler aimed at ripping apart the fabric and foundations of our remarkable nation. In more recent years, they've aimed their cannons at our Bible and Constitution. We've allowed this disaster — by inattention, by fear, by languor.

Liberal icons, past and present, have been paraded before us by their commune of prevaricators, about whom we were tutored that they held the answers to life's toughest problems: whatever ones existed at the time. We were told by progressive liberals to follow the icons for inspiration, guidance and direction, and that in doing so these pied pipers would lead us into the Promised Land. The depressing news is that as a nation we bought into their fables and have like mind-numbed robots dutifully followed, with horrid results. Each of them misguided us, one after another. Each one taking us further astray to the point that as a nation, we are so seriously adrift now. We are lost! These purveyors of treason — villains every one — were and are a threat to democracy, freedom, and free-enterprise. And all the time we have been told they were the intellectual "cream of the crop," the best leaders who could be found on Planet Earth. In reality, they were so lost themselves that their "leadership" brought on more destruction than most people would ever have imagined. Their destruction was so bad, it reached the point that virtually any good segment of our great country they touched has been corrupted, damaged beyond repair, or has in some cases has vanished altogether. The result — We are not only lost . . . we are lost in the land of the lost.

Case in point: Within the dominion of education, we were told nearly 100 years ago to heed and follow the popular instructor, the Socialist icon John Dewey. We did. We bought into "Deweyism," as it was called. Now we are so lost in education, we and our children are caught in a perfect storm of confusion, moral devolution, ignorance, corruption, filth, debt, plus mental and psychological exhaustion . . . all because we followed this self-proclaimed Socialist. The American tradition in education had long had the goal of building Christian individualists, who would learn by faith and self-assurance to take the hand of Godly teachers and pull himself above the dull level of mediocrity; to stand on a pinnacle of individual accomplishment, moral and spiritual growth. But no, this could not be allowed under Dewey and Deweyism. Dewey said all talk of an individual rising to the top was not only ludicrous; it was hideous. Dewey despised individualism and taught that the proper goal of the biological organism called "man" is to lose his individuality through a psychological neutering and by being absorbed into and finding acceptance in the great masses.

The kind of education Dewey recommended was incubated and hatched totally in the realm of socialism. Its goal was to devolve men and women into faceless creatures in a leveled-down mass of humanity. Education, or "Deweyism," as Dewey expounded, is his combination of psychology, coming from the child's experience, and socialist political theory, all coming from Karl Marx, the Communist Manifesto, and of course, the masses. His explanation is found in his book *My Pedagogic Creed*: "I believe the only true education comes through the stimulation of the child's powers by the demands of the social stimulation in which he finds himself. Through these demands, he is stimulated to be as a member of a unity, to emerge from his original narrowness of action and feeling, and to conceive of himself from the standpoint of the welfare of the group to which he belongs.... Education, therefore, is a process of living and not a preparation for future living.... We violate the child's nature and render difficult the best ethical results by introducing the child too abruptly to a number of special studies, of reading, writing, geography, etc., out of relation to the social life... The true center of correlation on the school subjects is not science, nor literature, nor history, nor geography, but the child's own social activities."[1]

While Dewey grew old, both in years and in his faith of socialistic collectivism, he left the University of Chicago to become head of Teachers College at Columbia University in New York.[2] From this position, his ideas were molded into the minds of disciples who followed in his footsteps, and sadly his ideas have amalgamated the thinking our American educationalists and unions since. Dewey retired from the university in 1930, and two of his closest colleagues and disciples at Teachers College — Dr. Harold O. Rugg and Dr. George S. Counts, were prepared to lead their mentor's dream child forward bearing the mantra "progressive education." That is a total misnomer; their idea of education is purely "regressive" in substance.

And in 1933, the same year Dewey was signing onto the Humanist Manifesto and supporting the FDR administration, his disciple Harold Rugg authored a book for teachers titled, *The Great Technology*. In it he basically told teachers that America must be converted into a socialist dictatorship. Those are my words; his words were, "we must have a "new government," with "all-pervading" powers to plan and regulate the lives of the people and the economy of the nation." He added, "... the teachers must disabuse their pupils' minds of any archaic ideas they might have about our history. They must be told that the American Revolution was not a revolt of men who wanted to be free against an all-powerful, tyrannical and tax-eating government. It was just a brawl between American landlords and the British nobility, and the men who led the Revolution were merely interested in their own property. The students must be taught that our free-enterprise system is a failure — it breeds poverty and inequality and the only fair system is a planned one, run by the government."[3]

Mr. Counts articulated his personal endearment for Dewey, for secular humanism, and for the liberal education that Dewey fostered in the following way: "In the collectivist society now emerging, the school should be regarded, not as an agency for lifting gifted individuals out of the class into which they were born and of elevating them into favored positions where they may exploit their less-favored fellows, but rather as an agency for the abolition of all artificial social distinctions and of organizing the energies of the nation for the promotion of the general welfare ... you will say, no doubt, that I am flirting with the idea of indoctrination. And my answer is again in the affirmative, or, at least, I should say the word does not frighten me."[4]

Dewey and his disciples, who followed him, swore allegiance to the socialist regimes prevalent in East Europe; critical to his core beliefs. He disdained the individualism of American thought: the very thought processes that made us great. Dewey rejected all fixed moral laws, eternal truths, anything to do with Christianity, and God Himself. How fitting, yet tragic in American Indoctrination Camps (aka, public schools) that he is hailed by Leftists as the father of modern education in America. The results we see today are sad; the seeds he sowed has brought madness, confusion, tyranny; anything but real education.

Race forward to September 27, 2014, and Dewey's disciples are "keeping the faith" by opposing anything Christian in a Temecula, California, school. It seems that the "educators: there and especially the superintendent of Springs Charter Schools said the school does not "allow sectarian materials on our state-authorized lending shelves." Therefore all Christian authors will be removed. They went about removing books they deemed inappropriate such as "The Hiding Place" by the well-known HOLOCAUST SURVIVOR Corrie ten Boom, who hid Jews from the Nazis. They removed it because of her strong Christian beliefs. Many others have been removed. Thankfully, the Pacific Justice Institute is taking the "super" on legally in court. I want them to defeat her, and watch her get fired from her job for such an Obama-esque move in her school. On the other hand, a good remedy would be simply to comply — Remove the works and books of Dr. Martin Luther King. The superintendent would never recover from the protests outside her residence. Yes, that would do it.

The sinister side of Dewey's attack on our culture is seen in full force. The humanists would love for Christians to shut their mouths, move to the back of the bus, and probably even drink from separate water fountains. The good news is that I believe the body of the Lord will awaken to this command to be quiet and not share our faith. They hopefully will soon respond in unison, "We must obey God rather than men."

Another icon hoisted into the air was one in economics and political theory: **Karl Marx.** We are told he was and is the epitome or penultimate of anyone to be found in the marketplace. So liberals set out to convince crowds to pay him homage, rather than paying it to what they called the "evil capitalism." A note of interest: the word "capitalism" was coined by none other than Karl Marx himself, who hoped, as he wrote, would help in his crusade to denigrate the system of private ownership of property, free-enterprise, thus helping to promote Communism. Virtually every hypothesis Marx put forth in his *Communist Manifesto*, has been proved wrong. Free-market capitalism, based on private property and peaceful exchange is the only authentic engine of civilization and the progress of the human race. But don't dare confuse progressives with facts. Adam Smith, in his work *The Wealth of Nations* succinctly identified how capitalism properly works, "Give me that which I want, and you shall have this which you want." Said differently, it's commerce in a "positive-sum game," of buyers and sellers both benefiting in the act of buying and selling in a mutually advantageous environment. Anything other than that, they should choose not to participate. In spite of the facts, tragically Marx is still espoused by Progressives as the spiritual godfather of economics. With his "guru" status, each day our free-enterprise system is condemned, attacked, taxed, waxed, beaten and left for dead in the dark alley of commerce by the American Media and the pundits of Progressivism. Result: Our free enterprise system has been verbally run over and "left for dead" by treason from within.

A lesser-known Progressive icon elevated to "Saint" status was Margaret Sanger. Sanger was an early 1900s political activist in America, a proponent for birth control and the founder of the American Birth Control League, started in 1921. Through the years, this group morphed into what later became an organization named Planned Parenthood, a prominent group still today. Women were coaxed to follow. Sanger was successful in recruiting many women to embrace her ideologies of birth control and what she called *"the imperative necessity of its adoption as the basis of national and racial progress."* This organization's influence has grown through the years embracing birth control and abortion. You can tell its prominence today: 55 million babies aborted and still counting. Planned Parenthood, Sanger's morphed dream child, has been project manager over many of them. Sanger's newsletter, an activist rag, was used nearly exclusively to pump Marxist ideologies and women's rights into the then modern female psyche. In a 1914 issue, her article *The Woman Rebel* carried the following message, *"I believe woman was enslaved by the world machine, by sex conventions, by motherhood and its present necessary child-rearing..."* She advocated negative eugenics, a collective philosophy which claims that human hereditary traits can be upgraded through social engineering and intervention. Sounds like Hitler and Stalin must have been avid readers, weaving and developing her thoughts into their own respective social engineering value systems. By the way, those were known as death camps, negative eugenics and all.

Sanger and her disciples believed in re-engineering and intervention connected to radical leftist methods in the past. She taught that by targeting "genetically unfit" groups, with selective breeding, euthanasia, and sterilization, the race could be improved. This was especially seen in her book *The Pivot of Civilization*. In a 1932 article, *"A Plan for Peace,"* Sanger proposed a congressional department to, "Keep the doors of immigration closed to the entrance of certain aliens whose condition is known to be detrimental to the stamina of the race, such as feeble-minded, idiots, morons, insane, syphilitic, epileptic, criminal, professional prostitutes, and others in this class barred by the immigration laws of 1924." Sounds like Hitler and Stalin were students.

Sanger got away with teaching that aboriginal Australians were "the lowest known species of the human family, just a step higher than the chimpanzee in brain development." Had she been a Republican or conservative, she would have been branded a "racist" for such comments. But liberals are given a pass when they produce such tripe. When an assassination attempt on John D. Rockefeller was made in 1914, the attack brought loud praise from Sanger, though the bomb exploded prematurely, killing three of the assassins. An innocent fourth person, Marie Chavez, not even involved in the conspiracy, but a renter in an apartment next door, was also killed. Sanger is just another example of a weird hero the Progressives told us to idolize. Unfortunately millions listened and still follow her ideology in lockstep today.

An extremely perverted icon which the Liberal Left and Progressives idolized and then trotted before us was Alfred Kinsey. While all their icons are despicable, he was the worst. Liberals said he held to key to sexual liberty for Americans. When that news hit the papers, he made many instantaneous disciples! He is the author of *The Kinsey Reports*, an extreme liberal post WW II rag, which hit American bookstands in 1948. Kinsey did "research" which produced lots of confusion, altering sexual perceptions in America for decades to come. Working from a platform of his education as a Zoologist and a loyal Liberal Progressive, all his work came from faulty and unscientific methods, as well as conclusions he reached by adding a liberal bias. The result was many Americans were being enticed to experiment with his weird and deviant sexual practice.

Kinsey was a typical liberal, basing his research on two unbelievably ludicrous lynchpins: The first were interviews he primarily conducted with felons, sex offenders, prison inmates, female and male prostitutes, pedophiles, and others of that ilk. All produced skewed results for obvious reasons. Regarding those dialogues with child molesters, he argued that most of the children involved actually derived "definite pleasure" from their experiences. That Kinsey would allow child molesters to dictate whether the children enjoyed being raped or molested speaks volumes not only about his character, but especially about his lack of devotion to any real "science," and especially to his liberal bias. Liberals lauded him so much that they created a bronzed image of him. His conclusions? The hysterical response created by parents and police was more harmful to a child than any damage caused by any molestation or rape. Throughout his work life, Kinsey continually did his interviews with child molesters and rapists. And being a good liberal he kept the confidence of his interviewees from the police, other authorities, and any conservatives.

The second warped lynchpin of Kinsey's research was in what he described as "laboratory" or "field" testing. From Daniel Flynn's credible research, we learned and now know, Kinsey "was a sometimes homosexual, a wife-swapper, a sadomasochist, and some suspect, a pedophile. . . . The real Kinsey lent his wife to other men and turned his attic into his own personal pornographic movie studio. His fellow researchers . . . also acted as his sex partners. One Kinsey researcher even bragged about bedding a dog. Others were committed sadomasochists. The common denominator among staff at [Kinsey's] *Institute of Sex Research* [still in business, located on the Indiana University Campus] was a "pursuit of sex that was outside of societal conventions."[5]

Kinsey's disciples and confidants kept his research confidential for years. His perversions were weird and strange, most were outright illicit; traits which seem frankly quite common for the Liberal Left. In fact, the Leftists of today view such perversions as resume enhancers. Suffice to say only close supporters and confidants within liberalism are allowed to view his original diaries and papers to mask the truth about him, deceiving the public about their hero. He had become so much a part of the fabric of America that the illicit findings made public resulted in Americans viewing neighbors with suspicion, fearing they might be involved in deviant behavior of all kinds, even though in truth they were not. The injury that a weird progressive can bring to society is overwhelming: their goal all along; and to make more disciples.

Paul Ehrlich is another Progressive icon of the 1960s. He was defined by a generation of liberals as an all-knowing, all-seeing philosophical guru. His disciples responded by placing him on a pedestal for worship. We were commanded to follow him too. The trouble was and still is, a person really did not know for sure how to follow him. Ehrlich became a professional doomsayer writing his first book of the 60s, *The Population Bomb*. It was closely associated with and planted in the "warmed up" soil out of which the climate change and global warming doctrine of today grew. In *The Population Bomb*, he predicted that "In the 1970's and 1980's ... hundreds of millions of people are going to starve to death in spite of any crash programs embarked upon now." Later he came up with any number of publications and predictions: all were doomsday prophecies. Leftists embrace him and his words as if he had discovered a cure for AIDS or cancer. One difficulty: while the Left views him an expert, his scientific training is in entomology: the study of butterflies. A second difficulty: none of his predictions to date came true. Yet, like most liberal ideologies that are floated like trial balloons, they have produced lots of cash for him and a myriad of environmental causes. If he had only predicted that hundreds of millions of deaths would have come because of Socialism, he would have been on target.

The list could go on but I will mention one more icon of Liberal Progressivism, the academic elitist, Peter Singer. Many liberal causes carry this Princeton Professor's signature, usually for being the outspoken godfather of the animal-rights movement. He's on record of having objections to humans eating animals — but not for humans having sexual relations with animals. Singer, this giant icon of the Left which they say we must also follow due to his "intellectual prowess," supports state-run infanticide (the killing of babies) and euthanasia (the killing of anybody else). Singer is on record of saying, "When the death of a disabled infant will lead to the birth of another infant with better prospects of a happy life, the total amount of happiness will be greater if the disabled infant is killed." It's as if the thirst for death by abortions isn't quenching enough any longer. Now it must be soothed by killing those already born who may have a physical defect; then move on to others like vets in the V.A., both an absolute outrage.

These are a few from the Liberal Hall of Faith: "Wizards of Leftwood." We have been commanded to follow them with both our thinking, but most especially with our tax dollars: the consequence of following these perverts and idiots has brought total disaster!

Add to this the list of other current liberal progressive icons. They are a witch's brew of career politicians, Ivy League scientists, social theorists, and Leftist theologians of our day. Liberals every one: they all live out past the outskirts of rational thinking. However, they preach social justice, gun control, environmentalism, and a hatred for democracy. This places them on a hot list for leadership within the Democrat Party. The politicians carry the brand of change agents; working to re-engineer the economy and tax system to match Karl Marx's collectivist theory. The Ivy League "scientists" are all tattooed on their backsides with global warming, which became climate change, now being called weather shifts. The social theorists travel the liberal talk show circuit using the same tired, worn-out clichés just to keep their liberal forces gassed up with phrases to use. The liberal theologians are an interesting sort. They live on the outskirts of a rational Christendom in our day — many liberal preachers tout whatever hot-button "ism" the liberal left pushes from their memos of the day. For example, we are consistently being told by them to abandon traditional Christian beliefs. In their place we are coaxed to follow the pied pipers who are with Churches who have been wooed away from truth of the Great Commission to preach the liberal propaganda. That Commission calls for Christians to go into the entire world making disciples and preaching the Gospel. But the liberal propaganda has "preachers" who have abandoned that high calling in order to pursue the social justice message. They carry forward pulpit-pounding themes like those shown below:

- Disarming law-abiding Americans through gun control;
- Universal Health Care for the purpose of controlling the population; this includes the elimination of the elderly through loss of benefits
- Promoting abortion on demand;
- Promoting the United Nations and its one-world government;
- Black liberation theology, an old Communist message;
- Pursuit of homosexual rights and gay marriages in the church;
- Global warming, aka – climate change, aka – climate shifts;
- Women's rights, and the supposed "War on women."

These are all part and parcel of the "liberal social justice gospel."

The sad thing is to hear the silence coming from the community of Christendom and conservative pulpits of America where once messages were "barked out" condemning the sins of the federal government. In today's setting, the IRS attacks private conservative citizens — and the pulpit is silent. The federal government refuses to protect its Libyan Ambassador — once again the pulpits are silent. The NSA spies on private, law-abiding citizens — the pulpits remain silent again. Illegal aliens are protected over citizens — and the pulpit remains silent. Preachers offer excuses that they must stay away from politics, keeping their message on "spiritual" subjects. But the same preachers today seem to have forsaken the way of the apostolic fathers, who in their time took stances against the evils in their cultures and governments. The preachers need to "man up," stop hiding and stand on truth against the evil of the day, just as Elijah did in days of old. Sharing of the "whole" Biblical message in and of itself, will address every social issue, and in proper context.

Case in point: The Apostle Peter and the Apostle John stood and preached "truth to power," against the government in their place and time, which was the Sanhedrin. They declared a counter-cultural revolution by stating "We must obey God rather than men!" (Acts 5:29) It would appear the bulk of the pulpits of America today have become firmly rooted in the liberal camp of obeying men.

It was also the Apostle Paul who spoke "truth to power" in his counter cultural revolution against the Roman Empire's political, economic, and social institution of slavery. The slave was not even considered a person. He was only a piece of "chattel," or property. He was deliberately held down. He was a thing — a tool that existed to be used at the whim of the master. Slavery was so engrained into the Roman Empire, that is has been estimated that there were over 60 million of them at the time.[6] In the Rome of Paul's day, slaves outnumbered Roman citizens. Some of the wealthy Roman land owners may have had 10-20 thousand slaves each working on their estates. The slaves outnumbered citizens so much so, that slave and master relationships were every bit as common then, as the employee and employer relationship is today. To collapse the social structure of slavery in the Roman Empire was to collapse the economy altogether. Paul could not unilaterally overthrow slavery but he sowed the seeds of rebellion in one instance by instructing Philemon to accept back his runaway slave, Onesimus, accepting him not as a slave but as a beloved brother. Paul didn't have the political clout to overthrow the system of slavery. So from a grassroots level, he taught that as a Christian, the slave was equal on a spiritual and physical footing with the master. Paul's revolutionary message of brotherhood between slave and free persons converted the slave from being a thing whose shoulders were bowed, whose back was slumped, whose knees were buckled, and who'd been driven into the ground. No longer did he have need to cower because of his loss of self-identity, self-worth, and self-respect. Instead, the slave was now a person who had a new identity not only in Christ but also in society. Paul's declaration on the equality between slaves and free persons was a principle that over time gained a foothold and ultimately tipped the balance of power, undermining the institution of slavery itself in the entire Roman Empire. Given the impotency in pulpits today, if America was involved in the slavery industry now, as it was in 18th and 19th centuries, there would be few counter-cultural revolution messages heard, as were heard in the antebellum period when pulpits rang loudly with sermons calling for abolition.

These images with the afore mentioned villains show a very clear picture that we are in the midst of a war for the hearts and minds of our young people — and for the soul of our country. That the war is raging is seen from many more examples of current liberal icons, as well as the carnage and wreckage seen on daily news programs: A tragedy from what was a once great nation. Abject crime, moral insolvency, economic bankruptcy, deteriorating schools and pitiful universities, depraved organizations, empty psychology, emptier philosophies, and now a wanton regime that wants only more of the same as the proposed answer to our problems. The landscape toward every horizon has no answers on morality; they have been stripped away. The truths of governing principles that work well have been hidden from view. This was all done by Liberal Progressives, as if an evil Halloween prank. Liberals have been about the business of shredding the tapestry of our existence. The landscape they have built for our children brings to mind two images. One is a barren desert with no sign of meaningful life and no guide or directional markers in any direction. The other is nothing more than an ocean with heavy seas and high winds to toss about any craft in its wake. The real picture of our health stands as a backdrop; crumbling infrastructure, rotten structures, vanishing services, empty promises within bedraggled administrative, financial and medical structures. All are the results of war the Progressives are waging on the morals and spiritual truth our founders left us.

All scenes have a common thread running through them. The thread is the Liberal thought which has destroyed the engine, oars, and credible sails of this ship called America, meaning that we are adrift in a wild ocean swarming with danger. Enemies circle like sharks, and are in a relentless attack. All this and no one seemingly is competent enough to take the helm. It is a horrible picture of us: We have become a people that love so much easy living, loose morals and bad habits that we are too fat, too lazy, too ignorant or too confused to fight for our diminishing freedoms. As Joseph Farah confirms in *Taking America Back*, there is a mad sleep that has overcome the country: "Americans as a people have moved from freedom fighters to comfort lovers... it's time to wake up and realize where our present state of affairs is taking us. It's up to Americans to choose the kind of country in which we want to live."[7]

What has transpired in America to make people nod off and have others say these things today? From around the world, many are observing America; commenting on our country's decline, both as an inspirational model and mentor for other nations in business, in finance, in work ethic, in faith, as well as in world supremacy. In my lifetime, Americans were known as being self-reliant, hard-workers who believed unfalteringly in the freedoms guaranteed in the Bill of Rights and Constitution. However in recent decades, the setting has changed. An ever increasing and record number of Americans depend totally and nearly nonstop on government for their income, housing, food, medicine, and entertainment. Many of them are third and fourth generation welfare recipients. Added to this group are those not working, mostly from unemployment, those institutionalized, and government employees. A growing preponderance of persons has acquiesced to become a breed of robotic disciples in behavioral lockstep with liberal politicians in order to keep receiving their sustenance from the government via a federal trough.

This tragic dark-side of the American persona has surfaced through our government that appears like a devouring monster with an insatiable appetite for the money and blood of legal Americans. Undoubtedly and irretrievably the government has become a devouring authority, impacting the reputation of America's leadership on the world stage. Just in the last generation, we created and possessed the most ferocious weapons known in mankind's history: highly-engineered, capable of mass destruction causing most of earth's peoples to quake in their boots. Sadly that is the only image of American power left, and it too is being stripped away by the Liberal Progressive regime. Stripped away also is any remnant of moral authority. Though the liberals claim to hold that ground, they are the worst offenders of the entire population. Under our feet, our nation is stockpiled with an unending treasure trove of natural resources on and under the soil: timber, minerals, coal, oil and natural gas; all the while due to liberal doctrines, we seem like clueless children, wandering aimlessly as if totally impoverished. Like a home that has the lingering aroma after a wonderful holiday meal with the food consumed and all gone; the U.S. is now only living off our earlier brand from the first 200 years.

While our nation has undergone an unparalleled collapse, there has been a lone survivor amidst the rubble. Though that survivor is a minority, it is important to footnote that it is the remaining number of American workers, dwindling as they are, who sit atop the most productive workers in the world. They do this despite the ever increasing number and percentage of Americans living from the trough of taxpayer funds. Look as you may, there is no other positive to find. Oh, the Liberal canard is that things are so much better now than before. But the non-politicized data does not lie. Those data charts tragically reveal the carnage of record unemployment, disappointment, immorality, crime, and death which Progressive Liberalism leaves behind in their wake as they move through neighborhoods and institutions of our land. One microcosm; the American education system is failing miserably compared to the rest of the developed world. Except for advanced degrees in engineering sciences and technology, it has totally collapsed. This translates into suffering for American businesses as they look for qualified and educated workers. As education goes, so goes the country and so goes its business sector. Looking further into this education data for the past few decades, it shows American students place near or at the bottom of annual mathematics and literacy tests. Shamelessly at the same time they score number one in their assessment of self-esteem. Said differently, our students are not learning much, but they sure feel great about themselves. Sadly, this failure impacts even our prestigious advanced degree programs. The evidence shows the proof. Going deeper in the silo, even in our top engineering schools, like Cal Poly, MIT or University of Missouri-Rolla, over half the students are now foreign-born. As complaints are registered about this result, academia, and in particular engineering schools say they have no choice: competing in the engineering business requires more math skills than American high school students are learning.

Data does not lie. It has an undisputable character about itself, even while politicians build colorful charts trying to diminish the truth. The picture painted by the facts, absent the political scene, is not pretty, when you add to the data the currently very low birth rate of native-born Americans, especially those from productive families. The cards are all on the table: The future of America, if Leftists get their way, appears to be coming down to a struggle between a diminishing minority of hardworking producers who pay the freight for an insurgent, rebellious, and recalcitrant underclass of negligent tax-dependents.

To thoroughly understand the level playing field that these Leftists are systematically manufacturing, the following elements, tragic as they are, need to be viewed through a proper lens. First, there are a growing number of persons who are both dependent upon government and who are unwilling to take a responsible place in society. They see the U.S. only as the source of the another paycheck, rather than an imperial and economic force in the world that it has been; providing opportunity to turn hard work into dreams come true. Due to the fact of being poorly educated in history, they lack the proper context essential to associate America with those great nations of the remote past, Egypt, Greece, Rome, or Great Britain. Secondly, many of these dependents of the state, lack the ability to understand events on the world stage since they have a juvenile view of foreign affairs. Democracy must be presented in simpler terms; for example they must be told that leading wars of conquest is really similar to a 1960s cause; a crusade against racism, or one for human or women's rights.

Unfortunately, Liberals seem equally as deficient when in any position of leadership, such as that of diplomats; in fact they are the worst possible. Take for example **Hillary Clinton and John Kerry**: they have been the worst two Secretaries of State in American history. Case in point — Clinton made her now infamous statement describing American support for the catastrophic "Arab Spring" in Egypt and the Middle East. She called it a campaign to liberate women from oppression! That was her public explanation in spite of the fact that the revolutions in Libya and Egypt were financed and led for the purpose of empowering Islamists. The stated pre-war goal of the Islamists was exactly the opposite — the subjugation of women. A second revolution was required in Egypt to turn that blunder around, and it occurred within a year of the Muslim government takeover — the citizens rose up to overthrow President Morsi and the Islamist thugs, called the Muslim Brotherhood. The sad point is that the wicked Islamist regime was helped into place by our self-proclaimed brilliant Liberal leaders in Washington just a year earlier. It appears Clinton was either too confused to understand the situation or she was following a script which was given her. No other explanation fits, and either one of these explanations disqualifies her to be a leader in the Western World. Frankly, it speaks of treason from within.

Couple that Clinton incident with her 2009 incident which the former Secretary of State pulled off with the aid of her senior advisor Philippe Raines. That is when she (Hillary) gave the Russian foreign minister the infamous "Reset Button" with a very poor translation in Russian. It had the English word "Reset" on it along with the Russian word *"Peregruzka,"* but was printed in Latin script. That translates not to "reset" but to "overcharge."[8] Gaffes like this should be seen for what they are — an ineptitude, a Freudian slip, and a total misunderstanding of how to negotiate anything, which are typical of her; showing she is not the smartest woman on earth as Leftists claim. She is after all one of the modern icons which Leftists hold up as nobility, to whom we must bow and follow. She is nothing more than her predecessors, an empty icon who promises to bring further demise.

Also at the bottom of the diplomatic bucket is John Kerry. He proved his lack of grasp on diplomatic history remarking about Putin's entrance into Crimea following the Olympics. Kerry's comments of Putin sound like a person who is expressing shock that this incident occurred: "It's an incredible act of aggression; it is really a stunning willful choice by President Putin to invade another country." Then he added, "You just don't in the 21st Century behave in 19th Century fashion by invading another country on a completely trumped up pre-text."[9] Such remarks seem unbelievable coming from Secretaries of State with the United States. How dare Progressive Liberals like these two and others from their entourage sit in judgment over the hard-working people of this country who love freedom! How dare they make fun of great individuals like John Foster Dulles! Dulles was probably one of the greatest Secretaries of State in this nation's history. In effect, Clinton and Kerry have through their politics been "preaching" to us what they claim to be the supremacy of Marxism and Fascism. Then suddenly when confronted with Marxism, they say they just simply don't understand. According to any reasonable job description for leadership in diplomacy — they have disqualified themselves — as have all Leftists.

This liberal "parade of fools" continues its procession from the home of political follies: the commune called the Democrat Party Headquarters. The foolishness is that every action they take results in hasty and enormous growth of a federal government and plutocracy, focused on the executive and judicial branches. Their actions have diminished the once sovereign states to the level of simply administrative districts, much like those of the former USSR; bound by more emerging regulations which results in them doing only the bidding of their masters in Washington, D.C. But it is not all the Democrats fault; though they are certainly the major holder of blame. The Republicans are at times appearing to be worthless. On balance the two national parties appear at times to be only one infantile party of immature persons; like the old Katzenjammer Kids cartoon strip. They are always rebelling against the will and the authority of the majority of the American people. Because at times they have a singular focus of placating the special interest groups who hoisted them into office, they can together appear like the ancient and giant one-eyed Cyclops. Bottom line, this translates into the current scene: a majority of American taxpaying citizens have become disenfranchised. They have been reduced to nothing more than peons force to serve the caudillo and the junta, while the picture of power is ostensibly transferred to a welfare-dependent underclass, under the mounting chant of "social justice." The reality is that the bureaucrats, working in tandem with some very sinister business interests, monopolize actual power and control people and commodities, maneuvering them like pieces on a chess board. Even once very influential people are like slaves, without power under this regime.

Another tragic result of this liberal treason that has occurred is cultural. Historically, our nation has been proud of its distinct regions, each possessing separate and unique cultures, vibrancies, and identities, like the South, the Midwest Plains, the Eastern Seaboard, or New England. All have been overrun with social justice and commercialization merging the regions. Bottom line — 320 million people have lost their distinctive identities with the touch of government's magic wand of tragedy, which has blended the various cultures down to the lowest common denominator. Look back in time at one simple microcosm. Fifty years ago when I was a teenager, there was a distinct variance between Country music, which was especially popular on kitchen radios in the rural South and Midwest, and pop music of the cities of the northern and western states. There were many similarities, but vast differences of that day went beyond form and style. Country music at the time depicted the everyday lives of small town and rural folks, men and women from farms, with lyrics and tradition that were very openly Christian, and though there were some songs about marital infidelity, throughout it tended to maintain a moralistic theme. Today, all those boundary lines of differences have been bagged up together, like they were prepared for throwing out as trash. Music is devolving into a similar theme and sound, to the point that it is no accident that the totally repulsive pop star, Miley Cyrus, and her father, popular country singer Billy Ray Cyrus could now be joined to perform on stage, father and daughter; as sellers of shameless, humorless, dour and repulsive pornographic material that even a slightly healthy society would bag up and pitch out as garbage.

The thoughtless among us cheer such "presentations" but there has been a huge and often unseen cost associated with fusing America's different cultures together: like those of New England, the Midwest, the Plains States, the East Coast, and the South; another microcosm. The fusing, or bulldozing style of commercialization and politics has first of all, usurped local power and placed it in the hands of Hollywood, New York Elites, and of course the ever-present and liberal media. Secondly, a similar process was started at work long ago within academia; in the "self-proclaimed" intellectual centers of a couple dozen or so universities. They are highly visible in the media, usually Ivy League, and can often be heard decrying statements like, "Only a bigot could ever possibly be a conservative or a Christian."

Chapter One — Lost in the Land of the Lost!

These self-proclaimed "academic centers" have through bigoted attacks, pressured most of the remaining universities to stand in unison with them. In this self-proclaimed elite trance, only positive remarks about mainline liberal ideologies such as gay rights, environmental causes, global warming, immigration, and Marxism will be tolerated on campus. All the classic liberal progressive clichés used in the 1920s and 1930s *avant-garde*, are resurrected by the elites in the claim their lifestyle is one that is normal and conventional in today's society. The result today is that on campus, any conservative viewpoint is viewed as eerie, out of touch, and unacceptable. Anyone supporting traditional capitalism or free-enterprise ventures is viewed as an idiot.

The progression which Progressives have made across the segments and institutions of our society can easily be tracked by the destruction they leave behind, much like following the trek of a tornado. Their elitist homogenization of America has claimed other victims. Two that come immediately to mind are the arts and the alternate lifestyle choices, such as free love which was renamed and sold to the public by the academia elite as "normal." All of this is then protected on university campuses and in public institutions by a political "cone of silence" as it were. The stated rule, which cannot be violated, allows for only positive speech about the arts and the other lifestyle choices, thus branding them as "normal and conventional." That is of course, except when an artist is willing to produce "art" that is ludicrous, violent and more obscene than any earlier works in the Western world. Mentally deranged "artists," who obviously feeling like secular humanist missionaries in a Christian land, get government grants and gain national applause for making ridiculous and horrid manifestations; like putting a crucifix in a Ball jar filled with urine, and labeling it "Piss Christ." These "works" are then applauded by the Leftist media as "remarkable," "earth-shattering," or "boldly original" as great works within the art world. All the crude attention and conversation given by the media and academia in celebrating such filth and garbage is simply this: It is like putting ear rings and a pearl necklace on a sow, then parading her around as a specimen of cleanliness. In true terms, this is a microcosm of liberalism; Progressives on parade floats. They are demonstrating the hostile takeover of our country and its culture; evil over good. Such celebrations made over Ball jars speak loudly of the mockery and war against traditional values in our nation. What is angering is to see family's tax dollars going to support such exhibitions that are called art by the elites, as opposed to the wonderful still-life paintings of a few generations ago, which have all but disappeared from the conversation today.

The flag of cultural rebellion against sturdy moral codes and behavior has also been run up the flagpole in elementary and high school too. The current American character is so corrupt that parents acquiesce when young children declare their intention of changing their gender. For example, when little Bobby, through pressure of the homosexual acceptance that is taught, decides he will be known as Sarah now, wants to wear a dress, and demands the right to use the girl's bathroom in school. It is all part of a true story that is happening on the streets of the good ol'

US of A. While some parents do object, they do not remove their children from a school where the government not only protects such children's wishes, but teaches the same. In California, liberal legislators are trying right now to pass hurdles in their attempt to place on the ballot a vote for having transgender bathrooms for school children in public school.

There is a complete, wide-spread, and total breakdown, not just of the morals, but of common sense and normal decency. Everyone feels the right to be a law unto himself, and all standards for public behavior have collapsed. One cannot go out for an evening to the movie theater or most restaurants without the possibility of facing rudeness and indecency that would be inconceivable in a civilized country. In cities like Kansas City, St. Louis, or Los Angeles, minority teenagers, in contact by cell phone, periodically form flash mobs in shopping malls or in fashionable shopping area to terrorize patrons. A responsible people who feel free would not submit compliantly to these outrages that most Americans meekly accept. The media and intellectual elites have, of course, built, encouraged, and promoted this decline in every standard. A significant percentage of the population goes along with enthusiasm, and the famous "silent majority" complains, and then submits, out of frustration; they do not know what to do.

Many "responsible" factors have facilitated this crash, along with them has been the mobility of the American people — they move several times in their life spans. People grow up in more than one place, 2, 3, even up to 7 different locations during a working life time. Mobility encourages irresponsibility. When I was a young father living in Southern California, helping my wife to raise our two daughters, I noticed something startling about the culture within the cities of our neighborhood. Most of the people moved to that location from someplace else, such as the Midwest or northern plains, and most of them quietly took on a demeanor of getting away from regulations; that is the rules of the former society from where they had been. That usually involved getting away from the wishes of grandpa, grandma, the Church, and philanthropic activity. They threw off the restraints of their past culture. The average term of residence can be 7 years or less. In Ventura Country where we lived at the time, the average length of residence reported by the chamber of commerce was only 6 months! People have moved away from their families and friends, sometimes never to see them again. They cannot put down roots in that type of environment. That can breed contempt for good qualities.

So the mobility culture can breed contempt for societal, spiritual, and moral underpinnings along with its ethics. Suppose a married man with children is caught stealing products from his employer, selling them and spending it on women and drugs? In a stable society, this activity would be unendurable. In America, he only needs to get divorced and move to California, where he can start out fresh. When Scott Fitzgerald said that in an American life there were no second acts, he was wrong in his own time and completely out of bounds today. Serial monogamy encourages some people to lead multiple lives, completely oblivious of the damage done to the children. Just as bad, the American transients are losing the ability to make friends or establish a stable home. With their much-vaunted individualism and hedonism, they can be perpetual adolescents, incapable of leading adult lives. This is seen even in our political leaders who behave like spoiled children. Vice President Biden is continually coming out with inappropriate and silly remarks, and the President himself could not resist the temptation to do a "selfie" (take a picture of himself on his phone) at the memorial service for Nelson Mandela. The narcissism of the "leader of the free world" was on public display as he flew all the way to South Africa to make a fool of himself by talking about himself.

To denigrate our culture further, the progressive left continues to spin their phony tales of this country's founding and heritage, saying it was different from what really occurred. The truth is colonists came here to get away from the religious regime in England and to be able to worship as they wanted. But liberals want to liberate America from that true history; also its citizens from the Bible, teaching that religious freedom and Christianity were not facilitators at all in the settling in this country. A closer look at our colonization and migration patterns reveals a different story from the Leftist's tale of rootless individualists. In many cases, towns along the Atlantic seaboard and later in the Middle West were settled by family groups and something like whole villages; these settlers maintained their religious heritage without pause. There was rugged individualism when one or two had checked out a region in an area. That's when they sent word back and were soon joined by their kinfolk and friends. Going west, American frontiersmen were always rugged in their individualism like Daniel Boone, but they worked within the context of being men of family and community. The actual historical Boone became the patriarch of a settlement made up of his own kinsmen and good friends. That was duplicated by others throughout the west.

The key is these early American people were not reliant on the government, but they were not irrational enough to face the wilderness by themselves. They relied, out of habit and of necessity, on relatives and neighbors. One of the important points made by Alexis de Tocqueville in *Democracy in America* was the cooperative spirit and collaborative endeavors of the Americans he found in the early 19th century. When necessity arose or trouble came, de Tocqueville observed, Americans did not wait for the government to solve their problems: they banded together to build barns and stockades, protect the village, gather in the crops, and even, when faced with an outbreak of crime and violence, enforce justice by means of lynch law and the vigilantism.

So while "rugged individualism" is what many have correctly used in starting and building family businesses, it was what some might call "individualism in context" that made America great. That context was a loyalty to self, God, family, to local communities and states with an individual and collective determination to resist any growth in the central government that would encroach upon the rights of the individual or the communities. That is the significance of the 10th amendment to our Constitution, reserving all rights not specifically enumerated in the document to the states and to the people. Without the promise of this guarantee, the Constitution might not have been ratified, and even if ratified, it would not have endured. Modern leftist historians do not admit this, but in the very first Congress of the United States under the Constitution, James Madison told his colleagues the government could not endure without the guarantees enshrined in the Bill of Rights.

Rather than take a circuitous path, we beg the basic question, what in the world happened to America to begin its decay? Some American leaders believe the U.S. can pry itself free from its moral foundation and simultaneously teach people to live lofty lives while avoiding criminal activity. Or continue to print and spend money, reducing the debt with the commotion. Or bluff its way through international incidents, rattling their sabers, sending drones to kill wedding parties in Yemen, while stockpiling advanced weapons. All these activities lead down a dead end road. Character is not built on a nation's cache of technology. The Soviet leadership discovered that in a war with Afghanistan: it became a grave-yard. The same could be true for America as we stumble through country after country on our way around the globe. Also the morale fiber of the culture, and with it the foundation of solid morality, is its best defense against enemies; not missiles, not armed forces. The ancient Spartans knew this and were known for saying "Our men are our walls" when challenged on their lack of walls around their cities. History shows that a reticent and sycophantic people will never hold on very long to their kingdom. The answer in America is that the decomposition we are experiencing is not only the loss of individual rights and liberties, but also the moral fiber of the culture; also with it, the rights and liberties of our communities, cities, and states, whose authority has been methodically smashed by a national government practicing expansion, mercantilism and, at times, fascism ever since the 1860s.

As stated, this picture of our nation was begun years ago, near the conclusion of the War Between The States, when by our resolute legislative determination, our federal government started shredding parts of and eventually throwing away whole sections of our "operations manuals." I call them manuals because they are similar to the "How To" books accompanying a product, that reads, "Warning! Read before operating." The manuals, of course, are the Bible and the Constitution. These manuals were transferred to us by the founding fathers so that we could run this society and keep it "operational." Of course, these manuals contain instructions and guidelines for keeping society and lives on the firm ground of moral and ethical foundations. However, we jettisoned whole parts of these ethical, moral and spiritual guidelines year by year. Not surprising is the result. As our society removed itself from the foundation of moral conduct, it started behaving as wild animals on instinct; and has totally collapsed.

A few years ago, Pat Buchanan, began his *Churchill, Hitler, and the Unnecessary War*, by describing what happened to the United States and the other western empires of the twentieth century: "All about us we can see clearly now the West is passing away.... What happened to us? What happened to our world? When the twentieth century opened, the West was everywhere supreme. For four hundred years, explorers, missionaries, conquerors, and colonizers departed . . . for the four corners of the earth to erect empires that were to bring the blessings and benefits of Western civilization to all mankind. . . . Whatever became of these men? Somewhere in the last century, Western man suffered a catastrophic loss of faith — in himself, in his civilization, and in the faith that gave it birth.... That Christianity is dying in the West, being displaced by a militant secularism, seems undeniable, though the reasons remain in dispute."[10]

Whether you are a Christian, a Jew, or claim no faith: if you despise Christianity and Judaism, the Church, the Synagogue, and God Himself, heed this: the action we are now taking as a nation would rank very high on the stupidity meter — to be written as a scene for a movie sequel of "Dumb and Dumber." The difference: there is no humor in it, no reason to laugh. The determinate act has left us without any credible guidance and extremely vulnerable.

For the past half century, it became increasingly apparent to me that all of these descriptions are a part of an image that's being painted into a lasting portrait in oils of an "emerging America." It is being framed by our laziness, callousness, ignorance, and the progressive march of socialistic destruction. We seem to have an inability to even superficially learn the basics from our recent or distant past! Abandoning the Constitution and moral principles as found in the Bible leaving us with no trustworthy leadership, no compass or map for directions while simultaneously, under a planned, systematic and inside attack of treason — that's become our oiled impression on canvas.

You would have to be some sort of philosophical Rip Van Winkle not to see this treasonous battle plan of the enemy causing decline in our country now. The headlines from the past twenty years tell the tale of a death spiral. The challenge and infiltration being made to our long-standing institutions of faith and action (Evangelical churches, Jewish synagogues, faith-based groups like the Boy Scouts of America, etc.) has been followed systematically with Muslim attacks on Christians. Strangely those being attacked are been labeled as terrorists, with governing officials in Washington taking a lead in assaults on conservative citizens and businesses. It follows that there has been steady erosion and loss of our rights, higher taxes conjoined to less representation, increased political criminal activity, huge decrease in educational output, high unemployment, higher underemployment, edicts from the aristocracy which reflect more of a Marxist dictatorship than a representative republic. All these things added together produce a resulting scene of a nation in grave condition, which from a Christian viewpoint has lost favor with God. What has happened?! Not to be overly simplistic in the answer; we have moved off our moral and spiritual foundation.

Our nation was blessed richly at its inception with 'the best of both worlds,' a deep Judeo-Christian heritage from the Bible and also a borrowed cultural enlightenment from the British empire of Europe, minus of course the damnation of their tyrannical regime. "[T]he transplanted culture of Britain in America," wrote Dr. Russell Kirk, "has been one of humankind's more successful experiments."[11]

We seemed to have over time adopted more than a few ameliorations of Great Britain. Reflect on this: when elected First Lord of the Admiralty in 1911, Winston Churchill entered the inner cabinet and every nation recognized Britain's military supremacy. No nation could match her in the weaponry of the new century, the dreadnoughts of the Royal Navy, or great battle fleets.[12]

Any serious student of history could see this is practically a mirror image of America in recent decades. Mark Twain once joked, "the English were the only modern race mentioned in the Bible, when the Lord said, Blessed are the meek, for they shall inherit the earth."[13]

Today's portrait is not a welcome picture of life for the many who love the bastion this nation once was. Some yell that this is "just politics," like we've had through many decades between Republicans and Democrats. While data can always be interpreted to fit one's pre-conceived ideals, the real evidence though points to a strategy of sabotage and a deliberate, systematic plan of betrayal of goodness and of God, a cult-like legislative ambush on His principles, combined with people goose stepping in place behind these betrayers, with the result: God has lifted His hedge of protection for the nation.

As Ben Stein might say, "Is there anyone who would argue this? Anyone? Anyone?" The silence is deafening. Despite the silence, we have lost our goodness, we've leveraged our future against all odds, we've thumbed our nose at God, and we're proud of it. And in doing so have lost God's favor and are reaping His judgment.

Being a student of the Scriptures, of Capitalism, of history, sometimes reluctantly of Islam, and also the Marxist/socialist ideologies, it is clear that this war I referenced is absolutely raging against America. It is raging against goodness, against western civilization, and most of all against God and any set moral code. Like a giant forest fire that is not contained, the heat is intense from this war. It has multiple sides, or fire lines, that must be addressed to gain control. There's the political side, which is more than just a veneer, but certainly the surface side most people see, recognize, and focus upon. It is vocal there, with loud shouting matches, name calling, threats of nuclear options, headlines of hate speech, shouts of racism. All these activities come with TV lights, camera, and especially ACTION!! The TV cameras attract groups of maniacal liberal characters who always seek a television audience. Sadly, it is a show that many watch while our culture burns.

Though a veneer, it is a representation, however of deeper, more fundamental levels or sides to this war front. One is the burning of ethical standards. On another front the moral foundation is charred rubble. Another fire assaults our identity and what we are. Another flame is cutting through to the deepest level, burning the spiritual front, and our conscience of a once national faith.

Enter Stage Right — More Progressives

Battles in this long war pop up daily in our current society, which is incrementally seen more often now than in years past. The landscape seems to change by the hour. More aggressive are these leftists, setting their fires with ideological attacks on Christians, and those who merely hold to values of Judeo Christian beliefs. Because of faithfulness to the founders' principles of freedom, the enemy now brands them as, extremists; those who "cling to their guns and their religion." The attacks are almost always on the news-film at 11. It is common now to witness a "verbal public lynching," of the latest law-abiding citizen or group, being branded as "extremists," done openly and without shame.

Our political system is rife with the disease called progressivism accompanied with its usual criminal activities in the highest places, lying, and betrayals. It's in both major parties, as we've said, supporting un-American and Marxist ideas. Seeming void of any positive value, these politicians are just as our nation, unknowingly adrift. "The System" that has developed now appears to be geared to reward treasonous, socialistic activity, to reward those whose performance supports vilest, the farthest leftist initiatives and enemy ideas. It's interesting how progressives aren't progressive at all with regard to positive targets for a society, but rather regressive installing freedom-loving ideals. In order to get buy-in, they lie repeatedly, and end up as welcome as a fourth showing of a bad "B" rated movie.

Sixty or seventy years ago, this would have brought about public debate and eventual hearings against such activities for treason and un-American activities. Come to think of it, there were hearings. The House Committee on Un-American Activities led the initiative, full of interviews and investigations including public hearings to dig out, arrest, and indict the Communists of the day. By the way, the Democrat Party despised, ridiculed, fought against, but finally joined in at least on a lip service level the search for those Progressives who were Soviet sympathizers. The problem is that those Progressives, or Communists, were in the White House for several presidential terms in a row, including those FDR years. Their goal was to win more elections so they could continue to transform the nation to look more and more every decade like an eastern European nation. Eventually the search for Communists within our country was put behind us. For every decade since, the Democrat Party has ridiculed any of those who would try to root out socialists, Communists, progressives. They of course branded that search, "McCarthyism." Ever since that day they have associated that term as being un-American, in particular when challenging any Socialist, or Marxist idea of their party. Actually, it was not un-American at all.

Each campaigner should be provided with a job description, a list of 3-5 goals, or some number appropriate for their region, to be accomplished during one term of service. At least once a year, each incumbent would be subject to a performance evaluation. They would be graded publicly, with performance judged objectively. All results would be kept on a score card which would be publicly available.

This is called "pay for performance" in the private sector. It's all a part of a managed performance system through which "positive" results are planned, cultivated and brought to fruition. We should demand the same from our representatives. We need to move from what 'sounds good' or 'looks good', to what is "genuinely" good, and productive based on a model of performance with which the Constitution harmonizes, no matter the look. Someone asked if I was serious. I said, "Yeah, I think so, because with some tweaking, though it sounds comical, this would be a whole lot better than the unbridled riff raff that we have now."

If we were a factory and politicians were our outputs, what we have today is similar to a train wreck within the lines of production, which occurred many decades ago: it ran off the tracks, into a canyon, with carnage around and in the train itself. Yet, it is upheld as a perfectly tuned machine still operating smoothly, making marvelous impacts upon society. It is trumpeted as the originator of the joys of freedom and democracy around the world. The problems with the train however are numerous. One, is that it is not operating per plan any longer; it is not on the tracks and cannot travel. Two, there seems to be no person in or around the train qualified to engineer a comeback. Three, the most obvious problem is our "servants" in Washington, D. C., are not serving anyone except themselves any longer. As a group, they are self-serving, seeking a will of their own — the rest of the world be damned. Four, and probably the most obvious problem, is that the position of "politician" was never intended to be career position; these guys and gals were to be business owners, farmers, etc., who went to Washington and represented us who stayed in the workplace. There should never have been a college curriculum offered under the title of "Political Science." Making a career out of the job has caused many administrations and congresses to run off the tracks and wreck because they don't serve us any longer. They have forgotten why they are there.

My point is that experience alone should teach us there are no political solutions, only political destruction that is occurring. Who wants to trust any of these political characters after seeing what they do both during work hours as well as after dark, sometimes with some female intern in a suite overnight. The aristocratic and plutocratic lifestyle of those hired to represent us, is a part of why we have a national crisis. Many politicians have promised the moon in 'returning the goods' to our true heritage. It sounded good, the sound of hope and change always does, but they have failed miserably. Mostly, they've lied. That's because they either abandon any loyalty to their professed values, they forget they have an electorate back home, or they want to be popular and "liked" by television cameras. So they quit their boss — that is you and me. The lies that politicians have told are too many to put into a history book. However allow me one. The strangest ones were told by Obama, and he has had many that were bad, but the one which I am thinking about regarded an event at which he was speaking. He mentioned from the podium there were 20,000 people in the building who had gathered to hear him. One man's account who was there said the building was 90 percent empty. He said, "If there were 20,000 people attending, most of them were dressed as seats!" Why Obama has to lie about everything is beyond me — unless his whole life is a lie.

More importantly, he promised hope and change, but he misled Americans with that one. The hope appears to be only that which HE and progressives had hoped for and the change was the kind of change we did NOT want. Others politicians are crass and bold in expressing an "I don't care what the people want" attitude. They openly promote what benefits their own dreams in building a political career rather than represent their constituency. It seems obvious; they bring no solutions, only destruction.

Ignorant, Mentally Lazy and Proud of It

When viewing this hill we have "to climb" in accomplishing our mission of taking the country back, it is distracting and frankly embarrassing to see and hear the lack of knowledge or drive among the "average" people. There seems to be little to no concern about what is happening in America.

A picture that comes to mind, are interviews with numerous average people, done by Jay Leno in his man on the street interviews when he did the Tonight Show. He called his segment, *"Jay Walking."* Frankly, I hope these folks are not average. If they are, we are in shoddier shape than I thought. While on the surface Leno's segment was obviously designed for humoring his young audience, there is an underlying and numbing shock. To see the multiplicities of human bodies who do not have even the barest knowledge of or facts about our time or place in the world is terrible. All these "contestants" seem to dwell in a "knowledge desert," lacking even the most basic information about government, current events, English, simple math, or any geographical markers.

If we added to this, questions on any part of American history, I am certain it would be absolutely jaw dropping. Possibly these "contestants" have memorized Sam Cooke's song lyrics of several years ago which had the emotional and gripping line, " . . . just say you love me; that's all I need to know!" If that is what you believe, you are so wrong: That is NOT all you need to know!

Couple with that, and this is key in understanding the problem, the obvious lack of knowledge among our newer generations, on how America was founded, what the value system used to be without even mentioning the spiritual base upon which our posterity once; when I view the absence of all this, it can be so discouraging. I contend this lack of information and teaching has been nothing less than a progressive party process (aka, liberal, Socialist, Marxist, Communist), a deliberate attempt by our enemies to take us away from our foundational beliefs and morals, thus derailing our great nation. I recall an ancient text, "a house built on shifting sand will not stand."

To even mention that a war is raging in our streets, our institutions, our schools, usually is received by many with dead silence, yawns, or "who cares!" One person responded, "That's nonsense, where is this 100 year war?" If you watch and listen, you will see and hear the sounds of this war. Rarely on this front are there any military, but usually citizens, illegal aliens, news broadcasters, and/or politicians who speak the language of this war, some with more sly oratory than others. But in their words are found the real drum beats of conflict. They contain flavorful rhetoric about rights, immigration, abortion, or whatever can be used as a hot social topic at the time. There is propaganda galore. Certainly there's name calling. You will see and hear civil unrest among some of them.

Though military framework is often missing in the Progressives' fight against America, her moral values system and her people, the war goes on. Even if you choose to ignore it, or characterize it differently, that changes nothing. Denying the war exists, or ascribing to it another title does not make it disappear. It still exists and has for decades been a devastating war. But with the right metrics, you will begin to measure the trends and regular casualties. At the end of the day, I believe in my heart and soul this war is not merely political, but it is an apocalyptic struggle for the heart and soul of this country, our way of life, and our Christian heritage so rich with spiritual wisdom. You will often identify it around a fight for portions of our constitution, about which a loud clarion call has been heard lately.

Hopefully, through the historical markers cited, current events, and past experiences you will be helped to frame this war, its battle cries, its progressive nature, and how we all must prepare for what is ahead. Maybe it is for the first time that you will see how the front of this war has been waged in our nation, evil against good. At times in the past it has been waged with different tactics. Sometimes battles in this war use many different tactics to draw attention and a fan base. Tactics like marches, loud speeches or burning bras. Or maybe next time with public unrest, rallies and painted picket signs that scream for free abortion on demand. Occasionally, the enemy will trot out a weak or misguided pastor to plead for acceptance and tolerance toward Muslims, gays or illegal aliens. Interesting how pastors seem to have no relevance or credibility except for promoting a gay, abortion, illegal immigration, or pro Muslim cause, isn't it?! Or there is always the ever ready progressive politician seeking a TV camera, in front of which is 'turned on' a china teeth smile, fast rhetoric and a continuous but false promise to lower casualty rates. And this is all delivered in a fake panic, pushing for changes based on the claim of some economic or social inequalities created by current evil conservative policy.

A school shooting performed by a deranged liberal, whose victims become the facilitators for a progressive politician — all to brand uninvolved, innocent and law abiding citizens as being dangerous, "clinging to their religion and their guns." There is an accompaniment of liberal voices in the local school, university, or national news, all instructing that our society cannot stand for, or upon, the same principles we have had for over 200 years. Reason given: a tragedy occurred to a minority. Therefore it is demanded that conservatives must adopt change. It is an often remanufactured scene with "messengers of progressivism" demanding we be tolerant of them with whatever they are selling in their wagon that day.

Through some of these voices, policies, activities such as the bra burning, gay rights marches, etc., from whichever city it takes place at the time, there is a message of hate. I contend with that evidence, there is and always has been an ugly but recognizable tenor to the voice they use. This leads me to agree with a writer of long ago, who said that we really fight not against flesh and blood but against principalities and the powers of dark spiritual places.

After all we often need to see the blessings we used to have and the direction from which we have come, in order to see where we really need to go.

So in feeling this urgency to help blaze a trail, or to follow in others' footsteps where a trail has been blazed earlier, it's a goal to identify what has caused the mess we are in and to find the way out.

There is far too much pressure from evil, wicked, and treasonous sources in today's political climate with its conjoined media as a lap dog. Leftist organizations hold marches and rallies, all shown on their media, demanding change and pulling away from the respectable and appropriate moral stands this nation has taken through the years. Those stands were taken on a platform of Christian values by our Framers in years past. It is considered chic now for a progressive moderator to be heard saying, "We live in a post-Christian nation." What they mean of course is that Christian beliefs are not needed; they believe society has evolved to the current level that as humans we have become our own gods now. They have at times pressured legislators as well as judges to order change in law to reflect these beliefs. But those changes have not usually resulted in correct or right positions in our practices. They have resulted in horrible choices driven by angry individuals wanting to thrust their opinions upon all of us. And this has been done incrementally, progressively through the years. For example, abortion was first won on the basis of an emotional moment, for only life-saving cases for the mother or for rape. Soon it progressed to any abortion at any time for any reason, on demand. In other words, what was allowed once in an emergency must now be allowed for any reason, at any time, and paid for by tax dollars. It's not just abortion, but many other practices that have abandoned spiritual, moral, and ethical underpinnings.

Now, a deep unrest, which seems much like a bottomless pit, has been established in the country. People from older generations are "longing for the good old days" when there was an air of innocence to the nation, there were practices cemented in place that honored set morals and Christian values. When the church had a credible voice in the nation, there was respect for individual freedom, and we all felt safer. Instead we see an "in your face" type of tenor about the people of the country with liberals and progressives demanding further and further distance between where we stand relationally to the Biblical principles.

To this, the left will forever proclaim, well we have rights too. "Why should we be forced to follow what you want?" they will ask. I'll answer that question gladly. I often remember the days when I was the head of a business unit within a global corporation. One man asked to meet with me in my office to discuss his projects. The day and time was set for 1 PM, just after lunch. The day arrived, and so did he in my office at the appointed time. No more than a couple of sentences were completed, when he quickly noticed that my Bible was lying on my desk. It was my practice to read it during lunch or to have a Bible study with others during the lunch hour. He advised me that he was very uncomfortable meeting in a room where there was a Bible and that a change was required or he could not meet with me. He of course was suggesting that I acquiesce and be 'tolerant' of his demand. I replied and simply said, "Then leave."

To this day, I'm glad I did that. Tolerance goes both ways, not just the way of liberals, or progressives, with conservatives giving up rights, shutting up, or yielding the road so that the loudest person, the liberal, can be heard. Besides, when it comes to what we have witnessed in the last decade of the establishment attacking Christianity and those who follow that belief, I know that I'm standing on the correct side of history. Our heritage in this country speaks loudly about the features of the foundation that made us a great nation. We have a rich birthright of moral and spiritual documents around us as mainstays of our society, such as the Bible, which our founding fathers used to build the fabric of our "philosophical guidance system." Need I repeat myself by reminding opponents that this common belief in our heritage trumps all on-comers, and all naysayers, since Scripture and Christian beliefs were selected by the founders' genius to be the platform which would serve as a conscience for our country?

*"I am sure that never was a people
who had more reason to acknowledge
a Divine interposition in their affairs,
than those of the United States, and I should be
pained to believe that they have forgotten
that agency, which so often manifested during
the Revolution or that they failed to consider of
that God who is alone able to protect them."*

~ George Washington, March 11, 1792

Chapter Two

America's Secret War

REMOVE THE DREAMERS FROM HISTORY AND there's not much left worth reading about. Some people's dreams have led to the invention of wonderful creations, machines and devices, some of which changed the manner in which life is lived as they have served individuals and communities for years. Through similar positive dreams, a nation called America was born. It was the result of dreams, of many good men, about what could exist for the purpose of God and the good of mankind. Stories of the dreamers and the dreams they had are seen chiseled in stone and recorded in writings in many places.

Here's one such dream. What was perhaps the weirdest auction in history was held in Washington, D.C. in 1926, and it dealt with many past dreams. By a special act of congress, 150,000 old patent models of odd inventions were declared obsolete and put on the block for public sale. They had accumulated in the U.S. Patent Office since 1800. Some of them had passed under the eye and hand of Thomas Jefferson when he served as Patent Commissioner. One quiet, reserved and respectful man attended the auction the first day and reported that he looked over the conglomeration of sticks, wheels, glued wood and iron contraptions. His first thought was, "Wow, how imaginative can people get?!" One by one, these inventions went under the auctioneer's hammer. Some were clever, some were clumsy, some amusing... there was an automatic bedbug buster, and another was an illuminated cat to scare away the mice! One woman had invented a gadget which enabled a mother to churn the butter and rock the baby in one simple operation. There was another gizmo to prevent snoring. Though an old remedy, if you're interested in building a replica, it consisted of a trumpet reaching from the mouth curling around to the ear designed to awaken the snorer instead of the wife or neighbors. One man, obviously bothered with cold feet, had invented a tube with a mouthpiece so arranged as to warm his feet with his breath while he slept. There was also an adjustable pulpit for short preachers, which was operated by a release spring lifting it up or down. The auctioneer, in building up his sales pitch, told how one preacher in Ohio, who using the adjustable pulpit while preaching a sermon on the subject, "Where Will You Spend Eternity?" happened to touch the spring at the wrong moment, and down he went!

Now, to some folks, the sale of 150,000 old patent models would mean 150,000 laughs. But the quiet, thoughtful man who watched the hammer fall again and again and heard the auctioneer's "Going — going — gone!" said he just couldn't laugh. He knew he was looking at 150,000 broken dreams. He was thinking of the long days and nights of tedious planning, the sweat and toil, of the people who first imagined, then made, then vainly waited for the child of their brain to bring some fortune. Some had died in poverty, still trying to market their inventions; the history showed that. He was thinking of the thousands who were dreaming dreams that could never come true, and he wrote it up in a heartrending story under the title, "The Shattered Dreams of a Century."[1]

However, not all dreams are positive or good ones. Some have been sad, some downright sinister and evil. The mind, when dissatisfied, has enormous capacity for dreaming up illusions and evil. Take the dreams of Karl Marx, or Adolph Hitler, or Joseph Stalin, or Mao Zedong. The visions of each, one at a time, turned into nightmares for hundreds of millions who were taken in by the illusions of these so-called dreamers. Marx's dream of Communism ultimately cost over sixty-three million innocent people their lives through his disciple Joseph Stalin, and enslaved hundreds of millions of others as he and his evil apostles of his ideology tried to rule nations with a version of his dream. Hitler is usually cited by liberals as being a conservative who killed millions with his perverted ideology. They were right, except for one thing. Hitler wasn't a conservative in any way, shape, or form. He was a liberal, who had an evil dream of his Nazi Party, the national socialist party ruling government (Third Reich) ruling over the lives of every person in the nation, through nationalized healthcare, nationalized religion, and nationalized economy, all answering to him. Eventually in his nightmare, the world would kneel in front of him, and he would sit atop the rubble created by thousands of death camps. But his goal met its death during the Second World War.

Stalin had a correspondingly menacing nightmare that ran parallel in many respects, positioning Marx's Collectivist ideas on the Bolshevik foundation; that was to make millionaires of himself and a few chosen disciples who were executives in his régime, while impoverishing many millions in his country. He also murdered a huge segment of the population, approximately 43 million of them in building his hallucination. In total, form 1917 to 1987, about 63 million were murdered or starved to death in the Soviet Union. It's interesting that his quest in building his version of social justice, brought only misery to his and many other nations.

Mao Zedong fostered a similar fantasy and made it his own, shoehorning the Marxist doctrines into his own country. It is interesting to note, today many of the liberal progressives in the Democrat Party speak of Mao as being their model of a perfect leader. I guess that makes sense, since Mao put over 70 million of his country's citizens into their graves, starving many millions and murdering the balance! A few estimates of those killed ranged upward over 100 million. What a pal, what a guy, what a leader!

Chapter Two — America's Secret War

Tired of oppression similar to this, the early colonists in America grew tired and exhausted during the vain dreams and illusions presented by their supreme leader, King George III. He placed egregious taxes and extraneous duties upon our forefathers even trying to force a wonton and nationalized religion upon their shoulders. They finally decided they had had enough. They also decided it was time to determine their own political destiny: to live on the popular consent of the people rather than a despot. It was time to make a change.

It must have been a cold but exciting night when those few thousand colonists quietly gathered to watch the 150 among their number in full Mohawk warrior disguise, so that not even their neighbors would know who they were for certain, board three ships from London and begin dumping nearly 100,000 pounds of tea into the harbor.[2]

Judge Andrew Napolitano wrote describing this act and its consequences:

> "After the Boston Tea Party, in which American colonists disguised as Mohawk Indians dumped a fortune of tea into Boston Harbor in protest of British economic policies, Parliament passed a series of heavy-handed laws to punish the colonists for their insubordinate attitude. The laws, dubbed the 'Intolerable Acts' by the colonists, closed the port of Boston to trade, made public meetings illegal, and barred Massachusetts courts from exercising jurisdiction over British soldiers. . . . In response, the Continental Congress met for the first time in September, 1774 . . . [in] an unsuccessful attempt to smooth over by petition to King George, it met again in 1775. By this time the colonists were already fighting scattered battles against British soldiers. The Revolutionary War had unofficially begun. . . . But independence was not enough to see them through the times ahead . . . meeting in June 1776 had another purpose as well: to draft as John Adams wrote, 'the form of a Confederation to be entered into between these Colonies.'"[3]

Full-blown, evil illusions are present at some point in every generation. We are living in the midst of such an illusion where a rebellious liberal segment of the population want government running nearly every portion of a citizen's life. That is having the usual result: shattered dreams of peace-loving citizens. How we have moved from being a representative republic that touted individual liberty, freedom and a right to practice your faith the way you wanted, to today being a socialist regime having tyranny and government control, nosing its way into every cranny or corner of life as its brand, is startling! I contend that it is all part and parcel of a secret war with America that has been going on for many years. The war has the pulse of a recusant evil spirit driving the progressive adversary which fights us. This enemy, inches along claiming lives, dreams, wealth, and territory by the inch, by the foot, by the yard, by the acre, by the mile, a little at a time. It has now quietly gobbled up so much territory, so many lives, and so many freedoms to the point that we have moved from liberty to tyranny, evidence of this secret war in our country.

A microcosm of this war is seen in the train of our elected leaders. <u>Said differently, how did we move from having a President like Ronald Reagan to having one like Barack Obama in just over 20 years? Reagan was a man who loved and embodied individual liberty, who fought Marxism, Communism, and Socialism with a passion, and now just 2 short decades later, we have a person in that office, who embraces those very same enemy ideologies which Reagan fought. And the current occupant of the office embraces those enemy idioms as being the glorious pathway to hope and change in this country.</u> What has happened under Obama is that government has taken mega leaps in taking control of huge portions of our lives. Look in your kitchen. See the blender, refrigerator, coffee maker. They all have a "Federal Regulatory Stamp of Approval" upon it. However with that stamp of approval but hidden from view comes federal regulations dictating how each can and cannot be used. For me, a boy who is the product of the Baby Boom generation, it seems we have traded 'isms' with our old adversaries from decades ago. On a deeper ground, we have sold our profound spiritual heritage, our deep-rooted moral truth with the associated freedom, only to replace both with a trunk of progressive lies that steals freedom; that enslaves.

The reality is that America has been in a raging war with the adversary for many, many years: It goes even back to the beginning of our nation, as we battled Progressive "mercantilism!" In the decades which followed, this war has had different faces, bore different names, had different front lines, announced itself with different battle cries, but always the same enemy was behind the fleshy masks, having the same destructive goal — to steal our freedom, our individualism, to destroy our legacy, underpinnings, and heritage.

View the War through My 50+ Year Lens

Events occurring just in my lifetime provide a good microcosm. First of all, I acknowledge that my life has been politically incorrect according to liberals, for the following reasons. I do not come from the Northeast. I did not attend Harvard, Yale, Princeton, or any other Ivy League University. Lastly, I am not an attorney, nor am I a medical doctor. While some would say the lack of those three credentials disqualifies one from speaking authoritatively about history, saying so is a remarkably short-sighted comment itself.

However, the story of who is and who is not qualified does not stop there. We have a bad habit in this country; that is in discounting anyone who does not have those three distinctions in their life. Lacking such, one is generally counted as amateurish, having anything they say discounted, as if they have a mental disability. While at one time it might have been said that the best and brightest lived in the Northeast, the truth is, the country has moved on from that point in time. However, liberals are stuck in the past; still believing the Northeast is the center for thinkers

Chapter Two — America's Secret War

in America. Why has the Northeast, and in particular New York, pushed the liberal mantra on the rest of America? As recently as 1941, 1 out of every 18 Americans lived within New York City. There are places to live which are as good as or better than Cape Cod, NYC, or Washington, D.C. These are places where people actually wear shoes and speak English fluently. Places where math and science are taught and learned. These are places where citizens have a firm moral and educational foundation under their feet; they can actually do critical thinking. That is the one true credential needed to understand both history and the world in which we now live. That said...

Los Angeles was my birthplace; a part of the postwar baby boom, with Southern California remaining my home for the first seven years. My parents were blue collar. My father a real country boy whose pedigree mostly rotated around his military experience, being an army sergeant, serving both Generals Omar Bradley and Anthony C. McAuliffe before, during and after the Battle of the Bulge in Europe during WW II. My mother came from polished parents, with her mother, my grandmother, attending finishing school as a young lady. And so I grew up in South Los Angeles. My parents moved back to Missouri to their hometown when I was young. In that dichotomy my childhood was spent during the formative years. Instead of Ivy League, my college education started in a Missouri University, toured through a Seminary and on to the California University System for work on my masters.

By my earliest recollections, growing up in the late 50s offered a life that was absolutely exceptional. It was a great time for America, arguably the greatest decade the nation has seen, despite what the Leftists try to say today. The economy rolled along. I have rich memories from the decade — one was when my father took me to the May Company during the Christmas season one year. That visit turned out to be my personal version of the opening scene from a Christmas movie. My nose, lips, and the balance of my face were obviously pressed up against the window watching the electric trains from Lionel run the various tracks, on various levels and through several tunnels that had been built. My mind still contains that personal movie, seeing the trains running on three different levels, going in different directions, which was pure excitement for a boy of my age. What a time to be a young boy in this country.

Compared to 21st Century America, there was an innocence in our nation in the 50s, even to some degree in cities like Los Angeles. Innocence was certainly in full bloom in smaller towns where people seldom locked their houses; fear and crime in many more parts of this country seemed to be in the rear view mirror like in my little town. "Blue laws" ruled; companies were closed on Sundays. In high school, some students drove to school. Many drove pickup trucks. Nothing unusual about that. What was unusual were the gun racks win the back window. Yes, there were rifles in the racks; and yes the guns were even loaded. What's even more amazing is the trucks were almost always unlocked. Sometimes with a friendly weather forecast, the windows were left rolled down. Nobody bothered the trucks, or the guns, or the tools in the back of the trucks. There were no school shootings. There was no theft. There were no worries about loss of property or possessions because there was a healthy respect for another's property and life. Oh, and yes, my friend, Lyndell, left his keys in his truck all day long. Sounds like Mayberry, but it actually happened that way. The reason why life was good? Because there was still a "national conscience" as I call it, certainly among the middle and lower classes. That conscience was often presented and guarded by local churches and synagogues — they spoke loudly to us and for us to "do unto others as you would have them do unto you." The reason why life was good: because while the war on America seemed to be raging in portions of our larger cities, in small towns it was not even in its infancy. It seemed the war against Middle America had not yet reached the city limits or even the outskirts of most small towns.

However, as the 60s came into view at the top of the hill just ahead, changes in our culture were starting to occur. There was a space race. And the launch of Sputnik in 1957 put the Soviet aggressors in the lead. There was also an arms race: America was engaged in a cold war with the same Soviets. There was a huge difference between the brands of those two nations. Fear ran through small towns and farm houses of this country the same way the news of a school shooting or the thought of an outbreak of Ebola does today. We feared the Soviets, who every May Day paraded their large ICBM's through Red Square in Moscow. Each was rumored to have the capability to reach even the interior fertile farm lands of the Midwestern plains with their nuclear payloads. Weekly air raid drills at school were routine and said to prepare us for their coming attack, and the feeling in the air of our country was "one of anxiety." Many families of this era were busy building lead-lined bomb shelters. Fear of and hatred for these foreign Communists was the buzz of the small town coffee shops around the country. Comedians and talk show hosts were busy with their patriotic speak and the imagery of these Communist missiles, in attempts to comically or realistically deal with the uneasiness most folks felt, having lumps that were rising in their throats. For some, every day brought new fears and grim visions of what might take place.

I remember as if it were yesterday, George Carlin appearing on "The Johnny Carson Show." It was 1963 and George was in his stage character, "Al Sleet, The Hippy Dippy Weather Man." He had a comical weather forecast (All weather forecasts are comical, but I digress . . .) but Carlin's routine was like nothing most of us had ever seen. It went something like this, "Hey Babe! What's happenin'?! Que Pasa! I know some of you were surprised at the weather over the weekend, especially if you watched my show on Friday night. There were some terrific storms. I'd like to apologize for the former residents of Ardmore, Oklahoma. Caught them napping! Tonight's forecast: Dark. Continued dark throughout most of the evening, with some widely scattered light towards morning. And I see that the radar tonight is picking up a line of thunder showers which runs from a line 9 miles north, northeast of Punxsutawney, Pennsylvania along a line and 6 miles either

CHAPTER TWO — AMERICA'S SECRET WAR

side of a line to a point 8 miles north, northeast of Chichaqua, New Jersey. [There was a slight pause for a moment, followed by the next statement.] However, the radar is also picking up a squadron of Russian ICBMs. So, I wouldn't sweat the thundershowers."[4] Of course, this was received with long, loud and raucous laughter from Johnny and the entire audience.

Two years earlier, Rod Serling saw an opportunity for urgent social commentary and rushed an episode into production that commented on prevailing anxieties.[5] In this episode of The Twilight Zone called "The Shelter," neighbors in a typical suburban bedroom community are meeting at a neighboring doctor's home for a birthday party. Suddenly a Civil Defense announcement is overheard stating that unidentified objects have been detected heading for the US. As the panic ensues, the doctor locks himself and his family into his back yard bomb shelter. All the previous hospitality and fun are replaced by vocal anger, shouts of racism and other pent up emotions which begin to boil. The guests want to be in the shelter but there is room for only three, the doctor and his family. The once friendly neighbors won't accept rejection, and they begin breaking down the shelter door with a makeshift battering ram. Just as they break the door in, destroying it, a final Civil Defense broadcast is heard stating that the objects have been identified as harmless satellites and there is no danger present. The neighbors dramatically apologize for their panicked behavior. The doctor is left with the poignant wonder if they have in effect destroyed each other without any bomb or missile attack being present.[6]

Both Carlin and Serling were openly addressing the nation's anxiety over this very real threat of attack during the cold war with the Soviets. They just addressed the fear in different ways endeavoring to ease the tension.

What we did not realize at the time, was that while this visual and loud frontal assault with its threat of missiles was being played out over and over on TV programs and national news, there was a second front to this war that our enemy had launched against us. It was a secret and quiet front; incremental. I guess you could say it was "progressive." As the fog of the threat from the Soviet missiles lifted, it became clearer each day that a second war, or more realistically, a second front of the same war, was entrenched and was in full throttle on American soil. The communists, the leftists, the progressives had infiltrated our schools and university campuses with their puppets who were teaching the tenants of Marx, Lenin, Stalin, and the Soviet regime.

For me, all this crystallized later by personal experience into a clear picture, when in 1977 while attending a part of the California State University System near Los Angeles. A class entitled "History of the Americas," was offered by the school and facilitated by a foreign-born professor, who as it turned out, daily expounded propaganda about "the perfection of the socialist and communist government," model, in places such as Cuba, where Castro was in charge.

The professor celebrated, expanding a daily diet of his diatribe stating there was no doubt the communist movement provided the most perfect setting for everybody in that country. On a map of the Western Hemisphere, he used his pointer going from country to country, citing dictators such as Manuel Noriega, Hugo Chavez and others; calling them great and wonderful world leaders. Of course, I recognized Noriega as being nothing more than an international thug. There was no question about Castro's thug qualities. But the lecturer stuck to his story of the greatness he saw in each of them, especially Castro. Several times he referenced Cuba again, contending its medical and business base as a prototype of a government system that was far superior to anything in the United States. Through his harangues we eventually learned he grew up in Cuba. He did eventually reveal himself to be what he called "card carrying communist."

After about two weeks of this dribble, I could not stand it any longer, and being the oldest member in the class by 10 years or so, asked aloud the logical question, "If Cuba is so wonderful, what are you doing here?" The class roared with laughter. A few classmates verbally affirmed their agreement to the question. I noted the professor had no comeback.

This war which the Left has waged on America is in the arenas of art, music, books, and even a study of war itself. These trappings are used because they are avenues into the minds of the youth, a way of educating them. This matters because as in art on canvas, in paint and in photographs they say something about who we are, what we think, and what we believe. Because these things are public, children see them and have takeaways from them.[7]

As Bill Bennett explained it, "The battle over culture reaches beyond art, music, poetry, photography, literature, cinema, and drama. The broader issue has to do with a growing realization that over the past twenty years or so the traditional values of the American people have come under steady fire, with the heavy artillery supplied by intellectuals. This all-out assault has taken its toll. In our time, too many Americans became embarrassed, unwilling, or unable to explain with assurance to our children and to one another, the difference between right and wrong, between what is helpful and what is destructive, what is ennobling and what is degrading. The fabric of support that the American people — families especially — could traditionally find in the culture at large became worn, torn, and unraveled."[8]

Liberals also used war, old wars to try and teach their twisted left-wing lessons which disagreed with America and American culture. Now about those our old foes, like Hitler and the Nazis, this nation's conservatives are branded as being "Nazi-esque." Conservatives are called right wing extremists. The progressives don't understand who the Nazis were and they surely didn't learn the right lessons from the war with them. Liberals learned erroneous lessons from the history of Nazism; practically all they claimed to learn from that history was wrong.

Lesson One as they teach it: Conservatives are evil, not merely wrong. The Nazi movement is labeled as being "right-wing." Every conservative has undergone character assassination by being compared to Hitler or Nazis. The labeling has gone on so long by the liberal media, people now believe it. That is why the Conservative Right is often branded as Fascists or Nazis. Vast numbers of people actually believe if conservatism prevails, Fascism will follow. The exact opposite would occur.

Nazism was not conservative or right-wing — certainly not in American terms. It could not have been. Conservatism stands for less government, not more. If anything, Hitler and the Nazis were left-wing; "Nazism" was and still is an abbreviation for National Socialism. Nazism was sui generis; it was everywhere. It was radical racism combined with totalitarianism claiming to be neither: that is Liberal Progressive. Racism has been a doctrine that historically and sadly has been embraced by individuals from both the left and the right. But racism is practiced so publicly by the Left, yet has been redefined by the Progressive Left to apply only to conservatives. That redefinition is the only application of the word that is heard in the media today. The association of Nazism with right-wing politics is one reason many Jews loathe the conservative right. In the Jewish psyche, to fight the Right is to fight emergent Nazism. But it is all built on a lie presented by the media. The lies of the Left have developed from their bad history lessons.

Lesson two from war with Germany is directly tied to their first lesson. The Progressives conclude that since Conservatism is "Right" on the political continuum and is evil, therefore because Nazism was evil, it must have been conservative. Their conclusion is this: The Progressive Leftist Way must be beautiful and noble simply because they oppose the Right. The Left sees itself as fundamentally beautiful and noble because they preach social justice; a battle for culture. In their circular thinking, anyone battling Nazism has to be a magnanimous soldier of truth.

Lesson three becomes the coefficient of the first two lessons. It simply states: Any group that loves nationalism is evil, and the Leftists loathe nationalism. Their reasoning goes this way: Since the Nazis committed their crimes in the name of nationalism (race-based nationalism, is what they did); thus nationalism must be stopped. Nationalists wave flags. The Leftists hold total contempt for citizens who wave the flag. They made a pejorative term out of the phrase "flag-wavers." Merchants trying to sell flags in liberal neighborhoods on holidays would go broke — you can tell who's who by who flies the flag on holidays. The trauma of World War I had already killed nationalism in much of Europe. Liberal reasoning says that whatever is good in Europe, especially in Eastern Europe, is good for America. World War II put the total kibosh to nationalism for Liberals — that war drove the last nails in the coffin.

The Fourth lesson gleaned from the Nazis by the Progressives: Do not ever judge another culture; it is evil to judge. They think it should be illegal to make statements about another cultural group. (Strange how they drop this lesson when they speak about believers in God.) They surmise all this from observing the Third Reich and Nazis in how they judged Jews and a few other ethnic groups as being worthless and inferior. Leftists declare they will not tolerate judgments of others. But of course, we are told we must tolerate their judgments. In the post-World War II world of the left, all cultures are equal, it is just the Communist, Socialist, and Muslim cultures which are more equal than the others! To say that the contemporary Islamic world, or that black inner city culture, has serious moral problems compared to the culture of the Midwest; that is a comment that would be labeled as racist, because the Nazis did the same. For the left, the only cultures one may judge adversely are white Americans, "religious" Jews, and Christians. The rules don't apply there.

One last lesson, Number Five: Liberal Progressives learned from the war that pacifism should be embraced as an ideal. Wars teach many lessons, but the most obvious one is to fight evil. Instead of learning to fight evil, the Left believes that fighting evil is evil. According to them, it is far better to appease an enemy, by giving them chunks of land. For example, notice in the Middle East, it is always up to Israel to give up areas of land to appease to a group of "Palestinians," or neighboring nation. Never is it required of another neighboring nation to give Israel land to seek a peace accord. We have two generations of young Americans who have been taught such garbage by the Left. The typical Leftist believes this: if our nation destroys its weaponry, disarms itself and waves a white flag, a utopian atmosphere will suddenly appear upon Earth, with other nations loving America. However, that is not only horrible judgment; it is a fatal mistake. Leftists also believe and teach that conservatives love to destroy kill people; they say that is why conservatives always want to develop more deadly weapons, bigger bombs, faster and deadlier fighter jets. They fail to understand a very elementary truth: Conservatives hate war as much as anyone. We want the most powerful weapons to be at our disposal as a deterrent hoping that we never need to use them. Deterrents are necessary since every century seems to produce a despot or dictator who must be either held in check, or put in his place. Think about it: if decent nations had not been militarily prepared as they were, and were not willing to use that might against Hitler, the Nazis would have conquered all and many millions more "non-Aryans" would have been enslaved and murdered.

Leftists in America today and those in 1930s Germany did not learn the "correct lessons" from the war. The lesson they should have learned is that the best defense against evil is power — power that is restrained but ready to roll when needed to obliterate the enemy. One can still hear cat calls when threatened by a foreign power, to unilaterally give up something, even real estate rather than fight. Liberals think enemies respect you when doing that. Historical truth shows the opposite, how those nations are now dust; they were conquered by the aggressor. Think Crimea. Think Russia. Think the Ukraine. Then think about how Obama and the Leftist regime in the U.S. convinced the Ukraine to give up its military defense. All the supposed wisdom of the Liberals turns out to be not wisdom at all. Giving away the nation's position of power does not bring peace in our crazy, mixed up world. It only invites disaster.

Good lessons can be learned from World War II, and from many other wars, but the Liberal Left did not learn them. They did not come close to learning; they seldom do. The correct lessons from that war and the instructions of that day, will only come to those who open themselves up to the truth, the whole truth. That means not looking at enemies, at life, or at history through the rose-tented lens of a current day American Socialist, a Marxist, or Communist.

George Santayana's famous precept applies here, but it should be edited slightly to include the Liberal, Progressive and Leftist crowd of today. It is those who learn the wrong lessons from history who are condemned to repeat it over and over again.

"A government is only to be supported
by pure religion or austere morals.
Private and public virtue is
the only foundation of republics."

~ John Adams

2nd President of the United States

Chapter Three

The Deception of Liberalism that Led to This Darkness

"There are two ways to be fooled. One is to believe what isn't true; the other is to refuse to believe what is true." — Søren Kierkegaard

IF TIME GOES ON, THE MEN and women who write the history books of our generations will have to include some chapters on the darkness of our deception, the lies we listened to, the mirages we believed in, and especially the treason which occurred from within our walls, here in America. They will put us down, not as the realists we imagine ourselves to be, but as at least a couple of generations of people who have totally dodged reality and responsibility. They will say we would not believe in unpleasant facts until they exploded in our faces; they will say we lived cheerfully in a world of make-believe and listened to illusion and false prophecy so long that it got into the grey matter in our heads. When they talk of the 1900s and the early parts of the 21st Century, they will talk of the secret war we ignored, about how many Americans were simply asleep to what was happening, about our isolationism, about paralyzing fear, about Mao Zedong, about Neville Chamberlain, about Adolph Hitler, about Joseph Stalin, our Pearl Harbors, our Battles of the Bulge, our Munichs, our 9/11s, our Barack Obamas, our PLO attacks, our Muslim Brotherhood attacks, our Fort Hood massacres, our Benghazi's, our NSA spy scandals, the battles of our war that crept up on us, with everybody meeting the immediate dangers with "too little, too late."

To illustrate the deep sleep that's overtaken this nation, step into a restaurant and observe a booth or table where a group of, let's say four people, are seated. Chances are excellent no verbal conversation will be occurring — the only communication will be the text messages that these four are sending to people outside the restaurant. The bigger point is this: so much of the technology today is used as an escape from the realness of the world in which we live. Facebook, Twitter, Linked In, can all be good tools, but they are usually used to ask the simple, wasted question of "What's up?" They are at times a distraction, or more often a drug to pull us from the stark realities of life into an escape; becoming as it were a six-pack or case of electronic adult beverages. These unreal worlds or escapisms they create are not good places in which to dwell for long periods of time or a rational place from which to deal with problems in life. The best forms of social media for these four persons in the booth is to put their hand-held devices aside for an hour, look into each other's eyes, listening and talking to each other. That is the original social media.

Once focused on our subject, it will become apparent that this secret war in our country has been raging much longer than just my lifetime. Go back further in time, to the turn of the 20th century, and you will see the battlefield and armament of this war, through a defining lens in a different age. What's visible is that we've been fighting this same enemy all throughout the entire 20th century. They all are wearing the same basic names; Marxists, Socialists and Progressives. They have the same agenda. But the faces, names and battle cries were different then. You will see that it was a time of prodigals, of progressives doing treachery and of propaganda all rolled up together seeking a perfect time for transforming America into a very dark place. But let's not just be spectators, go back with me to see, smell the ravages, and feel the heat of the battles waged against our way of life and the American dream.

The times, they had 'been a changin'. The year — 1900. It was an age of hope as the new century rolled over on the calendar. A great restless hunger was eating at the hearts of men, the kind of discontent that just won't let you be. And this appetite was transitioning people all around the cities, the suburbs, and little bergs of America! Look at some of the events that led to this sociological itch.

Charles Darwin had brought forward his theory of natural selection in 1838. That theory had been kicked around for years and was starting to take hold politically by the turn of the century, though many premier paleontologists had said earlier it lacked credibility and would not last as a viable theory to the year 1900. Even Darwin admitted the fossil record did not support his hypothesis. People were starting to question their origins and their basis for managing life and his theory seemed fresh and inviting. Two Scottish Scientists produced a scientific paper/theory in 1883 that was revolutionary and ran contrary to evolution's precepts speaking of the Biblical creation of the world. The first wave of the Industrial Revolution 1865-1900, with all that mechanization, had just drawn to a close. Machines were now making more clothes and more products than the world had realized possible. The assembly line was beginning to be a gleam in Henry Ford's eye. The Wright Brothers had planned carefully and were just about to take off on a wing and a prayer at Kitty Hawk. "And William Blake's picture of the little man standing at the base of a ladder which reached into the clouds, with his arms stretched toward the sky and yelling, "I want, I want," said all that needed to be said about this time period. An old copy of *Fortune Magazine* from that era had a full page picture of a boy looking up in the sky, a model plane in his hand, and a terrific gleam in his eyes. The caption read, 'The promise of the Sky.' This said it all. People were wanting something, a promise of something bigger and better."[1]

Chapter Three — The Deception of Liberalism that Led to This Darkness

Liberal Progressives had a hunger too: To feed the greed and anger of people's souls. They did so with a campaign slogan that repeated in essence, "Capitalism will not deliver!" It was definitive class warfare. These liberal progressives preached socialism as being the answer: the Sandman who would bring the dreams to fulfill life for decades to come. Implied if not openly stated by their ideologues was that all you will ever want comes by government; its oversight, ownership and provision to keep the playing field level and fair. So they began a campaign to strike out at greedy capitalists that through the decades started to take hold. These progressives promised the sky, but could never deliver. The fulfillment of the promises they made were always just out of reach, requiring another day, another dollar, another new tax. The theory of Marxism was to the progressive mind a fact that brought a favorable solution to society, much like Darwinism is and was to government education. **But note this: the fossil record of past collectivized nations has never produced a trace of success; not one recorded incident, rather only misery, failure, and death of millions.** Still the liberal progressive mind hails Marxism a success, verbally blasting anyone who dares challenge them.

"There's a sucker born every minute," I think is the way P. T. Barnum put it. For anyone who bought the lies and idioms preached against capitalism knew not what they were into until it was too late, and alas, they had been suckered. As cons go, what the Progressives do is a beautiful fleecing. Lots of promises; a lot of bait and switch; with just a glimpse and smell of what good might come your way, if you just keep following, only to see your life in a rut leading to destruction. A scene from the movie *Silverado* tells this legend. A covered wagon is driven by a couple with all their worldly goods aboard. As the wagon passed by, headed west, in tow are two pigs (the suckers) closely following a pan of feed dangling from the back of the wagon, swinging according to the bounces from the ruts in the road on the wheels; the feed always just out of reach of the continuous and growing hunger.

Oh, the carrot or feed trough which is hung in front of all us suckers. A tiny tax increase here and another there, both accompanied with the promise of more fairness, time ticks by slowly with a few more subtle vicissitudes made to the rules, all the time accompanied with the appeal to follow the emotional hunger inside each of us, and to do so by following the promise of ultimate satisfaction which is presented by a growing government in the covered wagon. With subtle tax and monetary changes happening beneath the feet that go unnoticed, liberals teach us to just keep swallowing their commitments and following the dangling feed trough down the road. Before you know it, the landscape has changed so much, and with it our lives, to the point that, like the pigs in the movie, you find yourself as being as a part of the omelet.

Following their own thirst for more power, Progressive officials have become more vocal demands for control in your life and most importantly to them, your money. Unfortunately their plan has taken hold as more and more people follow the government wagon with the dangling feed pan. Changes came in bits and drabs, very slowly, like watching the hem lines in skirts go up over decades. One such "bit and drab" used by progressives was the income tax, a perfect microcosm of their evil deeds. It started out so small but oh, how it has grown over the decades to claim the lion share of any income.

Anniversaries can be wonderful events, at least some of them. At this writing, we are standing on one now, the 100th anniversary, or century mark of important legislation, enacted in 1913. It is the income tax, or Revenue Act of 1913. Accompanying the act were several other liberal ideas handed down to us by Woodrow Wilson, one of the worst and destructive Progressives during the 20th century.

As we travel back seeing this legislation in action, one can almost smell the cigar and pipe smoke floating among all those wool suited liberals as they applaud the passage of their accomplishment, one of the pillars to support their overall agenda. Most alluring about this legislation to the public was that it came with the solemn promise that the law was just temporary (that is laughable) and that the tax was insignificant because it would never go above 1% of income for most folks (that is laughable too). Back up, clear the Prince Albert smoke from your lungs and examine this "insignificant" legislation. The incomes of couples exceeding $4,000, as well as those of single persons earning $3,000 or more, were subject to a one percent federal tax.[2] There was a sliding scale surtax of up to 6% for highest income folks with over $500,000 annual income.

Revenue Act of 1913			
Normal Income Tax and Additional Tax on Individuals			
Income	Normal Rate	Additional Rate	Combined Rate
0	1%	0	1%* Bottom Marginal Rate
$20,000	1%	1%	2%
$50,000	1%	2%	3%
$75,000	1%	3%	4%
$100,000	1%	4%	5%
$250,000	1%	5%	6%
$500,000	1%	6%	7% top marginal rate

* There was an exemption of $3,000 for single filers and $4,000 for married couples. Therefore the 1% bottom marginal rate applied only to the first $17,000 ($374,400 in 2010 dollars) of income for the single filers, or the first $16,000 ($352,300 in 2010 dollars) of income for the married filers, after the exemption was taken.

Camouflaged, was the operative word "temporary" used to pass the bill, "just to make up for the shortfalls of tariff duties," they said — so all believed it was going

CHAPTER THREE — THE DECEPTION OF LIBERALISM THAT LED TO THIS DARKNESS

to be just short-term for the years 1913, 1914, and 1915 only. In retrospect, they had to present this tax as a temporary act, since their earlier attempt to tax all Americans on every revenue stream, income from dividends, interest, and rent, by way of The Wilson-Gorman Tariff of 1894 had failed — it was declared unconstitutional by the Supreme Court. The Progressives were bitter but learned from that setback that you cannot get the whole ball of wax you seek with the first attempt. And besides, if you don't get all the money you want, change the law and tell lies, so you can get more of what you want. Half a pie is better than no pie. So they did just that. The Sixteenth Amendment was ratified early in Wilson's regime, February 3, 1913. "Start smaller to avoid the same objections next time and grow it slowly," they tutored disciples.

Taxation did have a very small start as most progressives learned to do with their ideas, with less than 1% of the population paying any income tax during those early years. This government act of reaching in your pocket while wearing a smile and a shoeshine has continued to expand each decade since, to grab for larger, and larger, and larger, and larger, and larger amounts of cash. Stretching a little more each year to eventually become a model of which even Karl Marx would be made to smile in an approving manner. It took 70 years for the tax to mushroom from 7 percent to 94 percent for those top brackets. (For those who are math challenged, 94 percent means you got to keep 6 cents of every dollar you made.) It then took a Ronald Reagan in the 80s to roll back the high tax rates from 80 percent of income taken, back down to 28 percent. Over the years, taxes have become equal to the mythological Kraken, having long tentacles to reach every victim or city that is in near proximity to the ocean. As Progressives wanted, the tentacles reach the bottom of even the deepest pockets, destroying more liberties and lives along the way. In modern-speak, their taxes have become like zombies which seem to be around every corner in current television shows. A microcosm of who they are for sure! A clear picture of how progressives and liberals really work! One step in their direction and your life becomes a slippery slide, with money being bounced out of your pockets at every turn and at every bump on the slide.

Over the years, inch by inch, yard by yard, mile by mile and year by year our tax rates and the number of them we pay have multiplied over and over exponentially. The scene of Maxwell Smart comes to mind, while he fights his arch enemy Norman Saint-Sauvage who possesses a dreaded "clone machine." Saint-Sauvage would run in one end of the machine; out the other end would come 2, 3 or 4 of him; exact copies or duplicates of him exited to battle Smart! That is the picture of taxes I see, all cloned by those who spend other people's money. Today, after decades of their lobbying, deal making in back rooms, and parading suckers in front of cameras pleading for increases in taxes to buy meals for the underprivileged, clothes for the poor, medicine for those who cannot buy, and checks for those who wish not to work. All was built into programs to the point now taxpayers buy cigarettes and cell phones for the poor, condoms for the children, or a Cadillac for some peon; all the while taxes are multiplying. Collectively they go well beyond 60% for many tax payers, when you add together income, gas, highway, vehicle, personal property, year-end business supply, sales, real estate, rent, interest, dividends, payroll, gift, estate, tariff, duty, inheritance, death, luxury, school, excise, aviation, inheritance, service, shipment of goods, farm, animal, farm animal, farm equipment, medical device, medical premiums, as well as consumption and value-added taxes! And today when things are so tough for most individuals and families, with national spending and debt at record levels, the ONLY solution these same progressives can offer is to — you guessed it — raise taxes again. New taxes have been designed in the name of cap and trade. Added to these are now the fees, for EPA inspections on automobiles, smog inspections, burn permits, pest control fees, thousands of fees that are not even considered by most as a part of taxes, but they really are taxes. They, the liberals, (aka, the enemy) just cannot get enough of what you have, to keep "improving" on what they want — the rate of destruction to this country and feeding their big machine of government (it could be called "givernment") answers. They call it "progress," as they get everyone caught in a tighter vise.

Though they claim differently, monetary matters are not the real forte for liberals in running an economy. They treat taxpayer money as if it were game show cash, as if it is coming from a bottomless, unlimited pool of money, with no out of bounds markers, "no house limits" and no taboos on how or where or when they can spend it. To talk of liberals and money's role in an economy, Ayn Rand had a grip on rightful thinking. Anne C. Heller explains: "A contributor, showed me the two-thousand-word text of Francisco d'Anconia's famous 'money speech' from Atlas Shrugged. 'So you think that money is the root of all evil?' . . . the capitalist hero Francisco asks a group of New Deal-style lobbyists and bureaucrats. 'Have you ever asked, 'What is the root of money?'' Rand's answer, in part, is that money is the 'tool and symbol' of a society built on mutual, voluntary trade rather than forced labor, duty to the state, or war. It is an engine of [free] economic progress."[3]

Fast forward a decade and a half from Woodrow Wilson and you find the progressive movement using monetary disasters like the market crash and the memory of the Great Depression to bring about, not free economic progress, but rather legislation which forced economic progress to carry more and more big incremental government on its back — all with dozens of new regulations and many new hidden taxes. They started with the federal income tax, then federalized social security; government programs by FDR, one after another and so on through the years, reaching even to today and the latest disaster, Obamacare. All of these were nothing more than outlets to bring on additional taxes. With FDR, the increased taxes brought about more welfare, more government services, followed by more tax increases, and the death spiral was in full swing. The picture is of us, being politically stuck in a revolving door for several years as it spins faster and faster, round and round. By the way, have you ever noticed how some things are just illegal unless the government is in charge of it? Social Security, for one, seems not much different than a Ponzi scheme in the way it is used. The mention of the misuse of

Social Security Funds to a liberal is equal to a root canal, since it involves a painfully negative jab to the legacy of Franklin Delano Roosevelt.

Mention FDR, how he was a Socialist and a Communist in his policies, and the leftists will come unglued as they race to his rescue. The record shows he is one who tried to push (my word is destroy) American Policy far to the left and over the edge. Packaging life into a "one size fits all can," as government preaches, does not answer needs, nor is it what the American spirit and the American dream is all about. It's about individualism; it's about freedom from the tyranny of government; it's about blazing your own trail, it is about morally doing your own thing, it is about freedom of expression, rugged in its nature.

A Little FDR History

During the presidential campaign of 1932, FDR was vague about his planned proposals except to say he was going to end the depression quickly and decisively. "When he accepted the Democratic nomination with a ringing acceptance speech, Roosevelt promised the people a "New Deal." After his election, in his first inaugural, he told Americans they had "nothing to fear but fear itself," and he promised a special session of Congress to deal with the national economic emergency. He came through on both promises."[4]

As he came to power in 1933, the first few months in office were frantic as he put one spending proposals after another in front of Congress for passage. They passed almost everything FDR put forth, which he called his "New Deal." Each legislative action fell into one of three categories: "Relief" (Short-term programs which promised to alleviate people's suffering), "Recovery" (Long-term programs promised to strengthen the economy), and "Reform" (Permanent structures put in place promised to never let a depression happen again). Each was a dose of big government carrying a huge price tag.

The New Deal was packaged and sold as a savior of capitalism and the fundamental institutions of American society from the disaster of the Great Depression. That's how it was sold — within the New Deal was framework, however, that existed to counteract and slow free-enterprise. The framework of the New Deal was built to look conservative, however, FDR and Congress passed so many policies, right and left, one after the other, the bulk of what was put in place was liberal within the framework. Because the 1st New Deal (1933-1935) failed to end the depression, there was a 2nd New Deal. The second followed "Keynesian economics," meaning the government pushed stimulus money down to the lower class pyramid, intending to "stimulate" spending and consumption. Keynesian economists call this "counter-cyclical demand management," believing that the government's massive financial impact can be used as a counterweight to current market forces. What this means is spending your way out of economic trouble. The proven fallacy was that borrowing and spending does not ignite any economic fuse. The simple truth is a nation cannot spend its way out of recession or depression. Though proven wrong in Europe, Leftists continue to believe the Keynesian approach the only credible path in an economic squeeze.

What the New Deal accomplished was better employment in two areas of the economy — in liberal and socialistic causes such as unions and organized labor, especially for unskilled workers with the steel and auto manufacturers — also with government employees, since government was exponentially growing very rapidly. The hidden truth is that women and minorities in nonunionized industries were largely untouched by this FDR action.

On March 9, 1933, Franklin D. Roosevelt called a special session of Congress telling the members that unemployment could only be solved via "direct recruiting by the Government itself." For the next three months, Roosevelt proposed, and Congress passed, a profusion of bills that attempted to deal with the problem of unemployment. This special session of Congress became known as "the Hundred Days" and provided the legislative basis for Roosevelt's New Deal. As Kenneth Davis records, "From March through June . . . Congress passed an extraordinary series of measures, sometimes without even reading them. [So this is where they learned to pass bills without reading them.] Roosevelt's approach was 'Take a method and try it. If it fails, try another'."[5]

FDR and the government established a plethora of government organizations and departments through this New Deal, which employed people for a wide range of project tasks. These organizations included:

The Civilian Conservation Corps (CCC), 1933-42, established to provide jobs for young men eighteen to twenty-five years old. Most jobs were infrastructural; concrete and dirt moving supervised by engineers.

The Agriculture Adjustment Administration (AAA), 1933, was started to pay farmers to take land out of production. The AAA suffered three major setbacks from poor planning. There were so many people starving, the nation became outraged to see pigs and hogs slaughtered and left to rot — then corn was plowed under by government decree to push up grain prices. Then the rule of supply and demand took over — prices shot up. "And thousands of mostly black sharecroppers and tenant farmers, lowest on the economic pecking order, were thrown off the land when farmers took their land out of production."[6]

The Tennessee Valley Authority (TVA), 1933 to present, was and is a federally run hydroelectric power program which competed directly across the country with privately owned industry. It was a major step by FDR attempting to federalize the electric industry, taking it out of the private sector across the country. "One man who did not like the TVA was future president Ronald Reagan. A spokesman for General Electric, Reagan was fired by GE in 1962 when he complained that the TVA was "big government." The TVA was also one of GE's biggest customers."[7]

CHAPTER THREE — THE DECEPTION OF LIBERALISM THAT LED TO THIS DARKNESS

The Federal Deposit Insurance Corporation (FDIC), was started in 1933, and was designed to build the people's confidence back from so many bank failures between 1929 and 1932.

The Home Owners Loan Corporation (HOLC), 1933, was started to refinance mortgages in default and was designed to help prevent foreclosures. This was poorly enforced, sometimes having the opposite effect. The government discriminated against poorer neighborhoods which eventually led to whole neighborhoods being blighted, or changed into "poverty deserts" by a practice that was later called redlining. The end result has been total disaster for many metropolitan areas. As Thabit says in his book *How East New York Became a Ghetto*, ". . . they practiced denying services or charged more of the services, such as banking, insurance, often racially determined by redlining areas of the city."[8]

The Federal Securities Act of 1933 began patrolling Wall Street activities. You all know how this has become a political football and how horribly it has worked.

The Securities and Exchange Commission (SEC), 1934 to present, was designed to regulate the stock market. It's interesting to note that FDR continued in the "liberal criminal" way by paying back huge political favors, or as Kenneth Davis says, " . . . and Roosevelt appointed Joseph Kennedy, a notorious speculator in his day, to be its first chief."[9] Back home, this practice is commonly referred to as having the fox guard the hen house!

The Federal Emergency Relief Administration (FERA) of 1933 was begun to provide huge amounts of monies for what is now known as welfare. This program, while wholesome and good on the drawing board, has developed into lifelong financial support and brought blight to the entire country through the years, building a dependence on government for the basic pay check a family gets each week.

The National Industrial Recovery Act (NIRA or NRA) of 1933 was very controversial because it aimed at having government take control over industrial production, labor and costs. It was liberal waste on parade as the act contained huge amounts of pork for business and especially for labor organizations, to win their favor and backing. "It also provided for business codes or legal price fixing that would be forbidden under any antitrust laws."[10] NRA became a typical governmental set of nightmarish and untenable set of regulations. In his book, *Franklin Roosevelt and the Making of Modern America*, Allan Winkler states, "The whole effort was a bureaucratic nightmare. More than 700 different codes regulated everything from the dog-food industry to the burlesque theatrical industry that for example, specified no more than four stripteases in a given performance. Hardware stores had to pay close attention to 1900 different codes, cork makers dealt with 34 different sets of regulations. An NRA staff of over 4,500 [government] employees was constantly busy with thousands of interpretive rulings."[11]

Liberals have a hard time understanding that adding government red tape, not only does not help private industry as they always think it will — it only hurts the private sector by piling meaningless weight and cost to what must be done in production to turn a profit. Besides, industry will normally make cut backs to offset the weight of government interference. As Winkler speaks about the NRA regulations, "The codes with their rigid stipulations led business interests to cut back on production as a way of maintaining prices ... those cuts encouraged further layoffs and discouraged much needed new investment."[12] Within a year, the complaints were running so loudly throughout the country about the waste of the agency that Roosevelt was at a crossroads, but asked Congress for a two-year extension of the program. However the Supreme Court settled the matter they "ruled unanimously in the case of "Schechter Poultry Corp. vs. United States" that the NRA was based on "unconstitutional delegation of legislative power;" with that ruling it ceased to function."[13]

FDR started the Projects Works Administration (PWA) in 1935, and it too was so poorly run that it got into early trouble. As a result it never had any serious impact helping the economy toward recovery. But FDR gets lots of credit, though Herbert Hoover's idea, because at least he was thinking of helping people.

Then there was the National Youth Administration (NYA) 1935-39, the Farm Security Administration (FSA) and the Public Works Administration (PWA) 1933. Other schemes administered by the PWA included the Federal Writers Project (1935-39) Federal Theatre Project (1935-39) and the Federal Art Project (1935-43). Davis adds, "The result was the "alphabet soup" of new federal agencies, some of them successful, some not."[14]

Other notable legislation enacted by Roosevelt in his first term was:

- 1933 — The Agricultural Adjustment Act,
- 1934 — The National Housing Act and the Federal Securities Act,
- 1935 — The National Labor Relations Act, known best as the Wagner Act, guaranteeing the right of workers to organize into unions within the private sector. This type of legislation has been a dream of liberals, since they believe it levels the playing field between educated and uneducated workers, as well as among those workers who perform good work, and those who don't.
- 1935 — The Social Security Act established a national system of old age pensions and coordinated federal and state action for the relief of the unemployed.

The New Deal, as engineered by FDR, was generally a bust, however, liberals believe it to be the crescendo to the work of a saint, since the talk was of helping the poor and restoring the economy. To a Progressive, talk is at a minimum equal to and generally greater than accomplishing anything, since it contains words of caring. The naked truth is many Democrats who had been faithful to Roosevelt, were fed up with his wasteful talk and little to no action; to many it appeared to be a political "rope-a-dope." Huey Long, a very visible and powerful liberal became a threat to FDR, because he saw through the wasteful spending, "... the New Deal, which he complained, took four hundred millions from the soldiers, and spent three hundred millions to plant saplings."[15]

During the 1936 presidential election, Roosevelt was challenged and politically attacked for not keeping his promise to balance the budget during his first term. In fact, many of FDR's acts ended up being very to extremely unpopular with the public; meaning they either did not work, or were perceived as not working. The National Labor Relations Act was unpopular with businessmen because it favored only the trade unions. That act actually harmed business by ultimately driving up labor costs which resulted in rising production costs, as well as dropping production quotas, something for which unions have been noted all these years. Liberals are usually there to help unions. It is not something they do to help business; rather it is and has been a back room political agreement to build power against capitalism and free enterprise. They call that partnering with business.

Following the 1936 election the Supreme Court stopped approving FDR's legislation carte blanche. This infuriated FDR and he went on a dictatorial tirade. He threatened to put liberal activists on the Supreme Court, and when time was not on his side getting that done quickly, he went so far as to insist the court be expanded to double its size to 18 judges. His goal was to stack enough socialist activist judges on the court so as to override the conservative judges; then he could enact any socialist legislation he wanted. However, he failed in this attempt also. But since he served four terms, <u>FDR did over time replace 8 of the 9 judges, thus building a solid liberal progressive base for future legal debates. And these liberal judges helped to solidify the progressive attacks on American society which included securing the removal of the Bible from school in 1948, as well as favoring many other leftist ideals in later court decisions.</u>

In foreign policy matters, FDR was an isolationist. In every way it seemed, except for in 1933, when he performed an unprecedented act in recognizing the Soviet Union. He knew the people of the US would never go so far as recognizing the Bolshevik government, but had no problem recognizing Joseph Stalin's regime. It was as if FDR had finally found his soul mate in Stalin. When talk of European war was in the air, he and Congress passed the Neutrality Acts of 1935, 36, and 37. Through this legislation, FDR barred any American company in providing armament to any of the European warring countries. When some ammo manufacturers did sell warfare to European interests, FDR called the management of these firms, "baby killers." With all the unpopular moves he made, he began to be accused of being a communist.

While some of his efforts helped to temporarily push back economic problems, they were not long lasting. By 1938, a hard recession had returned, thus making things even worse than what they had been.

Overall, FDR attempted the dictator role, but failed miserably because his programs were so financially disastrous to the country. But to liberals, mentioning those facts are words of treason!

Truth is truth. In April, 1933, FDR ordered gold and silver to be surrendered to the government. Surrender them or face the consequence of having it confiscated — it was now illegal to own either. This was done, I believe in an attempt to if nothing else, demoralize the average citizen, showing that the government could do anything they wanted, at any time, whether citizens liked it or not. In June, 1933, FDR also took the US currency off the gold standard, which freed him and the government to print new money as they wished.

Foreign policy for Roosevelt was just as disastrous. One of his worst decisions was framed at Yalta near the end of World War II in an agreement with Joseph Stalin, whereas my grandpa would say, "FDR sold us down the road." Two important things came out of that conference. One was a carved up Europe. FDR in particular thought he and Winston Churchill could appease Stalin by giving him Eastern Europe. That gift plus other concessions FDR made marked the start of a half-century long Cold War and the expansion of the Soviet Union and China. Westerners who were war weary coupled to the patented weak-kneed liberal approach was merely an empty hope that a ruthless tyrant would respond to our good faith decision. FDR's failure to understand Stalin resulted in unbelievable and unspeakable massacres, enslavement and human suffering. Giving land away to tyrants, terrorists, or communists does not soothe the savage beasts.

Today, Progressive liberals castigate Hitler while giving communist rulers a pass on that criticism, not realizing that they made Hitler's killing of 23 million seem amateurish in comparison. While FDR really liked Stalin, the only thing our two countries had in common for a half century was a common enemy in the 1930s and half of the 1940s; Hitler.

How FDR failed to deal with preparing the U.S. for the potential of entering the European War displayed his lack of planning. Roosevelt was not a stellar performer at following the trend line in world events. As one of my university professors used to say, "He couldn't connect the dots." Because he waited so long to act, if had not been for George Marshall we would have been totally unprepared to enter the war. The death tolls though terrible, would have been worse than they were. That WW2 wasn't a glorious win, Pat Buchanan agrees, "When President Bush flew to Moscow to celebrate the sixtieth anniversary of V-E Day, he stopped in one of the nations that was not celebrating, Latvia, . . . He told the world that while "V-E Day marked the end of Facism . . . . it did not end oppression," that what FDR and Churchill did to Eastern and Central Europe in collusion with Stalin "will be remembered as one of the greatest wrongs of history." Bush called Yalta a sellout of free nations as shameful as Munich."[16]

Though liberals praise FDR as deity, he was, as I have briefly tried to show, in

CHAPTER THREE — THE DECEPTION OF LIBERALISM THAT LED TO THIS DARKNESS

most practical measures of performance a disaster. He was so much of a disaster, that had it not been for WW II putting our economy back to work, we would have not come out of the great depression. And had it not been for George Marshall steering FDR's sites on Hitler's predictable goals, and our lack of preparedness in 1938, we would not have started those preparations for war. In his brilliance, Marshall saw what was coming; Roosevelt, planted in his socialistic beliefs, did not or would not.

"At 12:50 a.m. on Friday, September 1, 1939, a telephone rang in the darkened bedroom . . . . Franklin Delano Roosevelt, fifty-seven years old, the twice-elected president of the United States, stirred in his narrow iron cot and pushed himself up . . . On the line was Roosevelt's ambassador in Paris, William C. Bullitt, relaying a message from his counterpart in Warsaw. Germany's legions had breached Poland's frontiers. The Luftwaffe was bombarding Poland's cities. The greatest, bloodiest war in history had begun. "Well, Bill, it's come at last," said FDR. "God help us all.""[17]

When Hitler invaded Poland in 1939, to say Roosevelt was unprepared is a vast understatement — he was shocked, and caught totally off guard. He met with George Marshall and began making plans for Marshall to lead the armed forces and to better prepare the US for the potential of what lay ahead.

Unedited history demonstrates FDR's bland stance against international aggression; he was a garden variety socialist. Instead of strength, he responded by promoting doctrines fostering isolationism and anti-aggression. In 1934, he pushed through Congress the Johnson Act, prohibiting loans to nations behind on WWI debt repayments. His Neutrality Act of 1935 and 36, forbade the export of arms, ammunition or implements of war to belligerent nations — a 1937 amendment to the act forbade American citizens and ships from entering war zones or traveling on belligerents' ships.[18]

Thankfully, Marshall could influence FDR as shown early in 1939 Roosevelt asked Congress to repeal the Neutrality Act, so the U.S. could sell arms to the free European forces. Congress refused. In September, World War II began as Germany invaded Poland. Roosevelt spoke before Congress again, and on November 4, it approved the Pittman Bill, allowing America to sell arms to nations who could pay cash for their weapons.[19]

The Progressive Writers Attacked Free-Enterprise

We live in a time and place in this country when any absolute, such as truth being regarded as truth, has been tossed away with last week's leftovers and garbage. Ours is a pluralistic society where it seems anything goes, anything but a sacred or Christian truth of course. It would be humorous if it was not so tragic. Relativism, Atheism, Agnosticism, even Gnosticism (when used for liberal purposes and liberal definitions to claim special knowledge which by their 'definition' trumps any spiritual truth from our founders), rage like a giant volcano in our institutions and media outlets today, belching the smoke and ash of lies and deception.

A nasty conspiracy seems to follow this cast of liberals; that of redefining words and terms, in an attempt to usually push forth some artificial, abnormal or even offensive practice. They do this especially in picking those words which have been used for decades for noble purposes. Of course, I contend they do this because of the inferiority complex of their position.

But there was a time when life seemed to make more sense. If you go back just 50 years or so, you could still see if only a shadow of what our founders built. For our American institutions were anchored on Biblical morality, ethics, and truth in practically every instance. Those today who squawk for God to be removed from our entities of government because as their claim goes, this was never a Christian nation — they don't read well, they don't like evidence, or simply choose to close their eyes to the facts. It may too be just their age old attempt to remove the Deity's Name, thus feeling they have no responsibility to Him since there are no reminders of His name.

The most appealing and in some ways most comfortable explanation is that the tradition was undermined, destroyed, and replaced by alien infiltration and Communist subversion. Some historians cavalierly dismiss this conception by calling it the conspiracy theory of history, implying somehow that such a notion is disreputable on the face of it. Unquestionably, there has been and is a Communist conspiracy to undermine our true history. It is demonstrable; too, that many ideas of non-American origin have been propagated here. But such explanations attribute too much effectiveness to Communists and fail to account adequately for the massive help they have had from non-communists. It glosses over, too, the really difficult task of recovering liberty and individualism, for it ignores how deeply enmeshed in thought and ways collectivism has become.[20]

Discredited by Scholars

My contention is that much of the work of subverting (I use the word 'corrupt') the American tradition was all carried out by 'respectable' things, writers, academics, so-called scholars. They had grown up being taught of socialist methodologies and its associated level playing fields. Someone may argue that these ideologues acted behind the scenes. To me, they seemed to be very open and public in their criticism of Americana. Their motives did not appear covert at all. But in their classes and seminars some of them "paved the way" for collectivism in America. Their effects upon the culture have been identifiable and disastrous no matter what the intentions.

Before the American tradition was replaced, it was discredited. Odium was attached to it, logic was removed, and feelings were marshaled against it. It was not an easy accomplishment. There is every reason to believe that at the beginning of this century Americans at large were firmly attached to constitutionalism, government by law rather than by men, individual liberty, voluntary group activity, limited government, and personal independence.

Yet, "American" became a tainted word for many people in the course of the 20th Century. Several years ago, Karl Shapiro writing in The New Republic, referred to the "American way of life" as a "nauseating expression". This meant to him "the material life, the worship of the scientific mentality, and the belief that Americans are the best people on earth." A single instance of lynching is apt to call forth denunciations of the "American" penchant for swift and violent justice. Should a board of censors fail to license some obscene movie, it would be just another horrendous example of that latent Puritanism in America which has reared its ugly head once more. If a businessman were to question spending for foreign aid, he might find himself used as an example of that bête noire of the "liberals": the selfishly acquisitive American who stems in a long line from that vulgar preacher of penuriousness, Benjamin Franklin. "Americanism" is sealed off by quotation marks from too close a contact with it by the cognoscenti, who might otherwise be contaminated.[21]

It seems unimaginable that the simple expression "the American way of life" would be so hated and distasteful to any American. But liberals hammered on the gray matter of citizen's until today the term "Americanism" is used as a term synonymous with the word failure. The brow beating has continued to the point that it is easy to witness someone flinching or looking away in embarrassment when they obviously think the derogatory used of the word American will be soon followed by "ugly American".

We can admit that some individuals in their unwise and ungainly acts have wrongly become associated with terms like Americanism by thievery or other outrageous acts. We should not associate those acts as being "American." Church membership or doing good deeds to others is more centrally a part of the "American way of life" than crime, or atheism, or agnosticism, or scientism. Constitutionalism is much more deeply American than is materialism. The Constitution-makers took great care to guard the individual against falling prey to the bent of his neighbors to force him into conformity. Charity, both individual and organizational, is as much American as is acquisitiveness. Why then, in all fairness, does "American" not call to mind virtues as well as vices? [22]

Literary Denigration

The 1920s and 1930s brought on a large-scale denigration on the American tradition, a direct attack written into some literature: in stories and essays. Literature was under attack by the Progressive Left, subtly at first, then openly in history, politics, philosophy and theology.

H. L. Mencken, the sage of Baltimore, was likely the most uninhibited of the defamers in the 1920s. He not only pointed up the vices and failings of Americans, but he identified them with the American tradition. In the fourth volume of his vigorous *Prejudices*, Mencken asks: "What, then, is the spirit of Americanism? I precipitate it conveniently into the doctrine that the way to ascertain the truth about anything... is to take a vote on it, and that the way to propagate that truth... is with a club. This doctrine... explains almost everything that is indubitably American, and particularly everything American that is most puzzling to men of older and less inspired cultures...."[23]

Mencken attacked the Puritan thought, "There is only one honest impulse at the bottom of Puritanism, and that is the impulse to punish the man with a superior capacity for happiness—to bring him down to the miserable level of 'good' men, i.e., of stupid, cowardly, and chronically unhappy men." "New England," he declares, "has never shown the slightest sign of genuine enthusiasm for ideas. It began its history as a slaughterhouse of ideas, and it is today not easily distinguishable from a cold-storage plant." Mencken went on about Colonists: "What are the characters that I discern most clearly in the so-called Anglo-Saxon type of man? I may answer at once that two stick out above all others. One is the curious and apparently incurable incompetence—his congenital inability to do any difficult thing easily and well.... The other is his astounding susceptibility to fears and alarms—in short, his hereditary cowardice." Even free inquiry would appear to be a wholly non-American thing. "Thus the battle of ideas in the United States is largely carried on under strange flags, and even the stray natives on the side of free inquiry have to sacrifice some of their nationality when they enlist."[24]

And Mencken on faith and religious thought, "the average American is a prude and a Methodist under his skin.... Save in a few large cities, every American community lies under a sacerdotal despotism whose devices are disingenuous and dishonourable...." The *Boobus americanus* is taught by "oafs from the farms and villages of Iowa, Kansas, Vermont, the Dakotas, and other such backward states...."[25]

To say that Mencken stood above other liberal writers in pithiness would be an understatement. While many stood beneath him, they still shared his contempt for anything American — except of course their paycheck. Frederick L. Allen probably captured the classic progressive scorn for Americana with his 1931 book, *Only Yesterday*. He inscribed, "The typical American of the old stock had never had more than a halfhearted enthusiasm for the rights of the minority; bred in a pioneer tradition, he had been accustomed to set his community in order by the first means that came to hand—a sumptuary law, a vigilance committee, or if necessary a shotgun."[26]

Van Wyck Brooks, long-time chieftain of literary critics, calls the "traditional drag" of our culture "the main fact of American history;" writing in 1922. "If our writers wither early," he said, "if they are too generally pliant, passive, acquiescent, anaemic, how much is this not due to the heritage of pioneering, with its burden of isolation, nervous strain, excessive work, and all the racial habits that these have engendered?"[27]

CHAPTER THREE — THE DECEPTION OF LIBERALISM THAT LED TO THIS DARKNESS

Sinclair Lewis, a champion hater of the American way and lover of things Socialistic, described Mr. Jones, his most typical American, the businessman, in his introduction to *Babbitt*. Though it was published then, it captured his sense of his nauseating American, "Mr. Jones himself . . . votes the Republican ticket straight, he hates all labor unionism, he belongs to the Masons and the Presbyterian Church, his favorite author is Zane Grey, and in other particulars noted in this story, his private life seems scarce to mark him as the rough, ready, aspiring, iconoclastic, creative, courageous innovator his admirers paint him. He is a bagman. He is a peddler. He is a shopkeeper. He is a camp-follower. He is a bag of aggressive wind."[28]

George F. Nieberg pitched in with his description of the average American in an article in *The Forum* published in 1931. "I lean toward the heresy that the typical American citizen is, at best, an unpleasant go-getter, a professional back-slapper going through his dumb-show always a bit fearful of his job, of what people will say, of his wife—and of himself. To this heresy I will add another: that it is impossible for him to live like a civilized man, as it is impossible for him to die like one." More, "his blind, unwavering faith in 'success' stories, patent medicines, political platforms, his bootlegger's word of honor, and his boss's stupidity borders upon fanatical fervor."[29]

Yet another writer who embraced the rise of Progressive thought, Robert Herrick, in 1931, said that there "have been many instances . . . of American brutality, American tyranny, American intolerance, which have reverberated around the world." The same year Harper's carried an article by Katherine F. Gerould in which she associated Americanism with gangsterism, in an attempt to explain the alleged popularity of Al Capone. "It is not because Capone is different that he takes the imagination: it is because he is so gorgeously and typically American. . . . Of course he was born in this country: could anyone but a native American have adopted so whole-heartedly American principles of action? An immigrant would have taken years to assimilate our ideals; whereas Capone was born to them. . . . There are analogies for Al Capone among the American immortals."

Writers from the Leftist Camp left no aspect of the American way of life alone, denouncing it all as rubbish. Elsie Clews Parsons attacked even the sex life with her diatribes on American people with *Civilization in the United States*. She accused those in the US of a "lack of warmth in personal intercourse which makes alike for American bad manners and, in the more intellectual circles, for cheerlessness and aridity is due . . . to failure of one kind or another in sex relations." She preached that the American failures were due to "confusion between parenthood and mating."[30] She argued the French handled sex admirably. A serious history student should take note that since that time, Liberals, Democrats and Progressives have always compared Americans unfavorably with Europeans.

In 1931 the boldest collection of assaults on American traditional thought to date was published in a book called *Behold America*. It was edited in pure socialist and communist ideological fashion. In this book, the general defamation was narrated to a fever pitch. One writer says, "The United States is not peaceful: it's very geographic existence and its expansion in temperate North America is the result of a consistent policy of the slaughter of weaker peoples . . . and the expropriation of their property." V. F. Calverton declares: "Unfortunately, however—and if there is any single explanation of why America has had no great writers to compare with those of Europe, this is it—no traditions in America have ever been very genuine or very original, and never very long-lived. . . ."[31]

Karl Shapiro, using these as a sample of why he thought American "sucked," inadvertently gave us his explanation for his nauseating reaction to American life. He called up the names of the major American poets of the twentieth century, pointing to their "anti-American-way-of-life." Of T. S. Eliot, he wrote: "His entire literary output constitutes a condemnation of American materialism, economic greed, and cultural vacuity." About Ezra Pound, he penned, "is the most scurrilous critic of American life in the twentieth century." He mentioned Edgar Lee Masters as lamenting "the corruption of pioneer stock and the hypocrisy of small town American life." He included Robinson Jeffers, describing him as "chief of the self-avowed enemies of American society and civilization. His attacks on American materialism and the American savagery of character have become synonymous with his poetry." There are many more who could be included on this list, making it much longer. The point is made however, that Progressives had infiltrated the intellectual community and were heaping abuse on their country.

When the major novelists of the 1920s are mentioned, Henry S. Canby in support of socialistic thought pointed to the "dogged discontent of Ernest Hemingway, the mystic morbid discontent of William Faulkner, the strong lyric discontent of Willa Cather, the sharp scoffing discontent of Sinclair Lewis. . . ." He sharpens his beak with a vulture-like dissecting of America, claiming his list of those who despise the American way of life are nearly too many to count. Dramatists in writing about their land are to be compared to twelve year-old children who are being punished. They can find nothing positive to say about their parents. Seems that America is horrible; except of course for the pay check, the food, the luxuries, and the freedom these writers all have to write what they please. All this capitalism, money, and freedom to express oneself were afforded to them by the freedom fighters who built this land.

Objective: Tear Down the Country

Since the progressive movement writers set as its goal the destruction of belief in the American tradition. It turns out they did their work well. They portrayed the tradition as one of narrow-minded Puritanism, of low caste Anglo-Saxons, of intolerant busybodies, of rural oafs and hayseeds, and of vulgar democrats. Whatever good there was here was certainly sneaked into the country from Europe or the Soviet Union. It simply could not have developed here on its own, as they proclaimed. According to them, nothing in American thought was worth preserving. When you read that slowly, look to the school system and its teachings over the past 50 years and you see the seeds of progressive thought planted in the writers of the 20s, cultivated and watered in the FDR garden, the fertilized in public school by removal of any dogma or creed which is Christian. The harvest of this crop is in with two generations of younger people who proclaim there is nothing good about God, capitalism, Christianity, etc. They scream their mentor's words from years gone by — "Down with America!"

Judging from the writings of these authors, they were moved to this denigration by diverse aims. Some were unhappy about the unenthusiastic reception of the arts in America. Others wanted to awaken their countrymen to a more sensitive appreciation of "higher things." But at the base of all this, the Socialists and Communists were trying to arouse social-consciousness and prepare the ground they would plow and later plant their ideas. Besides, it has been fashionable in literary circles for some time now to discover decay and disorder everywhere, and to describe it in lurid detail.

It is important to note that the writers for the most part went on this defamation of lies about the country, but like H. L. Mencken, his only nation of loyalty was to America. There was no other place he could call home. Strangely, he said he admired the Constitution, the Founding Fathers. However, as one person put it succinctly . . . But bread cast upon the waters may return in strange ways, for once the tradition had been undermined the reason for which it had been done could become separated from it.[32]

The Church of Progressive Liberalism

Liberalism is, at its heart, a religion. They have their religious holidays, such as Earth Day, Gay Pride Day, May Day, Labor Day, etc. Then you add to those national days, the following specialty days: Save the Polar Bears Day, Spotted Owl Day, Save the Snail Darter Fish, Save the Turtle, or Jerry Brown's favorite, 'Save the Fruit Fly', ad infinitum, ad nauseam. These are political cause days, fund raisers, just in disguise. I love to save animals without the liberal politics. I do so all the time. To the liberal I say, "Yo Goofy! Why don't you save the unborn children?"

Listen to their talk, how they prance genially among the people, touting their ideology and hear their religion ooze out. Their ideology is constructed from companion volumes: Darwin's *Origin of the Species*, is the first which teaches what is commonly called "Darwinism" or what some refer to as evolution. The second is Karl Marx's Communist Manifesto from which they pull and try to practice the theory of collectivism (More on this later). They put more faith into these two books than any Christian ever put into the Bible. And that is the key word with these who claim they run on "reason" and "science" in having built their world view. It is not. It is faith. Faith is what we add to the evidences we have in order to provide our worldview. The less evidence there is, the more faith we need. Evolutionary scientists often admit that they, too, interpret the world in the context of their faith. And it takes a lot of faith to hold their worldview. Their faith says that everything and everyone got here by means of evolution, or as I said "Darwinism."

Prof. L. H. Matthews, a well-respected evolutionist, said he was honored by being asked to write a new introduction for the 1971 edition of Darwin's Origin of Species. In his introduction — speaking of evolution — he admitted, "Most biologists accept it as though it were a proven fact.... Although this conviction rests upon circumstantial evidence, it forms a satisfactory faith on which to base our interpretation of nature." At the end of the day, Liberalism is a tired, worn-out, and erroneous doctrine that is built not on reason, but on faith in two volumes that could not stand the test of time. That's why liberalism is a religion, and a bad one at that.

In the faith of the liberal there are sermons, or homilies — they will pound a podium, raise their octaves, wave their arms, in crying that we must "be tolerant" of them and their positions. They are speaking of their faith. After all they are the only ones who care for the down trodden, the poor, the under-privileged, or so they claim. But give them an inch and their fangs come out looking for more blood. The progressive fangs come out. All their efforts are used to move little by little; bit by bit to take away rights, swallow up territory, seize property, take over places of work, and extort dollars from the public to pay for their religion, through a means called taxation.

These liberals are like a church, they also have their gods, and FDR was certainly one of their deities. Their religion is wrapped up in idolizing some people, deifying others, harassing some, crucifying yet others — but also movements like environmental actions, government takeovers, labor actions and unions are their trademarks as well. And just like a religion, they have their own trinity to which they refer often they bow, which they have philosophically bronzed. While the Christian Church that has a holy trinity of the Father, The Son and the Holy Spirit, the Liberal or Progressive Church has theirs too: FDR is the father, John F. Kennedy is the son, and Karl Marx was and is their holy (unholy) spirit. Additionally in the Liberal Temple, "Satan" is played by George W. Bush.

One more small point: the offering plate is passed several times daily in the church of liberalism. It is called taxes.

Their Church Has Had Many Leaders

Viewing the last 125 years, there have been several architects of disaster who sat in the office of President, each one a Progressive. A few of them were most horrible. I mention them briefly now and will discuss them in more detail later. The first was Teddy Roosevelt who was a Republican Progressive. Later, he was also a Progressive in the Progressive Party, also known as the Bull Moose Party. Roosevelt's "'big

Chapter Three — The Deception of Liberalism that Led to This Darkness

stick" while being said it was used instead of conversation was in truth the Billy club used attempting to pound a strong federal government in on the top of all citizens. Big government for was the key for him; first, last, and always. He set the tone for all the others who would come along in his footsteps. When Roosevelt came into office following McKinley's assassination, he tried to assure America he would walk slowly in making changes. Then he announced his "Square Deal" addressing his concern for the big "c's" as he called them: control of corporations, consumer protections, and conservation. From that seemingly harmless beginning has come in the following years the biggest land grabs in human history. It all started with the founding of National Parks, federal lands, and the subsequent federal control.

Some folks are confused by the term "Progressive" as it usually stands for a positive object or initiative; history however has shown that these "Progressives" were not of that ilk. Their name is a misnomer since they are simply patient Communists campaigning for big government control in every area of life. The Liberal Left chose the word progressive because it is a non-threatening word, promoting thoughts and feelings of good will. The word by itself means moving forward "pro" = for; "gressive" = movement. It sounds on the surface that they are in favor of moving forward. In reality, in their movement the word "progressive" actually means moving backward. Look at the evidence; everything they touch is a failure, regresses, and results in misery. Their stand has always been for big continuous reform — just the wrong way. Through the years that has taken on the face of big taxes, big socialized medicine, a big EPA, big BLM, big secular humanism, big, big involvement in the private sector: aka, big centralized government in control of activity. That's the end result — progressivism was however always "sold" in a different package to voters; promises of big freedom, big choices, big protections to make individuals and families feel secure. Through the years that has brought growth of the fed in exponentially larger footprints and longer strides.

The second "Progressive" for review was Woodrow Wilson, who was what some called a "Diamond Progressive" — any angle through which he was viewed; he still looked like a Progressive, Collectivist, or Communist. FDR, a third socialist from the word go. Didn't matter what he didn't accomplish; it was his words of intentions that counted. The fourth person was one of the most destructive in my lifetime, LBJ. He started a war on poverty, which actually fed and expanded poverty. We watched it grow. Bill Clinton "was" and "is" a huge step backward for the country in many ways. (I know. It all depends on what my definition of the word "is" is!) He was a disaster legally, morally, ethically, politically, and in the end personally. Clinton had lots of cigars but smoked few of them. Lastly, the one "Progressive" who carries the radical socialist flag higher than the all the other Presidents, is Obama. Never has anyone pushed the socialistic balloon so high. There were and are others like Taft, Hoover; however, these are the worst. Each had a pretense of religion about them. In their hearts it was Karl Marx who sat on the throne.

When viewing Progressivism, Liberalism or Marxism; three closely-associated "isms," I not only see a religion in full bloom. I also see a cancer growing rapidly. It is a cancer of arrogance. It is an arrogance of believing nobody knows better or has the litany of great solutions. Once it lodges itself in the heart and mind, there is not much you can do as it begins to permeate the entire body with an inordinate sense of self-worth, significance, and position; claiming special rights for anyone who aligns with their "faith." In the 1960s, these progressives and liberals were front and center with marches, sit-ins, and riots declaring they believed in 1st Amendment rights: freedom of speech no matter how it may be disgusting to society. But when these same progressives and liberals began to come to power in the 90s, they began to realize they did not like people speaking against them. So they declared that freedom of speech should be allowed under "certain circumstances." Those circumstances were of course, when what anyone said was in lockstep with what the liberals were themselves saying. Otherwise, they did not like free speech any longer, and would prove through the coming years they would work hard to change to landscape to fit their views.

Case in point: Michael Sam is the first openly gay football player to be drafted in the NFL. In his official introductory press conference he indicated, "It's okay to be who you are." Later he said, "It's OK to be comfortable in your own skin."[33] I read his comments that he is proud that everyone can be open about themselves in public in their own skins. Except, of course unless you are an 82-year old NBA owner of the L.A. Clippers named Donald Sterling who made private "off color" remarks which became public. He told his girlfriend she should not be spending her time "with those black people" like Magic Johnson. The "Progressive thought Police" picked up on the comments. The end result in May 2014, they are trying to strip Sterling of his property: the ball team. This is all because Mr. Sterling was being himself, as Michael Sam suggested we all can be. However, Sterling was himself juxtaposed to the Progressive movement. The Progressives want you to "be free to be yourself," just so long as it in agreement with who they are. Add to this scenery, the fact that when Sam was drafted in the seventh round of the NFL draft, he was caught on camera kissing his boyfriend. After seeing that happen, Don Jones a defensive back for the Miami Dolphins "tweeted" "OMG" and "Horrible." Note that he was being himself, but he was immediately brought to bear by the "Progressive Tweet Police" for that brief comment, fined $10,000 by his team, forced to make a public apology for publicly disagreeing with Sam's position, and told he could no longer participate with team activities until he has gone through sensitivity training.[34] (Will the sensitivity training be conducted at a FEMA camp?) There are several bizarre points in this story, e.g., Sterling is a staunch Democrat supporting the liberal way; e.g., is there such a thing as free private speech where Sterling was having "no better feeling than being himself" in making his comments to his girlfriend. All of these events point to an exclusive progressive temple worship which requires strict adherence to the progressive doctrine on free speech. Speak only the doctrine that agrees with these Marxist, Progressive Liberals. If you don't, prepare for what comes next: excommunication, theft of your possessions and possibly worse.

CHAPTER THREE — THE DECEPTION OF LIBERALISM THAT LED TO THIS DARKNESS

Add to these bizarre scenes those which are becoming an everyday picture of a nation coming apart at the seams, another case in point. The Home & Garden Television (aka HGTV) network announced on Wednesday, May 14, 2014, it has decided to pull the plug on an upcoming real estate reality show. The reason? The huge firestorm of gay activist complaints and controversy from gay rights activists who accused the evangelical Christian hosts, twin brothers David and Jason Benham of being "anti-gay and pro-life."[35] Even their bank got in on the politically correct, public crucifixion by kicking the brothers out for their "pro-life" views. Then they reversed their decision saying they could stay. Hidden within these stated reasons is the real reason Liberals conduct themselves as wild animals. They hate Christians and anything to do with a faith which speaks against perversion.

Lucifer understood this firsthand after becoming so enamored with perversion and his own personality, so much so that he believed he was co-equal with the Creator. Some say that's arguable, but even Saul Alinsky believed this. Satan has been spending the balance of his days enticing mankind to join him in his misery. Contemporary Liberalism and Progressivism are headed for the same fate, traveling the same road, as it elevates itself to unnatural importance, having nowhere but downward to fall. Laws like the Affordable Care Act (I knew they were lying on that one), i.e. Obamacare, provides the yellow highlight to self-proclaimed superiority of liberals — they promote themselves to a place of superiority, telling us what we need and then redefining those needs as a "right." Life is a right. Liberty is a right. Pursuit of happiness is a right. Healthcare is not a right. Besides if it is a right, why aren't the politicians participating like the rest of the flock onto whom they inflict this pain?!

You will see much more about the scam of Obamacare in later chapters, but suffice to say it teaches us that liberals and progressives don't believe in true freedom or unalienable rights. They believe we are not smart; too stupid to make personal decisions. Instead, in their religion, they have promoted themselves as priests over us. They state they will make our decisions. They pervert the Constitution and misuse governmental authority to accomplish this. They have a strange sporting activity; we are forced to watch it. We become Guiney pigs as they play Russian roulette with their contrived healthcare. All the while, they watch from their luxury box seats. They even exempt themselves and their big money supporters, like labor unions, from their own laws. It's a religion of class warfare.

From their mahogany offices they shout at us to "move on" to another topic. "It is the law of the land." Anyone speaking out against their class warfare is called an "anarchist." Logically, it could be said that those who opposed once-legal slavery were also anarchists. By the way they did that. You will read about that in this volume too. Legality had proven to be a license for stupidity; at least if you are a liberal or progressive. It is interesting and also the height of arrogance these liberals and progressives do not label themselves as "anarchists." These crybabies are attempting to repeal another "law of the land," national sovereignty by the avenue aliens become citizens in this land. They are traitors, guilty of treason from within. Some of us are catching them in their betrayal and inconsistencies.

Go down Memory Lane with me. Remember when the global warming dragon slayer and former V.P., Al Gore was caught with his carbon footprint being huge in 2006. His 10,000-square-foot Nashville home used 191,000 kilowatt-hours of energy. The same year, according to Channel 5 News in Nashville, for a period of time from February 3, 2006 – January 5, 2007, the average home in Nashville used approximately 15,600 kilowatt-hours a year.[36] This is truly class warfare with no shame.

The microcosms of lies and hypocrisy are incarnate and growing within the Progressivette Liberalesque Church. Liberals love to spend time and energy pointing fingers at and demonizing people with their mouths wide open, as if from a scene from the movie *Invasion of the Body Snatchers*. That's probably not a bad analogy since they hound all people, especially the rich, trying take over their financial lives to spread their money around. That is, unless you're talking about their money and so many of them are "filthy rich." According to Roll Call, seven of the ten richest members of the 112th Congress are Democrats. They are immune from persecution since they occasionally speak about helping the poor and disadvantaged.

Another microcosm is the rich list in Washington. Number 13 on that rich list is House former minority Leader Nancy Pelosi (D-CA), badgered 2012 Republican presidential candidate Mitt Romney to release his tax returns. Note that she refused to do the same when McClatchy News asked members of Congress to release returns the same year. Incidentally, Romney had a higher tax rate than John Kerry did the year before Kerry ran for president. Secretary of State Kerry is Number 2 on the "rich" list, mostly due to marrying into "Big Ketchup" money. Wasn't it Senator Dianne Feinstein (D-CA), who said during the 2009 Baucus-Grassley jobs bill fight that it was her belief "that tax credits only go to people who are making money, and they generally keep it"? As Number 14 on the list, Feinstein didn't get there giving all her money away.[37]

As surely as the sun rose and fell today over the hills and plains of the Midwest, liberalism is going to fail. While it seems to be winning now, the rest of us are charged with speaking and spreading truth whenever possible. Anything less is arrogance.

Today, whatever label they wear; progressive, socialist, Democrat, Rhino, or mainstream-reporter, all are still the same opponent we faced since the 50s, or at the beginning of the 20th century. They are just in different style of apparel. Travel back with me a little farther. You will see that this war was on-going, long before this. Now let's go back farther to our nation's beginning.

*"Socialists cry 'Power to the People'
and raise the clinched fist as they say it:
We all know what they really mean —
power over people, power to the state."*

~ Margaret Thatcher

Chapter Four

The Illusion of Government That's Captivated America

THEY BEGAN GATHERING CAUTIOUSLY AT THE pre-appointed time, that evening, December 16, 1773. Quietly, secretly they came down the alleys and cobblestone streets of Boston. They came from the hills, and they came from the backwoods, and even the far countryside. All were making their way down by the sea to Griffin's Wharf. There were 7,000 of them in all that evening who did not know the magnitude of the history they were going to make. Suddenly from seemingly nowhere, out of that crowd appeared three groups of fifty men each dressed like Mohawk Indians, each group boarding one of the three ships anchored in port. These 'Sons of Liberty' had smeared black grease on their faces, or lampblack, some even with dark mud. All in full disguise so that not even friends in the crowd could recognize them for the liability they posed. Among the men boarding ships that night were some well-seasoned merchants and craftsmen — one who would forever put a footprint in American history books, a renowned legend and silversmith named Paul Revere. Most were very young apprentices, journeymen, and merchant seamen, all there to either watch or help destroy a life's fortune of tea. One sixteen-year old journeymen blacksmith, Joshua Wyeth was among those 150 who boarded the ships. His words describing their labor were preserved for posterity, "our most intimate friends among the spectators had not the least knowledge of us. We sure resembled devils from the bottomless pit, rather than men."[1]

Their hours of work were "holed up" for them as the task would take them long into the night. This was no childhood game. It was dangerous, even life threatening, since the action would be viewed as both expensive and treasonous. The tea they were about to destroy was worth a fortune, nearly 95,000 pounds in total. British East India Company tea was packed in 400 pound wooden chests; 342 of them housed in the ships' holds, carried up one at a time. With much hard work in front of them, and a wonderful economy of words, the chests were chopped open with broad axes and heaved over the sides into the bay. "Making so large a cup of tea for the fishes," remembered Wyeth brought joy to the men, as they risked their lives in this silent party. Samuel Nowell, another of the Mohawk band recalled later in his life, "I was then young, enterprising and courageous . . . my broad axe was never more dexterously used than while I was staving the chests and throwing them overboard."[2]

The activities that evening had been a spectator sport for the bulk of the crowd; they watched their patriots in Native American dress go about their planned work with no interference from the British enemy. They even formed their own security force which guarded the area against theft as they broke up for the evening. They guarded against any incidents outside of the planned agenda so they would not be seen as some kind of thieving, riotous mob. Breakage was held to a minimum; no other parts of the ships were disturbed. When one of the Mohawk players tried to make off with some of the loose tea hidden in his coat, his fellow collaborators grabbed and stripped him, covered him in dirt and mud. They were going to tar and feather him, but the assailant got off easy that night since heating the tar would have caused not only a disturbance that evening but would have led to questions about what else they were doing that night.[3] So while there had been lots of excitement, the town's people had maintained a demeanor of quiet and reservation. As the evening was coming to a conclusion, most were beginning to realize that something astonishing was transpiring in their country. They went to their homes quietly, solemnly contemplating the earlier work and activities of the evening. Few would have ever guessed that the chopping sounds of axes hitting the boxes of tea were some of the starting sounds of an upcoming revolution.[4]

Imperial authority's full weight was now beginning to rest on the shoulders of the colonists. The reason? It is something that has caused revolutions from time immemorial; taxes and money. England had run up huge debts in an expensive war with France and was looking to the American Colonies to pay their 'fair share' of the cost. Most of the Colonists did not see things that way — henceforth the Boston Tea Party for a start. And in 1764 and 1765, the British Parliament began levying new taxes, multiple taxes culminating with the "Stamp Act" in 1765. This act started taxing the daily business dealings of Colonists in order to pay for the British Empire around the world.[5] The British were just getting started with monetary demands. Next Parliament pressed Colonists to provide housing for the insurgent British troops now coming into the Colonies in large numbers. Each day seemed to present more new demands.

More vocal Colonists would not have it. That segment of the population drew the line in the sand. However, some wanted to keep the status quo; don't rock the boat, as many say even today, keep everything going as it is. They would say "we don't want a fight." In fact some Colonists were loyal to Britain and their demeanor would welcome new taxes if necessary. Today we have citizens like those loyalists of the 18th Century. They are comfortable with government's encroachment into almost every area of life. Most of the encroachment goes unnoticed since the 'end users' have been lulled to sleep, too busy with electronic devices to notice, or they have no historical benchmark against which to measure or understand the extreme danger that approaches.

CHAPTER FOUR — THE ILLUSION OF GOVERNMENT THAT'S CAPTIVATED AMERICA

Meet Bill and Carol: modern day Progressives, similar to some Colonials of yesteryear who wanted to keep Great Britain (big government) in power. Bill and his wife were travelers I met who use the smaller and younger Bob Hope Airport in Burbank, California. They were friendly, conversational, and seemed interested in going out of their way to meet people. I met them during the holidays while catching a flight to the Midwest; they were starting a vacation to southern Europe and Paris, France. Burbank's airport is the choice of many southern Californians now, since it is smaller and cozier than its older cousin LAX, and affords the occasion to have a slightly less stressful atmosphere, if there is such a thing in air travel these days. Because of its relaxed demeanor, Burbank has become popular for travelers on the northern side of Los Angeles, including the San Fernando Valley and some points west along the coast.

As we made introductions, Bill said he and his wife were both teachers; he taught 8th grade English while Carol is a yoga teacher in an inner city LA school. Without any further exchange of information, Tim surprised me by immediately asking, "Who speaks for you politically in America today?" Explaining that no one did now because of my disappointment with the political landscape, I did say that the last person who supported my position was Ronald Reagan. Bill and Carol quickly shook their heads in disagreement. Bill quickly said that he really liked Obama because he was a moderate, in fact he said, " . . . he's the most moderate president we've had over the past 100 years." Bill seemed nearly flabbergasted that I didn't respond, so he added, "The government has got to do something about the poor living wages of some people; bank tellers and restaurant workers being just a couple of them. The one thing I'm upset about is that even Obama has not said one thing about the poor in five years, and now finally he is starting to at least say something about it." Not wishing to disappoint Bill further, finally I did respond, adding that these people on "poor wages" as he called them, should probably do what I did when in college in a similar situation — look for better-paying job. Adding one more comment I said, "I know this is an unpopular opinion among some today, but it is my opinion that not all jobs are to be seen as lifetime employment opportunities with retirement benefits."

That got the ball rolling. Carol said, "You don't understand. These people need to have living-wage jobs, and I think the government has to do something to fix that." I added that the marketplace would take care of wage concerns in places where pay was low. "You think these people should look for other jobs that pay more," I asked? They emphatically said "NO," waiting for a response.

So I was about to oblige them. Every cause in life needs at least one ideologue: a purist disciple who beats the drum for a cause even when there is no understanding of what the details of the cause are, or what it takes to make the cause work. With that definition in mind, I told them, "You two certainly seem to be ideologues for social justice." Adding to that comment that the problem with social justice, as defined by liberal teachers, is they want to level the economic playing field — all by using other people's money; extracting money from a group of those who work to make it, run it through a government bureaucracy which spends a huge portion of it, and give the remaining pennies to those who either don't want to work or who say they just don't make enough. "It's all about using other people's money," adding, "It seems to me that social justice leaves out an important factor: individual responsibility and the idea of initiative to work on improving one's self."

Adding more to my earlier statements, "Next, I think we should try to get a better idea of how business works, how paying employees is only one part of the cost of any business. Asking questions about what to pay is appropriate, but what is the right hourly wage for these jobs? $15 per hour? $20? How about $30 per hour? What about $50 per hour? Pick a number and let's use it." Bill said, "I think $50 is too high; $25 per hour would be appropriate."

"Let's use that $25 rate in a restaurant example, I countered. "Take a man who owns a non-franchised pizza parlor. He probably invested $100,000 of his personal money, borrowed another $500,000 for equipment, lease, etc.; all to prepare and then sell $13.00 pizzas to families like the Smiths or Jones's, who dine there occasionally. The owner is paying his employees $25 per hour, as you propose, all to prepare and serve pizzas to these families. The first problem that becomes apparent is that Mr. Smith, the customer, is probably not prepared to drop $45-50 for the same 12" pizza. Believe it or not, the cost goes up when the hourly wages and other expenses are higher (it's called spiraling overhead). All of the costs, including lease, food costs, utilities, equipment, the increased labor costs, the increased worker's compensation, and increased social security have to be covered by the sales of pizzas. Above that, there should be a reasonable profit for the owner, and at best that won't happen for several months. The second problem flows out of the first. Since employee's hourly pay is this high, the pizza owner won't be competing favorable with other similar establishments in the business, if he has to pay a wage of $25 per hour. In other words, competitors can produce a pizza for less money. Third, if the government dictates hourly pay at this level for non-skilled jobs, you will find a great percentage of small business owners doing something different with their careers. They will most likely close their businesses. Others, who earlier planned on opening new businesses, will not. Very likely, for $25 per hour, the owner may choose to forego the headaches of opening a business where he would not make anything for several months, and simply work for another restaurant. As an hourly laborer, the hourly rate probably represents more than he will make during the first 3 years of owning his own business. Why would he want to have the headaches of owning a business with all the red tape, taxes, and government reporting, if he can make more money as just an employee? As I looked them in the eyes I added, "Anyone going into business, sinking their money into it, along with their sweat and long hours, deserves the opportunity to make a profit. Besides if people currently working in a pizza joint want to make more money, what's wrong with them finding another job, or preparing themselves to have skills that can be used

Chapter Four — The Illusion of Government That's Captivated America

in better-paying jobs? That can mean going to college, getting a degree, all while they are making pizzas. Or they could learn a needed skill in a trade school on an internship with other firms."

Then I challenged Bill, "Look at your retirement program. See if it contains investments in companies that produce products for public use or consumption. Investigate to see 'where' it is invested. If you have a retirement plan, you want your retirement program to grow don't you? That means you want your money invested in companies whose goal is to make a profit; not just be a place that pays their employees $25 per hour or more. The reason why, is so the stock price will have a better chance to go up and help your portfolio grow." They both argued saying I just didn't understand how the market should work. They also argued that it was simply important for government to help increase the pay for those in their current jobs so they could "feed their families." I did reply, "It appears that you have been behind your high walls at school so long that you may have forgotten how the free market place works. A simple fact in business is profit motive; if there is not profit, why do it." One of the most basic principles of owning a business is this: if a person has their welfare, their money, their time invested and at risk, they deserve to make a profit. They also deserve "the larger piece of pie" for those very reasons.

Ideologues often exhibit the following characteristic: they want to see the cause leveraged with other people's money even when they don't understand the inner workings of the cause or most of the principles driving the cause. This is clearly seen when demands are made that employees who have "no skin in the game" are demanding equal pay with management.

After more comments from them, I added, "Look next at how much you are really doing for the poor apart from your taxes or what you are saying in your classroom. Take me for example — I'm interested in helping the poor. I spent over half a week's pay out of my pocket, above my taxes, this last month to help ensure 1,200 poor people had food, a Thanksgiving Dinner, who wouldn't otherwise. We served those 1,200+ folks and it was wonderful to see them get to enjoy the holiday in at least a respectable setting in which they had grown unaccustomed to having in the last several years. What I am telling you is that I like to help the poor too, but I am willing to put my money on the line to make that happen, above the taxes, and above the talk. I don't just wait for someone else to do that."

Next Bill said he was upset with the number of American companies who had closed plants in the US and gone overseas. He didn't think it was fair, indicating companies should be taxed heavier if they operate plants of operation overseas. I said, "I don't think you understand some of the important factors in why business left the U.S. One reason they moved offshore was due to the egregious tax burden on them." "No," he said, "We don't pay enough taxes in this country as it is. That's especially true for companies. They need to pay more like in other countries." I told him, "If U.S. companies were to pay taxes at the rate of what other countries did, they would get a tax rate reduction. That's because U.S. Companies pay the highest corporate tax rate among the nations. The tax was too burdensome and was one element that put too much pressure on profit margins. Profit is one thing investors seek in a company or they sell the stock. So, in many cases, the companies have gone offshore to do the work, usually at a lower tax rate, and certainly at a lower hourly rate for their workers too."

Bill said, "That is one of the things that I think is cruel and unusual that companies offshore are paying only 50 cents to a $1 an hour for workers." I answered, "The international job market is different than here. However if you look at China as an example, American companies who went there and paid very little; they are now finding that due to competition of other American companies in the nation, and the market adjusting to competition, they are having to raise pay to higher and higher wages to compete with those other companies that manufacture in the country. There is an example where the market place took care of the hourly rates of workers. And it is still doing it. Some companies are now responding to that pressure by moving their manufacturing plants further into the inland provinces of China where labor is still very cheap. Over time the market will take care of pay in that region too, as competition in the area grows. The tax problem is still a key however." See chart below.[6]

Figure 1 – Corporate Income Tax Rate

Country	Central Government Corporate Income Tax Rate	Country	Central Government Corporate Income Tax Rate
Australia	30.0	Japan	30.0
Austria	25.0	Korea	22.0
Belgium	33.99 (33.0)	Luxembourg	22.05 (21.0)
Canada	15.0	Mexico	30.0
Chile	17.0	Netherlands	25.0
Czech Republic	19.0	New Zealand	28.0
Denmark	25.0	Norway	28.0
Estonia	21.0	Poland	19.0
Finland	24.5	Portugal	25.0
France	34.4	Slovak Republic	19.0
Germany	15.825 (15.0)	Slovenia	20.0
Greece	20.0	Spain	30.0
Hungary	19.0	Sweden	26.3
Iceland	20.0	Switzerland	8.5
Ireland	12.5	Turkey	20.0
Israel	25.0	United Kingdom	24.0
Italy	27.5	United States	35.0

Bill wasn't buying the data. But I wanted him to dig deeper with me into this discussion of cause and effect for cost of goods and labor cost in the U.S. I said,

Chapter Four — The Illusion of Government That's Captivated America

"Before we go any further, we must be clear that we are dealing with an economic theory of value and what it is supposed to do. Its task is to simply explain the exchange value of particular goods and services. Tax systems of the home country where manufacturing occurs have to be considered because they impact the cost of goods and services performed.

Similarly, a labor theory of value will claim that a good's natural price is proportional to the total quantity and type of labor required to produce it. It is my consensus that there is some cost within labor which unnecessarily increase cost of goods sold. Coming to mind immediately are union labor, union pensions, and paid retiree medical costs. These have been very visible in the auto industry as they priced themselves out of the global marketplace, forcing bankruptcy talks. The auto manufacturers were bailed out by taxpayers (aka, government), in large part because of salaries and pension funds, higher salaries, and very rich benefits plans that unions said were necessary; they were breaking the companies. Other industries with similar financials have reacted as they could; management in many instances moved production sites have offshore. There with a lower tax burden, lower wages, and less regulation, the cost of goods can keep products competitive and allow for profits too."

Bill said, "Well my wife and I disagree; government should force companies to stay in the U.S. and provide for higher wages for the working class. We are concerned for the poor people in this country. And we think conversations like this should be able to be take place across the country; liberal v. conservative like we have had, without either side becoming loud or angry. I appreciate your strong knowledge base and your civility during our talks. This type of discussion should happen often, don't you agree?" I replied, "Yeah, I agree that conversation should be free and open. Unfortunately, you are in a profession that does not allow the diversity of thought to be taught or even discussed behind the high walls of your school. If I were to share what I have just shared with you, on your school campus or in a classroom, I would be ushered off the property and possibly arrested for having a dissenting thought. Your union will only allow what you have been sharing today to be said in that environment. Check it out; I believe you will see that I am correct."

Finally, I said softly, "I want to challenge you and your wife. If you are really "all in" on taking care of the poor people in this country, especially in the inner city of Los Angeles, why not quickly consider doing the following: Get up, go home right now. Sell your tickets. Take the $7-8,000 it is going to cost to make your trip: Go to the inner city and give it to many of the poor and disadvantaged. Just give it to them, no strings attached. You will have a wonderful feeling. Don't fall under the illusion that this is government work. People need help, but they also need to learn how to fish for themselves; not by government programs and not in governments handing out food stamps or money. You could feed some people even this afternoon if you are really "all in" in taking care of the poor." Both of them just stared at me with their mouths open. I think that expressed their "true feelings." They really are not "all in" unless other people's money is being used. They talk about it; that is an illusion.

Someday historians will have to tell how, in our age, the powers of illusion were spread over America, how many of the people believed the words told them by government; that "government would take care of their needs." There was clever packaging to these words; they were told often. They were told so often that many people lost their sense of what truth is. And eventually they couldn't understand truth when they even saw it. The historians will also tell how one progressive after another taunted the people with promises until a Muslim found his way to Washington, who with an uncanny understanding of this weakness in human nature, adopted a whopping lie as his major weapon, believing the time had come for people to be fed a message of hope and change. Once elected, there was a bait and switch, with the real purpose of transforming the country into a socialized dictatorship. He counted on the unwillingness of the people to face unpleasant facts as his best ally. When confronted with accusations of being a Marxist, he simply stated what Karl Marx himself said in his time when he was accused of the same thing, "I am not a Marxist."

With a couple of young generations of Americans has come a lack of experience in knowing world affairs, economic principles, and moral policies; all necessary to guard freedom. The lack of these essential benchmarks has stopped the citizens from differentiating between true democracies and collectivized regimes. Without such benchmarks, they have been captivated by the cheap talk of hope and change, an illusion. And this illusion, if not stopped, will lead the nation down a terrible trail; to be forced to walk as the Cherokee Nation was forced to walk their "trail of tears," a path toward a thousand years of darkness. All because they could not recognize impossible and empty illusion of government; to take care of them and keep the playing field level.

These historians will have to tell their audience about the liberal Pied Pipers such as Obama who came with promises sounding rich; but were empty and never delivered. They were as deplete as dry thunder storm clouds; they promised rain, but never delivered, only teasing the dry parched land. By performing political tricks and fortune telling, the Liberals did nothing more than tell a lie. As historians continue their reporting, they will have to tell how Obama deflected condemnation for his actions, by craftily relabeling, repackaging and redefining terms. His term "transformation" comes to mind. It's a picture of a shell game, but there is not pea under any shell. Historians will say how he repeated his ideology in speeches until all the citizens had heard the terms numerous times. They had it beat into the stuff of their souls so much so that in one state after another in this great country people looked at his mirage, and believed it to be true change. Their belief lasted until they all had been bound secure in the dungeon of his wrongly defined terms until finally, they had lost their country.

Then if these historians are men of spiritual insight, they will go on and write

Chapter Four — The Illusion of Government That's Captivated America

even more penetrating criticism. They will show how the political misrepresentations of our age were the manifestations of a deeper moral and spiritual bankruptcy which caused deeper confusion and all were fooled by this one claiming to be one who would heal the nation. They will also write that the forces of destruction were working through him and succeeded in confusing much of the nation, because its' moral mind was already befuddled. They will say the reason why deception worked so well on us was because self-deception was already a set habit within our minds; that at the base of all the deceptions was the great lie of Secularism and Relativistic Humanism, which had been engrained into the people for over 70 years. They will have to report how men had lost their spiritual vision and turned away from the wisdom and sovereignty of God to substitute their own brand of thought, which was delusion. They will report the delusion was so great that liberals and progressives from our era claimed that God was never a part of our founding, that we should forget the heritage of a Christian beginning that some profess — and that we should after all be like other nations. They will also report how these Liberals concocted other lies claiming that Christians had fomented lies and manufactured a false story of our country to mislead anyone who would listen.

The concluding lesson of what historians should write is straight forward; in order for a nation to be successful in accomplishing its purpose and goals, reality must take precedence over the desired public relations of a political leader; for the laws of nature, such as cause and effect, cannot be fooled. Government cannot take the place of individual pursuits, dreams and energy, else all will be lost. All it takes is one generation waiting for government to place provisions upon the table, and those which follow will have lost their pride. Their drive to be exceptional will have dried up like a raisin in the sun; their dreams will have blown away like clouds on a windy day.

Thinking of illusions recalls a memory of a column in Rolling Stone magazine that revealed a recurring and disconcerting trend with young Millennials. They have been brain-washed by professors preaching the Progressive dream of a welfare state. In the column, "Five Economic Reforms Millennials Should Be Fighting For," Jesse Myerson, acknowledged disappointment with the current system and says his peers should demand guaranteed jobs, a universal basic income, the confiscation and redistribution of real estate and private assets. Those were very old ideas for such a young man — he doesn't realize all his ideas had been tried before multiple times in centuries past — they failed every time.

Many young people I have encountered agree with government mandates including the "old collectivism" with its welfare which marked the dark days of the Iron Curtain. These youthful ideologues have not heard or learned the lesson of history. When that lesson is comprehended, it taught us time and again that promises made by a welfare state are every bit as good as the dreams of Peter Pan: "So come with me where dreams are born and time is never planned; just think of happy things, and your heart will fly on wings in Never, Never Land." Nice movie and

Broadway play to escape reality for a time, but always untrue in this world. Welfare states never work because the material needs of those most vulnerable will always be a target that is ever changing. Governments always offer "one size fits all" solutions; these solicit causes which cost liberty and create more grief. However, the appeal in the growing welfare state of America is seen by some; when someone is hungry, the promise of a Peter Pan sure sounds appealing.

Jobs that are guaranteed by the government will always have some severe negative impacts,

- they destroy the innovative spirit;
- a universal basic income will start creating poverty and dependence where it did not exist before;
- confiscating private assets for public use creates an "Al Capone" type government;
- they nurture contempt, anger and laziness.

When my kids were little, they usually wanted what the other one had. Whether a new toy, a doll, a Cabbage Patch child; it made no difference — they would fight over each. There was lots of mopping up tears in that growing up process; screaming and fighting like all kids will do. And when a government starts the giveaways, the grown up kids want all they can get; they scream and yell, trying to conceive of methodologies for getting more than the other one, all without working for it. The huge challenge to parents in this giveaway society is to daily teach children the value of toys, money, things, and their appropriate place in life. Government sees itself as a parent, but does a lousy job of raising the kids in this country. The lessons government teaches are the wrong lessons.

We are a nation that has lost its way. We must learn the unvarnished truth from history. The real history, about the bloody boot of Communism; not the history taught in universities today. It can never do what it promises. It offers a utopia of box after box of candy; full of sweet chocolates, lollypops, goodies, clouds that taste like marshmallow crème, and full of Neapolitan flavored snow drifts. The problem is THEY ARE ALWAYS EMPTY BOXES.

Teachers in our primary, secondary schools, and universities need to learn the real world by getting out from behind their high walls so their ideas can be benchmarked and challenged in the real market place. Liberalism always works in the classroom — but not in real life. Survey results like those on the survey published in 2012 by UCLA's Higher Education Research Institute show why many professors prefer the Soviet-style Communism or that of Castro in Cuba to democracy. Among 23,000 professors who were willing to identify their political leanings, 50.3 percent identified as Liberal. 12.4 percent as far-left liberal. Only 11.5 percent self-identified as conservative, with 0.4 percent who said they were far-right.[7]

Chapter Four — The Illusion of Government That's Captivated America

More political balance among faculty in the classroom would produce smarter ideas, rather than the radical dreams we see today. This would result in children having a chance to see and hear the truth about what really happens when governments offer social justice at the end of a gun. They would hear the words of a Czech prisoner turned president, Vaclav Havel. He said communism "could never be tamed" and "socialism with a human face" is impossible. The only advice I have for those caught sleeping in the Progressive dream of a welfare state: Sweet dreams, kiddos; the only way to keep that dream alive is to keep hitting the snooze button.

Obama did not start the movement of Progressivism and Marxism in this country, but it seems to be reaching a crescendo with him. Teddy Roosevelt and Woodrow Wilson really started the ball rolling toward iron curtain socialism with all the loss of rights and freedoms that evaporate away under such regimes. FDR and LBJ tried to create new societies with wars on depressions and on poverty. Both wars brought a continual diet of new taxes and more government oversight in greater and greater areas of life. Then Bill Clinton, George Bush, and Barack Obama have been the icing on the cake, so to speak. They were pure Progressives in spending, raising the debt, creating more government oversight and creating an ultimate monster that is gobbling up dollars. It has been a relentless march by many Progressives that have pushed us closer and closer to going over the edge of a precipice.

The idea of social justice, social reform, and leveling the playing field to make sure no one is left behind, started this ball rolling. The leftists have been clever in their advertising campaigns, accusing anyone who does not agree with their tactics of being hard-hearted, cruel, and wanting to starve children and poor people. Conservatives have under estimated the lunacy or naiveté of some Americans; they have not responded to such idiotic attacks, thinking people were too smart to fall for the ruse. But the bottom feeders in the country have believed what the liberals have said in their attacks. Here is the truth: We are all concerned about the poverty, wanting the poor to succeed. But we believe in a different way to reach the goal. Rather than just give them a check each month, we want to help instill within them a drive toward excellence, a hunger to excel, a drive to work hard toward their goals, and the arena allowing them to dream big. Of course that requires help at various levels, but certainly not generation after generation of handing out checks and in doing so, developing more and more dependence upon big brother.

I was at a breakfast with some professional peers when one of the very outspoken liberals of the group began to accuse Republicans, conservatives, libertarians, et al, of deliberately trying to starve the poor, and create dirty water and dirty air for the world. I snapped back asking how stupid he really was to make such a statement. "Sure, I got up this morning trying to devise a better plan to take food away from poor children, continue my plan to poison the air and water," I sarcastically exclaimed! "How stupid are you people?" But it is not that they want to think we are that evil. It is just that the media and the Left has said it so long, so continuously, so vividly, that some people actually believe it now. Have we dropped to the sensibility level in our lives that cartoons like Underdog and the Bullwinkle Show express their idea of a perverted imagery of good against evil in this world for some?

If you recall, Underdog was continually fighting against the wiles of his arch-enemy, Simon Bar Sinister. An obvious liberal, Simon Bar Sinister was continually trying to devise a scheme to destroy civilization and blow up the world. He was always just inches away from doing so, when Underdog came to the rescue, saving his lady friend, Sweet Polly Purebred as well as the remainder of the world, and the day. In their cartoon, Rocky and Bullwinkle had to outsmart the likes of Boris and Natasha in every show; Boris was trying to destroy civilization, like the old Soviets waging war against capitalism.

Have we really become so dumbed down as a society that we truly believe that conservative people want to poison the water and foul the air?! Come to think of it, I guess we have. Except it is the liberals who are busy playing the real life role of Simon Bar Sinister and Boris, because they have loved the old Soviet style communism so much. They have complained that the world is unfair without them around to offset the effects of America. And if you notice, it is the Socialists, German Nationalists and Communists who have destroyed millions of lives. Come to think of it, there are some crazy people in the world who want to in effect blow it up, but it is not the conservatives. It is the liberals, like Nancy Pelosi, Harry Reid, and their gang that want to blow up civilization and capitalism, the path out of poverty. America was the answer.

America Started Differently

In contrast to what all these liberals, progressives, atheists, agnostics, Obama, et al are saying in profusion, standing in contrast to them are the speeches and writings of our American founders that point directly to a different kind of and unique beginning for this nation. Following that march on Griffin's Wharf by 7,000 that night and the Revolutionary War that followed, there were heroes in our country who stood head and shoulders above leaders today. These heroes of our country stand in strict contrast especially to what the liberal agenda teaches today, whether it is atheism, secular humanism, Marxism, Communism, Socialism, or whatever proponent they want to march out on a given day. Our founding stands in contrast to all that and in contrast to that of any other nation throughout world history and certainly in contrast to what liberals want.

America was dedicated to God early on, as is witnessed through the mountain of evidence in several sources, which once seen, is clear to a rational student of early American history. Obviously, not everyone who came to this country early on was a Christian; however, it is obvious that those who helped shape this nation and the core critical thinking had a faith in or a strong belief that God was starting a nation such as the world had never seen before. It was a grand experiment and those who came here, whose belief was not placed in God, nevertheless were able

Chapter Four — The Illusion of Government That's Captivated America

to clutch onto and ride along for the blessings of the faithful much like barnacles hold to the hull of a ship.

Any serious student who wants to understand the true origins of American history should read the works of Peter Marshall and David Manual, *The Light and The Glory* and *From Sea to Shining Sea*. Together, these companion works detail clearly how faith in Jesus Christ was involved in the founding of America. They provide evidentiary proof even back to Christopher Columbus that his intent was to bring Christ to the "heathen" in the East. Though you won't usually hear this when the story of Columbus is studied on educational TV or in the classroom, all this information is readily available in the personal diary of Christopher Columbus, and is frankly undeniable.[8]

Later in the early 17th Century, comes the evidence provided by the pastor of the Pilgrims who commissioned them with their real purposes in coming to this country. **Rev. John Robinson** was clear in his sermon on their whole purpose for coming to the new world (as he intended to do himself at a later time) and he gave his final sermon to them. Among other things, he said:

> "I charge you before God and His blessed angels, that you follow me no further than you have seen me follow the Lord Jesus Christ. The Lord has more truth to break forth out of His Holy Word. I cannot sufficiently bewail the condition of the reformed churches, who are come to a period in religion, and will go at present no further than the instruments of their reformation. . . . I beseech you, remember it . . . an article of your church covenant . . . that you be ready to receive whatever truth shall be made known to you from the written Word of God."[9]

There is also this, that when the Pilgrims finally landed in the new world, and they came to their final destination, they named that place, their colony, Plymouth. Once established in their colony, William Bradford, their governor wrote in his journal about the colonists as he led them for some thirty years. In his *History of Plymouth Plantation, Volume 1*, he wrote:

> ". . . they cherished a great hope and inward zeal of laying good foundations . . . for the propagation and advance of the Gospel of the Kingdom of Christ in the remote parts of the world . . . "[10]

Reading **The Mayflower Compact**, seeing its words and pledges that speak the undeniable evidence the Pilgrims named Jesus as their Savior in beginning their community:

> "In the Name of God, amen. We, whose names are underwritten, the loyal subjects of our dread Sovereign Lord King James by the grace of God . . .
>
> Having undertaken, for the glory of God and the advancement of the Christian faith and honor of our King and country, a voyage to plant

the first colony in the northern parts of Virginia, do by these presents solemnly and mutually in the presence of God and one of another, covenant and combine ourselves together and a civil body politic."[11]

Clearly, America's first political document openly stated the purpose and desire of those signing, was to glorify God and advance the Christian faith. Combined with Bradford's Journal they both say that the early settlers and colonists were unashamed of their faith in Christ. To say they were not bold and open with their statements of faith would be an understatement.

The liberal rewriters of history have been trying to make certain we do not hear this truth. Instead, a revision, or manufactured story of helplessness and other lies are put forward that our nation was never founded as a Christian nation. To visit any public school classroom today, you would never hear about how God was the central figure in our founding or that the pilgrims were nothing more than bumbling and helpless fools.

In total contrast to these new-age opinions, are the words of the first, official documents of the colonies, written with a commitment to God. The preponderance of the evidence is unavoidable. In honor of Jamestown, the first successful colony in America in 1607, the first charter of Virginia stated:

"We, greatly commending and graciously accepting of, their desires for the furtherance of so noble a work, which may, by the providence of Almighty God, hereafter tend to the glory of His Divine Majesty, in propagating of the Christian religion to such people, as yet live in darkness and miserable ignorance of the true knowledge and worship of God, and may in time bring infidels and savages living in those parts to human civility and to a settled and quiet government, do, by these our letters patent, graciously accept of, and agree to, their humble and well-intended desires."[12]

When **New Haven, Connecticut** was officially founded in 1638, their first general court recorded a set of laws for their colony, which were based solely on the Bible. Later, in 1659, seven appointees known as the "Seven Pillars," were selected for office to put in place a "civil polity where God's Word was established as the only rule in public affairs."[13]

The world's first written constitution, known as the Fundamental Orders of Connecticut, written in 1639, was put in place by those early colonists. Through their words, what they believed about the relationship between church and state becomes clear:

"For as much as it has pleased Almighty God by the wise disposition of His Divine Providence so to order and dispose of things that we the inhabitants and residents of Windsor, Hartford, and Wethersfield, and now cohabiting and dwelling in and upon the river Conectocotte [or Connecticut] and the lands thereunto adjoining; and well knowing where a people are gathered occasions shall require, do therefore associate and conjoin ourselves to be as one together the Word of God requires that to maintain the peace and union of such a people there should be an orderly and decent government established according to God, to order and dispose of the affairs of all the people at all seasons as public State or Commonwealth, and do, for ourselves and our successors and such as shall be adjoined to us at any time hereafter, enter into combination and confederation together, to maintain and preserve the liberty and purity of the Gospel of our Lord Jesus which we now profess, as also the discipline of the churches, which according to the truth of the said Gospel is now practiced among us."[14]

As if that is not conclusive evidence, add these other documents to make a stunning case of how God, religion and politics were all joined at the hip in the founding of our great nation:

In 1643 — The New England Confederation as it was called, which were articles of confederation between Conn., Mass., New Haven, and New Plymouth, were put in place. One sentence speaks volumes about their purpose:

"Whereas we all came into these parts of America with one in the same mind and aim, namely, to advance the Kingdom of our Lord Jesus Christ...."[15]

In 1695 — New York instituted state laws declaring the following in its preamble:

"Whereas, the true and sincere worship of God, according to His Holy Will and Commandments, is often profaned and neglected by many of the inhabitants and sojourners in this province who do not keep holy the Lord's Day, but in a disorderly manner accustom themselves to travel, laboring, working, shooting, fishing, sporting, playing, horse racing, frequenting tippling-houses, and the using of many other unlawful exercises and pastimes upon the Lord's day, to the great scandal of the holy Christian faith...."[16]

In 1705 — Pennsylvania, in its earliest legislative document, held every person in office to an oath by which the holder swore a commitment to Bible as the Word of God and to the Lord Jesus. In this year and following, all these selected office holders or magistrates, were required to:

"... profess to believe in Jesus Christ, the Savior of the world and swear that they profess faith in God the Father and in Jesus Christ, His eternal Son, the true God, and in the Holy Spirit, one God blessed for evermore; and do acknowledge the Holy Scriptures of the Old Testament and New Testament to be given by divine inspiration."[17]

William Penn founded the colony of Pennsylvania in 1682. That year he cited to his fellow Quakers, and the world, the Biblical basis for civil government, by referencing 1 Timothy 1:9-10 and Romans 13:1-5, which he read. Then he spoke:

> "This settles the Divine right of government beyond exception, and that for two ends. First, to terrify evil doers; secondly, to cherish those who do well."[18]

In 1775 — A resolution was passed by **the Provincial Congress** in that year, acknowledging a 'sin of failing to keep the Lord's Day holy.' It reads:

> " . . . there is great danger that the prophanation of the Lord's Day will prevail in the camp. We earnestly recommend to all the officers, not only to set good examples; but that they strictly require of their soldiers to keep up a religious regard to that Day, and attend the public worship of God thereon . . ."[19]

Today's progressive secularists would have everyone believing that our founders wanted to keep their religion and their public policies totally separate. Reading their writings, legislation and quotes shows the opposite: The magnitude of the purposeful lie which has been presented to Americans over the last sixty years has come all in the name of liberal progressive education.

Progressives are people willing to exploit anything and anyone to advance their agenda. Human props trotted out at every White House event to push gun confiscation, stimulus bills, Obamacare, or global warming. There's no line they won't cross, no lie they won't tell, to force their government religion on people who simply want to be left alone. Force is the cornerstone of the progressive philosophy. Hundreds of millions of people were slaughtered over the last century, all in the name of "progress." Lynchings, forced sterilizations and "work" camps may have morphed temporarily into "anti-poverty programs," speech codes and various marches for "rights," but the goal remains unchanged — control. Progressives have learned the lessons of the 20th century — public relations trumps all. You can do anything, no matter how despicable, as long as you couple it with flowery prose, staged visuals, and have the media carry the ball. Propaganda is king, and stated intentions supersede actual results.[20]

Judge for yourself. Based on only the small sample of evidence presented here, which faith system seems most feasible; Christianity or Secular Humanism? Which seems most plausible to you? Which one really holds water? Which one do you really want to trust?

"To the kindly influence of Christianity
we owe that degree of civil freedom,
and political and social happiness which
mankind now enjoys . . . . Whenever the pillars of
Christianity shall be overthrown, our present
republican forms of government — and
all blessings which flow from them — must
fall with them."

~ Jedediah Morse

*Patriot and Educator,
called 'The Father of American Geography"*

Chapter Five

The 50s:
They Were Something Special!

AS A BOY OF AGE FIVE I believe, one of my Christmas presents that year was a little record player that was two-tone red and grey; about 12 inches square and 8 inches deep. My other present was a little 45 record, one of the small ones you had to put a circle disk in the middle of the big hole on the record so it would fit and turn on the spindle correctly. The record was the only one I had. We were poor. It was a huge thing to get a record player like this! On one side of the record was the song "Davy Crockett." The other side had "Jim Bowie." I can still hear the music in my mind. That's the wonderful thing about memories; we can smell an aroma or hear a special sound that immediately opens a file drawer in the mind and out comes this great memory in full and living color from the distant past. In this case it was, "Davy, Davy Crockett, King of the Wild Frontier!"

As a 5 year old, you can never retain information to the fullest; it leaks out when you hear something only once. So with my record player warmed up, I played that record over and over again in my room, and was dancing to it around my bed. In retrospect, I played the song about 50 times back to back to back, as loud as the volume would go. I can still remember my mother finally stalking into my room, tired of hearing the same sounds over and over and over again. And she said to me, "TURN THAT THING OFF!" Not realizing the impact of a young 5 year old child's music can have on a parent until my daughters did the same basic thing from their room about twenty-two years later — of course, I was offered the chance to learn, but with a much louder sound system. Their song was different, about "Big Bertha" as I recall, but the repetition was about the same 50 times that I had done as a child. Prophetically, my words were nearly identical as that of my mom's from the quarter century earlier. I wanted to tell my mom after all those years I finally understood what she was saying that day. Unfortunately, my mom died of cancer when I was 19 and we never had that conversation. She did not get to enjoy her grandchildren.

I also remember my sweet mom gave me permission to decorate my room the way the way any boy of nine wanted in the late 50s. Coming of age, nearing 10 years old, I was ready to take on the world. She must have held her breath after making that promise and crossed her fingers behind her back. After a few weeks of work on my part, she came into my room and gleefully exclaimed, "My, this is a perfect boy's room!" She seemed at least a little happy and was talking about the replica solar system I had hanging from my ceiling, starting from the Northwest corner over my bed and proceeding "kitty-corner" across the middle of the ceiling to the opposite Southeast corner. It was laid out to scale and relative to size and color, according to the latest information according to astronomers, and the encyclopedias of the day. The earth hung over my bed with Mars and its curious canals a little further out. Pluto was in the Southeast corner and very small, but it counted because when I was a boy, it had not been stripped of its status as a planet, and it remains a planet today, at least in my mind. I was into anything outer space in those days and loved to think about someday becoming an astronaut. My 5th Grade teacher, Mrs. Robinson, knew that astronomy was going to be my avocation someday. My attention waned during school hours with some subjects, but during science class under her teaching, especially lessons on outer space, etc., I would hang on every word from my teacher and from the science book. My dream, my calling, my ultimate goal, and of course my patriotic duty to a nation, was to try and beat the Russians single-handed, by being an astronaut. My room was decorated for it; my pillow heard my dreams at night. I was ready to mount the rocket and travel to the moon or Mars, and in doing so, save America.

Even though I was only nine and one-half years old at the time, I was well aware that the United States was well behind the Soviets in the race for space. Soon after launching Sputnik in 1957, the Russians launched Sputnik II with its passenger Laika (meaning "Barker," also known as Little Curly), the Soviet space dog. She was a female stray found on the streets of Moscow, and those godless Soviets let her die in orbit. The United States had responded by trying to send up its own satellite; but it disastrously exploded on the launch pad, leading the media to call it "Kaputnik." In the following months and years, the United States tried to send up bigger rockets, such as the Atlas, but nearly every one of them exploded before reaching outer space. Now the United States was "behind the eight-ball," but was determined not only to catch up but to pull ahead. It was a national priority in those fervent days.[1]

Obligation to the citizens demanded that the US catch up with the Soviets. Necessity is the mother of invention; at least it was during the post-war boom into which I was born. Necessity had led the push to our nation had coming out with victory in the Second World War and as the dust cleared, we were the only major economy in the world that was not bombed back to oil lamps and tents; but we were behind in the space race.

Life was pretty exceptional during those 50s as I remember from my youthful eyes and saw much more evidence through the eyes of others who were adults then. Theirs was a similar experience, witnessing what is best described as a freshness and innocence about much of society. There was the naiveté, a more innocent time compared certainly to today, as we always hear as the descriptor of that time. You can see just a glimpse of the innocence through TV shows of that era. Several broadcast companies, like Retro TV, FETV, or COSI TV have started serving the public by playing those old programs reflecting the simpler times. Their current popularity has been growing among millions wanting to see the old shows that reflect that innocence rather than so much of the absolute stupidity and filth of so many current shows today, especially what is called 'reality TV.' If TV has grown up, I would rather it remained a child.

Also, there seemed to be more stability one could have in a job or career. A person could work for the same company for an entire lifetime; that was very common. Virtue was our national brand; money was not the only thing as it is now. That's at least according to my mom and the rest of her middle class family. Fred Siegel agreed, "Public opinion polls in the late 1950s and in 1960, one historian reminds us, reported that the American people were 'relaxed, unadventurous, comfortably satisfied with their own way of life and blandly optimistic about the future.'" [2]

Regarding more products in the home, magazines like *Life*, from the 50s and the previous decade were all promising the days of trouble all over — they were in the rearview mirror — at least according to the full page ads which ran inside. The picture of one ad said all that needed to be said — there was a full four-color ad for Libby's and their "family" of great canned juices (which included the new flavors of loganberry and kraut). In the ad, there was dad, seated at the table wearing his suit coat and tie. Beside him and smiling, was grandma in a flower print dress, and little sister, hair neatly braided. They had gathered around the breakfast table — they were each choosing from among Libby's ten different varieties to quench their individual thirst.

Advertisements in the 50s promised that hard work of housewives was going to be eased; improvements to daily life were on the way. The ads displayed gadgets which promised improvements to everyday life: pictures of electric irons, electric coffee makers, automatic clothes washers ("easy as turning on a light"); and electric sunlamps for tanning ("You too can have that winter vacation look"). Packaged foods offered both convenience and nutrition; frozen succotash; processed meats; cellophane-wrapped donuts, "dated for freshness"; canned chicken noodle soup ("a favorite among the simply homey dishes that built the men who built the nation"); and Dromedary-brand gingerbread mix, "made from the original recipe of George Washington's mother," promoting the down home goodness of Cream of Wheat and Aunt Jemima pancakes with grinning images of African Americans.

For men, there were several brands of whiskey; for women, slips, girdles, bras, hosiery, face powder, and diamonds; for everyone, toothpaste, mouthwash, and tobacco. Cigarette ads were prominent at the time. Lucky Strike was proudly declaring that it was searching the tobacco farms and paying top dollar "for the finer, lighter, the more naturally mild tobaccos."

But the biggest and most colorful were the automobile ads that testified in an alluring way to the promise that American life made — each ad was a full page, most were in vibrant color. There was a Chrysler in cerulean blue (with plaid interior), featuring a Spitfire engine and Vacamatic transmission. On another page, a dashing red Mercury roadster, "built according to aviation principles." Turn the page, and there was an Oldsmobile "Special Town" sedan, available in gleaming yellow. Another displayed a Chevrolet, with its Victory engine, "unisteel turret top," and "tip-toematic clutch," all offered at no extra cost. With more than 10 million female drivers cruising America's highways and byways, a Ford ad announced "it is the women of this country what needs the engineers must meet," and depicted a sturdy green four-door as the tangible response. Here was life, liberty, and the pursuit of happiness made manifest.[3]

My maternal grandfather, Hearl's brother, had spent his late teens, back in the Teens of the 20th Century, driving a street car in Kansas City, which was known at that time as "The Little Apple." After he married my grandmother, they moved back to a small town of 1,400 people in the Ozarks, close to where they had both grown up, and there he worked for the rest of his life. He started his career as a part-time independent grower of fruit trees and also worked at the grain elevator. One of granddad's customers there, who eventually became a mentor, told him one day he should be working with his mind rather than his back, because as he said, "he was meant for more than carrying sacks of feed."

Motivated by his customer at the elevator, grandpa researched business opportunities that seemed appropriate; then he took the gamble. He started an insurance business in 1937, sharing an office in those early days on the second floor over the Ferguson Dry Goods store building. By the 40s was rolling in his career. At first he sold policies for Kansas City Life and continued that practice as he grew a well-rounded insurance business for nearly four decades. He stayed with Kansas City Life, but added other companies in his brief case and officially became an independent insurance agent for the rest of his working life. While he could have gone on to do several other things, insurance was the career with which he stayed. He didn't build his business on big advertising or by being slick, but on credibility, trust, hard work, respect and his remarkable personality. Grandpa had the respect of everyone that I knew he ever met. He had a customer service model as a part of his demeanor and business that I've tried to emulate in my career. No matter how good mine was, I will always come in second to him. There was no one quite like him.

One thing he taught me was to make sure to be honest in dealings with others and have a "what you see is what you get" presence with people. "Everyone is a customer. Go out of the way," he would say, "to make sure you have given them the best service you can give, no matter how tired you might be. Remember that and it will take you far." I watched him in several different setting; having both business and personal friendships with many people, and I always found him to be honest to a fault with them all.

Chapter Five — The 50s: They Were Something Special!

Many of his generation could tell stories how they started working at a factory, manufacturing plant, a grocery store, or some other business, large or small, in their early 20's and stayed there for the rest of their career. There was more stability in common work then, and workers could provide for their families even with what some called a minimum wage job; even working at a gas station, or as they were sometimes called in those days, a "filling station."

My dad was one that had a similar experience. Having been a staff sergeant for two generals in World War II (Omar Bradley and Anthony C. MacAuliffe) he prepared the general's mess every day in Headquarters Company. That was for his division for the duration in France, Austria, and Germany. He even cooked a few meals for General Eisenhower on occasions when he would come to see the generals and review the situation. Coming home from the service, he went into the restaurant business, first with Mickey Canada in Mickey's Bar-B-Que House in South Los Angeles (Englewood), right on the corner of Western and Slauson Avenues. There he cooked and managed the place that had the "best little BBQ sandwich in town," as one man described it. He also said, "It falls all to pieces before you could get it in your mouth."

Dad had lots of tales of his own, real life accounts about some of the customers in what came to be known to me as the battles of Mickey's BBQ House. These were customers my dad found to be funny; they entered the restaurant in various stages of inebriation. One could not negotiate the sidewalk, but wanted some good barbeque to sober up. Even these hard luck stories had an air of innocence about them, similar to our friend Otis the drunk on The Andy Griffith Show. Given everything, it was probably the best decade in which to raise a child. The wholesomeness of family life was projected throughout the country. Everyone's experience was not that of mine, but was fairly typical for a middle class family in 1950s America.

One of Dad's customers, Jack, had become a friend to Dad over the years. I recall that the two used to go to the Friday night fights together in the mid to late 50s held at the arena in LA. Because the boxing matches were televised locally, my dad would always wear his Camel hair jacket, so as a boy I would get to recognize him on TV sitting ringside of the boxing matches as the camera would pan the audience once in a while; and get excited. To hear the old timers talk, there was an air of innocence in that day, even in this southern part of LA. My dad would walk me down to Mrs. See's Candy Store once in a while on a Saturday night to get some chocolate. It was a rough part of town in those days, but rough carried a milder, tamer definition in that decade than it does now.

Never to be satisfied, there were liberal "intellectuals" who claimed that the country was "going to hell in a hand basket" during the 50s. Their exaggerated claim was made because they were not in control of culture or government at the time. That infuriated the liberals. Anything they don't control, they will criticize and ridicule. When they control it, the result is typically total destruction, but like a spoiled child, they are proud of their results.

Some of these liberal progressives, all Ivy Leaguers I think, complained endlessly and held to, " . . . criticism of suburbia — and by extension of the 'American character' in the 1950s — there were deeper fears about the nation's psychological health. Buzz words and phrases exposed these fears: 'alienation,' 'identity crisis,' 'age of anxiety,' 'eclipse of community.'" " . . . Many of these words and phrases reflected the rising visibility of popular sociology, of psychological models, and of 'experts' — whether Norman Vincent Peale on the power of positive thinking or Dr. Benjamin Spock, who soothed nervous parents with immensely reassuring advice about child rearing. Psychiatry and psychology . . . boomed in the 1950s. The United States, it seemed, was becoming a 'therapeutic culture' in which 'experts' helped people to feel good."[4]

Other liberals ridiculed the country that runaway consumerism was absolutely undermining the American values, like C. Wright Mills who indicted the United States as having become, "a great salesroom, an enormous file, an incorporated brain, and a new universe of management and manipulation."[5] However, when one compares the 50s to our country today, Liberals are now in charge. Even with the shortcomings of those days, life was much better then. No comparison.

My parents told me their entertainment opportunities in the late 40s and very early 50s were limited. But when listening to them describe the time, it was more wholesome; mostly radio programs, classical music concerts in the park, attending art museums, reading, going to a drive-in movie, attending a live wrestling or boxing match at the L.A. arena, or a little later as they could afford it, watching television. (Pretty much the same as today, if you remove the reality TV shows.) Dad would attend live wrestling matches and the Roller Derby. My parents also took me to Disneyland, which opened in 1955, during its first few years of existence. In those days, it was a long drive of over an hour from LA out through the orange groves before arriving at our destination. The theme park's products spoke of the overall desire for wholesomeness in the country during the 50s. "Disneyland . . . was an enormously successful business enterprise, it testified to the power of affluence and of the consumer culture. Millions . . . traveled every year long distances to visit the park and enjoy the surroundings."[6]

Mom worked hard to make my "kid experiences" special. My mind becomes pregnant with all the memories of home; her ironing board and Maytag wringer washing machine. Her cake baking and salad making were treats for watching night time TV on our RCA Victor console I can still see in my mind. She took me "trick or treating" when I was five and six in Los Angeles. Door to door we went, I came home with two large bags (they seemed large but were probably pretty small) full of candy which we poured out in a pile on the kitchen table. My Dad smiled and sorted his favorites. In retrospect, I realize now he had a tough childhood, and in adult years rarely smiled. He really wanted to stay within himself, in a self-made prison of selfishness he had built. Mom made times, events, and holidays full of meaning and memories. It seemed she was always there for me, even when she

Chapter Five — The 50s: They Were Something Special!

was so ill and in tremendous pain. We did not know it at the time, but Mom was not going to be with us that many more years because of cancer. Her selflessness makes the perfect picture as seen in that she came to all my ballgames in high school, though she was sick all during those years, having illnesses which kept her bedridden much of the time. Recalling her words, "You need to be careful and don't get hurt." She was there when I was drug by my horse, an event which nearly killed me. She consoled me and protected me from Dad when I received the only traffic ticket of my teenage years, one for running a stop sign. She held me when my dog died; it broke my heart. Her love she provided in being there for everything has been a motivating factor to keep me going at times when life got too tough. As for many, Mother's Day always carries a bitter sweet meaning. It would have been wonderful to have her around in a portion of my adult years, to receive some of her home spun wisdom as I aged.

Movie goers had dwindled in the late 40s and early 50s, historians say. Movie producers, rapidly losing viewers, sought anxiously to bring people back to the theaters. Most responded, as usual, by playing cautiously to a mass audience. Westerns proliferated, many of them celebrating heroic men, submissive women, and treacherous and dirty Indians."[7] There were of course more serious subjects in the theater, "... Other movies played to Cold War obsessions by raising the specter of communism and glorifying strong military authorities."[8]

My perspective on that in the mid-50s: TV was a big thrill, with its 14" black and white screen in a large mahogany console. I could lie on the floor, getting up close and putting my feet on the screen. It was obvious TV was a marvel by the way my parents and all the adults in the living room watched programs, almost spellbound. In his offering, *The Best Years, 1945-1950*, Joseph Goulden explains the comments of Wayne Coy in 1948, a member of the FCC in how he saw the future of television: "Make no mistake about it," he said, "television is here to stay. It is a new force unloosed on the land. I believe it is an irresistible force."[9]

Coy's prediction certainly came true, as TV grew enormously over the next several months and years. Programs were limited and my Dad sarcastically said the only thing that was on was wrestling, with Gorgeous George and his opponents. "In 1949 it [TV] was in its infancy; few Americans had ever seen it. People relied instead on radio, which in 1949 had 1,600 stations compared to twenty-eight for television. Then the TV boom: 172,000 American households had television in 1948, 15.3 million by 1952. In 1955, there were 32 million sets in use ... by 1960 some 90 percent of households had at least one set..."[10]

Of course programming was what it should be now, no risqué programs, or at least the risqué part would be only suggestive for the adult audience. I remember in particular, the Roy Roger TV shows in the mid-50s had a moral for youngsters. Often Dale would quote a Bible scripture on living an upright life that was a lesson for all. As one advertiser put it, there were always great lessons for viewers to gain that would help build character. The Lone Ranger Show offered entertainment with stars Clayton Moore (The Lone Ranger) and Jay Silverheels (Tonto) leading the way against dishonesty and unethical behavior by the bad guys, working to maintain or restore truth and justice in the west. There was a moral code based on Biblical truth presented in many of the early TV programs. Young people hearing this today will often respond with "lame," "boring," "it's all in gray" or just "old." But the moral and especially the language content of the old, boring shows like Roy Rogers compared with some recent children's shows like "The Simpsons," "King of the Hill," "American Dad," the language differences become clear.

Mom and Dad moved back to the Midwest in the late 50s where they had grown up and started life over again. Dad initially worked at Rawlings Sporting Goods as a manufacturing foreman. Shortly thereafter he was into the food business again with a restaurant that was open 24 hours a day, a steakhouse that became known throughout the territory as one of the best places to eat. The restaurant stood alongside two national highways and was vibrating with a full house at least four times a day. And in that business, dad stayed for the balance of his working life.

Mom and Dad had a farm, and of course growing up there, my responsibilities expanded past being a kid; like immediately. It grew into managing that farm and the animals, since I had an absentee Dad from the time when I was 10 years old on. Then of course I was mustered into Dad's army, working at the restaurant on weekends as a dishwasher, a cook's helper at times and finally as part time book keeper. After seeing the restaurant business and how my Dad was married to it some 18 hours a day, I discovered in the 60s that college was calling my name.

Having moved to Missouri in our 1953 Mercury towing a tiny U-Haul trailer with a small Cold Spot refrigerator, a blonde colored bed room set and a sofa/chair and a console black and white TV, it was a huge change for me. There, close to my parent's original hometown of Willow Springs, we built a house in the country. There was only one TV station close enough that "came in," through the tall TV antenna on top of the roof. That made night time television programming so different in those days as we approached the 60s. For example, there were several situation comedies, like *Hazel*, some variety shows, like *The Smothers Brothers*, and the news was in a smaller time slot each evening, only thirty minutes total for both local and national. In many ways, TV was your only contact with the outside world, especially the nightly national news and that was just for a few minutes. In his book, *Grand Expectations: The United States, 1945-1974*, James Patterson explains, "Until September 1963, the evening news lasted only fifteen minutes. Newscasters — such as Chet Huntley and David Brinkley, who reported the news on NBC for almost fourteen years beginning in 1956 — lacked the technology of videotape... and mostly contented themselves with showing film footage and reading a script."[11]

Hand crank wall phones were popular in rural locations. We had one in our living room wall connecting us with sixteen families in the neighborhood. Our little telephonic world was held together by uninsulated wires strung through the

Chapter Five — The 50s: They Were Something Special!

woods on porcelain insulators. Once asked by a young IT professional later in my career if I remembered my first phone number and if so would I tell him what it was? I said "Yes, I remember it clearly. It was short – long – short." Following the laughter among the group, it took my young professional acquaintance a minute to grasp the meaning. He finally did with some explanation. Later we had two phones in the house — the latter connected us to the real outside world.

Homes were never locked in our part of the world; not for us nor my grandparents in town, even when we went back to California on vacation for two weeks at a time. We knew all our neighbors. They knew us. Neighbors would never bother anything, and they certainly wouldn't steal anything, and they kept their eyes out for any activity that would seem abnormal. It was a time of hard work, long hours, honest dealings with everyone with whom you had business, in particular neighbors and people you didn't know, as my grandpa used to say. I think that means everyone. We played hard: baseball in the summer league, basketball in the school gym on holidays. With no teachers around, or the police and guess what? No fights, nothing broken or stolen. Most people we knew had a good moral compass. If a friend didn't have a moral compass, there was usually a friend close by that had one to help keep others honest. The church was a viable voice in the community in those days, positively impacting the community morality.

Many words people have used in attempting to describe the 50s, while trying to speak of the exhilaration of the time. Young people were blowing past the threat of the cold war and living life in exhilaration because the whole world was beginning to open up to them. The music was fresh and brisk, new cars were exciting each October as we looked for the changes to next year's model. More products were available each year in the dry goods stores; mechanical machines were making life easier for homemakers. There were problems, but they seemed small and innocent in contrast to those of today.

Mostly the 50s brought a newness to life and culture. The youth were coming out with new expressions, which seemed numerous, and it seemed each month as if someone were coming out with the latest expression which you had to use to be cool! As one historian stated of the slogans, "Hear a few: gung ho, cool jazz, hot rod, drag strip, ponytail, panty raid, sock hop, cookout, jet stream, windfall profit, discount house, split-level home, togetherness, hip, hula hoops, Formica, and (in 1959) Barbie Dolls."[12]

Every little town was its own world in those days. Conservatively 90-95% of a person's time was spent in their own town, venturing out to another city rarely. Farmers came to town on Saturday to "do their trading." The whole town would swell those days to 5-6 times their size with the streets full of folks talking and laughing, everyone catching up on the latest news from their friends. Sundays were days for church, rest, family gatherings in a park, or catching up on chores and getting ready for the coming week.

One older church friend of mine said he remembered the fifties for the lack of inflation. Hearing his comment helped me recall the cars of the decade. At the forefront my dream car would appear, the 1957 Chevy Belair. You could drive one home for $2,700. That was brand new, fully loaded right off the showroom floor. It even had the "new car smell," as my mom would state. The perfect model was the two-door, two-tone in the now famous Indian ivory white, and matador red. A non-professional working man was generally making around $6.00 per hour. So buying a new car was always a challenge, but not nearly the challenge as in today's inflationary market.

Money was not the only thing that helped life be more relaxed. Families tended to be a little less stressed. Sundays were reserved at least early for church attendance. Not everyone went, but many did. Every Sunday it seemed was lunch (referred to as "dinner" to the elderly Midwesterners) at Grandma's house where everyone was usually in attendance. The afternoons were spent going to play softball or baseball in a school yard with neighbor adults and kids. It was truly a day of relaxation. And Sunday evenings were mixed between church youth meetings, dinner (super to the old-timers in the Midwest) and watching some TV together, like The Wonderful World of Walt Disney and Bonanza on the NBC lineup.

Parents did not spend as much time worrying about where their kids were. They knew for the most part they were safe. Due to the innocence factor again. In that culture, children were taught manners and respect for elders and others, and even their property. You were taught by osmosis to have ambition and drive. These attributes made for communities that had little to no anxiety.

Satisfaction has been called a byword for America in the 50s, a national feeling that the country was on the right road. Of course there were areas of American cities where horrible problems existed, but those societal problems seemed to be bottled up in specific places. We took responsibility for what we did, including our mistakes. The accepted motto in my mom's and grandparents' lives was "the decisions you make, dictate the lives you lead." We were taught that early in life; "When you make a choice, you choose the consequences that go with that choice."

The post-war boom brought continued focus on and involvement in synagogues and main line denominational churches. Families heard teaching and preaching that was Bible centered, usually in a "contextual, expository" message. The church voice in the community was obvious then. In 1959 I recall school assemblies where church hymns were sung by the student body. Teaching and school activities had a point; to help you learn lessons that would prepare you for life, not just the next test on the schedule. If a student got in trouble at school, there was a great chance there would be smoke up over the bushes at home that night, applied by the father's discipline. And that would be much worse than any discipline you had at school. I can still remember the empty, sick feeling of fear in my stomach when my mother had caught me in some mischief and said that one time, "You father is going to deal with this tonight when he gets home from work." The one time is all it took.

Chapter Five — The 50s: They Were Something Special!

The Christian faith was an active part in our school activities in those years. It was not perceived as a philosophical "Bubonic Plague" from which a child must be protected, as the government and others view it while operating the "indoctrination centers" which are nothing less than the brainwashing we were accustomed to hearing about during this time period. Nobody in school preached any faith, it was just a wholesome and healthy belief in God that was set forward, and in our need to make the world a better place than it was. Whatever else might be said about the Leftists in our society, they are vocal about wanting Christianity taken out of everything. A society cannot run away from it spiritual moorings at the breakneck pace which this society has done, without having serious moral and behavioral consequences. Historically, that is a proven rule, though the Leftists want to free us from all our good history.

We felt safe, because of the community moral code we had, which we were taught via the churches through family units. Much to the annoyance of the leftists today, those codes came from our religious, aka Christian and Judeo heritage, our spiritual roots. Your family might not have gone to church but you tended to have a healthy respect for people's rights, their property, and their lives. If you didn't you were not welcomed into the society at all.

And for those 50s and even through the 60s, for most of my junior high and high school years, we never were around drugs. Of course drugs were around; we were not that naïve! We just didn't go around them or keep friends who did them, because we were taught differently. The innocence of the age was rearing its beautiful head. Even the worst prank we ever pulled was at Halloween; that was usually to "soap someone's windows," or to let air out of a tire.

Another brand for which was famous in the 50s, was that "your word was your bond;" no need for pieces of paper with signatures. I recall my grandfather buying a Jersey bull from a friend of a friend in the cattle business. I stood there and watched both men discuss the deal; my grandfather asked him several questions, started to shake his hand, then pulled it back quickly to ask him one last question. Once they were in agreement on the last question, they shook hands and that finalized their contract. It was better than any notarized piece of paper today. Business was straight forward. If it wasn't, you weren't in business long. People were not money hungry as they tend to be today. There was a focus on providing great customer service; generally far better customer than what exists now. People lived quietly in their communities taking the responsibility to do the right thing, whether it made lots of money or not.

But that was then, and this is now. How in the world could we change so drastically as a society? We have moved from having communities with the school's greatest problem being students talking out of turn or eating candy in the classroom. We've traded that set of problems for those of today; the drugs, the beatings, the shootings and the murders in some of the same school buildings. It is so sad to see we have exchanged the safety and innocence of our schools, to now having metal detectors installed at every entrance attempting to keep the hallways and classrooms safe for our children.

If you really believe that the answer lies simply and solely in whether a Democrat in the White House instead of a Republican, or vice versa, then you are probably a big part of the problem. Politics in just a veneer that points out the sickness and turmoil that lies deep within our society. Our problems speak of a foundational problem; something has shifted or has been removed. Hopefully you will see in the following chapters not only many of the major problems facilitating our national decline. But you will view them against the backdrop of our nation's founding and even against the backdrop of what I call "the great decade of the Fifties." Possibly then at least a portion of the answers and solutions to those problems, aka the ultimate fix, will be visible.

Bill Bennett put it this way in *The Devaluing of America*: "The American people have overcome enormous challenges before. And I have seen; the difference that good, decent, and courageous men and women can make. Our cultural injuries are self-inflicted. The good news is that what has been self-inflicted can be self-corrected."[13]

"Before any man can be considered as a member of civil society, he must be considered as a subject of the Governor of the Universe"

~ James Madison

4th President of the United States;
Member of the Continental Congress;
Rapporteur at the Continental Congress in 1776

Chapter Six

Decades That Changed America

MY MOM AND HER MOTHER BEFORE her, kept lots of family pictures. They ranged from the then current Polaroid photos all the way back to the late 1870s close to when pictures were first being made I think, which had been passed down. Mom kept albums of photos. Grandma kept albums, albums, and boxes of albums. They were categorized by family groups in eras, or decades and stacked in the closet of her bedroom. What were not in albums, were piled in boxes. We are talking serious pictures here! Some older images had been taken using an old and early generation Brownie camera and some earlier cameras too. The yellowing on the edges from the years was telltale. Among the newer photos, were some which the camera dated as the shot was snapped. The oldest pictorials were from the mid-19th century and were extremely faded.

All of the photos, or a large portion was pulled out when relatives from out of state would visit. The pictures coupled with her comments when friends or relatives visited made up a huge portion of what I called "her generational library." As a child, of course they were not that important to me; I was too busy running, playing ballgames and building forts for us cowboys to defend against the neighborhood Indians. However, with the passage of time and at least a little maturation, it would be exciting to go through some of them at holiday times with Mom or Grandma to ask questions about older relatives whose images were still with us, long after they had passed away. Now, though it is too late, I would welcome an epoch or two to sit with her and ask for the story behind each person she had in pictures.

Mom's serious health situation dictated that we use time with her as a priority; we didn't know how much longer she would be with us. Photos became great friends to her, a nostalgic vehicle of time travel with the family, as well as books she liked. Technology was non-existent compared to today; no devices for texting, emails or browsing were around. And calling home from a far off hospital was not done without some extraordinary expensive.

My mind has forever captured the image of the coffee table in our living room upon which Mom kept a "photo cube." At least that is what I called it; containing pictures of her dad, my grandpa. They were pictures from various times in his life. They were snapshots from six decades of life, in one easy place to grab. Each picture showed this prince of a man as I knew him as being or doing something different, displaying his possession of various character strengths. One photo showed him as a teenager working in a barn pitching hay, another as a middle-aged adult serving food at church, still another sitting at his desk as president of his own company. Another one, proclaimed him as a new grandfather, as he held me at about two-weeks old. On they went telling the seasons of change in his life, a life story in visual brief. Recalling those photos and scenes just flood my mind with memories.

I started thinking about that "life cube" album with its various stages of life and decided decades are at times comparable; each has its own set of images, descriptors, seared into our minds, distinct from others that have rolled by. Unique traits from each become branded in our grey matter helping us remember them, good or bad. I believe that is why *Life* magazine historically sells so many copies of their end of year issue showing for example all the noteworthy people who passed away during the year.

The scenery of each decade brings a new season of life, whether, for example, they be the innocence of the 50s, or the tumultuousness of the 60s. Each stands frozen in time, with photos which can stir the heart, cause soul-searching, and even brand or cut its initials into the bark of the landscape. Over time, a brand will be ascribed for a decade, starting like wet cement, and then hardening into place. Usually that brand name couldn't be announced immediately when it rolls onto the scene. Nor are we usually aware of it right away, but becomes apparent as it seeps into the corners of life gradually, quietly, stealthily. Or sometimes it is suddenly upon you with no hesitation because of a tragedy or some events so great or so tragic, the one event branding the years immediately. And out of nowhere, suddenly the brand name will appear to describe it. Similar to a giant puzzle, with the pieces scattered around on a card table, over time the picture starts to take form, a panorama in the human eye. The brand is a word or words that "frame" a particular decade, like a frame on a family photo. Look at these seasons and see how they changed our lives.

The Fifties

Viewing the 50s through my "baby boomer" lens, through history books, as well *Life* and *Look* magazine articles, all added to the discussions with those who were adults during that time, I can see why most people truly called that time the "Happy Days" of America. So much so, that I committed an entire chapter just to those years. It became known as the decade of the Cunningham family with Richie and his friends. But those years really formed a time of hard work, earning, succeeding at work, earning still more, and materialism. It was a time to dream about great possibilities. What had brought America this way to this bounty?

World War II did more than usher in unparalleled prosperity for the United States. It transformed America's foreign relations. The war devastated the Axis nations, which took years to recover, savaged America's allies, including the Soviet

Union. Alone of the world's great powers the United States emerged immeasurably stronger, both absolutely and relatively, from the carnage. In a new balance of power it was a colossus on the international stage.

Few Americans at the end of the war fully understood how vast a role the United States would play on this stage in the future.[1]

With the wars over, America robustly went to work building upon the only economy in the world that had not been bombed out of existence. It was what some historians called the beginning of the good life for the middle class. New frontiers were opening up, such as outer space. Emphasis was made on not only staying in school, but getting a college degree, that is if you wanted to be part of the dream. You had to start getting ready; that meant getting your college degree. The talk of the day was "Our troubles are behind us," and they seemed to be, for a time disappearing in the rear view mirror fast, or so we thought.

The "Red Scare" seemed to some just to pop up on the scene, it is always attributed to the 50s but the Communist movement and scare started decades earlier in this country. During the late 40s and 50s, the open public search for communists of "McCarthyism" really changed the fabric of political campaigns in America. So much so that for over 5 years, as one historian outlined "... many events, while great in their significance were fanning the flames of anti-communism in the United States, have to be put into a longer chronological context. Joseph McCarthy was in fact a "Joey-Come-Lately" to the Red Scare, arriving much later — the roots of this scare require a quasi-archaeological degree and dig into the American past."[2] One could go back as far as to the time of the Bolshevik Revolution, or to Woodrow Wilson, with his pure liberal progressive desires in building a case. But certainly the turmoil surrounding the Depression and the legislation of FDR in that decade were a platform for the Reds in this country. The stormy years of the 1930s and especially those of the early decade of World War II did much to lay the foundation for the 1940s and 1950s. From the mid-1930s on, conservative leaders and philosophers associated the New Deal with socialism and communism. The House Committee on Un-American Activities investigated left-wingers following its establishment in 1938.[3] More of the foundation was laid during the war as it seems almost everyone became patriotic. In 1940, the Smith Act was enacted making it a criminal offense to teach, advocate, or encourage the overthrow or destruction of ... government by force or violence. People accused under the act didn't have to have acted, but only were seen advocating action. Simultaneously, Roosevelt had unleashed FBI director, J. Edgar Hoover to investigate subversive individuals and groups. In 1941, Congress authorized the army and navy to fire any federal employee who was acting contrary to national interest. "This was the start of government 'security risk' programs, which cost 359 employees their jobs in 1942. The Justice Department began developing, in 1942, the "Attorney General's List" of groups considered disloyal. By the middle of the year the FBI had helped the AG to name 47 such groups."[4]

Wartime patriotism still burned in the hearts of most Americans except for the die-hard liberals. Following the war, seeing film in movie theaters of the heroic deeds from our soldiers turned many to join the "get tough" chorus of the nation. The creeds of the atheistic Marxists were openly and vocally repelled by religious patriots. But in the midst of this nationalism, most Americans were simply trying to get ahead. They were going to college, raising families, moving to suburbia, acquiring consumer goods. They were all the more ready to believe fervently in the United States in its free and mobile society. They were seeing that Communism, which took away private property, was not only totalitarian but also a threat to their social and economic futures in the U.S.

More Americans had hopes for social mobility; that stimulated both grand expectations and nervous feelings about Reds. The quest for personal security and domestic security became inextricably interrelated.[5] Throughout the late 40s and into the 50s, anti-communist Democrats and liberals were concerned about the effects of communism in the Labor unions. Dems didn't think that communism was a threat to private property ownership in the US, but having tried to work with Communists in progressive causes, they were certain that American Communists got their marching orders from Moscow.[6]

Looking back at the ideas Progressives held in this era, it is clear to see they were Communist ideas. If they were not, a communist would have been proud to say he had put them into action. Some liberals, trying to disassociate themselves from the anti-communist conversations, said their people were too busy getting ahead to worry about Communists. A survey taken at the height of the Red Scare in 1954 found that only 3 percent of Americans had ever known a Communist, only 10 percent said they had known people they even suspected of being a Communist. The same survey concluded, "The internal communist threat, perhaps like the threat of crime, is not directly felt as personal. It is something one reads about and talks about and even sometimes gets angry about. But a picture of the average American as a person with the jitters, trembling lest he find a Red under the bed, is clearly nonsense."[7] Many Americans were becoming concerned that their neighbors might be communists, or that one might be under their bed. Even if they were not, they were ready to believe that party members and sympathizers were dangerous to the American Republic.

Americans should take note that in contrast to today, in the 50s universities and organizations took a strong stand against the Communist moniker. "Acting on these beliefs, liberal organizations made moves to purge Communists from their groups, which they knew were there. By 1949 labor unions, the NAACP, the Urban League . . . had largely succeeded in doing so, and in 1950 the NAACP decided to expel Communist-dominated chapters."[8]

"The academic world was also being shaken by this political earthquake. The campus in America became a frontline in the Red Scare as Presidents and Deans within colleges and universities started taking a stand against Marxists and Communists in their faculty system. In 1948, the University of Washington fired three teachers, two of them with tenure, when they refused to answer questions by state legislators about whether they belonged to the Communist Party . . . Later . . . the American Federation of Teachers, a leading union, voted against allowing Communists to teach, and the Board of Regents of the University of California system required its faculty to take a non-Communist oath. Faculty members who refused to sign got caught up in a long and internecine controversy. A total of thirty-one . . . were ultimately fired."[9]

Leaders of Ivy League universities followed suit, becoming outspoken against this Red Plague. It becomes obvious that Communists were already on campuses, leading classes, in spite of what the Presidents said. "Charles Seymour, president of Yale, announced, "There will be no witch hunt at Yale, because there will be no witches. We do not intend to hire communists." Presidents Conant of Harvard and Eisenhower of Columbia headed a blue-ribbon panel which concluded . . . that Communists were "unfit" to teach. The American Association of University Professors (AAUP) opposed teachers being fired for taking the Fifth Amendment, but it granted the right of university administrators to expect its professors to answer questions about their politics . . . the AAUP did not censure universities that violated civil liberties until 1956."[10]

It is interesting to note that the teachers unions did, in the 50s, adopt the view that to be communist and teach was an act that fell under the protection of "civil liberties," however, to be a Christian and teach, falls under the scope of being a traitor, which will lead to be summarily dismissed. Many felt and feel that anyone who was not open to having a communist professor stand on equal footing with a non-communist professor, was either a non-intellectual, lacked worldly wisdom, or was biased due to personal beliefs. I vote for the latter since when speaking with Communists, they tend to be very evangelistic about their "godless belief," but I am not to be given the same liberty of belief, since I am a Christian. All who took stern positions essentially endorsed the view that Communists, as minions of Moscow, had surrendered their independence of thought. Sidney Hook, a well-known philosopher . . . reiterated that Communists were not free to think for themselves: there was a party line "for every area of thought from art to zoology."[11] Against this tide, most universities — and many individual faculty members — defended academic freedoms.[12] Many on campus were embarrassed by the incident because they felt they should have the academic liberty to teach that which they wanted. The entire faculty had the assumption that communists were all the same. They believed that such communists should be given a screening question asking them ahead of time if they were planning on indoctrinating students in their classes. "It is thought that 600 or so public school teachers and professors in those years lost their jobs because . . . they were communists or communist sympathizers."[13] "Liberals always thought J. Edgar Hoover to be the number 1 villain of society since he openly searched the country for and kept a dossier on suspected communists throughout his career."[14]

Add to these scenes the Alger Hiss trials for espionage in the 1930s, the HUAC hearings which received testimony from Whittaker Chambers and other ex-communists, the Truman administration going after well-known communists, and the nation seemed in high gear to alleviate the country from its Communist problems. "However it was presidential appointments to the high court which slowed the tide. By the end of 1952 [the Truman Administration] had secured . . . convictions. Ultimately 126 were indicted and ninety-three convicted before . . . a more liberal Supreme Court discouraged such litigation in the mid- and late 1950s."[15] Liberals of this day still look upon these activities of the 40s and 50s as being a dark mark against the United States, because they implore free speech and civil liberties just so long as those speaking or acting are in favor of the liberal agenda. If not, they are the first to a podium to insist that free speech be taken away.

While leaders in the nation were disposing of Communists, nuclear testing from both The US and the Soviets was ratcheted up to a fever pitch. "Truman, while a Democrat, had more convictions about being prepared for future enemies than Roosevelt had been. Harry was courted by some interested in developing a thermonuclear bomb, much bigger than the atomic bomb used to end WW II, which became referred to as "the super." Going against the apparent direction of Harry Truman, J. Robert Oppenheimer, who was widely known for his scientific expertise . . . had many left wing associates . . . Their arguments carried the day in the advisory committee, which recommended against development."[16] Truman, however, decided to proceed in testing and building the super against the advice of Oppenheimer, who headed the General Advisory Committee, and the committee, plus the Democrats. Truman later explained to his staff, "[We} had to do it — make the bomb — though no one wants to use it. But . . . we have got to have it if only for bargaining purposes with the Russians."[17] The age of nuclear proliferation and of maximum possible destruction had arrived on the world stage was near at hand for use.[18]

While the 50s were a time that some Americans saw as carefree on one hand, the threat of conflict had started with the USSR and put people on the edge of their seats as we neared the end of the decade. One apocalyptic memo put it this way:

We must realize that we are now in a mortal combat; that we are now in a war worse than any we have experienced. Just because there is not much shooting as yet does not mean we are in a cold war. It is not a cold war, it is a hot war. The only difference between this and previous wars is that death comes more slowly and in a different fashion.[19]

If you listened to the homilies from the theologians, rabbis, and psychologists toward the close of the decade of the 50s, you would most likely hear a litany of complaints: the mass media was debasing public taste, sexual license was threatening traditional morality, juvenile delinquency was overrunning society, and generational change — a "youth culture" — was undermining the stability of family and community. A television series of the day, *The Many Loves of Dobie Gillis*, highlighted a character, Maynard Krebs, television's first beatnik. Maynard devolved into a life avoiding work at all cost, collecting tin foil and loitering with his bongos. His character was a soft version of the juvenile delinquents the late 50s and 60s saw.

Here are a few of the voices of the critics of the time:

- On the mass media, especially television: "The repetitiveness, the self-sameness, and the ubiquity of modern mass culture tend to make for automatized reactions and weaken . . . individual resistance."

- On sexual behavior, as described by a critic of Alfred Kinsey's book *Sexual Behavior in the Human Female* (1953): The book reveals "a prevailing degeneration in American morality approximating the worst decadence of the Roman Empire . . . the presuppositions of the Kinsey Report are strictly animalistic."

- On youth and juvenile delinquency: "Not even the Communist conspiracy could devise a more effective way to demoralize, disrupt, confuse, and destroy our future citizens than apathy on the past of adult Americans to scourge known as Juvenile Delinquency."

These complainers were not all prudes or reactionaries. The critic of "modern mass culture" was Theodor Adorno, a leader of the Frankfurt School of cultural criticism, which drew on Marxian and Freudian insights to lament the commercialization of American life. The critic of Kensey, one among many, was Henry Pitney Van Dusen, head of Union Theological Seminary, a prestigious religious institution. Critics of mass consumer culture also included shrewd and respected intellectuals such as the sociologist Daniel Bell and the historian Daniel Boorstin.[20]

In the late 50s, I started reading comic books — it was the cultural thing for a kid to do. I loved my super hero friends. Superman was my first favorite. Not only was he in the comic books, but he had his own TV show by the same name. My cousin had ulcers when she saw my stacks of comics later. She talked of the waste of paper that meant "zillions" of trees were cut down to hold the images. Today, environmentalists attack comic books as "garbage" or "codswallop." I use the same terms with them however in describing Al Gore's books, making us even it seems. My hero stood for truth, justice and the American Way. Theirs did not. That is why my comic book heroes and real heroes in life have never been Liberals.

Superman even had an antithesis of himself; a mirror image of himself but a supervillain named Bizzaro. This villain showed up in 1958 when my "man of steel" was exposed to a scientist's creation, a "duplicating ray" he was demonstrating. Different versions of Bizzaro show up in subsequent years, but they are all a defective clone of either Superman or Superboy. Bizzaro even speaks with an ugly form of broken English such as, "Me not human . . . me not creature . . . me not even animal . . ." Bizzaro's use of English was reminiscent of Tonto, the Lone Ranger's sidekick. (Those of you who were not around at this time missed something special! Life was so great, based on confidence, hope and limitless opportunity.) Bizzaro ugly and surly had the characteristic of being against everything Superman stood for.

Bizzaro eventually grew tired of normalcy on Earth and flew off to another planet called Htrae. (It was a cube-shaped planet and the name was "Earth" spelled backward.) Bizzaro was happy there because everything was ruled by his logic; that which was right was wrong, and that which was wrong on Earth was right on Htrae. Life on this planet was opposite of life on Earth. Vacuum cleaners for example there did not pick up dirt; they put dirt down. Bizzaro is strengthened by green kryptonite while Superman had a vulnerability to it. Everything was indeed opposite of Earth.

There is a powerful lesson in this story for us in America today. One writer says, "Now, let's look at today's USA, which increasingly resembles a 'Bizarro' version of traditional America — not just different, not just "transformed," but morphed in so many ways into the opposite of what it once was. First, for those who weren't around during the 1950s and early '60s, let me just say that the America of my youth, despite its shortcomings, was basically confident, unconflicted, prosperous, and full of life, hope and unlimited opportunity. People were patriotic and our culture was strong and essentially moral. America was the undisputed leader of the world — not just militarily and economically, but in terms of freedom and goodness. (To my liberal friends: Do me a favor, and don't tell me, "But the '50s had racial segregation." Yes, and today we torture, decapitate, dismember, vacuum and chemically burn to death 3,000 beautiful human babies every single day. So just drop it.) Compared with the vibrant nation it once was, today's America has become a weak almost paralyzed country, with political correctness reigning. Divided, angry, squabbling, the world's largest debtor nation, with rampant divorce, family breakdown and unprecedented sexual anarchy, 1 in 7 on food stamps, 1 in 9 on antidepressants — on so many levels America is disintegrating."[21]

To see how we got into this situation; it really did not happen overnight like it might seem. This has been a project of the Progressive Left taking several decades to complete.

Many intellectual and liberal critics voiced despondency about the 50s due to what they called the state of the arts, the rise in professional sales promotions, the changing styles of everything from year to year, but they exaggerate their case. Most of the complaints and exaggerations came from extreme liberals because they were not in control of government at the time. They did not control our culture and citizen's lives as they do today. It seems they really wanted more abortions, more murders, more crime, and more filth. They speak of the greatness of the new America which is the result of their leadership; all being run by a centralized government controlled by Liberals. It would be comforting to jump into Marty McFly's time machine and go back to the mid-50s. They were not perfect, but far better than today.

Much to the chagrin of the liberals and their poor image of this decade, the 50s gave rise to great culture. Artists and essayists came along; the likes of J. D. Salinger, Ralph Ellison, Saul Bellow, James Baldwin, John Updike, Philip Roth just to name a few. High culture seekers enjoyed recording of great classical music, art museums, theater companies, symphonies and orchestras did very well even in small market cities. Book sales and classic literature boomed as well as the new paperback rage. So as the 50s are judged in comparison to other decades which followed, it was one of the greatest times to be an American and experience of unlimited opportunity and freedom in keeping family values close in American life.

The Sixties (A 30,000 Foot View)

Major, sudden and tragic events create emotional and unforgettable images, mental snapshots that empower people, decades later, to recall where they were when they heard the news: the September 11 attacks, the deaths of John Lennon and Diana, Princess of Wales; Pearl Harbor. For me it was when I was home sick that day, close to noon on November 22, 1963, that I will remember forever when JFK was shot in Dallas when I was thirteen years old. As Tom Brokaw notes "The television set was . . . the centrifuge for the country. Everybody drew from it in some fashion."

The 60s seemed to arrive with anger, the frenzy, the riots, and the kids singing new songs that parents said were so different, horrible, and objectionable. And that new music had a heavy beat instead of the soft melodies of the 50s. Then the Beatles came to America brought to you on the stage of the Ed Sullivan Show, and later at Shea Stadium in New York in front of the largest to gather group to that point for a concert. Their 'success' was followed quickly by other "bug named" groups chartering flights to America. These and other rock groups, some quite talented, brought out the screams of the kids with the excitement you watched on the shows during the decade. The edges of our new frontiers we had planned in the 50s were seemingly becoming frayed from the campus riots, civil rights speeches and marches, political assassinations, the growing addiction to violence on TV, the drug abuse, sit-ins, the threat of nuclear attack, burning draft cards, the Watts riots, followed by the riots in Chicago and Kansas City. Of course the assassinations of Bobby Kennedy and Martin Luther King, Jr. were the headlines of the horrible nature of this decade. It all made governing a nation a nightmare of a job. Sitting atop this pile, was an extremely strange war called "Viet Nam," which became a political football for years. It was strange because it had this demilitarized zone, with all the holidays a modern UAW member would get. Draft dodgers were speaking and then running to Canada or Europe, and were center stage defiance to a government who said, "Uncle Sam wants you." There were the hippies, the flower children, with tie-dyed t-shirts all shouting their causes and strumming their guitars at sit-ins as the anti-war crowd was growing and getting angrier. The shootings, the beatings, the burnings, the riots; all this had replaced the calm and serenity of the 50s. Old timers were heard asking, "What in the world is going on?" There was certainly no quiet on this western front.

(A Detailed Look)

The 60s arrived and seemed to bring a new Dark Ages with them with the leftists coming into power. While the talk was of advancement, quite the opposite was true. Liberal historians have said the following about that decade: they were "the beginning of a more hopeful and Democratic time that lasted until the early 70s." Another one called the 60s "a modern Great Awakening which ignited a 'Burned-Over Decade' of cultural change. . . ." One called it an Age of Aquarius that heralded a new identity — a collective identity that will be blacker, more feminine, more oriental, more emotional, more intuitive, more exuberant — and just possibly, better than the old one."[22] These comments are typical of liberals, no data, no logic, just raw emotion and feelings. They percolate with desire in dividing people up by ethnic groups, race, sex, etc. Anyone not agreeing with their chorus is branded as racist, non-intellectual, or unpatriotic. However, it has been my experience that conservatives tend to more interested in looking at people based on the intent of their will based on their actions and words, not their color, not their race, or sex. Race, skin color, or the sex of the person has always been the territories into which liberals will attempt to divide individuals.

To the cultural conservatives 1960 and what followed brought a loathing like few decades have seen. Daniel Bell, the sociologist, was appalled by all the young people who were trying to "transfer a liberal lifestyle into a world of immediate gratification and exhibitionist display." This "counterculture," as he called it produced little culture and it countered nothing." George Will later dismissed the decade as an age of "intellectual rubbish," "sandbox of radicalism," and "almost unrelieved excess." Some, Braden in particular, worried that the Americans that were forging this "new identity" might be mistaking" vividness, intensity and urgency" for cultural sensitivity and responsible morality. They don't know what they like, but whatever they or other emotions like must be art — or must be right, and certainly righteous."[23]

There are two sides to this belligerent debate and both were correct in recognizing that unusually tumultuous events were shaking American life all throughout the 1960s. The changes to culture and society seemed to do nothing but accelerate rapidly in the early 1960s, to reshape public policies by the middle of the decade and actually helped to polarize our country in the next few years of the decade. By the middle of the decade, the thrust of activism was shifting directions: a backlash mounted quickly against public programs and ushered in a long and durable age of political conservatism that Americans had taken for granted before; including the vestiges of what the lack of a better word could be called "Victorian." Thereafter people seemed more ready to challenge authority. As Morris Dickstein, a perceptive scholar put it, "The sixties are likely to remain a permanent point of reference for the way we think and behave just as the thirties were."[24]

The view of the 1960s as viewed by Dickstein has much to be said for it. Signs of dramatic and gigantic change were gathering on the horizon in 1960 and were pointing toward terrible and prolonged problems that would move quickly. It started in February of that year with the sit-ins. SNCC (Student Nonviolent Coordinating Committee) came to life in April. Enovid, the birth control pill, was approved by the government in May that year. In June, the SDS (Students for a Democratic Society) later to be the most prominent of many "New Left" protest groups was born. In 1961 social change jumped to warp speed. The civil rights movement entered into a bloodier stage, with racists attacking "freedom fighters" who sought to integrate interstate travel; between 1961 and 1965, twenty-six civil rights workers were killed in the South. More than any other development of the early 1960s, the civil rights revolution spun off several other groups that claimed idealism, egalitarianism and the rights-consciousness that challenged the social relations in the United States.[25]

The early 1960s turned out to be the soil that brought forth liberal authors with extraordinarily provocative publications and influential books that questioned and challenged conventional conservative notions about American society and culture. 1961 saw Jane Jacobs author *Death and Life of Great American Cities* which skewered the grandiose pretensions of urban planners. Joseph Heller also published *Catch-22*, an unsubtle but hilariously disturbing novel about the inanities of the military World War II. It sold 10 million copies over the next 30 years appealing especially to those people who were against the Vietnam War. 1962 saw two other seminal books, sounding alarms for the liberal causes — Rachel Carson's *Silent Spring* sounded a warning bell against pesticides and environmental pollution, a first of its kind, which liberals widely acclaimed. Its theme served as a baton that liberals picked up to run in their ecological war against free-enterprise which was in high gear by the end of the decade. Michael Harrington's *The Other America* greatly dramatized the problems of poverty in the United States, with its theme used by liberal progressives to put pressure on the government to take action.[26] Then in 1963, James Baldwin produced *The Fire Next Time* alerting Americans to violence in the streets from racial confrontations. Betty Friedan's *The Feminine Mystique* also appeared on book shelves in 1963. It was a huge seller that helped inspire and launch a renaissance of feminism.[27]

Groups of protestors around the country who captured the anti-establishment spirit of those books appeared and garnered attention, starting in the early 1960s. In 1962 in Michigan, Tom Hayden and other young SDS radicals hammered out the Port Huron Statement, a long and at times contradictory manifesto that was much-cited by the New Left activism.[28] In Mississippi in the fall of that year, James Meredith who was an Air Force veteran, tried to become the first black person to attend the University of Mississippi. When segregationists retaliated with violence, President Kennedy had to send in the army. Also in 1962, Cesar Chavez and fellow migrant workers organized the National Farm Workers Association, thereby inspiring efforts that led to highly visible strikes and boycotts later in the decade.[29] This was followed in early 1963 as Martin Luther King staged a public protest against racial discrimination in the city of Birmingham — violence resulted with worldwide television coverage, and rising outrage against racism in the United States. Later that summer, in August, King and others held a march on Washington that drew over 250,000 protesters to participate.[30]

Simultaneously, there were many other unassociated events which when added to the other loud liberal voices, made it clear that times were changing rapidly for the worst at an ever-increasing speed. Some described the events as a political earthquake destabilizing the ground beneath their feet. Some of those additional events were as follows: the Supreme Court shocked conservatives — and others — in 1962 by ruling that public schools in New York could not require students to recite a State Board of Regents prayer in the classroom.[31] (The non-denominational prayer read, "Almighty God, we acknowledge our dependence upon Thee, and we beg Thy blessing upon us, our parents, our teachers and our country." Prior to the decision, schools had had the option of using the prayer or not. Students who did not wish to recite it could leave the room.) For Catholics, the Vatican Ecumenical Council, under the reformist leadership of Pope John XXIII, agree to authorize use of the vernacular in parts of the Catholic mass. Traditionalists were amazed and appalled.[32] Folksinger Bob Dylan, who had prophetically written "The Times They Are a-Changin'" in 1962, brought out "Blowin' in the Wind" in the spring of 1963. The version sung by Peter, Paul and Mary, marketed in August 1963, sold 300,000 copies in two weeks and became the first protest song ever to make the Hit Parade.[33] (These were forerunners of later songs of the decade, like in 1966 and 1967, "Day Tripper" and "Lucy in the Sky with Diamonds" respectively, both done by the Beatles. Paul McCartney admitted these were both about acid and LSD within the drug culture. Soon after the release of Lucy, it was banned by the BBC. Many of the songs during the later decade were cause music dealing with the drug culture.) Later in 1963, Timothy Leary and Richard Alpert, having helped to celebrate the virtues of drugs like LSD, were fired from their positions at Harvard University that spring. They did however continue to beguile their disciples, especially youthful ones.

Another year and in 1964, the beat went on with other noteworthy challenges to the normal lifestyle to which many Americans had grown accustomed. In January, the Surgeon General issued a report by the scientific community warning of the mortal dangers of tobacco.[34] Millions of Americans were shaken by the announcement since over one-half of men and one-third of women in the country smoked.[35] Movie-goers flocked the same month to see *Dr. Strangelove*, Stanley Kubrick's film, whose character, a crazed militarist, Jack D. Ripper who was convinced the "International Communist Community," was trying to "sap and impurify all of their precious bodily fluids." It was a movie that was effective in ridiculing the Cold War extremes. Just a month later, the Beatles arrived on the east coast of America from England, with full television coverage and became an instant sensation. More than 67 million people, a new record audience, watched them perform on "The Ed Sullivan Show." And let's not forget Malcolm X, who in March, started recruiting blacks from northeastern cities into his newly formed Organization of Afro-American Unity. He had left the Nation of Islam and was front and center in a recruitment campaign.

Young people were getting restless across the country and in 1964 had gained enough confidence to start a protracted "free speech" movement at the University of California, Berkeley. They gained immediate national attention. The activists, many of them who were veterans of protests against racism in the South, used their juice for demonstrating against a wide range of causes.[36] Some screamed against poverty; some against racial discrimination, lots against the escalation of the Viet Nam War, against the university, and at the end of the day, they even demonstrated against work and everything normal in free enterprise within the United States. The elite campuses in America were swarming with the most privileged cohorts the baby boom generation had to offer. Some of their leaders were shouting "If you're not part of the solution, then you are part of the problem." Their diatribes developed a following which gave energy to the leftists and progressives in their political ambitions in the U.S.[37]

In the sixties, Berkeley was a city at war. Students revolted against the University of California, blacks demanded their rights, radicals surged into prominence, and a counterculture of major proportions blossomed. White, black, red, and green — these movements coincided, fed into each other, and reacted against each other in myriad and sometimes surprising ways. The decade began with President John Fitzgerald Kennedy's Camelot; it ended amid chaos. Berkeley, no less than the country, went through a crisis. On the surface, the crisis revolved around turmoil generated by certain specific social issues.... The underlying issue however was one of gaining power. During the sixties, conservatives' hatred for communism was in full bloom, both abroad and at home, rejected socialism, distrusted all government, disliked labor unions, and abhorred the high level of domestic government spending that was called the welfare state; they admired Barry Goldwater, and later, Ronald Reagan. Liberals [said they] hated communism and [claimed they] rejected socialism, but they trusted the government, liked labor unions, and favored the welfare state; they admired Franklin Roosevelt, Adlai Stevenson, and to some extent they liked John Kennedy. The city's liberals built an unstable biracial political coalition, used government programs to maintain their power, but were spinning out of control. Radicals hated anticommunism more than communism, usually accepted some elements of socialism, were ambivalent about government, liked labor unions, and favored an expanded welfare state or a drastic reconstruction of society; they admired (in varying degrees) Martin Luther King, Jr., Malcolm X, Fidel Castro, Che Guevara, and Mao Zedong. They really loved themselves — in Berkeley, the self-promotion of black militants and white radicals took center stage as both angrily tried to seize control — failing that, they were determined to make it impossible for anyone else to hold power. (Not much has changed through the years as this is a descriptor of today's turmoil between left and right, throughout the various levels of our society.)

The social turmoil of the sixties was really a battle over power. College students, young blacks, members of the New Left, and hippies believed that power should flow from the bottom up, rather than from the top down — they were ready to take it to the top floors of society.[38]

All this and other developments did not add up to a coherent movement, there was not even a pattern to the protests, but changes were coming hard and fast. Television news coverage seemed to be present for all, which by then was being seen by virtually all Americans, and from other sources of news that reached a more highly educated population.[39] In the 1960s TV came into its own as a major force in American life. While promoting a more nationalistic culture, it focused an eye on the profound internal divisions. Americans could see that change was underfoot; society was being transformed in front of their eyes; it was a restless spirit that went against the political center of what had been considered normal for so many years. Early in 1963 activists were demanding racial justice and forced President Kennedy to come out for the civil rights legislation. Following Kennedy's assassination when Pres. Johnson came to power, there was increased tension for change. Johnson declared his "war on poverty" and began shocking the nation as a more liberal crunch was on. He provided federal-aid for education. Medicare was started for the aged and Medicaid for the poor. There was reform for the immigration law, there was a creation of the National Endowment for the Arts and Humanities, and there were two civil rights acts that were historic because they had brought about what was unimaginable just a few years earlier. Progressives, who had in the past been inching along with their wares, were now racing to gain more control in everyone's life through government, with more intrusion, higher taxes and more entitlements. It was as if the activists of the far left, who had clamored so loudly in their marches and sit-ins, were beginning to learn again the age-old lesson; the "squeaky wheel" gets the grease.

Culturally too, the political center seemed to be in disarray, especially after mid-decade. Large numbers of people, most of them young, began to find common cause in seeking relief from what they considered to be the vulgarity, impersonality, and overall dullness of middle-class culture. Some of these rebels adopted New Left political opinions, but many others resisted mainstream culture, not public policies. Millions found inspiration from rock musicians, especially (it seemed) from those who were loudly and angrily anti-authoritarian. A rock concert at a farm in Bethel, New York, in 1969 attracted some 400,000 people who wallowed happily about in the rain, some in various stages of undress and drug-induced haze, for three days. Traffic jams and police barricades prevented many thousands more from attending. "Woodstock" was the culminating event of [the] "countercultural" celebration in the 1960s.[40]

There were smaller numbers of young people who dropped out of the mainstream of American life to join the counterculture communes. They were a tiny minority of the overall population (which rose, a little more slowly than in the 1950s, from 180.7 million to 204.9 million during the decade), but they took pride in defying conventional mores. Many started openly smoking marijuana; a few experimented with harder drugs and engaged in various versions of free love. Between 1965 and 1975, when the communal movement lost momentum, some 10,000 such experiments blossomed in the country. They received lingering if sometimes snide attention from the often voyeuristic mass media.[41]

Nowhere was cultural change more clear than in the realm of sexuality among young people.[42] "The Pill" was invented and helped spread the already ascended sexual revolution, but there were other larger areas where personal freedom and "liberation" thoughts played a bigger role. In 1960 Playboy introduced its "Playboy Adviser" column which guided readers to new and imaginative methods of sex. (By the early 1970s, the magazine was reaching an estimated 20 percent of adult American men.)[43] This was followed in 1962, when Helen Gurley Brown wrote *Sex and the Single Girl*, a message of female liberation that she wanted delivered to the political center. Later in the decade, 1968 to be specific, Broadway staged *Hair*, a rock musical that featured frontal nudity. The actors were paid extra for disrobing. Due to the times, the play became a hit in New York and many other places on the road, off Broadway.[44]

American values were turned upside down in the 20th Century, and many observers had been aware of the trend all along. Some writers, for example have quoted Willa Cather's succinct observation, "The world broke in two in 1922 or thereabouts . . ." To more recent witnesses, the larger part of the change appeared to have taken place about midcentury. A University of Michigan researcher noted in 1979 that "norms about marriage and parenthood have changed dramatically over the past twenty years. Today, marriage and parenthood are rarely viewed as necessary, and people who do not choose these roles are not considered socially deviant." But the beginnings of the transformation tended to show up, as Cather suggested around the 1920s.

The change was so great that in public discourse people involved began . . . to speak of the conduct that had previously appeared "bad", as "good." More specifically, activities such as gambling and public swearing that had previously been considered deviant, frequently came to enjoy positive valuing. Conversely, to a greater and greater extent, the practitioners and advocates of common place virtues began to appear to other Americans to be the social deviants . . . Moral righteousness went out of style. A standard of no restraints — particularly in indulging the bad habits — came into vogue. . . . What is perhaps most striking is the fact in the mid twentieth century, sociologists found that the connection between the bad habits were neither fictitious nor accidental. High School students, who did not smoke, tended not to drink, either. Moreover, those who neither drank nor smoked virtually never used marijuana. And finally, as if to confirm popular prejudices, users of hard drugs had invariably come to them only by way of marijuana — or at least by way of drinking and smoking.[45]

Confrontation, violence, and social disorder indeed seemed almost ubiquitous in America during the mid- and late 1960s. In 1965 protestors at Berkeley proclaimed a "filthy speech movement," a degenerate form of the free speech demonstrations a year earlier, thereby hastening a trend toward open expression of profanity in American life.[46] More alarming that this scattered phenomena were broader and apparently related social indicators: rates of violent crime, drug abuse, and alcohol consumption, especially among young people, rose sharply after 1963.[47] So did divorce and illegitimacy rates, which had been stable since the late 1940s.[48]

Concurrently, changes were devastating the rules and taboos of the past. Many of the university parietal rules were crumbling away; administrators and authorities were so tired from earlier fights that they didn't even offer resistance on this piece of sexual revolution. Speaking of which, it was upon the college campuses that an unprecedented open and defiant tone among women became loud as they began to speak about the feminine mystique.[49] Some began flaunting miniskirts which was the new style that entered the United States from France in 1965. Many of them challenged their elders by living openly in unmarried relationships with men. William O'Neil reported in his book that the mid-1960s in a survey of sexual behavior concluded perhaps the greatest transformation in sexuality that the United States ever witnessed.[50]

The mostly optimistic and reformist Zeitgeist that characterized the early 1960s weakened rapidly after mid-decade.[51] Just five days after the August 1965 Voting Rights Act was signed blacks began rioting in Watts near USC in South Los Angeles. By 1966 the civil rights movement began splitting along racial lines, with blacks renouncing non-violence. Violent riots broke out in waves during the summers between 1966 and 1968 in several cities like Kansas City, Chicago, Cleveland and others, throughout the central US. An easy target for the rioters was the Viet Nam War which had been escalating between 1965 and 1968. Angry confrontations were commonplace on college campuses, with some of them being closed periodically between 1967 and 1970 because of the furor. Other ethnic groups entered the fray and along with feminists seeking television cameras and attention to promote their specific demands. Homosexuals going in during June 1969 in Greenwich Village with their own version of a five-day riot against police and shop keepers to garner attention to their cause.[52]

Violent confrontations and social may lays seemed to be happening everywhere in the late 1960s. Berkeley entered the headlines again in 1965, when protesters started a "filthy speech movement," a depraved takeoff of the earlier free speech movement. This was a stake in the sand so marking the emerging trend toward open expression of profanity in everyday American life. Hollywood produced the new films Bonnie and Clyde in 1967 and the wild Bunch in 1969 both of these house rebels in the choreography of killing. Rock musicians got rid of the "tame and calm" lyrics of Bob Dylan and Joan Baez they started playing "acid rock." Television shows responded with greater violence and "strong" language. These movies and shows were put into the after 10 pm time slots so children would not be as likely to watch. As some concerned clergy of the Midwest said, "Filth is filth. If it's not suited for a child, it is not suited for adults either." The most alarming and devastating of the trends among all of this phenomena were the rates of violent crime, drug abuse, alcohol consumption, especially among young people which rose sharply after 1963.[53] Simultaneously divorce and illegitimacy rates which had been stable since the 1940s began to rise sharply.[54] It's no wonder that about the same time in the fall of 1964 that the Scholastic Aptitude Test began to fall and I guess you could say that the decade was unraveling in every direction.

By the late 1960s, it seemed that anger was so rife with degeneration that even life itself was no longer sacred or even respected by many of the radicals; events hit an all-time low when Martin Luther King and Robert Kennedy were both assassinated in 1968. In December 1969 as the decade began to close its doors there was still another note of the unthinkable un-civilization, when a group of Hell's Angels working as security guards for the Rolling Stones concert in Altamont, California, savagely beat several concertgoers with pool cues. They stomped and beat an inebriated and naked young woman who tried to climb on the stage, and they stabbed to death a 19-year-old black man. News reporters said that featured performers looked on with an uneasy gaze, but kept playing; and the cameras — making a commercial film about the stones — kept rolling. Most of the fans in that huge audience of 500,000 seemed unaware of what happened.[55]

History had recorded rightfully that the 1960s were a breakaway from past culture in American life, and that society became polarized during those years. Most Americans had little to do with campus rebels, the counter-culturists, anti-war protestors, or the feminist movement. They watched the news and knew about the tumult — television had lavished attention on it — but they went about their lives in normal ways.[56] As in the 1940s and 1950s they celebrated traditional values and institutions such as the work ethic and monogamous marriage.[57] Though ever increasing percentages of women entered the paid work force, thus altering the dynamics of family life (and contributing to the falling off of the baby boom), most continued to do so to augment family resources; earning money for the home, not a deep dissatisfaction with life in the two-parent nuclear family, largely explained their behavior.[58]

As had been the case in the 1950s, millions of upwardly mobile Americans rejoiced at the ever-enlarging capacity of a thriving economy to bring material comfort to their lives. Actually the 1960s were the longest period of uninterrupted economic growth in all of US history. In spite of all the tumultuous activity, per capita income continued on its constant march upward moving from $2100 in 1960 to nearly $3100 in 1970. While income was increasing 41%, prices stayed steady until the last year of the decade. Unemployment among late teenagers was very high, approximately 19%, however the overall unemployment rate was very low falling to 3.5% in 1969.[59] Poverty, as measured by the government declined rapidly, from an estimated 22 percent of the population in 196 0 to 12 percent in 1969.[60]

All of these astonishing developments of the 60s seem to promote even more expectations among the people especially the Baby Boomers who were not around for the Great Depression or for World War II. Their outlook on life became much different than that of their parents. Not only was their outlook different, their numbers were different too. Near 20 percent of the total population were Baby Boomers. This was a record high for any generation; most of them were going to college. The Boomers by choice were the most education generation ever. They wanted knowledge and resources at record levels in order to build a better society, and change the world. They were a unique generation in all of history.

So while all these expectations were growing millions of Americans began to anticipate the role progress of the country, they felt like they had the rights to all sorts of blessings. What was always considered a lavish luxury in the 40s, was now considered an entitlement. These people, often narcissistically, felt that they would achieve great personal growth and self-actualization.[61] A revolution was about to start, the likes of which had not been seen in America before. Everyone it seemed was being "pressured" to become a part of a pressure group: labor unions, corporations, blacks, native and Hispanic Americans, feminists. All were starting organizations that screamed for rights. "Athletes even got in on the action. The major league baseball players Association was created in 1966."[62] Running in tandem with the rights movement, people were starting and joining interest groups which demanded legislation from the liberal movements to protect the environment and to improve our lives. The liberals cried for government help. Even elderly Americans became militant in their own way. They became known as the Gray Panthers. They established powerful lobbies in Congress.

Poverty-stricken people formed their own groups such as the national welfare rights organization. They angrily denounced Congress as failing to meet their needs. All these "activist" groups gave the appearance of only self-interest. At the heart of each organization, they were going after rights. From all appearances the United States was becoming a claimant's society. After all, most of these organizations were started to obtain utopian dreams with its expectations that life would become perfect. However it was a revolution that did not deliver. Expectations and the realities which followed created more distrust of government which has continued since the 60s.

Standbys of popular culture from the 50s and before offered glimpses and remembrances of the past, the way American life used to be; it seemed eons ago. Bulwarks of traditional values, like big-time sports coach Vince Lombardi talked of the virtues of hard work and daily discipline. He became a cult figure himself among many Americans because he stood for traditional values. Winning he would say wasn't an important thing, it was the only thing! Television tried to keep vestiges of the glory days past with violence free programs such as *The Lawrence Welk Show*, *The Lucy Show*, and *The Tonight Show* with Johnny Carson who took over in 1962 and became the "King of late night TV" virtually forever. Richard Nixon was sworn in as the 37th President of the United States in January 1969. Later that spring, he announced a planned withdrawal of 25,000 American troops from Viet Nam by August the same year. On July 17, 1969, Apollo 11 successfully landed on the moon, with Neil Armstrong's famous words of, "That's one small step for man; one giant leap for mankind." It seemed so long ago, but it was just earlier the same decade that John Kennedy put forth the challenge to put a man on the moon before 1970. We Americans took the challenge, it had happened just as predicted. Thus came a successful end to round one of the space race. And on December 1, 1969, the Selective Service System of the United States conducted two lotteries to determine the order of call to military service in the Vietnam War for men born between 1944 to 1950. "The draft" occurred during a period of conscription, controlled by the President, from just before World War II to 1973.

It is now clear that the 1960s America was living in the postwar era. When the era began in 1945, the northeast quadrant of the United States enjoyed a disproportionate share of wealth, power, and cultural authority. The big cities in the quadrant were home to the large mass-production industries and the multitude of workers who kept the machinery running. Since the New Deal, these workers and their new industrial unions were the foundation of the Democratic majority. The Republican Party was no less anchored in the region. Wall Street bankers and their corporate allies dominated the GOP on behalf of an internationalist foreign policy and a modest welfare state. Mainline church denominations, strongest in the North and theologically liberal, provided Protestants with their most authoritative voice. New York was the nation's financial, cultural, and intellectual capital, the place that published the books people read, that produced the radio programs they listened to, and that nourished a remarkable number of liberal intellectuals, whose ideas defined the nation's serious discourse. In an oft-quoted passage, the distinguished literary critic Lionel Trilling wrote in 1950, "In the United States at this time, liberalism is not only the dominant but even the sole intellectual tradition. For it is the plain fact that nowadays there are no conservative or reactionary ideas in general circulation."[63] While this has been the continuous claim of Liberals, it was a shortsighted view believing the Northeast had the ability to think for the nation.

During the next thirty years, profound changes transformed the northeast quadrant and subsequently the United States. The changes were above all, economic and demographic. Markets shifted, factories moved, and new modes of production rearranged the nation's economic geography. One consequence was that millions of people were displaced, remaking those regions they left and the places they settled. "By the early 1970s, beneath the surface tumult of politics, demography had prepared the way for the defeat of liberalism and the decline of the region where it once flourished."[64]

The chorus note of victory for liberals as the decade began turned sour toward the end due in large part to the extreme progressive spirit which Lyndon B. Johnson carried forth in his presidency. The Kennedy assassination on November 22, 1963 devastated and shocked the nation to its core. I recall as if yesterday that fateful day; having a fever, Mom had kept me home from school. I was playing with my Lionel electric train set in the living room floor and in the background I recall the phone rang. In just a moment, my mother starting crying aloud and she signaled for me to turn on the television. We couldn't believe the news from Dallas. There was so much uncertainty, so many questions. With the threat of the Soviet Union and questions of Cuban involvement in Kennedy's death, the assassination had many in the country fearful of atomic confrontation again. Some journalists thought there was even a possibility of war if either Cuba or the Soviet Union was found to have sponsored Kennedy's death. Johnson appointed a seven-man panel of distinguished public servants he thought had unimpeachable credentials.

A half century has passed since that extraordinary event, investigated first by the Johnson-appointed Warren Commission, just five days after the assassination. It was headed by Earl Warren, the Chief Justice of the Supreme Court. Other members included CIA director Allen Dulles and future president Gerald Ford, then House minority leader. Many Americans have felt through the years that there were still too many unanswered questions.

From the day its conclusions were published for public consumption, the commission was criticized for its methods, omissions, and conclusions, although several authoritative follow-up investigations confirmed the conclusion that the two bullets fired by Lee Harvey Oswald killed JFK. A House Select Committee report in 1979 professed the possibility of a conspiracy and another shooter, but it relied on acoustic evidence, which was later deemed faulty. Yet by 1992, less than one-third of Americans accepted that the Warren Commission was correct in finding that Oswald acted alone.[65]

History written by revisionists has been rather kind to Lyndon B. Johnson; kinder than his tortured presidency, and certainly kinder than the vociferous critics of his day would have suggested. "A power broker extraordinaire during his day . . . his vision for that 'Great Society' was counterbalanced and ultimately overshadowed by his doomed course in pursuing the war in Vietnam."[66]

The Seventies

The idealism, exuberance, and liberal turmoil that branded the 1960s, took a last eruptive gasp in 1968. It was the ground breaking moments for democracy to rebuild. Lyndon Johnson decided not to run for the presidency. There were protests and demonstrations at the Democrat Convention in Chicago. Student upheavals and riots were common at American Universities as well as in France. Coupled to them was the Prague Spring, those roller-coaster months during which the government of Alexander Dubcek and the majority of Czech and Slovak citizens challenged the limits of Soviet dissent. The year ended in chagrin for those who were dreaming of fundamentally transforming the democracy of the West and the Communism of the East. The American presidential election pitted liberal Hubert H. Humphrey against conservative Richard Nixon. They were two of the nation's most familiar political faces. The anti-liberal Nixon won. Once elected, he ordered authorities to crack down on the radical movement, especially students on campus. The French made the same move on their college campuses, as did the Soviets in a different more aggressive way. Soviet tanks absolutely crushed Czechoslovakian independence and its political dissent. Of course, a chorus of doom and gloom came from the liberals and progressive leftists everywhere. The world was quickly coming to an end according to several of their number.

Starting in 1969, there was a decade long concern about inflation. Rampant fear that global resources were running out; an escalation of the Viet Nam war, which the Democrats had politicized over the past decade, was at a stalemate. Leftists were voicing their disillusionment with our national institutions they no longer controlled. To them, our national pride was being injured.

The Viet Nam War is a pivotal point to understand the late 60s and early 70s, one has to see to understand many decisions that were made. Nixon wanted to end the war in Viet Nam quickly, but was not willing to unilaterally pull troops out and be seen as the only president in our nation's history to lose a war. He decided to reduce American commitment by what was called "Vietnamizing" the war. The ensuing Nixon doctrine enunciated in July 1969 said that America would maintain its "commitments" but future wars in Asia would have to be fought by Asians. It was a low-profile version of containment.

Nixon's approach differed from that of LBJ; Nixon was willing to do what it took to make this Vietnamization work. Nixon proposed to combine the withdrawal of thousands of troops with massive bombing of the North Vietnamese to such an extent as to make believers out of the enemy. One of Nixon's strengths in dealing with foreign negotiations was his air of unpredictability. With his strong, unpredictable demeanor, he thought he might force the North Vietnamese to end the war on terms favorable to the US. The race was on to see who would break first, North Viet Nam from horrendous bombing, or the US from the pressure of the riots in streets to stop the war.

In October 1969, I recall the largest of anti-war demonstrations to date, involving over a million people, which took place in Washington and other selected locations around the nation. The demonstrations accompanied by a flurry of books and polls claiming to show that "the system" was either tottering on the brink of destruction or invulnerable but so corrupt as to be beyond redemption, heightened the political mood of confrontation. Vietnamization, however, took the wind out of the sails of mass protests. By rapidly reducing the number of ground troops from a high of

543,000 in April 1969 to 60,000 by September 1972, Vietnamization dramatically reduced the student draft, which had mobilized the bulk of the demonstrators.[67]

Nixon's presentation of Vietnamization all but put an end to mass campus protests against the war. But withdrawals of troops escalated the war in a way few saw coming. The escalation of the war was a fuse which ignited an already smoldering racial tension and led to many ugly incidents in American streets and college campuses.

To say that we crawled or hobbled into the 70s, using crutches and canes leaving the storm-laden 60s would be an understatement. The "cause" music which rocked Woodstock for 3 days a few months before was pushed forward in some ways supporting racial unrest. Shouting matches between black and white students in April 1969 erupted into fistfights on half a dozen campuses, and at Cornell armed black students seized the student union and won concessions from the school's president. In May, the Kent State shooting gave a further bitter flavor to the decade. The massacre meant a little more to me and my family because my cousin worked with and supervised Allison Krause, one of the shooting victims on campus. Just mentioning the incident and the death of Allison and the other three students killed on campus that day, dregs up sad memories for my cousin and other family members; acidic scenes of the student protests that day. Starting in early 1970, bombs were set off at nearly 50 different campuses and businesses. In Vietnam, young, often black soldiers were involved in a number of highly publicized "fragging" incidents, in which troops sometimes shot their commanding officer rather than follow him into combat. "It was in the spirit of 'fragging' that the Black Panthers tried to 'bring the war home' by engaging police in low-level guerrilla warfare. Bombs were set off at the Manhattan offices of IBM, General Telephone, and Mobil Oil . . ."[68]

Depression songs became a norm at coffee houses and cause music was on the hit radio stations across the country everywhere. However, many young people possessed more passive attitudes. Because of the angry and energetic raucousness people were starting to rethink "work hard and get rich" moniker of the past in developing a materialistic mentality. Confusion replaced confidence. Young adults were becoming "disillusioned," and began saying so.

The 1970s had started and were marked by domestic division and international turmoil. This decade witnessed America's passage into which we were no longer predominant though still vastly influential. It was a painful transition, not . . . without achievement, that began the process of a new and in the long run perhaps even more seminal American contribution to the prospects of free societies. "The rift in the country had in large part been facilitated by Lyndon Johnson's failed attempt to build his 'Great Society.' His failure was complete, resulting in the division of America. Now Lyndon Johnson, who in 1968 would stride down the capitol steps for the inauguration of Richard Nixon; a picture of his total failure. Here was this . . . tragic figure . . . as he ended a term of office that had begun with soaring aspiration and finished in painful division. How had this man of consensus ended up with a torn country? Johnson stood like a caged eagle, proud, dignified; never to be tampered with, his eyes fixed on distant heights he would never reach."[69]

The Liberal Progressives had "Oval Office Hangover" following Nixon's inauguration in January 1969. They were angry and they got busy poking their heads into every part of society attempting to put question marks behind everything they could touch. They asked, the integrity of the Oval Office? No place for women in society? The place for men in society? National Defense? The need for the church? School? Capital punishment? Capital investment? Capitalism? Capital anything? Marriage? Education? Nuclear power? Rights? Work? Work rights? The questions were designed to leave a vacuum and create a foundation for no absolutes. This made a smoother route for them to move in and preach "down with the establishment." This is what happened in the 70s. Present day with Liberal Progressives in the White House, they use exclamation points instead of question marks. Either way, it's a replay of the same issues of the 70s. They rebrand words to carry only the meaning that they want you to hear. Said differently, questioning marriage in the 70s has turned into the demand, "You must now accept marriage of any kind." This is how progressives work in every generation.

With double knit slacks, suits, bell-bottomed jeans, and a rowdy spirit by the liberal left, Nixon tried to deal sternly with the bombings, the sit-ins, the racial marches, and the Black Panthers. To the White House, the "threat" to its authority and hence its policies were exemplified by the speech given by Black Panther leader David Hilliard at the October 1970 anti-Vietnam demonstrations in San Francisco. "Richard Nixon is an evil man," said Hilliard. Then drawing an analogy from Vietnam, he accused Nixon of unleashing counterinsurgency teams on Black Panthers. "We will kill Richard Nixon," he said. "We will kill any "mother___s" that stand in the way of our freedom." Hilliard was arrested for threatening the life of the President.[70]

Though Nixon was probably our best president in the realm of foreign relations by a factor of 10, his taping of conversations regarding the Watergate scandal brought to an end any hope of a great presidency he would have had. The media has for the past 40+ years used the spying on and the break in of the Democratic headquarters as a high water mark for them. So many books have been written on Watergate and the subsequent scandal, I will not devote time to that here, except for the following. The liberal, progressive portion of the Democrat Party, as well as the Republican progressives, have become so much a threat to this nation with treasonous activities that the American people deserve to have all their groups phone calls, memos, emails, and other communications monitored. Never in the history of this country has there been such a track record of treason within.

Though a genius in foreign relations with China, Nixon was extremely insecure. While his Vietnamization plan was moving ahead and keeping his critics within Congress at bay, the president wanted the North Vietnamese to think he might do anything to stop the war in favor of the United States; thus getting their leaders to surrender. In an effort to present himself as a man who would do this anything, and force them to that point, Nixon announced the unconstitutional American invasion of Cambodia. "That announcement set off a chain reaction of events that supercharged an already heightened and tense atmosphere. Cambodia was formally neutral in the war, but a weak government in Pnon-Penh... was unable to prevent the Vietnamese from using Cambodian territory as a sanctuary to attack the South. In March 1969, before the enunciation of the Nixon doctrine, the President ordered the bombing of the 4 Vietnamese positions in Cambodia, both for straightforward military reasons and as a signal to the North Vietnamese that a new hard-nosed player had entered the game. It was a sign of the weakness of Nixon's position, however, that he was forced to keep the bombing secret for fear of the public reaction if it was revealed that the American Air Force had extended an already unpopular war by bombing a neutral country without a constitutionally mandated declaration of war. In the midst of all the secrecy, Nixon was furious when someone in the Administration leaked information on the Cambodia operation to William Beecher of the New York Times."[71]

Anticipating the coming hostility, Nixon went on TV on April 30, just a day after news of the invasion had been made public. Claiming that an American defeat in Vietnam would unleash the forces of totalitarianism around the globe, he insisted that the invasion of Cambodia was a guarantee of American "credibility." "The most powerful nation in the world," he said, replaying to his critics could not afford to act "like a pitiful helpless giant." Appealing to national pride, he asserted that "it is not our power but our will and character that is being tested tonight." "We will not be humiliated, we will not be defeated."[72]

The invasion temporarily revived the nearly dead student anti-war movement. Campuses, coast to coast, erupted in passionate marches and violent protests. It was during one of these demonstrations that little known Kent State University in Ohio, became a household name. National Guardsmen initially called out because of a violent truckers' strike, were sent to the campus to quell disturbances which had included the bombing of an ROTC building. It had started with a demonstration of approximately 500 students was held on May 1 on the Commons (a grassy knoll in the center of campus traditionally used as a gathering place for rallies or protests). As the crowd dispersed to attend classes by 1 pm, another rally was planned for May 4 to continue the protest of Nixon's expansion of the Vietnam War into Cambodia. The growing and widespread anger had protesters issuing a call to "bring the war home." As a symbolic protest to Nixon's decision to send troops, a group of students watched a graduate student burning a copy of the U.S. Constitution while another student burned his draft card.

Trouble exploded in town around midnight when people left a bar and began throwing beer bottles at cars and breaking downtown store fronts. In the process they broke a bank window, setting off an alarm. The news spread quickly and it resulted in several bars closing their doors early to avoid trouble. Before long, more people had joined the vandalism and looting.

By the time police arrived, a crowd of approximately 120 had gathered. Some people from the crowd had started a small bonfire in the street. The crowd appeared to be a mix of bikers, students, and transients. Some in the crowd began to throw beer bottles at the police, yelling obscenities at them. The entire Kent police force was called to duty as well as officers from the county and surrounding communities. "Kent Mayor LeRoy Satrom declared a state of emergency, called Ohio Governor Jim Rhodes' office to seek assistance, and ordered all of the bars closed. The decision to close the bars early increased the size of the angry crowd. Police eventually succeeded in using tear gas to disperse the crowd from downtown, forcing them to move several blocks back to the campus."[73]

The National Guardsmen panicked after some rock throwing by the students and they fired indiscriminately into the crowd, killing four white students. On May 14 two black students were killed in a less publicized incident at Mississippi's Jackson State College.[74] All these killings came on the heels of the invasion and subsequent February 1970 revelation of the My Lai massacre and produced what one college president called "the most disastrous May in the history of American higher education." Protests broke out on more than 400 campuses, 250 of which had to be shut down before the end of the semester. A Harris poll in May found that 76 percent of the students felt that there had to be "basic changes in the system."[75]

Middle America had their fill with the bombings, marches, et al, and met the student anger with outrage of their own. A Newsweek poll found overwhelming support for the Guardsmen and a strong plurality in favor of the Cambodian invasion. New York Mayor "silk stocking" John Lindsay called for conciliation and personal reflection, which only highlighted the deep national divisions.

Due at least partially to President Nixon's paranoia and low self-image, and the continual harangue from the liberal left, he constantly pushed the edge of the envelope with regard to tracking these perceived enemies, which led to the bugging of the Democrat HQ. Now to the Leftists, this was the mother of all crimes to ever be committed, tantamount to Jewish feelings at the thought of a Gentile entering the Holy of Holies in the Jewish Temple. To be true, Nixon broke the law. He should not have and was punished by the media, Democrat party and even Republicans for the act. That he recorded many of the conversations dealing with the cover-up revealed more about his character. However, when looked upon honestly in the balance of history, his actions pale in comparison to many of the Democrat leaders both before and after his stay in the White House. Bill and Hillary Clinton's innumerable breakage of laws, criminal activity, insider trading, make Watergate look like a Sunday School picnic; to everyone except the Liberals of course. Then with the actions of Mr. Obama and most of the minions in his administration, he has made Nixon and even the Clintons look like angels in many aspects. Nixon was guilty of crimes; history has reported that. But through the lens of the pro-Marxist media, we are learning that some crimes are worse than others

Because of Watergate, the resignation of Nixon, and the weakness of Gerald Ford which followed in the Oval Office and Republicans lack of ability to affect positive advancements for conservatism in the country, the door was left open for liberals to once again push their socialist agenda forward. The lies of the Left coupled with the ineptitude of the Right, led to the election of Jimmy Carter. That was a very dark day for America as the next four years would prove out. The words Carter and other liberals saying, "We are the party that cares for the poor," sounds so good. If words alone could bring a cure for a nation, those words would. But the problem has been and continues to be that words don't fix things. And giveaways, non-ending welfare, with government running up the bill, only makes the situation worse.

While Jerry Ford was a nice guy, a liberal Republican, he was treated as a joke among the media, who was beginning to see the power they could sway over the American people by their reporting. They presented Ford as an impotent person politically, using his dry personality against him. He was displayed as an idiot, as when he played golf and always seemed to be hitting someone in the gallery with a tee shot. If he had been a Democrat, all these attributes would have been a resume enhancer. Republicans, afraid of their public image in the media, stood against Ronald Reagan in the presidential campaign of 1976. While Reagan stole the show with his convention speech, he narrowly was turned down by the convention to be their candidate. Following his narrow defeat by Gerald Ford at the Kansas City convention in 1976, Ronald Reagan was seen as a has-been. And Carter was presented by the media a fresh, come-of-age candidate; wholesome and ready to lead the free world in a new direction. And he was ready, to lead the country over a cliff. Once elected, Carter revealed a new definition to the term inept.

Carter's presidency was marked by continual disaster. His weaknesses were exploited by the Iranian Muslim regime. When radicals overran our embassy in Teheran, he was proven to be even weaker than the enemy thought.

Then came the Carter-Torrijos treaties of 1977, which gave away the Panama Canal; however, the old cowboy Ronald Reagan strapped on his guns: "We bought it. We paid for it. It's ours. And we're gonna keep it," he said. America loved it. Bill Buckley said we must recognize reality and transfer the canal. GOP Senate leader Howard Baker was the toast of the city as he led 16 Republicans to vote with Jimmy Carter. The treaties were approved.[76] Other than Obama, Carter will be viewed by true historians as among the weakest presidents in our American history.

Though he had been counted out four years earlier, Reagan had a consolation prize. What was it? The presidency of the United States. Voters in New Hampshire in 1980, remembering his lonely stand, rewarded Reagan with a decisive victory over George H. W. Bush, who had defeated Reagan in Iowa. When Howard Baker came in, the darling of the leftist media, he was greeted as "Panama Howie," and did not even survive the primary.

Chapter Six — Decades That Changed America

The Eighties

Let it be known that similar to an ambulance racing to the emergency entrance, the 80s arrived to save us from the 70s. They did not arrive a moment too soon. The medical answer it delivered was a campaign for the presidency. The first half of the decade was marred by the Nixon break-in of the Democratic headquarters and the subsequent Watergate hearings. The latter half of the decade was known as "those Jimmy Carter years" marked by Carter's political impotency. That was followed by Carter blaming many others for his results.

His policies and actions were among the most disastrous for Americans in history. The hostage crisis in Iran tortuously reached 444 days on the calendar. Each day was accounted for by Walter Cronkite as he ended his CBS Nightly News broadcast. Record inflation was eating away at that for which Americans had worked. Unemployment was reaching new highs for the post-war economy. An initial "misery index" was created by one economist to announce how bad monetary life was. Inflation actually hit 13.5 percent, prime interest rates hit a jaw dropping 21.5 percent, the poverty rate skyrocketed to over 30 percent, and disposable income for every income quintile dropped through the floor. The endless gas lines (cars lined up at the gas pump) trumpeted another high water mark for Carter's lack of ideas on how to run an economy. When he sought advice from his daughter regarding nuclear warfare, and then announced it to the world, he was in truth publicizing his inability to function. He created the Department of Energy (DOE) for the expressed purpose of reducing dependence on foreign oil thus reducing energy costs. What they do is actually unknown, but they do not drop any energy prices; quite the opposite. He gave away the Panama Canal. Carter's foreign policy debacles were shameless; he piloted a steady decline in American influence. The American military withered while he watched the Soviets go on a worldwide rampage. Carter's "attempted" military rescue mission of the Iranian hostages was at a minimum the most embarrassing during my lifetime of the 20th Century; a failure caused directly by his cutback in military spending impacting among other things, the manufacture of replacement parts for helicopters. While there are others, too numerous for this volume; suffice to say we have in an abridged manner come circuitously back to the Iranian hostage crisis.

What makes Jimmy Carter's presidency even worse — he continues to chirp about his self-proclaimed moral superiority as his "Carter Center" carries on the tenants of where his failed presidency left off; it is about waging peace, fighting disease, and building hope. Possibly the Arab Muslim world could stand a dose of Carter's misery index.

Like a bad Thanksgiving meal which had no turkey, no dressing no sweet potatoes, and no pumpkin pie, the 70s had sadly left a horrible taste in American's mouths. That for which the hippies claimed they fought seemed long gone and out of reach now.

And when Reagan did arrive, the giant resurgence of capitalism he brought was just the breath of fresh air the country wanted and needed. The fear of the 70s was being replaced by the American confidence of the 80s. We dared any foreign enemy to cross the line and knock the block off our shoulder. But while we were celebrating our independence the complexion of our nation was changing. The experienced war veterans were now at home watching a sitcom at night and working in an office during the day.

Like a morning rain, 1980 had brought a clean, crisp and promising feel to the air around us. Conservatism was on its way back into the streets and alleyways of American towns, and it brought the promising feel of positive change. No more status quo. We were moving ahead; Reagan was razing the old liberal convention of FDR from the past half century. Reagan confronted the liberal leadership as none before him had dared do. He was the new leader of a revitalized conservative movement which changed the way people looked at themselves, their governments, and the entire world. Reagan put the world in proper focus like no other president before him could do. "Reaganism" as it was called, had at first appeared like a wonderful oasis in the middle of a horrible desert called the 70s which we were now leaving and none too soon. As Craig Shirley said, "Reagan, the maverick populist, had wrought a fusion between the "Social Right" and the "Sociable Right," and the moderates in the party would have to get comfortable riding shotgun in the new GOP."[77]

A thorough look at the 1980 Republican primaries kept a 20th Century constant in place; the ever present Liberal media promoting weak, unstable, or upstart Republican candidates. It has been the media's custom ever since attempting to handicap the November ballot back in the days before WWI with a wishy-washy or weakling candidate on the Right; someone seemingly helpless to oppose their liberal Democrat champion. The media would always champion whoever was the liberal, no matter what the name, just so long as that individual would be a Progressive, leaning toward more Marxism. They would glorify that individual whoever it was since he wore a capital "D" for party affiliation. He was immediately placed on a pedestal in their story lines and news broadcasts as the icon that held "THE" answers to the nation's problems. All their primary and pre-election coverage on television and newspaper media would roll out positive press for liberals; simultaneously they would go on the attack whenever a Republican seemed conservative and strong. Certainly, the media attacked Reagan in that manner; doing it early and often. Case in point — right out of the gate in March that year, the Washington Post carried columnist's Lou Cannon's attack ad in its "Commentary" section. He penned, "Reagan has been depicted in this newspaper and by this correspondent as being old, tired, and hard of hearing." He then added his famous line, "His capacity to be president has been questioned."[78]

The media had done their homework searching long and hard for a bureaucratic, moderate, and weak candidate. They found who they wanted, and though they had more than one horse in this race they liked, they presented him at the Iowa Caucus as their darling, their Republican candidate of choice — George H.W. Bush. Bush feeling his oats after winning the straw poll in Iowa, proclaimed he had "Big Mo." By the time the New England primaries were in focus, the media switched horses going after John Anderson. Anderson, a real "liberal" Republican became the lead story and constant talk of the national media.

A debate was arranged just before the New Hampshire primary which Reagan ended up paying for out of his personal campaign funds. Moments before the debate was to begin, Bush refused to debate because he did not know the other challengers, all trailing Reagan and Bush in the electoral count, had been also invited to debate. Reagan tried to explain his position, but his microphone was muted on order of the editor of the Nashua Telegraph. Reagan, visibly angered by this declared, "I'm paying for this microphone, Mr. Green!" Only Bush and Reagan debated that day, Regan won the primary handily as his statement about the microphone dominated the news for weeks.

The exhilaration of media voices on regular broadcasts spoke of their "eureka" moment in finding another candidate to be their darling however. Anderson was their choice; he was liberal and held the low-information voters and the media temporarily in his hand; Conservatives were jumping into the Reagan camp; and Bush found himself deserted by the media, taking a long walk on a short pier. In fact, Bush's press secretary, Pete Teeley, said Anderson was getting, "the kind of influx of publicity, money, enthusiasm and support that we had before Iowa."[79] As the Republican primary campaign rolled on, most Republican candidates were dropping from the race. By mid-March, the campaign was picking up speed and just four candidates remained in the race; Reagan, Anderson, Bush, and Crane. With the campaign in high gear by April 1st, the marathon-like stamina of each candidate was being tested. The media, wanting to drag Reagan down, had publicly predicted his age would cut his campaign short. Bush thought his youthfulness would leave Reagan worn out and lying on the side of the road. But Reagan campaigned Bush into the ground. Though Illinois was a concern for Reagan — he was concerned about Anderson, who said he felt he would win the state. But as historian Craig Shirley says, Reagan "also had a "feeling," as he told reporters."[80] The media had been underestimating Reagan; they were listening to him this time — they were learning not "since they had covered since John Kennedy, had a politician had as much a feeling for the American people as Ronald Reagan." [81]

The time for the now-famous Chicago debate had come, just days before the Illinois primary. It promised to be a bare-knuckled event among the final four Republican candidates. It was all of that, even providing more "scorched earth" than promised. Though he was in attendance, Crane was not allowed to debate because he was basically broke and was being denied matching funds by the FEC; he was far behind in primary delegates and now he was off the stage. That meant only the three other candidates would perform in the "no holds barred" 90-minute debate.

The only promised interruptions would happen with a knockdown or from the lone moderator, Howard K. Smith. The bell sounded and Anderson and Bush tangled hard, attacking each other. The "darling of the press," liberal Anderson stayed on liberal message, as he "proposed a fifty cents per gallon gas tax."[82]

Most voters were just getting knowledgeable about the candidates in the campaign and did not realize how liberal Anderson was. The spotlight of the debates and the media coverage of the campaign were uncovering his position on abortion, his pro-choice announcement he made by signing a National Abortion Rights Action League (NARAL) petition. It was being made known that he could have been a candidate for the opposition party. This stance excited the media and they were almost totally focused on Anderson, Crane and Bush going into the next debate. I recall watching the Chicago debate waiting for Reagan's responses to issues but instead witnessed him being only of a spectator early on, watching the verbal brawling between Bush and Crane. Finally he was called on by Smith and did have a chance to speak — he spoke at first only of his victory in New Hampshire. Then smiling at the moderator, Reagan joked about having to sit and wait so long to speak: "Thanks, Howard, I thought that not having bought the microphone myself, I couldn't talk." The live audience laughed loudly.[83]

I briefly met the former governor in late 1977 and was impressed while watching and listening to him as he spoke at a public function in California. His relentless focus on and love for this country was impressive. He stayed on message when handling difficult, unrehearsed, and impromptu questions from the audience, something politicians will absolutely avoid at all cost. His demeanor brought an exceptional freshness dealing with awkward moments, those pregnant pauses that will come between questions, cracking jokes and staying in control. As I watched the debate on TV that night, the demeanor I had witnessed three years earlier was on full display this Chicago night when Anderson tried to attack Reagan. Anderson hit the Californian with everything he had. He said that Reagan's scheme of telling the Ayatollah Khomeini to release the American hostages or else by a "date certain" was far too forward and risky, trying to sway the crowd. "Wasting not a moment, Reagan responded powerfully that the Iranians must know that the United States meant business. Struggling to maintain composure, Anderson went further showing his liberal stripes by saying Senators George McGovern and Frank Church were 'good men.' Reagan said, 'You see, that's where we disagree. I don't think they're good men.'"[84] Speaking the unreserved truth brought conservatives racing in herds to Reagan; he spoke what they thought and he did it with conviction. When the moderator shifted to foreign policy, Reagan called out the weak-kneed politicians and candidates: "We seem to be able to only find human rights violations among allies. . . . We cozy up to and hug and kiss as he [Carter] did with Brezhnev — where no human rights exist at all. Let's thumb our nose at the Soviet Union."[85] Cronkite shifted to foreign policy. That segment ended with a question to Reagan about Henry Kissinger; asking what job he might have in a future Republican Administration. I remember Reagan almost skipping and laughing as he boldly told the audience, "Kissinger had a bright future back in academia."[86]

Reagan's protest to the liberal thought of wage and price controls was a penultimate moment of the debate. He had the crowd laughing heartily, so much so that Howard K. Smith had to halt the debate for the laughter in the ballroom to subside when Reagan gave an historical example of how they had not worked even for Roman Emperor Diocletian some 1,700 years earlier, even when the death penalty was threatened for those who violated that edict. The laughter came when Reagan said, "I'm the only one here old enough to remember it."[87]

Howard K. Smith ended the debate the same way all liberal media moderators end Republican debates. Follows is the classic liberal question asked during at least one of the presidential debates every four years: "Will you — can you support the other candidates if they are nominated?" As if on cue, Anderson and Crane quickly agreed with each other: they claimed loudly they could NOT support each other. Crane sniped at Anderson saying he should be in the Democrat Party. Anderson snapped back asking when the party started administering "saliva tests." Both spoke with poisonous accusations which pleased liberals. They love to see Republicans fighting. Bush gave the Bush family response; he could support anyone on stage. Reagan and Anderson had the camera on them for the moment, and I leaned forward in my chair waiting for Reagan's final responses — I recall that as if it was yesterday. If the debate had been a championship boxing match, Reagan would have been well ahead on points. He had knocked everyone down for the count at least once. In this last round, he did a political version of Cassias Clay's "rope-a-dope," covering up when asked if he would vote for Anderson if he ran as a third party candidate. It was a delay strategy that worked. Anderson however threw punches wildly and in a "bum's rush" tried to dismiss Reagan's comments. . . ." reiterating he could not support Reagan under any circumstances. During earlier days of the campaign, Anderson said that he would vote for Carter or Kennedy over any of the Republicans, even the Gipper."[88]

Reagan was known throughout his entire career for his pithy one-liners, learning some from his sports background, some in the movie industry, and the remainder in the world of cutthroat politics. Anderson's comment greased the skids for a haymaker. Remembering his comment from those weeks earlier in the campaign, Reagan turned to his fellow Illinoisan and deadpanned, "John, would you really find Ted Kennedy preferable to me?"[89] Anderson lost his composure and could not even respond. He did not need to for a time, since the crowd was roaring with laughter. In the silence of the aftermath, Anderson could not recover. That's when Reagan grinned, "I'm still waiting for John to say!"[90]

That night, Chicago proved to be Reagan's thoroughfare to victory in the Illinois primary, a very serious prize to fall his way. Some political prognosticators saw it as the microcosm of the election. But the perfect microcosm contrasting the leadership capabilities for this nation lay just ahead. This is the contrast of how the country had been run between the incompetence of liberalism and how it could be run if "the ship got turned around" with unfettered conservatism. That microcosm was first, the site of the debate, the city of Cleveland, and second, the exchanges occurring within the Cleveland Debate itself between Carter and Reagan held on October 28, 1980.

Blight in many inner cities resulting from the magic wand of liberalism, though normally hidden by media, are highly visible cities such as Detroit, New York, St. Louis, and a few others. But the city of Cleveland framed in 1980 Democrat policies, demonstrated the unembellished contrast between liberalism and conservatism as a backdrop for the site of the debate. Cleveland was not a blue screen upon which the liberals could post photographs of fresh construction; it was the most decrepit and dilapidated cities in the Rust Belt. What a perfect representation of the failure of Liberalism against which Ronald Reagan could graphically orate the wonders of free-enterprise when nesting within conservatism. Cleveland with its glut of dark, broken down buildings, crumbling infrastructure, mammoth crime rate, and huge gangs infesting the empty shells of downtown, and its river which had been on national news recently caught on fire from all the pollution problems were all picture perfect to show differences. No debate was actually needed.

Second, the atmosphere created by the throngs of media, their support staffs, and set-up crews converging upon the Cleveland Convention Center's Music Hall and subsequent swirling around the streets in chauffeur-driven limousines; attending "round-the-clock' pre-debate parties at every pub, bar and restaurant created a feeling similar to a heavyweight championship fight. Close to 2,000 reporters alone plus their media toadies ran the streets. The major national networks of NBC, ABC, CBS, and PBS were each installing TV cameras and microphones in and around the Hall. Add to this group the national, regional, and local radio station staffs, planting their microphones and sound equipment into the nooks and crannies available. Truly, the world was going to watch this championship event; four Intelsat satellites were going to be used to beam the debate to twenty-six countries. No self-respecting gang would have tried to commit a crime in this crowd, nevertheless law enforcement swelled to unprecedented levels so that safety seemed a certainty.

It promised to be such an exciting event, debate parties like the ones my friends organized in Southern California were being planned all around the country. After all, this would be the first televised presidential debate that would feature a live studio audience. The nation was getting ready, however, the liberal media was doing its part to dissuade conservative voters and was doing campaigning for their own candidate with the same stroke of the pen. That morning's *Washington Post* had a big story trumpeting "Carter Goes Into Debate With Lead in New Poll." Columnist Martin Schram seemed breathless as he detailed, "Their clash comes on the heels of a Gallup Poll report yesterday that voters have swung sharply toward Carter in the last two weeks — a six-point shift that now give the president a three-point lead over this Republican challenger."⁹¹

The third part of this microcosm, and most important, was the debate itself. As clearly as any single event can, it demonstrated the great gulf that exists between Modern Liberalism and True Conservatism. Drilling down and focusing on elements of this debate, encapsulates specific and detailed differences between the two opposing socio-political stances: capitalism and freedom vs. socialistic control and redistribution of resources. Today the gulf is even greater, but still illustrates the well-spoken positions of the two choices offering two diametrically opposed directions for America. Younger generations should focus on the debate itself; it is a time capsule showing distinct choices. A focus on the election is a waste; it was a blowout and boring, nothing close to what the media parlayed it to be the week before.

The Debate That Changed America

Our pizza and beverages had been served at our Southern California debate party as we watched the candidates enter the stage area. Of those watching at the Cleveland Hotel, Robert Rosenthal reported that Mondale said he worried that "Carter looked pale and drawn and sort of tense."⁹² Reagan looked youthful, robust, suntanned, his pompadour held in place with a lot of water and a little dab of Brylcreem. Only the veins in his hands betrayed his age. Reagan had had a light dinner and one glass of wine, "a little color for his cheeks," Mike Deaver said.⁹³ Reagan was ready.

The "Tale of the Tape" stood as follows. Carter — once known as "Jimmy Who?" — was the defending champion with a lifetime record of 126 wins and 46 losses. His wins included the presidency of the Future Farmers and Future Homemakers of America Camp Development Committee, the Georgia Crop Improvement Association, the Lions International, the Georgia State Senate, the Georgia Governorship, the Democrat presidential primaries of 1976 and 1980, and the U.S. Presidency of 1976. The champ weighed in at 155 pounds, and 5'9". The "Bantam Rooster" of the South had a deceptively good left uppercut but preferred body blows while sticking and moving, sticking and moving. Political pugilism was in his blood, though the word on the street was that he tended to overestimate his own strengths. He had won the title four years earlier when his opponent, Gerald Ford, made a critical mistake in the late rounds.

The challenger — Ron "The Gipper" Reagan out of the West; stood 6'1" and weighed 194 pounds. The East Coast writers knew less about him. His overall record was 86 wins and 31 losses, with his victories including his high school and Eureka College presidencies, the presidency of the Screen Actors Guild, the California Gubernatorial primaries and general elections, and the Republican presidential primaries of 1976 and 1980. The book on Reagan was that he coasted in the early rounds while taking the measure of his opponent. He sometimes used a "rope-a-dope" strategy, slipping punches and letting his opponents thump themselves weary, although he was often accused of tiring in the late rounds himself. When aroused, Reagan had a lightning-fast right cross. Though some thought he was not a terrific puncher, most agreed that he was a great counterpuncher. He was also more nimble on his feet, than most scribes gave him credit for.[94] Most observers expected the defending champ to wear down the challenger. But it was exactly one year earlier that Jimmy Carter had confided to Hamilton Jordan that he thought he'd be running against Reagan and that "it would be a mistake to underestimate him."[95]

In keeping with tradition, a liberal news anchor was in the position of moderator. Referee might be a more apt description since presidential debates are usually described in terms of a championship bout. Not being a member of the press, this liberal on stage was extremely nervous as she, Ruth Henerfeld, president of the League of Women Voters got the proceedings off and running. She introduced Howard K. Smith as the moderator, or referee. Smith then calmly went over the ground rules and introduced the panelists who would fire questions at the candidates. They were, William Hilliard of the *Portland Oregonian*, Harry Ellis of the *Christian Science Monitor*, Marvin Stone of *U.S. News & World Report*, and Barbara Walters of ABC. A coin toss backstage had determined who would receive the first question. Carter had won the toss, and in a bit of a surprise he chose to have Reagan field the first question and then go last with his closing remarks. As to why the president made these choices, Jody Powell joshed, "Good manners."[96]

The use of military power around the globe was the first topic or question tossed on stage by Marvin Stone. Reagan made two jabs at his opponent. When asked to explain specific differences between his approach to the use of military power and that of the president, Reagan said the following, "I don't know what the differences might be, because I don't know what Mr. Carter's policies are. I do know what he has said about mine. And I'm only here to tell you that I believe with all my heart that our first priority must be world peace, and that use of force is always and only a last resort, when everything else has failed, and then only with regard to our national security.

Now, I believe, also that this meeting, this mission, this responsibility for preserving the peace, which I believe is a responsibility peculiar to our country, that we cannot shirk our responsibility as the leader of the Free World, because we're the only one that can do it. And therefore, the burden of maintaining the peace falls on us. And to maintain that peace requires strength. America has never gotten in a war because we were too strong. We can get into a war by letting events get out of hand, as they have in the last 3¼ years under the foreign policies of this administration of Mr. Carter's, until we're faced each time with a crisis. And good management in preserving the peace requires that we control the events and try to intercept before they become a crisis.

But I have seen four wars in my lifetime. I'm a father of sons; I have a grandson. I don't ever want to see another generation of young Americans bleed their lives into sandy beachheads in the Pacific, or rice paddies and jungles in Asia, or the muddy, bloody battlefields of Europe."

Reagan then outlined his position on how a strong military would not invite aggression, and condemned the Carter administration for continually letting "events get out of hand" until the point that the United States was faced "with a crisis." Stone followed up, asking how Reagan could increase the military budget, cut taxes, and balance the budget all at the same time. Reagan's answer was a bit meandering and disjointed.[97]

Carter was given his turn to rebut Reagan. He too appeared nervous at first and halting. But he tried to score points by touching on all the right bases; peace, building up the military, and the treaty he'd negotiated between Israel and Egypt. He quoted H. L. Mencken, patron saint of cynical journalists, "For every problem there's a simple answer. It would be neat and plausible — and wrong." Of course, he was alluding to the well-prepared Reagan and his plans. Stone, in his follow-up, tried to pin the president down on how and when he might use military power. Carter calmly replied that he had worked for "security" in the Middle East and that he'd deployed two carrier task forces to the region. He restated that the military budget had gone up on his watch after going down during the Nixon and Ford administrations.[98]

Reagan, in response, cornered Carter on what he (Carter) had called shrinking military budget under Republican Presidents, saying, "Well, yes, I question the figure about the decline in defense spending under the two previous administrations, in the preceding 8 years to this administration. I would call to your attention that we were in a war that wound down during those 8 years, which of course made a change in military spending because of turning from war to peace. I also would like to point out that Republican Presidents in those years, faced with a Democratic majority in both Houses of the Congress, found that their requests for defense budgets were very often cut."

Reagan's answer was succinct, timely, and zeroed in on target. He rattled off a series of military programs Carter had canceled, saying, "Gerald Ford left a 5-year projected plan for a military buildup to restore our defenses, and President Carter's administration reduced that by 38 percent, cut 60 ships out of the Navy building program that had been proposed, and stopped the B-1, delayed the cruise missile, stopped the production line for the Minuteman missiles, delayed the Trident submarine, and now is planning a mobile military force that can be delivered to various spots in the world — which does make me question his assaults on whether I am the one that is quick to look for use of force." It was a strong swipe at Carter, but the president recovered when he accused his Republican opponent of "habitually" supporting "the injection of military forces into troubled areas" whereas he and previous presidents had exercised caution. Carter also got a dig in on the use of nuclear weapons. The president won the exchange on point when he said his military buildup would mean that defense forces would never be used and soldiers would not die in combat.[99] Reagan scowled at Carter; he must have wondered whether the Democrat had stolen one of his old speeches.[100]

Carter took the first question from Harry Ellis, one regarding inflation, and what, in the future, he would do for workers. The president faltered, blaming the oil-producing countries which he indicated started before he was elected, "Again it's important to put the situation into perspective. In 1974 we had a so-called oil shock, wherein the price of OPEC oil was raised to an extraordinary degree. We had an even worse oil shock in 1979. In 1974 we had the worst recession, the deepest and most penetrating recession since the Second World War. The recession that resulted this time was the briefest we've had since the Second World War."

He stumbled worse with his next sentences, "In addition, we've brought down inflation. Earlier this year, the first quarter, we did have a very severe inflation pressure, brought about by the OPEC price increase. It averaged about 18 percent the first quarter of this year. The second quarter, we had dropped it down to about 13 percent."

He was tap-dancing on the issue. Ellis followed up and gave Carter another chance to spell out what he'd do in a second term, but the president did no better, focusing on the "sacrifice" he had "demanded" from the American people. Carter came across as patronizing. He had just told the American people oil imports had dropped 33 percent, which was true, but around the bars and living rooms of America, voters knew why demand had dropped: because the bottom had fallen out of the economy.[101] At the time, a barrel of American produced oil was selling for $6.50 per barrel, but the fear was that it could rise as high as $36 if price controls were lifted.[102]

(What follows is a key part of this debate which explained then and explains now the basic difference between conservatives and liberals in this country: both in how they think and how they attempt to "solve problems." As to the liberal, it matters not which one is speaking; Jimmy Carter, Bill Clinton, or Barack Obama. One does not have to see the face speaking; the thinking and words are the same. So is their approach for fixing problems — Blame the people of the country who have succeeded in their work or in building a business; they have surely cheated the poor, building their success on the backs of others.)

Carter again answered the question of Mr. Ellis saying, "Yes. We have demanded that the American people sacrifice, and they've done very well." Carter's approach to America had been that of "conservation," and while saying he would drill more oil the next year than in any year in American history; most alert in the audience knew that was not going to happen. Carter then talked of a government jobs program for young Americans as well as tax credits for businesses. Now he was coming off as a scold. He wasn't really addressing the problems in a way that would resonate with the voters; the American people did not believe that inflation was their fault. Carter took a shot at the "Reagan-Kemp-Roth Proposal," calling it "irresponsible" reminding the audience that George Bush had once called it "voodoo economics."[103] Reagan, upon hearing this, caught his running mate's eye in the audience and smiled, giving him a friendly wink.[104] Reagan stirred and shifted, almost not being able to wait to respond to this claim.

As Ellis turned to Reagan, the Gipper was primed, ready to go. He hammered Carter, "I'm not sure that it means steadily higher fuel costs, but I do believe that this Nation has been portrayed for too long a time to the people as being energy-poor when it is energy-rich. The coal that the President mentioned: Yes, we have it, and yet one-eighth of our total coal resources is not being utilized at all right now. The mines are closed down; there are 22,000 miners out of work. Most of this is due to regulations which either interfere with the mining of it or prevent the burning of it. With our modern technology, yes, we can burn our coal within the limits of the Clean Air Act. I think, as technology improves, we'll be able to do even better with that.

The other thing is that we have only leased out and begun to explore 2 percent of our Outer Continental Shelf for oil, where it is believed by everyone familiar with that fuel and that source of energy that there are vast supplies yet to be found. Our Government has, in the last year or so, taken out of multiple use millions of acres of public lands that once were — well, they were public lands subject to multiple-use exploration for minerals and so forth. It is believed that probably 70 percent of the potential oil in the United States is probably hidden in those lands, and no one is allowed to even go and explore to find out if it is there. This is particularly true of the recent efforts to shut down part of Alaska.

Nuclear power: There were 36 power plants planned in this country — and let me add the word 'safety'; it must be done with the utmost of safety. But 32 of those have given up and canceled their plans to build, and again, because Government regulations and permits and so forth make it take more than twice as long to build a nuclear plant in the United States as it does to build one in Japan or in Western Europe.

"We have the sources here. We are energy-rich, and coal is one of the great potentials we have."[105]

Reagan had obliterated Carter's stance for what Reagan called Carter's suggestion "that inflation somehow came upon us like a plague and therefore it is uncontrollable and no one can do anything about it," calling the idea "entirely spurious" and "dangerous." Contrary to Carter's argument, Reagan calmly pointed out, inflation in Ford's last term was at a tolerable 4.8 percent, but by 1980, it was at an annual rate of 12.7 percent, not the 7 percent that the president had argued. Reagan agreed that there were a few new jobs created under Carter, "but that can't hide the fact that there are eight million men and women out of work in America today, and two million lost those in the last few months." He blasted Carter for saying that to get inflation under control; America would have "to accept more joblessness and less productivity."

Reagan laid his axe into the root cause of inflation: out of control government spending. He said Carter had blamed a host of other actors for inflation, including OPEC and the Federal Reserve; Carter, Reagan said, "had blamed the lack of productivity on the American people; he has then accused the people of living too well, and that we must share in scarcity, we must sacrifice and get used to doing with less." That would not do for Reagan: "We don't have inflation because the people are living too well. We have inflation because the government is living too well.[106]

Recognizing that his time was running short, Reagan summarized his position succinctly: "Yes, you can lick inflation by increasing productivity, and decreasing the cost of government."[107]

Reagan's answer was the right answer. Americans were not to be blamed, and were not to be charged to make sacrifices as Carter had said "inside the beltway" Washington was stating during the years of his administration. Reagan would not have it. He insisted sacrifices must be made, and Washington would make them. Inflation could be beaten. "Reagan had settled in . . . and was speaking to the American people — more than 100 million of whom were watching, with millions more listening on their radios."[108]

Clearly on the defensive, Carter chided Reagan again on the "Reagan-Kemp-Roth" Plan, saying even his running mate Bush said "it would result in a 30 percent inflation rate." Carter said Reagan's suggestion to eliminate the minimum wage was "a heartless kind of approach to the working families . . . which is typical of many Republican leaders . . . and accentuated under Governor Reagan."[109]

Reagan, the GOP nominee, homed in on Carter's savaging of his tax-cut plan. "I'd like to ask the president: Why is it inflationary to let people keep more of their money, and let them spend it the way they'd like, and it isn't inflationary to let him [Carter] take that money and spend it the way he [Carter] wants."[110] Bingo! Reagan had just driven a stake into the heart of the socialistic Progressive argument prevalent in the Democrat Party. It was common sense that struck home with viewers who were going to go to the polls and vote in exactly one week. The simplicity Reagan offered must have grated on Carter.

William Hilliard was the next panelist with a question, asking Reagan a question on the plight of the cities: "Governor Reagan, the decline of our cities has been hastened by the continual rise in crime, strained race relations, the fall in the quality of public education, the persistence of abnormal poverty in a rich nation, and a decline in the services to the public. The signs seem to point toward a deterioration that could lead to the establishment of a permanent underclass in the cities. What, specifically, would you do in the next 4 years to reverse this trend?" The Californian had a proposal for "development zones" as he responded, "... in cooperation with local government and with National Government, and using tax incentives and with cooperation with the private sector, that we have development zones. Let the local entity, the city, declare this particular area, based on the standards of the percentage of people on welfare, unemployed, and so forth, in that area. And then, through tax incentives induce the creation of businesses providing jobs and so forth in those areas." This he presented as a verbal mosaic for the audience to grasp about his recent trip to the Bronx in New York. "You have to see it to believe it. It looks like a bombed out city — great gaunt skeletons of buildings, windows smashed out, painted on one of them, 'Unkept Promises' on another 'Despair.'" Reagan reminded his audience that Carter had gone there in 1977, promising everything, delivering nothing.[111] Reagan's answer to Hilliard's follow-up question reminded Americans of the failed Carter record; four years of broken promises.

Carter, in his rebuttal, offered the usual liberal bromides of how we were a nation of refugees and immigrants wanting hope, a better life and how they brought their culture with them, their way of life, and their language. He of course, spoke of more government spending to get blacks into positions within the government. Speaking like a technocrat, he threw out statistics and big figures saying for example he had appointed more blacks, etc. that surely sounded like fingernails across a blackboard to those watching at home. At his conclusion, he accused Reagan of being insensitive to racism.[112]

Reagan's tranquil demeanor was clearly starting to agitate Carter. Reverting back to "liberal speak," Carter began describing America as if it was no longer a melting pot but rather a patchwork quilt, where immigrants could preserve as he called it "their ethnic commitments" and "their relationships with their relatives in foreign countries." It was a double shot of liberal speak followed by a pander mode for a chaser, as he spoke about the exclusion of minorities from "the affairs of government" and how he had appointed blacks, women, and Hispanics to government jobs. He did nothing but patronize by saying, "To involve them in administration of government and a feeling that they belong to the societal structure.... is a very important commitment."[113] (It is interesting to see how the "race card" is played by liberals, progressives, et al. They usually play the race card when they are losing a point, or challenged and taken out of their comfort zone.)

Reagan did not handle his response as well as I had hoped, watching from our debate party. Actually he could have hit a home run out of the entire park, if he had handled it better. He only touched on government jobs as being "dead-end" jobs. Carter viewed that as an opening and he took it, accusing Reagan of "insensitivity" to the plight of the poor. "This to me, is a very important difference between him and me," Carter said.[114]

Barbara Walters was the next panelist to ask a question. Walters 'always' reminded me of a dark-haired version of Lucille Ball, but with absolutely no humor; more of a Groucho Marks, without a bird or cigar, just bland and tasteless. For years, she had sought the spotlight by playing media shrink in asking her interviewee what type of tree they saw themselves as being. Thankfully, she did not do that in the debate, but she did open a can of worms no other panelist was willing to do. She boldly said, "Mr. President, the eyes of the country tonight are on the hostages in Iran. I realize this is a sensitive area, but the question of how we respond to acts of terrorism goes beyond this current crisis. Other countries have policies that determine how they will respond. Israel, for example, considers hostages like soldiers and will not negotiate with terrorists. For the future, Mr. President, the country has the right to know, do you have a policy for dealing with terrorism wherever it might happen, and what have we learned from this experience in Iran that might cause us to do things differently if this or something similar happens again?" Her question about the hostages was like a ticking time bomb. The silence could now be cut with a knife. Everyone had been avoiding the subject before but now the waiting was finally over.

Carter had spent a year negotiating with terrorists for the lives of over fifty Americans held in Tehran. He ducked the question and talked obliquely about how terrorism was "one of the blights on the world." He meandered in his answers and then took another shot at Reagan, accusing him of supporting the spread of nuclear weapons.[115]

Since Walters was visibly dissatisfied with Carter's responses to her question, she got more specific, asking whether "offering military spare parts wasn't [a] reward [to] terrorism." His answer was again very feeble, using just a few seconds of his allotted time.[116] He obviously was nervous about discussing the hostages and wanted to move on to other subjects.

As Craig Shirley comments, "At the debate's halfway mark, two things were clear. The first was that Reagan was the master of subtlety while Carter had all the subtlety of a blunderbuss. The second was that Reagan was getting under Carter's skin. Carter glared at Reagan periodically.[117]

The format changed for the second half of the debate. It moved more quickly and there were no follow-up questions, two chances by the candidates to rebut, and the opportunity to ask the opponent their own questions.

Following commercial break, the second half started by Reagan being asked about arms control and his suggestion to "scrap" SALT II. Reagan handled the question marvelously, with aplomb. He pointed out exactly what Democrats usually do, even to this day; that is to accuse a conservative of doing what they themselves do. In this case, Reagan said that while Carter and Mondale both blamed him [Reagan] for blocking their cherished treaty, it was the Senate Democrats, in particular the Armed Services Committee, totally controlled by Carter's party which had "voted ten to zero, with seven abstentions, against the SALT II Treaty and declared that it was not in the national security interest of the United States." Reagan again got in a dig on Carter when he reminded the audience; the response from the Kremlin was "nyet."[118] Reagan again brought laughter among the live audience with that statement.

Carter took the same question and he moved in on Reagan like a boxer throwing body blows. "There is a disturbing pattern in the attitude of Governor Reagan on the issue of arms control," Carter brusquely said. "He has never supported any of those arms control agreements.... And now he wants to throw into the wastebasket a treaty to control nuclear weapons." Then Carter got tough. "When a man who hopes to be president says, 'Take this treaty, discard it'... that is a very dangerous and disturbing thing."[119]

Following Carter's meandering statements, Regan's rebuttal time came. He took advantage of it, throwing Carter's comments back in his face. "If I have been critical of some of the previous agreements, it's because we've been out-negotiated for quite a long time. And they [the Soviets] have managed, in spite of all our attempts at arms limitation, to go forward with the biggest military buildup in the history of man." Carter had in his comments noted that the SALT Treaty had been negotiated "by myself and my two Republican predecessors," but Reagan dismissed this comment as misleading, pointing out that Gerald Ford "is emphatically against this SALT treaty." Reagan buttressed his case by telling the audience that it was two Democrat Senators, Henry Jackson of Washington and Fritz Hollings of South Carolina, who were carrying the fight against the treaty on the floor of the U.S. Senate. Finally, Reagan rejected claims that he supported "throwing away" the treaty: "I am not talking of scrapping. I am talking of taking the treaty back and going back into negotiations" with the Kremlin to press for real arms reductions.[120]

Reagan was no pushover; certainly he was not an empty suit, as many Democrats had claimed, saying "he was lost without his four-by-six note cards." Carter was finding this out the hard way. Reagan had deflected so many of his punches, "Governor Reagan is making some very misleading and disturbing statements," he said. Carter railed against Reagan's performance for wanting nuclear superiority over the Russians, even though recent polling showed that a strong majority of the American people wanted superiority, not the parity that Carter was advocating. (Democrats are never comfortable when the U.S. has superiority over other nations, or to be the lone super-power of the world. Their desire is to have a Marxist regime someplace else on the globe to offset our power; which is telling about where their real loyalty rests.) He [Carter] closed his rebuttal by saying that Reagan's "attitude is extremely dangerous and belligerent in its tone, although it's said with a quiet voice."[121]

Reagan began his rebuttal of Carter by saying, "I know the president is supposed to be replying to me, but sometimes I have a hard time in connecting what he's saying with what I have said or what my positions are."[122] Then Reagan simply restated his position on reopening negotiations with the Soviets.

The last response to this question was given to Carter. His response is one that he would regret for the rest of his life. "I think to close out this discussion it would be better to put into perspective what we're talking about. I had a discussion with my daughter, Amy, the other day before I came here to ask her what the most important issue was. She said she thought nuclear weaponry and the control of nuclear arms."[123]

The crowd snickered with mocking laughter. Carter's aids buried their heads in their hands. As he heard their laughter, Carter looked up at the audience. Americans all around the country, in their small groups and homes were laughing out loud. I know I was one of them. Reagan, understanding the rule of debate; if your opponent is shooting himself in the foot — stay quiet and allow him room to keep shooting. Hardly anyone heard the rest of Carter's answer; nobody was paying attention by then.

The questions moved on to energy exploration conversation. Carter was on the ropes and covering up. He continued throwing accusations at Reagan; "Governor Reagan says this is not a good accomplishment." "Governor Reagan's approach to our energy policy . . . is to repeal or to change. . . ." "The air pollution standards laws . . . were passed over the objections of Governor Reagan . . . and this is a very well-known fact."[124] Reagan simply brushed off the charges.

The moderator very quickly switched topics to Social Security, and with the new topic Democrats regained optimism. The Democrat rumor mill had Reagan very weak in the area of Social Security. He was not weak or dumb as some claim, which dashed the hopes of the supporters of Carter. Reagan was stronger in presenting the retirement program though his opponents had over looked this and his true credentials. Reagan led the nation that night in a quick seminar on the troubles of the bankrupt Social Security fund. All to the chagrin of Carter the Californian was able to quickly and thoroughly explain "how a program "trillions of dollars out of balance" must be "put on a sound actuarial basis." He even turned the tables on Carter, pointing out that he, Carter, was responsible for "the single largest tax increase in our nation's history."[125]

Carter swung wildly at Reagan again on his previous musings about making social security voluntary. Carter tried to appear patient, as if tutoring a slow student; then paused and put forth a broad smile on his face, being proud of himself. Reagan replied very simply, "The voluntary thing I mentioned many years ago was that [with] a young man, orphaned and raised by an aunt who died, his aunt was ineligible for Social Security Insurance because she was not his mother. And I suggested that if this is an insurance program, certainly the person who is paying in, should be able to name his own beneficiaries. That's the closest I've ever come to anything voluntary about Social Security."[126]

On the ropes and totally on defense with regard to Social Security, Carter pledged not to change the system or the relationship between Social Security and Medicare. Then he attacked Reagan again, and as it turned out it was one too many times. "Governor Reagan, as a matter of fact, began his political career campaigning around the country about Medicare." Carter made a few more perfunctory comments about national health insurance and then finished by saying, "Governor Reagan, again, is generally against such a proposal."[127]

Then in a moment which still lives in my memory, Howard K. Smith turned to Reagan and said, "Governor?" Reagan had had enough. With his patented chuckle, he turned to the right, gave that right-tilted grin that was his trademark, looked Carter straight in the face, and gave his immortal line: "There you go again."[128] The audience, given the earlier admonition to be quiet, had remained so. But with Reagan's comment, raucous laughter rolled through the Music Hall. Reagan had just thrown his famous thundering counterpunch.

Reagan finished his counterpunch by taking time to go through a plan which he favored more. By no accident it had been offered by physicians, totally based on market drivers rather than on incompetent government bureaucrats. But the crowd was hardly listening to very much of what was being said. They were instead watching other individuals with heads huddled close, whispering about the debate. Carter did not know it, but all was lost. He was given a chance to respond to Reagan, but he spent his time vilifying Republicans again He called them "heartless" stressing they were unlike Democrats who, according to Carter, were the group that really cared for people. Democrats, according to him had historical commitments "to the working families of this nation have been extremely important in the growth of their stature and in a better quality of life for them." Then he peevishly criticized Reagan for quoting Democratic Presidents, as if Reagan had taken his ball away on the playground. Reagan replied to this comment in his response, "I was a Democrat. I said many foolish things back in those days."[129] The audience just couldn't help themselves, rolling in laughter again.

As laughter subsided, Walters then asked Carter about leadership of the country and why he thought Reagan should not be president. Rarely had Carter smiled during the entire debate, but this was one of those times when he smiled. He said dryly, "Barbara, reluctant as I am to say anything critical about Governor Reagan, I'll try to answer your question."[130] There were waves of laughter which came again from the audience, this time at such uncharacteristic wit from Carter.

Throughout the evening, except for now, Carter appeared very rigid, as he attempted to portray a seriousness of purpose. But he again quickly returned to that mode of attack on Reagan, declaring that his opponent posed a danger he represented on several key issues "a radical departure . . . from the heritage of Eisenhower and others" in the Republican Party. Carter took yet another stab at Reagan commenting how he had "been running for president, I think, since 1968." Concluding, he circled back around to his warmonger theme, attacking Reagan once again for "careless" and "belligerent" attitudes.[131]

Barbara Walters then turned to Reagan and asked why he should be president and why his opponent should not. She publicly spoke for Reagan at that moment, stating that Reagan "may be equally reluctant to speak ill of your opponent." Reagan responded, "Well, Barbara, I believe there is a fundamental difference. And I think it has been evident in most of the answers that Mr. Carter's given tonight that he seeks the solution to anything as another opportunity for a federal government program." Reagan quickly spun into his federalism view of government, saying that Washington "has usurped powers and autonomy and authority that belong back at the state and local level. It has imposed on the individual freedoms of the people and that there are more of these things that could be solved by the people themselves if they were given a chance or by the levels of government that were closer to them."[132] (These remarks of the debate encapsulate the contrasts and approach to governing!) Somewhere, Thomas Jefferson was seeing Reagan and was smiling.

Reagan finished his responses strongly, stating his belief that "millions of Democrats . . . are going to vote with us this time around; because they too want that promise kept. It was a promise for less government and less taxes and more freedom for the people."[133]

Carter flailed in his rebuttal. "I mention the radical departure of Governor Reagan from the principles or ideals or historical perspective of his own party." He tried to attack what most Democrats thought were Reagan's weakness, his opposition to the Equal Rights Amendment. But Reagan answered showing his support for full rights for women while he was governor of California.[134]

As time ran out, there were a few more comments that meandered slightly. Then, at the end of questions, it was time for closing remarks.

Each candidate was given three minutes; Carter went first. He praised the League of Women Voters and the city of Cleveland. He tried to make clear to the American people his belief in "the stark differences" between himself and his Californian opponent. He talked of peace and fairness and the loneliness of the presidency and how he'd fought to keep America out of conflicts with other nations. He did not make mention once of the economy, jobs, or inflation.[135]

Carter made his best case, as the verdict of the American people was at hand. "The American people now are facing, next Tuesday, a lonely decision," he said. "Those listening to my voice will have to make a judgment about the future of this country, and I think they ought to remember that one vote can make a lot of difference." For a very brief moment, he seemed to regain his old form and almost had the people again, but then he reverted to the lecturing schoolmarm, talking about how one vote per precinct put JFK in office in 1960 and how the lack thereof kept Hubert Humphrey out of office in 1968.[136]

Carter concluded by speaking of human rights and American leadership in that world. "To stay strong, to stay at peace, to raise high the banner of human rights, to set an example for the rest of the world, to let our deep beliefs and commitments be felt by others in all other nations, is my plan for the future."[137]

If this had been twenty years earlier, or another era, another economy, it might have sufficed, but this was 1980 and the American people were hurting and couldn't save the world until and unless somebody saved their own country.[138]

But America was different now we had dropped into a valley of darkness, a time of incredible loss. Even Carter was forced now to admit it. America had been in a long dark 'drought' of incredibly tragic events and circumstances for nearly two full decades. This all began with the young prince of Camelot begin assassinate in Dallas; a horrible national tragedy. Added to this, a decade long war in the South East Asian jungle had not gone our way. In fact for the first time in our history there was quiet talk that we had lost the conflict in Viet Nam. Then another president had been cut down by a corrupt scandalous act. By this time Americans were frightened at the prospect of losing the Cold War with the Soviet Union. Now with Carter at the helm they had been losing their jobs in record numbers. They were also losing dream homes in a war of foreclosures. They were also losing the value of their paychecks due to hyperinflation; Carter's economic plan had dried up any extra money. And we had lost the battle to keep our international allies loyal to our cause.

Conversely Ronald Reagan had spent most of his adult life traveling the country, coast to coast, listening to the common people of the land. He had grown to know Americans; he knew their best times and their worst times. He knew the exhilaration of their hearts and he knew how their hearts ached when they had worked so hard and were losing everything. His love for the people and the desire to help them succeed welled up with in him. He was going to do something to help them.

As Craig Shirley says, "He hadn't only spoken with and listened to Americans. Other politicians sloughed off their mail to factotums to answer. Not Reagan. He read his mail. Not all of it, to be sure, but enough to gain an understanding and perspective that eluded other politicians. Reagan called himself a "citizen politician" and he really believed it."[139]

Those letters, Reagan read from fellow citizens; they spoke of joy and sorrow, of gain and loss, of hopes and dreams, of life and death. And to each, Reagan answered — not with a dashed-off note, but often with long handwritten letters, tender letters offering advice, offering counsel, articulating his philosophy, giving solace.

Every day, Reagan also read through a file of news clips which his staff had prepared for him each morning. The file contained the news of the day, coverage of Carter, himself, world events, and the like, but what he was most interested in were the other stories, often from small-town newspapers, about the American people. About blue ribbons awarded at livestock shows, about boys winning Eagle Scout, about the charity of Girl Scouts, about unselfish and heroic deeds performed by what he called the "quiet, everyday heroes of American life."[140] Reagan believed America was a very special and great country because in her heart, America was good.

Through all that he saw, read and witnessed, Reagan gained an insight and vision from which he hammered out a political philosophy that was based upon the most fundamental creed of the founders: That power should reside with the many people and not the few elites. That power should flow upward and not downward. That elected officials were truly "public servants" who had a solemn compact with those who put them into power. And that the first obligation of the national government was to secure the peace and freedom for those who allowed them to govern.

He understood the quintessential American because he was the quintessential American. He'd never forgotten the land from where he'd come. Ronald Reagan, age sixty-nine, now stood before the American people, exactly in the place he wanted to be and in the moment he wanted to possess. Now was his chance to make the case he'd always wanted to make since that time long ago when he was a dreamy boy whose ambition was to one day save others.

As the camera ever so slowly moved in for a close-up, Reagan began his remarks by thanking the "ladies" of the league and expressing his regret that John Anderson could not have been on stage that night. He moved quickly into his closing argument to the American people:

> "Next Tuesday is Election Day. Next Tuesday all of you will go to the polls, you'll stand there in the polling place and make a decision. I think when you make that decision it might be well if you would ask yourself:
>
> Are you better off than you were four years ago? Is it easier for you to go and buy things in the stores than it was four years ago? Is there more or less unemployment in the country than there was four years ago? Is America as respected throughout the world as it was? Do you feel that our security is as safe? That we're as strong as we were four years ago?
>
> And if you answer all those questions yes, why then I think your choice is very obvious as to who you'll vote for.
>
> If you don't agree, if you don't think that this course that we've been on for the last four years is what you would like to see us follow for the next four, then I could suggest another choice that you have.
>
> This country doesn't have to be in the shape that it is in. We do not have to go on sharing in scarcity, with the country getting worse off, with unemployment growing. We talk about the unemployment lines. If all the unemployed today were in a single line, allowing two feet for each one of them, that line would reach from New York City to Los Angeles, California. All of this can be cured. And all of it can be solved. . . . I

CHAPTER SIX — DECADES THAT CHANGED AMERICA

know that the economic program that I have proposed for this nation in the next few years can resolve many of the problems that trouble us today. . . .

I would like to have a crusade today. And I would like to lead that crusade with your help. And it would be one to take government off the backs of the great people of this country and turn you loose again to do those things that I know you can do so well, because you did them and made this country great. Thank you."[141, 142]

The debate was finished and just as in the beginning, Ronald Reagan walked across the stage to meet President Carter at his podium. Both families exchanged pleasantries as they came to the stage to support their heroes.

That night, the record shows that the Carters left the hall early. They forced a pair of smiles, but in his diary the night of the debate, Carter memorialized his contempt for Reagan forever: "Reagan was, 'Aw, shucks, this and that. I'm a grandfather, and I love peace' . . . etc. He has his memorized lines, and he pushes a button and they come out."[143] Gerald Rafshoon, Carter's media person, wrote a memo in the summer before the debate stating that the cornerstone of the campaign should be, "Carter is Smarter Than Reagan"; the president would not let the idea go.[144] Carter had believed it before the debate and had walked into that disaster thinking he would blow Reagan away, like so much soy bean fodder down on the farm, However, the morning after, when asked whether he had won the debate, Carter surprised many with his response, "It's hard to say."[145] Many years later, Carter soothed his ego, maintaining the debate was "a standoff," because "my folks thought I won. . . . his folks thought he won."[146]

Jimmy Carter's debate preparation team had convinced the president to make Reagan the issue. Unfortunately for Carter, he succeeded far beyond what he'd hoped. More than 105 million people had watched the debate, according to *Newsweek*, making it the most viewed debate in our American history.[147] Thanks to television and radio and to Carter himself, those many millions upon millions of viewers and listeners learned that night the former president of the Screen Actors Guild was not a mad bomber, he was not stupid, he wasn't as Democrats had claimed "an empty suit," he wasn't mean, he wouldn't throw old people under the bus, he wasn't a bigot. They discovered, much to the chagrin of the mainstream media and the Carter campaign, that Reagan was so different than what that media, the pundits, and the Carter campaign had portrayed him. Rafshoon's July memo had typically, as was the habit of Carter's men, dismissed this opponent, being contemptuous of Reagan, referring to him as "too old, not smart, too simplistic, doesn't read, naive [sic], inexperienced, right wing."[148] The result of the debate, instead, led the viewers to see a deeply humble man, very self-confident, a conservative who believed that compassion, real compassion came from home, the church, and the community where people lived their lives — and most importantly should never — be imposed upon the people by government edict. Carter never said truer words in his entire life when stating there were "stark differences" between Reagan and him.[149]

In the old black and white cowboy and western movies; ones with Roy Rogers, you could always count on the bad guys in the black hats to come riding into town with their version of the story. In this case the guys in the black hats were the elite media, or "the smart guys from Haavaad." They really "knoweth not" how to respond to the public about how the debate had gone. Surely it was not possible that Reagan, the actor, had beaten President Carter, could it? No way.

But the black-hatted liberal media did what it always does. They read the memo of the day from "on high" and noting their daily marching orders, then use identical key words as they are instructed. Therefore, like the townspeople in the tale of *The Emperor's New Clothes*, they scurried to the safety of their elitist friends to say that President Carter had won the debate because other members of the elites said Carter won the debate. "All the people throughout the city had already heard of the wonderful cloth and its magic and all were anxious to learn how wise or how stupid their friends and neighbors might be."[150]

The cover-up started with Dan Rather (aka, "Ol' Tell the Truth Dan), Leslie Stahl, and Bill Plante, the CBS correspondents doing the post-debate analysis; they chatted up Carter's performance as superior. The only positive comments for Reagan among the moguls that night, and they were backhanded comments, started with Walter Cronkite who expressed he was impressed with Reagan, but only because he hadn't screwed up. His comrades, Jack Germond and Jules Whitcover offered their agreement saying Reagan hadn't "done anything stupid."[151] The next day, Tom Brokaw, not to be outdone by his fellow liberals, said he was favorable of Carter's "handling of the SALT II issue."[152]

It should be remembered that the Liberal Media will always support the far left candidates; *The Washington Post* is in that fold. *The Post* came to the rescue of the Leftist Elites when David Broder wrote, "Carter on Points, but No KO." The title falsified the truth stating that Carter had kept Reagan on the defensive all night. "In a confrontation where most of the time was spent on Carter's preferred issues — and not on the economic record of the last four years, on which Reagan would have preferred to focus — the incumbent repeatedly managed to work in a partisan appeal to his fellow Democrats."[153]

A Potemkin village was built in written word by TV critic for the *Post*, Tom Shales. To follow suit with other liberal media he penned, "As TV personality, Carter looked. . . . basically unflappable. Reagan let himself be backed into corners by Carter punches to the face and body."[154]

Not to be outdone, Mary McGrory of *The Washington Star* fell in line with the rest and wrote, "Ronald Reagan showed the superficiality and insensitivity to such matters as the nuclear threat that makes people nervous about putting him in the Oval Office."[155]

The liberal chorus went on ad infinitum ad nauseam. Fred Barnes, then a reporter with *The Baltimore Sun*, watched the debate and said he too thought Carter won the debate. He left immediately after the debate to drive to Philadelphia to cover a campaign event. While driving he listened to the Larry King radio show during which he was stunned to learn that callers were saying that Reagan had won.[156]

The media elites did not want to listen to the results of the call-in poll, but the callers' responses were not a fluke. For example, the *New York Times* had assembled a focus group made up of a cross section of voters from the greater New York area including many who before the debate had planned on voting for Carter, or had been undecided. Not now! One pre-debate undecided voter, a woman from Connecticut, said Carter was "offensive and belligerent." She was one among those leaning toward Reagan. Even from those saying they planned on voting for Carter, praised Reagan's performance and panned Carter's. A Rutgers professor from Brooklyn, said of Reagan, "I had to hand it to him. He is very reassuring. He comes across so graceful. Without substance, though." She complained about Carter's "self-righteousness, his hyperbole." What's more, the group exploded in guffaws over Carter's assertion that he'd discussed nuclear policy with this daughter, Amy.[157]

In spite of the evidence, there was still such a gulf between the paper's coverage of the debate and what it heard and then reported from its little focus group. Bernie Weinraub's story which favored Reagan, was buried in the Section B of the paper, and then buried in that section, back on page 20.

The Associated Press did a poll right after the debate, which was even more lopsided toward Reagan. The poll showed that 46 percent of the respondents thought Reagan had performed better, while only 34 percent thought Carter had performed better.[158] The poll was done so late that evening, the east coast papers did not pick up on it immediately. Even when they did, they dismissed it, claiming that it had been slanted to favor Reagan from the beginning.

Standing nearly alone was R. Emmett Tyrrell, conservative columnist who saw the distinction between what he courageously called the "Wise and the Wisenheimers."[159] It took real backbone to stand alone, but he was right, because there was a big chasm between what the elite media represents and that for which the rest of the country stands (as there is today). There is no comparison, just a huge contrast. A union man said after the debate, "If Reagan was a Democrat; he'd have been in the White House in January."[160] Reagan was connecting with millions of Democrats watching the debate in 1980, using their language; he spoke simply from the heart.

One liberal elite broke ranks because he recognized what happened in the debate that night. He was Sam Donaldson of ABC News. When he left the hall that night, he saw Jody Powell and Hamilton Jordan back-slapping each other about how Carter had "won." Donaldson yelled at them as he left, "Your man blew it."[161]

Most news sources continued their attempt to hide the truth about the debate. But as the evidence became the talking points at coffee shops everywhere, frankly overwhelming, many news sources had to start conceding that Reagan was remarkably moving ahead of the incumbent. Two days following the debate, CBS news released a nationwide poll showing what the callers to Larry King and the rest of Middle America knew — Reagan had won the debate, 44 percent to 36 percent, and outperformed the president.[162]

Election Day finally arrived and in accordance with traditions, voting began in Dixville Notch, New Hampshire, just after midnight. And the sign of the times ahead pointed to Reagan, for he crushed Carter in this tiny New England village, 17-3.[163] Reagan had finally won Dixville Notch. He had lost there to Ford in the 1976 primary and tied Bush in the 1980 primary.[164]

The Democrat leaders began realizing their base was demoralized, while it was opposite news for Republicans as was seen in St. Louis County, Missouri. There, Chairwoman Pat Keyes, called Kenny Klinge and said, "I've got a problem." Klinge suspected she was going to tell him no one had shown up to work the twenty-five phones, but instead, she gasped, "I've got five hundred people, what am I supposed to do? A platoon system was very hastily arranged.[165]

About two hours after the old cranks of Dixville Notch voted, as Craig Shirley states, Jody Powell took a phone call on Air Force One as the big plane was on approach to the Seattle airport. It was from the White House. On the other end of the line were Hamilton Jordan and Pat Caddell. The connection was bad, but Powell could hear well enough to know the news was bad. "We need to talk to the president," his friend Jordan said. "The bottom has fallen out. It's all over."[166]

The day only got worse for Carter. Powell was keeping as much of the bad news away from the president as he could. Finally on their way to Georgia aboard the 707, Powell told Carter about the phone call and the way the polls were going toward a landslide to Reagan. Carter asked him specifically what they had found about the voting. "They say it looks bad," Powell told him. "It's probably all over."

Carter was first shocked and then disheartened. Cadell's latest numbers showed an utter and complete collapse for the Georgian, across the board, with nearly all groups and in nearly all regions. He was losing whites overwhelmingly, he was losing the Catholic vote, and Reagan was extremely competitive with union voters. Carter was being wiped out in the suburbs and in the rural areas. Reagan was scoring impressively with Hispanics and Jewish voters. Carter's beloved South had also apparently found a new hero in Reagan. Carter was running far behind in every category from four years earlier, even among the evangelicals he'd carried so handsomely in 1976.[167]

As the voting was coming to an end that day, from the earlier updates his staff provided, Carter knew he was going to lose. Reagan thought there was a chance he would win, but neither man was ready for the political earthquake that was sweep-

Chapter Six — Decades That Changed America

ing across this nation, from precincts, to towns, to counties, and to states. All the networks had huge armies of correspondents gearing up for an all-night election coverage. But it was not to be. Over at NBC, John Chancellor came on at 7 P.M. and predicted, "Ronald Reagan will win a very substantial victory tonight — that's our projection."[168]

Barbara Walters with her patented Rolodex came on at 7:12 P.M. to report on a startling phone conversation she'd just had with Cadell, of Carter's team. "He did say last night he told President Carter he was going to lose." She said she had pressed Cadell, asking him if there was any chance to which he replied, "Look up at the board and you can see it spelled out."[169]

NBC came back on at 8 P.M., and David Brinkley and John Chancellor called very quickly in rapid-fire succession Mississippi, Florida, Alabama, and in a few moments Michigan, Ohio, Illinois, New Jersey, and Pennsylvania all for Reagan. In the Keystone State, Reagan had taken 25 percent of the Democrat vote.[170]

At the same time, NBC had 295 electoral votes for Reagan which was twenty-five more votes than he needed to win. In a couple of minutes, Texas had gone Reagan, and the rout was on. What the media moguls had hoped would be an all-night study of the map and an ultimate Carter win, turned from a pipe dream into a nightmare. Only fifteen minutes later, at 8:15 eastern time, NBC called the election for Reagan, not just a state but the entire nation. Only 5 percent of the vote had actually been counted. Chancellor, unsmiling, intoned, "Ronald Wilson Reagan, former sports announcer, a film actor, a governor of California, is our projected winner."[171]

Reagan was preparing to go to the Century Plaza Hotel in Los Angeles, which by 8 P.M. Pacific Time, was jam-packed with a crowd chanting, "We want Reagan! We want Reagan!" And a few minutes later, the president-elect arrived, stage left of course. The family gathered on stage around him. What seemed like several minutes went by and finally it was time for Reagan to speak. He started slowly, but firmly, "There's never been a more humbling moment in my life." Pausing and reflecting, "I consider the trust you have placed in me to be sacred, and I give you my sacred oath that I will do my utmost to justify your faith." Reagan said many things in thanks to volunteers, staffers and so many across the nation. He reminded the audience of what Abraham Lincoln had told a group of reporters the day after his election: "Well, boys, your troubles are over now; mine have just begun." Near the end of his brief remarks, Reagan summed up his view: "I am not frightened by what lies ahead. And I don't believe the American people are frightened by what lies ahead."[172] *Time* later said the president-elect had given his remarks with "the same mixed tone of humility and boyish glee that so obviously had charmed American voters during the campaign."[173]

Reagan left no doubt about his priorities in his remarks, "Together, we're going to do what has to be done. We're going to put America back to work again!" Though his remarks lacked some of the rhetoric associated with the Gipper, mostly because the end of the election had come so quickly, he did say, "I aim to try and tap that great American spirit that opened up this completely undeveloped continent from coast to coast and made it a great nation, survived several wars, survived a great depression, and we'll survive the problems that we face right now."

A reverent mood came over Reagan. "When I accepted your nomination for president, I hesitatingly.... asked for your prayers at that moment. I won't ask them for this in particular at this moment, but I will just say, I would be very happy to have them in the days ahead." His voice caught for a moment. "All I can say to all of you is thank you." Then, revealingly, his thoughts drifted back to Tampico and Dixon, the two little towns in Illinois where he'd grown up. The old broadcaster had arranged to have his message aired on a small radio station in downstate Illinois to reach the folks there. He wanted to tell them that he was still thinking about them. "So to all of them," he said, "thank you, too, back there in the hometown."[174]

There — sixty years earlier — a wistful boy had dreamed of being a hero, of saving people, of saving his country one day when it needed him most. The little boy's dream had come true. He would get his chance to save America.[175]

RONALD WILSON REAGAN, THE president of the United States, departed the Century Plaza's stage to step shortly onto a much bigger stage — in, fact, the biggest stage of his life. He'd been on stages big and small his whole life — high-school stages, soundstages, convention stages — but this was something different, bigger, more vast, indeed all-encompassing. Ronald Reagan would finally get a chance to ply his trade. On world stage.[176]

Reagan kept his promise. He was a remarkable president. He restored the can-do spirit. He restored American morale. He revived patriotism, the idea of American exceptionalism, and of course revived the American economy from a horrible Carter recession. He did it with tax cuts and a tightened monetary policy, which reduced the record high Carter interest rates, reduced the devastating inflation, and put people back to work. He began an economic growth that ran for an unprecedented ninety-two straight months — oh, and by the way during which time nearly thirty-five million new jobs were created.[177] His conservatism was exactly what our country needed, not just for those two terms, but really for the next 1,000 years. He literally saved America at that moment from going over the precipice. Unfortunately, in the last few years, many of the other Republicans have since started looking more like the Democrats, becoming enemies of real progress. They are progressive, leaning to the left, in their approaches. All this was eating away at the freedoms and at our Constitution which the liberals of the 60s have been attacking.

There was a storm gathering — it was progressive and evil — it was being headed by liberals like Kennedy, Clinton, and their strong communist supporters, the professors of their past in the university system, and of course the media. Their goal has been to remove Constitutional Law, and replace it slowly with Socialism, a welfare state, and begin to make the city on the hill that was the hope of the world, an empty run down and bankrupt village.

Reagan hated Marxism, or as he called it Communism. He abhorred it to the core. In 1977 when he addressed the annual gathering of CPAC he told them, "When a conservative says that totalitarian Communism is an absolute enemy of human freedom, he is not theorizing — he is reporting the ugly reality captured so unforgettably in the writings of Aleksandr Solzhenitsyn."[178] When Reagan was reelected in 1984, the diplomatic tags on the cars used by the Soviet Embassy in Washington were changed to begin with the initials "FC." Nobody needed to guess what it stood for.[179]

None of the Communist nations liked Reagan either. "Probably no American policymaker at any time during the Cold War inspired quite as much fear and loathing in Moscow as Ronald Reagan," according to a definitive book on the Cold War, The Sword and the Shield. The Communists began tracking Reagan years before he was elected president. The East German secret police, the Stasi, maintained an ever bulging dossier on Reagan, while Soviet agents, beginning in the mid-1970s, were under orders to find "compromising material" on him. (Interesting isn't it how our media today works in the same way against true Americans? Surely it has caused many to question which side they are really on.) After 1976 the Soviets worked covertly in America to undermine his political career and to plant anti-Reagan stories in the world press, courtesy of "Service A" and the "Centre," two Soviet-based propaganda operations.[180]

History shows with absolute certainty that the Soviets wanted a different outcome in the 1980 election. Carter's presidency was frightening to blue-blooded Americans, but not Communists. Newt Gingrich recalled those years, "I think that the real risk was the Soviet Union winning the Cold War. They were in Nicaragua, they were in El Salvador, they were in Cuba, they were in Mozambique, they were in Afghanistan, they were paying.... partisans in Germany and Great Britain.... There is no reasonable way they would not have attempted under a Carter II to expand their capacity very significantly." Gingrich, the history professor, rated Carter as "the second most destructive president after James Buchanan."[181] Newt most likely would move those names down his "worst ever" list just a notch since Obama has come onto the scene.

Thankfully, the 1980 election was different and history shows that Reagan was the one who put the kibosh to the Soviet machinery, and won the Cold War. In doing so, he freed millions of civilians who were behind that Iron Curtain. From the time of the Bolshevik Revolution which started Communism in 1917 until 1991, no Soviet leader had ever willingly given up power. It is also interesting to note that from 1917 to 1980, the Soviet Union increased their territory against every American president, until Reagan came into the White House. His work in conjunction with Chancellor Margaret Thatcher and Pope John Paul II brought freedom where slavery and communistic rule once existed.

Perhaps the best estimation of the 1980 election is by writer R. Emmett Tyrrell, Jr., who founded *The American Spectator*. He summed up the differences which voters had in 1980 between Carter and Reagan. Probably the same differences are still seen between liberal progressives and true conservatives today. Carter, Tyrrell said, had an "antipodal view of mankind. Reagan is the optimist. Carter is the pessimist. Reagan sees us as capable. Carter sees us as inept and wobbling for skid row, were it not for the government's watchful eye."[182]

Oh, for sure, Ronald Reagan's election in 1980 was not welcomed by all Republicans, especially by the country club moderates under that tent. Actually, they loathed him and could not in their hearts forgive the man, who in 1977 said in a speech to conservatives, "The New Republican Party I envision will not be, and cannot be, one limited to the country club — big business image."[183] History shows that Reagan and these elites had little use for each other. Helene Von Damm, Reagan's long-time secretary in Sacramento, recalled an item from *National Review*, "It seems no one likes him . . . except the voters."[184]

Sad to say, it took a man who grew up in the Soviet Union — Aleksandr Solzhenitsyn, who was imprisoned there for ten years, starved by the Communists, all for writing a letter to Joseph Stalin which was critical of him, then he was finally expelled — It took him to express the prideful sorrow Americans felt in the days following Reagan's death on June, 5, 2004. "In July 1975, I concluded my remarks in the Reception Room of the U.S. Senate with these words: 'Very soon, all too soon, your government will not need just extraordinary men — but men with greatness. Find them in your souls. Find them in your hearts. Find them in the breadth and depth of your homeland.' Five years later, I was overjoyed when just such a man came to the White House. May the soft earth be a cushion in his present rest."[185]

The Nineties

Apathy was setting in as we saw the change in administrations and sailed on into the 90's. George H. W. Bush rode the coat tails of Reagan into the White House. However, it seemed that about the same time, the moderate Republicans started preaching again the "reaching across the aisle" mantra; which made John McCain so infamous. While the economy rolled, due to Reagan and the conservatives, America was forgetting its higher calling, to which Reagan had called us. Then another change of administrations, and with the entrance of Bill and Hillary Clinton, seemed to come a new moral direction downward as the 90's rolled on. The developing politics left a sour taste in the mouths of God-fearing and law-abiding citizens. The flavor of the decade spoke, "What difference does it make," and "I'll do whatever I want." The no restraint characters of the late 60s and 70s, with long hair and chaos as a monogram, were now taking charge in the country. The attitude of "Don't try to put your morality on me man," was on center stage. The strings which held our society together were unraveling more quickly now, as it had done in the late 70s. It seemed we were all headed in thirty different directions

— all the wrong way. Church was beginning to be totally out of the question for most. Religion was okay, so long as it was not Christianity. The time seemed to be without meaningful aim, no goals, no hope. The future as seen in the 50s which had been so promising had now dissolved. Events were not just frightening; they were earth shattering. While techy items and materialism rolled on, the world was becoming a dark place to live. Technology artificially took the place of meaningful communication; it was an empty box, except when used as a tool, rather than a god. But technology also showed us our weaknesses in the Y2K scare, with IT groups racing to their banks with millions, while supposedly saving the planet with Y2K solutions. What a joke.

When you look back on the nineties, one can ask how did Bill Clinton really enter the stage as president and create so much leftist change. It was due to the mundane demeanor of many Conservatives but also due to a strong third-party challenge by Ross Perot. Running as an "agent of change" who promised reforms, William Jefferson Clinton — Bill to most people, "Bubba" to some — and his running mate, Al Gore, became the first baby boomers to win the White House. Their victory followed a raucous election that was noteworthy, among other reasons for this third-party candidacy of H. Ross Perot.

Ross Perot, or "Boss Ross" as most called him, had built Electronic Data Systems (EDS) into a billion-dollar corporation with large, profitable government contracts servicing Medicare records. But his Reform Party platform was built on assailing big government and excessive government spending. He had deep pockets, and with them he financed an independent campaign aimed at overhauling government and opposing the North American Trade Agreement (NAFTA) which was favored by both major party candidates. Perot had so famously said that if NAFTA passed there would be a "giant sucking sound" as American jobs would migrate south of the border to lower-wage Mexico.

Perot electrified the campaign in more ways than one and actually had a lead in some polls through the early days of the campaign. He had a folksy style and a can-do approach which was a huge change from the politics as usual, and appealed to millions of American voters. They were totally turned off by the system, disenchanted with the two major political parties, whose differences seemed only marginal all the time. Perot appeared on Larry King Live, King's evening television talk show, and as one man put it, he completely altered the landscape of American politics at the time. But suddenly Perot canceled his unorthodox campaign, claiming he was being threatened by some opponent who had revealing pictures of his daughter. Many voters started dismissing him as an eccentric kook. Then, just weeks before the election, Perot shocked the political atmosphere by jumping back into the campaign battle. Perot, Clinton, and Bush participated in a series of three three-man televised debates. Perot again electrified many of the television viewers with his answers to questions; his answers were vague and general in nature, but certainly entertaining to many viewers who wanted a shakeup in Washington. I'll always remember his response to the moderator's question about regarding the economy, "We're going to lift that hood up and get over in there and fix this car, Larry, so we can get on down the road." This response was given many times to different questions. While extremely vague, his answers were seen as humorous. They were welcomed by some voters because in addition to other reasons, it made the professional political candidates on the platform a little uneasy or nervous.

Pessimism about where our country was going became a strong theme during this time. And why shouldn't it have been?! Without a doubt, up to the point, the election of Bill Clinton in 1992 should have been a wake-up call to every conservative and God-fearing man, woman and child. Of course that election would most likely not have had the same results if it had not been for Ross Perot running on an independent ticket. That pulled votes away from any conservative side of the ticket which existed. Something strange happened during the campaign of that year. In the course of the presidential debates, questions of character continually hounded Bill Clinton's bid for the White House. Accusations of marital infidelity threatened to derail the Clinton candidacy as Jennifer Flowers leveled her charges of their long-running affair while Clinton was Governor of Arkansas. The incident resulted in the now famous Barbara Walters' interview of Bill and Hillary Clinton which aired their marital difficulties to a national audience. In the ensuing days we were told, "It's the economy, stupid!" "Character doesn't count," and "Foreign policy expertise is not necessary. What matters is a strong and vibrant economy." "I still believe in Hope," the Hope, Arkansas, native told adoring audiences coast to coast.[186]

Gary Hart had his presidential campaign come to an abrupt train wreck due to his moral indiscretions aboard "Monkey Business," the now famous boat where the media found him and a female partner, who was not his wife. Clinton was different in that he survived the character assassination attempts by some of the media. In fact in his case, it was as if the extra-marital sex was a resume enhancer. At the same time, George Bush Sr. and Vice President Dan Quayle were reviled for addressing family values. It came to a head when Quayle made a speech attacking Hollywood's glorification of single parenting, such as seen on *Murphy Brown*, a popular sitcom of that day. He, they, and anyone who voiced a negative opinion about promoting that lifestyle were treated with ridicule and scorn from the mainstream media, Hollywood elites, and liberal progressives everywhere. As the election drew close, the Left, sinister in their own way, diverted attention away from Clinton, and did so by branding anyone who talked about moral issues as being "an extremist." The national media promoted Clinton stating his sex life was a private matter, and that the election was about matters of substance. Interesting how the word "substance" has fluid definitions and can be reverted back to private sexual matters, when any conservative is accused of an extra-marital affair. The mainstream media has always insisted at such a time when a conservative was charged with sexual harassment, "Saying the accusation of such acts are serious on their own merit and must be investigated." Bill Clinton was elected the 42nd President of the United States on November 3, 1992, though he received only forty-three percent of the Popular Vote. Meaning of course, that 57 percent of the American people did not want Clinton as president.[187]

Many presidents have iconic moments — images forever imprinted on the American psyche. FDR with Churchill. A jubilant Truman holding the newspaper that proclaimed DEWEY DEFEATS TRUMAN. JFK giving his ringing Inaugural Address. Ronald Reagan in Berlin, saying, "Tear down this wall!"[188] Unfortunately for Bill Clinton, in his most indelible image, he wags a finger as he indignantly tells America on January 26, 1998, "I did not have sexual relations with that woman, Miss Lewinsky."

It was almost a full year later, that this particular image came back to make the kind of history which Clinton and the Democrats do not really cherish, except for those who have either no conscience or a seared conscience. And that is on December 19, 1998, Bill Clinton became the second president in U.S. history to be impeached by the House of Representatives. (The first was Andrew Johnson, Abraham Lincoln's successor.) The Judiciary Committee sent four articles of impeachment to the House, of which two were adopted.

The impeachment case against Clinton dated back to when he was an elected official of Arkansas, and continued on through into his presidency. Hillary, who aided him, sat in the famous *60 Minutes* television interview (mentioned earlier) during which the couple admitted their marital problems. Clinton, in his 1992 campaign, maneuvered through the rumors of his "sex-capades," which were aided by fellow Democrats and the Elite Media, which said it was all about a matter of private sex. Then in 1994, in a lawsuit brought by Paula Jones, accused Clinton of sexual harassment while he was governor of Arkansas, which along with other women who came out of the woodwork at the same time with similar charges, said Clinton was aided by Arkansas State Troopers, and the rumored Arkansas Mafia. This all broke in the news as the Clintons were being actively investigated by Special Prosecutor Kenneth Starr. Starr was examining the tangle of Arkansas real estate deals known as Whitewater, along with two separate cases involving misuse of FBI files by the Clinton White House and missing billing records from Hillary Clinton's Little Rock law firm.[189]

The investigations by Starr basically went nowhere, due to the lack of cooperation from Democrats on the Hill and reluctant witnesses. Clinton's legal team was working around the clock to delay harassment suits until after the 1996 election — in which Clinton easily defeated the veteran Republican senator Bob Dole, who had votes siphoned off by Reform Party candidate Ross Perot, who did the same thing in 1992.

Totally ignoring the high-profile investigations, and in the midst of his reelection campaign, Clinton became involved with Monica S. Lewinsky, who then was a twenty-one-year-old White House intern. It was a sexual relationship that began in November 1995 and went through 1996. When Clinton was questioned under oath about this, in a deposition in the harassment suit, Clinton denied the relationship. Prosecutor Starr received word of this denial and began an investigation into possible perjury and obstruction-of-justice charges.[190]

Since the Democratically-controlled Senate voted to acquit Clinton on both counts, possibly it would have been best to consider some of the early acts taken by Clinton early in his presidency and even those done before he took office as president-elect. Dr. James Dobson, at that time heard daily on radio stations across America, while he was head of Focus on the Family, reported in a publication dated January 1994, that Clinton began his radical progressive-left agenda as soon as he was elected. Dobson offered the following overview of the first twelve months of the Clinton Presidency starting even before he was sworn in. Twelve days before Bill Clinton took office, the stage was set for what was coming. He received a letter signed by fifty-one members of Congress, including Patricia Schroeder and self-identified homosexuals Barney Frank and Gerry Studds, that contained the following paragraph:

> We were writing to express our support for an executive order prohibiting the ban on lesbians and gay men serving in the armed forces as soon as possible upon taking office in January. We will stand with you as you execute this historic executive order and will work with you to oppose any attempts to legislate this type of discrimination in the future.[191]

And on January 23, the third day of his administration, Clinton remembered their request. As they requested, he delivered. Clinton issued five executive orders that defined his agenda for leading the nation. They were designed to:

- Lift the ban on homosexuals in the military;
- Lift the ban on fetal tissue research that legalized treating preborn babies as tissue, not unborn children;
- Lift the ban on counseling in federally-funded abortion clinics;
- Begin the process of approving the importation of the abortion-inducing medication, RU486, ignoring the growing medical evidence of potentially dangerous side effects, and also making it easier to destroy unborn children; Provide funds for the first time in history, for abortions in military hospitals.[192]

When viewing Clinton's direction in his role of president, one cannot help but remember that his agenda was designed long before by his mentor, Saul Alinsky. Alinsky as you may recall, wrote *Rules for Radicals*, and dedicated his book to the one that appears to have been his personal mentor, the Devil. Though you may choose to laugh, don't yet, until you read on. In the first edition of his book he wrote a dedication, or forward, which was removed from subsequent editions. That first edition only, contains the following dedication:

"Lest we forget at least an over-the-shoulder acknowledgment to the very first radical: from all our legends, mythology, and history (and who is to know where mythology leaves off and history begins—or which is which), the first radical known to man who rebelled against the establishment and did it so effectively that he at least won his own kingdom—Lucifer."

—Saul Alinsky

Among the strictest disciples of Alinsky, were Bill Clinton, Hillary Rodham (Clinton), and now of course one of the purest disciples of that radical group, Barack Obama. When I have watched both men operate, Clinton and Obama, it is as if the ghost of Saul Alinsky is really the one who speaks.

The Communist doctrines which "Comrade Saul" taught were basically straight out of the Manifesto which "Comrade Karl" wrote in 1848. It speaks of the ever-escaping fairness that must be recaptured in our world, if it is to be a perfect progressive utopia. That, according to Marx and Alinsky, requires the overthrow of capitalism and free-enterprise. It requires government oversight in everything and of course extremely heavy taxation on all, so that every individual will be treated equally. Bologna!!

As Saul himself states, "Young people have rightly looked for from the beginning of time, a way of life that has some meaning or sense. A way of life means a certain degree of order where things have some relationship and can be pieced together into a system that at least provides some clues to what life is about. Men have always yearned for and sought direction, by setting up religions, political philosophies, creating scientific systems like Newton's . . . formulating ideologies of various kinds. This is what is behind the common cliché, 'getting it all together' — despite the realization that all values and factors are relative, fluid and changing, and that it will be possible to "get it all together" only relatively. The elements shift. . . and move . . . like the changing pattern in a kaleidoscope. In the past "world," . . . terms was much smaller, simpler, and more orderly. Today everything is so complex as to be incomprehensible." (And now, see the picture here on how wrong the world seems to a young, idealistic mind in his next statements.) "What sense does it make for men to walk on the moon, while other men are waiting in welfare lines, or in Vietnam killing and dying for a corrupt dictatorship 'in the name of freedom? These are the days when man has his hands on the sublime while he is up to his hips in the muck of madness. . . . The outcome of the hopelessness is morbidity. There is a feeling of death hanging over the nation. . . . Today's generation faces all this and says, 'I don't want to spend my life the way my family and their friends have. I want . . . .to be me, do my own thing . . . live.'"[193] And there you have the hook to get ideologues to bite on the principles of *Rules for Radicals*.

With Alinksy as his mentor in his rear view mirror, it no wonder that during the next twelve months of Bill Clinton's Presidency, with lightning speed, the most radical anti-Christian social agenda in American history was implemented. There was a conservative resurgence in November 1994, in the mid-term elections, which caused Clinton to try and reinvent himself as a moderate. But let's not forget that actions speak must louder than words. His record following his inauguration on January twenty-third 1992 reflects that his radical agenda did not reflect the values that the majority of Americans hold dear.

February 3 – Clinton nominated Roberta Achtenberg for a prominent position in the Dept. of Housing and Urban Development. As an avowed lesbian activist, she spearheaded an attack on the Boy Scouts in San Francisco because they promoted values that, as she put it, "provide character building exclusively for straight, God-fearing male children."

February 11 – Clinton attempted to lift the restriction on the immigration of HIV-positive individuals into the U.S. Thankfully, even the Democrat-dominated Congress rejected his proposal.

April 2 – Clinton initiated an attempt to repeal the Hyde Amendment which prohibits federal funding of abortions. Again, thankfully, even the Democrats rejected his proposal again.

April 24 – Clinton promoted a meeting which resulted in an estimated 300,000 homosexual and lesbian activists descending on Washington, D.C., to celebrate America's first president to promote their agenda. They chanted vulgar comments, the tamest of which were "We're dykes, we're out, and we're out for power."

April 26 – Clinton's nominee for U.S. Surgeon General, Dr. Joycelyn Elders, announced, "I['ll] tell every girl that when she goes out on a date to put a condom in her purse."

April 28 – Clinton abandoned 217 years of military tradition as he abandoned the ban on women in combat. He also abandoned any opportunity for Congressional discussion on the subject.

June 10 – Clinton signed into law a bill lifting the restriction on fetal tissue research. Most competent people realize that stem cell research on the unborn is wrong because it is not at all necessary for successful research. In reality this was just another attempt to build express lanes to abortion factories and make the act of abortion more palatable to the unthinking American public.

June 14 – Clinton appointed Ruth Bader Ginsberg to be an Associate Justice on the Supreme Court. As an avowed feminist and ACLU activist, she pursued lowering the age of consent for sexual acts to twelve years of age, and favored legalization of prostitution. She also advocated elimination of all sex discrimination in the Boy Scouts and Girl Scouts, including a forced name change.

June 19 – Clinton sent a thank you letter to Jon Larimore of the Gay and Lesbian Information Bureau. He thanked them for "selflessly giving their time and support to my administration. . . ." "All of you who joined our ranks are making a real contribution to the future of our nation."

June 26 – Clinton appointed Kristine Gebbie, an avowed lesbian, as the new AIDS Czar. Following four months in that position, she made the following statement, "[The United States] needs to view human sexuality as an essentially important and pleasurable thing. [Until it does so], we will continue to be a repressed , Victorian society that misrepresents information, denies sexuality early, denies homosexual sexuality, particularly in teens, and leaves people abandoned with no place to go. I can help just a little bit on my job, standing on the White House lawn talking about sex with no lightning bolts falling on my head."[194] It seems an evil trick that Clinton and Gebbie played on the American people.

These represent the most radical swing that any administration had taken in our history to date, moving away from Judeo-Christian values on which our American culture was built. Aside from the horrible legislative acts themselves, a very sad portion of this story is that the denigrating actions were accomplished in just six months; all the while 57 percent of the American people opposed and rejected them. Clinton made it a point to target many organizations in the government so they could be radicalized. As a start, he chose the military, the National Endowment of the Arts and the Office of Surgeon General.

And the hits, they "just kept coming" from the Clinton radical liberal machine.

July 29 – Clinton implemented the famous "Don't Ask, Don't Tell" policy in the military.

August 5–6 – Clinton's budget was passed by one vote. Al Gore's vote, in the Senate, tipped the scales. He hailed the vote a mandate. It was at the time the largest single tax increase pushed on the American people, ever in our history, which was opposite of his pledge during the campaign to reduce taxes.

August 27 – The National Endowment of the Arts funded three gay and lesbian film festivals. The Executive Director of the Gay and Lesbian Media Coalition called the funding, " . . . validation from the highest office for arts funding in the country." This is the same left-wing National Endowment of the Arts, which helped celebrate a thoroughly disgusting work called "Piss Christ." It was a 1987 photograph by the American artist and photographer Andres Serrano. It depicts a small plastic crucifix submerged in a glass of the artist's urine. The piece was a winner of the Southeastern Center for Contemporary Art's "Awards in the Visual Arts" competition. No wonder Clinton decided to use this organization for furthering his ideals.

September 4 – Plans were announced to invest up to $7 billion to reach ten to nineteen year olds with the failed message of condoms and safe sex. The same day, the Clinton White House diverted monies earmarked for abstinence based sex-ed curriculums INTO "safe sex" programs promoting condoms.

September 8 – Dr. Joycelyn Elders was confirmed as the new U.S. Surgeon General. She held the most radical views of any person to ever hold that office. After two years of her horrible gaffs and ridiculous handling of matters, even the Clinton Administration could no longer embrace her outrageous statements, and she was dismissed.

September 22 – Hillary began her crusade for "Hillary Care," a National Health Care Program.

September 23 – Janet Reno, Clinton's Attorney General redefined child pornography, in a brief she filed with the Supreme Court. Through this she disclosed her view that producers and distributors of such horrible material could not be prosecuted unless children were explicitly shown to be engaged in sexual conduct exposing the genitals or pubic area of the body.

October 9 – Clinton speaks against the "Religious Right," as they were called for the first time during a speech at Yale University.

October 18 – Clinton invited twelve evangelical leaders to White House meeting. In the days that followed, pressure was put upon pastors to preach sermons and write letters condemning Christians who were critical of the president's policies.

November 2 – Homosexual and lesbian appointees in the Clinton Administration held a "coming out" breakfast for the press. They announced during the meeting that twenty-two had been appointed within the administration, surpassing their goal of five. They applauded Clinton for his courage.

November 18 – Clinton granted $13.2 million to Planned Parenthood for overseas "family planning," today's euphemism for aborting unborn babies.

December 3 – Clinton, during an interview with Tom Brokaw, expressed agreement with Dan Quayle's Murphy Brown speech, which seemed other worldly.

December 7 – The Clinton Administration announced a new ad campaign to provide explicit information on how "to put on a condom." The same day, Jocelyn Elders announced that legalizing drugs would markedly reduce crime.

December 24 – Clinton announced he would require states to finance abortions for poor women who were made pregnant through rape or incest. (This seemed in the liberal mind a well-timed message to coincide with the celebration of Christmas Eve, the celebration of the birth of Christ.)[194]

Conservatives bitterly resented and despised Clinton, not just for the private affairs, but for signing into law legislation like NAFTA, which cost America millions of jobs. Moderates and liberals seemed to like him despite his affairs, which I suppose was likened to having a greasy sex maniac work on your car; you don't like it at all, but if you're stuck with no other options, you try to get something done. Pollsters tried to smooth over Clinton to help him have an ever-present "more favorably perceived legacy." In a 2005 post-presidency assessment, journalist John Harris concluded, "However heedless he could be in his personal life, Clinton brought a dutiful sensibility to his public life . . . Clinton had implemented a mild but innovative brand of liberalism that favored economic growth over redistribution, insisted that the government pay its way rather than rely on budget deficits, and embraced free trade rather than taking refuge in protectionism."[195]

However people may think his economics may have worked, it was really the conservative Congress elected in 1994, which drove Clinton to a more moderate position than he held earlier. The formula was certainly imperfect, as economic and other Clinton-era decision would allow the financial dealings that ultimately led to the financial crises and Great Recession of 2007. Chief among those Clinton decisions pushed by Barney Frank and Frank Dodd, who pressured banks and lending companies, including Fannie May and Freddie Mac, to lend to make very high risk loans based on ethnicity when there was no chance to repay the loan at all.[196]

What made matters worse was that the media and liberals then blamed Bush for this act, which he certainly stood against, but passively allowed in his fight with the progressives.

During his first year, Janet Reno at Clinton's direction, in February, sent federal law enforcement to surround the religious cult known as Branch Davidians, who barricaded themselves inside their compound outside of Waco, Texas. After a fifty-one day standoff, Janet Reno gave the command for the troops to "move in" with tanks and fully automatic weaponry. Shots were exchanged and it is still questionable who set fire to the building where the cult was housed; the government officials or the cult themselves. The American public was outraged by the government assault which left at least seventy-five people dead, many of them women and children. When pressed to give an answer for what happened, Clinton could only say, "I didn't order any of that."

Clinton also left a huge stack of unfinished business. On top was the growing threat of terrorism on the U.S. He had been too preoccupied with his sexual diversions to do anything about several off-shore attacks against U.S. interests. The World Trade Center was bombed on February 26, 1993 by individuals with ties to Islamic terrorists. Clinton had been advised by intelligence that Osama Ben Laden's al Qaeda was growing in power and was an extreme danger to Americans, but he seemed distracted by other personal matters and a domestic agenda. Al Qaeda was later believed to be behind the attacks on embassies in Africa in 1998 and the USS Cole bombing in October 2000. Though Clinton had authorized the CIA to capture Ben Laden, his attention was on more "personal issues" and the attempts to capture Osama were unsuccessful. The 9/11 Commission in its report, found that while the Clinton had taken steps to address terrorism, "the United States did not, before 9/11, adopt as a clear strategic objective the elimination of al Qaeda."[197]

The Clintons were very successful — in dividing the American people into camps and polarizing the nation. The result of having over 40 years of teaching Marxism in the public school system and the university system was obvious. The Clintons were both students of Marx in the 60s; later they were leaders of the same progressive movement. The effect has seen the raising of a group who are enthusiastic about leaving individual liberty behind while embracing socialist ideals. The Clintons and other Liberal Progressives could rejoice as they began to see their dreams inching forward more each year, embracing their mentor Saul Alinsky's radical teaching. One thing infuriated Clinton; that is he never won a majority of the Americans in voting for him.

Possibly, one of my most un-favorite commentators, George Stephanopoulos, said it as clearly as a Progressive could say, in pure "liberal speak." He detailed how Clinton was able "to achieve what no Democrat had done since FDR — two-full terms and a successful presidency."[198] In reading his book, one has to think that what he meant by "successful presidency," was this: marching the liberal, socialist, progressive ball, or agenda, down the field closer to the end zone than ever before. That of course requires slashing free enterprise, expanding the welfare state, and in growing dependency upon big government. He said in his book, *All too Human*, "As I write these words, a popular president presiding over an America prosperous and at peace has been impeached. Clinton's lawyers are skillfully defending him in a Senate trial against the charge that he committed perjury and obstructed justice to conceal his sexual affair with a twenty-two-year-old intern. The battle is all but over, and I'm still mystified by the Clinton paradox: How could a president so intelligent, so compassionate, so public-spirited, and so conscious of his place in history act in such a stupid, selfish, and self-destructive manner? I don't know how to answer that question, and I never thought I'd have to try. When I first considered writing about my time with President Clinton, I envisioned a political memoir shaped like a comedy — a story of good, talented... people acting on Vaclav Havel's hope that politics 'can be not only the art of the possible, especially if "the possible" includes the art of speculation, calculation, intrigue, secret deals, and pragmatic maneuvering, but that it can also be the art of the impossible, namely the art of improving ourselves and the world."[199] Because George is a full-blown progressive liberal, who failed to recognize the truth spoken by Andrew J. Galambos, the astrophysicist, "Politics is the destruction of, not the solution to any problem." He also missed the Democracy 101 course stating, "Freedom is the societal condition that exists when every individual has 100% control over his own property..."[200]

<u>Thanks to the Clintons, thanks to the revolutionary hippies of the 60s, and thanks to all those liberal progressives who through the last century sowed the seeds of dissent to gain more power and control over people's lives, as you can see through the decades in this chapter, there has been a gradual seizing of freedoms, thought processes and diminishing of our Constitution. All this has resulted in both moral poverty and the diminishing of material resources before our eyes.</u> Consider this example which the Clintons, the Stephanopouloses, and all their

CHAPTER SIX — DECADES THAT CHANGED AMERICA

liberal accomplices have used to exact tolls on our society through their ideology.

The budget crisis which appears in Washington every few months should be viewed through the lens of our founders. The political left says the shutdown was all about an ideological tantrum of a handful of Republicans. Certainly, conservative members have an ideology and vision about what ground rules would produce a more prosperous, freer and fairer America. But let's be honest. The gentleman in the White House, our president, is as hardcore in his ideological dispositions as any Tea Partier. Each side believes America would be better off if it were run according to their vision. What's the crucial difference? As a conservative, I'd like my neighbors to agree with me that personal responsibility, traditional values and limited government is the best way to build a healthy and prosperous personal life and nation. But if they don't agree, they can do what they want.

But the world according to the big-government, morally relative left is much different. In this view, yes, nobody is forcing me to agree that personal responsibility and traditional values don't matter. But in their view, it's also only fair that I pick up the massive costs of their failures.

Take, for instance, poverty. We all agree that we want to get as many people out of poverty as possible. The evidence abounds that a lifestyle that reflects personal responsibility and traditional values, like traditional sexual attitudes and marriage and family, reduces dramatically chances that an individual will wind up in poverty. I hope people live according to these values. But if they don't want to, that's their business; but not so with the left. They want to foster a culture that says do what you want. They think to promote traditional values in schools and popular culture is inappropriate and small-minded and at times even unconstitutional. But then they say that it is only fair that everyone pay the costs of the mess this culture of moral relativism makes.

According to Ron Haskins of the Brookings Institution, in 2009 the poverty rate for children in homes with married parents was 11 percent. The poverty rate for children in homes headed by a single mother was 44.3 percent. The incidence of homes headed by a single mother has gone from 6.3 percent of all households in 1950 to 23.9 percent in 2010. In a Gallup poll done this year, 71 percent of respondents between 18 and 34 years old said having a baby outside of marriage is morally acceptable.

A culture fostered by the political left has been promoted. It sanctions behavior and wealth. More poverty is more likely to occur. And then those that promote this culture say it is only fair that everybody pay the costs.

Worse, the evidence is overwhelming that government spending on poverty has little or no impact on the incidence of poverty. Again according to Haskins of Brookings, from 1980 to 2011, spending in constant (inflation adjusted) dollars on means-tested (poverty) programs increased $500 billion, with a tripling of the amount spent per person in poverty. Over the same period, the poverty rate was virtually unchanged.

Also worth noting is that over this same period, the percent of babies born to unwed mothers went from 18 percent in 1980 to more than 40 percent in 2011. In the first three years of the Obama administration, spending on these means-tested programs increased almost $150 billion, or 31 percent. Obamacare will add up to 20 million more individuals to the almost 60 million already covered by Medicaid, the government health-care program for the poor. Medicaid now pays for 40 percent of all babies born in the country.

"Price tag of big government, moral relativism — hundreds of billions. Price tag of limited government, personal responsibility — zero. Is this an ideological battle? Of course it is."[201]

The simplicity of logic seems to work with thinking people, except for the ones claiming the "Ivy League Liberal Way."

The 00s

As the new millennium hit, the excitement which was present for entering the 20th century before, was absent for this one. In its place was an "economic Disneyland" with money being given for loans on just about anything. This feeling that we were going to soar even higher, had settled itself on a large portion of the American people. Progressives had been the predominant political voice in Washington law making for fifty years, up until the mid-term elections in 1994. Substitutes for real character were being replaced by technology, especially the hand-held electronic devices accompanied by an "I'm non-committal" attitude which seemed to be everywhere. However the climate changed direction and ended being the "We Surrender" decade. The losses of retirement funds in crashes, banks closures, depression level unemployment and underemployment, all driven by a thievery styled mantra driven by government with lowered morals and ethics are being displayed in the remanufactured hippy generation leadership model. And it appears the ghost of Saul Alinsky is really in charge.

It is alarming to see the change trends over the past 50 years. The "free sex" slogan has morphed into the "free thievery" or "No room for good guys here" jingle. Losing touch, not caring, hopelessness were all marks as we neared the end of the decade. Hard to imagine how suicide would become a national pastime for members of our military as they look at a future which is growing dimmer by the minute. The "spend it all now, we may not have tomorrow" actions of our government's regime has left the nation with a pause, trying to understand what a future could really look like. You need to protect yourself from these thieves is an all too often spoken philosophy.

As the decade of the "Teens" has started, it's not totally unclear what history will say about it. For certain "Throw Caution to The Wind" and the ever heroic "I don't know what is happening" phrases seem to be repeated after hearing the exact same words from the White House, as with many in society.

Dr. Thomas Sowell, in *Dismantling America*, said in reference to President Obama,

> "That such an administration could be elected in the first place, headed by a man whose only qualifications to be president of the United States at a dangerous time in the history of the world were rhetoric, style and symbolism — and whose animus against the values and institutions of America had been demonstrated repeatedly over a period of decades beforehand — speaks volumes about the inadequacies of our educational system and the degeneration of our culture."[202]

Obama is by no means unique; his characteristics are being shared by a growing number of Americans, but what is unique is that no other time in our history would such a person been elected president. That says much about the degeneration of our culture, values, thinking abilities and acceptance of what's no less than tyranny. As Sowell says, "Barack Obama is unlike any other president of the United States in having come from a background of decades of associations and alliances with people who resent this country and its people."

In 2008, Americans voted for Obama's hope and change. Briefly, here is a peak.

Obama's Health and Human Services Secretary Kathleen Sebelius threatened that there would be "zero tolerance" for "misinformation" in response to an insurance company executive who said that Obamacare would create costs that force up health insurance premiums. That's not only an attack on our constitutionally guaranteed free speech rights but an official threat against people who express views damaging to the administration.

Not to be outdone by his HHS secretary's attack on free speech, Obama wants full disclosure of the names of people who were backers of campaign commercials critical of his administration, saying that there has been a "flood of deceptive attack ads sponsored by special interests, using front groups with misleading names." Disclosure would leave administration critics open to government and mob retaliation.

Obama and his congressional and union allies have lectured us that socialized medicine is the cure for the nation's ills, but I have a question. If socialized medicine, Obamacare, is so great for the nation, why permit anyone to be exempted from it? It turns out that as of the end of November, Obama's health and human services secretary has issued over 200 waivers to major labor unions such as the International Brotherhood of Electrical Workers Union and Transport Workers Union of America and major companies such as McDonald's and Darden Restaurants, which operates Red Lobster and Olive Garden. Keep in mind that the power to grant waivers is also the power not to grant waivers. Such power can be used to reward administration friends and punish administration critics by saddling them with millions of dollars of health-care costs.

Obama's health-care legislation contains deviousness that has become all too common in Washington. What was sold to the American people as health-care reform legislation includes a provision that would more heavily regulate and tax gold coin and bullion transactions. Whether gold and bullion transactions should or should not be more heavily regulated and taxed is not the issue. The administration's devious inclusion of it as a part of health-care reform is.

"Fighting to the death" against government intrusion into our lives is becoming increasingly a necessity or at least a label for the decade.

"At the time of the adoption of the Constitution and the amendments, the universal sentiment was that Christianity should be encouraged . . . In this age there can be no substitute for Christianity. . . .That was the religion of the founders of the republic and they expected it to remain the religion of their descendants"

~ House Judiciary Committee, March 27, 1854

Chapter Seven

Where's the Beef?

"I was born not knowing, and have only had a little time to change that here and there."
— Richard Feynman

SOMEONE YEARS AGO SAID THAT THE teacher's, professor's, and pastor's real business is to tell men and women who they are. People tend to forget that. We are a species that has lost its memory. It's a terrible thing to forget who you are. "There are times when it seems a whole generation falls into a state or moral amnesia and forgets. . . ."[1] We seem to be able to forget what it means to be human, what our plans are, or even our own history.

The written record of oral statements and early writings indicate clearly that the founders of America were men and women who knew who they were. They either had a relationship with, had a commitment to Christ as disciples, or they had a committed faith in God. A few were people with no personal faith, but they were certainly following or working with people who had that relationship. The original thirteen colonies were established by those who left religious and economic oppression in Europe. They wanted nothing more to do with such regimes — and their documents say so.

Atheists today attack the nation's Christian heritage. Their lay stated claim to a high ground of science and reason. However their claims are empty and their words are generally caustic. In particular, they insist we be tolerant of them, yet will not be tolerant of people claiming a Christian faith. Within their statements are demands that we jettison all parts and practices of Christianity existing in our nation; except for their faith system of course. Make no mistake theirs is a religion, the oldest religion in the world. It is called Humanism or Secular Humanism. That faith system simply replaces a spiritual deity with self, who then claims control. That faith was fully on display early in human history, even in the Garden of Eden. Loosely translated, an atheist's response to a statement of belief from a Christian will usually contain a statement of their own faith plus a condemnation of anyone in disagreement. Such a person will often say something as, "Nothing in the world has been created; it evolved. There is no god. Nothing is established or fixed. Everything in our universe is relative, in particular morality. I will do whatever I want, calling all the shots in my life." There you have the bedrock of secular humanism, or relativistic humanism, which is the oldest religion and faith system in the entire universe.

When hearing an atheist speak "evangelistically" about their doctrines, I will normally congratulate the individual for having more faith than me. It appears that way for it requires loads of faith to believe that the cosmos and everything in the universe including America and its very unique founding just happened by accident, with no guidance from a deity, in particular the Judeo-Christian God. If Christians and Jews had as much faith in God as atheists have in their "no-god" religion, they would turn the world upside down.

This poses the question for Christians and Jews, "Where's the commitment to your belief for that which America stands," or "Where's the beef?" When elected "servants" within the country are neglecting their constituency and in some cases committing treasonous acts, one after another, where is the courage of the pastors and the church to stand up like the colonists did against King George in the 18th Century? The pulpits should be ringing with courageous messages against such elected leaders, just as prophets of Israel spoke to the people and their leadership as recorded in the Old Testament books of history and prophecy. The problem appears to be that the religious "leaders" of today appear to fear government officials more than they fear their God.

When it comes to beef, these fledging colonies, though standing independent of each other, bonded together to form a shield of protection from further inflictions. This is an established fact shown in their recorded collective documents, by their college curriculums, and by their sermons demonstrating their faith in God, trusting He would shield the nation from harm or destruction by a regime such as George III. In turn, they swore their allegiance to God and Christ personally, professionally, and governmentally.

In spite of this mountain of evidence, modern revisionists, secular writers and the afore mentioned atheists, along with agnostics, humanists, et al — they all try to convince us that the founders never intended their faith to be a part of the American experience, especially their legislative processes. This is a lie which Liberals and Progressives have promoted in their lectures to so many of us over the decades. It has been a deliberate and coordinated action to hide the historical truth and replace it with their lie. Why? Because the progressives think the country will be a better place without mention or connection to Christianity, Judaism, or God. The atheists obviously claim there is no deity. (They mean to say, "no god except self.") Leftist elitists say that "thinking people" realize we have progressed to the point that we are a "post-Christian" nation. For Christian conservatives to not speak out on this, to be silent during this war against truth, is a huge offense to our heritage, to the faith, and to God. To not speak against evil, is evil. It is nothing short of a slap in the face to George Washington, Benjamin Franklin, et al, let alone the Heavenly Father. There is too much evidence, overwhelming in its detailed content, to say that we were not established as a Christian nation, by men of faith.

CHAPTER SEVEN — WHERE'S THE BEEF?

Ethan Allen, was a hero of the American Revolution. It is recorded that he was also commander of the famous Green Mountain Boys, who he led in 1775 in an attack on Fort Ticonderoga. When he surrounded the fort with "the boys," he sent an emissary in demanding its surrender. When asked by Captain de la Place in whose name and what authority Commander Allen made this demand, he simply responded, "In the name of the Great Jehovah and the Continental Congress."[2]

Samuel Chase was one that George Washington appointed him to the Supreme Court. He was also a signer of the Declaration of Independence. In 1799, Justice Chase displayed his faith when he opined the following in the case of *Runkel vs. Winsmiller*: "By our form of Government, the Christian religion is the established religion; and all sects and denominations of Christians are placed on the same equal footing, and are equally entitled to protection in their religious liberty."[3]

Why can't we find and have a justice or chief justice like this Judge Chase today?! I know that under his pen and gavel, there would have been no trashing of, or banning of the Bible, or of having prayer to God booted out of our schools, as is the federal law of the land today. Nor would he have allowed the removal of the Ten Commandments from any of our school walls or federal buildings as has been done today. Notice his words, "By our form of government, the Christian religion is the established religion." I do not see the so-called separation in that statement. If separation of religion and state is so vital to liberals, why are so many of them tripping over themselves to roll out a red carpet for Islam?

Samuel Adams, made a proposal, according to the official minutes of the first session of the Continental Congress in 1774, that the sessions be opened with prayer. Not everyone agreed. John Jay and John Rutledge opposed the recommendation claiming that the diversity of religious opinion precluded such an action. Their minority opinion did not carry the day. At the end of the debate over the proposal, Adams said it did not become "Christian men, who had come together for solemn deliberation in the hour of their extremity, to say there was so wide a difference in their religious belief that they could not, as one man, bow the knee in prayer to the Almighty, whose advice and assistance they hoped to obtain."[4] After the appeal by Sam Adams, the disputation ceased, and the Reverend Jacob Duche led in prayer.[5] Adams wrote home to his wife that the prayer "had an excellent effect on everyone here.... Those men who were about to resort to force to obtain their rights were moved by tears" upon hearing it. Following the prayer, the Continental Congress instituted four fast-day proclamations. Of special significance is the one fast day on July 12, 1775. All the colonies planned to participate. John Adams, writing his wife from Philadelphia, wrote, "We have appointed a Continental fast. Millions will be upon their knees at once before the great Creator, imploring His forgiveness and blessing: His smiles on American councils and arms."[6]

When the time came for delegates to be sent to Philadelphia to draft and write the Constitution, they were mired in a literary argument, having lost their direction for several weeks. Finally, **Benjamin Franklin** came to the rescue of the writers. We have been told by Leftists for years that Franklin was not a Christian, that he would have nothing to do with conversations on the topic of God, nor would he have anything to do with the church. In contrast to that notion, he said the following in 1787 to those delegates who were meeting: "In the beginning of the contest with G. Britain, when we were sensible of danger, we had daily prayers in this room for divine protection. Our prayers, Sir, were heard and they were graciously answered. All of us who were engaged in the struggle must have observed frequent instances of a superintending providence in our favor. . . . Have we forgotten this powerful Friend? Or do we imagine we no longer need His assistance? I have lived long, Sir, a long time, and the longer I live the more convincing proof I see of this truth; that God governs in the affairs of man. And if a sparrow cannot fall to the ground without his notice, it is probable that an empire can rise without His aid? We have been assured, Sir, in the Sacred Writings that except the Lord build the house, they labor in vain that build it. I firmly believe this. . . . I therefore beg leave no more that, henceforth, prayers imploring the assistance of Heaven and its blessing on our deliberation be held in this assembly every morning."[7]

In July 1776, when the Declaration of Independence was in final draft form, the colonies had officially moved into the first steps of political freedom and linked themselves to their Christian past. The Declaration is a Christian-based, or religious, document, because it bases its arguments on theological grounds. It openly states that "rights" are a gift from the Creator: "We are endowed by our Creator with certain inalienable rights." The logic is simple: No Creator, no rights.[8]

The moral issue of our nation is tied to this single phrase in the Declaration. Today, while people are clamoring for rights, they are typically rejecting the very standard by which those rights are secured; to their moral anchor. Progressives have taught us this, that rights come from the government, but this is a lie. Statements from the Declaration, "Nature's God," who is the "Supreme Judge of the world," make rights a reality, not any government. The religious phrases found in the body of the Declaration were easily understood in terms of the prevailing Christian worldview of the time.[9]

James Madison was known in my lifetime by the title "Chief Architect of our Constitution." Before he studied law, and before he became the 4th President of the US, he studied theology and prepared for the ministry. Based on his beliefs coupled with his legal and theological education he wrote: "We have staked the whole future of American civilization, not upon the power of government, far from it. We have asked the future of all our political institutions upon the capacity of mankind for self-government; upon the capacity of each and all of us to govern ourselves, to control ourselves, to sustain ourselves, according to the Ten Commandments of God."[10]

Alexander Hamilton is known not only for signing the Constitution, but when

I was in school he held the title of 'The Ratifier of the Constitution.' Of our national document, he wrote, "For my own part, I sincerely esteem it a system which without the finger of God, never could have been suggested and agreed upon by such a diversity of interests."[11]

Later in 1802, he wrote a letter to a friend, suggesting that he organize "'**The Christian Constitutional Society'** with the object to be in existence for 1) the support of the Christian religion, and 2) the support of the United States."[12]

Hamilton wrote, " . . . liberty is a gift from the beneficent Creator, to the whole human race; and that civil liberty is founded in that; and cannot be wrested from any people, without the most manifest violation of justice."[13]

John Jay was the first ever Chief Justice of the United States. He was appointed by George Washington. Among other titles, he was also elected President of the American Bible Society in 1821. In 1816, he wrote: "Providence has given to our people the choice of their rulers, and it is the duty as well as the privilege and interests of our Christian nation to select and prefer Christians for their rulers."[14]

Daniel Webster, famously known as the author of our first unabridged dictionary, wrote the following: "Whatever makes men good Christians, makes them good citizens."[15]

George Washington who is known as the Father of our Country is also known for his great faith and many communications in which he exalted Jesus Christ. In his book, *Enough is Enough*, Pastor Rick Scarborough said the following of President Washington, "The acknowledgments of his faith in Christ are enough to fill greater books than I am writing. His farewell address, given at the end of his presidency, is still one of the high points of oratory in our history. For years it was included in virtually every American history book. Not surprising, it has been omitted in recent years, perhaps because of its 'offensive' religious content."

<u>"I believe the "Father of our Country", the "Commander in Chief" of the Continental Army and our first President would be a good authority to consult when considering the intent of our founding fathers regarding the role of religion in civil affairs and the affairs of our nation.</u> His inaugural speech, given to both Houses of Congress on April 30, 1789, set the tone for his presidency"[16]

In that address, Washington said the following:

> "Such being the impressions under which I have, in obedience to the public summons, repaired to the present station, it would be peculiarly improper to omit, in this first official act, my fervent supplications to that Almighty Being who rules over the universe, who presides in the councils of nations and whose providential aids can supply every human defect, that His benediction may consecrate to the liberties and happiness of the people of the United States a Government insti-

tuted by themselves for these essential purposes, and may enable every instrument employed in its administration to execute with success, the functions allotted to his charge.

In tendering this homage to the Great Author of every public and private good, I assure myself that it expresses your sentiments not less than my own, nor those of my fellow-citizens at large, less than either.

No people can be bound to acknowledge and adore the Invisible Hand which conducts the affairs of men more than the people of the United States. Every step by which they have advanced to the character of an independent nation seems to have been distinguished by some token of providential agency; and in the important revolution just accomplished in the system of their united government, the tranquil deliberations and voluntary consent of so many distinct communities, from which the event has resulted cannot be compared with the means by which most governments have been established, without some return of pious gratitude, along with a humble anticipation of the future blessings which the past seem to preage. These reflections, arising out of the present crisis, have forced themselves too strongly on my mind to be suppressed. You will join with me I trust in thinking, that there are none under the influence of which the proceedings of a new and free government can more auspiciously commence.

We ought to be no less persuaded that the propitious smiles of Heaven can never be expected on a nation that disregards the eternal rules of order and right which Heaven itself has ordained; and since the preservation of the sacred fir of liberty and the destiny of the republican model of government are justly considered as deeply, perhaps, finally, staked of the experiment . . .

I shall take my present leave; but not without resorting once more to the Benign Parent of the Human Race, in humble supplication that, since He has been pleased to favor the American people with opportunities for deliberating in perfect tranquility, and dispositions for deciding with unparalleled unanimity on a form of government for the security of their union and the advancement of their happiness, so His divine blessings may be equally conspicuous in the enlarged views, the temperate consultations and the wise measures on which the success of this Government must depend."[17]

When it came time for Washington to leave the Presidency, he prepared a final address that he made to Congress on September 19, 1796. He made many, what would in this day of pluralism and relativism, be extraordinary and probably damnable declarations. They were all based on his knowledge and experience from the study of God's Word and from life. Our positive experience with Washington definitely provides proof, contrary to popular opinion in the 21st century that 'properly' vetting a candidate for public office, should be mandatory in selecting 'qualified' persons. Washington had dealt with so many difficult projects, and in doing so, proved the source of his strength and where his loyalty was. Hopefully, we will learn to go past the first gate, how pleasant his/her looks and voice are, in future selections to get someone who passes the muster in being a 'qualified' candidate, to weed out the masqueraders.

In his final address to Congress, Washington made some very noteworthy comments, the kind I wish current leaders could and would make. He said the following: "It is impossible to rightly govern the world without God and the Bible...."

Later he said: "Let us unite in imploring the Supreme Ruler of nations to spread his holy protection over these United States."

And finally:

> "The name of American, which belongs to you, in your national capacity, must always exalt the just pride of patriotism, more than any appellation derived from local discriminations. With slight shades of difference, you have same religion, manners, habits political principles... the habits which led to political prosperity, religion and morality are indispensable supports.
>
> In vain would that man claim the tribute of patriotism, who should labor to subvert these great pillars of human happiness, politician, equally with the pious man, ought to respect and to cherish them.... Let is simply be asked where is the religious obligation desert the oaths, which are the instruments of investigation in the courts of justice?
>
> And let us with caution indulge the supposition, that morality can be maintained without religion. Whatever may be conceded to the influence of refined education on minds of peculiar structure, reason and experience both forbid us to expect that national morality can prevail in exclusion of religious principle. 'This substantially true, that virtue or morality is a necessary spring of popular government.... Can it not be that Providence has not connected the permanent felicity of a nation with its virtue?"[18]

When reading these words the first time, my first impression was seared into my mind. That was to think how wonderful it would have been to have lived in a time in this country where the principles of those words were believed and practiced by the greater population. And that was the situation in America for almost 200 years. We were a people who held Christianity as the predominant faith, the underpinnings of political processes.

Evidences of our posterity being great people of faith are seen in other statements and actions they have taken. Our founding fathers knew that freedom was connected to something greater than themselves, or their words. In 1777, Congress issued a proclamation for a day of thanksgiving for November of that year. December 18 was also to be set aside for "solemn thanksgiving and praise." The proclamation called upon all citizens to "join the penitent confession of their manifold sins," and to offer "their humble and earnest supplication that it may please God through the merits of Jesus Christ, mercifully to forgive and blot them out of remembrance."[19]

Francis Marion was a man of courage and a Major General in the Revolution. His nickname, "the Old Swamp Fox," or so called by the English, especially British General Banastre Tarleton. Francis Marion was known to have said to his men on different occasions, "In short, the religion of Jesus Christ is the only sure and controlling power over sin."[20]

John Adams was the second president of the United States. In an address to the military, delivered on October 11, 1798, he stated: "We have no government armed with power capable of contending with human passions unbridled by morality and religion. Avarice, ambition, revenge, or gallantry, would break the strongest cords of our Constitution as a whale goes through a net. Our Constitution was made only for a moral and religious people. It is wholly inadequate to the government of any other."[21]

President Abraham Lincoln, on April 30, 1863, appointed a "National Fast Day," which read in part, "It is the duty of nations as well as of men to own their dependence upon the overruling power of God, to confess their sins and transgressions in humble sorrow yet with assured hope that genuine repentance will lead to mercy and pardon, and to recognize the sublime truth, announced in the Holy Scriptures and proven by all history: that those nations only are blessed whose God is the Lord."[22]

Prayers in Congress, the appointment of chaplains, calls for days of prayer and thanksgiving and fasting stand upright on the historical stage as actions not of mad men, but of humble, pious, and devoted men of courageous faith. The evidence is overwhelming that America has in its legislative past linked good government to both the Christian religion and its principles. The historians and constitutional scholars Anson Stokes and Leo Pfeffer have summarized the role that Christianity has played not just in the founding of America, but also in the lofty position Christianity has maintained until recently: "Throughout its history our governments, national and state, have cooperated with religion and shown friendliness to it. God is invoked in the Declaration of Independence and in practically every state constitution. . . . The sessions of Congress and of the state legislatures are invariably opened with prayer, in Congress by chaplains who are employed by the Federal Government. We have chaplains in our armed forces and in our penal institutions. Oaths in courts of law were administered through use of a Bible until recent years.

Chapter Seven — Where's the Beef?

Public officials take an oath of office ending with "so help me God." Religious institutions are tax exempt throughout the nation. Our pledge of allegiance declares that we are a nation "under God." Our national motto is "In God We Trust" and is inscribed on our currency and on some of our postage stamps."[23]

By 1862, many people were clamoring for our coinage to make reference to God. Some suggested "God Our Trust." In 1863 the motto "God and our Country" was proposed. The motto "In God We Trust" appeared for the first time in 1864; it did not receive formal Congressional approval until the following year. And in 1865 Congress enacted the following:

And be it further enacted, that, in addition to the devices and legends upon the gold, silver and other coins of the United States, it shall be lawful for the director of the mint, with the approval of the Secretary of the Treasury, to cause the motto "In God we trust" to be placed upon such coins hereafter to be issued as shall admit of such legend thereon.[24]

The events of the War Between the States had helped to create an atmosphere which led to repentance and a return of trusting in God, at least partially due to the hundreds of thousands of deaths and blood that was lost. This gave rise to the chants for themes of putting such a motto on our money which echoed around the country.

In 1907, **President Teddy Roosevelt** commissioned sculptor Augustus Saint-Gaudens to design new coins for currency. Roosevelt, in his commission of this project, instructed Saint-Gaudens to leave the motto "In God we trust" off his designs for the new coins; a desire even then from Progressives. Many people voiced their objections, being distraught with the absence of the motto. Roosevelt penned a letter, in November 1907, to a minister who had written the president a letter of objection about his removal of the motto. In his letter, Roosevelt told the pastor there was "no legal warrant for putting the motto on the coins." Roosevelt also added, "my firm conviction that to put such a motto on coins . . . is in effect irreverence which comes close to sacrilege."[25] Of course he was wrong, since the motto had been authorized and commissioned originally by Congress. As it should, the discussion came before Congress again on May 18, 1908. Legislation was passed to put the motto back on the coins again in spite of Roosevelt. "In 1955 Congress extended the act by requiring the phrase to appear not only on all coins but on all paper money thereafter minted or printed. The next year, 1956, enacted a law making the phrase "In God We Trust" officially the national motto."[26]

This continues to be a hotly contested topic in today's relativistic and pluralistic culture, a culture manufactured by the liberal progressive agenda. But in 1954 it was not so, as demonstrated by act of Congress that year, when the words "Under God" were inserted into the pledge of allegiance. The House and Senate adopted the measure without even one dissenting vote! On June 14th that year, President Dwight Eisenhower stood on the steps of the Capitol Building, and for the first time, recited the revised pledge to the flag that included the phrase, "one nation under God."[27]

Federal law provides the president to proclaim two days each year as National Days of Prayer. Public law 82-354 requires the president to proclaim a National Day of Prayer on a day other than a Sunday. And according to Public law 77-379, the president proclaims the fourth Thursday of November each year as a National Day of Thanksgiving.[28] Need we really deal with the questions some may have; "Pray to Whom?", and "Be thankful to Whom?" If so, then allow me to answer: The answer to both is not government but Jehovah God, the Almighty Creator.

The same year that Congress approved adding this phrase, "one nation, under God," to the Pledge of Allegiance, both houses of Congress passed a resolution directing the Capitol architect to make available "a room, with facilities for prayer and meditation, for members of the Senate and House of Representatives."[29] The seventh edition of *The Capitol*, an official publication of the United States Congress, provides the following description:

> The history that gives this room its inspirational lift, is centered in the stained glass window George Washington kneeling in prayer . . . is the focus of the composition. . . . Behind Washington a prayer is etched: "Preserve me, O God, for in Thee do I put my trust," the first verse of the sixteenth Psalm. There are upper and lower medallions representing the two sides of the Great Seal of the United States. On these are inscribed the phrases: *annuit coeptis* — "God has favored our undertakings" — and *novus ordo seclotum* — "A new order of the ages is born." Under the upper medallion is the phrase from Lincoln's immortal Gettysburg Address, "This Nation under God." . . . The two lower corners of the window each show the Holy Scriptures, an open book and a candle, signifying the light from God's law, "Thy Word is a lamp unto my feet and a light unto my path." [Psalm 119:105][30]

This prayer room is very decidedly Christian in its dedication. The Bible is featured, not the Book of Mormon. Citations are from the Bible, not the Qur'an.

It does make a difference that our coins are inscribed with "In God We Trust" instead of "In Allah we trust." It is also critical to note that the Library of Congress has a quotation from a Psalm of the Bible instead of a quote from the Qur'an. It's also significant to note that "every foreigner attests his renunciation of his allegiance to his former sovereign and his acceptance of citizenship in this republic as an appeal to God."[31] There is no quote from the Mahayana sutras of the Buddha; none from any other religious view. "But as true as these symbols may be, and as important as our structures may be, they are not, in, and of themselves, evidence of America's greatness — past, present, or future. National greatness does not spring from an accumulation of archival antiquities and archeological details, or from symbols and slogans. It does not spring from documents, precedents, constitutions,

Chapter Seven — Where's the Beef?

or legislation. National greatness springs from righteousness, goodness, character, and true spirituality."[32] References within the Bible bear this out, for it confidently declares, "Righteousness exalts a nation, but sin is a reproach to any people," (Proverbs 14:34), and "A throne is established by righteousness." (Proverbs 6:12).

The public education of young people has drastically changed in content since I was a youngster in school. For example, Civics classes were not only offered then, but required in school. Back then, we learned many details about the working of government; how it is supposed to work, and our associated rights and responsibilities of citizenship. American history is not taught in depth, at least regarding the material we were taught. The preponderance of our lessons focused in depth on how the nation began, the principles surrounding our founding, followed by in depth studies of the historical events and legislation throughout the centuries. There was minimal coverage of the previous two decades. Today, all the curriculum has changed. There are few to no civics lessons; students have a huge disconnect except for what a teacher might share. And given their propensity for teachers to be liberal progressives or Marxists, the chances of "good instruction" coming from those discussions would be minimal. And history lessons are totally bankrupt now, with only the last six decades in focus. This has facilitated a huge disconnect in our society; founding principles are generally unknown by citizens. Service institutions and even churches seem almost misdirected in our society, unaware of their critical and collective role to help educate. With the arrival of the Progressives in the classrooms over half a century ago, coupled with a union in charge of curriculum, the value for the educational dollar is gone. Churches and Synagogues not "plugged-in," must awaken, and let their views be known.

And so we have arrived to this, our day, to the makings of what Leftists call "the beginning of utopia." This liberal "utopia" has brought with it attacks on Christianity and people of faith, as well as attacks on most anything honorable and good. For the past century years, with a few exceptions, there has been a deliberate and orchestrated chorus of objections to anything Christian, or even righteous. The conservative Christians who for years were the literal backbone of this nation — have gone silent. Something is happening, apocalyptic in nature, and it is time for those millions who love the American of the past which is associated largely with integrity, justice and honesty of our origin as our nation to arise and say so. In the meantime, with such a mountain of evidence of the words of those who have blazed trails before us, we are left aghast to say, "Oh my God, how lost we truly have become! Where are the leaders with substance and integrity? Where are those who claim they love truth?

Have courage. Discover the truth, follow it and seize the moment. Or, we will be faced with having to ask in the darkness and quietness of the hour . . . "Where's the beef?"

"*Before any man can be considered as a member of civil society, he must be considered as a subject of the Governor of the Universe.*"

~ James Madison

*Signer of the Constitution;
4th President of the United States*

Chapter Eight

History Schmistory: Who Needs It?!

AMERICA, AMERICA — UNTIL ABOUT 40 YEARS ago, that name by itself would conjure a feeling of warmth and excitement. Whether it was pride, or gratitude, or hope, the response of the majority of people on earth was deeply confident. America's moral and fiscal currency was the soundest in the world. The common phrase was "sound as a dollar" — you could bank on it, and most of the world did. Abroad, we were the free world's policeman; an encouraging older brother to those younger nations struggling to achieve democracy; and the hope of all peoples still in bondage. Generally, we were the most steadying influence on an uneasy globe. Specifically at home, we were supremely confident that indeed we were making the world a better place in which to live. With our technology and diplomacy, we believed it was only a matter of time before the assignment of making the world modern and safe would be fittingly completed.

America itself [in the twentieth century] already was a better place to live. Despite the setbacks, there had been a gradual, sustained improvement that most men could trace in their own lifetimes, and there was every indication that this would continue. Technologically, we were on the brink of so many breakthroughs that it was difficult for science fiction writers to keep ahead of what was happening in the laboratories. Intellectually, we were developing radical, new, sensitive approaches to education, which were going to revolutionize the learning process and bring us into an earlier, fuller and more creative maturity. Medically, we were on the verge of conquering every disease in sight, while psychiatry would take care of the occasional aberrant personality which had trouble adjusting to it all. In a word, optimism summed up America. The American dream was about to come true.[1]

And then, with an abruptness that is still bewildering, everything went awry. Campaigns by our military ceased to go according to their prepared script. Our young president was assassinated in 1963. Our young people began to revolt on a scale that no generation ever had seen before — indiscriminately lashing out at citizens and authority, some plunging and escaping into the mindless self-destruction of drug abuse. The emerging nations, to whom we had given so much so freely, were almost unanimous in their hatred for us. Our foreign policy devolved again and again into being reactionary, rather than one of action. In effect we had no foreign policy.

Domestically, our economy waxed increasingly unpredictable; economists could no longer calculate its gyrations, let alone do anything to stabilize it. Our children's mathematics and English aptitudes were plummeting [year after year]; by college entrance standards they were two years behind a decade before. Our technologists, to whom we had gratefully turned with all our problems, seemed to create new and totally unforeseen dilemmas for each one which they were able to solve. And psychiatry could not begin to cope with the tidal wave of mental and emotional disorders which seemed to break upon the land, claiming one hospital bed in three. Our optimism was rapidly turning to despair.[2]

The loss of moral soundness was the most mystifying and disturbing indicator of our decline, which appeared regularly. There had always been pockets of dissolution throughout the country, appearing like little cavities, but we had thought of them as isolated situations; sometimes thinking of them as "city problems." The answer was to drill and fill those cavities. So we threw money at them. Looking further into those "drilled down" silos of problems, we discovered the remedy required greater work, similar to a root canal. Though we would not admit it, some problems were past repair. It was already too late.

Our problems became worsened because we did not learn from history. Knowing history, knowing the "cause and effect" of things often help to avoid mistakes. Certainly it helps to build character. Most of all we needed a knowledge base upon which to make decisions; after all, the best way to perceive outcomes, is to check outcomes from similar situations of the past.

The trend today is simple abstinence; many Americans just ignore history. So much so that large numbers of Americans don't even know who we are; we have an identity crisis. For example, results from a poll a few years ago showed that twenty-six percent of adult Americans did not know the basic question of from which country we had gained our independence. Of that number, six percent identified other countries. Those named were France, China, Spain, Mexico, and Japan. The remaining twenty percent did not offer a guess. Another recent poll asked the question, "Who were the first four presidents in the United States?" Only seven percent could identify them correctly; George Washington, John Adams, Thomas Jefferson, and James Madison. Thirty percent knew that Jefferson was the 3rd president; fifty-seven percent also identified Jefferson as the main author of the Declaration of Independence, the same percentage number said they knew Washington led the Continental Army during the Revolutionary War.

Polls are providing views to an alarming trend in America, such as the 2010 Marist Institute of Public Opinion Poll and a 2007 poll from the US Mint. These polls in effect tell how our little children are also not learning facts of our history and heritage. Without a working knowledge of history, aka, knowing who we are, it is difficult at best to avoid some crises or to plot a remedy for national crises as needs arise. Knowing history is also a part of the recipe for developing national dis-

CHAPTER EIGHT — HISTORY SCHMISTORY, WHO NEEDS IT?

cussions to plan decisions in avoiding the foolhardy traps made by bad decisions. To know American history is to prepare. It is in the preparing and testing of events, in the laboratory of life, that you can evaluate experience; to see what works and what doesn't work. Like finding solutions in the various fields of science, finding some solutions in everyday problems of life are made by guessing at a possible solution, then testing the solution against historical evidence and data.

There's an old proverb: *Good judgment comes from experience but unfortunately experience comes from bad judgment.* A modern translation would be, the shorter the learning curve one wants, and make no mistake about it everybody is going to have learning curves, the better it is to learn and use history.

As a nation, we are failing at learning history, world history, American history, Christian history, any history. As a nation, we indicate by actions that we want nothing to do with any history! Students with whom I have talked, as a collective group have made comments like; "I hate history, I tried studying that stuff before, but it just never worked for me." Or they would say, "That stuff is so boring; I hated my history class and can't learn anything from history." Statements like that are very revealing. They show some minimal grasp of learning, merely in what is not liked if nothing else. Further, such statements are made either from laziness, boredom, or a perceived waste of time while studying past events; possibly due to a poor teacher or curriculum, or simply a lack of understanding on how learning even occurs. As I recall, my "collective" responses to them was generally something like, "So help me to understand this. You are saying that studying history has taught you nothing, except that you "learned" there is nothing to learn from studying history! Have I got that right!?" Add to that, "You do realize by making that statement that you have revealed that you learned something, or else you could not make the statement!" I would argue that learning our American history and seeing our wonderful heritage as established by the Framers and the Colonists, can be among some of the most rewarding projects achievable in life. It can be life altering, leading one to change and improve his life in huge ways; even learning elementary lessons from events, experiences, and mistakes made by earlier peoples, helps us to collectively not to repeat the same mistakes.

So let's look at some of this history that could change your outlook on life. I'm betting that at a minimum there are one or two details in the following information you have never heard before.

There are many lessons from our past that will put a strong foundation under your feet.

In 1831 when the French philosopher Alexis de Tocqueville landed in this country to observe and report to his home country and subsequently the rest of Europe on the great American experiment of democracy as seen through her people and within her institutions, he started his work of discovery. His work was published in two parts in 1835 and then again in 1840 under the title *Democracy in America*, and was hailed as "the most comprehensive and penetrating analysis of the relationship between character and society in America that has ever been written."[3]

His work entitled, *Democracy in America*, contains other arguments, among them the following:

"The sects that exist in the United States are innumerable. They all differ with respect to the worship which is due to the Creator; but they all agree in respect to the duties which are due from man to man. Each sect adores the Deity in its own peculiar manner, *but all the sects preach the same moral law* in the name of God. . . . Moreover, all the sects of the United States are comprised within the great unity of Christianity, *and Christian morality is everywhere the same.*"

"It may be believed that a certain number of Americans pursue a peculiar form of worship from habit more than from conviction. In the United States, the sovereign authority is religious, and consequently hypocrisy must be common; *but there is no country where the Christian religion retains a greater influence over the souls of men than in America.*"[4]

Then there are these words. It would be remarkable to hear them spoken today by a Supreme Court Judge:

> "I believe the entire Bill of Rights came into being because of the knowledge our forefathers had of the Bible and their belief in it: freedom of belief, of expression, of assembly, of petition, the dignity of the individual, the sanctity of the home, equal justice under law, and the reservation of powers to the people . . . .
>
> I like to believe we are living today in the spirit of the Christian religion. I like also to believe that as long as we do so, no great harm can come to our country."
>
> Former Chief Justice Earl Warren, addressing the annual prayer breakfast of the International Council of Christian Leadership, 1954[5]

Approximately thirty-eight years later, in 1992, then Governor of Mississippi, Kirk Fordice made what was considered by the media an inflammatory remark for the time when he said, "America is a Christian nation."[6] His remarks were attacked by media, politicians, atheists, and Jewish leaders alike, with written comments being reported in periodicals and newspapers alike.[7]

A dispute ensued about the governor's "controversial" remarks which landed him "in the penalty box" on CNN for an interview. His comments were very perceptive and I believe irrefutable. He simply and calmly stated, "Christianity is the predominant religion in America. We all know that is an incontrovertible fact. The media always refer to the Jewish state of Israel. They talk about the Muslim country of Saudi Arabia, of Iran, or Iraq. We all talk about the Hindu nation of India. America is not a nothing country. It's a Christian country."[8] His comments went on

Chapter Eight — History Schmistory, Who Needs It?

target. Fordice cited current "surveys noting that 86 percent of Americans consider themselves Christian, but praised America's ethnic diversity. 'It's the true melting pot of the world,' he said. 'That's the strength of our country, and the strength is certainly not enhanced by denying simple facts that Christianity is the predominant religion.'"[9]

Though he was verbally assaulted by the media for his courage, history points out that Fordice was right. (See Chapters 2 & 3.) "Protestant Christianity has been our established religion in almost every sense of that phrase. . . . The establishment of Protestant Christianity was one not only of law but also, and far more importantly, of culture. Protestant Christianity supplied the nation with its "system of values.""[10] History bears this out as fact, which has been inscribed into law by the United States Supreme Court and in turn echoed by presidents and governors for more than two centuries. Now, amidst the assault on Christianity in the current pluralistic society by many liberal progressives, multi-culturists, atheists, secular humanists, agnostics, Marxists, and Communists with their ever ready media who pants to "carry water" for them all, our Christian underpinnings are being weighed almost daily on the skewed "balance scales." Weighed by these amoral, shiftless, and anti-Democracy liberals; their whole purpose is to destroy the foundation of our nation, the foundation which by the way stands in direct contrast to the Communist and Marxist Manifesto to which many of these rebellious spirits follow.

Liberals tie the view of America being a Christian nation to "demented" pilgrims and "uneducated" conservatives. They view Chief Justice Warren and Governor Fordice as if infected by an infectious disease. However, they conveniently forget or cover up the data which points to the truth that is an important part of our history, critical to this story.

"In 1931 the Supreme Court noted that the United States is a Christian nation. In a mid-Atlantic summit with British Prime Minister Winston Churchill in the darkest hours of World War II, President Roosevelt — who had described the United States as 'the lasting concord between men and nations, founded on the principles of Christianity — asked the crew of an American warship to join him in a rousing chorus of the hymn, "Onward, Christian Soldiers."

"In 1947, writing to Pope Pius XII, President Truman said flatly, 'This is a Christian nation.'" Nobody argued with any of them.[11] Where are the catcalls from Leftists saying that FDR and Harry Truman were "demented?" These would be the same taunts given to any conservative who dares to say the same identical thing. Possibly Harvard attorneys and revisionists will now scurry about to rewrite these historical remarks made by one of their own.

If the liberals were consistent to their dogma, they would hold their heroes accountable when their actions are the same actions of conservatives which is said to be so terrible. The pluralism and inconsistency is so thick, it could be made into a pudding. It is nothing short of political correctness gone berserk.

If the media were to have the decency to be honest both with themselves and the public trust they claim to represent, they would get tough with the anti-democracy activities in their party. In other words, they would stop doing what they are doing. But facts are not the problem for this crowd, nor do facts get in the way; they are just ignored. There is an overwhelming bias and hatred toward anything Christian. The press had a hay day reveling against former Governor Fordice in 1994. And they do the same today. Religion is okay, just so long as it is Muslim (Liberals are deathly frightened of Muslims and will never say anything negative about even Muslim terrorists), or if it is humanism, or even secularism, just as long as it remains "Socially irrelevant, even if privately engaging."[12] For as writers of today's, in the tank liberal print-world newspapers write, Mixing religion [Christianity] and politics is the ultimate social *faux pas*.[13]

The proposal that America is a Christian nation does not mean that every American is now or ever was a Christian. Moreover, it does not mean that either the Church or the State should force people to profess belief in Christianity or attend religious services. Furthermore, "a belief in a Christian America does not mean that non-Christians, and for that matter, dissenting Christians, cannot hold contrary opinions in a climate of a general Christian consensus. . . . Christianity presupposes that there are people who are not Christians."[14] Since so many of those in the media or of the liberal political stance today who despise Christianity, while at the same remain silent about Islam, I would encourage them to go to Riyadh, or to Egypt, or Jordan, or Iran, or Jakarta, or Kenya and publicly announce there that followers of Islam are "demented," "racists," or homophobes." It would be equal treatment, leveling the playing field. That would be fun, watching their demeanor as they would stand on a street corner and make such an announcement.

Jump ahead another twenty years from Governor Fordice's day to today. Witness attacks on Christianity not just one day, but every single day. We have heard the harangue spoken by the media as if they are reading from their memo of the day, "*The colonists who came to the New World and built the foundations of what now is the United States were "extremists." The discussions today that include mention of "individual liberties" are a danger to the future of this country.*" If you think that is far-fetched, just look at the news from among those who are in the majority in the U.S. government. At least these are the words now being used in educational materials that originate with the Department of Defense. A group called Judicial Watch, a government corruption monitoring group, obtained documents that are "training materials on hate groups or hate crimes distributed or used by the Air Force." The 133 pages make up a January 2013 "Defense Equal Opportunity Management Institute student guide" called "Extremism." <u>For example, the material warns:</u> "Nowadays, instead of dressing in sheets or publically (sic) espousing hate messages, many extremists will talk of individual liberties, states' rights, and how to make the world a better place." And it adds: "In U.S. history, there are many examples of extremist ideologies and movements. The colonists who sought to free themselves from British rule and the Confederate states who sought to secede from the Northern states are just two examples." The 9/11 attacks by Muslims who killed nearly 3,000 people are called a "historical event."[15]

"The U.S. military already had been caught teaching that the Founding Fathers, whose beliefs and political positions could accurately be described in today's terminology as conservative, were "extremists." According to their teaching, 'traits of extremists include attacking an opponent's character, name-calling, sweeping generalizations, no proof of arguments, viewing the opposition as evil, arguing through intimidation, using slogans or buzzwords, assuming moral superiority and doomsday thinking' (The traits sound like Democrat Party tactics).... Now, a report by Todd Starnes of Fox News Radio reveals U.S. Army soldiers at a Mississippi base were being instructed that the American Family Association, a pro-family and Christian-based organization, is a "hate group"... And according to a study at the West Point Military Academy, those who make up the right-wing segment in society constitute a danger to the U.S."[16]

This all sounds more like it comes right out of a Communists for America Handbook! What a change in direction from Harry Truman in the late Forties, to Governor Fordice in the early Nineties, and then to the collapse of spiritual morals and the blatant attacks by the current administration in government on Christianity today.

Our history, which goes unmentioned in the press, demonstrates we started as a Christian nation and were successful in maintaining operations on that platform for at least the first two hundred years.

American Institutions Point to a Special Founding

Our institutions were built designed to have wise leadership who would follow truth and foster ideals, providing work environments that are wholesome. The founders knew that God's will and righteousness must be central in our country's leadership, business and personal lives, in order to be rich in blessings and also to stay free from the bondage of kings and tyrants like they had seen in Europe. As such, our economy, our industry and whole national experience was designed to be free; free from government agencies and their intervention, free from tyranny and regulations. Built upon a foundation of morality, business could operate freely, hence the term "free enterprise system." Using these principles with open competition provided more positive outputs.

Our government buildings and landmarks display inscriptions indicating a Christian belief in the sovereignty of God, its overriding and guiding principles. In some cases, the special purpose for the building was signified.

The Liberty Bell bears an inscription from Leviticus 25:10 engraved in a prominent position around the band at the top. It reads, "Proclaim liberty throughout all the land, unto the inhabitants thereof."

The House and Senate chambers have the words "In God We Trust" inscribed on them.

The walls of the Capitol Dome have the following words on them, "The New Testament according to the Lord and Savior Jesus Christ."

In the Capitol Rotunda hangs the painting, "The Baptism of Pocahontas at Jamestown."[17]

The painting, "Embarkation of the Pilgrims" shows Elder William Brewster holding a Bible open to the title page which reads, "The New Testament of our Lord and Savior Jesus Christ." The words "God With Us" are inscribed on the sail of the ship. **This painting also hangs in the Rotunda of the Capitol.**[18] The painting portrays the Pilgrims' obvious devotion to God and His providential care.[19]

The Prayer Room in the U.S. Capitol Building, features a stained glass window that bears this prayer from Psalm 16:1: "Preserve me, O God, for in Thee do I put my trust."

A relief of Moses hangs in the House Chamber. Moses is surrounded by twenty-two other law-givers.[20] The relief of Moses is described by the Architect of the Capitol as a depiction of the *"unexcelled* Hebrew prophet and lawgiver."[21]

On the Great Seal of the United States is inscribed the Latin phrase *Annuit Coeptis,* "[God] has smiled on our undertaking." Under the seal is this phrase from Lincoln's Gettysburg Address: "This Nation Under God."

On the Walls or the Library of Congress, President Eliot of Harvard chose Micah 6:8, "He hath showed thee, O Man, what is good: and what doth God require of thee, but to do justly, and to love mercy, and to walk humbly with thy God."[22]

The lawmaker's library also quotes the Psalmist's acknowledgment of the beauty and order of creation: "The heavens declare the glory of God and the firmament showeth His handiwork." (Psalm 19:1)

The Washington Monument also has a special message engraved on the metal cap on its top, "Praise be to God." The walls of its stairwells are lined with several Bible verses: "Search the Scriptures" (John 5:39), "Holiness to the Lord," and "Train up a child in the way he should go, and when he is old he will not depart from it." (Proverbs 22:6).

At the opposite end of the Lincoln Memorial, words and phrases from Lincoln's Second Inaugural Address, allude to "God," the "Bible," "providence," the "almighty," and "divine attributes."

A plaque in the Dirksen Office Building has the words "In God We Trust" [engraved] in a bronze relief.[23]

The Jefferson Memorial includes these words of Jefferson: "God who gave us life gave us liberty. Can the liberties of a nation be secure when we have removed a conviction that these liberties are a gift of God? Indeed I tremble for my country when I reflect that God is just, that His justice cannot sleep forever."

The Senate doors (bronze) show George Washington taking oath with his hand on a Bible.[24] Upon this tradition from the Father of our Country, every president has taken his oath of office upon a Bible.

Several bas-relief sculptures adorn the Supreme Court Building. One which hangs directly over the bench shows two allegorical figures, "The Power of Government (left) and "The Majesty of Law" (right), flanking a tablet with two rows of Roman numerals, I-V and VI-X, an obvious symbol of God's moral law. The Curator confirms that the tablets refer to "ancient law," and the only ancient law which is clearly represented by ten laws is the Ten Commandments. Behind the two allegorical figures, and directly above the tablet, the American eagle spreads its wings, a universal symbol of protection.

The second bas-relief sculpture, "Justice, the Guardian of Liberty," portrays Moses holding the tablets of God's law. The shape of these tablets is similar to the shape of the tablet found in the "Majesty of Law" sculpture with its ten Roman numerals. In both sculptures, the tablets correspond to the universal depiction of the Ten Commandments; furthermore, Moses is almost always depicted holding the tablets which were given to him by God. Even though Confucius and Hammurabi are also portrayed in this sculpture, and even though each holds a copy of his law code, the carving clearly depicts these other figures standing in the background behind a central, elevated Moses.

Another sculpture is displayed on the south wall of the courtroom itself; this carving shows Moses, along with other noted law givers, holding a copy of the Ten Commandments inscribed in Hebrew.[25]

A rational thinking, evidence-driven human being should be fairly straight forward in arriving at a conclusive understanding; Understanding that God, the Bible and Christianity were a central focus of our founders in their personal, professional and governmental lives as they established and built this nation. These founders also thought those entities were critical for the further blessing and prosperity of this country. Not so for the Leftists of our day. They see the sovereignty of God, personal freedom, etc. as the big enemy, or embarrassment, in taking the country where they want to go. Where that is, should be clear after listening to these disciples of Marx, Hitler, Mao, and Stalin. They obviously seek to remove Christianity and its tenants only to have government reside as the sovereign in each of our lives.

Early American Documents Speak of a Heritage about which Few Have Heard

Our nation's heritage did not begin in 1776 as some current historians will teach, but over one hundred fifty years earlier in Europe, where you can see the emotional and spiritual roots. (Modern-day text books from Common Core only go back as far as World War II.) It was there in the hearts of a few Christians in tribulation, persecuted for their independent faith, discriminated against because they wanted freedom of thought, life and religion, that a new nation with a new start was conceived. Thirteen colonies had been birthed with constitutions of their own, and while true freedom from a stifling regime was still being sought, our Declaration of Independence was finally being drafted, inked and signed. The political ideals of those who forged this more unified nation were not developed within a quickly assembled Leftist "think tank" or in the vacuum of a liberal laboratory. Great ideas usually come from troubles in life. Those ideas have consequences. The colonists ideas had consequences for them, but as they forged their freedom from their beliefs, we should expect those same beliefs would influence the future unified nation. But the truth is, sadly, after over 200 years of unification, of greatness, of world leadership — our nation is being dismantled brick by brick, stone by stone.

Take your pick, Ronald Reagan, who in 1964 said "We can preserve for our children this, the last best hope of man on earth, or we can sentence them to take the first step into a thousand years of darkness." Or pick Senator Ted Cruz of Texas in 2013 who said, "What America needs so much now is a spiritual revival." Or choose, then Governor Kirk Fordice of Mississippi, who in 1992 said "the less we emphasize the Christian religion, the further we fall into the abyss of poor character and chaos in the United States of America."[26] All these men should be praised for making such unpopular statements in the era of the last 50 years when things religious, especially those associated with Christianity are being denounced as morally intrusive, and limiting of full potential of an individual. Whatever the current progressive rant, the historical record shows the foundation of America was constructed upon the Judeo-Christian heritage. The early Americans reliance on God's providence is not much more than a faded memory for most Americans. If we are ever going to restore what we are now losing, we must return to the discipline of learning of the real history and truth of our nation's founding. We can start doing that through looking at the early documents in America.

The First Charter of Virginia

There were attempts in the sixteenth century to colonize this country but each failed miserably. Nevertheless, in the seventeenth century, the London Company adequately planned and financed the attempt to place a colony in Jamestown in 1607. It became the first permanent English colony. Like other colonial charters, the First Virginia Charter emphasized Christian character of the purpose of the expedition:

> "We, greatly commending, and graciously accepting of, their desires for the furthering of so noble a work, which may, by the providence of Almighty God, hereafter tend to the glory of His Divine Majesty, in propagating of the Christian religion to such people as still live in dark-

CHAPTER EIGHT — HISTORY SCHMISTORY, WHO NEEDS IT?

ness and miserable ignorance of the true knowledge and worship of God, and may in time bring the infidels and savages living in those parts to human civility and to a settled and quiet government, do, by these Our Letters Patent, graciously accepting of, an agree to, their humble and well-intended desires."[27]

If you explore in detail the account of how this early expedition progressed, history shows that while it was well-financed, the Virginia colonists were not prepared to cope with the hardships that would confront them. First, most who were on the voyage were male adventurers. "There were no men with families. There were very few artisans, and none with any experience that would fit them to get a living out of the soil . . . Of them Captain Smith said, 'A Hundred good workmen were worth a thousand such gallants.'"[28]

In spite of their problems, according to Smith, their faith got them through tough times and long periods of despair. It was their chaplain of the expedition, Pastor Robert Hunt, "an honest, religious, and courageous Divine," who started worship services from the first hour of landing in May 1607. "There the first seed for English Christianity on the American continent was sown."[29]

Massachusetts and the Mayflower Compact

To correctly frame the formation of the American colonies in the 1600s, one must see this in context; England was a country of religious intolerance. Ministers and other Christians who would not comply were forcibly silenced, imprisoned, and sometimes exiled. Because of this great persecution, in 1609, a group of Christians left their homes and village of Scooby, England and moved to the Netherlands, where religious tolerance existed. There, under the leadership of their pastor, John Robinson, this group settled in Leyden, Holland, where they formed an English Separatist Church. This "separatist" group later became known as "Pilgrims" who were to take the famous voyage on a ship called the Mayflower and come to the new world. Short-term, their goals had been met in moving to Holland. They escaped the ravages of religious persecution; however, they were losing their English heritage, since their children were growing up learning Dutch rather than English. Their long-term concern was to live in a place where society was founded on the Bible and its principles, not just live in a place where they had freedom to attend the church of their choice.

But being poor and unable to finance their own trip to the New World, these Pilgrims developed a contract with some English businessmen for their support. The contract called for the English businessmen to receive any profits made by the Pilgrims Company during their first seven years in America. The Pilgrims also arranged with the London Company who had jurisdiction of Virginia, to settle north of Jamestown in Virginia. When the Pilgrims set sail for America in September 1620, because of bad weather the Mayflower was taken off course to a point well north of the Virginia Company's jurisdiction. The need for a governing document forced the ship's occupants to draft what today is known as the Mayflower Compact. This compact was drafted and signed by forty-one adult males while aboard ship in Provincetown Harbor, Massachusetts, close to the tip of Cape Cod, on November 21, 1620.[30]

The preparation of this Compact served as a temporary legal "agreement" for the arriving "saints and strangers." Non-revisionist history shows that. "By the terms of the so-called Mayflower Compact, the Pilgrims agreed to govern themselves until they could arrange for a charter of their own; they were never able to arrange for such a charter, and the Compact remained in force until their colony at Plymouth was absorbed in that of Massachusetts Bay in 1691."[31]

The preamble of the Mayflower Compact emphasizes religious and spiritual themes, all of which are reflected and spelled out in later charters and state constitutions in this country. These early settlers had brought with them their old cherished faith, one that was rooted in "the name of God … for the glory of God and the advancement of the Christian faith." All those on the Mayflower understood full well that they were acting "in the presence of God" as they penned this document that would later be called "the foundation stone of American liberty"[32] and the entire basis for representative government in the New World, or the "great experiment of freedom in the world. (Today's history revisionists attempt to leave out references to the Compact, an extremely important "American" document. They omit it for primarily one reason; it is an integral part of the foundation and what defines the United States of America as this unique experiment in the world, based on Christian beliefs.)

Plymouth Plantation

William Bradford (1590-1657), was the second governor of Plymouth, after John Carver following his death in 1621. He also served as the colony's historian, and in Book I of his *History of Plymouth Plantation*, Bradford chronicles the events that relate to the colony up to their landing at Plymouth in the winter of 1620. The reminder of the work completes the history of Plymouth up to 1650. As Bradford's work demonstrates, the Pilgrims were motivated by their faith in God and evangelism,

> "Last and not least, they cherished a great hope and inward zeal of laying good foundations, or at least of making some way towards it, for the propagation and advance of the gospel of the kingdom of Christ in the remote parts of the world, even though they should be but stepping stones to others in the performance of so great a work.[33]

Anyone who assaults Plymouth as not being first of all a religious society, secondly an economic enterprise, and thirdly, a political commonwealth governed by Biblical standards is either ignorant of the facts or chooses to misrepresent them. The religious convictions and spiritual beliefs are easily seen as expressions in the drafting of and the words of the Mayflower Compact.

Connecticut

The Dutch were the first to put a settlement in what is now known as Connecticut. The Dutch navigator, Adriaen Black in fact was the first European to explore the area in 1614. It was nineteen years later when the English settlers eyed the rich Connecticut Valley with great interest. The Dutch trying to protect their claim, built a fort on land that is near what is known now as Hartford, land they had purchased from the Pequot Indians. But the English pushed forward as if no one else was there by placing settlements in Windsor in 1633, and then Wethersfield and Hartford respectively in the next two years. New Haven was settled in 1638 by Pastor John Davenport and Theophilus Eaton. It was here that the first laws of the area were enacted when the first general court convened. "After a day of fasting and prayer, they rested their first frame of government on a simple plantation covenant, that 'all of them would be ordered by the rules the Scriptures held forth for them."[34] Davenport and Eaton guided the colony to success for some years to come, Davenport as pastor and Eaton as governor for twenty years until his death. Because the colonists wanted a more perfect form of government, just a year after the court had first convened a committee was formed consisting of Davenport, Eaton and five others. They were known as ""The Seven Pillars" and they enacted civil law where God's Word was "established as the only rule in public affairs. Thus New Haven made the Bible its statute-book, and the elect its freemen."[35]

After having a war with the local Indians, the colonists wanted to build more perfect political institutions and form a "body politic" that was based more on voluntary association. History was made when the "Fundamental Orders of Connecticut," generally known as the world's first written constitution, was adopted in Hartford by the colonists on January 14, 1639. Three men, John Haynes, Thomas Hooker, and Roger Ludlow in large part drafted this constitution. Notice the spiritual direction of this document as it reads in part,

"For as much as it has pleased Almighty God by the wise disposition of His Divine Providence so to order and dispose of things that we the inhabitants and residents of Windsor, Hartford, and Wethersfield and now cohabiting in and upon the river Conectecotte [Connecticut] and the lands thereunto adjoining, and well knowing where a people are gathered together the Word of God requires that to maintain the peace and union of such a people, there should be and orderly and decent government established according to God, to order and dispose of the affairs of all the people at all seasons as occasions shall require; do therefore associate and conjoin to be as one public State or Commonwealth, and do, for ourselves and our successors and such as shall be adjoined to us at any time hereafter, enter into confirmation and confederation together, to maintain and preserve the liberty and the purity of the Gospel of our Lord Jesus which we now profess, as also the discipline of the churches, which according to the truth of the said Gospel is now practiced among us."[36]

Reading further into depths of this Constitution, it is obvious that the colonists were animated about keeping the leadership of their colony in the hands of dedicated and solid Christian people. Gary DeMar notes, "The material that follows this preamble, similar to agreements in Rhode Island formed about the same time, forms a body of laws. The provision of electing a governor is particularly interesting: "It is ordered . . . that no person be chosen governor above once in two years, and that the governor be always a member of some approved congregation. . . ."[37]

New England Confederation

The colonists shared the idea of limited government and a common and collective mission which they described as wanting "to advance the Kingdom of God," and the cause of the Gospel. So on May 19, 1643, the New England Confederation was born out of love and hard writing,

> "The Articles of Confederation between the Plantations under the Government of the Massachusetts, the Plantations under the Government of New Plymouth, the Plantations under the Government of Connecticut, and the Government of New Haven with the Plantations in Combination therewith: Whereas we all came into these parts of America with one and the same end and aim, namely, to advance the Kingdom of our Lord Jesus Christ and to enjoy the liberties of the Gospel in purity and peace. . . . The said United Colonies, for themselves and their posterities, do jointly and severally herby enter into a firm and perpetual league of friendship and occasions, both for preserving and propagating the truth and liberties of the Gospel and for their own mutual safety and welfare."[38]

Once again, the Bible and its literature was used as the standard for developing civil legislation, Civil rulers and courts were considered to be "ministers of God for the good of the people," to "have power to declare, publish, and establish for the Plantations within their jurisdiction, the laws He hath made; and to make and repeal orders for smaller matters, not particularly determined in Scriptures, according to the more general rules of righteousness, and while they stand in force, to require execution of them."[39]

The colonists also built honest safeguards in to protect Christian beliefs in their government. So these early colonists set Christianity as the standard against those who "shall go about to subvert or destroy the Christian faith or religion by broaching, publishing, or maintaining any dangerous error or heresy. . . ."[40] (Liberal politicians protect Muslims today against any criticism, no matter how bad the terrorism, but they do so by hiding the truth, or by not allowing the truth to come to be clearly seen; thus in a "dishonest" manner they try to protect these entities.)

New Hampshire

Desiring to be independent like the other colonies, the first settlements in New

Hampshire were bogged down in Indian attacks. They lacked the resources and ability to defend themselves, so they tied their wagons, so to speak, to Massachusetts in 1641 and stayed connected to their protection and government until 1679. That's when "New Hampshire was constituted a separate province."[41] Their final declaration contained the following,

And, above all things we do by these presents, will, require, and command our said Council, to take all possible care for the discontinuance of vice, and encouraging of virtue and good living; and that by such examples, the infidel may be incited and desire to partake of the Christian religion; and for the greater ease and satisfaction of the said loving subjects in matters of religion, we do hereby require and command that liberty of conscience shall be allowed unto all Protestants.[42]

Cultures all throughout the last two millenniums have hated, despised and persecuted Christians for their faith. Subsequently congregations of followers, then and now, have suffered for their beliefs. In a limited way, this was certainly due to the migration of peoples from around the world even in the late seventeenth century. In 1680 laws were enacted to protect the Christian religion from those heretics who would "willfully presume to blaspheme the holy name of God the Father, Son, and Holy Ghost, with direct, express, presumptuous or high-handed blasphemy, either by willful or obstinate denying the true God, or His creation, or government of the world.[43]

New York

The New Netherlands, as it was first named by the Dutch Reformed, financed by the Dutch West India Company, and chartered in 1621, built laws protecting the Reformed Church. In 1644, the English defeated the Dutch and seized control of the colony and renamed it New York. While Christianity was held in high esteem, "under royal grants of James, Duke of York and Albany, 1664 and 1674, the Church of England became the established church."[44] Its colonial legislature meeting in 1665 passed the following in reference to Christianity: "It is ordered that a church shall be built in each parish, capable of holding two hundred persons; that ministers of every church shall preach every Sunday, and pray for the King, Queen, the Duke of York, and the royal family, and to marry person after legal publication of license."[45]

Later in 1673, each town was authorized to pass laws against "Sabbath breaking" and other immoralities. While the passion was righteous, I believe this had a negative long-term impact on society in the Northeast, that of ordering people to attend services rather than just drawing them there by great messages from the pulpits. However the preamble of a group of laws passed in 1695 shown below, shows the intent to hold Christianity at the center of its character and movement in motivating its colonists,

"Whereas the true and sincere worship of God, according to His holy will and commandments, is often profaned and neglected by many of the inhabitants and sojourners in this Province who do not keep holy the Lord's Day, but in a disorderly manner accustom themselves to travel, laboring, working, shooting, fishing, sporting, playing, horse-racing, frequenting tippling-houses, and the using many other unlawful exercises and pastimes, upon the Lord's Day, to the scandal of the holy Christian faith...."[46]

While there was obvious promoting of faith upon some colonists, which brought about some obvious dislike, it should be obvious to readers that Christianity was a cornerstone of life in the colonies, both in private life, public life, and was a driving concern to the early politicians. Every colony was founded on the precepts of Christianity. In some colonies, it was required to be a Christian to hold public office. As time went on, the Christian influence was over time removed from statutes as we have attested in the first three chapters. I am one that is thankful that we still have institutions with records of early constitutions, showing a trail of our true heritage. It should be clear that modern liberals have lied, and at a minimum falsified information, when they say Christianity played no serious role in our country. Many of the departures from the American tradition came with dramatic swiftness in the 20th Century, due to the progressive leadership of Woodrow Wilson and FDR. Any Rip Van Winkle who went to sleep in 1910 and woke again sometime around 1935 would have discovered many of his fellow citizens not as industrious as usual, but suddenly and strangely dependent upon government, the Constitution in many ways inoperative and grumblings about such restraints as it still imposed. There would be numerous laws of a type and character with which he was totally unfamiliar, and a trend of some to venerate leaders and to consider those who appealed to the past as being obsolete. He would rub his eyes in disbelief and conclude that a revolution had taken place, or that he had awakened in the midst of a revolution. At the least, assuming that he was a perceptive man and not too cautious in his pronouncement; he would have declared that the American tradition had been overthrown. Then if you had gone to sleep in 1910 and woke in 2013, he would have to suppose a coup d'état had surely taken place. When you listen to the lessons offered by today's teacher, professor, or politician, compared to the early American documents, it should be obvious that an anti-American revolution has taken place, somewhere in the past, that a cover-up of American ideals is in process, with citizens speaking of what more the government can do for them, talk of taking away rights, less talk of our Constitution, and as I tend to during all this political garbage coming from the White House and the progressives now, call it "treason from within."

Thankfully, it was not this way in the beginning, and we have the footprints of hero founders in the past to which we can reference. Our Declaration of Independence shows the footprints of the faith our framers had, which they held to be absolute when they penned: *"We hold these truths to be self-evident, that all men are created equal, that they are endowed by their Creator with certain unalienable rights, that among these are life, liberty, and the pursuit of happiness."* Those words speak truth to power that is definite, precise and absolute! Those words are not relative, they are not pluralistic, nor do they lack form!

American Education Was Started on a Different Road

If given the opportunity to overthrow, have a coup d'état, one of the quietest and most systematic methods to use would be the school classroom. The founders knew this, and if for no other reason, they never wanted the education system to be out of the hands of God-fearing and preferably Christian people. They knew that as goes the education of young people, so goes the nation. As Herbert Schlossberg put it, "One of the most useful tools in the quest for power is the education system."[47] This theorem has been proven true historically over and over again, "whoever controls the educational system will set the goals for the nation, especially in religious values, and ultimately control the future."[48] From Athens and Rome to Edinburgh and Yale, education is the facilitator of change its leaders wanted to bear in a nation. For 200 years in America, our education system was solid. For the past 50 plus years, it has been anything but.

The forefathers built a private system of education which was to be perpetuated and facilitated through channels that included home, school, church, voluntary associations such as library companies and philosophical societies, circulating libraries, apprenticeships, and private study. It was a system supported primarily by those who bought the services of education, and by private benefactors. All was done without compulsion. Although there was a veneer of government involvement in some colonies, such as in Puritan Massachusetts, early American education was based on the principle of voluntarism. If you wanted it, you used your energy and resources to go get it.

Roman leaders knew this principle and put it to use in teaching their form of democracy to the people in the university system of the day. Before them, the Greeks applied the same tools to use with their mythology, teaching their people through the years their version of gods warring against each other. They knew human nature well enough to apply the trade and get the people aboard their propaganda. So did Adolph Hitler. He knew that he could teach children his evil doctrines and get away with it before parents really knew what was going on. At that point, it would not matter what parents wanted, for the classroom teaching would rule. Through the centuries, ministers too knew that consistent week to week teaching was essential for disciples to really learn the precepts of Scripture; it would transform people with little knowledge into dynamos for the faith and advance Christian civilization. Ministers like Martin Luther in Germany, so critical to the Reformation Movement of the sixteenth century, and John Calvin in Switzerland, took great strides in developing Christian education and they tried to apply the Bible to every area of life. For these and other reformers, the teaching helped to reclaim much of life for an individual into positive good, not just salvation of the soul.

In 1559 John Calvin started "The Academy of Geneva," Switzerland that attracted students from all parts of Europe who wanted to fulfill the transformation of their whole life by the teaching of the Gospel. This was one of the great achievements of Calvin's last years. His high regard for the importance of good education is shown in his provision for a special rank of teachers in his church in the Ecclesiastical Ordinances of 1541. However, his educational plans were not fully realized, despite his constant efforts, for eighteen years. Since the council could not supply money out of public revenues to build the new building he wanted, he raised funds by soliciting gifts and legacies from private individuals. Calvin modeled his school after another famous school, the one at Strasbourg, which was developed by Johann Sturm, where Calvin himself had lectured. Based on this model, the school at Geneva consisted of two parts: the college (*schola privata*), and the academy itself (*schola publica*), which was a university, devoted chiefly to training ministers. Work in law and medicine was contemplated for the curriculum, but not actually offered during Calvin's lifetime. This was a great disappointment to Calvin personally.

The training in the college was specifically "humanistic" (Not the same 'humanism' as taught over the last century by liberal progressives). The pupils were thoroughly grounded in reading the Greek and Latin classics, and in speaking and writing good Latin. Also, special attention was paid to religious instruction. The teachers were charged with seeing that the students learned to know what it was to love God and hate evil, or as they called it 'vice.' Students in the higher school, or academy, were generally free from this discipline, although they had to subscribe to the confession of faith in order to be admitted. The "humanist influence remained strong in the academy, which had professors of Latin, Greek, and Hebrew." The school was a great success. It started with 162 pupils, mostly French, and in about six years it had ten times as many, with students from all over Europe. The effects were far reaching in several avenues: "It was not only the future of Geneva but that of other regions as well that was affected by the rise of the Geneva schools. The men who were to lead the advance of the Reformed Church in many lands were trained in Geneva classrooms, preached Geneva doctrines, and sang the Psalms to Geneva tunes."[49] As writer Sam Blumenfeld explained of the impact of Christian education on advancing the precepts of the Reformation,

> "Since the Protestant rebellion against Rome had arisen in part as a result of Biblical study and interpretation, it became obvious to Protestant leaders that if the Reform movement were to survive and flourish, widespread Biblical literacy, at all levels of society, would be necessary. The Bible was to be the moral and spiritual authority in every man's life; therefore an intimate knowledge of it was imperative if a new Protestant social order were to take root."[50]

In this same spirit of promoting both good education and the Reformation at the start of this nation, one of the very first actions taken by our forefathers was to establish schools and colleges; the very first colony to do so was Virginia, when the colonists chartered a college at Henrico in 1619. "Henricus College" as it was named was founded nearly twenty years before Harvard was started and its express design was built on the precepts of the Christian faith. As the founders had prescribed its purpose, it was there "for the training and bringing up of infidels' children to the true knowledge of God and understanding of righteousness."[51] The colonial colleges were designed to promote the Gospel of Christ in all the humanities and disciplines.

Notice please that our forefathers of all these early colleges knew the connection between a sound education based on Biblical absolutes and the future of the nation, something about which our current owners of education system in this country haven't a clue. The Reformation had taught our founders a valuable lesson which our peers in the 20th and 21st Centuries seem to have lost along the way; that is putting the Bible into the hands of the people (so that it can be read and understood) is the first critical step toward religious and political freedom. As Henry May stated, "From the very beginnings, the expressed purpose of colonial education had been to preserve society against barbarism, and so far as possible, against sin. The inculcation of a saving truth was primarily the responsibility of the churches, but schools were necessary to protect the written means of revelation."[52]

"Liberty" is the watchword. Americans forget that there is no way of regulating an economy without regulating men and women. We forget — all plans involve people — if governments attempt to enact plans, they must do so by the people's permission, by force, or the threat of force. We forget morality proceeds choice; choice depends on liberty.

And when you look further at the roots of our nation's founding, you find that this precise plan of following absolute truth of Biblical principles were used in the founding of our government, our institutions, our schools, and even our churches. Mentioning the church in this context may seem strange or out of context for a couple of reasons, however, (1) it was the church where the truth of the Gospel and freedom was to continue to be taught adults so that schools could be granted teachers of great freedom and great vision, all based on deep knowledge of Scripture and its lessons. And, (2) given attacks on Christianity, such as in today's teaching of relativism, it is common to see congregations or entire denominations of Christendom that flee teaching on any absolute truth, replacing it with political lies and social issues. This is called the 'emerging church' in our culture. The problem is an emerging church has given rise to an emerging culture. And it is a cheat, an illusion, a mirage. I do not apologize in saying this; when a local congregation gets away from the study of the Word of God using a grammatical, historical, contextual way of learning, and when they cease to disciple people into Jesus and The Word using this manner. I believe they lose their very purpose for existence, no matter how many social issues they may claim to tackle.

If godly people were in leadership within the churches and many of these individuals ended up in the educational system, by design that godly lives would be developed. In this way government work would be done by godly people and would further the goodness of God for all mankind. Said differently, as an example, when godly and wise people controlled the primary and secondary education system, the founders knew the purpose and agenda of the country would be protected and fulfilled. And that's because they were in godly hands. When I see the nationalized school system today, run by a union, with entities using our children as pawns to promote a dogma, transforming their minds with anti-American and anti-Christian curriculum, the result has been not only tragic in loss of the nation's ideals, but also has and is producing such pitiful results in learning. I wonder how angry the early Americans would be to see the current disaster we have on our hands.

One microcosm from our public school history shows the point. Since the Bible was removed from the school in 1948, as a reading book for the children, reading scores have continually dropped year by year. It is as if God said if you're not going to read His Word, there's really no reason to read at all.

An Education in the Colonies

A youngster attending school in the 17th Century in America was provided a quality education through a very limited curriculum, usually learning from just four books. The Bible was the first, with readings aloud and in silence. Vocabulary was increased in students via this method, as well as learning truths to be used in all of life. Second was the Hornbook, usually it consisted of one piece of parchment covered with a transparent substance, all attached to a paddle-shaped board, or piece of wood. The youngest of children used parchments with the alphabet, the Lord's Prayer, and other important Scriptural lessons printed or written on them. *The New England Primer* was the third book which appeared in schools in 1690 and was presented in different versions through the years. The earliest version had religious themes, including the names of Old and New Testament Books and 'The Lord's Prayer' all for memorization. Also included were "An alphabet of lessons for youth," the Apostle's Creed, The Ten Commandments and the Westminster Assembly Shorter Catechism as well as John Cotton's "Spiritual Milk for American Babes." The fourth reference tool was *The Bay Psalm Book*, which was the approved hymnal in the New England colonies, putting the Psalms into verse and song.[53] It is obvious that children were learning morals, ethics, manners, and proper conduct while learning the "3 R's." There were absolutes in the culture, as well as right and wrong were taught, which is absent today. There was an also obvious absence of pluralism which is taught today.

The Higher Education Life in Colonial America

Speaking of education, mention any of our Ivy League Universities and people would probably never guess that all but one started as a Bible College! One does not have to go back that far in time to see the footprints of our colonial culture in our university system. When Trinity University was endowed with the name Duke

University in 1924, the bylaws of this newly-named university stated, "The aims of Duke University are to assert a faith in the eternal union of knowledge and religion set forth in the teachings and character of Jesus Christ, the Son of God...."[54]

A study of Duke's founding and charter shows almost an identical character when compared to the founding of the colonial colleges nearly 200 years earlier in the 17th century. A friend and peer in management in another company in the same industry where we both worked for years, is a graduate from Harvard. On hearing me say several years ago that Harvard and most other Ivy League Universities were all started as Bible Colleges to train ministers, he shouted, "Are you kidding me — that liberal campus?!" Yes, that liberal campus!

The graph below demonstrates that these colleges were founded as Christian institutions to prepare students for Christian ministry. The curriculum was very comprehensive however and included more than just a divinity school. "Regardless of the vocation for which a student was preparing, the colonial college sought to provide for him and education that was distinctly Christian."[55] One exception was the University of Pennsylvania, founded in 1755.

Founded	College	Colony	Affiliation
1636	Harvard	Massachusetts	Puritan
1693	William & Mary	Virginia	Anglican
1701	Yale	Connecticut	Congregational
1746	Princeton	New Jersey	Presbyterian
1754	King's College	New York	Anglican
1764	Brown	Rhode Island	Baptist
1766	Rutgers	New Jersey	Dutch Reformed
1769	Dartmouth	New Hampshire	Congregational

Curriculum would vary slightly from one college to the next but they were distinctly Christian in their overall approach. For example, Harvard's curriculum emphasized the study of Biblical languages, logic, theology, and communication skills (public speaking and rhetoric). Churches expected and usually demanded their ministers read Scripture in the original languages. "Although each of the three earliest colleges, Harvard, William & Mary, and Yale, was chartered by the established church in its colony, each also held a direct relationship to the state and served as the center for training civic as well as clerical leaders for its region."[56]

Harvard

As stated, the purpose of each of these colleges was to train men for teaching and preaching the Gospel. Harvard was chartered by the Puritan Churches in Massachusetts. An early brochure, published in 1643, described the founding purpose of the college to be, " . . . to advance learning and perpetuate it to posterity, dreading to leave an illiterate ministry to the churches"[57]

Though it took some 230 years to remove Christianity as a chief tenant in its curriculum, evidence shows the school was started as a college to train people for ministry and learning the Gospel. Many modern progressives deny it.

It was John Eliot (1604-1690), also known as "the Apostle to the Indians," who first publicly proposed a college for Massachusetts Bay in 1633, and three years later his brain child came true. Harvard was actually named after John Harvard, who donated his entire library to the little fledgling school. The school's founding fathers wanted their college to continue the Christian legacy and precepts they had brought with them from England. They wanted to train ministers in their area since ministers were largely responsible for being the primary educators in their time.[58]

The evidence is clear that Harvard and all the Ivy League Colleges were founded by strong Christian people. Some of the schools had established student guidelines, indicating the foundation that the Scripture of the Bible was the absolute foundation to all truth for them. Isn't that a jaw dropper? You certainly do not hear about that today. Long erased from its current campus statements is the original Harvard motto, *"Veritas Christo et Ecclesia,"* or, "Truth for Christ and the Church." The motto has been abandoned for the shorter abbreviated version *Veritas* — "truth." Historically, Harvard called the Bible God's "Word is truth" — now Harvard asserts and teaches that truth is relative. The founders of Harvard were not delusional as their modern counterparts are. For the founders believed the converse.

The 1636 Harvard Student Guidelines, or Handbook, which every student received, as published later in 1643 in *New England's First Fruits*, had a clear message, *"Let every student be plainly instructed and earnestly pressed to consider well the main end in his life and studies is to know God and [Jesus] Christ which is eternal life (John 17:3) and therefore to lay Christ in the bottom as the only foundation of all sound knowledge and learning. And seeing the Lord only giveth wisdom, let every one seriously set himself by prayer in secret to seek it of Him (Proverbs 2, 3). [Every one shall so exercise himself in reading the Scriptures twice a day that he shall be ready to give such an account of his proficiency therein.]"*

New England's First Fruits also offered an explanation for why this college should be founded in the colony as shown here in its original spelling, "After God had carried us safe to New England and we had builded our houses, provided necessaries for our livele-hood, rear'd convenient places for God's worship, and settled the civil government: One of the next things we longed for and looked after was to advance *Learning* and perpetuate it to posterity; dreading to leave an illiterate minister to the churches, when our current Ministers will lie in the Dust."[59] Ari Goldman confirmed this creed, "Religion was so much a part of everyday learning in the early days of Harvard that for nearly two centuries no one thought of setting up a separate Divinity School. In the college, students gathered daily for prayer and readings from the Scripture. Hebrew as well as Greek were required subjects, because an educated person was expected to read the Bible in the original tongues."[60]

Based on current trends at the campus, it seems surreal to report of the early graduates, "fifty-two percent of Harvard graduates became ministers."[61] On a basis of what we've seen come from Harvard over the past few years, an estimate closer to zero would seem closer to the true percentage. But because of the very strong Calvinistic orientation of the Puritan colonists, they "did not distinguish sharply between secular and theological learning; and they believed that the collegiate education proper for a minister should be the same for an educated layman. They expected that the early colleges would produce not only ministers but Christian gentlemen who would be civic leaders."[62]

Unfortunately, time and the Liberal Progressives have taken a toll at Harvard, so much so that Christianity is now viewed as something of a roadblock to true intellectual thinking. To be free intellectually means to get rid of Christ and Christianity, according to the spirit that presides at Harvard now. What is interesting to see is that Harvard is not interested in being the only university to take this stand. The school has become "evangelistic" in trying to lead other universities in joining its staff in driving the remnants of Christian influence off all campuses. In a fit of political and anti-Christian humanistic rage, Harvard joined other universities some twenty years ago in publicly criticizing any campus of academia, such as Westminster Schools of Atlanta, Georgia, for having a policy that requires any teacher there to be a Christian and confess their faith in Jesus Christ.[63] And since that time, their demeanor against the faith which founded it, has led the school into a total prodigal sojourn. One wonders that if the original founders of Harvard, those colonists who loved freedom, both political and social freedom, could see the university now; how she has forsaken her first love, how she has betrayed her one trust, how she has wandered away from her original calling, if they would repent of every starting such a place, an institution, called Harvard.

Yale (in Connecticut)

History records that by the beginning of the eighteenth century, many New Englanders were convinced that Harvard was no longer doing what it was called to do because the school had forsaken its mission and goals. Harvard President, Increase Mather (President from 1685 to 1701) and his son who followed him, Cotton Mather, tried to correct the diversion that Harvard was taking by leaving its Calvinistic and Christian roots. But their efforts were to no avail. The college soon was embracing Unitarianism, the ultimate greased skids on the way to relativism. As a remedy to the theological shortcomings and abandonment of the faith by Harvard, Yale College was established in 1701 by the colonists of Connecticut. "The founders of Yale required the 'Westminster Confession to be diligently read in the Latin Tongue and well-studied by all the scholars,' 'for the upholding of the Christian Protestant Religion by a succession of Learned and Orthodox men.' The State of Connecticut in the Tale Charter in 1701 asserted its desire to support 'so necessary and essential an undertaking.'"[63]

Yale's founders wanted most of all to have a return to the Christian cause for which Harvard had been specifically established to address. Yale was therefore dedicated to Christian virtue in every lecture and every class, upholding the Gospel of Christ. This was also clearly seen in the bylaws, the letters which were written from the faculty, and even in the Student Guidelines from 1787 which read, *"All the scholars are required to live a religious and blameless life according to the rules of God's Word, diligently reading the Holy Scriptures, that fountain of Divine light and truth, and constantly attending all the duties of religion."*

A Christian foundation was laid at Yale by its founding fathers, the same that had been laid first at Harvard, and then deserted. Bill Ringenberg states, "Yale in the 1700s stated as its primary goal that 'every student shall consider the main end of his study to wit to know God in Jesus Christ and answerably to lead a Godly, sober life.'"[64] Yale demanded students have the same rigorous academic approach to study as Harvard did, as well as a religious commitment to the cause Christ and His Gospel: "All scholars shall live religious, godly, and blameless lives according to the rules of God's Word, diligently reading the Holy Scriptures, the fountain of light and truth; and constantly attend upon all the duties of religion, both in public and secret."[65] The 1745 'Charter of Yale' stated succinctly that the College, "Which has received the favorable benefactions of many liberal [generous] and piously disposed persons, and under the blessing of Almighty God has trained up many worthy persons for the service of God in the state as well as in the church."[66]

Figure 1 Picture of University Seal

Northeast liberal progressive trends overtook Yale, like Harvard before it and have moved on to other colleges since. Theologically, morally, and even educationally, it has failed to fulfill its stated goals. The father of the modern conservative movement and arguably one of most intelligent men who lived in New England, William F. Buckley, Jr. chronicled in 1951 Yale's fateful slide into secularism, progressivism, and collectivism in his God and Man at Yale.[67] Buckley's expose' on the college did little if any to turn the tide toward sin and decadence. Eventually the moral slide has produced the fruit which the progressives have been trying to attain: "Harvard and Yale have assembled Curriculum Committees to explore course material on 'Gay, Lesbian, and Bisexual Studies.'"[68] What a ridiculous tribute paid the founders of this university paid by decadent Leftists. It's no wonder that other colleges have been established in the last sixty years attempting to reestablish God's Word as the central theme of studies on their campuses.

Columbia (in New York)

On June 3, 1754, an advertisement appeared in the *New York Mercury* announcing the opening of King's College, with classes starting later that fall. Samuel Johnson (1696-1772), a graduate of Yale, had placed the ad in the newspaper. He had accepted the invitation and offer to be the first president of King's College, the position he held until 1763. In 1784 the college was re-named Columbia College, and later Columbia University.

Curriculum was very similar to what had been required at Harvard and Yale in their beginnings such as the requirement to know Latin and Greek. The college was founded by the Anglican Church, but they wanted to cast a larger net to Christians from other denominational churches. Their advertisement therefore assured students and parents that "there is no intention to impose on the scholars the peculiar tenets of any particular sect of Christians, but to inculcate upon their tender minds the great principles of Christianity and morality in which true Christians of each denomination are generally agreed."[69] The King's College advertisement went on to state:

"The chief thing that is aimed at in this college is to teach and engage the children to know God in Jesus Christ and to love and serve Him in all sobriety, godliness, and righteousness of life, with perfect heart and a willing mind, and to train them up in all virtuous habits and all such useful knowledge as may render them creditable to their families and friends, ornaments to their country, and useful to the public weal in their generations."[70]

Every day, students coming onto campus would see the King's College Shield (Seal) which was established in 1755. This shield would remind all who saw it of the stated purpose of the college that is evident from the shield's figure and inscriptions. Over the head of the seated woman is the (Hebrew) Tetragrammaton, YHVH (Jehovah); the Latin motto around her head means "In Thy Light we See Light" (Psalm 36:10); the Hebrew phrase on the ribbon is *Uri El* ("God is My Light"), an illusion to Psalm 27:1; and at the feet of the woman is the New Testament passage commanding Christians to desire the pure milk of God's word (1 Peter 2:1-2).[71]

Many years ago Columbia adopted a new shield, or seal. The only resemblance to the old shield is one line, "In Thy Light we see Light." All other references to God, His Word or His Son Jesus were not kept.

Princeton (in New Jersey)

New Jersey was the only colony that had two colleges, the College of New Jersey (Princeton) and Queens (Rutgers). The Log College, the predecessor of Princeton, was founded when Nathaniel Irwin left one thousand dollars to William Tennant to found a seminary.[72]

According to Alexander Leitch, author of "A Princeton Companion," Log College was the name given to a school that William Tennent, an Edinburgh-educated Presbyterian minister, conducted at Neshaminy, Pennsylvania, from 1726 until his death in 1745. There, in a "log house, about twenty feet long and near as many broad," Tennent drilled his pupils in the ancient languages and the Bible. At that time, however, only graduates of Harvard or Yale could become Presbyterian ministers — effectively prohibiting Log College graduates from the ministry. This rule led to a movement to charter new colleges, which in turn led to the creation of the College of New Jersey, or Princeton.[73] A bronze memorial plaque in the archway just outside the main entrance to Nassau Hall commemorates three names for Princeton, with their respective dates: Log College in 1726; College of New Jersey, chartered in 1746; and Princeton University as renamed in 1896.[74]

As the plaque indicates, the founding in 1746 in Elizabeth was led by the New Light Presbyterians and their members of Log College, to bring into being the *College of New Jersey*, or Princeton, as we now know it. It was one of the nine Colonial Colleges established before the American Revolution as well as the fourth chartered institution of higher education in the American colonies.[75] The purpose as stated in the charter was to train ministers for the Presbyterian Church until, John Witherspoon became president in 1768. He shifted the college's focus at that time from training ministers to a business curriculum. Witherspoon remained in that office until his death in 1794. The university moved to Newark in 1747, then to Princeton in 1756 and was renamed Princeton University in 1896. Today, anyone visiting Princeton could never tell that any religious group had anything to do with the college, since all traces of Christianity have been removed from campus, except for the plaque by Nassau Hall. I suppose it could be said the only religion honored at Princeton now is secular humanism.

Witherspoon's presidency constituted a long period of stability in that office for the college, since the five earlier presidents had all passed away in untimely manners. His presidency was interrupted by the American Revolution and particularly the Battle of Princeton, during which British soldiers briefly occupied Nassau Hall; American forces, led by George Washington, fired cannon on the building to rout them from it.

Until 1803, Nassau Hall was the college's sole building. The cornerstone of the building was laid on September 17, 1754. The school has a rich history that many do not know. During the summer of 1783, the Continental Congress met in Nassau Hall, making Princeton the country's capital for four months. James McCosh took office as the college's president in 1868 and lifted the institution out of a low period that had been brought about by the American Civil War. Nassau Hall was built in 1756 and named after William III of the House of Orange-Nassau. When built, it was the largest college building in North America. It served briefly as the capitol of the United States when the Continental Congress convened there in the summer of 1783. In 1896, the college officially changed its name from the College of New Jersey to Princeton University to honor the town in which it resides.

Based on the nation's primary principle of freedom, Princeton under Witherspoon produced some of America's most "animated Sons of Liberty." Many of Princeton's graduates, standing firmly in the Whig tradition of limited government, helped lay the legal and constitutional foundations for our Republic. James Madison, the Father of the Constitution, was a Princeton graduate. Following the change of curriculum in the nineteenth century, slowly the college started leaving its Christian heritage behind, except for the plaque by Nassau Hall which quietly speaks of the past.

William and Mary (in Virginia)

A full 114 years before the American Revolution, in 1662, the Assembly of Virginia enacted a bill to make permanent provision for a college in the colony. The Preamble of the college states the purpose for its existence which focuses on the great lack of preaching talent in the pulpits of America's churches and says in part, "... that the want of able and faithful ministers in this country deprives us of those great blessings and mercies that always attend upon the service of God"; and the bill itself declares "that for the advancement of learning, education of youth, supply of the ministry, and promotion of piety, there be land taken up and purchased for a college and free school, and that with all convenient speed there be buildings erected upon it for the entertainment of students and scholars."[76]

From the passing of the act, it took thirty-one years, or until 1693 until the college of William and Mary was actually founded. But like the other colonial colleges, its purpose was evangelical in that the school would supply the Church of Virginia with a "Seminary of Ministers" and that the "Christian Faith may be propagated amongst the Western Indians, to the Glory of Almighty God."[77] Making certain the college would remain faithful in the mission of training ministers, those and other evangelical goals were reiterated in 1727.

We Can Draw a Conclusion

The purpose of establishing schools and colleges in the colonies was a way of advancing and perpetuating the Christian faith. This is a fact with overwhelming evidence. "The schools were intended to form Christian men, Christian citizens, and Christian ministers, not as a by-product but directly. They were instruments of the Church, which was, at least in the beginning, virtually coterminous with the community. Education was an enterprise undertaken primarily in the interest of religion, with religion of course defined in terms of the Calvinistic orthodoxy then dominating New England."[78] Liberal progressive teachers denounce the Christian Faith despite the evidence. Would you not agree that their attempts to teach otherwise are a deliberate, premeditated, organized, and thoughtfully orchestrated attack?

Over the years, a huge philosophical shift has taken place. Those colleges and universities started in the 1800s were built by the money of wealthy entrepreneurs who had very specific and secular goals. "Ezra Cornell (telegraph, banking), Johns Hopkins (banking, railroads), Cornelius Vanderbilt (steamships, railroads), Leland Stanford (railroads), James Duke (tobacco), and James D. Rockefeller (oil) were only a few of the prominent businessmen who poured vast sums of money into the creation of modern universitites."[79] Some of the universities were more secular than others, and some stood as it seemed against American culture stating an objection about religion being involved in a person's education. Andrew Dickson White, for example, the founding president of Cornell University, committed that he would use the institution to "afford asylum for Science — where truth will be sought for truth's sake, where it shall not be the main purpose of the Faculty to stretch or cut sciences exactly to fit 'Reveal Religion.'"[80] It becomes obvious when listening to the voices from the past, as well as modern counterparts, that these individuals have "a bone to pick" with someone from their past who taught the Christian Faith, or just closed their minds to the Author of that Faith Himself. As a result they built a belief that anyone who would spend resources training ministers was a waste, as if truth from Scripture would stand against the free enterprise system.

From there it has been a downhill ride for these and other universities in actually taking stands against faith in God. America's institutions of higher learning have come a long way down the turnpike of "secularism" from Harvard's declaration that the main end of a man's life is to "know God and Jesus Christ which is eternal life (John 17:3)," to now Darwinian evolution as "a scientifically credible theory of random and purposeless change."[81]

Today, If you were to go to any of these universities, or take your pick of any other public university campus for that matter, and declare that there needs to be a return to the class structure for the study of the Bible, for serving God, teaching and searching the Scripture, all in preparing students for being stronger Christians, and that all classes be held on the campus — the end result would be that you would be mocked, attacked, laughed at, 'booed' or even arrested for a starting a riot. You could be charged with a criminal offense, since words spoken in support of the Christian Faith appear to be considered hate crimes now. And if you were to say that the current progressive curriculum (which is Marxist, socialist and communist), are to be banished on campus, there would be a riot by the student body, AND PROBABLY LED by the faculty.

Chapter Eight — History Schmistory, Who Needs It?

Despite what Marxist, progressive or atheistic principles professors teach at universities today, despite what students learn, and despite all the "anti-Christian fervor" that oozes from colleges today, many facts support the overwhelming evidence, to show the true founding of America's colleges. When combined with the statements from the inscriptions from our National Buildings, as demonstrated, and our early constitutions as shown, the combined evidence would stand in any unbiased court proving we were a Christian Nation dedicated to perpetuating the faith at one time.[82] When the historical record is left un-gagged and allowed to speak, it declares loudly that we were founded as a Christian nation. It screams that our institutions and learning centers were dedicated to the Gospel, the total opposite of what is taught in schools and colleges today. Our founders worked to please God and serve Him, God placed a protective hedge around them and the country.[83] Because of this, America truly became a bright and shining light to the entire world, as no nation had ever been before, all based on the blessing of His protective hedge.

It is so very clear to anyone who has eyes, ears, and the ability to "connect the dots" in a logical frame of thinking — no matter what their faith, even if they claim to have no faith — the evidence is clear that even an infidel can see as Romans 1:20 states, "For since the creation of the world God's invisible qualities — his eternal power and divine nature — have been clearly seen, being understood from what has been made, so that men are without excuse."[84] Finally, this thought was very prevalent throughout the founding of our nation, and existed in the top offices of government just 60 years ago, unlike today. Please read carefully the thoughts of one of the top legal minds in our land from the mid-50s, as he explained his belief about where the protection of our nation rested.

> "I believe no one can read the history of our country without realizing that the Good Book and the spirit of the Savior have from the beginning been our guiding geniuses . . . Whether we look to the first charter of Virginia . . . or to the Charter of New England . . . or to the Charter of Massachusetts Bay . . . or to the Fundamental Orders of Connecticut . . . the same objective is present. A Christian land governed by Christian principles . . .
>
> The entire Bill of Rights came about due to the knowledge and faith our forefathers had of the Bible and their belief in it; freedom of belief, of expression, of assembly, of petition, the dignity of the individual, the sanctity of the home, equal justice under law and the reservation of powers to the people. . . .
>
> I like to believe we are living today in the spirit of the Christian religion. I like also to believe that as long as we do so, no great harm can come to our country."
>
> - Former Chief Justice Earl Warren, addressing the annual prayer breakfast of the International Council of Christian Leadership, 1954 [85]

"*Is it not that in the chain of human events, the birthday of the nation is indissolubly linked with the birthday of the Savior? That it forms a leading event in the progress of the Gospel dispensation? Is it not that the Declaration of Independence first organized the social compact on the foundation of the Redeemer's mission upon earth? — That it laid the cornerstone of human government upon the first precepts of Christianity?*"

~ John Quincy Adams

Statesman; Diplomat;
6th President of the United States

Chapter Nine

Definitions in a New, Progressive Society

MRS. JESSIE MUMFORD WAS ONE OF the most "drill sergeant-like" English teachers who ever lived. Her reputation preceded her in being so tough that many freshmen basically believed the rumors that some of her poorer performing students were actually buried just outside her classroom: They "reportedly" had expired under the brutal assignments of "bench-pressing" her sentence diagrams, or sprinting away from her as she shouted displeasure about their incorrect work.

For four years, she had me in her "vice-grips" within her different English classes, English I, II, III, and IV, there in our small high school in Willow Springs, Missouri. And while I did not appreciate all she offered at the time, those "full terms of hell" amounted to both college prep language and even advanced college English: it all ended up being some of the best preparation for life afforded me in any classroom. I recall full well the day when preparing a final draft for state-wide English Comp competition, she threw my paper in my face saying, "This isn't your best work!" She was right, it wasn't. This was her "loving" way of challenging me to push myself to the next level, and then to the next. And it paid off in my case with a 1st Place Ribbon.

Her fortunate students should really have been called "survivors" rather than graduates since she touted that her classes "were indeed college level classes and were among the toughest English Comp and English Lit classes for any high school in the nation." Her expectation for excellence from her students was obvious and never needed to be repeated. More than once she proudly exclaimed about her college work, "In all my work at the University of Missouri, for both undergraduate and graduate degrees, I never had a correction on spelling, punctuation, or grammar for any paper turned in to my teachers while there." She expected the same level work from her students at Willow Springs High. And she got it from at least a few. The proof was seen in the parade of professionals who came from her graduates. One of her students, one she had in her first few years at school and in whom she had considerable pride, Rowe Findley, became a senior editor with National Geographic in Washington, D.C. Rowe had the most popular and widely-read article ever to appear in the Geographic; one featuring the eruption of Mt. St. Helens May 18, 1980. Three of her graduates became the heads of major city newspapers during their careers. She had several who became successful attorneys, writers, editors, authors and many, many business managers, executives, and some CEOs. Each year, one of her students it seemed was always winning 1st place in the state composition contests decade upon decade, and this from a high school with a total enrollment of about three hundred.

One of the most valuable lessons with which she gifted my gray matter, and there were many, was the simple lesson that "words mean things." Yes, they do. Language is a special tool which, when used correctly and efficiently, can afford people great satisfaction and peace of mind, including much leverage in a discussion. Mrs. Mumford's timing in my life was impeccable because she greased the skids for what I would face later in my career and for what we all collectively face in our culture today. We seem to be losing a war of language and of words on the basis of attrition. Those who cannot easily communicate grammatically, outnumber the ones who can — with many today lacking any ability to effectively converse through written words. And please don't even speak to me about the bulk of this culture's enunciation of spoken English words. It appears there is a sizeable segment of the population compounding the situation; they cannot spell to save their lives, they also can't enunciate appropriately, they do little more than grunt single syllables, and probably most importantly, they don't care to take pride in any of these tasks.

You may think this torques me — and you would be correct. But maybe it's for a different reason than you might think. Let me explain. Everybody has the right to learn or not learn as they see fit. Don't give me the excuse that some have better teachers; if you want to learn and excel, you will find a way. That is part of what is wrapped up in what I call equal opportunity and freedom. Freedom means taking the responsibility to do what needs to be done in your life, not waiting for someone else to do it for you. But that freedom, or rugged individualism, ends when some choose not to do the work to improve themselves. Ironically, life for them is self-professed as not being fair — a statement social justice experts (progressive liberals) use as reason to support their agenda. They make loud statements that the playing field must be leveled by taking from those who have worked hard and give it to those who refuse to do so. In education, the "no child left behind" slogan was created, meaning all students are taught at the level of the slowest student in a group. Therefore the true meaning is no child gets ahead.

I feel privileged now to have been "verbally spanked" by Mumford, arguably one of the best governesses in the language. Because of her coaching, I am better equipped for life. She could see the trend in this country long ago and saw what was coming; redefining words and language with a political correctness, before any of her students could even imagine it.

CHAPTER NINE — DEFINITIONS IN A NEW, PRIGRESSIVE SOCIETY

Beware, the PC Police Are Watching

Political correctness has affected our nation's culture as not even a huge tsunami could. No one understands the extent of danger and destruction until after the gigantic wave sweeps across the land and then slowly recedes — only rubble is left behind.

The rumblings of the "political correct" earthquake were felt, preceding the storm of his first term, when President Obama set the tone for that political correctness and how he expected sensitive issues to be handled. The Global War on Terror was soon renamed "Overseas Contingency Operation." The Department of Homeland Security (DHS) quickly followed suit, redefining terrorist attacks as "man caused disasters." This trickle-down idiocy, providing Liberal-speak name changes to events or crises is a game to appease Muslims, the chronically ill Left, and give only the pretense that things are different than they really are.

I learned the lesson of pretense as a kid. Having a mother and a grandmother who both loved me enough to make certain I was inoculated for polio, they took me to the doctor; there I screamed and kicked the nurse. When the shot was given by the doctor, I also kicked him. Following that first disastrous visit, my mother and grandmother decided to change the name "doctor's office" to "ice cream shop" to make the first leg of the trip in the car less traumatic. It worked once, up until our car pulled into the doctor's office parking lot rather than that of the ice cream store. Fool me once . . .

Within a day or two, my parents and grandparents sat me down for a grownup conversation, explaining it was going to be unpleasant, they would make it the least painful as possible, but it had to be done. To their credit, I never contacted polio — the reason for the inoculation. I still get a queasy feeling and smile sometimes when going to get ice cream, remembering those episodes. Too young to realize it then, that experience taught me a valuable lesson about political correctness. Switching labels doesn't change reality.

For the past several decades, the Left has been pushing to switch labels on almost everything in America to an opposite stance. Everything that made our country exceptional — relabeling all that is honorable, good and wholesome as inappropriate or racist by political correctness terms. They also label things once considered immoral, evil and anti-religious as now being good. Not realizing they are only trapping themselves in the process, more Americans are awakening to the gig, like me as a kid in the car, realizing that exchanging God-endowed freedoms for man-made rules is not a fair trade.

This scheme was recently on display in a smaller, but very toxic, military reservist sensitivity training workshop in Pennsylvania that would have Bill Maher crowing. The person in charge listed Jews, Catholics, and Christians as religious extremists alongside al Qaeda and the KKK. Inclusivity is not always a good thing. It can be a rotten thing, especially when put there by liberals.

The US military brass was quick to respond promising that the training class was an isolated event, but it seemed a bit misplaced considering the enormity of faith-filled military veterans out there who have balanced their love of God and service to their country without pulling a "Nidal Hasan" on fellow soldiers. In the name of political correctness, Obama jumped forward saying, "Don't jump to conclusions." Hasan's monstrous act was also kindheartedly labeled "work place violence" by the White House, which had the side-effect of denying Purple Hearts to well-deserving Fort Hood soldiers. The administration treated the massacre as if it were a random stabbing by a pencil rather than calling it for what it is.

It is a two-way street. When Obama was complimenting California's Kamala Harris last year as being "by far the best looking attorney general in the country," he should have just taken a selfie with her, since he got a tiny taste his own bitter medicine. A swarm of female PC police arrived, demanding Obama enroll in gender sensitivity classes. Following a staged apology, he created a larger tsunami which grew into free speech being threatened when journalists were told they should consider the term "illegal alien" kaput. There are only aliens now. No one should be discredited with an "illegal" adjectival modifier, is what Leftists are saying. The storm will only increase waving over even gay communities with an Oregon bakery owner refusing to bake a cake for a lesbian couple's "wedding." A civil rights complaint and suit were filed — their demand for service was denied. A monstrous storm is following which will swallow this country in legal red tape, drowning what little freedoms we have left. Liberalism will be in full bloom soon thanks to political correctness.

Unfortunately, the beautiful language of our land has been hijacked in this time by back alley hoodlum liberals, aka "political correctness thugs." Add to the political correctness the slashing and disheveled surgery done to our words, with nothing sewn back on before going to makeshift recovery. Some words have simply been kidnapped, redefined to a lower level of existence, never to be returned to their glorious place in history. Results have witnessed:

- unknown enunciations (e.g., Jesse Jackson's jive-slang Ebonics);
- mordacious elocution (e.g., Al Sharpton's, "DATS FO DAMN SHOW!" ["That's for __ sure!"]);
- syllable bastardization ("She's got capable of going places." ["She's got THE CAPABILITY of going places,"]);
- caustic verb misplacement ("He comical," ["He IS comical."];
- mordant syntax ("That cat quick catch it," ["Quick! Catch that cat."]).

There is also the syllable trenchant redefining, and at times, total eradication of syllables. These are serious sins in the business of communicating, since as language goes, so goes a nation. If individuals can't learn to communicate, they can't

Chapter Nine — Definitions in a New, Prigressive Society

learn how to advance in life. For some I have noticed today, it seems anything north of a four-lettered word, is too heavy to be lifted by brain or tongue.

Of course, many have tried hijacking a language on the stage of world history. Ours is not the first time it has been tried or even accomplished. Hitler launched his career by redefining words, such as "Aryan," from meaning the people of India and the subcontinent, redefining it as the people of Scandinavia — generally non-Jewish whites. While Hitler was neither of those, though it was his claim, his more learned contemporaries, as they learned this, must have guffawed at such nonsense. But the "Fuhrer" can make life very dangerous if you disagree with him. The sad fact is that his definition has inadvertently been accepted as truth. He redefined other terms like "Christian" in the Third Reich manner to mean "European neo-pagan" while all the while trying to destroy the real Christianity.[1] It appears his definitions stuck. Other definitions rolled out from his pen. He redefined himself as German, although he was not actually that either. All of which should serve as a lesson. Words, used properly can be very powerful instruments; a word spoken is a deed done.

The Soviets got in on redefinition. They redefined everything they touched. Their penchant for all this reclassification was pure overkill and became the springboard for lots of jokes, laughter, and cartoons about their ridiculous lack of subtlety. One Soviet Official described an unheated and uncarpeted dorm in Siberia as being "luxurious." For those who question it, this story has been preserved on "The People's Cube," the brilliant satire site of a man who survived real-life communism in the land where it first took root.

Other attempts have been made in ancient history in doing this redefinition for political gain. In Israel, it was "the shtick" of Ahaz and Jezebel as they redefined both "acceptable" holiness and "acceptable" sacrifice as something they were not; using their phony prophets of Baal to promote their misinformation campaign until Elijah called their bluff on Mt. Carmel.[2] Their New Testament counterparts, the Pharisees redefined "piety" associated with their gift giving to fit their blowing of trumpets or loud, public announcements of their intentions to draw attention to themselves as they gave, all of which was repudiated by Christ Himself in the Sermon on the Mount,[3] and as He would instill within true disciples, for in giving, everything like orientation is to be abhorred and avoided.[4]

The ancient Greek ruler Antiochus Epiphanies used hogs to drive home the point to his subservient peons, that sacred buildings could be renamed and the animals reclassified as "clean" to suit him because he was king and wanted to place his will upon his people. Roman rulers used politics to the utmost in redefining elements to suit them. Nero (*Nero Claudius Caesar Augustus Germanicus*) redefined the word "candle" or "torch" to include Christians whose bodies he coated with an oily substance and burned them at night to light his palace courtyard for his party guests.[5] He also gave a whole new definition to the term "government thrift," by spending money like it was water. According to ancient historians, Nero's construction projects were overly extravagant and the large number of expenditures under Nero left Italy "thoroughly exhausted by contributions of money" with "the provinces ruined."[6] Where have I seen this before?

In today's culture, "truth" has been redefined. "We are now, and have been for the past. . . . [three] . . . .decades, living in what has accurately been called a post-Christian, postmodern world. The modern era was defined by the belief in and search for truth. [Ironically, the "definers" were liberal and they immediately abandoned truth.] The postmodern era leaves that belief behind and no longer recognizes absolute standards of morality or truth. Whatever feels right . . . .is considered acceptable behavior, and truth has sadly become 'what you feel it is.' Defining truth in such an environment is a personal and subjective process. But this popular viewpoint runs contrary to all we see in the natural and physical realms. Science — whether astronomy, zoology, botany, medicine, chemistry, archeology, physics, or mathematics — these are all controlled by objective, fixed principles."[7]

In terms of morality and a worldview, however, these same pluralistic thinkers live by their own flexible standards, ignoring the existence of absolute laws in the spiritual realm. God incorporated moral laws into the fabric of life just as He established natural laws in the physical dimension. Denial of a spiritual law does not negate the consequences of disobeying it. Said differently, just because somebody does not believe in a spiritual absolute does not eliminate the negative consequences of violating them. One may choose not to believe in the law of gravity, but he will still fall to the ground if he jumps off a tower. "Likewise, one may believe biblical moral standards are wrong or outmoded, but he or she cannot escape the consequences of violating those standards."[8] Redefining moral absolutes does not make the absolutes vanish, nor does it negate the consequences of breaking them.

We are in one of those redefinition periods now, with the Obama "Drain-Train" pulling meanings away from words, redefining some words, and dropping language in many cases its lowest possible level. There's a new "top 10", with new hit definitions rolling in every few weeks from you guessed it — the self-appointed progressive guru and the liberal progressives.

Of course words are commanding entities — else why do you think the news media is able to convince so many among us that "that which is good is bad and that which is bad is good." By mere repetition of words, people can be moved to do things they would ordinarily never consider doing. And as our government schools do their job of "dumbing down" students, it is much easier to catch their agendas with their special phrases or words when repeated over and over again. Hitler did it and with his chants and phrases and a nation started moving toward a political precipice which they had been convinced was hope and change. Through the ages, those who have used a redefined language to push the masses in the direction he or she wanted are almost innumerable.

Chapter Nine — Definitions in a New, Prigressive Society

While much evil has been accomplished with the political reclassification of words used, much good has also been brought about by words using them in their wholesome state. People think of John F. Kennedy's Inaugural Speech of 1961; the speech which held the phrase what has been repeated millions of times, "Ask not what your country can do for you. Ask what you can do for your country!" No redefinition there. Often too, Ronald Reagan's great words come to mind, "Freedom is never more than one generation away from extinction. We didn't pass it to our children in the bloodstream. It must be fought for, protected, and handed on for them to do the same, or one day we will spend our sunset years telling our children and our children's children what it was once like in the United States where men were free." Reagan did not have to cheapen or redefine words to communicate a pure, prophetic message in his March 1961 Phoenix Chamber of Commerce speech — he knew how to communicate truth.

Because of the assault on our language by this liberal mob, language has obviously lost meaning and even a noble word like "freedom" has lost significance from one generation to the next. In my generation "freedom" was full of meaning, self-determination, our right to live our lives the way we wanted, which had been provided especially by those who gave their lives so we could have that choice. And freedom also meant you were personally responsible to take charge of your own life, not asking the government or leaning on the government to take the responsibility for you.

In the latest generation, it seems that "freedom" has been boiled down to the smallest of possible determinations, even being redefined; meaning now simply having the choice of a hand-held game to play while the government is sucking our life and money out of us: this word and others have been cheapened or poisoned in young minds by listening in classrooms to politically driven activists who seek to destroy the dream of liberty and religious freedom by teaching a deception of lies. They stand against the heroes of our past and others over the years and through time, and our heroes loved independence and self-determination, while taking personal responsibility, which is real freedom.

With the hippies and progressives from the sixties now running the government and making policy, it takes a new-age and progressive dictionary to be able to understand much of what is really meant by the re-forged dialect or printed material that appears to be immature or jejune, drawn up by some sophomoric group of Klingons from an alternate universe. Their language is certainly not steeped in the English once studied in our nation. As you discover the work that these liberal "progressives" have done in desecrating our dictionary, you need a "primer" to understand their swamp terminology.

A partial list of terms and their current "new-age" definitions in use is presented below. Other words can be added. However, with this list, possibly you can "wade through" some of the "Liberal Speak" and be slightly better prepared in navigating the swamp.

GLOSSARY: Liberal Terms with Their Liberal Definitions

Gay: (I know this is low-hanging fruit but . . .) One of the words that brought utter excitement to certain MSNBC news journalists. The word is used to describe those wonderful same sex individuals who have been shamefully beaten down by a society of white monogamists. Being gay is the preferred avocation of Hollywood elites. They want for the word to mean happy, cheery and glamorous, as it meant before they kidnapped the word. Now it just means homosexual, queer. A better word for the lifestyle would be "sour".

Too Controversial: A conservative person who is too outspoken.

Main Stream: This would be totally liberal in every aspect. Not a conservative bone to be found.

Joint Legislation: Beautifully prepared laws, really meaning totally liberal in every aspect. Not a conservative bone in the body.

Patriotism: Nothing, there is to be none of this, period; unless of course you are celebrating May Day.

Being "Open-minded": This has nothing at all to do with seriously considering other people's ideas. To the contrary, liberals define being "open-minded" as agreeing with or yielding to the liberal mindset. What could be more close-minded than assuming that not only are you right, but that you do not even need to consider another viewpoint because anyone who disagrees must be evil?

Racism: Only white people who don't belong to the Democratic Party can be racist . . . .at least that's the presumption of a liberal. For example, even if Jeremiah Wright can make it clear, "Hey, like you know man," that he despises white people because of their skin color or if liberals take an explicitly racist political position, as for instance suggesting that black people are too stupid and incompetent to get identification to vote, they cannot be racist. White Republicans, on the other hand, are generally assumed to be racist by default, no matter how much evidence there is to the contrary.

Fairness: To liberals fairness is an arbitrary concept. So, you could make the argument that no one could get "fairness" wrong. Still, liberals do because they don't make any effort to actually "be reasonable." As a practical matter, liberals define "fairness" in terms as follows: taking as much as possible from people who they do not think are going to support liberalism, then giving a portion of the money to people who may vote for them in return for their ill-gotten largesse. Certainly conservatives, libertarians, and moderates might disagree about how much money to take from the wealthy to redistribute to the poor or how to help the disadvantaged. However, the only liberal answer to the question, "How much is enough?" is "more."

Greed: Defined as a "conservative" trying to keep more of your hard-earned money instead of giving it to the government. In fact, to a liberal, if you believe that you pay too much in taxes or even opposing paying more in taxes that is total, unadulterated greed. In actuality, wanting to loot as much money as possible that someone else has earned to use for your own purposes, which is what liberals do, is a much better example.

Extremist: An extremist is a conservative who is leading a Christian, law-abiding and community-minded lifestyle. If an individual votes Democrat or liberal, there is nothing in their life they can do to be called extremist.

Hate Speech: Any disagreement with a liberal or their philosophy. Examples are issues such as gay marriage, abortion, taxes, education issues, et al. It does not matter how thoroughly a position is defined or the logical foundation and underpinnings supporting it. If the position disagrees with the Leftist position, it is hate speech. Meanwhile, liberals are always the angriest, most vicious, most hateful entities in the political arena, railing against what they say is "hatred." This irony is completely "Saul Illinski-esque."

Charity: Taking away your tax dollars and giving them to people who liberals hope will vote for them in return. Now that is charity.

Tolerance: A noted "One-Way" street whereby you are forced to accept anything a liberal wants to do, much like being run over on the freeway. No tolerance for conservatism. Liberals silence people who disagree with them at every opportunity which is, dare we say it, an extremely intolerant behavior.

Diversity: Lots of different races, colors, and creeds, all voting progressive and having the identical liberal political view point of Harry Reid. That is diversity to a liberal. A black or Hispanic conservative is not "diverse," does not contribute to society in liberal eyes because he/she disagrees with them, though he/she actually has diverse views.

Feminist: Liberal female who yells and screams her venom, burns bras, uses hate speech, etc., all for a liberal progressive cause, and as such they prove they care about people's plights.

Sex Scandal: Any conservative politician running for any office who has proven they will not immediately support liberal legislation, or an individual who could cause liberals problems AND who has been insinuated in touching a person's shoulder in a wrong way. Incredible role models for women like Sarah Palin are guilty of a sex scandal to liberals because she doesn't share the same liberal beliefs as sexist hogs like Anthony Weiner and Bill Maher. Anthony Weiner is not in a sex scandal because he is a liberal. Impossible for the terms Democrat and sex scandal to be linked or used together in the same sentence; so say liberals.

Treason: Voting against a liberal bill, praying to God in public, reciting Scriptures in public, these are all classified as treason by Progressives. No such word in the liberal or progressive vocabulary.

Freedom: Being watched via cameras everyplace you go, being spied on via drones, having your personal phone conversations recorded, personal email messages read; but having a Nintendo, X-Box, or hand held game of some sort to play, now that is freedom according to a progressive.

Karl Marx and Ronald Reagan: Sacred, wonderful, brilliant, having the perfect world system, and sees all are just some of the adjectives a progressive will use when describing Komrad Karl. He is also part of the (unholy [my word]) trinity for liberals or progressives. Ronald Reagan was garbage because he stood against Karl and the resulting communism.

Progressive: A true American bringing hope and change to America to help the down trodden, minorities and underprivileged. <u>In truth</u>, the word "communist" should be used most any time for the word progressive.

Narrow-Minded: A Conservative, need a liberal say more?

Terrorists: Tea Party member, Christian, anyone caught carrying a Bible to school, anyone voicing opposition to Obama. You get the picture? However, the dictionary provides a different definition:

1. a person who rises in forcible opposition to lawful authority, especially a person who engages in armed resistance to a government or to the execution of its laws; rebel.

2. a member of a section of a political party that revolts against the methods or policies of the party.

Hmmm, doesn't sound to me like the Tea Party, or Christians, or anyone carrying a Bible to school.

Insurgent: Tea Party member, Christian, anyone caught carrying a Bible to school, etc., you get the picture. But let's see some more examples given in the dictionary.

1. rising in revolt against established authority, especially a government.

2. rebelling against the leadership of a political party.

Christians, the Tea Party, or children carrying Bibles to school, do not qualify as "insurgents." We have an established authority in the USA. It is called the Constitution. Tea partiers universally embrace the Constitution. Christians I know do too. They hold in antipathy the many politicians and elected officials who don't follow its tenets. The movement seems to be far more geared to removing incumbents than targeting one party for takeover. There is another alternative definition: "a person who rises in raucous revolt against civil authority or an established government, in particular one not recognized as a belligerent." Don't look at me. That is Washington. That is not the tea party or Christians. That is Barack Obama, Nancy Pelosi and Harry Reid.

Alien: (1) An undocumented visitor to Earth likes ones involved in the crash at Roswell, NM in 1947. (2) Not an undocumented worker, or whatever else you were thinking; there are only visitors to our land from other countries who are in various stages of immigration processing.

Freedom: The right of a liberal to persecute someone.

Anthony Weiner: A true hero of our time (at least to the Liberals). He speaks his mind, does not apologize for it. His hand gestures and other signals in public however, were embarrassing; and appeared to speak to his very limited vocabulary. He does have sexual "inconveniences," which should not be counted against him because he is a progressive.

Bob Filner: A great man, who really put the progressive government in place in San Diego, and, oh by the way, a man who was SO misunderstood. Sure he fondled women, but that mattereth not if thou art a liberal! And besides, the women probably asked for it.

Liberal: Old term. New term is Progressive. Meaning? Well whatever the heck the liberals . . . I mean . . . Progressives want it to mean at any particular time. Really means a patient Communist.

Social Justice: Leveling the playing field of poverty by using other people's money.

Gay Marriage: A compound redefinition if ever there was one. It is still puzzling over how 2 percent of Americans can compel the other 98 percent to refer to them as happy and carefree when their stated life is normally one of anger. Shorter than normal life expectancy and excessively high suicide rates clearly do not support the joyous life that is claimed. Also, what these adults do in private with other consenting adults do not concern me, but requiring me to support the lifestyle with my tax money and my vocabulary certainly does.

Hyper-feminist: Post 1973 feminists who are carriers of bras, some of them burning. They are yelling, "We have the right to choose!" That whopping lie is about all they know to say, except for the phrase "emergency contraception!" But those phrases keep working for them, so why change?

Gay Marriage: To liberals, the purest form of unions, opening the door for weddings between people and animals. For this term, see **Alien redefinition**.

Illegal Immigration: No such thing, to a liberal. These two words "illegal" and "immigration" can never be placed next to each other unless you are a racist and a homophobe. People who should not even be here have not missed the lesson, either. If you think "undocumented workers" are Americans who left their ID badges on the breakfast table, you have not been paying attention.

Hordes of southern illegals have redefined our great Southwest as their "Aztlan," a kingdom in Aztec mythology, and some violence-prone easterners both inside and outside the country have taken an even bigger bite out of our language, bringing new definitions with them, with "resistance" now meaning imperialism, "honor" meaning ego and "marriage" meaning the purchase of a slave from her owner. "Modesty" now requires wearing half the yard goods department and implies with a sneer that women, but not men, who dress normally, are somehow *immodest*. "Martyrdom" has become suicide intended to take along unwilling victims. "Innocent" means belonging to their particular religious cult, and "racism," although they are not a race, is the questioning of any of their actions, religious doctrines or demands. The press in some civilized countries even helps them out by designating them "Asians" no matter what continent they come from. Real Asians ought to sue for defamation of character.

If you were taken in as a refugee to escape persecution, given personal liberty you had never imagined and fed at the public trough for an indefinite period of time, would you have the gall to tell your host nation to redefine its own words according to what you would like them to mean? I didn't think so.

Conclusion

The pillaging of the dictionary to grab words and redefine them continues at light speed by the enemies of free speech.. Liberal logic says, if unable to silence people, the next best thing is to redefine their words so meanings are lost. In this redefining venue, the word "tolerance" has been laundered to mean forced acceptance, "rights" to mean special privileges for those with highly paid lobbyists, and "freedom" to mean the legality to oppress those on the Right. The Constitution upon which our government is based has been blended into minutiae. The founders who signed it would be so proud of what their country has become. Proud: this is my new "liberal" synonym for the word "ashamed."

"I've lived, sir, a long time, and the longer I live, the more convincing proofs I see of this truth: That God governs in the affairs of men.
If a sparrow cannot fall to the ground without His notice, is it probable that an empire can rise without His aid? We've been assured in the sacred writings that unless the Lord builds the house, they labor in vain who build it. I firmly believe this, and I also believe that without His concurring aid, we shall succeed in this political building no better than the builders of Babel"

~ Benjamin Franklin

Signer of the Declaration of Independence and the Constitution

Chapter Ten

Those Robbin' Hoods of 'Rotting'ham Forest

"Socialism is a philosophy of failure, the creed of ignorance, and the gospel of envy, its inherent virtue is the equal sharing of misery."

— *Winston Churchill*

ALEKSANDR SOLZHENITSYN, THE LATE RUSSIAN historian, novelist and critic of Soviet totalitarianism came to the United States in 1974 after being expelled from the USSR. The history of that "Evil Empire" records how he had been imprisoned earlier in a Soviet gulag for many years. There he wrote several books, of which the best known in the West was *Gulag Archipeligo*. After receiving an honorary PhD from Harvard, he gave the Commencement Address there on June 8, 1978, condemning rationalistic humanism in western culture. Few Americans heard him then; most who did, disagreed at first with his tenants. Probably, the filters and barriers of liberalized rationalistic humanism (secular humanism) got in the way. No matter the position at school, frosh, to graduate student, to senior faculty, he had a message for all. And for those on a career continuum, from union apprentice to CEO of a global firm, he had a message for them all in his address. These are a few excerpts, if you missed his magnificent sermon to America:

"The communist regime in the East could endure and grow due to the enthusiastic support from an enormous number of Western intellectuals who (feeling the kinship!) refused to see communism's crimes, and when they no longer could do so, they tried to justify these crimes. The problem persists: In our Eastern countries, communism has suffered a complete ideological defeat; it is zero and less than zero. And yet Western intellectuals [meaning Liberal Progressives] still look at it with considerable interest and empathy, and this is precisely what makes it so immensely difficult for the West to withstand the East."

"This statement has proved to be not entirely unreasonable. One does not see the same stones in the foundations of an eroded humanism and of any type of socialism: boundless materialism; freedom from religion and religious responsibility (which under Communist regimes attains the stage of antireligious dictatorship); concentration on social structures with an allegedly scientific approach. (This last is typical of both the Age of Enlightenment and of Marxism.) It is no accident that all of communism's rhetorical vows revolve around Man (with a capital M) and his earthly happiness. At first glance it seems an ugly parallel: common traits in the thinking and way of life of today's West and today's East? But such is the logic of materialistic development."

"Humanism which has lost its Christian heritage cannot prevail in this competition.... Thus during the past centuries and especially in recent decades, as the process became more acute, the alignment of forces was as follows: Liberalism was inevitably pushed aside by radicalism, radicalism had to surrender to socialism, and socialism could not stand up to communism.... Of course, a society cannot remain in an abyss of lawlessness, as is the case in our country. But it is also demeaning for it to stay on such a soulless and smooth plane of legalism, as is the case in yours. After the suffering of decades of violence and oppression, the human soul longs for things higher, warmer, and purer than those offered by today's mass living habits, introduced as by a calling card by the revolting invasion of commercial advertising, by TV stupor, and by intolerable music."

"All this is visible to numerous observers from all the worlds of our planet. The Western way of life is less and less likely to become the leading model."

"There are telltale symptoms by which history gives warning to a threatened or perishing society. Such are, for instance, a decline of the arts or a lack of great statesmen. Indeed, sometimes the warnings are quite explicit and concrete. The center of your democracy and of your culture is left without electric power for a few hours only, and all of a sudden crowds of American citizens start looting and creating havoc. The smooth surface film must be very thin, then, the social system quite unstable and unhealthy."

"... We have placed too much hope in politics and social reforms, only to find out that we were being deprived of our most precious possession: our spiritual life."[1]

In 1978, he was exactly right. Thirty-five years later, he's still exactly right. These Leftists in this country must certainly have read about Robin Hood of Nottingham Forest, decided when they were young congressional servants to emulate in part his moniker; take from the rich, and give to the poor. They have given a real-live twist to the story: they take from the rich and the poor, and then keep it. This makes them "The Robbin' Hoods of 'Rotting'ham Forest."

Speaking of those on the Left; the socialistic thinkers have for several decades tried to change their manner of festivities so as not to offend others. For several decades they have wanted us to halt patriotic celebrations, flag-waving, saying "God bless America," and using other patriotic slogans in fear that a foreigner or their culture might be offended. This has been especially true in regard to Muslims and their culture following the 9/11 attacks in New York City in 2001.

U. S. Congressman Barry Loudermilk is one, who after hearing the "Be Quiet!

You will offend them" chorus by the politically correct crowd was livid. He said, "In the weeks after the September 11th terrorist attacks I'd been growing more and more outraged. . . . I was tired of hearing about how we have to be so careful not to say anything that might offend anyone of a different culture. I was sick of hearing about organizations ordering even the smallest flags removed from employees' cubicles."[2] He wrote and submitted his thoughts in an article appearing in his Georgia hometown newspaper, the *Bartow Trader* and later in the *VietNow* National Magazine, entitled: "This is America. Like it or Leave it". The subtitle explained his logic with a certain crispness, "If you don't like the way we do things here, you are free to leave any time." His words were:

At a high school in Oklahoma, school officials remove "God Bless America" signs from schools in fear that someone might be offended.

At a Long Island, New York television station, management orders flags removed from the newsroom, and red, white, and blue ribbons removed from the lapels of reporters. Why? Management did not want to appear biased . . . felt our nation's flag might give the appearance that "they lean one way or another."

Officials in a California city ban U.S. flags from being displayed on city fire trucks because they didn't want to offend anyone in the community.

In an "act of tolerance," the head of the public library at a Florida university ordered all "Proud To Be an American" signs removed so as to not offend international students.

Politically Correct Attacks against America

I, for one, am quite disturbed by these actions of so-called "American citizens"; and I am tired of this nation worrying about whether or not we are offending some individual or their culture. Since the terrorist attacks on September 11th, we have experienced a surge of patriotism by the majority of Americans. However, the dust from the attacks had barely settled in New York and Washington, DC when the "politically correct" crowd began complaining about the possibility that our patriotism was offending others.

I am not against immigration, nor do I hold a grudge against anyone who is seeking a better life by coming to America. In fact, our country's population is almost entirely comprised of descendants of immigrants; however, there are a few things that those who have recently come to our country, and apparently some native-born Americans, need to understand.

If You're among the Politically Correct, Here's What You Need to Know

First of all, it is not our responsibility to continually try not to offend you in any way. This idea of America being a multi-cultural community has served only to dilute our sovereignty and our national identity. As Americans, we have our own culture, our own society, our own language, and our own lifestyle. This culture, called the "American Way" has been developed over centuries of struggles, trials, and victories by millions of men and women who have sought freedom. Our forefathers fought, bled, and died at places such as Bunker Hill, Antietam, San Juan Hill, Iwo Jima, Normandy, Korea, Vietnam, and the Persian Gulf, for our way of life.

We speak English, not Spanish, Arabic, Chinese, Japanese, Russian, or any other language. Therefore, if you wish to become part of our society, learn our language!

And Yes, We Do Trust in God

"In God We Trust" is our national motto. This is not some off-the-wall, Christian, right wing, political slogan. It is our national motto. It is engraved in stone in the House of Representatives in our Capitol, and it is printed on our currency. We adopted this motto because Christian men and women, on Christian principles, founded this nation; and this is clearly documented throughout our history. If it is appropriate for our motto to be inscribed in the halls of our highest level of government, then it is certainly appropriate to display it on the walls of our schools.

If God Offends You, Here's What to Do

"God is in our pledge, our National Anthem, nearly every patriotic song, and in our founding documents. We ... turn to Him in prayer in times of crisis. If God offends you, then I suggest you consider another part of the world as your new home, ... God is part of our culture, ... we are proud to have Him."

It's Our Heritage

We are proud of our heritage and those who have so honorably defended our freedoms. We celebrate Independence Day, Memorial Day, Veterans Day, and Flag Day. We have parades, picnics, and barbecues where we proudly wave our flag. As an American, I have the right to wave my flag, sing my national anthem, quote my national motto, and cite my pledge whenever and wherever I choose. If the Stars and Stripes offend you, or you don't like Uncle Sam, then you should seriously consider a move to another part of this planet.

This is Our Culture — If You Don't Like It, You're Free to Go Elsewhere

The American culture is our way of life, our heritage, and we are proud of it. We are happy with our culture and have no desire to change, and we really don't care how you did things where you came from. We are Americans. Like it or not, this is our country, our land, and our lifestyle.

Chapter Ten — Those Robbin' Hoods of 'Rotting'ham Forest

Our First Amendment gives every citizen the right to express his opinion about our government, culture, or society, and we will allow you every opportunity to do so. But once you are done complaining, whining, and griping about our flag, our pledge, our national motto, or our way of life, I highly encourage you to take advantage of one other great American freedom, the right to leave![3]

Messages delivered in speeches from the current leader of the free-world, Mr. Obama run in contrast. Refusing to salute the American Flag is just a start. When an act of terrorism was leveled on one military bases in Texas by a Muslim, he said "Don't jump to conclusions," calling it "workplace violence." Paraphrasing, other messages from him are, "Government must expand in large measure to meet the needs of our people . . . Give me your guns, you are safe with me . . . Stop clinging to your guns and your religion — you don't need them as we are transforming the nation — I'll need your money for that job. If you don't give it — I'll take it through taxes anyway; Trust me - I'll take care of you. When we finish installing Affordable Care, it will be the best health care the world has seen, and at such cheap prices! You can keep your doctor. If and when you are attacked, don't stand your ground — it's not fair since you might injure your attacker who could be African American . . . I guess you can't keep your doctor . . . Don't ever question Muslims, and by the way, you can keep your healthcare plan if you like it. . . . Mine is the most ethical administration. . . . Oh, I've got to run and get out of town; my vacation awaits." Frankly, his speeches and his actions have starting building a sophomoric legacy.

On balance, the public has lost confidence in him and our "other elected leaders." This is due at least partially to the lack of patriotism seen. The feeling on Main Street in Hometown, USA is that these "servants" have overall forgotten their sacred trust. This political amnesia has emboldened some officials to publicly stand in opposition to the good folks who sent them to the capitol. Not only are Americans "assurance free" from their representatives but believe they are losing their right to speak publicly about what they believe privately. We have allowed our social and cultural institutions to drift away from their moorings. We have allowed the public square to become what Richard John Neuhaus termed, "naked." We ceased being clear about the standards which we hold and the principles by which we judge, or, if we were clear in our own minds, we somehow abdicated the area of public discussion and institutional decision making to those who challenged our traditional values. As a result of our neglect, we have allowed the lowest political denominators to take control and steer the country in a dangerous direction. Over time, we have suffered a cultural breakdown — in areas like education, family life, crime, and drug use, as well as in our attitudes toward sex, individual responsibility, civic duty, and public service. While we may hate to admit it, Putin, a hungry Communist leader trying to rebuild the USSR, seems more credible than Obama. It has become so very clear that Solzhenitsyn was on target about America in his statements in the 70s. It is as if the U.S. has lost its way due to horrible leadership, only to join forces with Russia against their populations.

Will the Real Enemy Please Stand Up

One of the oldest misdirected notions in homo sapien history is that some people were born to give orders and others were born to obey. The powerful progressive elite believe that their resumes fit the former. Believing they possess wisdom superior to the masses, this faith qualifies them to be ordained to impose their will forcibly upon the remaining percentage. The silent majority we have heard so much about over the years have allowed the loudest Leftists in the public square to control the conversation in settling the issue. Solzhenitsyn in effect was saying this about our nation's direction years ago. Using his address as a benchmark, one can see the revelation of the Leftist agenda, its real purpose for the past 100 years has been deconstructing our republic with its capitalism, free enterprise system and religious platform. They not only insinuate, they claim they have superior wisdom, they boast they have the key to unlock the door to "Utopia."

There are many campaign slogans, TV ads, and billboards associated with the political Left when advertising their utopia. Slogans such as "Level the playing field" are very common. Or the ever popular, "Do you know the conservatives are trying to take away your free lunch?" "Fairness is sureness" or "You're either with us or you're racist" speaks volumes. Two more are in this category: "Reducing America's carbon footprint... one job at a time" and "Jump on board for free healthcare. Gov't tested; Pelosi approved." This faux utopia is a cheap model of what they were able to copy after seeing and test-driving the Soviet model. The claim from Leftists is that they can build a better socialism leading to a Utopia obscures two historical realities — one is the Soviets and the other is the Bolsheviks.

The American Left signifies that they offer a better socialism (their utopia) than that of the Soviets. They must obscure two fantasies in holding out or presenting this mythical model. The first fantasy is the "Democrat or Obama alternative" to Stalin, a thesis that purports a non-violent, market road to Socialism. This is their yellow brick road leading to the wizard — Marx and his theory. They necessitate that government must suppress private property and profits, especially those of conservatives, including all free-enterprise. The second fantasy purports to find the impetus behind Stalin's bloody revolution. They say this will lead to a cultural revolution which is tamer, but ultimately leads to massive upward mobility of the poor and blue collar workers, reaching equality for all.

Once these fables are in place, a very real moral dilemma and blame is assigned to anyone not embracing the theory. This forces any serious citizen to view the hidden "ash heap of history," the global carnage of well over 100 million innocent people who were murdered, killed in a gulag, or died from starvation in the multiple political regimes of the 20th Century. There was Hitler and his "holocaust." The Russian Bolsheviks and their "Red Terror" had preceded him. Stalin built upon the Communism Revolution bringing about the collectivization famine of 1932-33, also his "Great Purge," followed by the gulags of 1934-41. Less familiar figures are those hidden victims who passed through China; the *laogai*, China's "hidden labor camps," and China's "Great Leap Forward" of 1959-1961, the single largest famine in human history. In Cambodia, Pol-Pot mimicked Mao's Great Leap causing one out of every seven citizens to die, the highest proportion of forced deaths in any Communist country.

The little known fact is that each of these regimes started with an initial phase of Communism that had the appearance of being benign, even friendly, before some mythical wrong turn was made by the political leader to put them on "the wrong track." Standing in opposition to this claim are examples of what Communist leaders really wanted. Lenin for example, expected from the start, and even wanted, a civil war to destroy the "class enemies," the poor people in his country. That war was fought for decades against these peasants, the very ones the Communists said they were going to save. That war continued until 1953. The Marxist model offers the most colossal case of political carnage in the history of the world. The Leftists in our nation believe that socialism, and Communism offers the best answer to America and her future. All the fables hide these important facts about Marxism from a low-information crowd who are looking for their next meal, but not from the serious student.

Here in a nutshell is the description of the contrast between the Socialist and Leftist utopia and the opposing conservative capitalism. The Left sees conservative Americans, the veterans of the armed forces, those who fought and made a sacrifice for this country, those who work hard to get ahead, and all these who believe in democracy — they see those as the threat to America. The Left will push their slogans of equality and aid to the poor downtrodden, while attempting to hide their systematic crimes against the psyche of the same individuals. The terror, theft, lies, cover-ups, criminal activity, and deaths speak of the true facts as they attempt to build their faux Shangri-La. America's actual enemies; these current liberals, progressives, and Democrats have more in common with these old Leninist anti-democracy forces, more than most in this country would want to admit. They are in effect, robbin' hoods.

What It Means to Be a "Robbin' Hood"

It is impossible for a Leftist or Socialist today to be honest with the public about who they really are. They must lie. They must deceive voters. They must cloak who they are, pretending and using the words of conservatism to gain votes. If they were honest about who they were, the American public would not follow them. They would never win an election, at least not in the United States. Theirs is a life of pretense voters, they have to pretend to be something they are not, they have to cloak who they are. They often say things like, "We are the only political party that cares for the poor." That is a lie. Even given their definition of the term "cares for" it is an enormous exaggeration in two ways; 1) they want to keep citizens dependent upon their public fund handouts, and 2) they want to put every citizen in that bucket, spreading the misery throughout, robbing from the poor, then robbing the wealthy for even more; misery for everyone. 'Masked thieves' is an understated term for their true character. Following their theft, and ride out of town yelling "Hi Yo, We got the Silver," the media those stupid Democratic "Tontos" praise the masked men not for what they do, but for what they claimed they wanted to do for the poor; "Kemo Sabe has saved them again!" It is all a lie. It is all rhetoric!

To understand a liberal progressive in today's America, it is best to keep Solzhenitsyn's comments in mind. He had experience with Communism, Soviet-style, which is very much like Communism American-style (aka, it is called Liberalism, Progressive-style). Whatever promotion they push and whatever tag they hang on the promotional item, be it education, healthcare, all the way to pop cycles, they tie the central government to it. Government must be the centerpiece of their agenda in every citizen's life, providing the regulations, penalties, sustenance, down to the very meals that you eat. The plan does not work, because government has no product — it never produces anything but misery. But don't confuse a liberal with facts.

Liberalism, Another False Religion

Human nature being what it is, "humans" will find something to honor and worship; it is inescapable. If God is not the deity, then up will go a wooden carving or a stone face of an idol, and if not that, then eventually they will put themselves on an altar. It is my contention that liberal Leftist philosophy, that includes Democrats, Progressives, humanists, American socialists, and Marxist, or Communist disciples, are all actually a part of an organized religious or faith system. It falls under the title of secular humanism and qualifies as an official religion where there are idols, where there is worship, and there are absolute quantifiable tenants of their faith. These humanists have been "evangelizing" for their religion through the decades. For example, the Judeo-Christian faith was dominant in the American classroom for nearly two centuries. That all changed in the 20th Century with the tipping point coming in 1962 with the push of the liberals, with the promotion of their religion called Secular Humanism, or Relativistic Humanism. That year, you may recall, the courts began the process to systematically secularize the nation, saying there was no place for the Judeo Christian God in the public arena. Any attempt to try to teach any principles in school which are Biblical, results in law suits, stating they violate the separation of church and state. But what they really meant was, in this case, Judeo-Christian thought violates the religion of the state, secular humanism.

These humanists will swear they do not adhere to any religion. Their claim is false. They do. One author explains: "Liberals love to boast that they are not 'religious,' which is what one would expect to hear from the state-sanctioned religion. Of course liberalism is a religion. It has its own cosmology, its own miracles, its own beliefs in the supernatural, its own churches, its own high priests, its own saints, its own total worldview, and its own explanation of the existence of the universe. In other words, liberalism contains all the attributes of what is generally known as 'religion.'"[4]

While one author sees the general framework to the religion, another one sees not only the structure, but the evil grip it has had on education in America going back to the 1930s, which still pronounces that there can be no other ideologies, and no gods allowed. That author states, "Humanism appeals to the intellect . . . Although endowed with great talent and creativity, [they] are apt to be idealistic, theoretical, and impractical, making them vulnerable to humanistic philosophy, even though it has a long history of disorder, anguish, and despair."[5]

The structure of Humanist religion is organized in the tenants or "doctrines" which have been taught publically ever since the 1930s. *The Humanist Manifesto I* was first published in the 1933 and was signed by thirty-four liberal humanists — their leader being none other than John Dewey, who is known as the Father of Modern American Education. For the secular humanist, this Manifesto is equivalent to the Bible. Among other things, it talked of a new religion (humanism) to transcend and replace faiths that spoke of a supernatural deity. Their guide book was revised in 1973, *The Humanist Manifesto II*, displaying five basic doctrines of the faith, proclaiming itself a "positive declaration for times of uncertainty." The following provides a summation of their quotes:

Tenant I: Atheism

"Religious humanists regard the universe as self-existing and not created. . . . We find insufficient evidence for belief in the existence of a supernatural; it is either meaningless or irrelevant to the question of the survival and fulfillment of the human race. As non-theists, we begin with humans, not God, nature, not deity. Nature may indeed be broader and deeper than we now know; any new discoveries, however, will but enlarge our knowledge of the natural. . . . But we can discover no divine purpose or providence for the human species. While there is much that we do not know, humans are responsible for what we are or will become. No deity will save us, we must save ourselves."

Tenant II: Evolution

"Humanism believes that man is part of nature and that he has emerged as a part of a continuous process. . . . Holding an organic view of life, humanists find that the traditional dualism of mind and body must be rejected . . . Humanism recognizes that man's religious culture and civilization, as clearly depicted by anthropology and history, are the product of a gradual development due to his interaction with his natural environment and with his social heritage. The individual born into a particular culture is largely molded to that culture . . . science affirms that the human species is an emergence of natural evolutionary forces. As far as we know, the total personality is a function of the biological organism transacting in a social and cultural context. There is no credible evidence that life survives the death of the body. We continue to exist in our progeny and in the way that our lives have influenced others in our culture."

Tenant III: Amorality

"We affirm that moral values derive their source from human experience. Ethics is autonomous and situational, needing no theological or ideological sanction. Ethics stems from human need and interest. To deny this distorts the whole basis of life. In the area of sexuality, we believe that intolerant attitudes, often cultivated by orthodox religions and puritanical cultures, unduly repress sexual conduct. The right to birth control, abortion, and divorce should be recognized. While we do not approve of exploitive, denigrating forms of sexual expression, neither do we wish to prohibit, by law or social sanction, sexual behavior between consenting adults. The many varieties of sexual exploration should not in themselves be considered "evil." Without countenancing mindless permissiveness or unbridled promiscuity, a civilized society should be a tolerant one. Short of harming others or compelling them to do likewise, individuals should be permitted to express their sexual proclivities and pursue their life-styles as they desire. We wish to cultivate the development of a responsible attitude toward sexuality, in which humans are not exploited as sexual objects, and in which intimacy, sensitivity, respect and honesty in interpersonal relations are encouraged. Moral education for children and adults is an important way of developing awareness and sexual maturity."

Tenant IV: Individual Autonomy

"Human life has meaning because we create and develop our futures. Happiness and the creative realization of human needs and desires, individually and in shared enjoyment, are continuous themes of humanism. We strive for the good life, here and now. The goal is to pursue life's enrichment despite debasing forces of vulgarization, commercialization, bureaucratization, and dehumanization. . . . Reason and intelligence are the most effective instruments that humankind possesses. There is no substitute: neither faith nor passion suffices in itself. The controlled use of scientific methods, which have transformed the natural and social sciences since the Renaissance, must be extended further in the solution of human problems. . . . To enhance freedom and dignity the individual must experience a full range of civil liberties in all societies. This includes freedom of speech and the press, political democracy, the legal right of opposition to government policies, fair judicial process, religious liberty, freedom of association, and artistic, scientific and cultural freedom. It also includes a recognition of an individual's right to die with dignity, euthanasia, and the right to suicide."

"We oppose the increasing invasion of privacy, by whatever means, in both totalitarian and democratic societies. We would safeguard, extend and implement the principles of human freedom evolved from the *Magna Carta* to the Bill of

Rights, the Rights of Man, and the Universal Declaration of Human Rights.... The preciousness and the dignity of the individual person is a central humanist value. Individuals should be encouraged to realize their own creative talents and desires. We reject all religious, ideological, or moral codes that denigrate the individual, suppress freedom, dull intellect, dehumanize personality. We believe in maximum individual autonomy consonant with social responsibility. Although science can account for the causes of behavior, the possibilities of individual freedom of choice exist in human life and should be increased."

Tenant V: Socialistic One-World View

"We deplore the division of humankind on nationalistic grounds. We have reached a turning point in human history where the best option is to transcend the limits of national sovereignty and to move toward the building of a world community in which all sectors of the human family can participate. Thus we look to a development of a system of world law and world order based upon transnational federal government. This would appreciate cultural pluralism and diversity. It would not exclude pride in national origins and accomplishments nor the handling of regional problems on a regional basis. Human progress, however, can no longer be achieved by focusing on one section of the world, Western or Eastern, developed or underdeveloped. For the first time in human history, no part of humankind can be isolated from any other. Each person's future is in some way linked to all. We thus reaffirm a commitment to the building of world community, at the same time recognizing that this commits us to some hard choices.... The problems of economic growth and development can no longer be resolved by one nation alone; they are worldwide in scope. It is the moral obligation of developed nations to provide — through an international authority that safeguards human rights — massive technical, agricultural, medical and economic assistance, including birth control techniques, to the developing portions of the globe. World poverty must cease. Hence, extreme disproportions in wealth, income, and economic growth should be reduced on a worldwide basis.

The principle of moral equality must be furthered through elimination of all discrimination based upon race, religion, sex, age, or national origin. This means equality of opportunity and recognition of talent and merit. Individuals should be encouraged to contribute to their own betterment. If unable, then society should provide means to satisfy their basic economic, health, and cultural needs, including, wherever resources make possible, a minimum guaranteed annual income."[6]

Reading the manifesto, certain terms and terminology stick out like a sore thumb; phrases like "we believe" in connection to evolution, speak of a faith system, but one that attempts to destroy individualism, something tenant 5 claims to uphold. It should be noted that secular humanists believe their agenda should be accepted by all, and then financed in totality by other people's money. The tenants and their entire platform sound strangely like they came out of the same box as the tenants of the Communist Manifesto. Phrases like "we believe" also seem strange within a movement that claims not to possess a religious path.

Exclusivity is the desire of humanists when they teach their doctrines, all the while saying they will not tolerate religion to be taught to children, in public places, or on government property. "Under the guise of not favoring religion, liberals favor one cosmology over another and demand total indoctrination into theirs. The state religion of liberalism demands obeisance (to the National Organization for Women), tithing (to teachers' unions), reverence (for abortion), and formulaic imprecations ("Bush lied, kids died!"; "Keep your laws off my body!" "Arms for hostages!"). Everyone is taxed to support indoctrination into the state religion through the public schools, where innocent children are taught a specific belief system, rather than, say, math."[7]

Humanism is not only a religion that hates most other faith systems, Humanists especially hate Christianity. They do this under a guise of deception, as they fear one religion, Islam; and they attempt to mask the terrorism within the faith. Also, they never want to be questioned about their stances, or else they might turn violent, as they accuse Christians of, or like those practitioners of Islam, the so-called "Religion of Peace, who ransacked Danish embassies worldwide because a Danish newspaper published a cartoon of Mohammed. This is something else that can't be taught in government schools: Muslims' penchant for violence. On the first anniversary of the 9/11 attack, the National Education Association's instruction materials exhorted teachers, 'Do not suggest that any group is responsible' for the 9/11 attack."[8]

The absence of an apparent divinity makes a liberal's statements about humanism seem credible at first, but it is no less religious. Liberals define "religion" as only those belief systems that subscribe to the notion of a divine being in order to dismiss other religions as mere religion and theirs as something greater. Shintoism and Buddhism have no Creator God either, and they are considered religions. Curiously, those are two of the most popular religions among leftists — at least until 9/11, when Islam became all the rage.[9]

Then, gaze into the worlds of Karl Marx, Saul Alinsky, and George Soros. While all of them claimed they hated religions, they were all members of this Church of Liberalism, wanting government and self on a throne that ruled in their own lives as well as other's lives. And what Marx was to theory, Alinsky and Soros were and, are to application. Once you understand just some of the major tenants of Marx and Alinsky, you will become aplomb of how progressives work, how they mislead others, to eventually force their agenda into place for this country.

Karl Marx

Being a German philosopher, Marx spent most of his life in exile within Great Britain and France. After watching what he called the "proletariat" work long hours and become ravaged financially by greedy overlords, he put pen to paper and began to write his solution for their case in what became the Communist Manifesto in 1848. The political theory of socialism, which gave rise to communism, had been around for hundreds of years by the time Marx was on the scene. Socialism was tried in many different settings throughout history. Marx's "Manifesto" was the icing on a cake and connected some of the dots that later served as the inspiration for the formation of the Communist Party.

The Marxist Precepts

Marx believed that a truly utopian society must be classless and stateless. (Marx died well before any of his theories were put to the test, but to an ideologue, ideas are the crucial thing on which to hold, not the testing of them.) Marx's main idea was simple: Free the lower class from poverty and as he said, "give the poor a fighting chance." It sounds great on the surface, which is why so many are suckered by today's Leftists. How he believed it should be accomplished, however, was another story. Marx believed that the government must have control of all production if the lower class is to be liberated. Labor must be organized; no one makes more than another in their class. The theory sounds good, but will not work long term due to human nature.

In Marx's "Communist Manifesto", he described three essential phases which must be achieved to reach what he called his idea of utopia. They are:

Phase 1: A revolution must take place in order to overthrow the existing government. Marx emphasized the need for total destruction of the existing system in order to move on to Phase two. It can be called just about anything, including transformation, but the key is to destroy what was there before.

Phase 2: A dictator or elite leader (or leaders) must gain absolute control over the proletariat. During this phase of transformation, the new government must exert absolute control over the common citizen's personal choices — including his or her education, religion, health care, employment, housing, and even marriage when possible. "**Collectivization**" of property and wealth, aka, government taking control, must also take place.

Phase 3: Achievement of utopia. In a Marxist utopia, everyone within the bounds of the country, the "utopia," would happily share property and wealth, free from the restrictions that class-based systems require. This phase has never been attained because it requires that all non-communists be destroyed in order for the Communist Party to achieve supreme equality. Too many upper-class individuals are also unwilling to release their wealth, though they preach this precept for everyone else. The key is for those in control; it always involves other people's money. In other words, everyone participates or there is no utopia. Theoretically, the government would control all means of production so that the one-class system would remain constant, with no possibility of any middle class citizens rising back to the top.

Marx also detailed his ten (10) essential earmarks of communism, namely the following:

- Central banking system
- Government controlled education
- Government controlled labor
- Government ownership of transportation and communication vehicles
- Government ownership of agricultural means and factories
- Total abolition of private property
- Property rights confiscation
- Heavy income tax on everyone, at a rate of 80 per cent
- Elimination of rights to inheritance through taxation, etc.
- Regional planning

Of these ten principles, modern Progressives and in particular Mr. Obama appears to believe in each one wholeheartedly.

In the Communist society of which Marx dreamed, the government is supreme through land control and all production. Because the government distributes land and property among the people, Communism sets a standard of equality — both economically and socially — among the citizens. This allows for the spreading of misery as witnessed in the Soviet Union.

Communism, like many liberal dreams, sounds attractive at first; it has a published face which seems friendly and benign. It is needed to satisfy this demented idea of fairness which is only emptiness.

Meet George Jetson

Among my favorite television shows as a pre-teen and even as a teenager, was The Jetsons. George Jetson was the luckiest man in the world I thought. He had everything at the touch of his fingers or at the end of an automatic walkway. Even the dog walk was motorized! The progressives must have watched the Jetsons back in the 60s on Saturday morning, as I did. It was great to see this family, living in that futuristic society which was supposed to be before the beginning of the 21st Century, with conveyor belts running through the house to take you from room to room. Taking trips through the solar system was really groovy, stopping at the snack bar and shops on the Moon, Mars, or the rings of Saturn for a refreshing space burger, topped off with a Moon Crater Shake!

Especially, I loved George Jetson's car, the glass bubble car which appeared to run on hydrogenated water. These cars folded up into a brief case at the push of a button, for an easy carry into the office. They could fly about anyplace, with the little exhaust bubbles coming out the back, which I believe were made of water vapor. Upon arrival in this new century where they are supposed to exist, my question was, "Where are they? Why don't we drive cars like that? The Leftists have been screaming about carbon footprints. What better way to reduce the size of your print than with a car that gets 2,000 miles per drop of water!! George Jetson's job was cool too; he only pushed one button periodically with his feet on his desk. Where are those jobs?" Simple answer; the world does not work that way. It was a cartoon, pretty, but an empty a dream; not realistic.

Utopias are a great dream too. It would be great to have one, where no one wants for anything, but listen carefully, it will not work in this lifetime. Why? There will always an occasional Obama or another liberal elite who believes themselves above citizens in society. They will take their $180,000,000 week long vacations and expect the underlings to work harder and to sacrifice so he can take more expensive vacations. That's why! Evil, greedy people will keep a utopia from working. Government cannot govern the evil out of society, mostly because they start fostering the evil themselves.

Back to School

Marxist theories taught by professors in colleges sound great to the professors teaching them, and to many of the students because they are all in a classroom — without real application, they are just theories. This past summer, we went to eat at one of our favorite eateries in a suburb having a major university, which is very liberal of course. While waiting on our table to open, we sat at the bar getting some liquid refreshment until the table became available. Within the first minute of our arrival another couple came to the bar too, accidentally bumping into us, as they were ordering drinks. This gave us an opportunity to exchange pleasantries and get acquainted. The gentleman's introduction included a confident remark, almost egotistical in manner, that he was a professor of economics at the university. He seemed disappointed when I did not feign a reverent response, like saying, "Oh, my! How brilliant you must be!" He asked about my profession, and I shared my story of heading a business unit for a global engineering firm. We immediately jumped into a discussion as he asked me what I thought was the most expensive cost item that was holding back engineering and manufacturing firms. I quickly replied, "Funding pensions, high salaries, and expensive benefits packages, and corporate taxes." He quickly replied, "On my no; that is incorrect. Those have nothing to do with the problem." He then stressed how critical it was for government to take more control of the business sector, unionizing it, thus making it fairer and more profitable. This comment opened a major can of worms for our discussion, as I told him he didn't seem to understand at least some of the basics of economics in business. I asked where he researched his data. There was no answer.

Toward the end of that little discussion (aka, debate) in the pizzeria eatery, I suggested to the professor that he take a sabbatical from his teaching, take a job in private industry, preferably in a large firm, possibly in the marketing department, and try his theoretical ideas as a real world experiment. I also told him that he would sadly discover that in the real world where products have to be delivered on time and under budget, his ideas would not be accepted, because they will not work, unless price is no object. I would prefer these "think tank" gurus to stop teaching their Marxist, Communist propaganda. I would prefer they teach their students to apply their skills in the real world first. Marx's ideas sound very appealing to a young student; the ideology is safe from harm because he is on a campus, where the theoretical reigns have no challengers. The Mr. Professors of the world build their ideology everyday calling it the great equalizer and savior for mankind. But the problem we have seen in this case, is not a solution at all. It is a lie, a fake, similar to the world of the Jetsons. But it sure is fun to pretend sometimes and watch those bubbles coming out of the tailpipe of his car.

By the way, our professor could learn in a real job for a year or two, that in industry, something has to be "produced." Government fails on that point. It can only take things away from people, like money in taxes. And the professors will find out their theories are just that — theories, which are insulated from the real world behind the walls of a college campus. If honest with themselves, they would try their theories in the real world of free enterprise and discover they are not the utopia builders for the future, but just theories, and bad ones at that. My advice dear doctor, stick to the curriculum of finance, leave government ownership out, because Marx was wrong.

Saul Alinsky

Alinsky had a level of brilliance, though genius can be evil, as it was with him. Multiply his brilliance by 20X and you are approaching the level of evil. Under the guise of wanting to help people, everyone on the Left (especially the progressive arm of this movement), from the president on down through the senators and representatives are playing by Saul Alinsky's "Rules for Radicals." This is performed in this squared circle called the political arena.

If a Martian were to land in America and set out to determine what official rule book was being used in the country, he would have to conclude that it was Alinksy's Rules for Radicals. Most liberals follow it step by step. Conservatives are spanked by the tenants from that book daily. Not all liberals have read his book or even know his name, but his tactics have become universally used by Communists and Socialists. Sadly for conservatives, when two evenly matched forces go head-to-head outside of a fairy tale, the side that tries to play nice usually ends up with its head in a box. What is also angering is that most conservatives either have not read Alinsky, have not even heard of him, or they do not care to get acquainted with his instructions. Every conservative needs to learn from Alinsky, for he provides

CHAPTER TEN — THOSE ROBBIN' HOODS OF 'ROTTING'HAM FOREST

marching orders for the Left. Keep your friends close and your enemies closer; that is the motto of a wise man. Besides, if the tenants of Alinsky are learned by the Conservatives, they can in turn provide the Leftists in this country a dose of their own medicine. This is the leveling of the playing field I would prefer.

Alinsky wrote *Rules For Radicals*, a must read in understanding the current progressive mindset. Of course, he is famous for having dedicated his work to what some call his hero, Satan himself. (Text of dedication shown in Chapter Six) This text is proof of a religion.

These tenants are:

1. **Power is not only what you have but what the enemy thinks you have.** Boycotts have fallen out of favor on the Right because the Left has used that tactic to target conservative radio. This is a mistake. That's because there are a lot more conservatives than there are liberals and we're much more capable of using the tactic effectively. There are roughly 160 million people who identify with conservatism in this country and roughly half that many are Christians. Threats that Christians and conservatives will refuse to go see movies, stop buying products, or cancel subscriptions, will scare some people straight. That threat should be used and carried out much more often.

2. **Never go outside the experience of your people.** When an action or tactic is outside the experience of the people, the result is confusion, fear and retreat . . . [and] the collapse of communication. Liberal Progressive politics starts at this point on a platform of divide and conquer — meaning they will always address Americans not as a whole, but as ethnic groups, e.g., Hispanics, African Americans, Whites, etc. This is called "identity politics." Conservatives and especially Republicans historically have not been good in identity politics; at reaching out to minority groups — they tend to see Americans through a color blind lens. Because identity politics works really, really well in the 21st Century culture but on principle, conservatives tend to oppose its use. The media builds a brand of white Conservatives or Republicans as hating minorities — their experience in reaching out to minorities has not usually been well-received because of the brand of negatives about them on TV, radio, and written press. Recalling a conversation with a relative who listens only to NBC News verifies this premise: She said, "Well, the Democrats are the only ones who care about poor people — the news said so." In a nutshell, that's the problem. Conservatives as a whole, and especially the GOP needs to accept and adopt the reality and tactics of the Democratic Party. That is, to get their own versions of Al Sharpton and Jesse Jackson to reach out to minority groups with talking points. When they do they can show

the Democrat Party to be the racists they really are — the end result will be making inroads with minorities for the first time in decades.

3. **Wherever possible go outside the experience of the enemy.** Alinsky taught to look for ways to increase insecurity, anxiety and uncertainty. (This happens all the time. Watch how many organizations under attack are blind-sided by seemingly irrelevant arguments that they are then forced to address.) This simply means Liberal Progressives will drag arguments outside the realm conservatism, *per se*, into the social arena or into anti-religious topics. Social issues are not the strong point of the GOP or conservatives — they tend to avoid them. And conservatives historically do not defend Christianity well — they avoid that subject also. A huge percentage of the country claims Christian beliefs their avoidance of the issue is a huge mistake. Christianity and Christian beliefs are repugnant to liberals. While Progressives view Christians as being akin to a scene from the movie *Elmer Gantry* with the wagging fingers, loud rhetoric, or sermons. We don't have to be a Ned Flanders, but we shouldn't be afraid to talk about our Christian beliefs, certainly stick up for Christians who are under attack, and hammer the Left for its anti-Christian bigotry. Conservatism is contained in a pro-Christian ideology. <u>**Liberalism is an anti-Christian ideology**</u>. We should never be afraid to drive that point home.

4. **Make the enemy live up to their own book of rules.** Alinsky's disciples have been defeating many conservatives with this — for they can no more obey their own rules than the Christian church can live up to Christianity. Liberal Progressives have owned this territory for 70 years — conservatives have gotten much better the last few years, but seldom go far enough. Being a liberal means you hold conservatives to a strict set of rules, always trying to enforce them. However, the same liberalism gives you *cart blanch* to avoid the liberal rule book. In fact being inconsistent in not walking the talk is a resume enhancer. The proof is revealed in the Obama Administration — a tax cheat advocates higher taxes for the masses from the Office of Treasury Secretary, Barack Obama associates openly with race hustlers like Al Sharpton, a "one per-center" like Warren Buffet gets away with his tax homilies, and Al Gore's mansion has every light on in the place as he lectures Americans on carbon footprints. Note he continues to be the leader of the cult on climate change (formerly global warming) while the polar ice caps grow larger and larger the last few years. Liberals focus on conservative sins.

5. **[4b] Ridicule is man's most potent weapon.** It is extremely difficult to counteract ridicule. Also it infuriates the opposition, which then works to your advantage. Liberals always attack logic — the reason

is that logic is never supporting their argument. Liberals use emotion, e.g., dragging a wheelchair bound and paralyzed Christopher Reeve on stage to attack Conservatives for not supporting fetus stem cell research. Right wingers have a tendency to try to win every debate with logic and recitations of facts which, all too often, is never seen or heard by average viewers — they are too busy feeling sorry for the guy in the wheelchair. The really good news is that liberals almost never have logic on their side, in fact they have to mask who they are, and they lie about their platform, in order to get any appeal. First, if they told the truth about themselves, nobody would buy their arguments. So while incapable of using rational arguments, they will follow old Saul's remedy — attack the opponent's most potent arsenal — and that's reason or logic. Conservatives can become considerably better debaters by simply adding some emotion-based arguments and emotion to their discourse. Listen to Dana Loesch, Glenn Beck, Laura Ingraham, or Mark Levine. They are all conservatives who don't mind "calling a spade a spade." They don't play Mr. Nice Guy, nor should they.

6. **A good tactic is one that your people enjoy.** Allinsky taught his liberal disciples they should stay in the arena of fun, like having loud rock and roll band members assisting with a fund raiser to support their cause. I'd like to see the Conservatives get big body suits characters made into the likeness of Nancy Pelosi, Harry Reid and Barrack Obama — the suits being much in the same character of past presidents who run races at baseball games. Wouldn't it be great to photo-shop them onto old films like using Abbott and Costello to meet the Marxists?! Or tripping them up as they run the ballpark race?! A little controversy and fun would draw in the eyeballs and get people excited. Besides that's turning around rule number 6 around on them for a change.

7. **A tactic that drags on too long becomes a drag.** A person can sustain militant interest in any issue for only a limited time.... This one seems self-explanatory, but in practice, it can be tough to keep things on a timeline. This is what happened to the Occupy Movement, the wars in Iraq and Afghanistan, and the Republican race for the presidency, too. If it goes on too long, people sour on it whether it's a war, an election, or a tactic.

8. **Keep the pressure on.** Liberal Progressives are good at keeping the pressure on Conservatives — they know how to keep especially the GOP jumping back and forth on one issue after another. The diversion of all this is that while the pressure is on and the Conservatives are doing jumping jacks, the liberals are free to move ahead with creating

more destruction by starting another scandal, or shielding something shameful they have committed. Case in point — The murders in Benghazi; while an investigation is almost started, Democrats keep the pressure on by starting a scandal about women's pay packages. This if followed by another scandal involving supposed "prisoner swaps" of Taliban generals for what appears to be an American Army deserter. All the while Benghazi is left in the dust by the Republican dogs chasing the sticks that Democrats throw. And Conservatives, Republicans, etc., never seem to learn to play the game from their opponents. For example, just when Obama's SuperPac was starting to feel real pressure over taking a **million dollar donation from Bill Maher in 2012**, conservatives dropped their discussion of the topic — like getting the dog to chase another stick. This is why liberal film stars feel so comfortable trashing conservatives, Christians, and Americans in general — even right before their film comes out. It's because we get offended, shrug our shoulders, and then almost immediately let it go.

9. **The threat is usually more terrifying than the thing itself.** Alinsky knew that Conservatives usually don't have the stomach to follow through on fixing problems caused by Leftists. He knew their threats were hallow. We should treat the Leftists with good doses of their own medicine. Like, every time they make an accusation against a Conservative, take out two of their leaders by revealing their activities publicly. When they post addresses of gun owners in New York, for example, we should post addresses of Liberal Senators and Representatives including private phone numbers — then start calling and visiting them. If they hold a protest at someone's house; then we hold 5 protests at Liberal network news owner's homes. They hit one of our politicians with mud; we hit 5 of their politicians with real scandals. Liberals have a mentality that says, "Everything we do is harmless, but everything conservatives do is potentially dangerous." Yet, in this war, we've been too well behaved to respond to their tactics. Now is the time to stop that. There's a prescription that works. When the Liberals throw one pie, conservatives should throw 10 or more back at them. Respond to their tactics once or twice in such a manner and the Libs will cry foul, because it will be too costly for them to continue their tactics.

10. **The major premise for tactics is the development of operations that will maintain a constant pressure upon the opposition.** It is this unceasing pressure that brings reactions from the opposition essential for the success of the campaign. The Clintons and the Obamas certainly followed in their mentors dictates on this rule. They never stop hammering on a theme in the press — that keeps the pressure on Conservatives. Their theme says, if it is working, keep doing it. We need to

respond in kind, following the same rules. John Kerry is a flip-flopper, Bill Clinton is a liar, Barack Obama is a liar and is bankrupting the country economically and morally, wrecking the country. Learn from the liberals — tie your attacks into themes that can be picked up on social media, talk radio, cable TV, and in the blogosphere over the long haul. Where do you think the term "drive-by media" was coined? By Rush Limbaugh; now almost everyone uses the term to show the shallowness of the press. Notice how Obama always calls people who love the 2nd Amendment, "extremists." Why does McDonald's keep running ads? Because it may be that 50th ad or 100th ad you see that gets you to go buy a Big Mac, just as it may be the 50th or 100th time someone hears that Obama is bankrupting the country and wrecking the economy before it sticks. People tend to be like sheep, totally asleep; that's when rote learning comes happens by constant repetition.

11. **If you push a negative hard and deep enough it will break through into its counter side.** This makes the point every positive has its negative. The winner in a political race is almost always the one who is on offense. Liberals understand this in an intuitive way that most conservatives don't. We think because we have this wonderful, honest, logical response to a charge made that we're scoring major points with voters — but, except in rare cases, it's not true. If you're spending all of your time refuting the charges that you're extreme, racist, hate women, and despise the poor — you're losing, at least in the eyes of the public. That's because some people will assume where there's smoke, there's fire — they choose to believe that something is true because it is on the news so often. Additionally, if you're busy defending yourself, you can't go after the other side. Defend when you absolutely have to, but make sure most of your time is spent attacking relentlessly attacking.

12. **The price of a successful attack is a constructive alternative.** Notice that when liberals attack long enough and hard enough, some alternative action is usually taken by those being attacked. Typically, it is with legislation being withdrawn or massaged into something that it was never intended to be. For example, Liberals always clamor that the thousands of gun laws already in place aren't enough. Their continual beating of drums usually leads to some new legislation to take guns away from law-abiding citizens. They would call that constructive — ripping out some functional necessity of American society so they can replace it with an ill-defined hodgepodge of ideas that they think will shift power their way or be less "mean." Conservative ideas are best. We should use the same rule to attack with goo legislation.

13. **Pick the target, freeze it, personalize it, and polarize it.** In tactical war, there are certain rules that should always be followed. One is that the opposition must be singled out as the targeted person and "frozen." ... When you freeze the targeted individual, that person will usually cry for help saying, "Why are you focusing on me when it's not really my fault ... there are so many others who caused this?" In freezing the target, the rational argument is negated, but arguments in war are distracting and need to be negated. Then, as one zeroes in and freezes the target, continuing the attack, others for the cause will come out of the woodwork very quickly. They become visible in their support for the target, and become a target themselves.

Conservatives tend to do well with this one until they get to the last part. Polarization is at the core of the Left's strategy. According to liberals, if you're conservative, you hate blacks, Hispanics, gays, Jews, Muslims, women, the poor, the middle class, the environment, and probably a half dozen other groups I've forgotten. Even when something is in front of our face, conservatives shy away from polarization. What's wrong with pointing out how hostile the Democratic Party has become to Christianity? Why not point out the truth: that most white liberals are racists who think black Americas are too stupid and incompetent to compete with white Americans, which is why they push Affirmative Action and racial set asides? Why not note that liberals want poor Americans to stay poor and dependent, because as long as they do, they'll keep voting for the Democrat Party? There's a reason Barack Obama bows to foreign leaders, is constantly apologizing for America, attended an anti-white, anti-American church for 20 years, and it's why <u>his wife was proud of the country for the FIRST TIME</u> because she saw it elected her husband. The sad truth is that these are people who hate and despise what has made this country great. Why do you think "hope and change" appealed so much to Obama that he made it his theme? When you look at America as an evil, racist, unfair, horrible place to live, inhabited by ignorant trash and "bitter clingers," what else would you do other than hope for change? If you love this country and the values it represents, the people in the White House not only don't share those values, they hold such people in utter contempt.

Always remember the first rule of power tactics. Here they are in more abbreviated format: "One acts decisively only in the conviction that all the angels are on one side and all the devils on the other."[10]

Reading the rules designed for attack upon society and its ultimate destruction, remember those who embrace them. They are the same ones who promise to take care of the poor, to care for the sick and heal the blind. In reality they wear masks and speak lies, hiding their true identity.

George Soros

While many Americans will still say "George Who?" when Soros' name is men-

Chapter Ten — Those Robbin' Hoods of 'Rotting'ham Forest

tioned, CBS' "Sixty Minute's" Steve Kroft did a four-month research project into George's past that revealed critical facts about George Soros; his early years and background, his beliefs, his world view, and what he'd like to see done in the world. During an interview with Kroft, Soros was asked about his youth, growing up in Hungary as a Jew, and working with the man who took the property of fellow Jews in 1944. Soros has repeatedly called 1944 his "best year," in fact, "the best year of his life." What makes his statement more interesting and disturbing is this: "70 percent of Mr. Soros's fellow Jews in Hungary, nearly a half-million human beings, were annihilated in that year, yet he gives no sign that this put any damper on his elation, either at the time or indeed in retrospect."

The text below is an excerpt from a transcript of the actual exchange between Kroft and how Soros responded to each question during his interview. The Soros storied background is important in understanding both the questions and the Soros responses. Kroft questioned Soros regarding his life in Nazi occupied Hungary. At the time of the interview, Soros was 68 years old. He had been born to wealthy, "well-educated" Jewish parents. At the time of the Nazi occupation of Hungary, his father was a "successful" attorney who lived on an island in the Danube. Understanding what lay ahead for the Jews in Hungary, his father "split" the family, purchased forged papers and paid to have George sent to a Christian family whose bread earner's job was to confiscate Jewish property. This is what Soros said on the Sixty Minutes interview about what he, Soros, called "the best year of his life."[11]

KROFT: "My understanding is that you went out with this protector of yours who swore that you were his adopted godson."

SOROS: "Yes. Yes."

KROFT: "Went out, in fact, and helped in the confiscation of property from your fellow Jews, friends and neighbors."

SOROS: "Yes. That's right. Yes."

KROFT: "I mean, that sounds like an experience that would send lots of people to the psychiatric couch for many, many years. Was it difficult?"

SOROS: "No, not at all. Not at all, I rather enjoyed it."

KROFT: "No feeling of guilt?"

SOROS: "No, none at all. Only feelings of absolute power."

Glenn Beck said, "Soros has admitted to having carried some rather "potent messianic fantasies with me from childhood, which I felt I had to control, otherwise they might get me in trouble." Be that as it may. After WWII, Soros attended the London School of Economics, where he fell under the thrall of fellow atheist and Hungarian, Karl Popper, one of his professors. Popper was a mentor to Soros until Popper's death in 1994. Two of Popper's most influential teachings concerned "the open society," and Fallibilism.

"Fallibilism" is defined as the philosophical doctrine that all claims of knowledge could, in principle, be mistaken. (Then again, I could be wrong about that.) The "open society" basically refers to a "test and evaluate" approach to social engineering. Regarding "open society" Roy Childs writes, 'Since the Second World War, most of the Western democracies have followed Popper's advice about piecemeal social engineering and democratic social reform, and it has gotten them into a grand mess.'"[12]

If you really want to know what fills the empty suit of Barack Obama, here he is. Imagine this type of pathological personality this type of Gnosticism and this type of narcissism, all wrapped up in one mentor. Every bit of secular humanist, all atheist, all deceit, and all social justice wrapped up in one neat, little package. That at least is the analysis of CBS writer, Steve Kroft:

"Some time ago I wrote an article questioning who might be the power behind Barack Hussein Obama. It has to be someone because of his meteoric rise to power, with experience at virtually nothing, with questionable wisdom, and with a mysterious past that has been carefully erased and hidden where no one can check it. The puppet master apparently paid for Obama's education and his travels to Pakistan for some mysterious purpose, and promoted him into Illinois, then national politics. I once suggested it might be billionaire George Soros. I now believe that to be the case more than ever. George Soros might be the most evil man in the world, with intent to destroy America and every value we have held dear. Obama seems to be in lockstep with Soros' philosophies and simply a tool in Soros' world-changing strategies. The main obstacle to a stable and just world order is the "United States" -- George Soros

What we have in Soros, is a multi-billionaire atheist, with skewed moral values, and a sociopath's lack of conscience. He considers himself to be an elitist world class philosopher, despises the American Way and just loves to do social engineering (change cultures).

"Gyargy Schwartz, better known to the world as George Soros, was born August 12, 1930 in Hungary. Soros' father, Tivadar, was a fervent practitioner of Esperanto a language invented in 1887, and designed to be the first global language, free of any national identity. The Schwartz's, who were non-practicing Jews, changed the family name to Soros, in order to facilitate assimilation into the gentile population, as the Nazis spread into Hungary during the 1930s. When Hitler's henchman Adolf Eichmann arrived in Hungary, to oversee the murder of that country's Jews, George Soros ended up with a man whose job was confiscating property from the Jewish population. Soros went with him on his rounds. Soros has repeatedly called 1944 "the best year of his life." "70% of Mr. Soros's fellow Jews in Hungary, nearly a half-million human beings, were annihilated in that year yet he gives no sign that this put any damper on his elation, either at the time or indeed in retrospect."[13]

Soros moved to New York City in 1956, where he worked on Wall Street, and started amassing his fortune. He specialized in hedge funds and currency speculation. Soros is absolutely ruthless, amoral, and clever in his business dealing — he quickly made his fortune. By the 1980s, he was well on his way to becoming the global financial powerhouse that he is today.

In an article Kyle-Anne Shiver wrote for "The American Thinker" she says, "Soros made his first billion in 1992 by shorting the British pound with leveraged billions in financial bets, and became known as the man who broke the Bank of England. He broke it on the backs of hard-working British citizens who immediately saw their homes severely devalued and their life savings cut drastically, almost overnight."[14]

In 1994 Soros crowed in "The New Republic", that "the former Soviet Empire is now called the Soros Empire." The Russia-gate scandal in 1999, which almost collapsed the Russian economy, was labeled by Rep. Jim Leach, then head of the House Banking Committee, to be "one of the greatest social robberies in human history. The Soros Empire" indeed. In 1997 Soros almost destroyed the economies of Thailand and Malaysia. At the time, Malaysia's Prime Minister, Mahathir Mohammad, called Soros "a villain, and a moron." Thai activist Weng Tojirakarn said, "We regard George Soros as a kind of Dracula. He sucks the blood from the people."

The website Greek National Pride reports, "Soros was part of the full court press that dismantled Yugoslavia and caused trouble in Georgia, Ukraine and Myanmar [Burma]. Calling himself a philanthropist, Soros' role is to tighten the ideological stranglehold of globalization and the New World Order while promoting his own financial gain. He is without conscience; a capitalist who functions with absolute amorality." (It sounds like he subscribes to the Humanist Manifesto!)

France has upheld an earlier conviction against Soros, for felony insider trading. Soros was fined 2.9 million dollars. Recently, his native Hungary fined Soros 2.2 million dollars for "illegal market manipulation." Elizabeth Crum writes that the Hungarian economy has been in a state of transition as the country seeks to become more financially stable and westernized. Soros deliberately driving down the share price of its largest bank put Hungary's economy into a wicked tailspin. They still are to recover.

Soros is a planetary parasite. His grasp, greed, and gluttony have a global reach. But what about America? Soros told Australia's national newspaper *The Australian*: "America, as the centre of the globalised financial markets, was sucking up the savings of the world. This is now over. The game is out," he said, adding that the time has come for "a very serious adjustment" in American's consumption habits. He implied that he was the one with the power to bring this about." (Do you hear Obama in this one?)

Soros: "The world financial crisis was "stimulating" and "in a way, the culmination of my life's work." To quote the Left's favorite father, Franklin Delano Roosevelt, "In history, nothing happens by accident. If it happened, you can bet someone planned it." Soros obviously planned it, with a one-world government in mind.

Back in this country, Soros has been actively scheming and working to destroy America from the inside out for some years now. People have been warning us. A few years ago, news sources reported that "Soros [is] an extremist who wants open borders, a one-world foreign policy, legalized drugs, euthanasia, and on and on. This is off-the-chart dangerous." I find it interesting that George probably learned this one-world thing honestly. Soros' father, Tivadar, was a fervent practitioner of the Esperanto a language invented in 1887, and designed to be the first global language, free of any national identity.

In 1997, Rachel Ehrenfeld wrote, "Soros uses his [mask of] philanthropy to change or more accurately deconstruct the moral values and attitudes of the Western world, and particularly of the American people. His "open society" is not about freedom; it is about license. His vision rejects the notion of ordered liberty, in favor of a PROGRESSIVE ideology of rights and entitlements."

David Horowitz and Richard Poe, in their book "The Shadow Party" outlines in detail how Soros hijacked the Democratic Party, and now owns it lock, stock, and barrel. Soros has been packing the Democratic Party with radicals, and ousting moderate Democrats for years. The Shadow Party became the Shadow Government, which recently became the Obama Administration. While the goal is the same with the Republican Party, he's not quite there yet, almost, but not quite.

DiscoverTheNetworks.org (another good source) writes, "By his [Soros'] own admission, he helped engineer coups in Slovakia, Croatia, Georgia, and Yugoslavia. When Soros targets a country for "regime change," he begins by creating a shadow government, a fully formed government-in-exile, ready to assume power when the opportunity arises. The Shadow Party he has built in America greatly resembles those he has created in other countries prior to instigating a coup."

November 2008's edition of the German magazine "Der Spiegel," carried a story in which Soros gives his opinion on what the next POTUS (President of the U. S.) should do after taking office. "I think we need a large stimulus package." Soros thought that around 600 billion would be about right. Soros also said that "I think Obama presents us a great opportunity to finally deal with global warming and energy dependence. The U. S. needs a cap and trade system with auctioning of licenses for emissions rights."

Soros is a partner in the Carlyle Group where he has invested more than 100 million dollars. According to an article by "The Baltimore Chronicle's" Alice Cherbonnier, the Carlye Group is run by "a veritable who's who of former Republican leaders," from CIA man Frank Carlucci, to CIA head and ex-President George Bush, Sr.

In late 2006, Soros bought about 2 million shares of Halliburton, Dick Cheney's old stomping grounds. When the Democrats and Republicans held their conventions in 2000, Soros held Shadow Party conventions in the same cities, at the same time. In 2008, Soros donated $5,000,000,000 (that's Five Billion) to the Democratic National Committee, NC, trying to insure Obama's win and wins for many other Alinsky-trained Radical Rules Anti-American Socialists. Soros has been contributing a $ billion plus to the DNC since Clinton came on the national scene.

Soros has spread the dirt on both sides of the aisle, trust me. And if that weren't bad enough, he has long held connections with the CIA. We must also mention Soros' involvement with the Main Stream Media (MSM), the entertainment industry (e. g. he owns 2.6 million shares of Time Warner), and the various political advertising organizations to which he funnels millions. Bottom line, George Soros greatly influences most of the MSM. Entities like the Tea Party and the NRA are an absolute nemesis to Soros.

As Matthew Vadum penned, "The liberal billionaire-turned-philanthropist has been buying up media properties for years . . . to drive home his message to the American public that they are too materialistic, too wasteful, too selfish, and too stupid to decide for themselves how to run their own lives."

Richard Poe wrote, "Soros' private philanthropy, totaling nearly $5 billion, continues undermining America's traditional Western values. His giving has provided funding of abortion rights, atheism, drug legalization, sex education, euthanasia, feminism, gun control, globalization, mass immigration, gay marriage and other radical experiments in social engineering."

Some of the many NGOs (Non-Government Organizations) that Soros funds with his billions are: MoveOn.org, the Apollo Alliance, Media Matters for America, the Tides Foundation, the ACLU, ACORN, PDIA (Project on Death In America), La Raza, and many more. For a more complete list, with brief descriptions of the NGOs, go to DiscoverTheNetworks.org.

Poe continued, "Through his global web of Open Society Institutes and Open Society Foundations, Soros has spent 25 years recruiting, training, indoctrinating and installing a network of loyal operatives in 50 countries, placing them in positions of influence and power in media, government, finance and academia."

Without Soros' money, would the Saul Alinsky's Chicago machine still be rolling? Would SEIU, ACORN, and La Raza still be pursuing their nefarious activities? Would Big Money and lobbyists still be corrupting government? Would our college campuses still be retirement homes for 1960s radicals? America stands at the brink of an abyss, and that fact is directly attributable to Soros. Soros has vigorously, cleverly, and insidiously planned the ruination of America and his puppet, Barack Obama is leading the way.[15]

The Evil Game

They lie, they cheat, and they steal to gain more control over citizens' lives.

Remember the lies: "We are the only party that cares for the poor"; "There are no death panels with the new medical care act"; "you will be able to see every piece of legislation on C-Span before it is acted upon"; "you can keep your medial plan if you like it"; "those who oppose us are extremists"; "you can keep your doctor if you like him"; "a woman has the right to decide what she wants to do with a fetus, since it is part of her body"; and the best one, "you must agree with us in order to be bilateral." But America is in the balance.

When viewing what has been transpiring in this nation politically, it is obvious that while the country is getting sicker, the average people who make this nation run and operate are fairly healthy; it is the "doctors" so to speak in Washington who are sick and so corrupt. And that illness comes at least in part from our representatives seeking and following the guidance of individuals such as Alinsky, Marx, and Soros. To see Marx, Alinsky, and Soros is to see their truest disciple — Obama. Said differently, Obama is best seen in "the context" of his true character through these three gurus of Marxism. **All these men share the idea of 8 levels of control that must be obtained to create a social state.**

The first is the most important.

1. **Healthcare** – Control healthcare and you control the people.
2. **Poverty** – Increase the Poverty level as high as possible, poor people are easier to control and will not fight back if you are providing everything for them to live.
3. **Debt** – Increase the debt to an unsustainable level. That way you are able to increase taxes, and this will produce more poverty.
4. **Gun Control** – Remove the ability for people to defend themselves from the Government. That way you are able to create a police state.
5. **Welfare** – Take control of every aspect of their lives (Food, Housing, and Income).
6. **Education** – Take control of what people read and listen to — take control of what children learn in school.
7. **Religion** – Remove the belief in God from the Government and schools.
8. **Class Warfare** – Divide the people into the wealthy and the poor. This will cause more discontent and it will be easier to take (Tax) the wealthy with the support of the poor.

Does any of this sound familiar?

Sharing the data and information has a purpose; to be heuristic. Behind every decision made, are also the consequences tied to that decision. I realized long ago you will save time and energy if you discover the mindset, philosophy, and underlying world view of those asking you to vote for them so they in turn can shape legislation within the country. There are also lessons to be learned from making "blind choices" based on party affiliation. Our culture, our children, our country are in an extremely troubled condition because of bad choices already made. Too many of us have not properly evaluated those we have chosen to represent us. Vetting candidates, their positions and backgrounds on issues takes work. But bad choices of the past now require "rework," which is more work. It will take hard labor to turn this country around. Doing things the same way as we have in the past and expecting different results, will not work; it is truly the definition of insanity. Our nation and the associated values are headed the wrong way, and will not be turned around by followers of a Karl Marx, a Saul Alinsky, a George Soros, or a Barack Obama. We must choose better mentors than these and do it quickly.

The words of Patrick Henry are apropos: "Is life so dear, or peace so sweet, as to be purchased at the price of chains and slavery? Forbid it, almighty God! I know not what course others may take, but as for me, give me liberty, or give me death!"

*"If a nation expects to be ignorant and free
in a state of civilization,
it expects what never was and never will be."*

Thomas Jefferson, 1816

Chapter Eleven

"No Gods Allowed in Here!"

IN 1859, CHARLES DARWIN PUBLISHED HIS now famous book, *On the Origin of Species*, based on his visit to the Galapagos Islands and his research of animal life there. He used the pages to state his belief in what he called "Natural Selection," his theory that all biological life on earth came from one common ancestor. Liberals immediately hailed the book and its theory as "the" earth-shattering answer to the fundamental question of how all life appeared and now exists on earth; attempting to answer the ultimate question you still see on television science programs presenting evolution today, asking "What are we doing here?" Though unstated, the answer to that question, from the professors on the TV program's viewpoint is basic and simple, "We are trying to explain away God and the creation account found in the Bible."

Though a huge number of top paleontologists and scientists at the time said the theory was baseless and probably would not last until the year 1900 as a credible thought, it continued to be hailed by the liberal community as the answer to the riddle of life. Never mind that 160 years of digging fossils has produced absolutely nothing, nada, zip in the arena of evidence to support Darwin and his theory. (Darwin said himself that the fossil record didn't support his thought, but encouraged the world to dig and find the "links" necessary to support it which he thought would be discovered in a few years.) So the digging has kept going on and on, always with the same results — Nothing. But facts never get in the way of a liberal. No sir! Facts be damned, not only do the Liberals keep believing in Darwin, but they preach his faith system (aka, Theory) as unquestionable fact.

The liberals, never ones to quit beating drums to support their cause, used spokesperson at the time, Julian Huxley, who in 1942 invented the term "modern evolutionary synthesis," a term used in putting more liberal spin on "ideas" they got from genetics and cell life study in botany. Basically Huxley said among other things that "All evolutionary phenomena can be explained in a way consistent with known genetic mechanisms and the observational evidence of naturalists." That word "mechanisms" refers to the study of cell structures and how a cell is built internally. The problem is this, Huxley, nor any of his liberal scientist buddies could tell anyone what a cell resembled internally. "Until relatively recently, scientists didn't know what the inside of a cell looked like. The cell was a mysterious "black box," as Lehigh University biochemist Michael Behe puts it. Darwiniacs prefer to ignore modern scientific knowledge so that they can pretend the cell is still a black box and tell us the mutation god created it. In his 1996 book *Darwin's Black Box*, Behe used discoveries in microbiology to refute Darwinism on Darwin's own terms. Darwin had set forth this extremely self-serving standard for himself: "If it could be demonstrated that any complex organ existed which could not possibly have been formed by numerous successive, slight modifications, my theory would absolutely break down."[1]

Facts be damned, evolutionary synthesis, along with Darwinism, took root in the public school system (government-owned by the way) in the 1950s, thanks to the liberal and progressive professors, and has been treated there as absolute fact ever since. Over the past 65 years a plethora of other theories have been submitted by liberals attempting to support Darwin's theory of evolution. All this was presented as keys to getting closer to answering the question, what are we doing here. But realistically, all this project work was being done in an attempt to explain away God, which would by default dismiss the creation account for the existence of our world and universe, because God was presented as creator. One theory, very popular now, says that comets seeded the earth over billions of years bringing the elements of life, amino acids, dipeptides, etc., which were the building blocks of elementary life. The secular humanist holy scroll must certainly ring out the following (historical or hysterical?) doctrine:

> "And the comet looked at its completed work, which it brought to earth, and seeing that it was good, blessed it; thus was the evening and the morning of the first era of evolution." – 2 Hesitations 1:7

Another supporting idea has been floated by the secular humanist scientists. You've seen it — it says that asteroids have brought bacteria or germs to earth, seeding our planet from other planets like Mars and the deep recesses of outer space, thus kick-starting life here. Their philosophical stance is also covered in other liberal sacred texts:

> "And the Senior Meteor said to the meteorites, 'Let us go down and build dry ground and bring with us seeds and have the land produce plants and bear their own seeds and blend with other life to conglomerate and synthesize.' Let us leave our marks upon the earth so they will know that we were here. When we do they will give us the credit we deserve. And thus it was so, thus they were pleased with their work." - 1 Orbituary 2:2

Another theory, held by "ancient astronaut theorists" says that ancient aliens came to earth from a planet near the star Sirius and planted life and the seeds of evolution here. There have been some in the scientific community who have jumped at one or more of these ideas, massaging them into "facts."

> "Build the stone houses and structures with laser guns that melt the stone and other

Chapter Eleven — "No Gods Allowed in Here!"

constellation tools preparing the paths for anthropoids which we will make in our own image. And we shall give them tools to build great structures but let not them have assault weapons; taketh them away along with whatever amendments they buildeth. Thus shall the population be savaged and unable to accomplish much." — Dreams from My Ancient Fathers 19:11

Well you get the picture of how things "evolve." These "professors" and some "scientists" jumped joyously at these ideas because it kept a creating God out of the picture for them. They thought of these ideas, they believed the ideas; therefore the ideas became facts which cannot be questioned. So in the minds of the liberal theorists, when one or more of these supporting theories stick to a liberal educator's hopes it becomes "scientific" fact that makes Darwinism true, despite the lack of any supporting data. But don't confuse them with facts, since they are too busy crowing that they have a working slogan with the uneducated, "You KNOW God is a Myth." This is whom they need to be rid of since His presence would speak of creationism.

Humanists accepting Darwinism will normally add to their cart "amorality," as well as "situation ethics." Removed from school long ago is the book that taught a "fixed" moral code and ethical standard. It had that guiding principle "Do unto others, as you would have them do unto you." Add to the cart, a biology, which having removed all the creational aspects, makes fertile ground to just teach the lowest common denominators of what is now called sex education; with zero morals. Imagine the unlikelihood that as all these theories and doctrines are percolating in separate test tubes at various lab table stations all at the same time in one laboratory. What would be the odds of them exploding at the same moment in time with the conglomeration of each of them landing in government education centers and being taught alongside each other in school, all as fact and normal? The odds are bad, but in this case this long-shot has come in to break the tape and be given preferential status as "fact" at least in textbooks. Looking at this list of what goes on in school now, all one needs is to add liquor and some controlled-substance drugs, a t-shirt and a leather jacket and you have a James Dean starter kit. Now that is "edumecation!"

Liberals invoke their sanctity and authority to keep the classroom free from the ultimate crime of mentioning anything of the Christian faith (Islam is okay however). Classrooms are typically kept "pure" so as not to threaten the tenants of evolution or their own religion of secular humanism. William Provine, an evolutionary biologist at Cornell University, calls Darwinism the greatest engine of atheism devised by man. His fellow Darwin disciple, Oxford zoologist Richard Dawkins, famously said, "Darwin made it possible to be an intellectually fulfilled atheist."[2]

Teacher training is aligned with humanism, demanding there be no toleration of any religious faith alongside their own humanist beliefs. The ACLU sued a school district in Cobb County, Georgia merely for putting stickers in biology textbooks that urged students to study evolution "with an open mind, studied carefully, and critically considered." According to the ACLU, an open mind violates the "separation of church and state, . . ."[3] Lebec, California is the town where parents represented by the Americans United for Separation of Church and State sued to prevent the school from even offering an elective philosophy class on intelligent design, creationism and evolution.[4] In Dover, Pennsylvania, a small group of parents backed by the ACLU and Americans United for Separation of Church and State sued to prevent any discussion of intelligent design in a ninth-grade biology class.[5] As seems the case in today's judicial pluralism, "the judge ruled in their favor and ordered the school district to pay the plaintiffs' legal fees, which . . . exceeded $1 million."[6]

Joelle Silver, a seven-year veteran science teacher in the Cheektowaga Central School District in the western part of New York was told that the Bible Study Club she advised at school was against school regulations and therefore was "illegal." "She received a 'counseling letter' from her superintendent that ordered her to remove all religious materials . . . from her classroom or she would be fired. She was even forced to remove a sign in class that had a quote from former President Ronald Reagan, which read in part — 'If we ever forget that we are One Nation Under God, then we will be a Nation gone under.'"[7]

The super's eight-page letter informed Silver that "your rights to free speech and expression are not as broad as if you were simply a private citizen."[8] The school's war with their teacher insisted that among the items that had to be removed from her room was a poster with an inspirational Bible verse superimposed over an American flag and various inspirational messages she had written on small sticky notes she usually kept on her desk, and a prayer request box that students had placed in the room, which Fox News reported.

One independent voter said, " . . . Joelle Silver has been singled out because she is a Christian . . . is unfair, un-American. Why aren't other teachers required to remove items? This is against God, the USA, our Founding Fathers and the Constitution."[9] Historians point out that American schools were designed to disciple our nation in Christ. The Bible was the first and only textbook in public schools. Children prayed Christian prayers in school for 355 years until 1962.[10]

This is targeted discrimination against Christianity only. If the teacher had been a Muslim and had been posting Islamic religious themes round the classroom, the school superintendent would not have rebuked her at all. No letter of chastisement would have been sent; no order to cleanse the classroom. There would have been no threats of firing. There could have been a letter, if written, most likely would have been a complimentary one, hailing courageous behavior. In fact "the super" may have even come down to the classroom and helped put up the material. The extremism and bullying tactics of this superintendent and the whole public school system cannot be tolerated. The only reason why this lady was singled out is because she is a serious Christian.[11]

Apparently secular humanism can be joined in the classroom by Islam, not only prominently welcomed into public school, but both taught there. Both are ancient faiths. A note of interest: "Christian" thoughts promoting peace and unity cannot be posted in public school classrooms; it is considered worse than any pornography. Humanism however, teaches atheism, only the material universe exists, ethical standards are totally flexible at any given point, and that morality is not discovered, it is made. This humanism leads to killings, riots, mass destruction by their followers — this faith is heralded, uplifted, and embraced as wholesome. It is also a religious faith.

One of the twists de jour to secular humanism is Darwinian evolution, which while taught as fact in science classes around the country, is nothing more than a faith system in and of itself. It treats doubts about evolution as religious heresy. Darwinism, as philosopher and mathematician David Berlinski says, is "the last of the great 19th Century mystery religions." The real reason a lot of Christians reject evolution is that we're taught to reject big fat lies. You can look it up — we have an entire commandment about the importance of not lying.[12] Teaching evolution as science is not science, it is a system of faith not even based on fact. Nevertheless, Humanists and other liberals teach this as science and accepted fact. Sadly, we are told that is never to be questioned. Even sadder; Christians in mass do not challenge it.

A full century of intimidation by Humanists and evolutionists threatening everyone in earshot to say that evolution is a fact, and that lawsuits will follow if disparaging comments are made of this official state religion. If having an appetite for truth, the story of Colin Patterson, a highly respected anthropologist at the Natural History Museum in London will be of interest. Like Diogenes searching for an honest man, Patterson was on a quest to find someone who could tell him — as he puts it — "anything you know about evolution, any one thing you think is true." Patterson said, "I tried that question on the geology staff at the Field Museum of Natural History, and the only answer I got was silence. I tried it on the staff of the Evolutionary Morphology Seminar in the University of Chicago, a very prestigious body of evolutionists, and the only thing I got there was silence for a long time."[13]

Labeling evolution as "change over time," Darwiniacs, will discuss about anything except evolution; they pretend evolution means something utterly uncontroversial. Author Joe Sobran states, describing "evolution" as "change over time" is like describing abortion as "choice." Aren't we all for "choice?" Don't animals change over time? The boring point that organisms "change over time" is not what the Darwiniacs are teaching schoolchildren, and that's not what the fuss is about.[14]

Darwin's Theory Must Be Challenged

While Darwinism is a theory, and a bad one, it's being taught "as fact" in schools. Those who teach it, the Darwiniacs, atheists, agnostics, secular humanists, progressives, liberals, et al; they demand that we be tolerant of them, as they control the school since "the public schools prove crucial to the advancement of the tyranny's agenda."[15] While this Humanist religion is being taught, they and the courts have blocked all access to the same stage within schools for creation, let alone allowing Christianity to even be mentioned.

Evolution has more than a few proponents who have an "in-your-face" and egotistical type of presentation. Take Evolutionary Biologist, Ernst Mayr, "No educated person any longer questions the validity of the so-called theory of evolution, which we now know to be a simple fact."[15] They are supported by a litany of professors in various universities who have been teaching these tenants of the theory for years. The problem with their theory; nothing close to 100 percent of scientists agrees with the theory. There is a fast-growing number of paleontologists and other scientists embracing creationism. That has seriously reduced the number of Darwiniacs within the science community who believe in evolution to around half the scientists. In fact, it may not even be half now, since the number of those who are seriously questioning what is being taught as evolution is growing so fast. "Scientists who utterly reject evolution may be one of the fastest growing controversial minorities.... Many of the scientists supporting this position hold impressive credentials in science."[16] "Doubters of Darwin" are a formidable and extremely impressive group of scientific minds within that community.

A Growing Group of Elite Doubters "Proclaim" Another Account

It was a photograph to behold. All one hundred of them gathered in one place at one time; biologists, chemists, zoologists, physicists, anthropologists, molecular and cell biologists, bioengineers, organic chemists, geologists, astrophysicists and other scientists.

Their credentials were impeccable beginning with their doctorates being earned at such prominent universities as Cambridge, Stanford, Cornell, Yale, Rutgers, Chicago, Princeton, Purdue, Duke, Michigan, Syracuse, Temple, and Berkeley. Their teaching credentials included professorships at Yale Graduate School, the Massachusetts Institute of Technology (MIT), Tulane, Rice, Emory, George Mason, Lehigh, and the Universities of California, Washington, Texas, Florida, North Carolina, Wisconsin, Ohio, Colorado, Nebraska, Missouri, Iowa, Georgia, New Mexico, Utah, Pennsylvania, and elsewhere. Among the prestigious positions among the group was that of the director of the Center for Computational Quantum Chemistry and scientists at the Plasma Physics Lab at Princeton, the National Museum of Natural History at the Smithsonian Institute, the Los Alamos National Laboratory, and the Lawrence Livermore Laboratories.

Here they stood together, communicating a simple message: They are extremely skeptical of Darwin's evolution in particular, "skeptical of claims for the ability of random mutation and natural selection to account for the complexity of life." And they challenged the contention of designated spokespersons of the PBS series to answer the claim contending "virtually all reputable scientists in the world" support Darwin's theory of evolution.

In 2002, Public Broadcasting System (PBS) aired their seven-part television series *Evolution* throughout which spokespersons asserted "all known scientific evidence supports [Darwinian] evolution" as does virtually every reputable scientist in the world." Following that program, these professors, laboratory researchers, and other scientists (mentioned above) published a two-page advertisement in a national magazine under the banner, "A Scientific Dissent to Darwinism." Their statement was succinct and defiant. "We are skeptical of claims for the ability of random mutation and natural selection to account for the complexity of life," they said. "Careful examination of the evidence for Darwinian theory should be encouraged."[17]

It is obvious what producers of the series were doing. They used their contentious statements to keep any scientific criticism of Darwinism from being acknowledged, discussed, or examined in any length within the series. "They want people to think that the only criticism of Darwin's theory today is from religious fundamentalists," the Discovery Institute's president, Bruce Chapman, said. "They routinely try to stigmatize scientists who question Darwin as 'creationists.'"[18]

One of the problems we face with some believers of Darwin is that they lower their standards in viewing evidence for the support of evolution which as scientists they would never accept in other circumstances. That inconsistency of scientific approach is the conclusion of chemist Henry Schaefer, a five-time Nobel nominee. Another problem: Rather than being gatekeepers who cut off dissenting opinions, it is time that those "scientists" who support Darwinism enter serious dialogue and debate, if they are as secure in their beliefs as their programs indicate they are. True science must be able to be challenged by evidence and hypothesis, otherwise it is not science. However, the producers of *Evolution* refused to cover any of the scientific objections to Darwin's theory. Instead they offered dissenters the chance to go on camera to tell what was called "personal faith stories" in the last episode of the series. The series also accepted normally challenged hypothesis of Darwinians as accepted fact. Producers of the show are clearly at odds with some scientists who wanted to point out where the series used inaccurate history or flawed reasoning. The viewing public agreed in a Zogby Poll taken following the series. Responders to the poll indicated, "71 percent of Americans say biology teachers should teach Darwin's theory of evolution along with scientific evidence against the theory."[19]

A quick look at the photo of these top 100 scientists posing together, one is reminded of their credentials. That immediately lifts them out of the mold of barefoot hillbillies, uneducated, religious fanatics; all of which liberals group together as being from some swamp or tarpaper shack on a country mountain side. What the protestors are: "highly respected, world-class scientists like Nobel nominee

Henry F. Schaefer, the third most-cited chemist in the world; James Tour of Rice University's Center for Nanoscale Science and Technology; and Fred Figworth, professor of cellular and molecular physiology at Yale Graduate School. Together, despite the specter of professional persecution, they broached the politically incorrect opinion that the emperor of evolution has no clothes."[20]

When a high school student studying science, my teacher cared enough for truth and for us that when teaching "theories of origins" he went past the approved curriculum to discuss creation, or intelligent design, on at least an equal footing. Attending most any college today, one would have never known that some credible scientists do not buy into Darwinism theory, which is natural selection. Today if you listen to government sanctioned educators you would think that only hick pastors or misled non-union teachers object to the theory of evolution on the grounds that it contradicts Biblical claims. We were kept in the dark that, according to historian Peter Bowler, substantive scientific critiques of natural selection started so early that by 1900 "its opponents were convinced it [Darwin's theory of evolution; i.e., natural selection] would never recover."[21]

The Graven Images Which Liberals Want You to Worship

Despite evidence which stands against "the theory of evolution" and the many giants within the scientific community who on scientific grounds seriously question the tenants of Darwinism, the "theory" continues to be taught in schools as an absolute fact. It is typically promoted in textbooks with the use of four very famous images. Anyone who has looked through a high school science or biology textbook has seen them. The images have been used for so long that they have become hallmarks seared into the minds of many current and former students; all regarding the promotion of the theory of natural selection and evolution. They were published together in 2000 in a book entitled *Icons of Evolution*. The book offers a scientific and clear-headed look at those visual images, the Miller experiment, Darwin's tree of life, Haeckel's embryos, and the *archaeopteryx* missing link — all together with other symbols of evolution, which are being used to convince people of Darwin's theory of evolution. The book subtitle points out the thesis and its direction, *Why much of what we teach about evolution is wrong*.[22]

Books on the subject of discounting Darwin are not that hard to find. Most book stores carry both books that advocate evolution and those that deny it scientifically; book store managers are trying to make a living and will sell you either brand. One book in particular, however, is Jonathan Wells' *Icons of Evolution*. That volume digs deep into the truth behind each of the four images in question. Wells serves as senior fellow at the Discovery Institute's Center for Science and Culture. His credentials are not weak; he earned his undergraduate degree the University of California at Berkeley in geology and physics, with a minor in biology. His doctorate is from Yale in religious studies where he specialized in the 19th Century controversies surrounding Darwin; his resulting book, *Charles Hodge's Critique of*

Darwinism, was published in 1988.[23] At Berkeley, where Wells graduated in 1994, he focused primarily on vertebrate embryology and evolution. He also worked at Berkeley as a post-graduate research biologist. Wells has written on the scientific and cultural aspects of evolution in such journals as *Origins & Design, The Scientist, Touchstone, The American Biology Teacher,* and *Rhetoric and Public Affairs.* His technical articles are just that — with such scintillating titles as "Microtubule-mediated transport of organelles and localization of beta-catenin to the future dorsal side of Xenopus eggs" — [and] have appeared in *Proceedings of the National Academy of Sciences USA, Development,* and *BioSystems.*[24]

A serious student digging for the truth will find Jonathan Wells' work very encouraging as well as fulfilling. My purpose is to show truth from a lay person's vantage point, exposing evolution for what it is. I do not pretend to be a scientist but have read scientific authors to whom a serious student could go and find truth. Wells establishes truth in *Icons of Darwinism*. Though all four images are used as "the examples of evolution," Wells will through the data and true scientific approach demonstrate that each of them are either false or misleading.

What a shock it is for an inquisitive student to hear that for the first time. It is so shocking that such statements have been outlawed in a government mind control centers, called public schools. What any rational person should do when confronted with this conundrum, or one similar, is to propose, or postulate, an "if this, then that" hypothesis. So, let's postulate an "if this, then that" challenge to evolution. Here goes: "If" these four icons (images) which are cited by scientists so often are the best evidence for Darwinism — and "if" they are either false or misleading, "then" what does that tell us about the evolutionary theory? Also, "if" and particularly when a person witnesses this theory being taught as fact "with fervor and threats against any opposing views," which is seen at times in high schools, universities, and on television specials, "then" one is left with a few questions: If evolution is such a concrete fact, why bar all opposing theory or conversation? After all, any supposed facts would instantly reveal the opposing views to be baseless. That is "if" they are facts. Another question; what are the science classes in high schools, universities, and TV specials, really trying to teach? Is it science — or is this a kind of mythology? Myths are often used in place of truth, because truth can be difficult to swallow.

Look closer at the four images, these famous icons of evolution.

Image one; Stanley Miller's 1953 experiment. It is an experiment that every science student in America has seen at one time or another. The description of Miller, arms folded, looking into the camera over the tubes, flasks, and electrodes in a lab will help recall the picture. This scene shows him shooting electricity through an atmosphere which he claimed was similar to the one on primitive earth, creating amino acids, the building blocks of life. The picture is absolutely significant, because it is still used by proponents of evolution in biology textbooks. An "if, then" hypothesis is applicable; especially when the viable question is whether Miller's atmosphere was an accurate simulation. In other words, one should ask, "Did Miller's atmosphere resemble the proper mixture of oxygen, hydrogen, carbon dioxide, and other various gases present on "early earth?"

To answer that question, there is a horde of not only credible, but outstanding scientists and researchers, including Wells himself who stand as a testament saying that there is no credible way to tell for certain what that atmosphere was like. "Miller chose a hydrogen-rich mixture of methane, ammonia, and water vapor, which was consistent with what some scientists "believed", was present then. But scientists don't believe that anymore. As a geophysicist with Carnegie Institution said in the 1960s, 'What is the evidence for a primitive methane-ammonia atmosphere on earth? The answer is that there is no evidence for it, but much against it.'"[25] "By the mid-1970s, Belgian biochemist Marcel Florkin was declaring that the concept behind Miller's theory of the early atmosphere "has been abandoned."[26] In fact, two of the leading origin-of-life researchers, Klaus Dose and Sidney Fox, confirmed that Miller had used the wrong gas mixture.[27] And Science magazine said in 1995 that experts now dismiss Miller's experiment because "the early atmosphere looked nothing like the Miller-Urey simulation."[28][29] Conducting the same experiment using an accurate atmosphere, you do not get amino acids. Some textbooks try to hide or fudge by saying even if you use an accurate atmosphere, you get organic molecules. But those molecules, as reputable scientists point out, are actually formaldehyde and cyanide. This is an embalming fluid. So, what evolution teaches about results from Petri dishes or glass vials is actually quite contrary to reality.

Our "if, then" hypothesis leads us to a result; a living cell cannot be "naturally" generated. When getting one's mind around that result, it becomes clear that evolution is in reality a materialistic philosophy masquerading as empirical science. The position which evolutionists take is that life HAD to have developed this way because there's no other materialistic explanation. In their minds only the material is in existence. By inserting another explanation, such as intelligent design, evolutionists will literally scream "you're not a scientist if you hold that opinion." Regardless of what one believes on that subject, within the realm of science alone, "Science doesn't have the slightest idea how life began." That is according to Gregg Easterbrook, journalist who wrote about origin-of-life field. "No generally accepted theory exists, and the steps leading from a barren primordial world to the fragile chemistry of life seem imponderable."[30]

Another scientist and former professor at Texas A&M University, Walter Bradley, is considered by many an origin-of-life expert by many scientists. In 1984 he co-authored a landmark book *The Mystery of Life's Origins*.[31] Bradley discussed all the various theories that have been advanced by scientists about how life first appeared on earth; theories how it could have generated naturally with no divine spark. Those range from random chance, chemical affinity, self-ordered tendencies, comet-seeding from outer space, deep-sea ocean vents, and even using clay to encourage pre-biotic chemicals to assemble. For each individual theory he demonstrated that not one of them can withstand the scrutiny of true bench work science.[32]

Bradley and a growing number of scientists see overwhelming evidence pointing to intelligent design behind life's creation. The reason is fairly simple to Bradley. Moving from "nonlife" to "life" is so far removed from any natural causes — bridging that gap becomes not only impossible, but incredibly impossible.

Second image - Darwin's Tree of Life. This image is one of the most recognizable icons that represent the theory of evolution, Darwin's sketch showing his idea that all life came from just one common ancestor. Through the years I grew up with this image and believed it for a time. Looking back now, given just this image alone, I can see why it was so compelling in school. No rational explanation for the world is "legally" offered in school except for evolution; therefore it is eventually accepted by most students since it seems to offer an explanation for all natural life. While the "Tree of Life" image is a good representation of Darwin's theory, it is a failure for explaining origins of life; it is not supported by the physical evidence scientists find in the fossil record. "In fact," Jonathan Wells said, "Darwin knew the fossil record failed to support his tree. He acknowledged that major groups of animals — he calls them divisions, now they're called phyla — appear suddenly in the fossil record."[33] The problem is, "that's not what his theory predicts."[34]

Darwin's theory predicted there would be a long history of gradual divergence from a common ancestor, with differences appearing slowly. The fossil record showed exactly the opposite in Darwin's day and shows the same today. Darwin knew the fossils did not support him, but thought that in some future day, he would be vindicated by a reversal of the trend. "THE FACTS are compelling," as Lee Strobel states. "Nobody can claim that Darwin's tree is an accurate description of what the fossil record has produced. Protests from Darwinists aside, the evidence has failed to substantiate the predictions that Darwin made. Yet when I encountered the drawing as a student, I walked away with the conclusion that it illustrated the success of his revolutionary ideas."[35]

If education is about presenting facts, it would seem obvious that Darwin's drawing or image would have been removed from school text books. Wells says, "Not only is it included in the textbooks, but it's called a fact. . . . What I mind is when textbooks call it a fact that all animals share a common ancestor . . . it's not a fact. If you consider all of the evidence, Darwin's tree is false as a description of the history of life. I'll even go further than that: it's not even a good hypothesis at this point."[36]

We have arrived at a moment in American history where the truth can be defined as "that which you choose to believe in spite of evidence and facts. Replacing facts by simple repetition is the methodology and facilitator for creating beliefs today." Replacing facts are the methodology and facilitator for creating beliefs today; simple repetition. Say something enough times and it becomes, for millions of people, the truth. This is why control of the education system equals control of the populace. The heavy repetition of lies and smears for political gain are by no means inconsequential. Unfortunately, we have been in the habit of vetting scientists like presidential candidates. When evolution is vetted, there is very strong reasons why we can claim treason from within.

The third image is Haeckel's Embryos. I remember seeing Ernst Haeckel's comparative drawings of embryos he did, then in 1868 called the best evidence for proving Darwin's theory. Scientists today however see different evidence when working on vertebrate embryology. Ernst Haeckel's embryos are "his drawings" not photographs, and as drawings that will make a reasonable thinking person conclude that Darwin was right. However, as Dr. Wells states, "There are three problems with these drawings. The first is that the similarities in the early stages [of the embryos] were faked." He went on to say, "You can call them fudged, distorted, misleading, but the bottom line is that they were faked. Apparently in some cases Haeckel actually used the same woodcut to print embryos from different classes because he was so confident of his theory that he figured he didn't have to draw them separately. In other cases he doctored the drawings to make them look more similar than they really are. At any rate, his drawings misrepresent the embryos."[37]

The teaching of Haeckel's embryos to support evolution is absolutely maddening for this reason. While this image and other images are taught as fact, his drawings (not photographs, but detailed drawings) were exposed in the late 1860s as frauds by his colleagues. Why are the drawings still included in curriculum textbooks and used to teach evolutionary biology when the drawings were proven a fraud? The teaching of a 150-year old fraud is not education. It is rather another reason why I say that we are experiencing treason from within. Believing in Haeckel's synopsis is to stand on incredibly thin ice. But this is extraordinarily common in education today. There are still more reasons why I believe portions of our science curriculum in our schools is not only an empty philosophy but also dangerous.

Then image four, The Archaeopteryx Missing Link. Pronounced (ar-key-OPT-er-icks), this is the most famous and recognizable of the images. It is and has been used in many textbooks and TV specials. Evolutionists call it the awe-inspiring picture that is designed to silence any Darwin critic. With the publishing in 1859 of his book *The Origin of Species*, Darwin was forced to concede that "the most obvious and gravest objection which can be urged against my theory" was that the fossil record did not back up his evolutionary hypothesis. However, Darwin postulated that though the fossil record was inadequate and incomplete because not enough fossils had been unearthed, some day he would be vindicated along with his theory by a eureka moment in a future archeological dig. All that was needed was more time.

And "as if on cue, two years later scientists unearthed the *archaeopteryx* in a German quarry. Darwin's supporters were thrilled — surely this missing link between reptiles and modern birds, unveiled so promptly after the appearance of

Darwin's book, would be just the first of many future fossil discoveries that would validate Darwin's claims."[38] Through the years there have been many following the lead taken by the scientist who "actually fell upon his knees in awe" when first glimpsing the archaeopteryx at the National History Museum in England.[39] Even as a junior high student I remember being in absolute awe of that picture that just had to, as I thought it proved at the time, be as representative of facts as the solar system hanging on my bedroom ceiling.

Over time however, in clinging to the theory I discovered I was wrong. In determining to study for myself, I discovered that the fossil record in the last 150+ years has spoken loud and clear. It has said plainly that Darwin was wrong. Author, Michael Denton in his book *Evolution: A Theory in Crisis* summed up the desolate record this way, "[T]he universal experience of paleontology . . . [is that] while the rocks have continually yielded new and exciting and even bizarre forms of life . . . what they have never yielded is any of Darwin's myriads of transitional forms. Despite the tremendous increase in geological activity in every corner of the globe and despite the discovery of many strange and hitherto unknown forms, the infinitude of connecting links has still not been discovered and the fossil record is about as discontinuous as it was when Darwin was writing the *Origin*. The intermediates have remained as elusive as ever, and their absence remains, a century later, one of the most striking characteristics of the fossil record."[40] As a result the fossil record provides a tremendous challenge to the notion of organic evolution.[41]

Said differently, the missing link is still missing. Translation; it will always be missing because there is really no link to find. Paleontologists have been racing to locate an actual reptilian ancestor for birds. They drank the humanist cool-aide and have "bought-in" to the evolutionary theory. Their zeal has both consumed them and has also over the past twenty years proved to produce some embarrassments for the field of science. For example, as Jonathan Wells states, "A few years ago the National Geographic Society announced that a fossil had been produced at an Arizona mineral show that turned out to be 'the missing link between terrestrial dinosaurs and birds that could actually fly. It certainly looked that way. They called it the '*archaeoraptor*,' and it had the tail of a dinosaur and the forelimbs of a bird. National Geographic magazine published an article in 1999 that said there's now evidence that feathered dinosaurs were ancestors of the first bird."

Going on the assumption a picture is worth 1,000 words, they were able to convince the world for a time that evolution was very real. It seemed to be the critical link long sought for over a century; then the fraud was revealed. The fossil was proven to be a fake. As Wells put it, "A Chinese paleontologist proved that someone had glued a dinosaur tail to a primitive bird. He created it to resemble just what the scientists had been looking for. There was a firestorm of criticism — the curator of birds at the Smithsonian charged that the Society had become aligned with 'zealous scientists' who were '<u>highly biased proselytizers of the faith</u>' that birds evolved from dinosaurs."

Fakes come out of the fossil beds all the time, because the fossil dealers know there's big money in it. Read what ornithologist Alan Feduccia, an evolutionary biologist at the University of North Carolina at Chapel Hill stated in an interview regarding the *archaeoraptor* fraud. Feduccia said: "*Archaeoraptor* is just the tip of the iceberg. There are scores of fake fossils out there, and they have cast a dark shadow over the whole field. When you go to the fossil shows it's difficult to tell which ones are fake and which ones are not. I have heard there is a fake-fossil factory in Northeast China, in Liaoning Province, near the deposits where many of these recent alleged feathered dinosaurs were found."[42]

There is very little surprise that faked fossils are appearing. Cash is king in this market, plus the desire for fame. Combine those two and it becomes irresistible for some who are greedy. According to Feduccia, "The Chinese fossil trade has become a big business. The fossil forgeries have been sold on the black market, for years now, for huge sums of money. Anyone who can produce a good fake stands to profit."[43] Evolutionists are the ones buying the forgeries, hoping they can get their name in the journals as "the one" who first produced the missing link.

Many, many other frauds have "surfaced" through both scientists and the public. They are all bizarre in their own right, that have come out about the same time that *archaeoraptor* appeared. Take *bambiraptor*, a chicken-sized dinosaur with supposed bird-like characteristics that popped up at a scientific conference. Evolutionist paleontologists jumped on this exhibit heralding it to the media as the missing link. This fossil turned out to be another fake — a reconstructed animal with feathers or substances that looked like feathers on it. The problem was revealed however by evidence that when the specimen was originally unearthed it did not have feathers on it. But because evolutionist scientists thought the feathers should be there, they added the feathers! And the dinosaur looked even more like a bird because the man who did the reconstruction used the same artificial eyes that taxidermists put in stuffed eagles.[44] National Geographic Magazine eventually got around to writing a disclaimer, though it was bad, cryptic, and very brief.

Because they "itch" to have Darwin's theory be true, some scientists will help manufacture and promote fossils to meet the criteria, resorting to about anything, knowing that the find will be reported. For example, one group of scientists reported that bird or turkey DNA was found in dinosaur bones. Turns out, it was not just turkey DNA; the bones were actually that of a turkey. While the announcement was an obvious hoax, it didn't stop the disciples of Darwin from rushing to publish the story of the fossil in Science magazine as being a missing link.

The king of all the icons used to support evolution is the picture of the left to right parade of ape-like creatures that morph into a upright human as they all walk across the dust cover of the 1995 edition of *The Origin of Species*.[45] The picture has

Chapter Eleven — "No Gods Allowed in Here!"

been shown repeatedly seen over the many years to the point that it is no longer theory in many people's minds, but absolute fact.

The repetition of seeing all these frauds in classrooms built a certain brand of bold certainty among young students; the type of certainty that witnessed the igniting of a revolution of those becoming disciples speaking of the theory as fact. Eventually, statements similar to the following were an everyday occurrence. "If you go back far enough," the news icon Walter Cronkite crooned in a documentary on evolution, "we and the chimps share a common ancestor. My father's father's father's father, going back maybe, a half-million generations — about five million years ago — was an ape."[46]

There were several fraudulent ape-man fossils: There was **"Java Man,"** especially prominent in the 1940s World Book Encyclopedia. Java Man was found on the island of Java in 1891 by Dutch scientist Eugene DuBois, who touted immediately that his find was a half million years old which as he said "represents a stage in the development of modern man from a smaller-brained ancestor."[47] The "fossil" hit the papers being advertised once again by evolutionists as the missing link for humans, but most are haphazardly ignorant of the full Java Man story. "What is not so well known is that Java Man consists of nothing more than a skull cap, a femur (thigh bone), three teeth, and a great deal of imagination," one author would pen.[48]

The fossil that became known as **Piltdown Man** was discovered early in 1912 within Pleistocene gravel beds at Piltdown in Sussex, England. Amateur archaeologist Charles Dawson did the digging and made the find. What Dawson actually discovered were some pieces of human skull cap, a jawbone with two attached teeth, a variety of animal fossils, and some primitive stone tools. Contacting Arthur Woodward the keeper of Geology at the Natural History Museum, the two teamed up to dig further. They unearthed more fragments. Piecing them together, they believed the skull fragments and the jaw bone were from the same fossil. In December of that year in a press conference, they presented the world with their discovery of Piltdown Man. The story went absolutely wild in the newspapers, with pictures running in papers around the world. For forty years this fossil was used by evolutionists to boast they had finally done it — discovered the true missing link of mankind to vindicate Darwin! Over those 40 years, over 500 scientific essays were written about it. For forty years it was upheld in science books as the genuine link in evolution. Finally, as the evidence began to make Piltdown Man look suspect, in 1953 three scientists tested the fossils revealing the fossil to be a hoax. "Pilty" had been found out; it had been made from two human skulls, an orangutan jaw, an elephant molar, a hippopotamus tooth, and a canine tooth from a chimpanzee. It had been assembled by Dawson and Woodward.[49]

Storming in came the Roaring Twenties, and with them came storming in another fossil discovery into front page headlines; it soon became known as **"Peking Man."** It brought a welcome catharsis for Darwinists and new hope as they claimed this newly dug fossil was finally the true missing link between ape and man. It was found near Beijing, called Peking at the time, and most people think it was an entire skeleton which was unearthed. In truth, the fossil consisted of a piece of skull cap and one tooth. During World War II, the fossil was lost in a transportation mishap and was never seen again. There was a plaster model made early on of the fossil, and the model has been studied through the years. However, later discoveries of several skull caps and jaw bones have revealed that Peking Man was very much human-like. However, it too was a fake, and was reclassified as *homo erectus pekinensis*.[50]

The evidence for evolution within the fossil record, or essentially the lack of fossil evidence, reveals something obvious. We are dealing with religious belief systems, that of Secular Humanism and one of its tenants, Darwinian evolution that runs counter to Christianity. Christianity is considered a serious threat to the huge majority of Darwinists. Given the lack of evidence in the fossil record, it takes great faith, actually a faith against faith, to accept it as truth. It also becomes obvious that our public school system, is actually teaching this religious belief on its own in spite of the lack of scientific evidence to support it. So taking one more step, it becomes obvious in science classes in school that deal with the origin of species, that whatever else is being taught in these classes, it sure as hell is not science![51]

When taking another look back at cases in schools such as Joelle Silver in New York in light of all this evidence against Darwinian evolution, suddenly an evil religious twist becomes visible which Humanists are using in schools. According to Silver's attorney, Robert Muise, he's never seen a more egregious example of religious hostility in a public school. He said, "It's like they're treating those posters and inspirational sticky notes like it's some sort of pornography . . . I find that offensive."[52]

"Be on guard. Stand true to what you believe. Be courageous. Be strong. And everything you do must be done in love."
- 1 Corinthians 16:13-14

Muise went on, "When they launched the investigation, they literally went through her classroom . . . and removed anything that had anything to do with Christianity. I've never seen anything like that. Ms. Silver does not cease being a Christian nor does she shed her constitutional rights at the schoolhouse gate."[53]

Official instructions were also given to Silver that if she needed to look at inspirational messages for her personal use she would have to "keep such material in a discreet folder" that only she would have access to. In other words, keep that horrible stuff locked up, girl! She was also told to never disclose the contents of that folder to any parents or students.[54]

"Our nation was founded to promote religious liberty," added AFLC co-founder David Yerushalmi when he was interviewed. "Yet, for years our public schools have been bastions of religious hostility." To make sure that Christians' views are kept

CHAPTER ELEVEN — "No Gods Allowed in Here!"

out, the "liberal judiciary vigorously enforce the spread of 'tolerance.'"[55]

"Tolerance" is one of the latest buzz words in the tyrannical one-way agenda legalized by the courts to ensure that schools remain firmly in the control of Humanist doctrine. Tolerance is legally a one-way street which forces anyone in objection to humanist doctrine to surrender while strangling any reform movements which stand on  constitutional grounds. It also ensures that courses containing basic moral principles are not taught, especially any course mentioning Christianity or patriotism. "The movement to turn schools into hotbeds of political correctness began with the deliberate exclusion of God, and it threatens to end with the deliberate exclusion of country. In between, the courts have seized control of curriculum in the name of desegregation and free speech (yet speech codes have even filtered into elementary and secondary schools), and have made the simple task of maintaining order and discipline virtually impossible."[56]

Actions taken against Christian individuals, including Ms. Silver, in our public schools, and other parts of our society, resemble "The Obsolete Man," a 1961 episode of the television series *The Twilight Zone*. Though he predicted that it was not necessarily our future, but could be, Rod Serling began his episode with an ominous tone:

> "You walk into this room at your own risk.... This is not a new world, it is simply an extension of what began in the old one. It has patterned itself after every dictator who has ever planted the ripping imprint of a boot on the pages of history since the beginning of time. It has refinements, technological advances and a more sophisticated approach to the destruction of human freedom. But like every one of the super-states that preceded it, it has one iron rule: logic is an enemy and truth is a menace. This is Mr. Romney Wordsworth... who will draw his last breaths in The Twilight Zone."[57]

Obsolete Man dealt with themes of Orwellian totalitarianism, euthanasia, relativism, progressivism and religion, in some future totalitarian state, (possibly the USA in 2014). A man, Romney Wordsworth, is put on trial for being 'obsolete,' in the state. His occupation as a librarian is a crime punishable by death because the State has eliminated books and literacy. (Well, we're half way there.) Yet, his real crime that infuriates the State is that Wordsworth believes in God, also punishable by death. The State claims they have long since proved that there is no God, therefore anyone believing in God should die, unless they retract their beliefs in a publicly televised confession. Wordsworth is prosecuted by the Chancellor of the State, who takes time to announce to the court, assembled in the building and with a television audience, that Wordsworth is not an asset to the State, and must therefore be liquidated.

Serling had written this story to present his television audience with the dangers of an authoritative dictatorship, a result of continued liberal progressivism. Wordsworth compares the Chancellor to Adolf Hitler and Joseph Stalin, asking the Chancellor the ultimate question of the episode, "Does history teach you nothing!?" The Chancellor, perched at his judge's bench some 20 to 30 feet above Wordsworth scolds him, "On the contrary, history teaches us everything." The Chancellor argues that Hitler and Stalin had all the right ideas but they mistakenly did not go far enough with ruthlessness to teach the subjects the necessary lessons. He then points to Wordsworth indicating relics who believed in art, philosophy, literature, free speech, and freedom of religion, all of which had been stripped away and banished by the State, would have to pay the price of disobedience. Great question that Wordsworth asks the Chancellor and his television audience, "Does history teach you nothing!?" That timeless question screams for an answer.

While the Chancellor's charge of "Obsolete" is leveled against our hero of this Twilight Zone episode, strangely, it is the identical charge of government officials leveled against students and teachers while in school for any expression of a personal faith in God. Conversely, the term obsolete is most fitting as a charge to be leveled against the same officials for cultivating and teaching their choice in belief system within the confines of school. That belief system is secular humanism. (See Chapter 2 for a full description of the secular humanism and its beginnings in modern America) Reason for saying that? Humanism is the "oldest" belief system in the world. It even predates any of the polytheism of the ancient world. What government officials force to be done when attacking students and teachers for their personal beliefs in God, is an act of replacing a wonderful and reasonable belief with one which is a counterfeit. If the Founders of America could see the country's education system now, they would be about bringing change once again, up to and including a revolution. The scenes rising from charges being made against children demonstrate that individuals such as Mr. Wordsworth living in a totalitarian state, may not be so far away. As this treason grows unabated, sooner rather than later culture will arrive at that point.

The 'Jack-Booted Thugs' in the America of today are not just the KKK, the Skin Heads, the Biker gangs, or the ethnic gangs running some cities as the liberal media wants you to believe. Those groups have been overtaken and superseded by gangs of government officials directed by the DOJ and the Obama administration. Their courts, the universities, the media and Hollywood all react similar to Pavlov's dog. Action is taken when a bell rings, that bell being the indication that a comment has been heard in school or a note found supporting some Christian thought; All the forces prepare for battle and respond in kind, beginning with threats and intim-

CHAPTER ELEVEN — "No Gods Allowed in Here!"

idation. Their actions speak of a deep-seated fear as they flinch at the mention of Christianity, similar to Superman cringing at the presence of kryptonite, or Dracula shielding his eyes from a Christian Cross, or Mr. Obama wrestling his hands into his pockets at the sound of the Pledge of Allegiance.

More of the hatred some school officials are having for Christians is seen as reported by David Limbaugh in his book; *How Liberals are waging war against Christianity*. "In a **public school in St. Louis**, a teacher spotted the suspect, fourth-grader Raymond Raines, bowing his head in prayer before lunch. The teacher stormed to Raymond's table, ordered him to stop immediately and sent him to the principal's office. The principal informed the young malefactor that praying was not allowed in school. When Raymond was again caught praying before meals on three separate occasions, he was segregated from other students, ridiculed in front of his classmates, and finally sentenced to a week's detention."[58]

"Before snack time in her kindergarten class in **Saratoga Springs, N.Y.**, little Kayla Broadus held hands with two of her classmates and recited this prayer: "God is good, God is great, thank you, God, for my food." The alert teacher pounced on Kayla, severely reprimanded her, and reported her to the school administration. In short order, the principal sent a sternly worded letter to Kayla's parents advising them that Kayla was not allowed to pray in school, aloud or with others. We are left with the definite impression that God is not allowed on campus. The school board then issued a triumphant press release crowing about its victory over a kindergartner praying before snack time. A creeping theocracy in Saratoga Springs was stopped dead in its tracks! Kayla's mother brought a lawsuit, winning Kayla the right to pray out loud. But she was still prohibited from holding hands with others while she prayed. "Hearing the G-word in kindergarten might interfere with the school's efforts to teach proper sexual techniques in the first grade."[59]

Consider the wonderful display of tolerance at **Lynn Lucas Middle School, in Willet, Texas**. Here school administrators snatched students' books having dust covers displaying the Ten Commandments. "In a lawsuit filed in U.S. District Court in Houston . . . [legal counsel] alleges that a Lynn Lucas Middle School teacher . . . .threw away Bibles owned by 15-year-old Angela and 13-year-old Amber Harbison, saying, 'This is garbage.'" They tore the covers off, threw them in the trash can, and told the students that the Ten Commandments constituted 'hate speech.'"[60] Apparently, it is insensitive to expose little children to the Ten Commandments when they are learning to count from one to ten. Possibly counting ten new Obama executive orders or ten Muslims would be acceptable.

Columbine High School brings back memories of tragedy from the 1990s. One of the scenes that most people missed were pictures and video of teachers leading small groups of surviving students in circles of prayer on school grounds immediately following the tragedy. Don't get me wrong. I was not against the teachers leading prayers, just confused. The school had been spending years drilling into these children's minds that mentions of God and Christianity were to be compared to horrible hate speech: the prayers to God spoken in school. Mentions of Jesus, God or Christianity before the tragedy would not be tolerated! Now suddenly, during a tragedy the staff, including some teachers, was leading the pupils in prayer on the school grounds? Should I read into this a picture of an educational aristocracy which is saying 'we will do what we want, but you cannot?' Or could it be that not even those who teach against Christianity do not really believe what they are teaching when 'push comes to shove!?'

Good old-fashioned double standards are admissible occasionally, but if that is the game we are playing, then we should ask Alex Trebek to skip this round, and go straight to Final Jeopardy!

After seeing the prayer circles that day at the Columbine School, what the School District did next added to the scenery, confusing many adults, let alone the children who attended classes there. Following the massacre at Columbine, the district had taken the recommended precautions by assigning several squadrons of grief counselors armed with teddy bears to be in school. Students and family members were invited to paint messages on tiles above student lockers. However, some students took it upon themselves to paint messages and remarks that contained "objectionable" thoughts, that by some were said to be equal to "hate speech;" messages such as: "4/20/99: Jesus Wept" and "God Is Love." This would not be tolerated school officials announced. The school removed some 90 tiles that had these offensive religious messages.[61] Not to worry, a progressive federal court came to the rescue of the school, when the school was criticized for their heartlessness, on the subject of the censorship of the religiously messaged tiles. They upheld the school's decision to rip them down.[62]

Not All Gods Are Banned from School

The last decade has witnessed Christianity being kicked out of the American classroom, and with it God Himself. Mentioning God, etc,, are now classified as hate speech. However, not all mentions of religion constitute "hate speech" or "terrorism." Down south, in Tupelo, Mississippi, school administrators recently purified all Christmas carols from any religious content, at least of the Christian messages. Then they led the children in a chant of "Celebrate Kwanzaa."[63]

Similar scenes have become all too familiar in recent years. Local news video fills a slot with an ACLU attorney in the front of some school building as a backdrop, similar to Cheektowaga Central School. The scene is all too common of such a government barrister explaining in a monotone that prayer and Bibles are not allowed in public school because they are against the law. A broadcaster will usually shoehorn in some statement that we are a 'post Christian nation' now, to accompany reinforcement of the authority of the video clip. Can anyone say "Obsolete?" Or "Romney Wordsworth?"

CHAPTER ELEVEN — "NO GODS ALLOWED IN HERE!"

The stories zoom at us these days like mortar attacks launched by an army, except the attacks are against some quiet reserved student carrying a Bible in his backpack, or targeting two parents who dared to bow their heads with their child on the school building steps in a prayer; or wearing a religious theme on a shirt. (See court case 393 U.S. at 511.) Or what seems even more typical in today's "Assault the Christian" fervor, is a school principal from a respectable middle class neighborhood in the suburbs who is being legally bludgeoned and forced to surrender to the will of a "No Gods Allowed" agent of the government.

It Is the School Property; Don't You Get It?!

School districts officials have gotten in on the act about what can and cannot be placed on the property. I could tell you of the city of New York — how the district is working to cancel the leases of all church and religious groups that rent city facilities. It is the policy of many school districts around the nation to lease building space to church groups meeting on Sundays. But space for this story allows this one glimpse: "Our view is that public school buildings, which are funded by taxpayers' dollars, should not be used as houses of worship," stressed Marge Feinberg, a spokeswoman for New York City's Department of Education. "Public school space cannot and should not be used for worship services, especially because school space is not equally available to all faiths." (I bet space is available to Muslims if they want to use it!)

Some court cases show the persecution: Herds of court cases could be cited displaying the current trend to persecute Christians and cement secular humanism in as the official religion at school. Here's a reference to whet your appetite:

"The seeds for these attacks were dropped in the Supreme Court opinions in the 30s and 40s, and it really began to take off in the 1960s, circling around keeping order in class and disciplining children at first.[64] During the long era following the War Between the States and the adoption of the 14th Amendment, or as I like to say, Once upon a time, in an altogether different era, the disciplinary powers of schools were quite clear. There was a seamless line between parents and teachers-the latter serving, literally, as in loco parentis. The teacher's authority began when the student left home in the morning and lasted until he returned home. Thus "most parents would expect and desire that teachers would take care that their children, in going to and returning from school, should not loiter, or seek evil company," the Vermont Supreme Court held in 1859.[65] The courts almost never intruded into school administration, except in extraordinary cases, such as when teachers inflicted brutal beatings, and then only by way of actions for damages against the perpetrators.

The start of the Supreme Court and Anti-Discipline: The Supreme Court got in on the act in 1969, with the case of *Tinker v. Des Moines School District*. "For the first time," the Court has granted to the judiciary "the authority to determine the rules applicable to routine classroom discipline."[66] The Court decided that public school authorities could not discipline high school or junior high students for wearing black armbands. That would be to violate the students' First Amendment rights. The justices decreed, with delicious irony in light of contemporary speech codes, that "state-operated schools may not be enclaves of totalitarianism."[67] The Court went on to say that discipline could only be administered if the school could 'demonstrate' that students materially or substantially interfered with the requirements of "appropriate" or invaded the rights of others. Of course, *Tinker*, transferred the decision about what was appropriate in discipline, from the school to the court.

Tinker did a lot to destroy authority in school, and set up a revolution of rights for children. Backlash was setting in-indeed, had already set in. In 1966, the Republicans gained 49 seats in the House of Representatives and six in the Senate; eight governorships also switched from Democratic to Republican hands. A September, 1968 poll found that 81 percent of the public felt that "law and order (had) broken down."[68]

But later cases that relied on the Fourteenth Amendment's "due process" clause did much worse mutilation to authority in school. The Due Process clause had originally been put in to ensure that proper notice and an avenue of protection via a hearing is provided when government threats are made against a citizen's life, liberty, and property. But with liberals brandishing the clause, they rebranded it with a new meaning: Now being extended (I'm sure you can guess what they did) to embrace welfare benefits, driver's licenses, and public education. Observant citizens will see that the intent of the law has gotten lost in the malaise, with welfare recipients getting more protection than property owners, who have been savaged by a dictatorial arm of the law through eminent domain.

Once the courts established that "free speech" was the order of the day at schools, they used the due process clause to do for school discipline what they had done for criminal law using the same clause: create new procedures out of whole cloth to protect rights discovered for the first time by liberals. Students who faced temporary suspension from the public school have property and liberty interests that are protected by the due process clause of the Fourteenth Amendment, Justice Byron R. White argued, writing for a majority of five. Public education is a property interest-a right to a benefit embedded in Ohio law-and the state "may not withdraw that right on grounds of misconduct, absent fundamentally fair procedures to determine whether the misconduct has occurred." [69]

The scandalous thing for those of us, who are old enough to have witnessed much of this trend within the courts, is that we are able to verify much of what has been reported in the Wall Street Journal, World Net Daily, and a few other reputable websites, periodicals, and papers that dare to report truth. We see our schools, our country, and our way of life being destroyed by "treason from within." We have seen school discipline run the gamut, from the days when teachers and

CHAPTER ELEVEN — "NO GODS ALLOWED IN HERE!"

principals used paddles to drive home a point, to now, seeing we are snookered by the liberal courts that have taken the classroom from the teachers, principals, and even the parents, just to turn it over to unruly student punks and jerks. Control in these classrooms has been snatched up by the same people who took control of the prisons away from guards, the same people to whom objective standards of conduct have no meaning; they are the radical progressive liberals, who have been for so long working with their buddies in the courts to bring about this chaos.

And the court said "It must be fair in the land": It all started with black armbands, then the courts moved their attention to school discipline. Once the courts turned their sights on school discipline, all bets were off. Babbling of "liberty interests" and "fairness," the Supreme Court decided that the Fourteenth Amendment's due process clause applied to public school suspensions of any high school students. Among the rights the statute ensured was entitlement to due process hearings when the school sought to change the classroom placement of an emotionally "disabled" child. Moreover, unless totally incapable of learning, even with prodigious supplemental tutoring, such children were entitled to instruction in a "regular education environment."[70] Well, it doesn't take much to turn a hearing into a nightmare, once the lawyers get their noses under the tent. Before long, it became almost as difficult to suspend students as it did to fire public employees. Seeing their goal of total control almost accomplished, next on the court docket, was ridding the schools of mentions of the Christian faith. They did that by ridding the classroom of what they called the evil of religion.

One must remember that the trappings of anti-Christianity in school had long before been built and put in place with the Supreme Courts' actions of 1948 and 1962, those were the removal of the Bible from the classroom and dropkicking prayers off the school property. From there, as designed by the liberals and their ACLU, it has been nothing more than a slippery legal slide. For anyone daring to step out of line, they found themselves on that slide, a very steep and greasy slick ride to a lawsuit, with a big government basket at the bottom for principals, teachers and any parents daring but dumb enough to voice an opposing opinion about school.

Control is the key word: The next step was to seize and expand more control in the classroom for the liberal progressive agenda over every individual student. Disability entered the school as a special right. With attorneys swarming this country, schools have become inevitably ensnared in the legal web woven not only by judicial rulings but also by the statutes and regulations drafted to interpret them. The legal rights and prohibitions resulting from legislation, aka, the law, have arguably become the true impediments to school discipline. But keeping with their liberal progressive path, in 1975, Congress passed the Education for All Handicapped Children Act, and since then, students with a multitude of disabilities, including those with a "serious emotional disturbance," have been nearly exempted from standard disciplinary procedures.[71] What this meant was federal protection for disabled youth, now extensive and costly, got a quiet and innocuous start in 1966, when Congress added Title VI to the Elementary and Secondary Education Act (ESEA), passed the year before. The amendment was mainly an appropriations measure, providing money to the states for plans designed "to meet the special educational and related needs of handicapped children," such as wheel chair access, handicapped restroom facilities, etc. But already, "handicapped" was starting to include the "seriously emotionally disturbed," a decision that would be used to change the landscape in the future.[72]

Three years later, in 1972, a federal district court ruled that nearly all children had the right to attend school. Public education, even for children with a "mental, physical or emotional disability or impairment," had become an entitlement. A child suspended for more than two days was entitled to a hearing, legal representation at the hearing, diagnostic services, and the provision of an alternative education.[73] The education of the "disabled" was maneuvered to include a category of children with behavioral and emotional problems ranging from the merely hyperactive, the common trouble makers, and to the violent. They are protected under this basic civil right.

This also meant now the liberal judiciary could expand their control in classes, past telling teachers how they would keep control in classes, but also to intrude into academic decisions. That meant determining who could not be flunked in a subject. A federal court of appeals opined that a teacher could not have student's grade one another's papers. The appeals court cited "privacy laws" to make even this simple classroom task subject to judicial scrutiny. Is this what judicial review is all about? No. In fact the Supreme Court rejected this nonsensical idea. Still it's a testimony to the powerful liberal assault that such a case could be carried all the way to the highest court in the land.[74]

Activists for liberal causes find candidates they can use in teaching their socialist activist lessons which they call "liberty interests." These are people who are prohibited from expressing themselves in lewd, sexual, or unorthodox manners. School children are often the pawns in their game. Children, who are in school, must logically be viewed as subordinate to and in a special relationship with legal authority. This is because they are children attending school being run by adults. Since these students are lawfully subject to school authorities, routine matters of discipline simply do not implicate "liberty" in the constitutional sense. The student's liberty is lawfully curtailed as soon as he sets foot in the schoolroom. Not according to liberals. They want children to have freedom of expression in school; to exercise lewd, sexual, anti-democracy, and even demonic behavior. According to them, the only people who have no "liberty interests" are people who want to pray in public schools.

Periodically, there are attacks made upon some student's freedom as they express their belief in God. The media will normally sweep most of these under the rug, but they will certainly report on some person who has been trampled upon

CHAPTER ELEVEN — "NO GODS ALLOWED IN HERE!"

because they are protected under the discrimination act. A couple of cases follow to demonstrate how real they are:

In 2011 a New Hampshire school district was bullied by a Wisconsin-based Freedom from Religion Foundation, forbidding the mother of two high school students from "giving speeches" which was really praying on the front steps of her kids' high school building. She was monitored for over two years and accused of praying for 15 minutes each morning. What seems to have upset the Freedom from Religion Foundation worker the most was that the mother often wore a white necklace displaying a cross, bearing the name of Jesus. The school board was threatened with a letter — they chose to force the mother to leave the steps rather than fight for the right to pray outside school.[75]

In a Southern Missouri school, there was a dispute that arose over a student, a boy, just carrying a Bible into school in his back pack. What made this dispute so controversial is that while the Bible was suddenly outlawed by the school district, other religious material, such as what they called "Islamic material" was not. This went to the Missouri Court of Appeals where the judge wrote the opinion saying materials such as the Qur'an and I Ching could be allowed in school, but the Bible could not, because as the judge wrote "the Bible was unique among all religious material."[76] It should be obvious to anyone who can fog up a mirror with their breath the obvious conclusion: "No Christian God allowed in our school!"

In a Maryland school district, the Gideons were banned from giving away Bibles to the public elementary school there. The Gideons have placed the Bible in 181 nations in 82 different languages over the years. The organization focuses on hotels and motels, hospitals and nursing homes, schools, colleges and universities, the military and law enforcement and prisons and jails. But, the school board banned the distribution after a woman complained about the activity to the American Civil Liberties Union and the school district. The woman said the action blurred the separation between church and state. Even when the school board said no child was forced to take a Bible, letter writing followed with screams of "the Supreme Court has said this is unconstitutional! You can't argue with the Supreme Court!" While this case is still being bantered about, you can see clearly the message from 'the authorities', "God is not allowed in our schools."[77]

In Katy, Texas at Pattison Elementary school, Christmas songs were forbidden by the school to be sung by the children. This was done apparently because many of the students had refused to sing songs celebrating other religious faiths, like Islam. The school board claiming to rescue the day and teach a level playing field as well as tolerance communicated the message to parents that students must participate in the songs of other world religions or face academic punishment. What a way to teach tolerance.[78]

New York School Districts through the pen of the Chancellor of the Department of Education prohibited the display of Nativity scenes in public schools. The

Chancellor wasn't heartless however — he directed that the Jewish menorah and Islamic star/crescent moon could be displayed instead of the manger of Jesus. I suppose this is at least consistent with the decision of New York City to become the world's largest display of Islam at Ground Zero with the building of a mosque.[79] While the Chancellor has made his decision, at the time of this writing, it is not a done deal. In fact, there are many persons behind whom I would have to stand in protest and prohibit an Islamic center to be built on Ground Zero.

Regarding the California School District, the California legislature has announced their latest liberal foolishness — while prohibiting discrimination against transgendered individuals and running up a huge deficit — has mandated public schools to present a three-week immersion course in Islam for all seventh graders. According to the course direction, students have to adopt Muslim names, dress in Muslim garb; plan a pretend trip to Mecca and among other things chant "Praise Allah, Lord of Creation!" They are encouraged to dress in Muslim garb.[80] Ironic, isn't it? All of this is okay, but mentioning the name of Jesus in school brings out the threat of riot gear and a jail term. Whatever else might be said, this is not education; it's indoctrination.

And in Louisiana, the ACLU has asked a judge to hold members of the local school board in contempt for allowing an elementary school student to recite the Lord's Prayer before its meeting. The contention is that public prayer at school-related functions is "un-American and immoral." Further the leader of the ACLU said "The school board and its superintendent cannot get away with a shell game that mocks the judiciary and its role of interpreting and upholding the rule of law." The same outrage was expressed when an adult, Shane Tycer, used the PA system and said a prayer before a baseball game between Loranger High School and Sumner High School, on school property. The state ACLU director also had a moment of liberal interpretation of our heritage when he said, "Public schools should be kept inclusive and secular in keeping with our founders' ideas for religious liberty for all." If that was not enough, he also added, "We need to have a welcome mat in our schools to welcome all. Children and parents whose beliefs are different from the majority must not be made to feel like outsiders in their own schools."[81] If you really want to make children more comfortable, just throw out all their English, science and math tests. Tests and test scores are making "outsiders" of some in their own school. Besides, the children don't feel welcome when you test them.

While our high school campuses have become virtual battle grounds, the ACLU has fixed its sights not on the perpetrators of violence but on those who would allow or offer prayer. Take note — when school shootings take place like in Columbine, the students, dazed teachers and administrators didn't turn to the ACLU or the courts to be consoled. They turn to local ministers who are usually summoned to the school to pray and counsel with the students.

CHAPTER ELEVEN — "NO GODS ALLOWED IN HERE!"

At Lakeview Elementary School in Mount Juliet, Tennessee administrators told parents that the posters which students had prepared for a special prayer event, had to remove the words "God," "God Bless the USA," and "In God We Trust" from the hallways of the school.

It's Not Just High Schools, but Colleges and Universities, Too.

While I did not have the following experience in college, a friend of mine did within a state university in the east. She said that in the first day of a history class, the professor made clear in his opening remarks that he was an atheist, and that he would approach history from an atheistic standpoint. He added, "And if there are any Christians in this class, you may want to think about leaving this class because I will chew you up and spit you out! Your ideology cannot stand up under the pressure of what I have to say." She said she stayed in the class and kept quiet because she needed the course and did not want 'to be flunked' because she tried to argue with the professor.

Suffice it to say that in the university system there are professors who are trying to indoctrinate their students with Marxism rather than teach the curriculum of the course. Who isn't insecure when they are without the psychology of God? G. K. Chesterton must have been right; "Without education, we are in a horrible and deadly danger of taking educated people seriously."

Some Curriculum Is Horrible.

The popular school student textbook, "Across the Centuries," presents the Inquisition and Salem witch-hunts and trials as symbolic of Christianity. I disagree. They are exactly the marks of people who are not Christian. However, it is strange that this book never gets around to mentioning the Muslims bloody conquest of Spain, the crimes of the Ottoman Empire, the Battle of Tours, or the execution of Jews in Quarayza. What is worse, the book doesn't even mention 9/11.

To support other textbooks, a school board in Florida, which wields considerable influence on the curricula of public schools nationwide, has decided to keep a controversial world history textbook that has been criticized for sanitizing Islam's violent history while diminishing Christianity. The decision in November 2013 by the Volusia County board, without a formal vote, came after hearing four hours of public comment, the *Daytona Beach News-Journal* reported. The comments from parents were anything but kind either. One person at the hearing, Walter Hanford, said it "whitewashes" the history of Islam, including the involvement of Muslims in the 9/11 terrorist attacks and the shooting at Fort Hood, Texas, which the Daytona Beach paper reported. A later rally was called by parents over the dispute of the textbook *World History*, a textbook published by Prentice Hall. Of course a response was filed by the Florida chapter of the Council on American-Islamic Relations which called protests against the book "un-American." An attorney for CAIR-Florida, has insisted that opponents "just want to create an environment of intolerance toward Muslims and an environment of hate against Islam."[82]

There are several inconsistencies found both in the science and history textbooks which are used in classrooms across the land. The remarks, more often than not, end up being pro-Muslim, anti-Christian, and pro-Darwinism. Need I remind you that Darwin's theories are just that, theories. But they are taught as absolute iron-clad facts in school. Need I remind you of the Islamic dream — that of converting every individual to Islam or else! So, there is inconsistency, there is discrimination, there is fear pandering, but mostly, that is a sign of the treason from within that is being disseminated from within our schools to rebel against the great heritage of our education system. Progressive liberals will promote these doctrines because they have learned that teaching students within our school system is the most-assured avenue to grow a crop of secular humanists to lead this nation to say loudly, "No Gods allowed in here."

In Case of Illness, Remove the Bag from the Seat Pocket in Front of You — Unfold and Use

To display the myriads of claims filed against students by school boards and the ACLU would take several books to do just that. Over 100 new charges are made each month in our culture today. Hopefully, with the few cited in this volume, it will be enough to drive home the point.

We are in for a rude awakening if we don't heed the warning signals and see the tragic reality of what has been happening in our schools for the past 50 plus years. It is a train wreck that is destroying the culture of our nation. Reviewing a short history of the world should suffice to point to the danger ahead. We are not smarter than God, never have been, never will be. If we kick Him out, we will have expelled the only protector we have had in our nation. And as He is removed, how do we protect what we have and who we are? History teaches that every nation that did what we are doing, did not survive. The list is long, Phoenicia, Samaria, Assyria, Persia, Mede, Babylonia, Judah, and so on. All those nations are now dust. To those professors of engineering, chemistry, English, etc., in schools who would say we must have Christian-free school, I simply point you to G. K. Chesterton's remarks in this context; "**Without education, we are in a horrible and deadly danger of taking educated people seriously.**"

Historian Arthur M. Schlesinger Jr. once wrote, "History is to a nation . . . as memory is to the individual. As an individual deprived of memory becomes disoriented and lost, not knowing where he has been or where he is going, so a nation denied a conception of its past will be disabled in dealing with its present and its future." In that vein, the National Assessment of Educational Progress tests school children every few years in the 4th, 8th and 12th grades on many subject areas. In the 2010 exams, American history was shown to be an obvious problem — only 20% of 4th graders, 17% of 8th graders, and 12% of seniors were at grade-level proficiency.

Chapter Eleven — "No Gods Allowed in Here!"

Students who don't learn our true history one day turn into adults who don't understand our liberties and heritage, who get run over rough shod by politicians due to poor education. And the history of current educational trends in America point this out — in a 1990 survey, almost half of college seniors could not identify the correct half century of our War Between the States (aka, Civil War). Since then, other surveys show over 60% of American adults could not name the president who dropped the first atomic bomb — 20% didn't even know where, or whether, the bomb had been used. The same folks did not know which nations were our enemies during World War II (Germany, Japan, and Italy). However, take heart — in another survey, more teenagers could name the three stooges than the three branches of government. Most disturbing however, were responses to the question on the origin of the statement, "From each according to his ability, to each according to his need". A third of adults said it came from the Bill of Rights; it actually is a core statement of the *Communist Manifesto*. It becomes obvious when viewing such statistics, that public education has been deliberately steered away from teaching our true founding principles, our real heritage — for in that heritage comes true freedom.

There has been a progression of attacks upon students and schools which have come from a few different directions. There are a few villains supplying the assaults. But initially, we must establish that there are many great teachers and administrators in our schools, as well as many great and responsible parents in parent teacher associations who all feel victimized by "the system."

The first mark of the system is that schools are a selected target in which to position Leftist agitators. Second, the Progressive agenda of spreading humanistic theory and Marxism has been carried forth by the agitators, many teachers and administrators; they castigate capitalism in a classroom that allows only one political party to speak. Third, is the brand carrying a steady stream of needless government regulations. No matter how well the intent many regulations are not well thought out. Subsequently, they are used as lightning rods of destruction by Leftists and the media. Fourth, the teachers unions are saddled with a great deal of the blame, with their activist members and outspoken leaders. Take for example the statement made by the past president of both the United Federation of Teachers (1964 to 1984) and the American Federation of Teachers (1974 to 1997), "When school children start paying union dues, that's when I'll start representing the interests of school children." This is the statement of a "so called" leader, proving they are not true leaders at all. The purpose of school is to help children, not help a union.

Some of our public schools have been spared from a portion of the various troubles we have all seen displayed on the local news broadcasts. They have been spared because of good administrators, teachers, and PTA groups who have become a part of the solution in their areas. Collectively, they have put in place many of the following actions in their primary and secondary schools:

- They have implemented practices that make it harder for the wrong thing to happen;

- They have remembered that less is more, e.g., they tred cautiously so as to not allow a mountain to be made out of a molehill; they have recalled that it is possible to needlessly beat a subject to death before truth is revealed.
- They have made the student the worker and the teacher the coach.

At the university level, a few Boards of Regents have left their directives stating each school class must remain above political indoctrination.

To support these good educators with their best intentions and hard work, guidelines and other positive principles have been constructed to provide an environment that helps students think carefully, critically and for themselves. Working against this tradition in primary and secondary schools as well as in universities, it is obvious that thousands of professors across this country go to work every day with the strict intention of indoctrinating their students in their personal liberal political views and prejudices. Many of these activists make no bones about their objectives.

At USC, in Los Angeles, a school which touts its intellectual vitality, the nearly 35,000 students have the opportunity to sample or plunge into portions of this activist propaganda, each an offering from one of the over 3,200 full time faculty. Take "Middle East International Relations: Colonialism, Nationalism, and Identity," a class "organized around Professor Laurie Brand's pro-Arab view of the Israeli-Palestinian conflict ... devoted to a one-sided analysis.... All of the texts assigned, have an anti-Israeli point of view ..."[83] Or consider "Introduction to Feminist Theory and the History of the Women's and Men's Movements." The class is offered from the department, *Barbara Streisand Academics: The Gender Study Program*. In a self-description, this program explains that among its primary goals are those to examine the "functions and images of women and men from the feminine perspective." As to the class "Notwithstanding the word history is in its title, this is not a history course but an instruction in feminist ideology.... [It] calls for 'feminist political solidarity'.... Not only is the course composed solely of feminist political texts, it also discusses subjects (Capitalism and its Discontents) that the professor, whose background is in 'gender studies,' has no competence to address."[84] One could also be severely tempted by the class "Radical Critiques of Penalty," as offered the University of California at Santa Cruz by the always popular professor Angela K. Davis. This Communist and former Black Panther teaches this Leftist course " ... whose major goal according to the catalogue description, is to 'identify ways of disarticulating crime and punishment using race, class, and gender as principal analytical categories' ... [Her teaching on imprisonment is very interesting saying in effect] prisons do not exist to serve justice by punishing individuals who inflict injury on others but rather to carry out the sinister agendas of capitalist elites against minorities and the poor. Even Marx did not believe nonsense like this."[85] One last course to consider on campus is "Racism and Imperialism." The professor and course claim that practices of modern imperialism are motivated by racism. The course claims that "emergent global capitalism is also racist. Both these views are staples of Marxist theory, and, not coincidentally, reading assignments for the course consist mainly of writings by Marxist writers like Lenin, C.L.R. James, Frantz Fanon, and Aime Cesaire, among others."[86] "Classes" cited above are a very few of the hundreds being facilitated within the university system in the U.S. It appears that the curriculum of a pre-Marxist state is in high gear and moving forward ever faster.

Common Core Has Its Hands around the Throat of Education

In American education, we have been led down a path by the federal government coaxing states to come to the trough and receive money if the state would accept certain "standards" in education. It started with "no child left behind," and the associated waiver. The coercion of the federal government has continued with the offering of large grants of money to states which would sign on with Common Core standards. Most people are ignorant of what is contained in the curriculum of Common Core. Many teachers were totally unaware of what was in it, until they received their first instructions on how and what they were to teach. Make no mistake about it; the evils contained inside are manifold. Big Liberal Progressive money and those behind the adoption of Common Core are very strong. They are Marxist in their intentions. The tentacles of Common Core are far reaching into even home schools and private schools, letting no child escape its grasp by standardized tests. The hour is late and past time for good people to stand and fight to eradicate Common Core lessons from our children's future.

Some states have "pretended" to stop Common Core by simply renaming the curriculum. In Iowa for example, Common Core has been renamed Iowa Core.

An example of the egregious actions in standards is the College Board's redesign of AP U.S. History Framework (curriculum) which according to proponents allows for the teachers and students to have a "balanced" coverage of American History. There is no balance however. There are unbelievable statements which the College Board Framework make in their material, plus they have omitted many seminal documents. In my mind, both offer proof that the Framework is nothing but a biased and deeply flawed view of the American experience.

Below is a list of just a few egregious statements:

- Teachers can explore the roots of the modern environmental movement in the Progressive Era and New Deal, as well as debate the underlying and proximate causes of environmental catastrophes arising from pesticide use and offshore oil drilling. (Page 12-13)

- Many Europeans developed a belief in white superiority to justify their subjugation of Africans and American Indians, using several different rationales. (Page 34)

- Reinforced by a strong belief in British racial and cultural superiority, the British system enslaved black people in perpetuity, altered African gender and kinship relationships in the colonies and was one factor that led the British colonists into violent confrontations with native peoples. (Page 36)

- The New England colonies, founded primarily by Puritans, seeking to establish a community of like-minded religious believers, developed a close-knit, homogeneous society and — aided by favorable environmental conditions — a thriving mixed economy of agriculture and commerce. (Page 36. Note that this is the Framework's sole statement about the New England colonies. It omits the Pilgrims, Mayflower Compact, Winthrop's "City Upon a Hill," Roger Williams and religious toleration, New England town meetings and the birth of democratic institutions and so much more.)

- The demographically, religiously, and ethnically divers middle colonies supported a flourishing export economy based on cereal crops . . . (Page 36. Note that this is the Framework's sole statement about the Middle Colonies. It omits William Penn, the Quakers, Pennsylvania policy of religious toleration and the fact that is economic prosperity attracted a diverse mix of ethnic and religious groups.)

- The colonies along the southernmost Atlantic coast and the British islands in the West Indies took advantage of long growing seasons by using slave labor to develop economies based on staple crops; in some cases, enslavbed Africans constituted the majority of the population. (Page 37. Note that slavery is the sole focus. This omits the House of Burgesses, the Maryland Act of Toleration and much more.)

- Although George Washington's Farewell Address warned about the dangers of divisive political parties and permanent foreign alliances . . . (Page 43. This is the Framework's sole reference to George Washington.)

- Lincoln's election on a free soil platform . . . Lincoln's decision to issue the Emancipation Proclamation . . . (Page 57. These are the Framework's sole references to President Lincoln. Note that the Framework omits Lincoln's Gettysburg Address.) There are many more statements in the Framework one should view to see the egregiousness of their position.

A List of the omitted Seminal Documents
- The Mayflower Compact
- The Northwest Ordinance

- Federalist Paper Number 10
- Frederick Douglass's Independence Day Speech at Rochester
- Excerpts from the writings of Emerson, Thoreau and other Transcendentalist writers
- Alexis de Tocqueville — excerpts from Democracy in America
- Lincoln's Gettysburg Address and Second Inaugural Address
- Emma Lazarus, "The New Colossus"
- Woodrow Wilson, "Peace Without Victory" speech
- Theodore Roosevelt, "The New Nationalism" speech
- Excerpts from Steinbeck's Grapes of Wrath describing the Dust Bowl
- Franklin D. Roosevelt, "The Four Freedoms" speech
- Harry S. Truman, The Truman Doctrine speech
- George Kennan, The Sources of Soviet Conduct
- John F. Kennedy, Inaugural Address
- Dr. Martin L. King, I Have a Dream Speech and Letter from Birmingham City Jail
- Lyndon B. Johnson, Speech to Congress on Voting Rights

Common Core is at best a tool intended to uncouple our nation's children from their heritage. At worst it is an egg that was hatched in Marxist philosophy to divert children away from any moral underpinnings, Christian ethic, and into enslavement by an evil central government.

Conclusion

Courts and government regulators have taken over the game, launching restrictions against the mention of Christianity in our learning institutions. Based on all these actions, people are now asking, "Is this even American any longer?" The answer is "No, it is not." <u>The action taken by this country to flee its Christian heritage is unprecedented. Never in history has a nation run away from its religious heritage as quickly as America has.</u> It is enough to make you cry in wanting to get your nation to come to its senses. In the face of right becoming wrong, we have the task of taking our country back. Witness the treason from within, that liberal agenda that is creating the depravity of our school, our culture, our institutions, our government, and of our people.

We must face this challenge and begin the task of taking our universities back. If we do not start now, then when? If not here, then where? If you are tempted to start praying about these problems, heed this message: "Warning! Warning! If you pray for America, do so in the solitude and quietness of your living room. Never pray in the classroom, on the school house steps, or any other place on school property. You will be arrested if you do."

"One of the beautiful boasts of our municipal jurisprudence is that Christianity is a part of the Common Law . . . There never has been a period in which the Common Law did not recognize Christianity as lying at its foundations. . . . I verily believe Christianity necessary to the support of civil society."

~ Joseph Story

U.S. Supreme Court Justice; "Father of American Jurisprudence,"
Placed on the Court by President James Madison

Chapter Twelve

Honey, I Shrunk the Morals

"THE ULTIMATE TEST OF A MORAL society is the kind of world that it leaves to its children."[1] Dietrich Bonhoeffer said that. He is credited with saying it in the midst of imprisonment in a German hell hole called Buchenwald; at the time a hidden and supposedly secret part of the society Hitler built. For a time the world thought Pre-World War II Germany was most civilized for its day in Europe. Of course, history has uncovered the lies and substructure of the Third Reich. Buchenwald was one of the many concentration camps, or "Death Camps" in Germany, operated by the master mind of the Third Reich. Other death factories were there, more than twenty in all. Still discussed today were the most notable ones: Auschwitz, Dachau, Buchenwald, Peenemunde, and Nordhausen. Each was designed to make life a veritable hell for a select slice of ethnicity before they were ultimately killed. The camps, when later exposed, were commonly found having rat-infested dorms, being fenced with concrete and barbed wire designed for forcibly containing, then murdering hundreds of thousands of the German population, mostly Jews. Bonhoeffer "lived" in three prison camps the last days of his life. The first was Tegel military prison in Berlin, where he spent eighteen months. He was moved to Buchenwald near Weimar, for six months, a guest of the Fuhrer. Finally he was moved to Flossenburg concentration camp. There he was executed. Where else would a Christian fit in a nation which makes itself god?

Dietrich Bonhoeffer had said he would stand against the tyranny, which had obviously reached the point where he said enough is enough. While the rest of the churches in Germany melted in fear under the threats of Hitler, Bonhoeffer used his strength to write and warn the church not to submit to political pressure from this evil dictator. He did so until he was executed in April 1945. Bonhoeffer was one of four members of his immediate family to die at the hands of the Nazi regime for their participation in the small protestant resistant movement. They wanted to have a church where the theology was not dictated by the government, but rather the Bible. He wanted a church that would stand firm, keeping the faith while persecuted. The letters he wrote during his final two years of his life were posthumously published under the name "Letters and Papers from Prison" by Edberhard Bethge, his student and friend. Bonhoeffer wrote many papers which were discovered after his death; they were salvaged and then published into books. Interestingly, two of his books carry the titles of what he wanted the church to courageously display; "Grace" is one and "Ethics," is the other. An earlier book, *The Cost of Discipleship*, was published before he went to prison in 1937. Among his many now famous statements, Dietrich is probably best known for his lesson; far too many of his fellow Christians believe in "cheap grace." He coined the term while observing little to no visible difference between a member of a church and they typical person who was of the culture and claimed no faith. Jude 4 says it best, "For certain individuals whose condemnation was written about long ago have secretly slipped in among you. They are ungodly people, who pervert the grace of our God into a license for immorality and deny Jesus Christ our only Sovereign and Lord."

There comes a time, when faced with severe adversity, persecution and physical threats of injury or worse, and sharing at least this one characteristic with Bonhoeffer, some men will finally say, "Enough is enough. I am not putting up with this any longer." Every boy or man will at one time stare into the teeth of decision time. For when one feels alone in the dark, a demon will come. Whether a childhood bully on the playground, a gang member expressing his insecurities and inferiority complex while in some movie theatre or restaurant, an inebriated and violent attacker on a street, or even an over-bloated government that wants "control" of everything in one's life. The Nazis of Germany were just such a demon; the Communists the USSR, in China, and in the banana republics of the Western Hemisphere were also. They wanted whatever a citizen had that had value. Now it is clear that a regime, the U.S. Government is in the same diabolical mood. The end goal is clear, a Socialistic or Collectivist State. Among the various action steps for achieving the goal has been to grab hold of the media, of the school. And one of the last steps to finish off the quest is to break the spirituality and morals of the country. Slipping into socialism, Communism or Marxism is so much easier when the morality codes are broken.

The word "morals" is derived from the Latin word *"moralis"* which has been translated into our English word "behavior." The Latin phrase *"socialis morilas"* is then translated as "social behavior." Morality is then *defined* as "the principles" that govern the distinction between right and wrong or good and bad behavior. Therefore, when we speak of a person having good morals, we are generally referring to that person's standards of behavior or belief system governed by principles that enable him to determine what is or is not socially acceptable.

From that point, society has attempted to define morality even farther by illustrating activity according to what can be called a "moral compass." Everyone knows a compass is an instrument containing a magnetized pointer that shows the direction of magnetic north with bearings shown from it, south, west or east. A traveler, who may be lost and is desperately seeking the direction that he should go in order to reach his desired destination, finds a simple instrument such as a compass to be indispensable. However, the instrument which he holds in his hands will only serve its purpose of directing him if he is willing to go in the direction that its needle points for him to go. If he chooses not to trust the guidance of the instrument, then the instrument will be rendered useless, and he is left to his own means of finding his way. From that analogy, we then will describe a person as either having or not having a "moral compass," which is used to determine at any time an internal tool for finding his way to choices which shores up the beliefs.

As a devout Christian might say, our life is a journey, and in order to find our way to our desired destination, which is back home to our loving Heavenly Father who awaits us, we need guidance and direction. Within each of us is a moral compass that is designed to guide our decisions based on morals and virtues. It is our morals or behaviors that determine the magnetic north of our compass. Choosing wrong or bad behaviors will cause our compass to be off by even the slightest of degrees, and we will find ourselves traveling down paths that often lead to destruction, misery, and woe. However, if we choose right or good behaviors, our moral compass will guide us along the paths that we should follow, and if we endure the journey to the end, we will reach our desired destination. And of course if you don't have a good moral compass within you, make it a priority to find someone who has one.

It Starts with Kids in School

"Old-style" or "Biblical" morality is under assault like never before in America. Because this morality has been thrown out of school, kids are wondering what is right and wrong, how to identify either and what the definition of morality really is. Is it a strict intolerant attitude? Liberals push such questions aside saying society will deal with morality issues over time. We just need to tolerate those who are "running against the grain" and learn to "understand" all their actions. Really? I don't think so. Liberals embrace immorality. They have created a new perverse subculture that has crept into nearly every home and every portion of society. There is the plain truth about immorality and where it is going! Let me show you.

For several decades, "pop psychologists" have followed the guidelines laid down by John Dewey and the secular humanist manifesto suggesting that children need the "seeds of tolerance" planted in them at an early age, allowing them to blossom into well-rounded, tolerant adults making society better. Complying with those dictates, most school curriculums have been replaced to allow alternative lifestyles and viewpoints to not only be expressed, but to be taught as the lifestyle of choice by many of the so-called "intellectual" members of society. Usually this has been done without the parents' knowledge. Parents are usually shocked when they discover these facts and see the pictures and diagrams in books of the Common Core curriculum. Common Core is nothing but the outgrowth of runaway secular humanism.

One area of supposed expertise school officials have been "teaching" is sex education. The schools have both the classroom instruction, followed by unsupervised underneath the stairway activity which has flourished exponentially on many school campuses; this due to the moral turpitude which liberals promote. A real problem for this author is that children are supposed to remain children during their childhood: however the new school curriculum focuses great effort on sex early on in grade school.

A statistical picture reveals the sexual state of the world and our schools. Although it will not supply you with answers, it will show you the dire straits in which we live. In today's world, it is common to lose one's virginity by age 16. However, this is tame in comparison to the problems across middle schools in America. Instead of learning math and English, reports regularly appear about students caught having oral sex in the classroom. This is now generally considered to be at epidemic levels. A child caught underneath stairways during recess engaged in sexual activity is also an epidemic now. Reports of fifth grade graduation parties featuring scores of children "freak" dancing, a form of dancing in which they simulate the sex act while keeping clothes on. The new Common Core lessons and material should be indicted along with their liberal promoters since the authors of this material are promoting sex to young school children. The mind of the liberal seems to assume that teaching children about sex helps them to make right choices. That is wrong for a couple of reasons. First, children cannot see past the end of the day and understand the consequences of their decisions. Second, teachers who believe that immorality and alternative lifestyles are flexible are not the best candidates to teach children, let alone this subject. Based on what we have already seen, with the lack of moral truth in school, it is no place for children to learn about sex. But under the guise of government being correct, this activity continues, almost unabated. Result? Little children's life experiences are gained within a philosophical swamp.

If All Else Fails Be a Bully

However, using the venue of government school and public education, the liberals have gained control of huge portions of society and they have shredded the moral fabric of our culture. They started this process, and if it is not immediately accepted by adults, parents, etc., they begin bullying techniques on parents and others to shut them up, intimidate them. Those tactics have stayed a favorite of theirs for decades.

Highlighting this tactic of the Progressives, consider that on March 10, 2011 President Barack Hussein Obama led a White House conference on what he called a very serious crisis that is plaguing America; a crisis of bullying. (This is like the pot calling the kettle black) In the middle of the greatest economic collapse since the Great Depression, with American soldiers involved in two wars overseas, with Iran on the brink of nuclear weapons development, and with a new White House Scandal every two weeks, Obama focused like a laser on kids getting threatened or being thrown up against student lockers.

Chapter Twelve — Honey, I Shrunk the Morals

Everybody in America hates bullies. Even bullies hate being bullied. But over the past several years there has been no increase or uptick in bullying activity, except by the Liberal Left and Progressive movement in America. Yet, Obama felt the necessity to call leaders from across America together to denounce bullying. He could have denounced the Benghazi decisions, or the lies being told by government. But he did not. The real question is why this, now when there has been no jump in bullying activity in the land? In fact, bullying has been on a decrease and there are so many other fiscal items which need attention. It is my observation that we needed many things during March 2011, but a mega lesson on bullying was not one of those things we needed, especially not from a well-known bully like Obama.

However, if you look at his strategy, he is simply building upon the foundation Progressives have laid in the past. Some will proclaim his innocence indicating he was only trying to protect little children. However, while the media and Obama further joined forces in leading this bullying conference, it is obvious the purpose was to name the bully they want to make certain the world will identify: **anything conservative**. Follow the Obama logic here. The Tea Party: a bunch of hillbilly bullies. Religious fanatics, with the exception of Muslims of course: are all viewed as pure bullies. Fans of traditional marriage: now are considered some of the biggest bullies around since homosexuals are made to suffer so terribly with traditional marriages going on. Anti-union advocates: bullies. Anti-Common Core: real school bullies. The list goes on and on. It turns out by this new definition that anyone who does not like Obama: they are bullies; anyone who disagrees with Obama: bully; anyone who is not black: they are a big bully too. But of course, liberals, progressives, Marxists, Collectivists, we are told by Obama and his media they are true anti-bullies in the world.

The scene of Obama on stage embracing this anti-bullying cause, it was a surreal scene of a true Chicago thug, tricking "some" watchers by associating anti-bullying as anti-conservatism. It was all a big lie. While it appears to be the single best bully tactic in the history of American politics, it is not a new tactic at all. The Democrat Party, which is filled with Marxists, Fascists, Progressives, Liberals, the EPA, the BLM, Leninists, Environmentalists, and anti-Capitalists; they have been in the bullying business for a century. They do what they accuse their opponents of doing and they do it in profusion. They own the brand on identifying victims in society, who as we're told, are always those who have been bullied and run over by the evil conservatives. Victims have held a special place in the heart of a liberal. In fact the emotionalism churned up by seeing the victims they present is the only way most people can put up with liberal politics. When things get rough politically for liberals, there is another victim just around the corner. **With victims by their side, comes the perceived moral high ground; power. With that power, the liberals have attacked the morality of America and the associated people of faith who hold those moral codes as a necessity to good living.**

The interesting, recent twist to this 'victim-ology' is how Barack Obama has hopped back and forth like a spring toad on both sides of the issue. First he is a bully stabbing conservatives and their morality in the back. Then he claims to be a victim by playing the "race" card when anyone disagrees with him. And he loves being the bully while he prepares to play the victim; the race card is in his hip pocket. When talking about his mother, he said she was a "typical white person," then claimed people make fun of him because of his funny name. He says if he had a son, he would have looked like Trayvon Martin. Then he points to the rural people of Pennsylvania saying they are clinging to their religion and their guns. He trots out media talking heads like the 9/11 Truther Touré suggesting that white people, while they were the ones to vote him into office, are angrily opposed to him now because, he, a black man has finally made it. Then Obama had Tom Hanks narrate a 2012 campaign video suggesting Obama's failures were due to this naïve, beautiful waif of a man facing down the harsh realities of evil Republicans who oppose "Glorious Change." The message of the video was obvious: the only way to deal with the poor victim of these Republican attacks was to vote for Obama and get even with the bullies.

This anti-bullying stance of Obama and the Left is at best a huge lie. The dirty little secret beneath their supposed hatred for bullying is their passionate love of bullying. Their second nature is to bully someone and use power to force those who disagree to shut up, back down, or face crushing consequences up to and including loss of reputation, career destruction, and in some cases, death. And in their diatribe, they bully their way to change the landscape of our morality, the spirituality and ethical codes of our nation.

That has been their goal and if they were to receive a grade for how badly they have impacted the culture, it would be the letter grade A+. It has been an all-out assault in every corner of the culture too. Look at a few of the venues of attack.

Hollywood's Impact on Morality

Statistics of immorality in our schools are eye-opening; the fruits of that education system are obvious. Young adults' activities today are alarming. Adults are involved with many dangerous lifestyle choices. They open themselves up to sexually transmitted diseases, addictive lifestyles, with no thought of any prolonged impact. Douglas MacArthur (1880-1964), our top commander of the Allied forces in the Pacific during World War II, stated: "History fails to record a single precedent in which nations subject to moral decay have not passed in to political and economic decline." These insightful words point to the moral decay that is rotting the underpinnings of our nation around us. Legislators have introduced bills and statutes that would give pedophiles and other "alternative lifestyles" legal standing. Our society is failing; the results are in. And no place is that more obvious than in Hollywood, in television and movie industry.

Movies over the past twenty years have been exhibiting an increasingly and ugly tenor of anti-Christian, anti-morality theme. They indoctrinate the audience in despising conservative thought, presenting it as evil, warped, weird. In effect they present an alternate morality built on having sympathy for who they identify as victims. Take the themes of the winning movies from the Academy Awards; there is this theme of political 'victim-ology'. Take the Academy Award winning film from 2014: *12 Years a Slave*. "Everyone deserves not just to survive but to live," said the British filmmaker. "I dedicate this award to all the people who have endured slavery . . ." Well, there is a victim. The big winner of the night was the lost-in-space thriller *Gravity*, which won seven Oscars. That tally included directing honors for Alfonso Cuaron, who made history by becoming the first Latin American filmmaker to win in that category. Notice how the liberals break out ethnicity to create a victim. In 2012, it was *The Help*, focusing on the evils of slavery of years gone by. The message is clear. It should be clear that I thoroughly enjoyed each of these movies. The focus on the story line was exceptional. However, the focus the message that was received loud and clear is that these people are still victims because one or more of them had family members who were persecuted in the past because of their race. In 2005, *Brokeback Mountain* was hailed in its graciousness as being such a gracious, gracious movie, honoring the true victims of Hollywood, the homosexual lovers, or the LGBT/LGBTQ young people, to be politically correct. Now we are talking the redline middle of what Obama believes are the true victims of our society: anyone who displays courage in coming out of the closet to tell of their victimhood, they are hailed as true heroes.

Bottom line, the message which Hollywood sends out in the films they cherish as award-winners, are generally those that carry a theme of societal victims or where a victim is found in a starring role, in the middle of a field picking cotton, being bullied on the ranch because of their LGBT lifestyle, decry they are victims. While I love to see the down trodden get ahead, and will almost always cheer on the underdog, I will admit it; the problem with the most of the Hollywood presentation is they either substitute immorality in place of good morals, or they just continue to beat the same drums for the same group of "victims." It is always slaves, gays, and liberals.

For the objective viewer, Hollywood has declared war on the cherished morality of yesteryear and the citizens of this nation. Other examples are rather obvious. Take the one regarding how a Christian believer or a Christian minister has been stereotypically presented in movies over the years. Sixty to seventy years ago, movies having a character of a "preacher" in a starring or support role, presented that character in a fairly straight forward manner. A person who would provide counsel when there was a serious problem, or that of trying to help when the chips were down. Over time, that same role became a confused, misguided person who bordered on pathological behavior. Then over the next 20 years the role has taken on a sinister persona, for example one who is now a terrorist in some movies. It is interesting to note that producers, while showing Christian characters as pathological weirdoes or terrorists, will produce movies having the Muslim or Middle Eastern character be a quasi-hero, if not clearly stated hero of the flick. This is all done in spite of the fact the exact opposite has usually been the real life script. And by the way, does anyone identify the victim in this scenario?

It is true that the Hollywood Left hates Christian actors, Christian believers, Christian morality, and all things Christian. What is behind that hatred is a true hatred for that which Christian people try to exhibit: that which is good, pure, forbearing, kind, respectable, honorable, gentle, and of good report. They will bully these people anytime they get a chance. They will search out opportunities, i.e., hunt down actors or others in society who have these characteristics and attempt to harass them. This is why some of the few actors who are Christians wish to "conceal" their faith. If it were common knowledge, or if they were outspoken about their faith, they would run the risk of never working in major motion picture industry again. I grew up close to Hollywood, and had relatives in Burbank, North Hollywood and in surrounding 'burbs like Encino, Sherman Oaks, and Woodland Hills. I say all that to say this: there is not much of any redeemable character in Hollywood. I will go on record saying there are a few actors past and present for whom I have great respect and admiration. Even those who are not may not be Christians but exhibit strong views supporting freedom, or 1st and 2nd Amendment rights, they will be attacked. Among those who are no longer with us are Ron Silver and Charlton Heston. They stood for stable American values and the Left did not like that. Currently, Tom Selleck, Jon Voight, and James Ballwin come to mind. There are a few like these who speak for morality and patriotism from their vantage point in Hollywood, but they are few.

For years, Hollywood has held defiance for the spiritual-oriented life, unless of course it centers on something similar to a Ouija Board teaching something against traditionally good morals. In the movie *Dead Poets Society*, (which was hailed by Leftists as a marvelous projection of the way life should be) John Keating, a prep school English teacher played by Robin Williams, challenges his students with these words: "Carpe Diem, lads! Seize the day. Make your lives extraordinary!" In this bold statement he is telling his prep school students to seize the moment or enjoy the day, trusting as little as possible to the future.

Robin Williams' acting was brilliant; he has been one of my favorite "actors" for years; the message of the movie was my concern. One of the major questions in that film is, "What is the meaning of life?" To understand that properly, one must look first at the context. The school is upper, upper class supported by wealthy and socially respectable parents. The school is definitely what one would call establishment oriented. Keating, the existentially-inspired English teacher, chases an agenda to instill within his boys a sense of passion for poetry and the arts that goes well past understanding the verse. So, he turns his and their attention to the human feelings, and like a true existential, he totally ignores the spiritual ramifications and morality beyond the physical life.

CHAPTER TWELVE — HONEY, I SHRUNK THE MORALS

Leftists have difficulty seeing past the fallacy of a "Carpe Diem" philosophy of life. They say they wish to rely solely on the physical senses, unless it is by chance focusing on the walking dead, tantalizing demons with the Ouija Board or the like.

Another fascinating film that put theatre goers into a morality blender and on the existential midnight train to Georgia was Woody Allen's *Crimes and Misdemeanors*. The story, centering on Allen's philosophy of life says there is no meaning to our universe unless we give it meaning. By default we are nothing more than the sum total of our choices, resulting in hopelessness. The only hope is our offspring will somehow learn from our mistakes to get a deeper meaning of life.

Hollywood has been preaching doctrines of choice through their flicks which are reminiscent of the old Let's Make a Deal Doors on the game show. Depending on which door you get, there is a theorem on life, or poison, waiting for you: from "there is no God; live it up," to "our moral code will remain flexible based on our environment," on to "might makes right." The existential life becomes sexy and appealing to young viewers, based on any of the choices made. Over time, this has taken a toll on America's hold of the moral high ground. Because it is difficult to prove cause and effect, i.e., linking murder rates, existential behavior, control substance abuse, and godlessness to the movies, lawyers have kept the movie business in business. They continue to make movies, and I might add to that, TV shows which collectively speak of throwing anything with Judeo-Christian morals attached either into prison or out of the nation. Their substituted morality does not resemble anything close to what a civilized society would even accept on its soil, deserving of only a cussing as they are kicked out of the country. Bottom line, the moral code substituted in society by Hollywood truly takes us farther and farther from any reasonable and life-loving morality.

The Broken "Vertical Hold" on the TV Has Blurred Morality

Children and adults are bombarded on television today with advertising, television shows, and the story lines of stormy social issues that simply did not exist a few generations ago. Each year, the standard of what is considered acceptable entertainment drastically degrades. Hollywood pushes immoral concepts through television, because it pays. And the fashion industry and magazines take up the baton in offering clothing to suit these roles. Such drastic social changes have not occurred without a dramatic effect!

American society does in many ways resemble a forest fire. It started with a small match flame of smut and sex and eventually growing to catch the entire forest on fire. Take for example how the trend has gone from Hollywood and television; it started driving the poor moral standard years ago. Now, Hollywood and television appear in many ways to be trying to keep up with society as a whole as it burns with lusty immorality. They helped set the fire; now the fire is out of control. So Hollywood and their media now merely reports and reflects a snapshot of the condition of society last year; and they blame conservatives for setting the fire with hate. Hollywood has taken some serious lessons from Nero.

In 2002, a survey in the United States showed what children believe and consider being moral. It was a kind of moral gauge, or barometer, to see where the country stands. It found that 30 percent of adults in America did not even believe in morality.[2] Catch your breath for a moment to think about that statistic. Almost one in three adults does not feel that morals shape the way he thinks or makes decisions. Just as startling as reported is that only 9 percent of teenage Christians believed that there was any absolute moral truth.[3]

The American Heritage Dictionary defines morality as "a system of ideas of right and wrong conduct." Unless those surveyed do not understand the meaning of morality, one-third of Americans do not believe in a concept of right and wrong conduct. Television has had a huge negative impact on this conduct, but still we must ask, how could this happen?

It was not too many decades ago that surveys showed totally different results, more positive ones I would add. Can the blame be laid at the feet of the entertainment industry? Analysts have argued for years: "Adults can resist the pulls of television and society. They can watch televised acts of murders, sex or deceit without it affecting their moral compass."[3] While I would argue that garbage is garbage, there seems to be a portion of their thinking that is partially correct. But for children it is a different story. When they are young, they are very impressionable. The most effective way to instill wrong morals into a person is to teach him wrong morals as a child. The key is education!

For example, there is no such thing as a born racist, as some liberals have declared in bullying some persons; a person might be accused of that, but must be educated in particular ways to reach that point in life. It is a learning process that must be cultivated over time in an environment that fosters that thought process. You can see this in very young children, who do not even see the difference in skin color of their playmates or others around them. The same impressions are formed over wealth or the lack of wealth or any other element in life. It has to be developed over many years, in an environment that reinforces or drives these wrong concepts into his mind, supplanting what should have been proper and balanced concepts of racial equality.

Also, the younger a person is when wrong thoughts and concepts are introduced, the more likely he is to be open to them and parrot what he hears and sees. Attitudes must be programmed before a concept of right and wrong solidifies. And so is the case with morality. People must be taught morals when they are young to have them transfer to adulthood. But if they are not being taught proper morals, what are they learning? This is exactly why the Progressive Liberals have been succeeding at teaching young pupils in school about socialism, Marxism; that they are the answer for social justice. When these young children age into young adults in their thirties, they still hold those thoughts as being true.

Television has been called the window into our society. It truly shows the "state of affairs." There was a time when society reflected television, when good morals were taught by the characters showed up in real life. It was the stimulus for change in society. Popular culture once reflected what was seen on television — and so did morality. The early years of television saw programs such as *Leave it To Beaver* and *The Donna Reed Show*. These programs represented wholesome families, and were good examples for the viewing audience. Even later shows like *Gunsmoke* and *Bonanza* had characters who taught doing right was the right thing, and the culture reflected that morality. But, like so many things in our culture, human nature prevailed. What sells became more important that the content of programs. And a society being loosed from its moorings started demanding more sensuous story lines, more sex, and more lust. The competition unraveled the moral direction of producers and their TV programs. The writing became a second thought and was poorly done. Just get it out for sale. So over time the basest elements of humanity are visual each week on favorite shows. Not much brain power is needed to understand what is happening.

How did this happen? Just a few decades ago would have shown completely different results. Can the blame be laid at the feet of the entertainment industry? Many will argue: "Adults can resist the pulls of television and society. They can watch televised acts of murders, sex or deceit without it affecting their moral compass." This thinking is partially correct. The most effective way to instill wrong morals into a person is to teach him wrong morals as a child. The key is education!

For example, few suggest that people are born as racists. It is learned, developed, over many years, in an environment that drives these wrong concepts into his mind, supplanting what should have been proper and balanced concepts of racial equality.

Also, the younger a person is when wrong thoughts and concepts are introduced, the more likely he is to be open to them. Attitudes must be programmed before a concept of right and wrong solidifies. And so is the case with morality. People must be taught morals when they are young to have them transfer to adulthood. But if they are not being taught proper morals, what are they learning?

Morality on television has had far-reaching effects on the whole of society, on how it views the value of life, on weekly murders viewed on favorite shows, and subsequently even on abortion. Nearly two of every three babies aborted are not white, the pro-life movement, which is mostly white, are constantly tarred as racists for trying to save their lives. If pro-lifers are racists, and pro-choicers are non-racists, then how come so many non-racists support population control and abortion among non-white and black families? "More black babies are aborted in New York City every six weeks than all the blacks who were lynched in all the rest of US history."[4]

We have seen this go even farther today. Society no longer reflects television on important moral issues. Society is now regressing at a faster rate than even this popular medium can sustain.

The old cliché, "sex sells," is very true in the world of television for young people especially. TV shows, music videos on several channels, and Hollywood films all glorify sex which strikes a blow against the moral values and leads our very young astray. Today, teens are hearing and seeing sex through different media outlets which contributes to early and unsafe sexual practices. As seen in the area of rap music, "Rap music has had a lot of controversy about the negative lyrics about sex and drugs." The women in these videos appear scantily dressed, usually are berated by men while performing sexual moves.

Children today watch these images for hours, becoming apathetic with the passive assumption that this is how life truly is. A Rand Research Study has now provided hard evidence (proof) that "youth who are exposed to high levels of sexual content in TV are twice as likely to initiate early sexual intercourse and other sexual activity such as "making out," "hooking up," or having "oral sex."[5] Consumption of these wasteful and unproductive media images of these unhealthy messages have become the norm.

Unfortunately, Hollywood has an effect on public opinion. Hollywood has played an active role in desensitizing our youth. Entertainment media, in all of its forms, have a huge impact on how we should think, perform and desire to be. Society seems to have lost the realization that values and ethics must be established at home. By doing this, we can abolish these negative beliefs.

The Intolerance of Tolerance

We now live in a world where our societies have been overtaken by the exponential growth of immorality, violence and hatred. The liberals who have joyously brought these loads of filth, crime and immorality wear them proudly like a new shirt on TV shows today. Things that were once considered taboo by society are rapidly becoming accepted as the norm in many circles, and those things which have always been accepted by society as the norm, are slowly being downgraded to a matter of individual choice or suitability. After the liberal mob has tormented the world with their smut, get lots of disciples, change the moral code in the country over time, then all they can do is tell us we must tolerate both the new morality and those who practice it.

At first blush, the concept of tolerance we are told seems logical. However, it seems to me to be illogical from the very beginning. Why should I tolerate everyone who practices an immoral code? They do not want to tolerate me, even with a Biblical moral code we try to keep. Tolerance goes two ways or it does not go at all. We should tolerate people who are a part of the human race, but not those who are not even remotely human. Tolerance is similar to self-respect. I will respect anyone who respects themselves and others. But when they start preaching sermons about how they are due tolerance, that dog just won't hunt. Tolerance must be based on the noble idea that those for whom we are supposed to be tolerant are honorable and have their lives built on the underpinnings that are not distorted or perverted. That is especially true when it comes to a moral concept.

Liberal and Progressive educators go well beyond simply teaching that we should tolerate and accept others. They insist to their students that acceptance of others is necessary "because" those others are American Indian, African, Hispanic, South Sea Islander, or white; with that then comes the step stated need to accept the associated cultures from each person. And with that we have reached the point where our society and our schools are teaching that we should be tolerant of every action that we encounter, except one: the action of a conservative. Tolerance as the story goes is that we are unaware of what that individual has been through: skin color, nation of origin, and sometimes even religious preference become reasons why we should tolerate even the most questionable activity.

For example, when a child throws a temper-tantrum, the child is not said to be unruly, he is merely a "child expressing himself." Or later when the older child steals cigarettes from the local convenience store, he is not really guilty of breaking the law. He has been misunderstood and is trying to "work out his anger against society." Then even later, as a teenager who drives while under the influence of alcohol and wrecks his dad's car, he is not a disobedient teenager. He is viewed as someone who is a "victim of an evil society." And when this person armed with a knife and gun later breaks into a home to steal money, jewels, and the TV set, when he is shot he's not a burglar. He is again "the victim of an unfair capitalistic system." Therefore, the homeowner is guilty of taking advantage of someone whom he should have been tolerant of in the beginning. Farfetched? Not at all. Our society has reached that point and gone beyond, all due to the stated need for tolerance.

When a country attacks another, it is not blind hatred or lust. It is our "mismanaged foreign policy."

There is now always a reason, an excuse, for what is simply wrong conduct. "Being tolerant" has become that excuse.

An often-heard mantra of tolerance advocates is, "As long as we are not hurting others, what we do to ourselves is our business."

This is a prime example of watching the new morality as taught by the liberal culture take effect and precedence over the Biblical morality on which our country was at least founded. Not only are the shows immoral in much of their content, many of them are ridiculous. Most shows which are referred to as Reality TV make a display of, for example, how many worms a person can eat while on an island. Another Reality TV show corrals four married couples in a house to witness how many staged fights can be filmed. Another show swaps wives. One has hillbillies in Hollywood, yet another has moved Survivor candidates into a home to see who will survive the longest. To call such things real is ridiculous. Whatever these shows are, they are not Reality TV. And while you can easily see I reference a few shows of the "Reality' genre, each new reality show seem to become more insulting to the intelligence; and the moral code is horrible

There is at least one exception in the 2013-2014 schedules; that deals with real Cold Case crime files. The hosts of the program review the files of actual crimes and begin a reinvestigation involving the witnesses and suspects. If some cases, they able to work with local law enforcement officials and resurrect the case to a point that the perpetrator is brought into the justice system. Now that is a good example of true Reality TV.

According to a new Gallop Values and Beliefs poll which is conducted each May, "Some 72 percent of Americans said moral values in America are "getting worse," compared with 20 percent who said they are "getting better" and 6 percent who said they are "the same,"[6] The results of the poll further revealed: But the discontent is palpable. Only 19 percent say U.S. moral values are "excellent or good," while 44 percent say they are "poor" and 36 percent say "only fair." "The net result of these two trends is that seven in 10 Americans have a negative view of moral values in the nation," said Alyssa Brown, author of the Gallup report.[7]

A separate Gallup Poll report, issued on Monday, May 20, 2013, indicates an increase in the social acceptability regarding the issues of same-sex relationships, use of birth control, getting divorced, sex outside of marriage between a man and a woman, having a baby outside of marriage, and using human embryos for medical stem-cell research. Interesting enough, according to the poll, Americans rated adultery as being highly taboo.

While some may argue that television programming has nothing to do with the drop and trend of morality in America, a strong case can be made that it has been a facilitator of the movement. A person must look at a minimum of two points of data. First, looking at television programming over the past 60 years shows just in that short time period a vast change in the "ethical" and "moral" standards of what is acceptable by society to be heard by adults and children. Forty to sixty years ago, it was not possible to hear any of the four-letter words we hear today on an everyday basis. Over time the language has changed. Liberals call it a healthy change. I do not. Also changing in concert with the language has been dress codes, nudity, and what is now called "adult content" movies and TV shows. This is all called the content. It has changed over time.

As the mind, eyes and ears are exposed to more and more violence, sex, bad language, nudity, etc. this content becomes like a drug to that mind, eyes and ears. More is required each time to get the same stimulation that was reached the last time. If not, the viewer will usually feel dissatisfied that it was not enough. A microcosm of that is easily tracked in the area of what we call special effects. At one time, special effects were very limited if there were any. Movies used to depend upon good acting which is sorely lacking in most films today. Now the more special effects one sees the more are required in the next movie; and the next to hold your attention. The threshold has to go higher, the crashes bigger, the explosions more gigantic or they aren't satisfying. The mind is an interesting instrument and must be carefully managed. The survey data in question certainly points to it. It is fairly obvious by a data-driven person, or reasoning person, that morality is driven by an educational process, and not just any education. One thing is for certain. They should not be driven by movies.

The Hollywood entertainment industry has become increasingly influential so that society now looks towards them to develop their standards, teach values, and provide morals. One would ask however, "Is this truly beneficial?" Is society helping us or hurting our current and future generations? Certainly, we have mimicked people in Hollywood by copying dance moves (e.g., Michael Jackson), dress styles (e.g., Don Johnson in *Miami Vice*) or action movies (e.g., *Spiderman*). However negative images are now being portrayed as cool so much of our younger society is not only imitating these Hollywood figures, but also endangering themselves. People talk about Hollywood and how influential it is but the truth is for many years, Hollywood, while having many talents for good, has unfortunately forced negative images on society at large.

This is precisely why morality cannot be fluid or situational or relativistic. As children we needed parents who knew the difference between right and wrong, who would teach us that no matter what the disguise, what the situation, or even how relative it was to current life, however appealing, it cannot be changed. Then children grow up, mature, become parents themselves and start the cycle over again. The only way this cycle continues uninterrupted is to have a basis for ethical and moral behavior that is fixed. Our Founders knew that, because they had been taught that. Therefore they built our society on the Bible, not on relativism, not on movies, or video games, or anything else. The truth is that the character of transgression remains the same over time. Liberals from the 1960s have been subscribing to the "if it feels good, do it" morality. The problem with that approach is that there is an internal personage that is living within your physical body. Even the hedonist and world famous psychiatrist Sigmund Freud talked of the internal person, but denying the spiritual elements of the human soul, he identified the "soul" in terms of an id, an ego, and a super-ego.

If your so-called friends urge you to do anything you know to be wrong, you need to have the moral compass and internal strength to make a stand for right, even if you stand alone. Having the moral courage to be a light for others to follow is a wonderful attribute. There is no friendship more valuable than your own clear conscience, your own moral cleanliness. What a glorious feeling it is to know that you stand in your appointed place clean and with the confidence that you are worthy to do so. That is where the morality of Hollywood falls short. It fails to pass the test of time. But it is so appealing since it comes in Technicolor with all the special effects. Takes a moral compass to be able to segregate what is truly garbage from what is truth and to keep the two separate. Liberals cannot do that. They prove it through bullying and through the products of Hollywood.

Then There Are the "Bullies" from School

Turns out there are big bullies in school but they are not the James Dean student type that teases another child that poses the largest threat. Rather they are the elite teachers and their union of elitists, the curriculum of Common Core, and sometimes the events which all facilitate the removal of both religious liberty and the religious morality which this country has held dear for 240 years. Replacing these morals are brand new ones presented by the professional staff at school; ones associated with secular humanism. One of them came to us via the Elite Progressives, John Dewey, and believe it or not, mainly through the Scopes Monkey Trial. The liberal elite have hated religion of the Christian sort; hated the morality that came with it; hated Jesus; hated the church; and hated Southerners, because many of them were religious, seemed backward or strange compared to their Ivy League friends, and they hated whites who were conservatives.

It was that Southern religiosity that led to one of the most vicious literary assaults on any single group in American History. H. L. Mencken became a hero to generations of elites through his newspaper reporting on the "Scopes Monkey Trial." Uninterested in the subtleties of the debate over evolution, completely indifferent to the concerns of those who felt their traditional religious teachings to be in danger from teachers who despised them and their culture, Mencken gleefully seized upon the case to mock and ridicule everything he could find in the South. We owe the popularization of the phrase "white trash" to Mencken. He also coined the phrase "Bible Belt" to describe the "bigoted" South. In true elite fashion, Mencken approved of the elitist antebellum South, where power had devolved to the despised white trash.[8]

The 1925 "Monkey Trial" was ostensibly about the battle between teaching creationism versus the theory of evolution, and in particular the theory of natural selection, in Tennessee schools. When the schools banned the teaching of evolution, the ACLU kicked into action. It advertised for volunteers to get themselves arrested for teaching evolution, and then offered to pay for their defense. John Scopes, a math teacher turned biologist, accordingly violated the statute, and the ACLU sent Clarence Darrow to represent him. The prosecutor was William Jennings Bryan, a devout Presbyterian and three-time Democrat presidential nominee. Bryan was sometimes known as the Great Commoner for his outspoken defense of populist ideas against the elites of his time, and spent most of his career crusading for many causes we think of as liberal. He spoke out against the distribution of wealth resulting from laissez-faire capitalism. He pleaded with Americans not to use their power to bully smaller countries. His pacifism was so strong that he resigned as secretary of state for President Wilson because he feared Wilson

Chapter Twelve — Honey, I Shrunk the Morals

would lead the country into World War I. But Mencken, who despised the poor people Bryan fought for, saw him as nothing more than a cartoon figure.[9]

To Mencken, the trial was a clear-cut case of tolerance, progress, urban sophistication, and secularism (Darrow) versus country backwardness, religion, tradition, and conservatism (Bryan). Mencken's "reporting" from Dayton, Ohio reeked of [bullying] prejudice and elitism:

- About Bryan: "[H]e has been oozing around the country since his first day here, addressing this organization and that, presenting the indubitable Word of God in his caressing, ingratiating way."
- More about Bryan: "He has these hillbillies locked up in his pen and he knows it . . . They understand his peculiar imbecilities. His nonsense is their ideal of sense."
- He referred to "the so-called minds of these fundamentalists of upland Tennessee," and at other times, dismissed the townspeople as "morons", "yokels", and "Neanderthal".[10]

Reading these quotes, you have to wonder whether Mencken and the elites who laughed over his insults were motivated by love of science or love of snobbery. In reality, it was a love of bullying people different from themselves into accepting their form of morality: the elite kind. Speaking of evolution, why is it the elites have not evolved much in their own stale thinking? Anyone of Mencken's insults from 1925 would work perfectly in a cocktail party conversation among the bullying elites today. They repeat the same snickering about religion, the same slurs about stupidity, and the same lies about bigotry. So much for having a monopoly on tolerance.[11] They wear their hatred, their bigotry, their fake morality like a flag.

While these liberal elites practice self-actualization and preach tolerance with one breath, in the next breath they will not allow anything to be spoken other than what amounts to be their own spiritual tenants. Tenants of their religion, secular humanism, which they proclaim will be the only prophetic voices heard in school; the voices of Darwin, FDR, John Dewey, Marx, and anyone else who agrees with them. With all that has come a trade out of our morality.

The Family Unit Suffers with the New Morality

Sexualizing children with the grown-up clothes which many of them wear now has contributed in bringing a toll to the family unit. There is a whole generation of adults now that have been spawned into delving into every perversion under the sun. Relationships have in many cases become twisted and perverted with the result that marriages are devastated, many of them ending in divorce.

The influence of Hollywood, television and the Internet with their associated exploding morality has attacked the family unit. Take the Internet for example. An

American Academy of Matrimonial Lawyers survey of 2010 showed statistics from the previous twelve months. They reported Internet-related issues as being blamed for 62 percent of all divorce cases, from meeting partners off dating-sites for affairs, to delving into suppressed perversions, all the way to addiction to pornography. The American family is being destroyed by the immoral framework established by the liberal element that runs rampant in society today. Other studies show that over 80 percent of marriages in the US have an unfaithful partner who gets caught.[12] Children learn by example and capture more information than most adults wish to admit. Trends are set early in life. Children who are abused tend to become abusers. They likely look at marriage with their parents as an example.

But there are even more extreme forms of behavior which the new morality has brought into the home. While soft drugs are said to never be a problem by the users, they mostly lead to heavier drug use; into experimenting with pornography, which in turn leads to other perversions. The child who grows up in a home like this must truly be confused by blatant immorality. And our friend, the TV, gets in on the act. Look at how far we have come in looking at TV families. There was *Ozzie and Harriet*, that wonderful TV family from the 1950s. That seems to have been replaced in some ways by the Osbournes in the last decade. Speaking of Ozzie and Harriet, I was watching an episode of this show and one of the people who happened to be visiting at the time said "How ridiculous! They are so square. It's not even in color!" Square or not, they held a moral value that was wonderful. A retrospective look at the TV shows of the day made the time period "safe" as one acquaintance said. Watching an episode or two sure brings back memories. It would be wonderful to return to that type of morality. One thing is for certain, we can never get that atmosphere back in our land with the new liberal morality at the helm.

Just two generations ago, couples would date and get to know each other. Getting involved intimately meant having deep meaningful conversations with each other. Being involved in a sexual relationship was not considered until they got married, and any ideas of living together before marriage just was not in the equation. Today we see more of a reversal of that; couples "live together" giving the appearance of a married couple with no firm commitment of marriage. Children growing up in the home learn their parents are not married. This feeds into the moral failures we see around us. Children with the foundation of sound male and female role models do best in life. It is wholesome and sound.

The old-fashioned two-parent family has over the centuries proved to be the sturdiest and most prolific environment in which to raise children who will one day grow into sound, well-rounded adults. Because the atomic family has become "the enemy of the state" it has all but disappeared. When you get down to it, the nuclear family unit has been much of what is the foundation that made this country a beacon to the rest of the world; the foundation that held up the freedom and justice and righteousness which have been the trademarks of this nation. Because of the hatred for this righteousness associated with this family unit, it has become

Chapter Twelve — Honey, I Shrunk the Morals

the target of the Left. There is such a wide array of "families," the new "normal" family structure is nearly impossible to define with the current morality definition.

Proof is seen in that four out of every ten children are born to an unwed mother in America. This data comes from Single Mother Guide Initiative. And this number is skyrocketing. Many believe that the odds of a marriage surviving are so low that they should forgo marriage altogether. This results in cohabitation becoming the precursor to marriage.

What has resulted is not conducive to building a country. Researchers in Washington, D.C., wanted to start a program to prevent sexual activity in youth. After initially offering the program to seventh-graders, they found it ineffective because too many seventh-graders were already having sex. The program was then re-worked and offered to fifth-graders (10- and 11-year olds). The study followed these students from 1995 to 1999, and the results were nothing short of eye-popping. While it said that most simply talk about sex, 20% of the students had sex before they were 15 years old: one in five. A notable fact was the change in girls. The 1999 results showed that 19% of girls reported having sex. This was a 42% increase from 1988.

A recent U.S. president added to this confusion. In the course of denying his act of adultery with an employee, he declared that oral sex is "not sex." This mentality has solidified itself in the minds of many youths. Adults often define sex as *any* sort of arousing activity between a couple. Young people believe that only intercourse is sex. Oral sex, petting or touching is not defined as sex by them.

This explains three stories below. The explicit nature and graphic wording of the articles are far too detailed to be quoted directly. Keep in mind the ages of the children involved in these incidents.

(1) A *14-year-old* reported to USA Today that two students were caught in a washroom in the midst of a sex act.

(2) A *13-year-old* told ABC News that a female student had sexual relations with nearly a third of their school's football team. This from the Huffington Post, March 8, 2013.

(3) Another story involves two *12-year-olds* in Baltimore, Maryland. While a movie was being shown to the class, these *children* were in the back of the room committing a sex act.

There is simply not enough space to mention all the increasing news reports of *children* caught in the act of sex. It should then be no wonder that a New York Times writer stating way back on February 9, 1989 in an article "some studies indicate three-fourths of all girls have had sex during their teenage years and 15% have had four or more partners." It is much worse now.

We were sold a bill of goods by the liberal elite that sex education was going to fix all of these problems. After all liberals have refused to allow teenagers to be taught that abstinence will be the ounce of prevention that diverts the pound of cure.

It is absolutely no surprised in our culture any longer when it comes to the amount of sex demanded in shows, reading material or movies. Society has become so infected that before marriage the average person has had up to five sexual partnerships. Marriage no longer holds the fascination, the excitement, or the mysteries that it held for our older generation. What should be one of the holiest, purest, and most powerful expressions of love has been reduced to a cinder. Therefore, it is no surprise that something so under-valued is so easily marred.

Our culture, our permissiveness, and our lack of discipline, has created what has become known as the most sexually active generation of children, and I might say the most confused, the world has ever seen.

Charting Our Path with a Clear and Consistent Moral Compass

Through the last forty years there has been a regular assault on what could be called Middle American morality. Each of the various movements has brought their own individual attacks. The Hippies of the 1960s were a huge statement against establishment. I am convinced now that it would not have mattered what the political landscape would have been at that time. The Hippies would still have been active in pickets; anti-war, anti-poverty, anti-racism, anti-job, anti-money was just what took center stage at the time. With the free love, free sex, abortion, and drug abuse came a new wave of immorality which took a toll on our mid-American morality. The Flower Children, the acid rock, and the entire free love generation brought more new morality into town, which caused more problems. We now live in a time where daily it seems there are rocket and mortar attacks against Judaism, Christianity and the respective moral code.

Progressives will try to pump more of their immorality or situational morality our way. The best way to attack that in my perspective is to not apologize for using Scripture, but use it often and wisely to remind ourselves of the moral code we follow.

The Apostle Paul in his letter to young Timothy must have looked forward to our day when he recorded the words found in 2 Timothy 3:1-7: "But mark this: There will be terrible times in the last days. People will be lovers of themselves, lovers of money, boastful, proud, abusive, disobedient to their parents, ungrateful, unholy, without love, unforgiving, slanderous, without self-control, brutal, not lovers of the good, treacherous, rash, conceited, lovers of pleasure rather than lovers of God — having a form of godliness but denying its power. Have nothing to do with them.

They are the kind who worm their way into homes and gain control over weak-willed women, who are loaded down with sins, and are swayed by all kinds of evil desires, always learning but never able to acknowledge the truth."[13]

We cannot cope with the confusions and the challenges of this world unless we use a clear and consistent moral compass that will unerringly take us through our own personal trials and the tugs and pulls of our own temptations. Progressives tell us we cannot use them for fear of warping a person's mind. However, a compass that will chart our way to peace of mind, self-worth, and joy is worthwhile in every way.

There are Absolute Truths to Which We Should Cling

The moral compass for a Christian is built upon absolute truths. I will list four simple ones:

The first absolute truth is that there is a loving Father in Heaven, and His Son, Jesus Christ, who can be our personal Savior. This is a more certain truth than any worldly fact. This concept is expressed with unmatched eloquence in 1 John: "This is how we know what love is: Jesus Christ laid down His life for us. And we ought to lay down our lives for our brothers." (1 John 3:16.) Nothing else could provide a truer "north" for every person's own moral compass.

The second absolute truth is that there is an adversary, Satan, the tempter, who would lead us away from God and His infinite peace. Note that the Hebrew translation for devil is the "destroyer." Satan is the destroyer because he would wreck our moral compass and end our journey back to a loving Father in Heaven. Said differently, he wants to sink your ship. You might note that while some Progressives will make fun of someone believing in a personal devil, they and Barack Obama follow a man, Saul Alinsky, who dedicated his book *Rules for Radicals* to Satan, the devil. Interesting how they want their faith, but they do not want us to have ours.

The third absolute truth is that all of us have freedom to choose the path we will walk in life. Yes, who we are is the sum of all the choices we make. We should always remember that our choices do not begin with the act, but in the mind with the idea. As Ralph Waldo Emerson wrote, "Sow a thought, and you reap an act; sow an act, and you reap a habit; sow a habit, and you reap a character; sow a character, and you reap a destiny."

The fourth absolute truth is that the temptations of the devil can always be overcome by renewed faith in God and by repentance. Yes, when we stray from that narrow and straight way, marked by our moral compass, our footing can be restored on the road that surely leads to salvation and eternal life. When Christ went to the Garden of Gethsemane, clearly knowing of His impending Crucifixion, He prayed to His Father for His Apostles as well as for each of us. In that prayer, He commands us to avoid evil, but in His infinite compassion He also asks the Father to "... protect [us] from the evil one." (John 17:15.)

Wisdom, peace of mind, a feeling of self-worth, and joy in life can be true when following the Savior's footsteps, guided by a compass that is unfailing, since it is calibrated to these eternal and absolute truths.

The words of the Apostle Paul are so comforting: "For God, who said, "Let light shine out of darkness," made his light shine in our hearts to give us the light of the knowledge of the glory of God [displayed] in the face of Christ.

But we have this treasure in jars of clay to show that this all-surpassing power is from God and not from us. We are hard pressed on every side, but not crushed; perplexed, but not in despair; persecuted, but not abandoned; struck down, but not destroyed." (2 Corinthians 4:6-9; NIV.)

Look now at the events in which our government has been involved over the past few years; stripping freedoms away on a regular basis, involved in sinister activities, supporting evil regimes in the Middle East, and lying to the American people. Morality has consistently been getting worse with every action. As a backdrop to this, I can see our old enemies, the Soviet Communists from 50 years ago, standing behind these current events. They were indeed enemies of our country and our way of life. They must have leapt into the air for joy that day long ago when they finally figured this out. They knew they could not defeat us militarily but they did not need to. All they needed to do was learn our language, put teachers in our schools, give new meanings to our words, and manage the implementation of those meanings into textbooks and the curriculum. Once the ingredients when complete and in place, one only need wait for those hearing the daily message to become adults. Then they could sit back and wait a generation until the children would begin to adopt their meanings. They would graduate, get into government and voilà. In 20 or so years our young graduates would do their work for them.

Eventually their definitions would be accepted, because the media would use these new definitions. That is because the media learned from them while in school and transported their tenants into the workplace. Meanwhile, the Americans known as "the greatest generation", who built the nation and culture of freedom and personal responsibility, who wrote the dictionaries would retire, die off or otherwise become irrelevant.

Human beings are marvelously adaptive creatures, but that can sometimes work against us. That is because we tend to be so focused on adjusting to our present circumstances that we often forget to ask the bigger questions. How did we get to where we are now? Would we be in a stronger position today if we had made some better decisions upstream? What lessons from the past can we use in the future? This is the case for individuals, but it is even more applicable to nations.

Many people thoughtlessly assume that all societal changes are for the better. Certainly, we should all be grateful that the Democrat Party finally joined the Republicans in opposing slavery, segregation and Jim Crow laws. How wonderful that the Democrats at long last agreed with Republicans that women should have the right to vote. It is also great that both parties worked to help Americans become more educated, end child labor and make our society more affluent.

Ways We Are Worse Than in the 1960s

That being said, while it is wonderful to celebrate all the progress we have made as a nation, we should not lose sight of the fact that we in our current generation are also inferior to previous generations of Americans in some crucial areas. Only by recognizing where we've fallen short can we take steps to try to get back what we have lost as a people; and as you are about to see, culturally, we have lost a great deal.

1. "To get a sense of how different attitudes and morals were in the 1960s, perhaps this will do it. In that day, never-married women were asked, "In your opinion, do you think it is all right for a woman to have sexual relations before marriage with a man she knows she is going to marry?" Eighty-six percent said no."[14]

The early sixties was a different time, when morality was fixed. A young lady named Dawn Eden wrote a book on chastity and it was considered to be so unusual that she was scheduled for numerous "Can you believe there are people who still do this?" on a few TV interviews. Would society be better off if more people were chaste before marriage? Unquestionably, but again, how do you put that rabbit back in the hat without a spiritual reawakening in our country?

2. "Today, about two-thirds of U.S. households with children are led by a married couple, down from more than nine in 10 in 1960."[15]

Studies also consistently show not just that children turn out better in two parent families, but that people who are married are happier than those that are single. Because of a soaring divorce rate, high profile break-ups and gay marriage, we have stopped treating holy matrimony with the reverence it deserves in our country. However, marriage really is the bedrock of our society and as it has turned to pumice, we've paid a terrible price.[16]

3. "In the decade after 9/11, China built the Three Gorges Dam, the largest electricity-generating plant in the world. America still thinks of China as being the cheap place for an assembly plant for just about anything carried at Wal-Mart. Dubai, a mere sub-jurisdiction of the United Arab Emirates, put up the world's tallest building and built a Busby Berkeley geometric kaleidoscope of offshore artificial islands. Brazil, an emerging economic power, began diverting the Sao Francisco River to create some 400 miles of canals to irrigate its parched northeast. But America, the super power can't put up a building to replace the World Trade Center."[17]

America put a man on the moon in less than a decade; yet we cannot put a man on the moon today. We are more than 13 years out from 9/11 and we STILL have not completed 1 World Trade Center. Yet when you look at our illustrious history, it took only 16 months to build the Pentagon, 4 years to complete the Sears/Willis Tower and we knocked out the Hoover Dam in just 5 years. If we were to get into another fight like WWII that depended on America's ability to produce massive amounts of military equipment, we count not win it because for all of our advanced technology and know-how, we are just not as good at building things as we used to be.[18]

4. "If filmmakers in 1963 wanted the approval of the Production Code of Motion Picture Association of America, which almost all of them still did, the dialogue

could not include any profanity stronger than hell or damn, and there had been dramatic justification even for them. Characters couldn't take the name of the Lord in vain, or ridicule religion, or use any of form of obscenity — meaning just about anything related to the sex act . . . the plot couldn't present sex outside of marriage as attractive or justified. Homosexuality was to be presented as a perversion. Abortion? 'The subject of abortion shall be discouraged, shall never be more than suggested, and when referred to shall be condemned,' said the code."[19]

There are cartoons aimed at children and even video games that do not come close to living up to this anymore. In fact, these "Leave it to Beaver" standards for entertainment seem almost bizarre today; yet they were the norm fifty years ago. Are we now better off as a society because your kids hear video game characters dropping F-bombs, listen to music glorifying murder and are regularly exposed to themes that were considered too racy for adults half a century ago? Absolutely not. Could we go back to rules anywhere near this strict? Realistically, no, but that says a lot about how much our society has degraded morally since then.[20]

5. "Going back a hundred years, when blacks were just one generation out of slavery, we find that the census data of that era showed that a slightly higher percentage of black adults had married than white adults. . . . As of 1940, among black females who headed their own households, 52% were 45 years old or older. Moreover, only 14 percent of all black children were born to unmarried women at that time."[21]

Fast forward to today and we find that, "Half of all children born to women under 30 in America now are illegitimate. Three in 10 white children are born out of wedlock, as are 53 percent of Hispanic babies and 73 percent of black babies." If the problem were fixed, the poverty rate would plunge, drug use would plummet, prison populations would drop, the suicide rate would dip and we'd be healthier as a society in almost every way imaginable.[22]

In Federalist 2, John Jay looks out at a nation of a common blood, faith, language, history, customs and culture. "Providence," he writes, "has been pleased to give this one connected country to one united people—a people descended from the same ancestors, speaking the same language, professing the same religion . . . very similar in their manners and customs . . . " Are we still that "one united people" today? Or has America become what Klemens von Metternich called Italy: "a mere geographical expression"?[23]

In *Suicide of a Superpower*, Patrick Buchanan holds firm to the idea that the America we knew as children and young adults is now "disintegrating, breaking apart along the fault lines of politics, race, ethnicity, culture and faith; that the centrifugal forces in society have now become the dominant forces. Our politics are as poisonous as they have been in our lifetimes."[24]

A clear example is Sarah Palin who was maligned by a poisonous politics that

Chapter Twelve — Honey, I Shrunk the Morals

is as morally complicit with her as with the murder attempt on Rep. Gabrielle Giffords. Venomous terms like "terrorists" and "hostage-takers" are routinely used on Tea Party members who one congressman said want to see blacks "hanging on a tree."[25] Our nation has not progressed in race relations over the past fifty years. We were promised that the election of Barack Obama would take the country into a "post-racial" stance; race riots were over. A full half century after the civil rights revolution, it is sad to see terms like "racist" and "racism" in regular use. "We remain, said Eric Holder in calling us a 'nation of cowards,' as socially segregated as ever."[26] Arguably, this is a massive misinterpretation by Holder, since he and other liberals are serving as bullies when they play the race card.

"Outside the workplace, the situation is even more bleak in that there is almost no significant interaction between us. On Saturdays and Sundays, America ... does not, in some ways, in some places, differ significantly from the country that existed some 50 years ago," said Holder. Holder is not altogether wrong in that synopsis. In California's prisons and among her proliferating ethnic gangs, a black-brown civil war has broken out.[27]

If history is a prophet for what is coming, it indicates there will be 66 million blacks in America, outnumbered by 135 million Hispanics, who will be living in southern states close to Mexico.

What has held us together through the many years? There is a thread that runs through all these years. It is the consistent and fixed morality built on Biblical truth. Neither prejudices nor pop-psychology have held us together. It is truth built into the moral code seen in phrases like "Do unto others...."

We are not now and will not then be "descended from common ancestors." We will consist of all the races, cultures, tribes and creeds of Earth, a multiracial, multicultural, multiethnic, multilingual stew of a nation that has never before existed, or survived. The parallels that come to mind are the Hapsburg Empire that flew apart after World War I, and the Soviet Union and Yugoslavia that disintegrated after the Cold War.

No more will we all speak the same language. We will be bilingual and bi-national. Spanish radio and TV stations are already the fastest growing. In Los Angeles, half the people speak a language other than English in their own homes.[28]

As for "professing the same religion," [in 1990 85 percent of Americans were Christians, now in 2011 that number] is down to 75 percent and plummeting. The old line churches [Presbyterian, Methodist, Lutheran and especially Episcopalian] are splitting, shrinking and dying. Where three in four Catholics attended Sunday Mass in 1960, it is now one in four. One in three cradle Catholics has lost the faith. The numbers of priests and nuns are plummeting; religious orders are dying; Catholics schools are closing.[29]

We have avoided and rejected the fixed moral code Christianity gave to us; it has collapsed in our society. Since the great cultural-social revolution of the 1960s, there has occurred what Nietzsche called the "transvaluation of all values." Morally repugnant things in the 1950s and 1960s — things like promiscuity, abortion, and homosexuality are now broadly accepted as not only normal and natural, but also healthy and culturally-advanced.

Socially, too, America is breaking down. Where out-of-wedlock births in the 1950s were rare, today, 41 percent of all American children are born out of wedlock. Among Hispanics, it is 51 percent; among blacks, 71 percent. And the correlation between the illegitimacy rate, the drug rate, the dropout rate, the crime rate and the incarceration rate is absolute.[29]

Warning alarms have been sounding off over the last forty years, getting louder every decade as the test scores of American school children plummet and the prison population quadruples. With this chorus of failures, the government has joined in, failing in its own way, growing more Fascist, Socialist, and Marxist.

Our southern border has all but vanished; we cannot control it or the tidal wave of illegals flooding our land. Wars which we were told we won, now suddenly we are being told they are almost lost, all due to a decadence in the leadership at the top and refusal to fight evil. Confidence in politics, politicians and the future of the country has been plunging; it has never been so low.

Less than sixty years ago, our nation was united around mutual objectives; the same faith, morality, history, heroes, holidays, holy days, language and literature. Because those are all contested, it is clear there is and has been a war on America. Even the Constitution which has held us together is being attacked, though liberal leaders are chiseling at it daily. Liberals use a mocking chuckle to try convincing us that their proposed changes to it would not be just another failed spinoff.

Even the Amendments of the Constitution all based on Biblical principles are being attacked. They were so pure, solid and secure, that we just forgot about them for a few generations. Funny thing about living in the paradise the Constitution provides. Every day is so special and yet amazingly unique, that it is very possible to allow years to go by unprompted. That is why we have holidays to remind us of how special a place this has been. Now that attacks have come, we can hopefully agree that the amendments do not mean the same to all of us. For example, the First Amendment says about the freedom to pray in school and celebrate Christmas and Easter are all protected. Not according to Leftists. How can we be the "one nation, under God" of the Pledge of Allegiance, or the people "endowed by their Creator" with inalienable rights, if we cannot even identify or discuss or mention that God and that Creator in the schools of America?

Each amendment is being challenged by radicals wanting to change the meanings. We need to learn the lessons of this war. No matter how many times you have to defend the freedom, you are still never quite prepared for it when the next attack comes around. For example, the Ninth Amendment's protection of the right to life has been hammered to mean only sometimes, and for only qualified persons. Likewise for the 14th Amendment which protected affirmative action. According to Leftists, it only applies to a select group. Then there is the Second Amendment guaranteeing the necessary armament to protect ourselves and way of life from tyrants within and enemies from outside. It even covers the right to carry a concealed gun. Not according to the attacks it comes under by the Left.

There is a new secession that is on the way. It is not going to be like the secession of 1861. It will rather be a secession of the conservative from the liberal and progressive; the heart seceding from the wickedness of liberalism. Dietrich Bonhoeffer was a part of a secession like that. He was a true trail blazer who learned firsthand and how progressives work. He lived and died speaking out loud that what he believed in, a moral code, was worth living for, and worth dying for. That is the difference between him and the Progressives of today. They are not willing to die for their faith. It is all in the moral code by which you live.

Look around today and see what the lack of good morality has done in America today. Almost everywhere you look, something has gone wrong. You do not want to believe it is true, but you feel it in your heart, you know it in your gut. Something has gone terribly wrong. The core values we believe in, the things we care about most are changing and eroding before us.

We did not realize it but our loss of morality in this country affected our rights. Our right to speak freely, our right to assemble peaceably, our right to privacy, our right to practice our religious faith, our right to protect our families the way we deem best; these are all going away because we allowed our wholesome Christian morality to be usurped by an evil liberal immorality. These values are our core freedoms. They are what have defined us as a nation and we feel them slipping away.

In every section of our country people are saying for the first time they are worried about the future of our country now like never before. We are all worried about the economic crisis that is attacking our future and shrinking our retirement. We are worried about our children's education and their college education; worried about the safety of our families as gangs take over our cities and towns. This loss of morality was a much bigger thing than we ever imagined; it was a train wreck headed our way that we didn't see coming; it was the light at the end of the tunnel that turned out being what we would fear most. And this is why our neighborhoods have changed so much; why our streets which were once filled with kids on bikes and scooters are now filled with gunfire and murder. The price is higher than we thought.

In virtually every way, for the things we care about most, we feel profound loss. We are sad not because we fear something *is* going wrong, but because we know something already *has* gone wrong. The loss of morality has brought about many reactions. People are now building bunkers and storing food for coming problems.

The entire fabric of our society seems to be coming apart as it were "at the seams." Everything that we once counted on is now in jeopardy. And the terrible new moral code which the culture accepts as normal has led to a political train wreck. Our politicians and our media lie openly to us without apology. Our government puts forth reckless policies that bring consequences of destruction. Because of the loss of this morality, the government corrupts the truth and breaks faith with the American people. Departments of the government designed to serve us are now weapons used against citizens; all because of a loss of morality. The NSA, the IRS, the FCC, the court system, the judiciary, even the so-called scientific community in some ways, have been crafted with an agenda in opposition to the America we used to know.

With this loss of a solid Biblical moral code, those who proclaim themselves to be wise have become fools and try to regulate our religion. They collect cell phone and email data. They create massive unemployment and huge debt and horrible scandals. While they through their new morality tell us all is great, they are lying through their teeth as they give us Solyndra, Benghazi, Fast and Furious, and Obamacare.

Because of the immorality of the media, rather than exposing the dishonesty, the scandals, and the perversions that go on in government offices, the media chooses to hide them, to lie about them, to whitewash them, and to tell us "there is nothing to see here." The greatest threat to our society by this media is that they do not provide a level playing field for truth. They present an agenda which is full of lies. All was created by destroying our morality.

The lying and the cover-ups by the politicians and media have become so numerous and horrible, that Americans are turning off the news and not even listening any longer. It is why we see poll after poll saying the people have grown weary and do not trust the White House, they do not trust the Congress, and they do not trust either political party. Why? It is because they have lost their morality: they lie; they cheat the citizens of their freedom; they steal rights and money. A 2014 poll states that 90 percent of Americans disapprove of and do not trust Washington.

We trust our freedom. What we do not trust are the lies and corruption of an uncertain world. There is no greater freedom than the right to survive, to protect our families with all the rifles, shotguns and handguns we want. We know, in the world that surrounds us, there are terrorists, home invaders, and drug cartels. There are car-jackers, knock-out gamers, rapists, and campus killers. There also exist airport killers, shopping mall bombers, road-rage killers, and inner-city killers. These and terrorist killers scheme to destroy our country with massive storms of violence against our businesses, power grids, and other infrastructural points with vicious waves of chemicals, disease, or an EMP that could collapse the society that sustains us all. And all of this happened because some were not happy with our culture and the moral code associated with Judeo-Christianity.

Chapter Twelve — Honey, I Shrunk the Morals

Which is more desirable: a Judeo-Christian ethic that brings some serenity and a morality which makes your streets safer? Or the new flexible morality and situation ethic of secular humanism that has brought all the killing and the sickness in society? These questions are answered by the moral choices we make.

"We are a Christian people . . .
not because the law demands it,
not to gain exclusive benefits or to avoid legal
disabilities; but from choice and education;
and in a land thus universally Christian,
what is to be expected, what desired,
but that we shall pay due regard to Christianity"

~ Senate Judiciary Committee Report,
January 19, 1853

Chapter Thirteen

Who Moved the Hedge?

ON JULY 8, 1741, THE GREAT New England Pastor, Jonathan Edwards, of the Congregational Church named Christ Church, Northampton, Mass., preached what has been arguably called by some modern theologians "the greatest sermon ever delivered on American soil." It was entitled, "Sinners in the hands of an angry God." Greatness aside, it certainly is the most famous message delivered in America. It is credited as being an integral part of the start of "The Great Awakening" in America; Edwards played a pivotal part in that revival. Because Edwards' eye sight was poor, he wrote his sermons in large hand written print and read the words loud as his throat would allow that day.[1]

Some of what he said in his famous sermon that day was as follows,

> "There is no want of power in God to cast wicked men into hell at any moment. Men's hands cannot be strong when God rises up . . . The devil stands ready to fall upon them, and seize them as his own. Then they shall be left to fall, as they are inclined by their own weight. God will not hold them up in these slippery places any longer, but will let them go; and then at that very instant, they shall fall into destruction; . . . There is nothing that keeps wicked men at any one moment out of hell, . . . And let every one that is yet out of Christ, and hanging over the pit of hell, whether they be old men and women, or middle aged, or young people, or little children, now harken to the loud calls of God's word and providence. This acceptable year of the Lord, a day of such great favours to some, will doubtless be a day of as remarkable vengeance to others."

And at the conclusion of his message, "Therefore, let every one that is out of Christ, now awake and fly from the wrath to come. The wrath of Almighty God is now undoubtedly hanging over a great part of this congregation: Let every one fly out of Sodom: Haste and escape for your lives, look not behind you, escape to the mountain, lest you be consumed."[2]

It was reliably said that those in attendance that day were cut to the heart. Loud crying and wailing in fear of the punishment of God for their wayward lives, was heard throughout the congregation, by all those in attendance. This one sermon was credited as the reason for the start of a great spiritual revival in America, called 'the Great Awakening' of the reform movement, which swept over the country and lasted for well over a quarter century in America.

An interesting sidebar to this story: Jonathan Edwards who was born in 1703, started his college education at Yale in 1716 when the school was just two years older than he was and completed his graduate level studies there in 1722, at the age of 19.[3] Yale was established 1701 by the Congregational Church and was dedicated to the furtherance of the Gospel by its Founders. In 1727, Edwards left his position as a tutor at Yale to become the associate minister at his grandfather Solomon Stoddard's church in Northampton. Two years later, after Stoddard's death, Edwards took over the congregation.[4]

Like many of the leaders from Israel throughout the Old Testament era were protected by God's hedge as established by Scripture, early Americans were in the same manner protected by God's hedge which He promised, as they obeyed. This is seen in the Founders' statements of spiritual determination and their separated lives in submission to His Will, and the direction of this country for approximately 200 years.

God Has Removed Our Hedge of Protection

Given the history of times in Israel's history when God lifted or removed His hedge of protection, it appears He does so, there and here, for a few dissimilar reasons.

First I believe, the hedge has been removed by God to gather our collective attention, as an act of discipline and punishment. Nations, just like people can and do get out of control through rebellious acts against goodness. When that happens things change, because God will discipline us by sending us problems. The purpose of course is bringing on a return to His goodness. Even for individuals or nations who choose not to believe in God, it is interesting to see how they talk about 'violating the goodness of the universe.' Some may call it karma, but whatever name is applied, it is clear through Scripture this universe who is trying to help keep us on our path and get our attention is none other than God Himself. Whether it is a U S President, a 'subterranean sanitation engineer' like Edward Norton, or a 'bus driver' like Ralph Cramden, individuals can become too self-absorbed with bloated egos, and self-imposed narcissism so as to forget morals, ethics, goodness, etc. More self-discipline is often needed.

Beginning in 1831, Alexis de Tocqueville, the famous French Statesman, philosopher, and historian toured America in a quest to discover why America was so good. He wanted to know the secret. When I was a young man, teachers, preachers and officials used to describe our country as good. That of course has certainly changed over the past century.

Chapter Thirteen — Who Moved the Hedge?

The dire problem in America today is the huge pile of results from choices the nation has made over the past century. 'We' have rapidly been abandoning the commitment made by Founders. Never before in the history of the world has a nation run away from its spiritual heritage as fast as America has. It is most likely true that America went through a similar process before the start of the War Between the States (Civil War). Due to the arrogance of the nation toward slavery, treating others as you would want to be treated, service to God, and many other things, I believe God lifted His hedge at that time. The result was economic and societal trouble, war, and eventually a destruction that brought about a forced long look into the national mirror. This eventually brought about a repentance of the country in returning for the most part to a goodness of Godly principles.

Europe came close to following that trek of events and ultimate repentance, but substituted poor economic reform in the name of the European Union instead of a long soul-searching and repentance for abandoning their spiritual heritage. They may come around some day but it will probably be too late, and certainly it will not be quite as fast as America did following the War Between the States. The EU should be a lesson to us in seeing what happens when you abandon your ethical and spiritual heritage. Forming alliances with other destitute and sinful nations is no substitute for true soul searching and repentance. Some will argue that Europe is wonderful with the beautiful architecture, the cities with fountains, the socialized organizations, the ancient stained glass church structures, with all the ornate work of centuries it took to finish some of them. But those are aesthetics and speak rather to what "used to be" rather than to what is. Look at the church buildings in Europe, many of them are beautiful, but they are empty. The buildings make wonderful photos for greeting cards or vacation pictures. But they are void of disciples of the Lord, such as existed centuries ago when these edifices were constructed. We should carefully look and learn before it is absolutely too late here in this country. Substitutes do not work well with national planning.

In the United States, through decades of horrid and misguided government legislation, poor education, the wrong education, a long tiring war with progressivism, and just simple neglect, our nation does not begin to even cast a shadow of what the magnificence it once held. The design of steel and glass in downtown edifices may speak of great architecture and engineering feats, but they are hollow without the ringing conscience and declarations of what once made this nation so astute. No wonder our Founders placed within our government buildings the pronounced quotations, the art work, and the reliefs which spoke of God's guidance; the Ten Commandments, the Exodus led by Moses and many other wonderful references: to remind us who we are.

These national holidays are intended to remind us of who we are and whose we are, including the blessings under God; not just to be treated as days off from work. They were embedded on our calendar to guide our thinking on those days, for pause and recalling events of the past that changed our nation. Think about these holidays. They were once celebrated differently than now.

Holiday	Original Purpose	Current Typical Practice
Washington's Birthday	Celebrate the life of the father of our nation	No longer observed except for day off from work in a few places
Lincoln's Birthday	Celebrate the president who saved the union	Currently replaced by President's Day
Memorial Day	Honor those who died in wars to preserve our freedom — remembering its high cost	Typically viewed as 1st day of summer vacation
July 4th	Celebrate Independence day and the birthday of our nation	Mixed celebration of summer and national birthday
Labor Day	Day honoring workers in USA	Union celebration holiday
Columbus Day	Celebrate discovery of America	Day off from work
Veteran's Day	Celebrate Veterans groups with their accomplishments	Rarely observed except in small towns with active veterans groups
Thanksgiving Day	Day of national thanksgiving to God for His blessings on nation	Day off for turkey, football, and family togetherness
Pearl Harbor Day – December 7th	Commemorate the day of Japanese sneak attack on Pearl Harbor base	Seldom observed; occasionally observed by active veteran groups

The Spiritual Conscience

After all this evidence add one more reason for the hedge being removed. That would be the church, as a whole, not just some individual congregation, but collectively the body of Christendom, which seems today so overly involved with social issues, that it has forgotten its calling, which is to go into all the world and make disciples. Examples of the social and political issues that seem to have used to sidetrack and shackle pastors are the move by liberals to disarm America, the move by liberals to insure gay liberation rights into all areas of life, and racism; all these things have preempted the church's real work and the playing of politics has also caused the church to often melt in the face of opposition. This is opposite of what a student of Scripture sees from key members of the body of believers in the first century during days of persecution from the government or the Sanhedrin. The reformed church's voice has been drowned out by their activity in these so many social concerns, basically having its voice and the voice of the culture stating the same things. All this similarity with the culture makes the church meaningless. It has lost respect and is no longer the conscience for our nation as it should be.

Years ago, I attended a Christian men's conference with over 10,000 in attendance. The lectures and messages ranged from good to great. I recall one pastor who spoke, Ed Bousman. While I did not agree with his entire message, he made a point that is certainly applicable in the arena of the church having basically the same message as the world. Bousman, in this context, gave an example of the worthiness of a minister who would deliver a sermon. He said, "If a preacher says more than the Bible said, he says too much; if he says less than the Bible states, he says too little; and if he says exactly the same as the Bible states, what good is he?!" That is the dilemma of the church today; it seems to be saying exactly what the world says, and in doing so, what good is it?

The overall result is this — Due to the long lingering war with the progressive agenda, the loss of faith in God, and the lack of leadership in the country, America does not even cast a shadow of its former self regarding the principles our Founding Fathers put in place. While you may not care or even say it is a non-issue, I beg to differ. The church needs to as a voice of conscience in a world gone wrong. The loss of that conscience now demonstrates how far we have moved away from our moorings and touchstones. This should be a red flag telling us we are in dangerous waters far from protection. We have come to a point where all will soon be lost. Through the accumulation of these many indignant sins, God has lifted His protective hedge around this nation. That leaves us with numerous calamities from which we may not be able to recover. There are mountains of evidence to arrive at this conclusion.

In his book, *Enough is Enough*, writer Rick Scarborough says the following:

> Not only does God build hedges around individuals and their families, but He also builds hedges around nations that fear and acknowledge Him. Deuteronomy 28 records a covenant that God made with Israel. In the chapter, He guarantees the nation success as long as they acknowledge Him. 'If you fully obey the Lord your God and carefully follow his commands. . . .' Furthermore He promised in Deuteronomy 28:1-2 to set them 'high above all the nations on the earth', if they would simply obey the Lord. God also made a second guarantee; He guaranteed their destruction . . . If you do not obey the Lord your God and do not carefully follow all his commands and decrees I am giving you today, all these curses will come upon you and overtake you. Deuteronomy 28:15
>
> "God made a number of specific promises to Israel that were conditional upon their obeying and acknowledging Him. The Founders of America believed that those promises would be equally applied to them as they sought to glorify God in the building of their new nation."[5]

Most, if not all of the offending charges, have been lightning rods within our culture which liberals and progressives have politicized and pushed upon society to get legislation in place, all to lead us further down this road farther and farther away from the statutes where we started and where we need to be. Ironically, at the same time, the church as a whole has mounted nothing but a deafening silence as an opposition to this war of the progressives or even the sins of America.

Removal of the Bible from Schools

To lead a leftist revolution within a country, probably the place to start is to remove God, the text books, the morality, and demoralize the religious followers as best you can; move them all from the scene. That is exactly what the progressives started doing in the modern era, in 1948; they removed the Bible as a reading tool in public schools. The stated reason was that Scripture did not help students learn English. The subliminal reason was of course an attempt to remove God's influence from the learning factories. The goal was to hopefully remove what could earlier be called 'violations of conscience' from what would happen at school. The result has been catastrophic for the children and in turn the nation. When the Bible is replaced in school with books like, 'Slaughterhouse Five,' and others much worse, learning will lose the moral out of bounds markers that goes with reading good wholesome books like Scripture.

Prayer Removed from School

There is a progression that goes with the progressive movement, which is anything but progressive; it is regressive and destructive to all it touches. Though it promises freedom, enlightenment, and fun, the end is quite opposite. When you start making changes to your course, such as removal of the moral and ethical boundary lines; i.e., the removal of Scripture from schools and then prayer, the course of things requires more and more change to satisfy the greed to get away from God and His good. So, it leads to making another evil change, then another, and another, and another. The cycle becomes what I call a 'death spiral.' Lower and lower the morality and goodness and positive results go, while evil results such as theft, murder, and other baggage increasing in greater proportion. There is sort of a numbing affect that needs to go deeper than before, therefore the fall continues.

And so it was when school prayer began to be hotly debated in 1955 and was outlawed in public school in 1962. It did not come overnight. That too was gradual. First there was avoidance and neglect, then suggestions that prayer go away. This was followed by law suits, and more law suits. Finally, it was a law. No more prayer, at least to God. Interestingly, the legal tenant used to legislate prayer out of school; it was the First Amendment. I guess you reframe the Amendment in a way to suit you, then get rid of the Amendment altogether.

When I was becoming a teenager in the 60's, one could see the progression of this happening in real time. We used to start every day with the 'Pledge of Allegiance', then that was suddenly outlawed because God was mentioned. Before that, in my earliest school years, a prayer was offered each day in school, but that was outlawed because it was deemed criminal activity. During the same time period there were Bibles left over in the library where study hall was held. It was not long until the thought police arrived to remove that type of "brain washing" material, because it was declared to be dangerous to young minds. In looking back on all this activity, I believe I can see the reasoning behind these moves by liberals. It seems appropriate to hate anything that is wholesome and good. We do not want young students' minds poisoned with morals. Better to have wild, unsupervised sex under the stairways rather than have clean, wholesome thoughts. Yeah, I got it now.

Progressives have always attacked godly attributes, insisting all must be removed as if it were contraband. But at the same time they insist on our tolerance for their ungodliness. Whatever they have in their wagon on that day they take on irrational behavior in insisting we have tolerance for them. Sometimes, it comes through tears of a campaigning California politician saying that "young children are dying because of these extremist Christians." As stated earlier, tolerance is a two-way street. Christian people must stand firm, not surrendering any of their rights, lest all rights be dissolved one at a time. The hatred for God and anything religious is incredibly amazing, and also sad to watch. The end of course, proven in history over and over again, is total destruction. It is as if God is saying, if you are not going to have a country that allows people to freely worship Me, then maybe you do not need to have a country.

So prayer was dissolved in the schools. Over the years it is now interesting to see the looks on the faces of younger people when they watch older individuals pray in a restaurant before a meal for example.

Abortion's a Wrapping Paper

Over the years, progressives have inched closer and closer to their goal, abortions on demand, all nestled under the guise of 'women's rights'. That goal is to have abortion on demand at any time during a pregnancy, and as our current president has touted, he wants post-birth abortions to be readily accepted. What we need is the same sense of responsibility our Founders had. The older generation used to have a term that applies, 'you made your bed; now sleep in it.' When you read Scripture, a basis in this country for making decisions, life begins at conception. Many references are made about the individual being a living being before birth.

Here's Where the Rubber Meets the Road

To this I have often heard proponents of the left say, " . . . that's your opinion. You can't throw your morality on me. I will determine for my own life what is right and wrong." When listening to a common criticism of leftists in their pluralism or relativism, such as this, I always like to offer a slight challenge. "If you do not want any one, such as God, His Word, or legislation made based on Scripture, to dictate a level of morality in the culture, and you want morality to be determined by what is right in a person's eyes, then you had better hope that your neighbors and all with whom you come in contact have at least the same level of moral conduct as you, or higher. If not, there is a real possibility some individual, possibly your neighbor, may decide that he thinks it is okay according to his moral compass, to steal from you, or even rape your wife while you are gone, because in his relativistic world, he has decided on his own what is moral for him. True relativism, don't you see. And when you say, 'Wait a minute. That is why we have laws against such acts", I will remind you that such laws were legislated by wise people and based entirely on what? They are based on God's directives from Scripture, such as the Ten Commandments, the Golden Rule. You should note that all our original laws in this country had their benchmark drawn from the Bible. Our Founders knew that not everyone would have a good moral compass within themselves, therefore they built a code for the basis of our society, a moral compass if you will, to hold society together. They used the very best compass that could be found, the one designed by The Almighty and tested by time.

Relativism, secular humanism, or progressivism is neither a good model nor a benchmark to use for making decisions. Typically, there are no absolutes strong enough within any of these schemes to support a consistent moral or ethical code. Being in this turf and making a decision about substantive issues could lead to a disaster, as has happened throughout our history. Frankly stated, if there are not absolutes, then you can convince yourself eventually that killing someone, who disagrees with you for example, might be acceptable. If you think not, look at history. Mao, Stalin, and Hitler: they all did it.

The Real Problem with Progressives

Leftists do not seem to understand that we are granted freedom, not to do just anything we want, but to do what we ought. Our Creator knew that if left alone, we have the ability to eventually destroy anything and anyone around us, including ourselves. Our Framers realized this and wisely built our society on those ancient and time-tested principles which incorporated morality along with science and math to ensure that children would have the tools necessary to grow into wise and productive citizens. True education, must combine moral and spiritual lessons with the hard disciplines of math and language study.

Our Framers also followed the principles of the Bible to build laws to protect the weak, the innocent, the meek, all against attacks from individuals AND governments who try to destroy or steal their rights. Every right you and I have what the Founders realized were granted by our Maker, not by any government. Every law, every principle, and every institution in the beginning of this great country were all here to protect what God had provided. Progressives, liberals, Democrats (Oh, these wise sages) they just cannot figure this out. They think government is the provider of all rights. And therein lieth the problem.

Progressive Liberals or Secular Humanists have made it their business to attack all those rights, laws, and institutions, attempting to take them away or halt their original purpose. And being filled with such anger, they believe any guiding principle provided by our Founders should be wiped away because they were based on Biblical ideals. Progressives speak of freedom, fairness, social justice, and liberation, but their results smack of slavery, indentured servitude, unbelievably high taxes, loss of rights, morals tossed out, and an evil, sick end to society. In spite of what these "Humanists" orate, we all need to be reminded on a regular basis that we often fail, that we need good moral constraint, Godly principles, and a safety net to protect our culture from the evils that seek to destroy us. Unfortunately, often the enemy we face is worse on the inside of our country than it is outside our borders. Make no mistake about it, liberals, progressives, et al, are true enemies of Godly justice and freedom.

Biblical history, world history, American history, all history teaches us that when leaders come along who thumb their noses at righteousness and at God, eventually they witness the hammer come down on their economies, their health, their agriculture, their weather, their relationships, their agreements and eventually every decision they make.

Let me show you how that trend line works. Our history shows there have been several in national leadership who have chosen the low road in life, but in the last half century it is easy to see that among those who are close to the top of that list are Bill and Hillary Clinton, both of whom bought into the culture of anti-righteousness demonstrated in their lives. They are both products of the sixties when the departments of most universities, especially the political science and legal departments, were already extremely liberal. History shows that professors had an "in your face" demeanor in presenting the Marxist ideologies and chasing God and Christianity out of the class. Professors were trained I suppose by memos of the week, to teach such things as what Karl Marx said about religion, "It is the opiate of the masses." The agenda of the liberal professors and by their acquiescing silence, the university too, was to shatter the faith of young students making more disciples for Marxism. They too had read the words of President Lincoln, "The lectures in our colleges in one generation become the laws of the next."

The Clintons are products of that era. They thoroughly bought into the liberal thinking and the anti-American ideology that was taught then and is taught now. Clinton has long acknowledged his opposition to the Vietnam War. On December 3, 1969, while in England in his 2nd year as a Rhodes Scholar at Oxford, he wrote a letter to Colonel Eugene Holmes who headed the Reserve Officer Training Corps. In it he said, "First, I want to thank you, not just for saving me from the draft, but for being so kind and decent to me last summer.... Because of my opposition to the draft and the war, I am in great sympathy with those who are not willing to fight, kill, and maybe die for their country.... Two of my friends at Oxford are conscientious objectors.... One of my roommates is a draft resister who is possibly under indictment and may never be able to go home again. He is one of the bravest, best men I know. His country needs men like him more than they know. That he is considered a criminal is an obscenity...."[6] He helped organize an anti - war protest in

November of 1969. Clinton also conducted protests against his government while he was in Europe. We know what he thought of military service and the selective service draft; his comments have been numerous. In his first six months of his presidency, he identified himself with the extreme left wing ideology, naming himself a liberal social activist signing executive orders authorizing abortions of the unborn at military complexes around the world and at the same time legitimizing homosexual behavior. He also became the first president in US history to place homosexual activists in key positions in several positions throughout his administration.

Barack Obama has entered the theatre of the Oval Office, making Bill Clinton look very conservative in comparison. While in office, he has held total disdain for people of the Christian faith. Ironically, while he campaigned, he feigned a Christian faith and relationship with God, which along with almost all his other statements as president, have been proven to be dishonest. He said as a campaigner that he thought about joining the military; but reality shows he loathes the military of the U.S.

Obama has not only supported abortion, he has signed legislation authorizing post-birth abortions against helpless children. He has lied about his statistics while in office. When unemployment was officially reported at 7 percent, economists using U-3 government data noted it was north of 18 percent. What is troubling is the report from White House staffers who say the numbers are just "made up" in order to hit proposed targets. Weekly jobs reports are revised downward every week, and even those reported are anemic. While saying that more Americans are working now than ever before, the truth is nearly 100 million Americans are no longer in the workforce. The only statistic that looks good is the Dow Jones Industrial Average; but alas, that is only because the Federal Reserve (The Fed) is propping it up. Obama has indeed attacked every conservative pillar of the Constitution of the United States, while lovingly clinging to Marxist policies. Some have said he appears nearly star-struck when speaking from his teleprompters about Muslim practices.

Deuteronomy 28 describes the blessings that follow national obedience to God's law. As shown in the first part of this presentation, God's hedge of protection has been removed. When the hedge is down, the enemy is able to run rampant through the country destroying that which is good. As much as many want to deny it, God is our greatest hope. But He is also our greatest threat. We will either see a national spiritual revival or we will see the end of America as we know it, losing freedom and everything else that is positive about the country.

Another book of Scripture was written in warning of what will happen if a nation forsakes its original charter to honor God. Isaiah is that book which was written to record and show the trend line of unfaithfulness of God's people at the time, and the spiral of judgment that came their way because of their actions. In Isaiah chapter 5, the prophet records the question that God ultimately asks, "What more could have been done for my vineyard than I have done for it? When I looked for grapes, why did it yield only bad?"

Chapter Thirteen — Who Moved the Hedge?

Given the war of progressives on Christians, the same question could be asked of us today. A great number of our founding fathers believed the conditional promises of Deuteronomy 28 applied to them as much as to the nation of Israel. They understood that the conditional curses of that chapter applied to them along with the prediction of Isaiah, if they abandoned their commitment to honor God.

We are a nation currently under the judgment of God. That explains why our nation has failed so badly in the past few years. I also believe that the judgments listed in Deuteronomy 28, have not only surfaced in our nation, but are expanding upon us daily. Have we passed the event horizon; are we too far gone for this ship to be turned around? No, it can be turned around. I believe that whole heartedly, since history also shows us examples of how God has spared Israel and Nineveh in the past.

If reading the words of Deuteronomy 28 is new to you, please consider the words carefully and brace yourself. Start with verse 15, "However if you do not obey the Lord your God and do not carefully follow all His commands and decrees I am giving you today, all these curses will come upon you and overtake you . . . " Then notice the promises in the balance of the chapter that seem chilling as you realize the trends in our nation over the past fifty years.[7]

Promises in Deuteronomy 28	Status of these promises in America
V. 17 – "Your basket and kneading trough will be cursed"	Failing industry, food prices are increasing monthly
V. 18 – "The fruit of your womb will be cursed."	Rise in childhood disease and a loss of fertility due to many sexually communicated diseases & abortion. This may apply to youth violence, at epidemic stages now.
V. 18; 38-40 – "The crops of your lands will be cursed."	Fires, droughts and floods in America's fertile heartland. Also California valleys that grow food, only weeds now.
V. 18 – "Your lambs and calves will be cursed."	Falling wages and rising costs of raising stock.
V. 20 – "Confusion surrounding everything you do."	Rise in emotional illnesses and disability claims; 1 in 3 hospital beds taken by mental health patients.
V. 21-22 – "The Lord will plague you with . . . the Lord will strike you with wasting disease."	Venereal disease including AIDS is increasing at a record rate in America. Cancer and viral infections are on the increase.
V. 22 – "Scorching heat and drought."	Water tables in many parts of the country are declining
V. 24 – "The Lord will turn the rain into dust . . . it will [then] come down until you are destroyed."	Think of hurricanes and the record number of tornadoes, floods and violent weather patterns in the past decade.
V. 25 – "The Lord will cause you to be defeated on the battlefields."	Vietnam was first

continued on next page

Promises in Deuteronomy 28 cont.	Status of these promises in America cont.
V. 27 – "The Lord will infest you with tumors and festering sores."	Cancer, skin cancer, AIDS, and shingles are all on the rise.
V. 28 – "The Lord will inflict you with madness... confusion of mind."	Mental disorders are rising. The number of mental patients freely walking our streets now is shocking.
V. 29 – "You will be oppressed and robbed."	Robberies and home break-ins are quickly rising
V. 30 – "You will be pledged to be married... but another will take her."	The continuing breakdown of marriage and infidelity is now past epic proportions
V. 43 – "The alien who lives among you will rise above you higher and higher."	Need we say anything about illegal immigration in America? It is an epidemic.
V. 44 – "He will lend to you but you will not lend to him."	Our national debt is roaring out of control and will eventually sink the nation.

Moses must have distressed his audience as he ended his message with a warning by driving a grave statement in the sand for them, "All these curses will come upon you because you did not obey the Lord ... Because you did not serve the Lord joyfully and gladly in the time of prosperity." (Deut. 28:45, 47)

As mentioned as almost a companion passage to Deuteronomy, Isaiah predicted what would happen to Israel, Judah, and Jerusalem if God removed the hedge of protection from them. As our Founders believed the promises of Scripture applied to America just as it did to Israel; we can also see from Isaiah's predictions how the hedge of protection of America is being lifted or has been lifted so that we are no longer protected by God.

An Economy That Is Faltering (Loss of an Economy)

Because Judah went back on its promise to honor God, Isaiah predicted that his nation's economy would fall, and that it would become so bad that God would withhold water and bread from the citizens. (Isaiah 3:1) In similar fashion, I believe the case can be made that progressives and their war on America have taken a horrible toll in our time, over the last 100 plus years. So much so that these stances have driven the country into at least two oppositional financial positions that seem almost impossible when you look at them side by side. First, there is their exorbitant taxation that's been legislated in place to deal with their "social justice" programs which they created to "level the playing field." There is a simple lesson to learn here. If I give my money to help the poor, that is compassion. If I give your money to help the poor, that is theft. Should we help the poor? Of course, but not through never-ending government giveaways that encourage more of the same. The progressive politicians in this country have made careers out of confiscating money from law-abiding citizens to legitimize their unscriptural habits and to support their horrible infrastructure of countless government subsidies.

Politicians and banks have created an out of control national debt that has largely made our economy fail. The end result, when it comes, will not be as simplistic as stated in Isaiah's third chapter; it will certainly end with horrible circumstances; hunger, starvation and death; the nation has forsaken its calling.

Progressives have no set value system; whatever values they have move and shift based on whims and political causes; they shift based on elections. The end justifies the means. They oppose righteousness in whatever name or form is taken, and become violent when the righteousness has a Christian foundation. They scream for women's rights as an example, then protect entities like Ted Kennedy when he steals those rights away, even when it costs a young woman her life. This current legislators and their relativism date back to the 60's and early 70's when they were doing drugs and screaming against the establishment. Now they scream for more intrusive government than they fought when they were young and foolish. Now they are just foolish.

Loss of American Character

Isaiah said that God was about to take from Judah and Jerusalem both supply and support ... the hero and the warrior, the judge and the prophet, the soothsayer and the elder, the captain of fifty and man of rank, the counselor, skilled craftsman, and clever enchanter. (Isaiah 3:1-3)

Due to the abandonment of our nation in honoring God, we see something of the same happening to us. As America has lost its character, it has negatively impacted us in our institutions, our military, and our courts. You may remember a faithful saying that I too remember, from not so long ago, "A man's word is his bond." That was true for so many years when the signing of a legal agreement or contract was a mere formality, and in most cases was nonexistent. Most dealings were done on a handshake. But today, practices have grown so bad, that not even the contract is worth the paper it is written on. The need for having a team of attorneys is now considered a normal business practice, to exact language so that people can be forced to keep their commitments. Integrity and character, the supply and support of the nation, like with Judah, has flown the coop.

Our heroes and military champions of the past have come under assault in this day by the progressive left. Even Santa Claus has come under assault as if he were a Christian symbol. Come to think of it, for some in Christendom, St Nicholas is a Christian symbol. The heroes of society today are a breed all their own. No more selfless sacrifices to help someone as heroes of the past did. Today's modern hero, as viewed through the progressive lens, is one who indulges himself, with little thought for anyone else. The Left will attack anything good, righteous or solid. They will also change directions based on how it serves them at the time.

What is stunning, as someone who lived through those decades of time, is not just how the warped ideas have triumphed and now dominate the mainstream culture. It is however incredible to witness how the leftists and Humanists have turned 180 degrees in what they support and in what they hate. The inconsistency is should dominate the nightly news. Everything seems to be flipped completely; so that the things the so-called "progressives" were for in the 1950s and 1960s, they are now totally against and of course vice versa.

I love Marty McFly; he was a great "history facilitator." He and that stainless steel time machine he drove. Just 88 MPH is all the faster he had to go to engage the flux capacitor, and violá; he was plowing under a mailbox and pine tree, back in good ol' 1955. If we could get in that DeLorean and go back with him, oh say, just to the late 50s and early 60s, you would find some startling facts about the time, especially as it involves these liberals; things I am certain you do not know or do not recall. Get this. Back in the 1950s and 1960s, leftists, progressives, they loved guns. They just could not get enough of them. That is right, guns! They carried them, they used them quite a bit, praised those who used them, and preached the doctrine of possessing them. And guess why? It was because they wanted a revolution and wanted to end the establishment that was in power at that time. That is why. They threatened violence; they posed for pictures with their hog leg (aka, gun) and talked of what they would do some day. Fast forward to today, they have seized power. They are the establishment, and presto, their story has conveniently changed.

One of my favorite editors tells the true story, "As a former leftist revolutionary during my misguided youth, I recall with crystal clarity when the radical left of the 1960s brazenly bore arms in public, boasted about firearms training, stockpiled arms and ammo and even engaged in armed violence against police.

The Black Panther Party, originally, by the way, the Black Panther Party for Self-Defense, is a case in point. The organization, led by Bobby Seale and Huey Newton, were often referred to in the 1960s as "the vanguard of the revolution."

They were known for ambushing police. Newton himself, after being freed from prison for the killing of Oakland police officer John Frey, boasted of murdering him. James Forman, Black Panther Party "minister of foreign affairs," called for blowing up police stations, killing Southern governors and mayors and murdering 500 cops. They took full advantage of the Second Amendment and California laws that permitted the carrying of loaded rifles and shotguns in public, as long as they were not concealed or pointed at anyone. In May 1967, the Panthers literally invaded, fully armed, the State Assembly of the California Legislature. Later they organized an armed march on the state Capitol when lawmakers introduced legislation banning the carrying of loaded weapons in public. All of this made them the heroes of the left. So-called "civil rights attorneys" like Charles Garry and William Kunstler and the American Civil Liberties Union defended them for their brazen calls for armed struggle, armed attacks and armed intimidation tactics."[8]

Guns are now 'anathema' and they are fighting for massive gun control. Imagine that? You can tell they feel they are in control of society because they want to take away your right to protect yourself from them. And besides, they know if oppressed enough, bitter clingers will decide they are going to use their hog leg today for the same purpose that they, the liberals, were going to use them back in the 1950s and 1960s. They do not want to be overthrown. They are afraid. They have Flexible beliefs. Flexible values, flexible morals, but what they do not have is a Moral Compass. I think they are just opportunistic liars.

Pile in our DeLorean time machine again, fasten your seat belt and go back with us to the sexual revolution, same 1960s and even the 1970s. The same bunch of progressives, with the bra burning, marches. You can hear them yelling, "people need privacy in their own bedrooms; the government must stay out." Now back to today again, and presto, they have changed their mantra. Now it is everyone's business what people do in the privacy of their own bedrooms. With liberals now in charge of government, they are trying to find out every fact they can about your habits even in your home. In fact, progressives have enacted hate crime legislation, through their judge friends, against anyone who objects to the lewd or flagrant displays of sexual deviancy wherever it is, especially in public. Alternative sexual lifestyles are now considered protected by some affirmative action programs. Gay or homosexual has become the new 'black' and the rage of the Hollywood elite. It is preferred over heterosexual lifestyle, which is so ancient, and considered so square and boring. Isn't it crazy, back in the 1960s and 1970s, Progressives mocked marriage saying it was so out of style and so square. And God forbid if you were monogamous. I mean sex is Free, man! Today, they insist the marriage is for everyone, no matter if it is male and male and female and female. I am certain if God allows this culture to survive, it will not be long until farmer Ned Perkins and his faithful dog, Queenie, can legally get married. Cool, don't you know to have leadership that is so flexible. Not!

Back then, they claimed women and minorities had everything stacked against them. Now the deck is stacked in favor of women and minorities, which includes any kind of relationship you can imagine to have going on. However, they still complain.

Back in 1968, the progressives rioted at the Democratic National Convention in Chicago and tore both the city and the convention apart. Today, after these progressives have given up their hippie clothes and cut their hair, they run the Democratic Party and protest anything and everything conservative, normal, straight, freedom-loving, Godly, and yes, Christian. By the way, they usually do not complain about the Republicans because the Republicans for the most part have joined them in their efforts.

Back in the 1960s and 1970s, when the "progressives" were promoting abortion on demand, they insisted it was because women had an absolute right to make decisions about their own bodies. Today, those same progressives and their disciples have 'progressed' to defend the murder of babies *outside* the mother's womb — even female babies! Flexible beliefs can take you far — from the truth that is.

Back in the 1960s and 1970s, the progressives said they had a right to protect their own children from prayer and Bible reading in the public schools. They and their parents succeeded at eliminating it by liberal legislation. Today, the progressives say that parents are not really the guardians of their children. They really belong to the entire community. After all, "it takes a village to raise a child." That slogan is so sickening to me because I have seen their villages they want to raise these community children within and they are nothing more than a Potemkin Village, like the ones built for Katherine the Great to see when she rode through the area. Those were empty hallow shells.

Back in the 1960s and 1970s, the progressives screamed, and I love this one, that the conservative minority was imposing their will on them, the majority. They at least claimed to be the majority then, but were not. Today, the progressives never miss an opportunity to impose their version of morality on others, though they are still an absolute minority. Situation ethics has its benefits when you are a liar.

I could go on, and on, and on, and on. However, just from all these examples, I see the following takeaways:

- The so-called progressives have no respect for the rule of law. They will use the law when it is advantageous for them and discard the law when it no longer suits their objectives.
- The so-called progressives have no fixed values. They're spitin' in the wind.
- The so-called progressives are actually rebelling against God, His universe, and His fixed morality.
- The so-called progressives are not for progress at all. Progress was what America's Founders gave the world in the form of self-government and limited government. Progressives are really "retrogressives" who want to return to the old system that dominated most of world history, before American, in which the state was supreme, not the individual.
- The so-called progressives, while they claim to represent the interests of minorities and the oppressed, actually seek to keep minorities and the oppressed in chains of government control because they make good subjects for them to use when necessary.
- The so-called progressives hate just about everything that made America the greatest experiment in liberty the world has ever known.

By the way, where are the prophets? Isaiah said that Judah would lose theirs. It seems we have too. You would expect that the preachers of today would be speaking overtime about the sins of this administration and this nation. In irony, they are almost silent doing what appears to be "internal sensitivity training." Preachers are afraid of offending someone, thus they build churches that are fashioning themselves after the world rather than after the Word of God.

CHAPTER THIRTEEN — WHO MOVED THE HEDGE?

Loss of Statesmen in Leadership

Isaiah said, "I will make boys their officials; mere children will govern them." (Isaiah 3:4) The prophecy is shocking and at the same time almost seen as a natural progression in the loss of statesmen.

America has had great statesmen in the past. Our history is rich with them. Sure there have been real scoundrels in political positions in the past, but recently that has become more the norm than the exception. But statesmen were the mark of our past; that is men and women who put the concerns of the people above their own interests, and their own incomes. Not anymore. They are in the business for themselves, campaign be damned. So with the loss of integrity, we see in effect, selfish children who are governing, boys and not men. Children lack the polish and poise to stand on their own. They need a gang mentality; someone to protect them.

If we are to survive as a nation, we will have to regain the image of having men of conviction and character in leadership. To not change, as the prophet has spoken, our future, our national securities will be in the control of self-interested children and lobbyists are directed by evil who try to control them. When God withdraws his support, the nation then and now finds itself being ruled by men who act like little children. Children want to be accepted. Children will do only what is expected of them or demanded of them, usually no more. Children can be manipulated by cheap rewards or bounties. Children mimic other children. Children scream aloud or throw a fit when they do not get their way. Children can be very cruel and inhumane. Children act irresponsibly. Children lack discretion. Children blame others for their own failures. Sounds like our politicians of today who are in power. They spend so many resources on themselves and run several polls every day to see which way the wind is blowing; much like a child does in finding out what the "Top 10" songs are of the day or week.

Something else we need to add here. A nation that loses its support from God begins to lose value for many things; especially their senior citizens. Ronald Reagan, probably one of the greatest presidents we will ever have, was constantly criticized for his age. Children do that. Children also attack more helpless senior citizens, like the knockout flash mobs we are hearing about in our culture today. Children run in gangs, because they lack the impetus to stand on their own. Children; children; isn't it interesting that Isaiah's prophecy is true here today like in Judah in his day?!

Possibly you are able to see it now? If not, especially those of you who were around in the 70's, remember how the liberals or progressives felt about the Soviet Union? They loved the Soviets and what they represented. They thought communism was the answer and that America was the dangerous nation in the world. Do you remember what the media did when Gorbachev was put in power? The American media worshipped him. Now that the Soviets are gone, the same media is threatened because we are the only super power and are no longer held in check by the Soviets. Progressives want to cut this country down to size. They want the

Soviets back to balance this country. They think we are too dangerous on our own.

There are very dangerous narcissistic ways about these Progressives. Whatever cause they are hawking at the time, it is actually a sales pitch that is all about them and what they want at the time.

In this light, progressives or liberals on one hand are not really confusing in their decision making. They usually are in a death spiral which they refuse to acknowledge. What they destroy, they blame on others. They will create many inconsistencies in the various stands they take. Their attempts to cover these up lead to lies; more cover ups and then more lies. All to support a world view of socialism and communism that cannot hold water on its own.

Examples of this can be seen daily in news reporting. Many news worthy stories are not reported at all in liberal media. They are not there because they do not fit their political agenda, but also because they have over time built a world view based on lies and half-truths. To report a particular story 'might' destroy the foundation of their prior lies and deceptions. So in their mind and make-believe world in order to support their position, it is better to manipulate the real facts of the story to make it fit your wishes, or not report the story at all.

Loss of Community and Togetherness

Isaiah said "People will oppress each other, man against man, neighbor against neighbor." (Isaiah 3:5) As the progressives have grown in power within our nation, the secular humanism which most of them embrace as a religion, gives rise to unpredictable behavior as we have shown. While they embrace the ideology of social justice, that means using your money to accomplish their goals, not their own. So there is much about them that lacks integrity. Notice how this humanism has moved among our nation and changed the culture over the years. Magazines that were popular years ago such as *Look* and *Life* have been replaced by *People* and then *Us* and ultimately *Self*. We have a society that is vastly populated with individuals who have no active concern for neighbors or for others and focus almost exclusively on themselves and their own personal rights.

I remember so well in 1961, how our neighborhood felt about all the neighbors. The country telephone we had connected the sixteen families together like an extended family. They were almost as much a part of our family as our own parents or children were. When the McAllister girls in the neighborhood were in a horrible car wreck, it was devastating to the whole neighborhood. All of us felt the loss and went to work to help the family, because they were a part of our family. Years later, when my family and I moved to California, it was as if we were in medieval times, with high walls and motes to keep the neighbors out. Sure there was warm sunshine, but neighbors were afraid to get acquainted. I forced my friendship on some of the neighbors, and had lasting friendships because of the initial action taken. Others wanted to remain distant behind their walls; some just afraid because of

Chapter Thirteen — Who Moved the Hedge?

crime rates; some just pointed inwardly, wanting to serve self only.

Sadly the current American scene has lost its neighborliness. Not only are we not good neighbors, but we are looking to sue those around us. One report claims one of every 300 persons in America is an attorney. (Source: American Bar Assoc., 2012)

Court Cases Provide the Proof. There are many real stories. Os Guinness wrote many in the 80s that "Only in America could a man try to commit suicide by jumping in front of a train and then successfully sue the New York City Transit Authority for $650,000 for the injury suffered in his unsuccessful attempt on his own life. Another equally ludicrous involved a fireman who sued the city for $5 million for the pain and suffering caused by a fleabite in the firehouse. The same report from the 80s stated that in 1986, New York City was forced to employ 120 full-time personal injury specialists and to pay out $938.9 million to resolve claims, including $17 million for sidewalk falls alone."[9]

Then take another real story of partial birth abortions conducted by the doctor, Gosnell, who was on trial in Philadelphia in 2013. The progressive media, who really supports the legalization of partial birth abortions, did not want to even cover the story because they said "it was not news worthy." To cover the story in a truthful way would do damage to their political cause. Of course they could not print the pictures of the little babies whose heads were being cut off by scissors, nor report the laughter the doctor practiced while he was doing it. To report such "news" would have created a condemnation of their entire position and would have steered people away from where they want society to go. Their response? First, they said it was not news worthy. Then when the torrents of pressure were applied to them, they only mentioned the trial in passing, that it was on-going, and reported bare facts and half-truths. Most interviews that were done were with and of supporters of Gosnell. Actually as I recall our current Oval Office occupant stating his support of the doctor's positions.

When I saw the real story of what this monster abortionist had done to these little children, I was overtaken by such grief that I could hardly bear it. I cried, "Oh My God, how far we have fallen and sinned against you!" In my heart I know that the preponderance of sin against God has caused him to lift his hedge of protection for this country.

In 2013, the George Zimmerman trial reached its conclusion, with an acquittal. You may recall that this surrounded the death of Trayvon Martin, a young black man. The reason I mention this here, is that the news sources have for decades been chasing ghosts in reporting what they call 'racism' by whites on blacks. (Interesting that black on white crime is not called 'racism.') When the NBC reporter received a copy of the 911 tape of Zimmerman calling for help, he could not hear anything substantively in his voice that pointed to this 'racism.' Zimmerman was asked by the 911 operator what color the intruder after he had described the young man in several other ways, but not by race or color. When finally asked about what color he was, Zimmerman said, "He's black." The NBC reporter, and I'm sure he did not do this without approval from management above on NBC's mahogany row, had the tape edited with words changed around to make Zimmerman say immediately on the call, the race of the intruder. Note, this was all done to, fit within their political aim in society. It was also done, because to report simply the truth would not have supported their view of white on black crime, they have been reporting for decades. They also did this to drum up headlines and to start a frenzy to keep the story going, and thereby keep selling their product.

At the end of the day, the wrong person was put on trial. The media person(s) who edited the tape and concocted a lie, should have been on trial. It's not too late for this to happen. I know this is risky to say this, because as Samuel Clemmons said, "Never pick a fight with a man who buys ink by the barrel." But it is not too late to take the filth out of the news business and start getting back to telling the truth about news worthy events. Let the chips fall where they may, Truth, it is an interesting concept that the media of today might want to consider.

But in order to keep their story going early on, there were only claims of racism. This followed a full year of incredible hype and yells of racism. The moral is, progressives will manufacture a story if necessary to push a lie on down the road, kick the can so to speak and keep it going. By the way, over 200 black children were murdered in Chicago in 2012, as in the past by black thugs. When asked if he knew any of their names, the National Director of the NAACP said he could not, but he sure remembered the name of Trayvon Martin. He is an embarrassment to an organization claiming to seek equality based on the content of the heart, not the color of the skin.

For 200 years decency and morality were the standards of our nation, until of course the progressives and secular humanists got ahold of power in the country. When God became irrelevant and morality became situational, everything changed. History revisionists are striving to convince unsuspecting citizens that the Founding Fathers were something other than Bible believing Christians who intended that the government they founded was to be guided in perpetuity by precepts of the Judeo-Christian Bible. Agenda-driven history revisers do not want Americans to remember their spiritual roots; they plan to take the country in a secular humanist direction never intended by the Framers.[10] That is what the Left wanted and they got it. Now people are afraid to leave their homes not knowing what will happen. America is quickly becoming a jungle; amazing what post-modernism will do

It seems very confusing to see the inconsistent behavior of Leftists and listening to what they claim are the decisions they would have us make. They will parade for animal rights (dogs, cats, spotted owls, snail darter fish, fruit flies) but it is all cosmetic. By the way, do not turn your animal over to the ASPCA to have them find a home for the pet. The data shows they many times put them to sleep. Those commercials on TV which are so touching are often reported to be all about raising money for progressive political causes. Bet you did not know that! Sickening, isn't it? But they talk about saving those animal lives, and that pleases the low information progressive base of voters so much, because the right words were used, the right buttons were pushed. Talk is more important it seems than action for this bunch of hypocrites. But notice in turn the same group will march to promote death to the unborn, or to even those who may have just been born, as Mr. Obama has done on different occasions the last few years. They see no inconsistency here at all.

Making sure the record is straight, I love animals. Anyone who knows me knows how I have worked hard to rescue small animals all my life, to give them a home or find them a home, where they can be loved and give love to those around. My pets are treated as my children; their lives are precious, because they are a part of my little family. But they are not nearly so precious as those little innocent babies who had their lives snuffed out before they had a chance to run, play, learn, grow, go to school and even learn how to vote and get involved in society.

Given the evidence of both history and Scriptural records, God certainly stands opposed to the wasteful slaughter of animals, or the cruel and inhumane treatment many of them receive. But God certainly hates abortion and will not allow a nation that practices it to stand for long. There are more than just moral reasons to reject abortion. Of course, morality based on Scripture is first, but there are also economic reasons.

Good People Must Step Up to Lead

When things went bad in the country of Judah, Isaiah challenged the men about the lack of good leaders, "A man will seize one of his brothers at his father's home and say, 'You have a cloak, you be our leader. Take charge of this heap of ruins!' But in that day he will cry out, 'I have no remedy. I have no food or clothing in my house; do not make me the leader of the people.' Jerusalem stagers, Judah is falling; their words and deeds are against the Lord, defying his glorious presence." (Isaiah 3:6-7)

Talk about a prophecy being relevant to our society in America in 2013! There is a lot of truth here for where we are. Someone grabs his brother; "You be the leader." Any conservative in America today knows that the nation is in serious trouble. No one has answers, but everyone wants a piece of the pie, whatever is served. Notice the excuses offered by the brother. First there was, "I have no remedy." I don't have a clue what to do with this crisis is another way of putting it. Next the brother said, "I have no clothes," which is another way of saying he couldn't afford to get involved. Finally the brother says, "Don't make me the leader," another way of saying that he really doesn't care to get involved. No one wants to take the lead in changing the outcome of things, but they want it changed. "I don't care," probably sums up the American scene about as well as anything statement that could be made. In our last presidential election there were several million Christians who didn't even bother to vote.

It seems that many people just don't care and they will jump on some bandwagon that does not impact them personally, financially or with a commitment of time to be levied. As a result, they seldom understand the full ramification of what they are supporting. Let me show you what I mean.

As a young middle management professional in Corporate America, I attended a national conference of some 1,200 similar professionals in San Francisco in 1986. Without knowing the details of those speaking at the conference, many of us were surprised to see Gloria Steinem and the lady noted as being the first woman to burn her bra for the cause of women's abortion rights in the 70's. When she was introduced, most of the crowd in the hotel ballroom was electrified, providing her a standing ovation. I had forgotten until that moment most of the people in my professional circle were liberals, progressives, and over 50% were women. I noted that only three of us in the entire hall did not stand and applaud when the speaker entered the stage. Of course, she noted that, looking at me with my arms folded on my chest. While I am not always consistent, I do not like to be found applauding what I consider to be totally immoral causes or the associated people. Once she started speaking, she made sure to say to the audience, " . . . and gentlemen, I was doing this for you just as much for you ladies," as she looked again directly at me.

Following her 'political speech', the next speaker on the agenda was a professional person, a metrics statistician who followed in the same vein but did offer through PowerPoint® slides facts about our American workforce. She demonstrated through bar charts how the Baby Boom Generation had approximately 72.3 million in the workforce. She exclaimed that the next generation, Generation X, only had 32 million. She said as far as her group was concerned nobody really knew why there were so many fewer workers were in that generation. Following about three minutes of her telling of all the pondering that other professionals had done in trying to solve the riddle, I swallowed hard, held my breath and raised my hand to make a comment. She recognized me. I calmly said, "I know where they are." She chuckled and then said sarcastically, "Oh really, well then enlighten us if you would." I calmly replied, "We aborted them." This, as I had calculated and feared, was met with many loud 'boos' and a very small smattering of applause. The speaker said she was not going to allow her time to become a "religious presentation." I simply added, "There is nothing religious or spiritual about what I said," (though I can see from this historical place where we stood, it would be interpreted that way.) I added, "It is nothing but the facts about what has taken place over the past 35 years."

The facts do speak loudly about 40 million babies being destroyed, actually murdered as I would put it, in America over the past two generations. Since the 80's the number of abortions has swelled to 55 million. Remember, that though this is a lightning rod and emotional issue, the preponderance of evidence from our history speaks of taking life as being immoral and murder. The progressives, as they call themselves, will give thunderous applause to a law allowing abortion on demand. But raise a hand against a frog or a fruit fly and watch them go nuts! It's not just inconsistent, it's immoral and in our nation it has been an economic disaster.

I too noted recently that abortion rights activists were marching in Texas to criticize proposed legislation outlawing some forms of abortion in that state. It is interesting to note that these youthful pro-abortion activists were screaming. And though most of them claim they hate religion, I noted that they were screaming "Hail Satan!" It seems they are not opposed to all gods, just the good ones! Their words give them away for what they really are.

Their screams and chants were of course in response to the Christian supporters of the legislation. No further comment is necessary, except to say that the flexible morals and situation ethics are on parade again among the progressives and secular humanists.

The New Morality Is a Curse to the Nation

Notice that in Isaiah's sixth judgment coming from God, he articulated, "Jerusalem staggers, Judah is falling; their words and deeds are against the Lord." (Isaiah 3:8)

In a strictly literal interpretation of his words, it is similar to envisioning a man trying to negotiate a sidewalk while inebriated, Isaiah seems to point to America's current condition of physical, emotional and spiritual drunkenness. Both the *Humanist Manifesto* of 1933, and the *Humanist Manifesto II*, of 1973, which was the updated version, dreamed of today it appears. They both affirmed that ethics were situational and come from no absolute source, they ended up effectively wiping out any reference points that society or culture could build as an acceptable norm for behavior.

After years of watching their dream child grow into a monstrosity, having moved from decent rules of behavior in public to now seeing the pornography, wild sexual acts and just about anything being acceptable, the humanists have succeeded in their revolution against righteousness.

The so-called "music" of this day is anything but decent and in truth anything but music. It would take pages of paper and bottles of ink to describe in limited detail the number of groups today who have songs about various parts of the human body, how to turn tricks as a prostitute, how to take the lives of cops or other citizens. Isaiah sure did nail this one. A society that is staggering on its own drunkenness. Need we say any more than this: we need leaders in this country who have moral courage. We have an enemy; the progressive liberals are just the marching army of this enemy whose name they have screamed in loyalty as they by their disobedience to things moral and clean, state what they want: they want a Satanic society where anything goes at any time with no restraints. And that is a society that is staggering and ready to fall.

Coming Out of the Closet

Isaiah adds statements to the judgment, "The look on their faces testifies against them; they parade their sin like Sodom; they do not hide. Woe to them! They have brought disaster upon themselves." (Isaiah 3:9) It is interesting to me how wise Isaiah is in identifying the parade of man's sins and how he progresses from bad to worse. Here Isaiah focuses on that progression of life as people continue to forget God and put their trust in only the human spirit.

Gay Rights and Gay Marriage — As politically incorrect as it is to say so, I believe that embracing the abortion and homosexual rights as our nation has been doing are as condemning as anything has been in the history of mankind. It is true that there have been active homosexuals in societies for centuries. Why else would the literature speak of the indecency of the act and the sin against God as described many ancient secular texts, notwithstanding the Bible. To scream that God and the rest of the world are prejudiced is a ridiculous argument. But it appears to be true that God's hedge is being lifted because of these and other offenses against what is right, true, just, honest, and of good report. There have been times in history when the 'gay rights' individuals have paraded their activities over the thousands of years, but all examples of such in the cultures of the past arguably have brought on disaster from the Almighty. Rome and Sodom are only two examples.

When you look at all our human history, it is sorrowful to view the progression of what is considered "acceptable to society" as it starts to spin out of control when God and/or morality is eliminated from the culture. A few decades ago, our path began being downhill, an insult to the many great leaders we have had in our nation's storied history.

Recent legislation in bell weather states such as California, Colorado and New York, all controlled by Democrats, or progressives, or Humanists have mandated that 'gays' actually have more rights in what they call marriage than in a 'normal' marriage between a man and a woman. The extra rights come in more than one arena. For example, if a gay couple want to have a wedding cake done and the baker says he will not prepare one for them, they are ushered legally to the front of the line in a tort trial because their 'rights' were violated. Find out just how far you can go with a court trial if a baker decides he/she does not want to bake a cake for a straight couple. This couple has no rights to sue for damages as do the gays. It just goes on from there.

Also, it is noteworthy that in California the voters, by referendum in 2010, legally mandated marriage to be a union between a man and a woman only, not a woman and a woman and not a man and a man. The noteworthy part is that the 9th Circuit of Appeals, controlled almost totally by progressives, overturned the voters saying the referendum was not 'legal' therefore voters will would not be allowed to stand.

The truth is, there has been another front to the war which progressives brilliantly started putting in place years ago. It promised to give them an advantage even when people voted against progressive ideas. And over time, they have finally reached the point where they can overcome even the will of the majority of the people and overturn their votes. They did so through the courts by appointing liberal progressive judges over time and thus stacking the deck against freedom. As this trend grows, a progressive will be able to find an appeals court some place that will be able to overturn any conservative referendum from a vote of the people calling it illegal.

If you were a Martian who had spent the last year in America trying to absorb the news and find out what really are the driving causes in our country, he/she would have to surmise that the reorientation of Americans to accept homosexuality is one of the most critical issues in front of us. The evidence bears this out as students in schools now are mandated to do sensitivity training dealing with sexual orientation.

Americans continue to be made the victim of liberal causes and movements who make speeches stating "we just want equal rights." What they really want is to be able to evangelize and recruit new members into their way of life, and to do so with no barriers whatsoever. And they have come out of the closet to parade their lifestyles for the world to see.

What to Do with the Youth

Isaiah adds to God's judgments on Judah by saying, "The young will rise up against the old, the base against the honorable . . . youths oppress my people." (Isaiah 3:5; 12)

Recently visiting a local high school, I was asked by the superintendent to be a panel member at a school assembly. Upon arrival, seeing the police cars in the parking lot, at first it appeared I had gone to the police station by mistake. The picture is a common one today with officers present in the halls attempting to provide security and safety as an answer to the gang violence, the threats of physical assault, and that is just the ones against the faculty from some of the student body. Things in school have certainly changed since I was a student. The secular humanists have been victorious in their agenda to control the public education program in America. The tenants of the *Humanist Manifesto* are being taught both in the primary and secondary schools, as well as the university system. Along with that is the theory of Darwin, namely that we all have a common ancestor, the ape. Having been taught in an uninterrupted fashion now for 50 years, it always seems amazing to me that the public is so shocked when violence occurs in school. Children have been taught their ancient ancestors were apes. Thinking that they came from apes, and are nothing more than apes, morality and ethics are viewed as situational. Given the lessons in Darwinism, Why should we suddenly be surprised when the children behave like apes?! Witnessing the poor conduct and at times criminal activity coming from some out-of-control students in a few schools, it is obvious those kids are measuring up to those lessons about apes. Actually they give apes a bad name.

Consider the message our society, namely liberal humanists, has given young people about what is important in education by the decisions listed below over the past half century,

1. In 1948, prayer in public school was outlawed, and in 1962 was actually declared unconstitutional, when the US Supreme Court ruled 6-1 against the use of what was called the "Regent's Prayer" in New York public schools *(Engel v. Vitale)*.

2. In 1963, Bible reading in public school was outlawed, declared unconstitutional again by the US Supreme Court, 8-1. No devotional readings could be done in school from the Bible *(School District of Abington Township v. Schempp)*.

3. In 1973, killing preborn children, legally classified later as "fetuses," was declared to be a right, absolutely guaranteed by the Constitution, in a 7-2 vote by the US Supreme Court *(Roe v. Wade)*.

4. In 1980, the posting of the Ten Commandments in public school was outlawed, declared unconstitutional by the Kentucky Supreme Court *(Stone v. Gramm)*. (My word is outlawed, because the word seems more fitting with a renegade society.)

5. The decisions made in the eighteen-year span have come back to haunt America. The Supremes decisions, in my opinion, have done more to devastate the youth of this country than anything other single set of actions by any particular body. In the span of just under twenty years, over 200 years of American culture was overturned and declared illegal. Our schools became "God-free" zones, just what the progressives and secular humanists wanted.

Look at our high schools of today,

What's "Thrown Out" of School	What's been "Put In" School
Prayer is outlawed	Police officers are in
Bibles and Bible reading are out	Flexible morals and values are in
The Ten Commandments are out	Rape, armed robbery, gang warfare, murder, gun violence, cheating, and making threats are all in
Creationism, Intelligent design are out	Darwin, natural selection and evolution are all in
Corporal punishment is out	Rebellion, destruction of property and disrespect are in
Righteous values are out	Drugs, booze and unwed motherhood are all in
Sexual abstinence is out	Condoms, sex in the janitorial closet and abortion – all in
Learning is out	Social engineering and programming are in
True American history is out	Revisionism of everything the last 50 yrs

Chapter Thirteen — Who Moved the Hedge?

As strategy goes, the secular humanists were brilliant. They targeted the one area of society, public school, to become their indoctrination center, where just about everyone over time attends. They must have thought in their strategy sessions, if we can remove all vestiges of the Christian faith and influence, then we can isolate young people for six or so hours a day to do our philosophical instruction in secular humanism, and do it every day. They must have thought, the parents will not even have a chance since we will have them longer than they do. From a planned performance perspective, these liberals have been absolutely successful; beyond what I bet even they thought they would be able to accomplish. What a resume of achievements they can boast!

What an accomplishment by the progressives, the liberals, the secular humanists! Makes one believe with a record like this, they should be in charge of everything in America. Oh, but they are and that's the reason it has gone to hell.

Spending in public schools in constant dollars has increased from $67.5 billion in 1960 to $205.3 billion in 1989, and then upward to $687.7 Billion in 2010, which is more than doubling twice over.

It appears the statistics show that Generation X, Y and the Millennials have every right to feel a sense of betrayal and distrust toward the earlier generations, especially the "Boomer" generation. Generation X, in looking back, witnessed the extermination of wholly one-third of their classmates and peers. The two-thirds that managed to survive arrived in a culture where by age fifteen, 60 percent of them were living in single-parent homes because of the no-fault divorces and lack of commitments of their parent generation. While they are told they were better off if they parents just went their separate ways, we have discovered the reverse to be true, they are not better off. No wonder many of them have turned into criminal activity, and at a minimum antisocial trend or at minimum antisocial trends. Frankly, given how they have all been treated, I do not blame them for being angry. Their anger has brought about a whole backlash of anti-Christian behavior.

World Net Daily reported in August 2011 on the Houston, Texas, veterans' cemetery director who issued an order banning God from military or veteran funerals at the facility. A pastor and family members of deceased veterans eventually filed a federal lawsuit alleging that the Houston National VA Cemetery is discriminating against their religious freedoms. The suit alleges that cemetery administrator Arleen Ocasio required Pastor Scott Rainey to edit a Memorial Day prayer so that the prayer was "general, and its fundamental purpose [was] nondenominational in nature."

Christian civil rights organization ACLJ senior counsel David French says the exact rate of increase is hard to determine, but many of the new cases come from colleges. "Our knowledge of incidents is only as good as the reporting," French says. "However, it's clear that — particularly on college and university campuses — we have seen a significant rise in attempts to silence Christian organizations by the misapplication of nondiscrimination laws."

French adds that many public facilities are also covering over Christianity. "One of the most strident examples: the misuse of the Establishment Clause to attempt to ban any mention of God from historical markers, monuments or even museum exhibits," French says. "This represents an effort to whitewash God from American history and change our national identity." Shackleford says the attacks are becoming violent, too.

"The recent attacks on the faith-based Family Research Council and the attack on the Sikhs are recent examples alone," Shackleford says. He also cites an example of a city trying to push out its Jewish residents. "In one case I was involved in, a city literally tried to zone out Orthodox Jews from the city. An official city meeting perpetrated this," Shackleford says. "Some said, 'Hitler should have finished the job.'"

The acts of persecution point to a deeply rooted psychological and spiritual issue. "Religious hostility is the red light on the dashboard that tells us we have a problem and that violence will come next if not fixed," Shackleford says.

French says although the Obama administration has contributed to the problem, the problem didn't begin in 2008. "While the Obama administration launched its own unprecedented assault on religious liberty through Obamacare," French says, "the attack on Christian expression is the result of cultural changes that have been taking place for decades." Shackleford agreed, saying, "The Obama administration has been very hostile, from the HHS mandates to the VA case to many, many more; but it has been getting worse and worse with each administration. Government always tries to increase its power, and freedom has been fading in the process. It has been a steady and consistent."

French says the current crisis has been brewing for decades. "No, the trend began with advent of the sexual revolution and the mainstreaming of the 1960s counterculture," French claims. "As leftist radicals have progressed through the academy, media, churches and government, the trend has only accelerated."

It is obvious that some key court cases may have accelerated the trend. Isaiah was visionary as he was able to see not only into his own culture's demise. He provides us with a glimpse into our national trek too.

The Rise of Crime against the Family

Isaiah gives us one last judgment from God in his prophecy, "Women rule over them. O my people, your guides lead you astray; they turn you from the path" (Isaiah 3:12).

Isaiah unfolds something interesting for the future of nations that forget God, something sad if you have been watching his words. It is easily missed however; like a drunken man first stumbling trying to negotiate the sidewalk, then falling. That is a picture of the nation that begins trusting man rather than God. There is the attack on manhood and an eventual perversion of his manhood, homosexuality. As a result there is an attack on children and the state of childhood, until the children become frustrated and rebellion occurs. If you look at this whole section of Scripture in its entirety, Isaiah is talking about an attack on the family and the family unit. In the absence of a good God-fearing father in the home, the appropriate leadership for the family is absent or gone. In his absence, there is a rise of all sorts of cheap substitutes that are attempted to replace the husband, the dad, but they all fail. Just as if the mother is gone, all substitutes to replace her results in tragedy too.

During my lifetime, I have witnessed more than one of these substitutes. Feminism is the first that seems to come to mind. It was a lie drummed up by secular humanists that told women they would become fulfilled when they threw off the chains of subjugation, including marriage, children and any sexual inhibitions. Then they were promised they would experience real womanhood. All of these false promises have helped to ruin family units, frustrate children and rob the women themselves of real womanhood. Feminists claimed that this time in history was the worst time for women to be alive regarding dominance from men; pregnancy was declared to be the ultimate surrender of personal rights. Abortion rights were demanded; Roe v. Wade, which came to fruition in 1973. Over the past twenty years, we have been averaging 1.5 million abortions per year in the United States.

While it is the law and millions cheer its existence each year, it is not a good law. After looking at a few years of the results of the landmark legislation in the abortions performed, in 1979, C. Everett Koop, former Surgeon General and Francis A. Schaeffer coauthored a work in which they state among other things the following, "Of all the subjects relating to the erosion of the sanctity of human life, abortion is the keystone. It is the first and crucial issue that has been overwhelming in changing attitudes toward the value of life in general."[11] Dr. John T. Noonan, professor of law at the University of California Berkeley added, "By virtue of its opinions, human life has less protection in the United States today than at any time since the inception of this country. By virtue of its opinions, human life has less protection in the United States than in any country in the Western World."[12]

There was a time in this country, before this nation turned its back on God and its cultural faith, when aborting or slaughtering unborn children was inconceivable. Things have changed. Today it is not only conceivable, but now tens of millions of Americans think denying a woman access to an abortion is not only inconceivable but criminal.

There was also a time in this nation before it turned its back on God, when it was unthinkable that the Bible would not be allowed in school as a reading book for children. Things have changed, today it is not only conceivable, but now there are tens of millions of Americans who believe that reading of the Bible in school, or even having the Bible carried into a school in a backpack is unthinkable.

There was also a time in this nation, before it turned its back on God, when it was unthinkable that Scripture verses or the Ten Commandments would not be a part of the public and government landscape on buildings, on school walls, and in front lawns of government buildings. Things have drastically changed, today it is not only thinkable, but now there are tens of millions of Americans who believe that any part of a Judeo-Christian Scripture like the Ten Commandments that might appear on any school ground or government building is not only unthinkable, but now is also criminal.

When Isaiah looked at Judah and Jerusalem, what at one time was a vibrant righteous city and countryside, was now decaying, and rotten to the core because they had gone back on their commitments to be a righteous people. After several warnings of urging and nudging the people to come back to him, Isaiah had to stand and deliver the horrifying news that God would no longer protect them from their enemies, that they would start collapsing as a society, and the end result would be ruin. And through a series of judgments, God lifted his hedge of protection, and the nation started coming apart at the seams, just like was promised.

America, as I have tried to show, is standing in the crosshairs of judgment, very similar to where Judah and Jerusalem were. As a nation, we have turned our back on righteousness and God, and now He has lifted the hedge of protection against our enemies. We are wide open for attack. As Judah, we are stumbling and ready to fall. It is up to each one of us if we are willing to accept this fate or want to decide that we want to have another chance to do what is right. Wouldn't it be great to have safe streets again? To have no debt? To have families and children who were honorable and kept commitments? If it is not too late, that might happen again. But it starts with one person at a time. Unless things change quickly, we will be down the drain just like Judah, Jerusalem, Rome, Assyria, Egypt, Chaldia, Greece, Mesopotamia, and the list goes on. They were all judged because they would not change. The question of the day is, "Will we in America change?"

"The Bible is the best of all books,
for it is the word of God and teaches us the way
to be happy in this world and the next.
Continue therefore to read it and
to regulate your life by its precepts."

~ John Jay

*Co-author of the Federalist Papers;
1st Chief-Justice of the U.S. Supreme Court*

Chapter Fourteen

There's Nothing Legal about Illegals

AT THE CENTER OF WHAT MANY call the greatest story in all of literature; the story of the prodigal son, there is an intense truth that is usually overlooked. This boy who was weary of the rules under which he lived, who wanted things to be less obtrusive, different, and be free to do what he wanted, left home one day for the far country, eagerly searching for something, only to return home another day and find there exactly what he had been seeking. Right there in his father's house, what he had so vainly sought in the far country; it had been there all along, from which he had run away.

In many different ways and many different manners, this is a truth that is the experience of many people today. James Hilton poetically illustrated what many are vibrantly underlining in the experiences of their lives, the loneliness and homesickness of our day in his book called *Random Harvest*. Hilton certainly knew how to encapsulate the moods, thoughts, and hopes of a generation and weave them into a story such as he had done earlier with *Lost Horizon*, with its mythical Shangri-La, which seems to be an exacting symbol of our day, with its escapist mood. *Random Harvest* exposes the picture of loneliness and homesickness of our day.

The story is that of a soldier in World War I who lost his memory as a result of shell shock and combat fatigue. When he comes to himself, he could remember nothing of his life due to amnesia. Everything about his life is gone. He meets his wife, does not know her, and has absolutely no memories of her. And she, while her heart is breaking for him, leaves her identity a mystery to him. Fortunately, he is drawn to her, falls in love with her all over again, and marries her. She guards her secret closely, hoping that someday he will find a way to remove the cobwebs and discover it for himself. Together they build a home, become successful in business and prominent in public life. But still his mind is haunted by that unremembered past, the life that he is sure that he has lived, and the woman he had loved. There are times when vague shadows float before his eyes, when bits of forgotten memories come, only to vanish before he can lay hold of them and piece the past together. He is always searching, searching, searching for a face, for the woman he had loved.

And then one wonderful morning, drawn by some strange impulse, he makes his way back to a half-remembered town and a half-remembered house, and there he finds her waiting — his wife whom, with his now clearing mind, he recognizes as the one he has always loved, though for a while he was searching, as he thought, for someone else.[1]

Something like that is happening in America today, in the experiences of many thoughtful people. Shaken and shocked by the tragedy to this nation by decade after decade of liberal attacks, from days long ago to the current day, seeing unspeakable and repeated tragedies to our way of life and Constitution, much of the nation has slipped off into a quiet state of shell-shock. We do not even know who we are. Some people are making their way back to half-remembered things, finding out that the joy and happiness which they have been taught, which they were seeking to find in faraway places and strange lands filled with ideologies of Marx, Socialism, Communism, and open borders. They are discovering that the joy they were seeking far off in something else, is something they had always really known. Though lost for a while, the truth was here all along to be rediscovered in our heritage; in the pillars of our society. Those are the Constitution, the Federalist Papers, the Bill of Rights, etc., all there at home where they had been all along.

Whittier once expressed this exact sentiment in verse:

> We search the world for truth; we cull
> The good, the pure, the beautiful,
> From graven stone and written scroll.
> And all old flower-fields of the soul;
> And, weary seekers of the best,
> We come back laden from the quest,
> To find that all the sages said
> Is in the Book our mothers read.

-John Greenleaf Whittier [2]

Decisions we make dictate the lives we lead. Said differently, making a life choice means also choosing all the consequences that are tied to that choice, good and bad. That applies to a person as much as it applies to a nation. Moving off the moral and spiritual foundation our fore fathers built was a choice which led to consequences, many of them we do not like. That resulted in other choices, which did more of the same and eventually devolved into horrible situations; exit stage left an example from school, the banning of the Bible and prayer. These choices that we signed on to, led to terrible consequences, that I guarantee most did not see coming until they arrived. In science, you call this cause and effect. Other areas of life have the same law. Elections have ramifications. Spiritually we say that whatever we sow is what we will reap. It is a universal law that for some unknown reason we cannot seem to learn from an earlier generation without going through the process ourselves.

CHAPTER FOURTEEN — THERE'S NOTHING LEGAL ABOUT ILLEGALS

The conclusion is in. The choices and resulting consequences have been poor and poorer in today's American education. Reading scores over the years when shown on an Excel spreadsheet show a consistent downward spiral. Plus all the violence and teacher-student sexual acts you would ever want year after year. Lack of money, need for stronger unions, these are always blamed for the poor results. But the true conclusion is unavoidable. Take the morality map out of the classroom then morality and learning leaves too.

Then down the path we have gone with more billions of dollars thrown at the school house wall, more horrible legislative choices and more bad consequences with which to deal. And they get worse each year.

This leads us to our official position on Illegal immigration, which is nothing at which to sneeze. It is one of those bad choices that had many evil consequences tied to it. The resulting explosion of illegals in the country is but one snapshot of our national death spiral and a portion of a suffocating crisis. One result of this crisis - we have lost our national identity. the immigration problem is that we have lost our identity as a people. We do not know who we are in America anymore.

Throughout history, immigration in other foreign countries has been viewed through various lenses. For example, some nations used immigration or the transplant of peoples into a country as an act of war, to destroy the culture of a particular place so that it became weak. Two of many examples throughout history are seen in the particular history of Israel and their then neighbor to the North, Assyria. In approximately 720 B.C., Sargon II, the king of Assyria captured the people in Israel and deported them to many locations in Assyria.[3] Moving the Israelites out and moving foreigners in was Assyria's post-war resettlement policy to prevent revolt in that region. Said differently, spreading the captives across Assyria prevented their reuniting; and repopulating Israel with foreign captives made it difficult for the remaining Israelites to unite for revolution. This mixture of peoples, who settled in Israel, came to be known as Samaritans who were despised by the Jews in the South. (These people had not even recovered from this resettlement policy at the time of Christ.) Inter-marriage took place all over, Jews with Assyrians and the eventual acceptance of the culture of Assyria: their idols, their eating habits, their way of life. Years later during captivity, when a Jewish man named Ezra led a group of Jews back to their land from Babylon to rebuild their temple, the half-breed or Samaritans wanted to take part in this construction project in Jerusalem. The Jews rejected their offer outright because of their diluted culture and practices of foreigners, which in effect had made them non-Jews. As a result of their anger, the Samaritans built a competing or rival temple on Mount Gerizim to stand in competition to the temple in Jerusalem.[4] The cultures had competing systems; there was no unity — it led to a continual state of discord. The Samaritans twisted both Scripture and history to favor their own people and their own nation. This is almost identical to what is happening in America today.

During the time of the Roman Empire, the Caesars dealt with immigration problems in a similar yet unique method. They were usually the immigrating force into other territories. They established colonies in conquered lands.[5] In doing so, they mandated that in order to be a colony, the people there would have to dress like Romans, speak the language of Romans, and act like Romans. The city of Philippi is a perfect example. It was a proud Roman colony. It was famous for being a miniature of the city of Rome. In those times, a city became a Roman colony in one of two ways. First, Rome founded colonies throughout the outer reaches of the empire to keep the peace and to guard against invasion from Barbaric hoards. Veteran soldiers ready for retirement, were usually granted citizenship if they would go out and settle these colonies.[6] Later on in history, there was a second way a city was granted the distinctive title of Roman Colony for loyalty and service to the empire back home. The distinctive thing about these colonies was their fanatic loyalty to Rome. The citizens kept all their Roman ties: the Roman language, the titles, the customs, the affairs, and the way they dressed. They refused to allow any infiltration of local influence whatsoever. They totally rejected the influence of the world and the culture around them. They were Roman colonists within an alien environment.

The example of Roman colonies is eerily similar to what we see happening in America today with the migration of Mexicans from the southern border. They are fanatic in their loyalty to home. They have brought their culture with them, the language, the title, the customs, the affairs, and the way they dress. They indicate they will never adopt the culture of America.

Immigrants from other countries have in effect come to this country and established foreign colonies within our nation. They have done so by following the exact same pattern:

- They keep their close ties with their homeland.
- They speak the clean and pure language of their homeland.
- They bear the title of their homeland, and do so proudly.
- They bear witness to the customs of their homeland.
- They carry on the affairs of their homeland.
- They dress as citizens of their homeland.
- They allow no infiltration of American influence whatsoever.
- They live and conduct themselves as a colony of their homeland, promoting their own culture over the American culture, which they believe to be a polluted and dying environment.

In summation, what we see today is that when some people immigrate here, they really do not immigrate at all; e.g., they continue to be all things Mexico, or all things Islam. In every word, thought, and deed they never become American. There-

Chapter Fourteen — There's Nothing Legal about Illegals

fore we cannot unite under the current banner of immigration as is being run and operated by the Liberal Left. We are really being filled and divided with colonies from other lands. The old Roman Government strategy is being played out on us. . .

When reviewing our immigration policy today, we are implementing legislation which foreign governments of the past used as strategies of war to conquer other nations. In other words, by the liberal left policy on immigration, we are at war with ourselves.

Being a native Californian, it was extremely easy 35 years ago to see the illegal immigration problem growing from bad to worse as I was perched in the middle of it on the left coast. The 'check point' on I-5 near Oceanside was always a 'bone of contention' for some friends and especially my uncle every time he would drive from San Diego north to Los Angeles. He had a ritual of grumbling and complaining about being forced to slow to a stop, so that officers could visually check for possible illegals in every car. We kids did not pay attention to this at the time.

Today, California stands on the top of a pile of states with overwhelming floods of illegal immigrants. The start of the consequences: the state's huge deficit and other resources that are drained like the lakebed at Furnace Creek. Now the term illegal is being phased out in favor of "undocumented worker" to create a milder, calmer tone for those here outside the law.

The problem is not just the illegality of some immigrants; it is all the associated baggage. The clamoring by progressives, for tolerance, acceptance, multiculturalism, and all their recent associated cries for amnesty, just to add more liberal voters are all bad ideas, even for them. California's issues in this arena are so over the top now, that when you add to it the continued and worsening legislation that comes from a totally Democrat or Socialist State Congress, as resulted in a state being a catastrophe racing down a freeway looking for a place to happen. We should not have patience for a person driving the car, racing at record speed, leaving no skid marks in front of the brick wall into which he is crashing. Nor should we have patience with illegal immigration.

Today, few states are left that are not riddled in some way with the problem of illegal immigrants. Granted, most are on a smaller scale than California. All of the associated baggage with this group of states, cause huge problems that, when combined with associated baggage we have discussed in the earlier chapters, bring the smell of death for the nation. Here are the associated marks of death which go with illegal immigration.

<u>One is the bilingual, multi-lingual and bi-cultural demands</u> put on the nation's back. No nation on earth can stand the strain, the bad blood the competition that two languages and cultures create and demand. It is remarkable for an individual to be bilingual, but for a society, it is a curse. The historical scholar, Seymour Lipset, put it this way: "The histories of bilingual and bicultural societies that did not or

do not assimilate are histories of turmoil, tension, and tragedy. Canada, Belgium, Malaysia, and Lebanon all face crises of national existence in which minorities press for autonomy, if not independence. Pakistan and Cyprus have divided. Nigeria suppressed an ethnic rebellion. France faces difficulties with Basques, Bretons, Corsicans and Muslims."[7]

 <u>Second</u>: <u>Multi-culturalism is a dangerous trek and a disaster to any nation.</u>[8] In America today immigrants are encouraged to maintain their previous culture and not to assimilate into the nation's culture and way of life. An "Idiot's Guide on How To Kill A Country" would probably contain this advice: maintain your past culture and never assimilate into the nation's culture. The current leadership of this nation, the Progressive Left, in fact, has made multi-culturalism an article of faith that all cultures are equal; that there are no cultural differences. In fact, I would say they have taken a step further in saying, " . . . any culture beats the American culture." Another article of faith of the progressives has been that the Black and Hispanic dropout rates in school or society are due solely to prejudice and discrimination by the majority white culture; or as reported by one "what colleges do for students of color powerfully impacts the futures of these young people and that of our nation." [She tried to say that the white culture is not doing enough for black and Hispanic students. Conveniently she omitted statistics on Asian student graduating rates, which were extremely positive.] [9] Any other explanation that is mentioned is branded by liberals as being 'out of bounds.' The truth is, as much as somebody may not want to hear it, all cultures are not equal. Some should be viewed as better than others. American culture of the first 200 years was one such culture that was supreme. It was not because of the "brain trust" in the Socialist Progressive party. It was due to the supremacy of the Judeo-Christian pillars that serves as a foundation to the wonderful Constitution of this United States which was a guide to citizens during that time period.

 <u>Third, in immigration, to not stress uniting in the American culture will continue to break the country into pieces.</u> One of the attorneys with whom I worked in the 1990s, made it a habit to continually emphasize that her reference point on dealing with a work issue was as she said "unique, because she was 'African American.'" Following several meetings where she provided me with this the same repeated position each time, I finally asked her rather excitedly one day, "Really? Where in Africa were you born?" After she said she was born in Pennsylvania and had never been to Africa, I concluded with, "Well, I've got bad news for you — you're just a plain old American, just like me." She became angry, and she rebutted me. Apparently when she got home and talked to her husband about the issue, it was quite a discussion. The next day, she came and apologized for her demeanor. She said her husband, who was also black, told her that I was right. One of the problems, he told her, is to continue to draw distinctions between herself and people of different color or culture. She said that she had thought about it and was going to change her reference point starting immediately, and just call herself an American, with no

prefixes of any kind. She saw the point of focusing on unity rather than diversity. My advice to corporate America is to have all the true diversity you want, but to focus on unity. Collectively, as a people, we will learn to survive and excel when and only when we focus on unity. Someone might say, "Well, you're saying all this as a "White-American!" My response is simple. "I write and say this as an American, no prefixes, no dashes, no special connotation needed."

Fourth, focus on education which assimilates people from all walks of life into the workforce. Within the immigrant groups in this country, the second largest demographic group remains relatively undereducated, unassimilated, and antagonistic toward the majority. The differences have been exploited by Leftists, creating class warfare. The result: strife, riots, destruction, all creating an extra "tax" on each citizen.

Fifth, we have built a society of "instant victims" by not stressing unity. This is measured by what one person called, the Left's 'Victimometer,' which is basically the network media. Having worked in industry for years, I can tell you for certain that the government has put "the squeeze" on large foundations and business of all shapes and sizes to provide what they, the government classify as "victims" of a conservative culture with clubs, midnight basketball courts, organizations of all sorts and of course colleges; all with gobs and gobs of money. The result: what we commonly call minorities, all think or at least do this "victim speak" about their lack of success and how that was all created by the majority, the white business culture. There is a blaming culture alive and well in this country which has become nothing less than an outright industry which is expanding and that is being trumpeted by progressives. Could be women one month, next month African Americans, the next Hispanics, oh, and don't forget about Native Americans, and so on. If you check the headlines, you will see the victim movement has followed this basic roadmap, having reached the gay and lesbian movement last. And the media races to collect the latest vocal rendition from some poor soul every week in order to announce the play by play on this "blame game." It is advertised with salty adjectives, all the bells and whistles, and all waiting for you on the 6 PM or 11 PM news. The promise of "you've got to see what they did to this guy" is a tease that cannot be missed. The only thing missing from the lynching of American Culture is a daily Soap Opera by Al Sharpton with his comments like, "White folks was in caves while we was building empires.... We taught philosophy and astrology and mathematics before Socrates and them Greek homos ever got around to it." Later Sharpton also uses the N-word to describe David Dinkins.[10] Sharpton must feel he is a well-paid victim.

Several years ago, a Missouri Congressman received immediate national news attention from all the networks when he emotionally pleaded that white Americans everywhere write letters of apology to African Americans for the slavery to black Americans. I have a black friend who asked me a question that coincided with this Senator's appeal of letter writing. My friend, Glenn, asked me when I was going to write my letter apologizing for slavery. I responded that I would write the letter when he wrote a letter apologizing for wasting the welfare dollars. His immediate reaction was that of righteous indignation, "What makes you think I have ever been on welfare?" he snapped. I simply replied, "What makes you think I ever owned slaves?" Victimology is alive and well on this planet, at least in this country. (You might want to read the chapter on Prejudice, Discrimination, and Slavery in this book before you start writing your letter.)

Sixth, we are busy celebrating diversity instead of unity. True diversity is much, much different than the skin color, which is usually presented as a modern version of diversity. The fashion statement that came forth from this movement has developed into trends of dual citizenship, and has promoted divided loyalties. Differences are stressed rather than similarities. Diverse people worldwide are mostly engaged in hating each other; that is, when they are not killing each other. A diverse, peaceful, or stable society stands in contrast against the historical precedent. People undervalue the unity it takes to keep a nation together. The ancient Greeks are a prime example. The Greeks believed that they belonged to the same race; they possessed a common language and literature; and they worshipped the same gods. All Greece took part in the Olympic Games. A common enemy, Persia, beat the drums of war and threatened their liberty. Yet all these bonds were not strong enough to overcome two factors: local patriotism and geographical conditions that nurtured political divisions. Greece fell. "E. Pluribus Unum" — From many, one. It is a historical reality, if we put the emphasis on the 'pluribus' instead of the 'Unum,' we will, as one has said, "'Balkanize' America as surely as Kosovo."[11]

Seventh, the Leftists are saying it is immoral to speak critically of illegals. To use any critical lends in viewing or discussing our illegal immigration and diversity problems is considered politically incorrect and taboo. It is now considered political suicide and off limits for any politician to name diversity as that which stands against unity. In the 16th century, the word "heretic" was drudged up to stop discussion on politically taboo subjects. Today we have invented other words to stop discussion; words like "racist", "xenophobe," "homophobe," or "extremist," and as they were designed, they stop discussion and debate. I have heard Leftist politicians use these terms often. Having made America a bilingual/bicultural country, having established multi-culturalism, having the large foundations fund the doctrine of "Victim-ology," one is pressed to ask, "Does anyone know where we are going?"

Where we are headed right now, should be clear to a thinking, reasoning person; that is over the edge of the cliff and into the drink below. Victor Hanson Davis's book *Mexifornia* exposes what he calls a plan to destroy America. America deserves to be saved in this immigration battle, if you agree this book would be a good read.

Eighth, is the enforcement of immigration laws in our states. It has become illegal to enforce immigration laws in our states, at least according to the regime running the Federal Government at this writing. Can you imagine that? The one purpose of the Federal Government as designed by our Constitution, the one obligation they have to the citizens is to protect the borders, to protect this nation from outside enemies. That is the ONE thing they refuse to do. The Feds want instead to listen to every phone conversation of law-abiding citizens, read all their email messages, promote Muslim doctrines, take away rights, raise taxes, but "Heck No! We are not going to watch the borders." I contend this is a natural 'progression' down the path of tyranny, a death spiral, that leads in the end to a pile of rubble.

Mantras have been developed by leftists to preach what they term the righteousness of illegal immigration. People today believe that because legal immigration has been good for America, illegal immigration must therefore be even better. "Individual immigrant" has been made symmetric by the Democrats and some Republicans to ignore the cumulative impact of millions of them. It is so unfortunate that we have made our decisions which have led us to the brink of disaster. Arnold Toynbee has studied and observed that all great civilizations rise and fall; he contends, "'An autopsy of history' would show that all great nations commit suicide."

Ninth, is closely associated with number eight, to take away the vote from illegals, and others not eligible to vote. Do this by requiring voters to produce the same state-issued picture ID you need to rent a video at a video store or to obtain a fishing license. In August 2013, Ari Berman from *The Nation* was frothing at the mouth and in ink over North Carolina's levelheaded and correct decision to require official identification documents to register voters and then permit them to vote. This "voter suppression law," he positively shrieks, is "the worst in the nation."[12]

Nearly everyone who is not a leftwing aficionada is aware, first, that North Carolina's law is hardly different from existing laws in a majority of states, and, second, that North Carolina's constitutional rights to pass such legislation had been abridged by the infamous Voting Rights Act that stripped Southern states of the last vestiges of the rights explicitly granted by the 10th Amendment.

During that summer, one could not turn on NPR or CNN without hearing the same complaints over and over. "These laws are designed to deprive major segments of the Democratic Party of their right to vote: Blacks, Hispanics, the elderly, and the young." They should have thrown in criminals and mental defectives who constitute a majority of that party's rank and file. The NAACP actually went to the length of posing as the defender of the elderly, as if anyone was going to believe this.

It is really quite simple to tell the truth on this issue, but Conservatives are naturally reluctant to tell the truth, at least in public. Here's a simple rule: If someone is too lazy or too dumb to get an ID, then we should take far more active steps to prevent that person from voting. In California I know a man who on election day would always pick up two mentally handicapped veterans who were patients in a private residence — he would take them to the polling place and go into the voting booth with each of them to show them how to vote, pulling the lever for a straight liberal party vote.

If politics is ever going to matter in this country, the conservatives will have to set one initial and all-important priority: They have to take away the vote from people who are not citizens. This would include people who cannot learn to read or understand the Constitution, people who commit major felonies, people who dodge the draft or betray their country. All of these have demonstrated their unfitness to vote on measures affecting the common good. A larger and more important group is composed of government dependents: people on welfare, people currently employed by any level of government (including school teachers, bureaucrats, politicians in office, and members of the military on active duty). All of these take money from their neighbors and fellow citizens and should not be able to vote themselves raises and benefits by voting for the bribe-takers otherwise known as legislators. Before you yell, "Racist", take a look at the Framers who built this country and how they established voting rights. Owning land was a requirement to have the right to vote. Their reasoning was sound. Anyone not involved with the business of being functionally leveraged and operating in this country, were deemed as probably not having enough "skin in the game" to make a voting decision.[13]

With this one simple measure, elections would be decided forthwith in a business manner. The back of any party who tries to buy votes would be broken permanently.

While you say it is impossible to change all nine points I raise, maybe it is; but I like some pipedreams. Otherwise why vote at all. Why get involved in any manner with the process of correctly transforming this nation back into the country it once was. Keeping conservatives away from the process is what the Democrats wanted to do long ago, simply disenfranchising me because I can think and chew gum at the same time. Laugh if you will, but at least my impossible scheme is one that addresses the real evil of our woes with illegal immigration. Considering the history, the Liberals have had this goal all along: the enfranchisement of non-citizens who are far more disastrous drones than any computer-controlled flying machine.

America, with liberals and progressives leading the way, are proceeding methodically, quietly, darkly, and pervasively across the United States today to take responsible citizens out of the picture. Discussion is being suppressed. Tolerance is being preached. While illegal immigrant children have been encouraged to cross our borders, Democrat leaders have raced to the border to welcome them, encouraging others to come. It is clear there has been a concerted effort by Leftists in promoting this latest immigration nightmare. Who would have dreamed a decade ago that in our life times we would be witnessing refugee tent cities throughout our nation, especially during the reign of the Leftist hero, who six years ago was hailed as "The One," "The Black Jesus," "The Savior." Conversely, one word comes to mind, "empty."

Over 100 official languages are ripping the foundation of our educational system and national cohesiveness. Even barbaric cultures that practice female genital mutilation are growing as we celebrate their 'diversity'. American jobs are van-

CHAPTER FOURTEEN — THERE'S NOTHING LEGAL ABOUT ILLEGALS

ishing into the Third World as the government and some corporations create a Third World here in America. Take note of California and other bell weather states. According to World Net Daily, in 2013, there are thirteen to twenty million illegal aliens roaming the country, and the number is growing fast. This is all too reminiscent of George Orwell's book *1984*. In that story, three slogans are engraved in the Ministry of Truth building. Do you remember them? They were, "War is peace," "Freedom is slavery," and "Ignorance is strength."[14]

Just another thought on the prodigal son and James Hilton's *Random Harvest* as they both relate to us. By our ineptitude, we have moved off our ethical, moral and spiritual reservation attempting to find happiness. It was G. K. Chesterton who once said, "There are two ways of getting home; one is to stay there, and the other is to walk around the whole world until you come back." It should be obvious to loyal Americans that with regard to in effect going to the far country in the attempt to find a way to produce happiness by opening our borders and legalizing illegal immigration. We should have just stayed home.

Though the road ahead seems treacherous and dark, we should remember the words of one of our greatest leaders. "If we ever forget that we're one nation under God, then we will be a nation gone under." — Ronald Reagan[15]

"*If there is anything in my thoughts or style to commend, the credit is due to my parents for installing in me an early love of the Scriptures. If we abide by the principles taught in the Bible, our country will go on prospering and to prosper; but if we and our posterity neglect its instructions and authority, no man can tell how sudden a catastrophe may overwhelm us and bury all our glory in profound obscurity.*"

~ Daniel Webster

US Congressman; Senator; Secretary of State under Presidents William Henry Harrison, John Tyler, and Millard Fillmore

Chapter Fifteen

The Trouble with Islamists

THEY WERE BILLED AS "THE GAMES of Peace and Joy." Those were the 1972 Olympic Games to be held in Munich, a southern German city. They were going to be the absolute biggest and most expensive ever in the history of mankind, with more athletes competing from more countries than at any previous sporting event.

The world was watching as at 3:00 PM local time, August 26, 1972, as ranks of tall Greek athletes marched into the packed Olympic Stadium on the city's north side, to thunderous applause, signaling the start of opening ceremonies at the XXth Olympiad. The 10,490 athletes jockeyed for the best positions in which to watch the opening ceremonies. These featured hordes of Bavarian folk-dancers, 5,000 doves released into the blue skies above Munich, and sixty men clad in Bavarian national costumes fired antique pistols into the air, all signaling the arrival of the hallowed Olympic flame from Peloponnese, the site of the ancient Olympics in Greece. With the Munich flame lit, the games could begin. All the opening events had gone without a hitch which thrilled West German officials, since they had fought to get the games back to Germany. Bavarian officials hoped the event would confirm Germany's rehabilitation as a civilized society, expunging memories of the Second World War and the infamous 1936 Berlin Olympics, which Hitler used to glorify Nazi ideology. They invited massed ranks of the media, a greater concentration than ever before, to witness the festival of sport and the redevelopment of West Germany.[1]

Over the years, I have studied the Qur'an. I have observed several of the disciples of this 'religion'. I came away from my study with the firm conviction there have been few religions in the world as deadly to mankind as that which Mohammed started. Allow a further explanation.

There are a couple of handfuls of persons with whom I have worked in a corporate setting over the last decade who indicated they were practicing Muslims. Knowing half that group well, I can say with certainty they were meek and mild persons; one of them was probably one of the finest, truest gentleman I have ever known. He continues to be over several years one of the meekest men I have ever met. The whole group of individuals seemed to truly represent their beliefs as a religion of love. That being said, I believe their representation is irrelevant given the huge radical arms of Islam that have taken control of the public discourse and destructive activities within Islam today. Additionally, peaceful Muslim leaders seem unwilling or unable to deal with the Islamofascism, radical Islam, or Islamism within itself. These groups appear a progeny of Islam itself.

In fact when exploring in depth the obvious impacts which these radical groups have had in wrestling away the controls on the dashboard for the public discourse of faith, there have been disastrous results not only in the Arabic and Muslim world but also in the West. If the statements of faith made by these "Islamists" mean anything, it certainly speaks that their aim has been to steer destruction, pain, and death in the path of innocents. As any individual explores openly the faith, the overall impact it has had on humanity over the past 1,300 years must be weighed in the balance.

It may be less absurd than the polytheism of the Hittites of old, with their many gods and goddesses. However its social and political tendencies are in my opinion to be spurned and feared.

Four Views

To assist in getting a better grasp on Islam from a high level, we will look at views and statements from people of today, as well as people from the past 300 years. We will also consider a snapshot of the actions from those professing to be true followers of Islam, but identified by others as "Radical Islam." We will also examine in a cursory fashion some details of their prophet Mohammed.

Modern Day

Prior to 9/11, a broad sweep across our country would reveal that most Americans knew or understood few details of Islam, its factions, or their actions; benign or terroristic. There also appears to be a general fear expressed in words and demeanor when the subject is broached. Examples have been seen regularly. Today, it is not uncommon to see a politician make a passing reference to Islam, using not only favorable, but glowing terms. Conversely, more than a few radio commentators over the past decade have shared the fear they feel when speaking spoken of Muslim hostilities. More than one has commented they believe death would come to them or anyone who speaks openly and succinctly about Mohammed or Islam in truthful historical terms. Another example is hearing the questions asked by the general public regarding the dress of Muslims.

Daniel Pipes, American historian and president of the Middle East Forum focuses much of his efforts on American foreign policy and the Middle East. While being unwilling to identify Islam with Islamism, he has said, "Islam, unlike Christianity, contains a complete program for ordering society . . . Islam specifies exact goals for all Muslims to follow as well as the rules by which to enforce them . . . Along with faith in Allah comes a sacred law to guide Muslims, in all times and places. That law, called the Sharia, establishes the context of Islam as a political force. . . ."

Mr. Pipes changed his tune with the events of the modern Islamic movement. Great Western Orientalist Scholarship, from the late 19th and early 20th Centuries, supports his understanding of how Islam is linked politically and religiously. Interestingly however, the scholarly analyses tend to debunk some of his statements and current views. Pipes has more recently indicated,

- Muhammad was really a jihadist, (his word is "Islamist") waging aggressive proto-jihad campaigns to conquer the Jews, Christians, and pagans . . . to bring them under nascent Islamic law;

- Orientalist scholars who long ago established the inherently political nature of Islam and saw the modern Islamic revival starting at least four decades earlier than Pipes did, who said that it started in the 1920s;

- It is agreed by both that Sharia is a religio-political totalitarianism of Sharia — which includes eternal institution of jihad against infidels, as well as dehumanizing laws and punishments for non-Muslims and Muslims alike;

- Contemporary polling data demonstrate the overwhelming appeal of Sharia states to ordinary Muslims — 77% of Muslims from the most populous societies, i.e., Indonesia, Pakistan, Bangladesh, Egypt, and Nigeria, pooled — debunking Pipes assertion that only "10-15%" of Muslims are Islamists. (Source of these 4 points: Andrew Bostom, "Daniel Pipes and Islamic 'Essentialism'", May 26, 2013)

Bernard Lewis, famed British-American historian and doyen of Islamic culture wrote and spoke about Islam; many times in glowing terms. While he did talk negatively of "Islamic rage," he often listed Islam as a sister faith in the world of religions. Possibly due to being a true historian, he appears to have given way to "historical relativism" in many of his views; he often stopped short of pronouncing judgment upon Muslims.

In his essay "Communism and Islam," he highlighted differences of socio-political life in the West vs. socio-political life in Muslim countries, focusing on the time period from the decline of the Ottomans to the post WWII. He wrote, "I turn now . . . to essential factors . . . of Islamic society, tradition, and thought. The first is . . . authoritarianism . . . we may even say totalitarianism of the Islamic political tradition . . . the political history of Islam is one of almost unrelieved autocracy . . . [I]t was authoritarian, often arbitrary, sometimes tyrannical. There are no parliaments or representative assemblies of any kind, no councils or communes, no chambers of nobility or estates, no municipalities in the history of Islam; nothing but the sovereign power, to which the subject owed complete and unwavering obedience as a religious duty imposed by the Holy Law. In the great days of classical Islam this duty was only owed to the lawfully appointed caliph . . . but with the decline of the caliphate and the growth of military dictatorship, Muslim jurists and theologians accommodated their teachings to the changed situation and extended the religious duty of obedience to any effective authority, however impious, however barbarous. For the last thousand years, the political thinking of Islam has been dominated by such maxims as 'tyranny is better than anarchy' and whose power is established, obedience to him is incumbent.... the Ulama [religious leaders] of Islam are very different from the Communist Party. Nevertheless ... we find certain uncomfortable resemblances. Both groups profess a totalitarian doctrine, with complete and final answers to all questions on heaven and earth; the answers are different in every respect ... and in the contrast they offer with the eternal questioning of Western man. Both groups offer to their members and followers the agreeable sensation of belonging to a community of believers, who are always right, as against an outer world of unbelievers, who are always wrong ... the content [in Islam and Communism] of belief is utterly different, but the aggressive fanaticism of the believer is the same. The humorist who summed up the Communist creed as 'There is no God and Karl Marx is his Prophet' was laying his finger on a real affinity. The call to a Communist Jihad, a Holy War for the faith-a new faith, but against the self-same Western Christian enemy — might well strike a responsive note" (Communism and Islam [International Affairs, Vol. 30, No. 1(Jan, 1954), pp 1-12]

It may be of interest to note that Islamic societies have for the most part forsaken democratic experiments in their nations, rejecting western democracies as a fraud and delusion, being of no value to them.

Past Leaders Comments

Alexis de Tocqueville, the French social scientist, had an extraordinary mind, penetrating and magnanimous. Anyone who has read his *Democracy in America* knows this well. He said of Islam, "I studied the Quran a great deal. I came away from that study with the conviction that by and large there have been few religions in the world as deadly to men as that of Muhammad. So far as I can see, it is the principal cause of the decadence so visible today in the Muslim world and, though less absurd than the polytheism of old, its social and political tendencies are in my opinion more to be feared, and I therefore regard it as a form of decadence rather than a form of progress in relation to paganism itself."[1]

It should be noted the context of his statement. True, his statement was made during the middle of the 19th Century, when the Ottoman Empire was in rapid decline. There were not the "Islamists" in de Tocqueville's time period as we see today, nor were there the suicide bombers whose barbarism is hailed in large parts of the Islamic world.

The Framers of America saw emptiness and refused Islam as a system of religion or faith. These Founding Fathers had no problem pointing out what they determined to be the evil and the grave error of 'the cult of Muhammad.' They loved freedom and people enough, to express the truth.

Chapter Fifteen — The Trouble with Islamists

Ethan Allen, Revolutionary War patriot and hero, wrote the following in his infamous book, *Reason, The Only Oracle of Man*: "Mahomet [Mohammed] taught his army that the "term of Every man's life was fixed by God, and that none could shorten it, by any hazard that he might seem to be exposed to in battle or otherwise," but that it should be introduced into peacable [sic] and civil life, and be patronized by any teachers of religion, is quite strange, as it subverts religion in general, and renders the teaching of it unnecessary... We are liable to be imposed upon by impostors, or by ignorant and insidious teachers, whose interest it may be to obtrude their own systems on the world for infallible truth, as in the instance of Mahomet (Mohammed)."[2]

Joseph Story, Father of American Jurisprudence, in his Commentaries on the Constitution of the United States, primarily concerning the First Amendment:

> "Probably at the time of the adoption of the constitution, and of the amendment to it, now under consideration, the general, if not the universal, sentiment in America was, that Christianity ought to receive encouragement from the state, so far as was not incompatible with the private rights of conscience, and the freedom of religious worship. An attempt to level all religions, and to make it a matter of state policy to hold all in utter indifference, would have created universal disapprobation, if not universal indignation... the real object of the [First] amendment was not to countenance, much less to advance Mahometanism, or Judaism, or infidelity by prostrating Christianity; but to exclude all rivalry among Christian sects and to prevent any national ecclesiastical establishment which should give to a hierarchy the exclusive patronage of the national government."[3]

James Iredell, a U.S. Supreme Court judge appointed by George Washington, who was in the debates of 1788 on the wording of the Constitution:

> "But it is objected that the people of America may perhaps choose representatives who have no religion at all, and that pagans and Mahometans may be admitted into offices... But it is never to be supposed that the people of America will trust their dearest rights to persons who have no religion at all, or a religion materially different from their own."[4]

This article is the first installment of a two-part critique written by James Hutson, Library of Congress Manuscript Division Chief, on the Founding Fathers' attitude toward Islam. He was the Father of Classical Liberalism (NOT today's liberalism), was an English philosopher and physician. In his, "A Letter Concerning Toleration", 4 of the 5 exceptions he mentions inarguably describes Muslim behavior across the world, as it clearly resembles the precise intolerance that characterizes Islamic countries:

> "Those whose religious opinions are contrary to "those moral rules which are necessary to the preservation of civil society" (1796, p. 53);

The religion that "teaches expressly and openly, that men are not obliged to keep their promise" (p. 54);

[T]hose that will not own and teach the duty of tolerating all men in matters of mere religion . . . and that they only ask leave to be tolerated by the magistrate so long, until they find themselves strong enough to [seize the government] (p. 55);

All those who see themselves as having allegiance to another civil authority (p. 56)."[5]

Specifically, John Locke gives the example of the Muslim who lives among Christians and would have difficulty submitting to the government of a "Christian nation" when he comes from a Muslim country where the civil magistrate was also the religious authority. Locke notes that such a person would have grave difficulty serving as a soldier in his adopted nation (cf., the 2009 Fort Hood shooting spree by a Muslim soldier who shouted, "Allahu Akbar" as he opened fire, killing 13 and wounding 32; see Stewart, 2010).

"[T]hose are not at all to be tolerated who deny the being of a God" (p. 56)

Ezra Stiles (Yale College president from 1778-1795), from his sermon, "The United States Elevated To Glory and Honor" in Connecticut in 1783:

"The more Christianity prevails in a country, civil society will be more advanced, ferocious manners will give way to the more mild, liberal, just, and amiable manners of the gospel." He stated his belief that "[a] time will come when six hundred millions of the human race shall be ready to drop their idolatry and all false religion, when Christianity shall triumph over superstition, as well as Deism, and Gentilism, and Mohammedanism."[6]

John Quincy Adams, sixth President of the United States (son of our Second President, John Adams [a primary, quintessential Founder]) knew much about the problems with the Islamic faith, documented it, and kept a copy of the Qur'an in his library for ready use. He spoke from his heart in, *The American Annual Register for the Years 1827-1829*:

In the seventh century of the Christian era, a wandering Arab of the lineage of Hagar, the Egyptian, combining the powers of transcendent genius, with the preternatural energy of a fanatic, and the fraudulent spirit of an impostor, proclaimed himself as a messenger from Heaven, and spread desolation and delusion over an extensive portion of the earth. Adopting from the sublime conception of the Mosaic Law, the doctrine of one omnipotent God; he connected indissolubly with it, the audacious falsehood, that he was himself his prophet and apostle. Adopting from the new Revelation of Jesus, the faith and hope of immortal life, and of future retribution, he humbled it to the dust, by adapting all the rewards and sanctions of his religion to the gratification of the sexual passion. He poisoned the sources of human felicity at the fountain, by degrading the condition of the female sex, and the allowance of polygamy; and he declared undistinguishing and exterminating war, as a part of his religion, against all the rest of mankind. **THE ESSENCE OF HIS DOCTRINE WAS VIOLENCE AND LUST: TO EXALT THE BRUTAL OVER THE SPIRITUAL PART OF HUMAN NATURE.**[7]

The precept of the Muslim is, perpetual war against all who deny, that Mahomet is the prophet of God. The vanquished may purchase their lives, by the payment of tribute; the victorious may be appeased by a false and delusive promise of peace; and the faithful follower of the prophet, may submit to the imperious necessities of defeat: but the command to propagate the Moslem creed by the sword is always obligatory, when it can be made effective. The commands of the prophet may be performed alike, by fraud, or by force.[7]

Speaking specifically about Muhammad, he concluded his thoughts regarding any possible comparison with Christianity:

> "Between these two religions, thus contrasted in the characters, a war of more than twelve hundred years has already raged. That war is yet flagrant; nor can it cease but by the extincture of that imposture, which has been permitted by Providence to prolong the degeneracy of man. While the merciless and dissolute are encouraged to furnish motives to human action, there never can be peace on earth and good will toward men. The hand of Ishmael will be against every man, and every man's hand against him."[7]

General George S. Patton, obviously not a Founder by approximately 200 years, did make considerable observations of the impact of Islam on the countries of North Africa in 1947. They are worth noting; in spite of the fact our current leadership does not see the same trend that continues:

> "One cannot but ponder the question: What if the Arabs had been Christians? To me it seems certain that the fatalistic teachings of Mohammed and the utter degradation of women is the outstanding cause for the arrested development of the Arab. He is exactly as he was around the year 700, while we have kept on developing. Here, I think, is a text for some eloquent sermon on the virtues of Christianity."[8]

Thomas Jefferson had a copy of the Qur'an in his library that he had purchased. He was fascinated with the idea of having religious freedom for all people, no matter what that religion was. He did find out however over his life as he fought wars with Muslim pirates who lived by the Qur'an, there was another side to many within that faith. That is why he kept a copy of it. The wars he fought were called the Barbary Wars, from 1801-1805; his aim was to free Americans taken as slaves from American merchant ships. The government spent millions of dollars to get them back at a time when private citizens were financing much of the government from their own pockets, with little or no reimbursements! AND it was the first time a President (Jefferson) initiated a war without Congress approval, so it was very controversial. He did it while they were adjourned. But the Americans were freed in the end. Jefferson knew the reality from 1801-1805.

The essence, the presence, the cleanup, and manifestation (or rather, infestation) of the devoutly followed ideology of Islam is wafting up into the nostrils of freedom, once again, as it has done over the course of our history. The dehumanizing of women, the slaughter of anyone who will not convert to Islam, and the relentless push to take over any properties in view have built a strong case against the faith which Muslims choose to practice. Most of our Founders got it. They knew it was not right for the new nation of America. The question is, will we continue to ignore the results or will we finally get it?

Snapshot from Radical Islam

In the modern era, Islamists have carried on in Mohammad's absence. Despite what the politically correct media would have you believe, Islam is actually an enemy not only of Christianity, but also any civilized society that has a democratic base. Anyone who will not bow the knee in Muslim prayer has a potential target on their back. Just in the last half century, look at the evidence of how warm, cuddly and cool their religion of so-called love is:

1. In 1968, Bobby Kennedy was shot and killed in Los Angeles — by a Muslim.

2. In 1972 a Pan Am 747 Airliner was hijacked and diverted to Cairo, Egypt where a bomb was lit and the plane blown up shortly after landing. This was all done by Muslims.

3. In 1973 a Pan Am 707 Airliner was attacked in Rome, Italy, killing 33. The attackers used grenades and they were Muslims.

4. In 1979, the American embassy in Tehran, Iran was overrun by thugs and 52 Americans were taken and held hostage for 444 days. This was all done by Muslims.

5. In April, 1980, an attack was launched on Misgav Am, a Northern Province kibbutz within Israel. The attack was directed at a children's dormitory with several toddlers and young children taken hostage. Two of the children and one Israeli soldier were killed. The attack was led by PLO militant Muslims.

6. In April, 1983, the American Embassy was bombed killing 63 and wounding an additional 120. The bombing was done by Muslims.

7. In October, 1983, the US Marine barracks in Beirut, Lebanon was blown up using two truck bombs: 241 US Marines, 58 French Paratroopers, and 6 civilians in these barracks were killed, totaling 305

CHAPTER FIFTEEN — THE TROUBLE WITH ISLAMISTS

deaths. An additional 75 were injured. The attack was planned and carried out by Muslims.

8. In June, 1985, TWA flight 847 was hijacked at Athens, Greece. During a two-week hostage ordeal, passengers were beaten and a US Navy diver was shot and killed. The attack and murder were carried out by Muslims.

9. In October, 1985, the cruise ship Achilles Lauro was hijacked off the coast of Israel and a 70 year old American passenger was murdered and thrown overboard in his wheelchair. This was done by Muslims.

10. In December, 1988, Pan Am Flight 103 was bombed in flight over Lockerbie, Scotland killing 243 passengers and 16 crew members. This was done by Muslims.

11. In January, 1993, the World Trade Center building was bombed for the first time. Six were killed. This was done by Muslims.

12. In August, 1995, the Ramat Eshkol bus bombing took place in Jerusalem, Israel. Five were killed and over 100 wounded, with one of the victims being an American teacher. This was carried out by Muslims.

13. In June, 1996, the Khobar Towers Building in Khobar, Saudi Arabia, housing US Air Force personnel was blown up using a truck bomb. It resulted in killing 19 US service men and wounding 498 civilians. This was done by Muslims.

14. In August, 1998, the US embassies in the East African capitals of Dar es Salaam, Tanzania and Nairobi, Kenya were bombed. Twelve Americans in total were killed in the bomb blasts, with another 211 locals being killed and over 4,100 injured. The simultaneous truck bomb attacks were carried out by Muslims.

15. In October, 2000, the U.S.S. Cole Navy Destroyer in the Yemen port of Aden, was bombed killing 17 American soldiers and injuring 39. This was done by Muslims.

16. On Christmas Eve, 2000, 8 churches in Jakarta, Indonesia were bombed during worship services, killing 18 and wounding many others. This was carried out by Muslims.

17. On September 11, 2001, forever more known as 9/11, four airliners were hijacked by 19 men. Two of the planes, American flight 11 and United Air flight 175, were crashed into the North and South towers, respectively, of the World Trade Center. The other two planes were planned for the same type of use, one, American flight 77, was crashed into the US Pentagon and the other, United Air flight 93 was diverted from crashing into the US Capitol building, by passengers and instead

crashed in field near Shanksville, Pennsylvania. Approximately 3,000 civilians were killed in the buildings, including 227 civilian passengers on the 4 planes. Hundreds of fire fighters were injured in the subsequent rescues and cleanup with many of them dying as well. The attacks were planned and carried out by Muslims.

18. In January, 2002, Daniel Pearl bureau chief in South Asia with the Wall Street Journal was kidnapped and later murdered in February the same year. It was all done by Muslims.

19. In July, 2002, the cafeteria at Hebrew University in Jerusalem was bombed, killing 19. Five of these were American students. This was done by Muslims.

20. In October, 2002, a Bali nightclub was bombed during busy hours, killing 202, 7 of which were Americans. Over 300 more were severely injured. This was done by Muslims.

21. In October, 2002, the Moscow Theatre Hostage Crisis was orchestrated taking some 900 hostages. While a very few hostages escaped, there were 75 western visitors who remained hostages in the theatre that night, some of them American. During the rescue attempt by Russian police officers, 40 of the attackers were killed and 130 hostages died. Approximately 700 were injured. The theatre takeover and hostage crisis including subsequent murders were carried out by Muslims.

22. In August, 2003, at the Marriott in Mega Kuningan, South Jakarta, Indonesia a car bomb was detonated outside the lobby. It killed 12 and injured 150, mostly local. The hotel was used by the American Embassy at times and was targeted as such because it was seen as a symbol of the West. The bombing was done by Muslims.

23. In August, 2003, a Shmuel HaNavi bus was bombed, killing 24, 7 of which were little children. Two Americans were killed, one was three months old. The bombing was done by Muslims.

24. In October, 2005, a series of bombing attacks were made in Bali. Twenty were killed and 130 were injured. Six Americans were among those injured. The attacks were done by Muslims.

25. In November, 2005, coordinated bombing attacks were made on three western hotels in Amman, Jordan. The Grand Hyatt, Radisson SAS, and Days Inn, were hit, where many activities were on-going, including a wedding at the Radisson. First reports showed a total of 67 killed and over 300 injured. Among them a Hollywood film producer and his daughter who were guests at the wedding. The attacks were carried out by Muslims.

CHAPTER FIFTEEN — THE TROUBLE WITH ISLAMISTS

26. In April, 2006, Rosh Ha'ir shawarma restaurant was bombed killing 11 and seriously injuring 68. One American was among the dead. The attack was planned and done by Muslims.

27. In July, 2006, pressure cooker bombs were placed on 7 trains in Mumbai, India and all exploded over an 11 minute time frame with each train either in or close to a train station. A total of 209 people were killed, 700 others were injured. It was reported at least one American was among those injured. The attacks were carried off by Muslims.

28. In November, 2009, the Fort Hood Massacre happened, on base near Killeen, TX. Thirteen service people were killed and 30 injured in what has now been identified as the worst attack on a military base in the US. We were told at the time not to . . . "jump to any conclusions." But you guessed it, the attack, the act of terrorism was carried out by a Muslim.

29. In May, 2010, a foreigner attempted to ignite a car bomb in Times Square in New York. The bomb did not detonate and bomber was captured. He was a Muslim.

30. In April, 2013, coordinated bombings were carried out in what is now known as the Boston Marathon Bombing. Four civilians including one small child were killed, and 264 injured. This was done by Muslims.

Keep in mind as you read this list of killings above, it is abridged. It has been cut down to highlight just a category of Muslim attacks. If I were to list all the attacks and attempted bombings by Muslims over the past 30 years, it would take a book by itself just to list the accounts, let alone tell an abridged story of the thousands killed in Israel, Africa and other areas of the globe. Therefore, I have limited my offering to you of only those which directly involved either injury or loss of American lives.

Pause for a moment to put the attacks in context. While the media and secular humanists would have you believe that Christianity is the nest for terrorism in America today, and thus the real problem the modern world faces, it is not. These attacks were not planned and carried out by Baptists, Presbyterians, Anglican, Nazarenes, Christian Church, Church of Christ, Methodists, or any other denomination of Christendom. The American media would have you believe that Christianity is the real problem in the world. However, these attacks were carried out by Islamist Muslims. Any religious group can have some malcontent coming forth endangering or taking life. But no other religion in the world, of which I am aware, fosters the killing and massacres that Islamic followers foster. Political correctness aside, the truth is what it is.

Evidence Usually Points to Cause/Effect Issues

The Qur'an enjoys a sanctimonious standing, since Muslims believe it was written by Allah himself. They believe Allah (Lit. "the God") handed down the Qur'an to Archangel Gabriel, chapter by chapter, to deliver to Muhammad over the course of some 22 years. Muhammad could neither read nor write. So he said Gabriel had to whisper the chapters to him and Muhammad in turn would reveal them to a scribe or in some cases any literate person who happened to be around to write them down on anything he could find. To Muslims, every word of the Qur'an is a literal perfect immutable eternal word of Allah himself. Therefore, no man or divine is ever to revise, much less dispute, the Qur'an.

The Muslims believe that the Qur'an is written and exists only in the Arabic languages. The truth is the Qur'an exists as a transliteration in other languages. Some of the English editions are less forceful than the original Arabic and some have omitted the warlike sections. There are some scholarly editions that appear to be a close translation to the Arabic. The Qur'an teaches a systemic way of works through which the follower, or disciple, can over time please Allah. It is through these good works that the believer hopes someday he can become good enough to please Allah and be able to enter into heaven. While it is not a "Twelve Step Program" it does teach the essentials, such as a series of prayers and times of fasting on this avenue of growth. The fasting is sometimes familiar to non-Muslims, since disciples of Islam participate in a month-long fast between the crescent moons during the month of Ramadan. This fasting is done between daylight and dark for that month. Nothing is swallowed during the daylight, not even saliva. Pregnant women and people who are sick are exempt; but have to observe the fast at a later time.

The License in the Qur'an

One of the features that interests many non-Muslims are any references to the dealings with infidels, in particular any teaching that allows the killing of them. Mohammed both taught this violence and practiced it himself, leading in the beheading of anyone who disagreed with Islam and those who would not convert. Those who resisted conversion, he branded as 'infidels.' Those in that number which he could reach, he killed.

When it comes to violence, self-defense is not often the position we see proponents of Islam in. It is probably a safe bet that most Americans don't know the Arab version of the Qur'an promotes violence. Take for example Surah Nine. The first part of 9th Surah, is considered the most bellicose part of the Qur'an. It was revealed shortly after the Muslims had established military dominance in Mecca. Consider one of these verses which is interpreted to promote violence:

"But when the forbidden months are past, then fight and slay the Pagans wherever ye find them, and seize them, beleaguer them, and lie in wait for them in every stratagem (of war); but if they repent, and establish regular prayers and practice regular charity, then open the way for them." (9:5)

The words, "when the forbidden months are past," point to the fact that this violence is not a matter of self-defense. The Muslims had already been given the divine right to fight during the sacred months, and it is simply implausible that they would have suffered attacks over a four month period without defending themselves. That they were not under attack is consistent with the historical evidence, in which the *Haj* period was a traditional time of peace and tolerance throughout Arabia.

Muslim wars and infidel beheadings have been regular activities, beginning in the 7th century era of Muslim conquests, starting in 622 A.D., and continuing to today. Muslim violence on non-Muslims is done in the name of "Jihad", causing many to debate whether Islam was fundamentally a religion of peace, of violence, or perhaps of some combination of the two.

Truth is truth. Islam promotes through the Qur'an an evangelistic life of violence. When you reflect on who dictated the book, Mohammed, he was a killer, who practiced his trade on a regular basis. The "Muslim extremists" as they are often called, are merely following in his footsteps. The US has been fighting two wars, Iraq and Afghanistan, against Muslims. In total, over 800 service personnel have been killed in action during these wars. And that by Muslims.[9]

Some in ignorance of what the Qur'an says cannot believe a religious people could do things like this, so they deny that these Middle Easterners hold such a view. However, they do not realize what is in their "holy book." The Qur'an has what are called '*Sword verses*', called such because Muslims are advised to, ". . . kill the polytheists wherever you find them and capture and besiege them and sit in wait for them at every place of ambush. But if they repent . . . [then] let them go on their way . . . Fight those who do not believe in Allah or in the last day and who do not consider unlawful what Allah and his messenger (Mohammed) have made unlawful and who do not adopt the religion of truth [Islam]".[10] Down through the ages, it becomes apparent that, while there are obvious texts of community care and concern that are written, they are written to and about other Muslims and Muslim sympathizers. But the violence and "turn or burn" passages taught in the Qur'an were due to the author's (Mohammed) bent in spiritual things, which was frankly shallow. Threats of violence are how many Muslims are "kept on the reservation," and use is an emotional tool to "change the world." And for whatever else someone might like to say about this religion of works, the violence is a huge deterrent for even some faithful believers. The apparent ambiguity between such Qur'anic verses has left room for a multitude of differing interpretations of the final or ultimate meaning of the texts, mostly by those who choose to operate from a basis of fear.

Seeking a Rational Directive

The emerging and current culture in this country of secular humanism, atheism, and progressivism ridicules and makes frequent attacks upon Christianity and Christians with claims of them being "extremists" and "terrorists." At the same time, it appears they are in the midst of a romancing with the Muslim faith. It would be good to compare the two faith's books of guidance: the Bible and the Qur'an. One note of interest, while Christians are being hit with the title of terrorist, it is self-proclaimed Muslims who are clearly the ones behind the innumerable attacks where multiple deaths occur.

Upon looking briefly at the Qur'an, one can begin to see the thread of activity that many Islamists cling to, today. First of all, there are sections of the book calling for the massacre of all people who will not convert to the Islamic faith. This is probably one huge reason why our liberal leaders as well as many citizens fear Muslims. While claiming it is a book written by Allah, it is not. There is no reason why it should be considered a sister religion either. There's no reason for our culture to kowtow down to them for they have a philosophy which was written by a man, told that it was from a god, but was actually hatched by the same individual to whom Saul Alinsky dedicated his book, *Rules for Radicals*, to Satan himself. In the true Word of God, the Bible, Titus 1:16 clearly states, "They claim to know God, but by their actions they deny him. They are detestable, disobedient and unfit for doing anything good." Matthew 12:33 adds, " . . . for a tree is known by its fruit." And Colossians 2:8-9 would seem to ice the cake, "See to it that no one takes you captive through hallow and deceptive philosophy, which depends on human tradition and the basic principles of this world rather than on Christ. For in Christ all the fullness of Deity lives in bodily form . . ." The "elementary principles of the world," in Alinsky's work are exactly what is built into the backbone of Islam; it is a "works" religion. It's entirely true that the world does not understand Christianity at least in part because they do not understand "the work" of it. The elementary principles of the world always contain a scale of working to get forgiveness and earning grace. "Earning" is clearly taught in Islam; not so with God in Christianity. The Bible teaches there is no way a person can work hard enough and become good enough to earn merit.

If this were a nation built on reason as it was at our founding, strong families would be instilling historical facts like these in their children's minds. Our nation would not now be facing many of the problems we face, if we had not lost our reason and logic in decision making. It is also fair to say that this nation would not have elected officials of the brand we now have, if we made decisions based on reason. We would not have a president who at a minimum is a Muslim sympathizer, as witnessed in his activities when he 'circles the wagons' to protect Muslims when one of their own commits an act of violence against American citizens. But with a sympathetic administration, we hear remarks such as "don't jump to conclusions" when a Fort Hood Massacre occurs. Their remarks of "stay calm" and "don't jump to conclusions" are made from behind security guards or concrete walls topped with barbed wire. Often, we hear the subject change, and unfortunately, it

CHAPTER FIFTEEN — THE TROUBLE WITH ISLAMISTS

is common to hear a reprisal against racial profiling, water boarding and the need to provide special rights to certain people among us.

It can get rather ridiculous. With the removal of logic and reason, critical thinking is lost. As critical thinking leaves, the ability to "connect the dots" is lost, in critical areas of life. One of those is in the spiritual realm; sometimes we fail to see that which is really a wolf in sheep's clothing. It is a time when we cannot separate what is bad about religious thinking from the good.

The region of the world where Mohammed started his religion in the 7th Century was not rational either. Reasonable law would require that anyone practicing rape, murder, pillaging would be stopped, charged and arrested. Without reasonable law in existence there, history shows that the Islamic prophet carried on sexual assault, rape, pedophilia and even murder. That was never declared in a court of law there, but certainly if true, it is quite a resume for a leader of a world religion. Whatever response is heard to that news, facts are facts. Truth should not be swept under a rug, truth should not be silenced by fear of reprisal. Due to so much political pressure and paralyzing fear that is placed on anyone trying to report the truth about him, all that is reported as loving and positive things about him, much of history is negated, and the truth is not told.

In the background of all this information, is the media who is having a field day going after Israel who is trying to protect itself from missiles being fired upon the people in their country from Hamas; aka Muslims. What is off the screen is media coverage of ISIS Muslims in Syria who have been murdering Christians at will from 2012 through 2014. The worst appears yet to come as the Muslims now threaten an entire nation. No media coverage is offered, and Mr. Obama, will not even mention the distress in any public announcement. To this we must ask the question, "Why?" TV shows which put a critical focus on the Bible and Christianity, all produced in New York and Hollywood, will often put forth unproven theories to attack the dignity of religious leaders in Scripture. They will attack the stated position of Christ; they will place doubt into the minds of young viewers about the reality of historical events in Biblical days. We must ask, "Why?" They will take great efforts to either denounce Christian beliefs, or fill marginal listeners with questions of integrity. Again, we ask, "Why?" At the same time, when the subject of Islam is discussed during a similar or same show, no question will ever be asked as to its integrity at all. You need to ask the question, "Why?"

There are reasons. They center on both political posturing and fear. The political posturing is being done by the Obama administration which has sided itself with various groups of Islam throughout the Middle East. The media has sided itself with the administration and falls all over itself in making certain to never as a challenging question of Islamic leaders.

The fear is mostly centered in Washington politicians and the media. The media does not fear Christians; they fear Muslims. And probably for good reasons — the

Christians are not the terrorists today; the terrorists are coming from among the Muslims. The media knows that Christians do not respond as Islamists do. Until the courage to investigate and report on such things is developed, we will be seeing the same news events and the same television programming.

One Last Truth

One of the features of Islamic teaching is particularly disconcerting. That is lying. Like most religions, Islam in general, forbids lying. The Qur'an says, "Truly Allah guides not one who transgresses and lies," Surah 40:28. In the Hadith, Mohammed was also quoted as saying, "Be honest because honesty leads to goodness, and goodness leads to Paradise. Beware of falsehood because it leads to immorality, and immorality leads to Hell."

However, it is evident through historical incidents that Mohammed made lying a practice. He often lied and instructed his followers to do the same. He rationalized that the prospect of success in missions to extend Islam's influence overrode Allah's initial prohibitions against lying.

A good example of sanctioned lying is the account of the assassination of Kaab Ibn al-Ashrf, a member of the Jewish tribe, Banu al-Nudair. It had been reported that al-Ashrf had shown support for the Quraishites in their battle against Mohammed. This was compounded by another report that infuriated Mohammed. It was alleged that al-Ashrf had recited amorous poetry to Muslim women. Mohammed asked for volunteers to rid him of Kaab Ibn al-Ashraf. As Mohammed indicated, al-Ashrf had "Harmed Allah and His Apostle." At that time Kaab Ibn al-Ashraf, and his tribe were strong, so it was not easy for a stranger to infiltrate and execute the task. A Muslim man by the name of Ibn Muslima, volunteered for the murderous project on the condition that Mohammed would allow him to lie. With Mohammed's consent, Ibn Muslima, went to al-Ashrf and told him fabricated stories that reflected discontent about Mohammed's leadership. When he had gained al-Ashrf's trust he lured him away from his house one night and murdered him in a remote area under the cover of darkness. (Source: Abdullah Al Araby, IslamicReview.com)

Within Islam there are certain provisions that demonstrate that lying is not only tolerated, but actually encouraged by past and current leaders. The book *The Spirit of Islam* by the Muslim scholar, Afif A. Tabbarah was written to promote Islam. In it Tabbarah states: "Lying is not always bad, to be sure; there are times when telling a lie is more profitable and better for the general welfare, and for the settlement of conciliation among people, than telling the truth. To this effect, the Prophet says: 'He is not a false person who (through lies) settles conciliation among people, supports good or says what is good."

Christianity and Islam are NOT sister religions. Christianity is not truly a religion at all; it is unlike any religion on earth. Christianity operates on a basis of grace; that cannot be earned. Islam operates on a basis of deeds; it can only be earned by

Chapter Fifteen — The Trouble with Islamists

good works. Although Christianity and Islam share some terminology and some history, Islam is fundamentally different than Christianity in every other way.

As a works-oriented religion, Islam requires that its adherents strive to possibly earn their way to heaven by performing five pillars of their faith. Those are,

1. Say the confession of faith;
2. Pray at five specific times a day;
3. Give alms of 2.5 percent of their wealth;
4. Fast during Ramadan, and;
5. Make a pilgrimage to Mecca, if financially able.

Completing these acts still does not guarantee salvation. The works of a person are stacked up and evaluated. <u>If bad works outweigh good works, Islam teaches the person will probably go to hell. If the reverse is true, the person might go to heaven.</u> But there is still no guarantee of heaven for a Muslim, as Mohammed taught.

The one exception providing a guarantee is found in "jihad." Though it is often translated "holy war," it means "exerting force for God" and could mean many things; like writing a book for Islam, or sharing their religion to others, or the seemingly most popular one, fighting infidels. This is popular with Islamists as seen in terror bombings throughout the world today. An interesting note: if a Muslim dies in jihad he is taught that he is guaranteed salvation and a trip to heaven.[11] There are far too many differences between Islam and Christianity for the two to be sisters of anything.

The report card on Muhammad and the Muslims is in. It is up to anyone to read it, interpret it, and then make a rational, reasonable decision. Our Founders made a reasonable decision; they got it. They chose not to have Islam as the basis of our nation. Hopefully, our current citizens can wake up and smell that coffee.

"For almost two centuries we have proved man's capacity for self-government, but today we are told we must choose between left and right, or, as others suggest, a third alternative, a kind of safe middle ground.

I suggest to you there is no left or right, only an up or down. Up to the maximum of individual freedom consistent with law and order, or down to the ant heap of totalitarianism, and regardless of their humanitarian purpose, those who would sacrifice freedom for security have, whether they know it or not, chosen this downward path . . ."

~ Ronald Reagan

A Time for Choosing, October 27, 1964

Chapter Sixteen

Having the Right to Own and Bear Arms

"A free people ought not only to be armed and disciplined, but they should have sufficient arms and ammunition to maintain a status of independence from any who might attempt to abuse them, which would include their own government." — George Washington

WASHINGTON, D. C., NEW YORK CITY, DETROIT, Chicago, and St. Louis top the list in 2014 as the most dangerous cities in America. These locations have either the strictest gun laws, or are among the strictest gun law locations in the nation. In fact in Chicago, guns have been totally outlawed on the streets, yet crimes using guns is off the charts there, as it is in all the above cities; they all remain the most dangerous places in the nation. On a regular basis we are told that new and additional gun laws are required to ease armed criminal activity in the same places.

Contrast with that reality, the scene in Switzerland where crime is practically unknown, yet most Swiss men are required by law to keep in their homes what amounts to nothing less than automatic and portable machine guns.[1] All Swiss men are required to serve in the military and to retain their guns after their required service is complete. The "gun in every closet" tradition was challenged by the local liberals in 2001 when a disgruntled person opened fire in a regional parliament, the only mass shooting in that country in many decades. The Swiss are very serious not only about their right to own weapons but also to carry them around in public, so they soundly defeated the push for removing of military weapons from homes.[2]

Guns are ubiquitous there; they are accepted as a part of the landscape. The acceptance has created a steady "culture of safety and support" that is adopted from generation to generation in owning guns. Young and old alike are constantly seen with rifles and handguns, single shot and semiautomatic alike. The only national group in America that consistently fosters a similar culture of safety and support is the National Rifle Association (NRA). However, they are consistently excoriated by liberals, progressives, and the media as being extremists, homophobes, and even racists. How silly, when the data indicates that the extremists are really the liberals and their media. Nobody bats an eye in Switzerland at the sight of a civilian riding a bus, bike or motorcycle to the shooting range, with a rifle slung over the shoulder.

Israel is another country where practically the same circumstances exist, having a Swiss model military where the common citizens make up much of the militia in the country. And here you find many citizens keeping military-style weapons, both rifles and semiautomatic pistols in their homes, such as the famous Uzi submachine gun and the Desert Eagle 1911. And street crime in Israel is extremely low by U.S. standards. It becomes evident as one looks at the data, that possession of firearms does not automatically nurture crime.

The Progressive Left is always screaming for gun control. Following a shooting at a theater they will seek out TV cameras to call for confiscation of guns. They have the same pre-packaged diatribe prepared for the television audience following a crime with a knife or a screwdriver. They kick into automatic overdrive and call for more gun laws and confiscation of guns again. Then some boy slashes another with a razor or box cutter. The liberal response is always predictable; they dust off the same gun control speech and begin screeching again. The predictability of the liberal promises go past the words; they guarantee that gun control will stop crime dead in its tracks. In the meantime, every policeman and peace officer I know says that confiscation of guns will put no dent in crime whatsoever. In fact it will have the reverse affect. One simple reason is taking guns from the hands of law-abiding citizens, does not remove them from the hands of thugs and criminals. Second, no gun has ever killed anyone by itself unless directed by someone's idiocy, madness, anger or revenge. The one exception to this, the scene I witnessed on Looney Tunes in the 1960s, when a gun actually cocked itself and fired at Elmer Fudd, hitting him in the seat of his pants.

A cartoon legend seems to carry more weight with our elected officials who sadly seem to believe the image rather than real data from the street. Some way or another, guns themselves, just hunks of metal and hardware, has become the source of all evil in the world. Accusations are made about the gun, while the background stories of persons full of hatred or having confused minds are conveniently swept under the carpet. Surely this could not be done to support a political agenda! Ah, but it is. Our liberal government wants to confiscate guns from law-abiding citizens, while they maintain a stockpile of their own. Leftists know that criminals will always have guns while yours have been locked away. Some early evidence is seen in Chicago, that in the first three months following the passage of concealed-carry, major crimes of murder dropped significantly. More solid evidence is seen in the data presented by a 20-year study by John Lott book, *More Guns, Less Crime*. While the work set off a firestorm with liberals crying "Foul; flawed study," author and criminologist James Q. Wilson calls Lott's work "the most scientific study ever done . . . using facts from 1977 through 1996 and controlling for just about every conceivable factor that might affect the criminal use of guns." Wilson's endorsement continued: "Of the many scholars who were given Lott's data and did their own analyses, most agree with his conclusions. States that passed these laws experienced sharp drops in murder, rape, robbery, and assault, even after

Chapter Sixteen — Having the Right to Own and Bear Arms

allowing for the effects of poverty, unemployment, police arrest rates, and the like. States that did not pass these laws did not show comparable declines. And these declines were not trivial—he is writing about as many as 1,000 fewer murders and rapes and 10,000 fewer robberies. Carrying concealed guns reduces—it does not increase—the rate of serious crime and that reduction is vastly greater than the generally trivial effect of gun-carrying on accidental shootings."[3]

It should be noted that of thirty-four criminologist peer reviews and studies, twenty agreed stating crime went down, eleven indicated crime increased slightly, and three said crime remained static. Actually, the burden of proof should not be on the shoulders of pro-gun advocates. They have the majority of data supporting their conclusions, plus they stand on the side of freedom. The burden of proof, if it lays any place, must rest upon the liberals. Non-manipulated data just does not support their conclusions.

Stripping Second Amendment rights away from any law-abiding citizen does not make good sense. It is a good time to review where the right to self-protection comes from — it comes not from the government but from God. Therefore it is important to learn what the Second Amendment does and does not do. It does not give us the right to have protection by guns. It prohibits the government from trying to take away a natural right which God has already granted. Many, many people own guns in this country for hobbies, shooting at ranges and personal enjoyment. There is now a much larger and growing number who collect them for self-defense, more than in any other generation. I contend there are many collecting both guns and the appropriate ammunition in case it needs to be used against any criminal element, foreign or domestic, much as our Founders used weaponry against the English Crown, the government of their time.

Whatever a felon may decide to do with a gun in Chicago or Detroit, when statistically it has been illegally obtained, should and must be considered irrelevant to my right to own a gun for my personal enjoyment or self-defense, or both. Owning a gun in America has a history older than our nation itself. The tradition is certainly much older than the current bunch of Marxist progressives. My grandfather had a gun behind his door that spoke of his preparedness to put game on the table and to defend his family against would be robbers or thieves. That was a tradition which was passed down for five generations; his father, grandfather, and great grandfather, all the way back to his great, great, great grandfather before him. The tradition has survived through to the current generation with the same applications: personal independence and a sense of self-defense against enemies foreign and domestic. Many liberals have great fear of firearms and therefore wish to punish the rest of us for their fright. Since their angry demeanor in decision-making does not easily lend itself well to having a semi-automatic handgun in their hands, it is best they remain frightened.

Not allowing any good news to stand long, Obama, Liberals and the U.N.

are singing harmony about confiscating personal guns. Welcome to President Obama's dream for America, the transformed country where reason and absurdity supplants raison d'être, and a self-proclaimed dictator wishes to gift us with presents like gun control á la United Nations. Liberals and Progressives certainly know how to bulldoze straight ahead trying to get what they want, kicking laws and ethics to the curb. You will recall that in 2010, when former House Speaker Nancy Pelosi described how liberals would circumnavigate their constituency to pass Obamacare. Pelosi said they would "... go through the gate. If the gates closed, we'll go over the fence. If the fence is too high, we'll pole vault in. If that doesn't work, we'll parachute in." And they parachuted on us like wicked commandos.[4]

Second Amendment rights are not safe with Mr. Obama alone. He and the Liberals are ready to "shoot down" the Amendment. On one hand, we have the administration telling us they are committed to protecting our Second Amendment rights. On the other hand, the president is joining alliances with UN gun grabbers by giving them the green light for the Arms Trade Treaty (ATT). In the real world, presidents work in conjunction with Congress to pass laws, but in Obama Land anything goes.

The administration claims ATT primarily applies to exporting weapons, thus posing zero threat to gun ownership domestically. Looking at ATT's verbiage, a different message is received; instructing nations to "take the necessary legislative and administrative measure to adapt, as necessary, national laws and regulations to implement the obligations" of this treaty. That is too gray, hence leaving room to dilute or supersede the Second Amendment.[5]

It is clear Obama has been a gun control advocacy in the past has been for re-election purposes. According to the Washington Post during the campaign, Obama told gun control activist Sarah Brady, whose husband Jim was shot during the Reagan assassination attempt in 1981, that gun control was "very much on his agenda... but under the radar." Since Jim Brady passed away on August 4, 2014, his shooting was ruled a homicide since it was the result of the assassination attempt. History will not be kind to America's 44th president who promised transparency, but governed mostly under the radar.[6]

Liberals want us to believe that global gun control is for our own good, just like registration of our guns is for our own good; as if that will prevent crimes. Since gun control will not remove guns from the "wrong people's hands," the question is, "For whom would it be safer?" The easy answer is street criminals, as well as political criminals.

Today, government is the real problem when it comes to guns, in at least two ways. First, there are enough laws on the books to choke out any criminal element if enforced. Second: that little scandal affectionately codenamed "Fast and Furious," speaks that we cannot trust a regime. The Fast and Furious involved the Justice Department making the injudicious decision to sell weapons to those members and others linked to the Mexican drug cartel in Arizona. Their plan backfired when the weapons "walked" across the border into Mexico and into the hands of cartel thugs. It should have been codenamed "Dumb and Dumber."[7] Lastly, the U.N. has no business telling us what to do. If the UN is given an open door into our personal lives by way of the ATT, gun confiscations will, at some point, follow.[8] Even if that treaty is never ratified, Obama has shown his stripes to confiscate on his own if allowed to do so.

History Tells the Tale

History in America contains numerous accounts of individuals, usually liberals, afraid of some legal activity, then working to leverage laws against people who do like that legal activity. Earlier in the 20th Century there were many people who disapproved of drinking alcoholic beverages and so liberals decided that no one should consume alcohol. Given the practices from the previous two centuries, standing against alcoholic beverages was truly un-American and their fight of prohibition actually caused much more harm than good, giving gangsters, criminals, and moonshiners many special opportunities to grow an industry even bigger than it normally would have been. Because liberal government wanted to participate too, they just decided to tax it, for $Trillions in taxes. Interesting how revenue streams will help legalize products.

This is closely related to the action I witnessed on a much smaller scale several years ago. Senior management within a company where friends worked took unilateral action against the entire employee base for the actions of two employees. In order to squeeze every minute of work out of every professional who was laboring on billable project hours, department heads were told to keep all employees working with few breaks and little to no down time, thus hitting important deadlines with critical clients. One morning at approximately 10 AM, a supervisor found two staff professionals talking while drinking coffee in the cafeteria. Regardless of the fact that no one else was there, and that these two were probably discussing a project issue in a quiet area, senior management used their action as an excuse to send a message to all employees and close the cafeteria during off hours. They sent a message to the entire workforce in no uncertain terms. Because there had been no discussion at all before this unilateral action, there was a response certain and to the point given by the employees. The message sent back to management was in the form of emotional sabotage that continued for several years, all revolving around and responding to managements actions in closing the cafeteria. While management made their point, the employees made a more lasting one.

What did the employees do? Several things were done that became much more costly to the billable hours on projects than was two employees taking a 20-minute break in the cafeteria. Extended lunch hours were taken, no more free overtime given to the company, no more early to work and late to leave; rather lots of coming in a little late and lots of leaving a little early. These were all messages that management began to see over a two-year period that were very expensive.

What do these stories have to do with the Second Amendment and gun control? They show us exactly what gun control laws in this country have done while trying to curb criminal activity by taking guns from law-abiding citizens. These laws have done nothing more than increase the very criminal activity they said they wanted to stop.

Politicians seem to have a huge blind spot; either that or they are deceitful. They do not learn the lessons nor see what so many rational people see with gun violence. So with their feigning legislation against criminal activity, they focus attention on the inanimate objects, the guns, and in doing so, use their loud, vocal prejudices against the general public, not the criminals. This results in two dangerous practices; first, crime actually increases since fewer people have the chance for self-defense, and second, the real issue of crime is focused on the guns, which are not the real problem. If this continues, laws will be changed to take away guns. That is when the criminal element on the streets and in government offices in Washington, D. C. will have a huge advantage against God-fearing peoples.

A third reason this could be dangerous, I believe, is that there are millions of pro-active Americans who possibly have drawn the line for revolution at this point. Given that legislation is passed, or even executive orders signed outlawing gun ownership, an atmosphere will be created which will be met with resistance. Any time those resisting believe in their cause enough to die for it and those they are fighting do not have the same depth of loyalty and are afraid, no matter how bad the odds are stacked, the end will favor those with the courage. In case you are wondering which side is courageous and which is not, notice the high walls the legislators are behind, notice their desire to listen to phone calls of normal Americans, or to spy on families in their homes. That is all driven by fear. They know what the KGB knew long ago when the Soviets discussed and then gave up on the idea of trying to fight a conventional war on American soil against Americans. They knew their trek inland would result in so many casualties of their troops; there would be no army left by the time they made the central plains.

While some may claim such a stance as mine as naiveté, saying that I do not understand the harm guns bring to our streets; that I am twisting the data to make it say things it really does not say. However, for the 900+ of the 2013 former residents of South Chicago, I wonder how many of them would like to have had a weapon in hand to protect their families and themselves before they were shot by a criminal and lost their lives to those neighborhood thugs who were supposed to be the ones who were unarmed.

In 2012, more young people in Chicago died at the point of a gun than did all Americans during the years of the Iraqi War put together. That is according to Michael Thompson of World Net Daily, January 16, 2013. Someone said to me, "Take their guns away in Chicago!" The answer back was, "They already did; 30 years ago!"

The big problem, they took the guns away from law-abiding citizens. They did not go after the gang members, the thugs, or the progressive politicians, which liberals always have a habit of forgetting. But who in their right mind wants to approach anyone who's mean and vicious to take their guns away?

Rare is any shooting in Chicago that ever makes the national news. The reason? It is usually black on black crime, meaning there is no political point of reporting that, for media executives that is. It does not further their agenda of tearing down what was built by the Founders. To qualify for the national news, it has to involve a "white" person who is shooting a black person, which they reframe as an "African American." There is a difference between the terms black and African American to the media — mainly political correctness. If anyone other than a black person shoots a black person, it does not matter if the person who is shooting is defending himself or not. It is reported as a crime of racism. Just listen to the media hounds, Jessie Jackson or Al Sharpton when an "African American" is shot by someone who is not black, and they are trying to defend themselves. Better to get smashed into the pavement or the floor than to defend yourself. Hence, the Department of Justice Chief has spoken to challenge the law of the land, "Stand Your Ground," will not stand. It has been changed to "Thou shalt run, when approached by a person of color with a gun," is the mandated law of the regime now. What kind of foolishness is this? What kind of hypocrisy is this?[9]

We Americans have held guns since we first landed in this great land. While the progressives have an agenda to take guns from the law-abiding citizens, that action will not reduce crime because criminals will always have a black market through which they can obtain a weapon to use upon some defenseless citizen. Whatever their stated reason, the liberals' argument in their mind is not eligible for discussion; they insist we must just be tolerant of their view and accept it as reality. That is ridiculous! Liberals never have a solution that works for good. They do not have one here either.

Do not bother a liberal with facts like 'having a weapon of equal fire power evens the odds between a 69 year-old grandmother and a 28 year-old would-be felon who just broke into her house.' Victory is for the taking when the equalizer exists in the hands of the weaker of two opponents. That is between two nations or between two individuals. As Howard Zinn illustrates, "The American victory over the British army was made possible by the existence of an already-armed people. Just about every white male had a gun, and could shoot . . ."[10]

Rule 1: The Script is This: Find a Victim to Whip Up Emotion

The real point the Leftists have is not to save a life, though that is their cry on the "Left". The truth is to get traction for using calamities like "racial" shootings to whip up an emotional panic of the public so as to collect more guns from law-abiding citizens. Here is an example,

Paul Bedard of the *Washington Examiner* has uncovered a fascinating document: an 80-page "talking points" monograph titled "Preventing Gun Violence Through Effective Messaging," written by a trio of Democratic political operatives. *The Wall Street Journal* recently ran the story of how the Left plans to follow these talking points to use tragedies for their political gain.

The document, as Bedard writes, instructs politicians and advocates "to hype high-profile gun incidents like the Florida slaying of Trayvon Martin to win support for new gun control laws." Essentially it is a how-to book on inciting a moral panic:

> "The most powerful time to communicate is when concern and emotions are running at their peak," it advises. Antigun advocates are urged to seize opportunistically on horrific crimes: "The debate over gun violence in America is periodically punctuated by high-profile gun violence incidents including Columbine, Virginia Tech, Tucson, the Trayvon Martin killing, Aurora, and Oak Creek. When an incident such as these attracts sustained media attention, it creates a unique climate for our communications efforts."

The booklet explicitly urges foes of the Second Amendment to abjure rationality in favor of the argumentum ad impromptu, or appeal to emotion. "When talking to broader audiences, we want to meet them where they are," the authors advise. "That means emphasizing emotion over policy prescriptions, keeping our facts and our case simple and direct, and avoiding arguments that leave people thinking they don't know enough about the topic to weigh in."

The do's and don'ts are consistent with this advice. "Examples of power language" include: "It breaks my heart that every day in our country (state or city) children wake up worried and frightened about getting shot." "Just imagine the pain that a mother or father feels when their young child is gunned down." "The real outrage—the thing that makes this violence so unforgivable—is that we know how to stop it and we're not getting it done."

And here are examples of "some ineffective language to avoid": "There's a clear body of research demonstrating the high social cost of gun violence." "The policy outcomes we're after are the ones that can have the most beneficial impact on the rates of violence among the most affected populations." "Of course, gun violence affects people's lives. But, it also has a devastating economic impact to the tune of over $100 billion a year. That's a number that should get every American taxpayer's attention."

The monograph was published before the December massacre at Newtown, Conn., and its advice, as Bedard puts it, was "likely followed by top Democratic leaders including President Obama." Whether the post-Newtown campaign was propter hoc or merely post, there's no question that the book describes with great accuracy the approach Obama and his fellow antigun zealots took. The paradigmatic example, as we noted in April, was a *New York Times* op-ed carrying the name of Gabrielle Giffords, which was a model of unreasoning vehemence.

The campaign proved remarkably ineffective. A few states, Colorado, Connecticut, Maryland, New York, enacted new antigun laws amid the post-Newtown panic. But it was hardly a national trend: Democratic Party dominance of state government was a necessary condition. On Capitol Hill, the big gun-control effort ended with a whimper in April, as even the mildest measures failed to win approval in the Democratic Senate. In fact, that Giffords op-ed was a reaction to that outcome, not an attempt to prevent it.

Why didn't these cynically manipulative tactics work? Maybe because the anti-gun zealots aren't as cynical as they imagine themselves to be, which is to say, that they themselves are the most susceptible to these sorts of emotional appeals.

After all, Obama was genuinely furious when he appeared at the Rose Garden in April and raged impotently against the Senate for thwarting his efforts. No doubt the president was, as the monograph advises, trying to manipulate others by playing on their emotional weakness. He ended up playing on his own weakness instead.[11]

Rule 2: Exaggerate, Embellish, Exaggerate, and Embellish Again

Liberal academia and the media can falsify or mislead the reality of statistics with their erasers. Take for instance during a January 27, 2014 ABC News segment titled "Young Guns," Diane Sawyer claimed, based on a Yale University study called "American Children and Guns" says, "Every hour, a child is rushed to an emergency room because of gunshots." Her co-anchor David Muir took it even further and claimed that "453 of those children die at the hospital." They bolstered their claims with the introduction and testimony of a study in the *Journal of Pediatrics* to show how many children find guns in their homes, or the homes of friends and neighbors, and accidentally shoot themselves or others.

However, in building their case against guns, the Yale study, ABC, and Diane Sawyer ignored critical facts by falsifying and/or reporting the data. Fact one: The *Journal of Pediatrics* study they introduced actually covered statistics for "both" children and teenagers who were victims of gunshot wounds; with the latter opening the door to deaths tied to gang activity and criminal misuse of firearms. Fact two: According to the Centers for Disease Control, the number of accidental firearm deaths for children ten and under in 2010 was 36. That is 36 too many deaths, however, but far short of the 453 Diane and David wants you to believe is true. And then there's fact number three: *National Review* reported that "two thirds of these accidental deaths . . . [were] not shots fired by other little kids but . . . by adult males with criminal backgrounds."[12]

Diatribes and other emotional responses to discussions on guns are heard almost every day. I am reminded of an incident involving a young woman in a restaurant several years ago. Her emotional demand that everyone must surrender their guns or else children were going to die was quite remarkable. She took a few seconds to lecture all within earshot of how evil they were if they owned a gun. A couple of the people tried to calm her down, one man tried to reason with her, but she was having nothing to do with it. Finally, one fellow whom I learned later was concealed carry holder asked her, "Have you ever thought of how you would defend yourself if someone broke into your house?" She said she had a ball bat by her bed. "How will you defend yourself if the intruder has a gun?", he asked. His question at least pulled her off script long enough to get her to stop talking. The obvious answer to anyone asking why have a gun for self-defense, is "I'd rather have a gun and not need one, than to need a gun and not have one."

Possibly liberals should take vacations in places like South Chicago, of course with no weapons. If they survive for a week, they "might" quickly learn that continued survival depends upon having a firearm for protection. It is no different than a nation like the U.S.; even though a super power and no other nation is equal in power, we still want armament to stand off enemies

Help with Home Security Systems

If protection from home invasion is not present, then perception of a home alarm and firearm readiness may be the answer. In either case to follow what one reader suggests below in building that "perception of protection" in his "southern home" the directions of the security system guide shown below could be a first step toward the real thing. When first reading it, I smiled at the humor, but realized that eventually threat is not meaningful unless the system has the teeth to back up what is promised so as to stave off real attack. There is one statement I would add to this notice if I purchased the system obviously AFTER the teeth were in place; something to the effect that, *"We shoot first, then call the police. If you have questions, inquire within!"*

"HOW TO INSTALL A SOUTHERN HOME SECURITY SYSTEM

1. Go to a secondhand store and buy a pair of men's used size 14-16 work boots.
2. Place them on your front porch, along with a copy of Guns & Ammo Magazine.
3. Put four giant dog dishes next to the boots and magazines.
4. Leave a note on your door that reads:

"Bubba,

Bertha, Doc, Doogie, & I went for more ammo and beer. Be back in an hour.

Don't mess with the pit bulls; they attacked the mailman this morning and messed him up bad. I don't think Boomer took part, but it was hard to tell from all the blood all over each dog. Anyway, I locked all four of 'em in the house.

Better wait outside. Be right back.

Signed - "Big Jim"

CHAPTER SIXTEEN — HAVING THE RIGHT TO OWN AND BEAR ARMS

The "teeth" of the system would come in the form of a 12 or 20 gauge shotgun loaded and ready, plus semi-auto hand guns and rifles loaded and ready in the following calibers; .45, .40, .223, .308, and 556. If you are trained in safety and the use of each, plus attentive to the surroundings, you should be okay with any challenger or challengers who want to test your resolve.

When Journalists and Academia Join Forces

In November 2013, Mary Margaret Penrose, a full-time professor on the faculty of the newly-minted Texas A&M University School of Law called for the repeal and replacement of the Second Amendment. In the safety of a day-long, well-guarded panel symposium on gun control and the Second Amendment at the University of Connecticut School of Law in Hartford, attended primarily by law students, law professors and attorneys, Penrose made her declaration.

Noting her own outrage in her perception that Americans continue to tolerate gun violence, Penrose asked audience members to raise their hands if they thought laws intended to prevent gun violence have been successful. No one raised a hand. "I think I'm in agreement with you and, unfortunately, drastic times require drastic measures," the professor said. "I think the Second Amendment is misunderstood and I think it's time today, in our drastic measures, to repeal and replace that Second Amendment."[13] She launched into her misinformed explanation of the Second Amendment; implying that our enumerated right to possess a firearm is largely responsible for the mass shootings that have cropped up in recent years.

Her argument and blatant contempt for the Constitution (which she admits to describing as an "obsolete" document in her classes) is nothing new among the Left, aka, the Progressives. Among her ramblings about the uselessness of our Constitution she managed to make a "state's rights" case for the repeal of our Second Amendment right. Penrose argues that States should be able to make their own gun laws, without the burden of complying with that document from the 1700's. She should be applauded on attempting to grasp the idea of Federalism, though her attempt was very inadequate. It should be considered a dangerous thing to have someone with so little grasp of the law teaching the law in a university system. A glimpse of our founding document whose Framers added the Second Amendment, shows that they did so because they feared there would be a violation of citizen's rights if left up to local legislation and local governments. Believe me, Ms. Penrose has not thought this through; I do not believe she would be in agreement with individuals states deciding independently if women could vote in elections. Nor do I think she would favor the states deciding independently on naming a state religion. Like most liberals she has not thought this through. I believe it would be good for her to spend a summer as an intern in South Chicago, an area that is strictly restricted concerning guns and do research door to door, at night preferably, and without any armed protection of course. Possibly she would see that outlawing guns does not make the guns go away.

With her words, "desperate times call for desperate measures," the following is possibly a better and more honest solution based on data. That would be to outlaw guns: in the hands of just the Democrats and Progressive liberals. Out of the five worst and recent mass murders in America, all five were carried out by Democrats. They are:

- Fort Hood – Registered Democrat/Muslim;
- Columbine – Too young to vote, but both parents were registered Democrats and Progressive liberals;
- Virginia Tech – Wrote hate mail to President Bush and to his staff;
- Colorado theatre – Registered Democrat; staff worker on the Obama campaign; Occupy Wall Street participant; Progressive liberal;
- Connecticut school shooter – Registered Democrat who stated he hated Christians.

When liberals travel, such as Ms. Penrose, all have hired personal body guards, and all the guards carry loaded gun(s) to protect her personal safety and life. That is the same thing all concerned citizens want to have we do not have the wealth to hire guards; we must rely on ourselves. As Eric Owens wrote, "You have no intelligent suggestions Miss Liberal, so go away ... shoo ... shoo! The name of the game in America should be freedom, not more despotism like you suggest."[14]

Liberal progressives have learned through the years to be crafty, **to avoid facts about guns and to use only emotional arguments** in their public presentations. "Guns kill our children; take them away," is an example. In spite of their emotion it is only true that thugs, gang members, felons, etc., will always have access to getting a gun through a "black market." The emotional arguments of liberals appear in editorials to "preach" through the power of the printed word their liberal agenda to grab your guns. The newspaper print makes them appear to be more powerful than they actually are.

A prime sample is an editorial which appeared around the county's newspapers written by super-liberal editor Mary Sanchez, and appeared In the *Kansas City Star* on February 22, 21013 under the title "*Gun Lobby defends a cynical business model, not the Constitution.*" Searching through past census data, Sanchez or associates found information about the "General Social Survey" and its data which she fashioned into a handle on the idea that gun ownership in America is on a severe decline.

In summary, she wrote, "There's a little-known fact about guns in America, the firearms industry and its political allies don't like to dwell on ... Gun manufacturers, the National Rifle Association ... want to shore up a market that has been slipping away for decades ... A declining proportion of the public is involved in gun culture ... This should lead us to an alarming conclusion. The marketing ... is not about defending the Second Amendment. It is about defending a business model — a sick, cynical business model . . . the gun industry . . . has lost its credibility . . . Gun ownership's place in American culture is withering . . . Industry and political efforts to resuscitate it need to be understood and, when appropriate, challenged in that context."[15]

The response offered by yours truly, which still has not been inked to hit the page of the Star op-ed, appears below as a conservative response to those in the elite media who want to take the Second Amendment away just from law-abiding folks. Please read her editorial above first to better understand my printed response below.

> *Thank you, Ms. Sanchez for your editorial of 2/22/13. It seems to represent a continuing mind-numbed robotic drum beat from the progressive left in its cries against guns, self-defense and the Second Amendment of the US Constitution. Your opinion has the scent of what I believe to be the talking points from your party's memo of the day. Please accept the following as a response to your "data" and "opinion."*
>
> *First, given the lies which are continually presented by the current regime when tabulating numbers for whatever is the topic of the day; unemployment, support polls, disapproval polls, supposed creation of jobs, and now the results of the "General Social Survey", there has to be a question mark following the "data." Behind your "excitement" in reporting that gun ownership is down, the data of such a survey is not scientific and is therefore highly questionable. While it is true there is a changing demographic in this country, the recent uptick in gun purchases is not readily available in any survey or census data, especially the "General Social Survey." Also, many people, including gun owners, who come from military, ex-military, law enforcement, sportsmen, collectors, etc., most likely provide inaccurate data in the general social survey, and many do not respond at all. The reason: it is certain that some do not wish to share private information with any despotic regime or members of the press who run addresses of gun owners in their publication (such as in New York in 2013]). Certainly the respondents are wiser than calculated for they question who would be asking things like "who owns guns, who doesn't and why?" Also, when regimes state there needs to be a national registry of those who owns guns, then later deny they said that (aka, lie), many people choose to follow suit and respond in kind.*
>
> *Second, your comment about younger people is of interest to me; "Younger people are more likely to play soccer than sit in a duck blind or deer stand." Could be, but your comments bring forth word pictures and visual landscapes from cities like South Chicago, Detroit, NYC, DC, just to mention a few. In Chicago for example, whether it is from a soccer field, a duck blind, a deer stand, or a grass hut, the shootings are coming from someone, someplace. I don't think it is all "old white guys" which you referenced in your column, who might be just cruising through those neighborhoods. (The real data in Chicago for example shows it is generally young black men who are in possession of illegal or stolen guns. And this in a state which has historically had fierce gun control laws already. These young men, I suspect, would probably not complete a general social survey honestly either even if their lives depended on it!)*

Third, you mention "zombie shoots". These may be the referenced target shooting by young people whose parents will not take them to a gun range. However, many gun owners use the word "Zombie" as a rather common colorful metaphor (aka, a figure of speech used to refer to something else. By the way, have you watched a TV show lately that does not have at least a zombie or two in the show?). Anyway the metaphor is used in this case for "stupid", brain-dead", "lacking any logical reasoning ability", "out of touch" type individuals, also known generally as the enemies of America and its free enterprise system. This includes some in your own profession who "feel" rather than "think" as they write columns, and who proudly tout themselves as, "progressives, communists, socialists, leftists, etc. There are also synonyms for these named individuals, "terrorists", "traitors", "the enemy," "brain dead editors", et al").

Fourth, you mention declining numbers of people purchasing firearms as a group having a lack of credibility because the group is on the decline. I doubt this decline is actually for the mentioned reasons. However, your reasoning is sound and true, and serious questioning of judgment should be placed on statements from groups that are waning. We can suppose that for a minute. If we do, don't look now, but you might be condemning your newspaper and the liberal press in general with that judgment. Talk about declining numbers of individuals purchasing your product (the newspaper) across the nation, as well as total sales dropping through the floor. I guess folks have grown tired of your news reporting, editorials, etc. Your own words in the next to last paragraph of your anti-gun editorial could very well apply to your editors, rather than gun owners; <u>"Americans HAVE become fed up with its paranoia and its rank influence peddling. It has lost its credibility."</u> Just how many people did your paper/industry lay off over the past 10 years? Last report was over 75% of support staff lost their jobs. Talk about a declining cultural icon. Guess the demographics are truly changing. Or possibly, liberalism just does not work. Anyway, I did not see those numbers represented in the "general social survey." At the end of the day, your readership has flown the coop. I guess we SHOULD question very seriously the judgment offered in a portion of the editorial page.

Last, you mention: "This much is clear. Gun ownership's place in American culture is withering on its own. Industry and political efforts to resuscitate it need to be understood and, when appropriate, challenged in that context". Sounds like real hope on your part. However, if you really believe this, why did you not challenge the regime in your editorial? You see, the real data shows the government is increasing its purchases of ammunition and weapons at an alarming rate of speed, stockpiling 1.6 Billion rounds of hollow point ammunition over the past two years (by the way, those are illegal according to the Geneva Conference and the NATO Accord) and purchasing 70,000 fully automatic rifles with those dreaded 30-round extended magazines you so hate. And all this in the name of FEMA? I hate to think about who FEMA intends to fight. All I heard from you on this subject was silence. Oh yes, but I forgot. You must "feel" it is okay for government organizations to have lots of weapons, just not private citizens. Can anyone say "sieg heil?"

Chapter Sixteen — Having the Right to Own and Bear Arms

In summation then, it appears you are against groups who are on the decline, especially gun owners. But, as mentioned earlier, members of your profession are in decline and doing so very rapidly. Your liberal editorials and others, have "gone the way of disco balls and bell bottom jeans", as well as tie died t-shirts. People are still reading but not necessarily your press. According to your own word and definition of such, your "place in American culture is withering on its own. Industry and political efforts to resuscitate it need to be understood and, when appropriate, challenged in that context." Is your opinion applicable to gun owners only? The answer is NO! So I am challenging you, taking you to task, scolding you for getting so excited in your attempt to prevent private citizens who want to legally protect themselves and their property; the practice of which, I suspect is NOT now withering, mostly due to liberal leader. I know that is my opinion, but it was also the opinion of the country's Founders. I trust their opinion very much, and frankly much more than yours, mostly due to the respective value system which they used. How long will you publish such tripe, attacking lawful citizens and yet protecting your party's desire to make that which is right, wrong and that which is wrong, right? At the end of the day, most reasoning people see guns as a means of protecting themselves against a criminal element. This President does too; else he would drop his Secret Service detail. Thanks for your opinion, but as Harry Callahan once said, opinions are like another part of the human anatomy; everyone has one. You can keep yours. End of OpEd

Thomas Jefferson wrote in the Declaration of Independence that we are "endowed by our Creator with certain inalienable rights." As he wrote, he was acknowledging that God provides natural rights which originate from the "natural law." Therefore, he was acknowledging that freedoms are pre-political and come from our humanity and not from the government, and as our humanity is ultimately divine in origin, the government, even by majority vote, cannot morally take natural rights away from us. A natural right is an area of individual human behavior like thought, speech, worship, travel, self-defense, privacy, ownership and use of property, consensual personal which is immune from government interference and for the exercise of which we do not need the government's permission.[16]

The right of the people to keep and bear arms is an extension of the natural right to self-defense and a hallmark of personal sovereignty. It is specifically insulated from governmental interference by the Constitution and has historically been the linchpin of resistance to tyranny. And yet, the progressives in both political parties stand ready to use the coercive power of the government to interfere with the exercise of that right by law-abiding persons because of the gross abuse of that right by some crazies in our midst. When Thomas Jefferson wrote in the Declaration of Independence that we are endowed by our Creator with certain inalienable rights, he was marrying the nation at its birth to the ancient principles of the natural law that have animated the Judeo-Christian tradition in the West. Those principles have operated as a break on all governments that recognize them by enunciating the concept of natural rights.[17]

We have been created free. Thus, the natural law teaches that our freedoms are pre-political and come from our humanity and not from the government, and as our humanity is ultimately divine in origin, the government, even by majority vote, cannot morally take natural rights away from us. A natural right is an area of individual human behavior like thought, speech, worship, travel, self-defense, privacy, ownership and use of property, consensual personal intimacy is immune from government interference and for the exercise of which we do not need the government's permission.[18]

Today, the limitations on the power and precision of the guns we can lawfully own not only violate our natural right to self-defense and our personal sovereignties; they assure that a tyrant can more easily disarm and overcome us.

The essence of humanity is freedom. Government, whether voted in peacefully or thrust upon us by force, is essentially the negation of freedom. Throughout the history of the world, people have achieved freedom when those in power have begrudgingly given it up. From the assassination of Julius Caesar to King John's forced signing of the Magna Carta, from the English Civil War to the triumph of the allies at the end of World War II, from the fall of Communism to the Arab Spring, governments have permitted so-called nobles and everyday folk to exercise more personal freedom as a result of their demands for it and their fighting for it. This constitutes "power permitting liberty."[19]

America is Different

The American experience was the opposite of every other nation. Here, each human being is sovereign, as the colonists were after the Revolution. Here, the delegation to the government of some sovereignty, the personal dominion over self, by each American permitted the government to have limited power in order to safeguard the liberties we retained. Stated differently, Americans gave up some limited personal freedom to the new government so it could have the authority and resources to protect the freedoms we retained. **Individuals are sovereign in America, not the government.** This constitutes "liberty permitting power."

But we did not give up any natural rights when we became a new nation; rather, we retained them. It is the choice of every individual whether to give them up. Neither our neighbors nor the government can make those choices for us, because we are all without the moral or legal authority to interfere with anyone else's natural rights. Since the government derives all of its powers from the consent of the governed, and since we each lack the power to interfere with the natural rights of another, how could the government lawfully have that power? It does not. Were this not so, our rights would not be natural; they would be subject to the government's whims.[20]

CHAPTER SIXTEEN — HAVING THE RIGHT TO OWN AND BEAR ARMS

Disarming Is Not the Answer

To assure that no government would infringe the natural rights of anyone here, the Founders incorporated Jefferson's thesis, fundamental to the Declaration, into the Constitution and, with respect to self-defense, into the Second Amendment. As recently as two years ago, the Supreme Court recognized this when it held that the right to keep and bear arms in one's home is a pre-political individual right that only sovereign Americans can surrender and that the government cannot take from us, absent our individual waiver.

There have been practical historical reasons for the near universal historical acceptance of the individual possession of this right. The dictators and monsters of the 20th Century from Stalin to Hitler, from Castro to Pol Pot, from Mao to Assad, all disarmed their people, and only because some of those people resisted the disarming were all eventually enabled to fight the same dictators for freedom. Sometimes they lost. But sometimes they won.[21]

The foremost reason the colonists won the American Revolution is that they possessed weapons that were equivalent in power and precision to those of the British government. If the colonists had been limited to crossbows that they had registered with the king's government in London, while the British troops used gunpowder when they fought us here, George Washington and Jefferson would have certainly been captured and hanged.

We also defeated the king's soldiers because they did not know who among us was armed, because there was no requirement of a permission slip from the government in order to exercise the right to self-defense. (Imagine the howls of protest if permission were required as a precondition to exercising the freedom of speech.) Today, the limitations on the power and precision of the guns we can lawfully own not only violate our natural right to self-defense and our personal sovereignties; they assure that a tyrant can more easily disarm and overcome us.[22]

The historical reality of the Second Amendment's protection of the right to keep and bear arms is not that it protects the right to shoot deer. It protects the right to shoot tyrants, and it protects the right to shoot at them effectively, thus, with the same instruments they would use upon us. If the Jews in the Warsaw ghetto had had the firepower and ammunition that the Nazis did, some of Poland might have stayed free and millions would have survived the Holocaust.

Most people in government reject natural rights and personal sovereignty. Most people in government believe that the exercise of everyone's rights is subject to the will of those in the government. Case in point: U.S. Attorney Eric Holder despises citizens having guns to even protect themselves in their own homes, let alone the millions who now carry legally on the street with the various concealed carry licenses. But, Holder knows that a politician does not normally get everything he/she wants on the first legislation; he is now primed to follow a private citizen's lead in development of what is called "Smart Guns." Once that private citizen, Silicon Valley's venture capitalist Ron Conway, offered a $1 million "prize" to privately fund this smart gun development, Eric Holder jumped on board. He is proposed dumping $2 million seized from taxpayers into smart gun development.

The so-called smart gun syncs itself with a radio-frequency identification (RFID) chip in a bracelet, meaning the gun will not fire unless the shooter is wearing the bracelet. For several reasons this is a bad proposal:

1. It is expensive technology that has been conservatively estimated will add approximately an additional $1800 to put it in the gun and bracelet.
2. This makes homeowners more nervous in thinking about relying on some RFID technology for self-defense in life and death situations, just as it is with iPhone 5S fingerprint identity sensor technology. There is no reason to have to use these technologies in a crisis.
3. Federal government researchers and bureaucrats will develop any such technology to help government track gun owners in the worst possible scenarios, like NSA spy scandal, like drone technology gone wild.
4. Bracelets can be more easily stolen than a gun; we know that criminals do steal guns.
5. Since bracelets would be required to be worn at all times, it would be a sinister way to mark patriots, much like 1930s Jews were marked with a tattoo.

You think this is too far-fetched to ever happen? Think again. Leaflets were passed out in the East Ukraine city of Donetsk ordering Jews to register with the "pro-Russian" militant forces who took over area.[23]

Did you empower the government to impair our freedom all because of the mania and terror of just a few that fear the sight of a gun? I doubt it. Nor would we give up our automobiles because some crazed drunk crashes into and kills or injures members of a family of four. Cars might frighten survivors for a time, but common sense says we would not confiscate all automobiles because of the fear of a few. When we make it more profitable for attorneys to keep criminals in jail, rather than in getting them out, our streets and homes will be much safer, much like they were in Colonial days. Penalize the criminal, not the law-abiding citizen.

[The New Atheists] are not open or willing to go where the evidence leads, unless that evidence sustains their own naturalistic assumptions. They have covertly reduced all philosophical thought and deduction to—ironically—faith!

Ravi Zacharias

Chapter Seventeen

Your Invitation to Sit Down and Shut Up!

"When even one American — who has done nothing wrong — is forced by fear to shut his mind and close his mouth, then all Americans are in peril." — Harry Truman

MANY YEARS AGO I CAUGHT A flight from Chicago to Los Angeles and with a few of my frequent flyer miles was able to bump up to the first class section, seat 3B as I recall. Having settled in with my refreshment I was gradually slipping off into a nap. Just before the door on the plane closed, a young man rushed in, tapped my leg saying, "Excuse me," and took the window seat beside me. I was already half asleep, so just moved my legs as he sat down, my eyes closed, having already had a healthy swig of my grapefruit juice, and prepared for some rest. As my grandfather would say, I was going to watch the movie on the inside of my eyelids. But this guy who got on late and sat next to me wanted to talk, and talk and talk. And so he rattled on. After complaining about how he was treated in a restaurant in some Midwestern town, he started expounding on the evils of what he called the "white regime," who were trying to keep certain types of people "down." He did mention being a minority at one point. I opened one eye just a bit to catch a glance so as to put in context his comments, attempting to see why he thought he was different. With no comment, I tried to go back to sleep but he kept talking, I suppose thinking that I was a fit target or audience for his diatribe. After complaining about the outcome of the latest national election, he started in on free speech and as I dreaded he might do, he said something that I could not let go. Sure enough he did, saying, "I don't care what a person might think just so long as I don't have to hear it." My initial thought was, "I wish I could say that right now."

    I could not withhold giving an aside now, so yawning and grasping some extra oxygen for my lungs to force my eyelids awake, I said, "So you really don't believe in free speech, do you?" "Sure I do," he said. "I just don't want to hear someone say things I don't like." I repeated, "So you really don't believe in free speech do you?" Adding, "That is what free speech is all about. It's having a license to say something, speak a minority opinion, or yell out something that might be unpopular to the people around or to the culture. I mean after all, I am sitting here listening to what

I don't like. Why should you be so special as to avoid the same from me?"

Wanting to be in the right, I thought the First Amendment was put in the Constitution so that you, I, whoever, could say things that are unpopular. Think about it. If conversation is allowed for only complimentary opinions with which one agrees, why would we have an amendment on free speech in the first place? Our Framers knew that to grow a country, one had to be open to hear other dissuading thoughts, so as to have the best results. Restricting thought or speech to only what the bully likes, no matter what the stated reason, reveals insecurities within the bully, but it also limits others to be at the whim of the bully. For a socialist to hear stories of democracy and free-enterprise should not be threatening, if the socialist is secure in his belief. I certainly am willing to listen to stories socialists and Marxists tell. I do not agree with them but do not feel threatened by any of them since I am secure of my footing within freedom of speech.

Unfortunately, we have walking among us today, liberal "constitutional rights narcissists." Do not get me wrong. They may appear normal people from discussions on a limited range of subjects. They are among blue collar workers, teachers, all the way to PhD law school graduates from Ivy League Schools. I call them narcissists when it comes to our rights, in this case the First Amendment, because they believe strongly and wholeheartedly in their right to say whatever it is they want to say. When it comes to a dissenting opinion, they stand opposed to those rights. For those with whom they disagree on bellwether subjects, such as on abortion, homosexual marriage, or immigration, you must be quiet. They are not familiar with the two-way street upon which the First Amendment of our Constitution is built. They can be seen on television quite often, usually in a diatribe "talking down" to a group of American conservatives saying they should "Be quiet." And when you follow the bread crumbs of the liberal reasoning as to why conservatives should sit in the corner quietly, it is very simple. They disagree with them. Whether it is Michael Moore, Nancy Pelosi, Sean Penn, the *New York Times*, or some academic professor there is a growing segment in this country who feel authorized to wage war on conservative's rights to free speech. Because they are the socialists, they believe they are in a majority. Loud volumes of speech do not constitute a majority. It never has, except in the bully's mind. Nor is a Michael Moore in a majority simply because a media bent on socialism chooses to follow him everywhere to catch his comments. No, a majority is simply what it sounds like: a true number that is bigger (hence, the word "majority").

A prime window to a view of this hypocritical deportment, given that donations are considered free speech, consider this: Brendan Eich was forced to resign as CEO of Mozilla in April 2014, after it became public knowledge he donated money many years ago opposing same-sex marriage. This is the same, identical position which President Barack Hussein Obama held just a few years ago, before his pretentious conversion and current stance. Now he is the darling of the LGBT, but to be consistent in their treatment of individuals, the LGBT should insist that Obama resign.

They will not ask for a resignation since they probably know Obama's earlier stance of being opposed to gay marriage was just a political stance of a campaign to gain votes from a majority of Americans in the election.

This politically correct control over speech, donations, and even thoughts is way beyond being out of control. Freedom does not matter for a huge portion of people on the Liberal side of the aisle, unless they are speaking of course. They have no tolerance, compassion or willingness to listen to a dissenting position, but everyone must listen to theirs. When anyone stands opposed to their "correct" views, i.e., if a person believes and supports the position that marriage should be defined as it has been, between one man and one woman, then according to the liberal, that person will not "have standing." It results in receiving no respect or even losing the right or freedom to speak. As in the case of a CEO who has an opposing view, he is branded as "intolerant" and "full of hate," a varmint who must forfeit privileges of speech and being tolerated. The activists from the LGBT group amount to nothing less than Nazis or mafia members. Their actions are in line with those groups. The solution is to provide them the same treatment in return over time, since that is all they seem to understand. Someone in the media will eventually be forced to take notice and call their bluff.

In case you have not read it:

> "Congress shall make no law respecting an establishment of religion, or prohibiting the free exercise thereof; or abridging the freedom of speech, or of the press; or the right of the people peaceably to assemble, and to petition the Government for a redress of grievances."[1]

Product commercials on television often point to some pitchman calling out the "wisdom of crowds" the appeal to follow a large group of people who usually make a better decision, rather than what an individual will do on his own. The commercial is obviously full of compliant throngs who have chosen their product to use. The line around two corners on a block waiting to see a movie makes "the flick" much better than others according to reasoning of a commercial. Seasoned movie goers know that is not true. The reality tells them many shows have been "sleepers" that catch fire later after it has been out for some time. Large does not always equate to good, with crowds, restaurants, movies, big gulps, or even with ships. Of ships, the Titanic was one that the crowd ballyhooed, "Not even God can sink her," but she didn't even finish her maiden voyage. The message then is individualism — the kind my mom and grandmother taught me to have. Decisions, they said, should be made on sound reasoning, not emotion. Mom always said, "Set aside your emotion right now; you can come back to it later." She added, "I suppose just because your friends said they were going to run off a bridge in the dark, you would want to do the same?" Enter stage right the Constitution — it favors individualism. And reason within that document says that just because the crowds on television are supporting some ridiculous political stance doesn't mean you need to do the same. Our friend the Constitution and the Bill of Rights provides us both company and protection for the thug crowds.[2]

Many among liberal groups in Hollywood and Washington are now claiming the country has outgrown our Constitution. Wishing to maneuver some rights guaranteed in it, taking them away from groups they despise, liberals are often seen and heard making statement in support of stripping away parts or all of the Constitution. PBS ran a series where the host, Peter Sagal, set out to determine how the Constitution applies to modern life in America. As part of this series in the final segment, Sagal journeyed far beyond our borders to Iceland, where citizens have been drafting what he called a new, "crowd-sourced" constitution.

Sagal offered this, "Is our Constitution up to the challenges of the 21st century?" After all, "national constitutions are like cars. After enough wear-and-tear they can break down." That is certainly true for most constitutions. Law professor Mila Versteeg has read every national constitution drafted since World War II and found they are rewritten, on average, every 19 years. Some cars do indeed last longer than that. But the beauty of the American Constitution is that it predates automobiles and many other modern conveniences. Today's governing documents read like a laundry list of "rights" the government is required to "give" to you. South Africa's constitution guarantees a "right" to "adequate housing," "reproductive health care," and "to receive education in the official language or languages of their choice in public educational institutions where that education is reasonably practicable."[3]

Not made for political correctness or voyeurism, our Constitution is dissimilar. Its architecture and structure were made for a free people to confront the political questions and treasonous acts of their times. As Heritage's David Azerrad puts it, "Its words and principles, anchored in the Declaration of Independence, categorically rule out certain laws — e.g., bills of attainder - and create a system of checks and balance between different levels of government. But within the confines of these restrictions and delineations, it leaves the people free to deliberate via their elected representatives on the questions and problems of the day."[4]

Its simplicity was genius. As Sagal later admits, "it has lasted . . . because it is brief and allows for occasional "repairs" through amendments. . . ."[5]

Ridiculous statement! Constitutionalists are viewed by Leftists as amateurish, archaic, and old-fashioned. Leftist Richard Stengel, *Time* managing editor penned a lengthy article on the Constitution; it was defective with this self-evident chronological platitude; "Here are a few things the framers did not know about: World War II. DNA. Sexting. Airplanes. The atom. Television. Medicare. Collateralized debt obligations. The germ theory of disease. Miniskirts. The internal combustion engine. Computers. Antibiotics. Lady Gaga." Reading through his piece, it soon appears there are a few things *he* doesn't know. Let's begin with the basics. "Citizens of all political persuasions who uphold the Constitution are not pining to turn back the clock on technological advances and social progress and return to the late 18th century to live in a world where men wore powdered wigs and doctors "still used leeches." Constitutionalists aren't hapless characters in a political remake of Woody Allen's latest movie *Midnight in Paris*.[5] More research would have helped Stengel; an article in the January 23, 2011 issue of the *Baltimore Sun* says trauma doctors at Johns Hopkins, University of Maryland and other U.S. hospitals are using leeches as a temporary measure to keep blood flowing as new vessels grow in a damaged area.

That the Constitution has an enduring relevance for all times was the argument of the Framers. They are dead and gone, but their principles, thankfully timeless in nature, can endure forever. These principles, although first articulated centuries ago, are not tied to the material conditions of a bygone age. They rest on that most solid and enduring of all foundations: human nature. Madison's rhetorical question in *Federalist* 51 rings true as ever: "But what is government itself, but the greatest of all reflections on human nature?" The miniskirt, sexting, and collateralized debt obligations haven't put much of a dent on good ol' human nature. Until men become angels, let's stick to the Constitution's healthy distrust of concentration of power and unfettered mob rule.[6]

Time rolls on and with each new decade, new crises arise, then wane. New phenomena are delivered; science and technology continue to amaze. And with each new political challenge of any day, our Constitution is structured ready to answer each one, not with policy prescriptions. "Its words and principles, anchored in the Declaration of Independence, categorically rule out certain laws, — e.g., bills of attainder, — and create a system of checks and balance between different levels of government. But within the confines of these restrictions and delineations, it leaves the people free to deliberate via their elected representatives on the questions and problems of the day."[7]

Stengel almost shockingly attacked the Constitution very openly in his article. Shown below, are a few of his off-the-wall attacks, yet each is a part of the mainstream Liberal Progressive posture:

> "The Constitution works so well precisely because it is so opaque, so general, so open to various interpretations. Originalists contend that the Constitution has a clear, fixed meaning. But the framers argued vehemently about its meaning."

Being what it is, human nature created some very heated disagreements over some issues such as the chartering of a national bank. However, for the underpinnings of the nation and government they agreed; the Constitution was the solution. It was to be of the people, by the people, and for the people. Most importantly, they agreed that there must be limits to the powers of government to avoid tyranny. Stengel's "constitutionalism" recognizes no theoretical limits to the scope of government. The debate that the Constitution should foster concerns its proper limits — not whether there are any limits.[8]

"[The Framers] also gave us the idea that a black person was three-fifths of a human being."

There are many brazen lies which liberals peddle, this arguably the worst. Likely it originates from an Ivy League Constitutional Think Tank. Liberal media will never challenge or vet statements from one of their own; they fear losing voters who depend on news from them. In contrast, here is a true and unbiased statement: "The Constitution does not classify people according to race. While the Constitution does compromise with slave-holding interests, free blacks in the North and the South were counted on par with whites for purposes of apportionment and black citizens were voting in five of the original 13 states at the time of the Founding. As for enslaved blacks, it was the Southern states that wanted to count them as full persons, thereby inflating pro-slavery representation in the House. The three-fifths compromise was aimed at preventing Southern states from magnifying their own political power."[9]

If the Constitution was intended to limit the federal government, it sure doesn't say so. Article I, Section 8, the longest section of the longest article of the Constitution, is a drumroll of congressional power.

There are many ludicrous statements; that is one of them. Stengel did not learn definitions, syntax or hermeneutics it appears. From the wording of the legislative vesting clause — "All legislative powers *herein granted*" — to the specific restrictions placed on Congress in Article I, Section 9 and in the Bill of Rights, including the unambiguously constraining language of the Tenth Amendment, the Constitution creates a government of limited enumerated powers.[10]

"George Washington once signed a bill asking Americans to buy a musket and ammunition. There's nothing in the Constitution that restricts the government from asking us to do something . . ."[11] There is however a difference between the government "asking" citizens to make preparations for being in a militia to help protect the nation, and the government today mandating that we pay a tax to purchase a service under the commerce clause; that would be health insurance. One feature that makes the Affordable Care Act illegal in my opinion is its mandate to particular segments of the population, yet other segments all loyal to the political left are provided an exemption altogether. Then too, once the legislation was "approved" by the Supreme Court, the president has unilaterally altered provisions of its rollout; each alteration is unconstitutional.

The law which President Washington signed was made pursuant to Congress's specific and enumerated power to "raise and support armies . . . provide for calling forth the militia . . . [and] provide for organizing, arming, and disciplining, the militia." There's a world of difference between that and arguing that Congress can invoke the commerce clause to compel citizens to purchase health insurance.[12]

Because they lived two centuries ago, the Framers did not watch MTV, CNN or ESPN sports. They were therefore not aware of Lady Gaga, or Wolf Blitzer, or that Major League Baseball had swollen to thirty teams. Stengel on the other hand probably does know quite a bit about Lady Gaga as the managing editor of the country's largest news magazine. However, most are unaware that he is the former president and chief executive officer of the National Constitution Center, where he launched the Peter Jennings Project for Journalists and the Constitution to "help both professional journalists and students interested in journalism understand constitutional issues more deeply." He has no excuse for knowing so little about the Constitution.[13]

Threats to the First

To qualify as a full-fledged representative republic, America must have a viable two-party system. Unfortunately, we are directionally headed toward one political party, which means we cannot remain operational. Tyranny happens when government devolves into one party, freedoms, justice, and respect for human life melt away into totalitarianism. When government gets out of control and cockeyed as it is now, our Bill of Rights come under fire by lop-sided political comments. Exampling this, Nancy Pelosi said in 2014, "Can any one else imagine how much more fun 2015 and 2016 will be if we could control all three branches of government and show the American people what a functional government can look like in the hands of Democrats . . ." With her statement obviously pointed toward one-party control, one needs only view a dictatorship for a few minutes to understand her meaning of "functional." Also, the former and disgusting Representative Barney Frank (D-MA) told Sagal in the PBS special that "the entire system is weighted toward inaction." But commentator P. J. O'Rourke countered that that's a feature, not a bug: "Tyranny was more worrisome to the Framers than legislative deadlock." They wanted it to be difficult to enact national laws, so that most of the power would be left in the states.[14] This translates into more control at a local level. The genius of states' rights, separation of powers, and the Electoral College all make great sense. After all who wants people wandering the streets of Manhattan, New York and Chicago deciding on what rights we can have in Timbuktu, simply because New York can out vote my particular state on an issue at the time?

Today, in the current political travesty going on in America, it would be impossible to write a limited constitution, such as our Framers gave us. Every special interest group under the sun, such as the former ACORN, the LesBiGay Community Action Group, the Global Warming Catastrophe Initiative, Vote Hemp, Sierra Club, and the MoveOn.Org, would all demand "rights" to be included. A constitution should not read as a governing document, not a menu. Guess Mom was right after all. All the more reason we should avoid following the crowd of countries that are constantly reworking their constitutions. Instead we should rededicate ourselves to defending the one with which we're blessed, and keep protecting our right to speak freely.

Traits such as passivity, a lack of courage, or weak ambition, we have not defended our documents in the appropriate manner, and most of our rights are under assault. As will be seen, the First Amendment is being challenged by the Leftist, Socialist regime. An interesting twist to these attacks upon the right to free speech, is what is currently happening to the press. Even the media, which has led the charge for years in trying to undermine the right for free speech among citizens, is now under the same vice grips of a national government who is trying to squeeze their rights to free speech too.

Even the Media's Right to the First Amendment Is Being Challenged

The *New York Times* published a blog on September 28, 2013 from James Risen about the NSA scandal as it applies to the "free press." It focused on the bipartisan backlash President Barack Obama's administration faces in the wake of revelations about the domestic surveillance operations of America's National Security Agency (NSA). "Lawmakers from both parties called for the vast collection of private data on millions of Americans to be scaled back," he wrote.

The ruling shows a trend now of protecting the administration's unilateral moves to spy on citizens is going to be protected by federal judges in many cases. The Feds are pulling out all the stops with Edward Snowden revealing more of what the NSA has been doing. The Risen trial sheds further light on the Obama administration's unparalleled clampdown on official leakers. The 118-page judgment, which sets a precedent that could create significant hurdles for investigative journalism, has dealt a further blow to First Amendment protections for reporters within the boundaries of the US.

Unrelenting Pursuit to Destroy the First Amendment

Many conservatives believe President Obama has declared war on Snowden, the whistleblower the battleground shows the fight on multiple fronts, in the Russian capital, where Snowden was granted temporary documents of asylum. He was holed up at the Moscow airport for months, but wants to go to South America, where he wants to seek permanent asylum. The battle has been waged in Maryland, where Bradley Manning, a former U.S. Army private, currently faced military trial for passing documents to WikiLeaks. It also took hold in Virginia's fourth circuit appeals court, where Risen is being compelled to give evidence. The government wants to be able to press Risen, "Who is your source?" It is interesting to note, that in the days of Deep Throat, reporting on Nixon; all stops were pulled out, by the press, by the Democrat Party, by Hillary Clinton, and the court, to protect anonymity for a correspondent per the First Amendment. So here comes the liberal narcissism again. The same troop who fought to protect the First Amendment back then, are now on the prosecution side, trying to wipe it out. Liberalism is a narcissistic illness. This is proof.

Whatever it is worth, Risen has piled up several awards for his writing, including two Pulitzers for exposing been the CIA sins and carelessness in the past. His book *State of War* was written because *The Times* would not publish his story. He exposed of the CIA's attempts in 2000 to channel flawed blueprints to Tehran's weapons designers; Operation Merlin, the aborted mission that misfired, involving a Russian double agent who tipped the Iranians. The abortive mission, dubbed Operation Merlin, misfired when a Russian double agent on the CIA payroll tipped off Iranian officials about the defects. In his book, Risen describes the mission as "grossly negligent," and brands it one of the most ridiculous gaffes in CIA history.

Right after the book hit book stores in 2006, the Bush administration, progressive in its own right, embarked on an unrelenting pursuit of Risen. The same pursuit, yet different and more heinous was done by Obama, who renewed the Risen subpoena. Obama's tactics of spying on citizens and writers is highlighted in *The Obama Nation*. Its emphasis is the whistleblower crackdown and the growing tension between the administration and news organizations. Risen was pursued relentlessly by government intelligence organizations. He, his phone calls, emails, bank statements were all scrutinized in the government blender in order to get to Jeffrey Sterling.

Contract employee, Edward Snowden uncovered the NSA's secret work of listening to private citizens. The uproar created in 2013 captivated a nation; one person daring to speak up. Judged by many Beltway insiders as being a traitor, that view was not shared nationally about Snowden who said in part, "The very first open and adversarial court to ever judge these programs has now declared them 'Orwellian' and 'likely unconstitutional.' In the USA FREEDOM Act, Congress is considering . . . reforms. And President Obama has now confirmed that these mass surveillance programs, kept secret from the public and defended out of reflex rather than reason, are in fact unnecessary and should be ended."[15]

Enemies Will Be Jailed

When Sterling was indicted in 2010, Risen refused to testify, though subpoenaed, citing the irreconcilable damage it would do to his work for future reporting, if he were to finger his sources. An appeals court ruled with Obama stating that Risen must testify since he was the "only witness" who could provide a "firsthand account of the commission of a most serious crime indicted by the grand jury." Ignoring the subpoena, can have the same outcome as it did in a slightly similar situation with fellow *Times* reporter Judith Miller who in 2007 refused to testify and spent 85 days in jail. That scandal surrounded CIA agent Valerie Plame.

Standing Strong

The legal ground beneath U. S. journalists is similar to an earthquake. Journalists would do well to remember a critical element. The same liberals, who are attacking them and their rights now, are attacking the identical same journalism that was silent during assaults on free speech of conservatives and Christians. "In most instances, the journalists "piled on" as they helped in the tackling of the same conservatives and Christians — supporting the progressive agenda by working overtime to dig up dirt or write fake news stories — all in support of the regime that is not out to barbeque their rights."[16]

Hardly waiting for the court decision to be announced, the Justice Department publicly announced its support, and immediately announced next steps in prosecuting the case. An interesting note; the Justice Department had just published "new guidelines for leak investigations designed to protect the interests of reporters. The revision was a response to public outcry . . . including subpoenaing Associated Press reporters' phone records."[17]

Regardless of the court ruling and any announcement the Obama administration made, Risen said he would protect his sources. He previously said that he would not shy away from taking the appeal to the Supreme Court. In 1972 another reporter took a similar case to the country's highest court in 1972 — and lost. The court invalidated the journalist's use of First Amendment freedoms as special protection from a summons to testify before a grand jury on a case related to the radical Black Panther movement.[18]

Touché Away and Here Is Dum Dum

While liberals and particularly the Obama Administration want to limit conservative free speech, not all legal decisions have been reported going their way. In 2011, the Supreme Court ruled in favor of Westboro Baptist Church, and strangely, some conservatives were encouraged. In reality But this is probably a mistaken opinion since it appears to me that the court was paving the way to destroy the Bill of Rights and the Constitution in this move. Let me show you what I mean.[19, 20]

The Westboro Baptist "Church" as many have observed is a group who sends loud demonstrators carrying picket signs containing "rude, crude statements." The activities are certainly unbecoming of Christian virtue. They regularly picket funerals of soldiers killed in action as a statement of protest of the Defense Department's policy of tolerating and/or encouraging homosexuals in the military. Seeing their group carrying indecent signs at a funeral, signs that read "God Hates You" or "We are glad your son is dead," are not appropriate messages for a funeral. There is nothing remotely Christian about either their stated views or their behavior.[21]

Regarding freedom of speech, in a March 2011 case, the Supreme Court ruled 8 to 1 against a Catholic family whose son's funeral had been disrupted by members of the Westboro Baptist Church who carried signs saying "You're going to Hell," and "Thank God for dead soldiers." People carrying these signs are not displaying a faith belonging to Christianity. They have a right to speak against homosexuality. The preferable place for them, if they really have the courage they pretend is theirs, is to express their anti-gay message in San Francisco, hoisting their signs in the Haight-Ashbury District. They want feedback; they will get it there. They want TV cameras to record their actions; they will get that there also. May be more action than they sought, but it will sure show their daring by going into the lion's den. Besides, they can picket against a whole host of "sins" and touch the lives of those they so want to save.[22]

But the Supreme Court's expression of their theory on democracy and universal human rights, seems to say that any group of ruffians, hoodlums, and vigilantes has a right to invade your private life, no matter how difficult the time. Writing for the majority, Chief Justice John Roberts based his decision on the fact that they were on a public street — not bothering to consider that the protestors were not local residents of the town whose taxes paid for the streets. "Speech is powerful," he said. "It can stir people to action, move them to tears of both joy and sorrow, and—as it did here—inflict great pain. But under the First Amendment "we cannot react to that pain by punishing the speaker."[23] The inconsistency is that the media, the Supreme Court and the Liberals do not really believe that. Otherwise they would not restrict the First Amendment rights of conservatives, Christians, school children, or any other decent citizens. They would not restrict Christian messages in public school nor would they try to restrict those voices who in speaking of Obama say, "The king has no clothes!" They certainly would try to restrict criticism on the basis of what they term "extremism" or "racism."

Under the First Amendment, as it was originally drafted, the Federal government has no jurisdiction over even rational political speech. The local town or the State of Maryland could have put the protestors in the calaboose for the rest of their lives. Under the incorporation doctrine, the First Amendment is now included in the 14th, but even with this legal fiction in place, it is hard to see how the Federal government in any of its agencies is morally or legally justified in protecting these disgusting people. Is there nothing I can do on a public street that can be outlawed? If the court felt the family's case against the so-called church was without merit, because, for example, it was up to local authorities to keep order, they might have said so or not taken up the case. But that is not what they did. They have armed every Jerk in these United States to intrude into other people's private lives.[24]

The irony ran deep here — the ACLU, the *New York Times*, and other groups conspiring against public decency filed briefs supporting the so-called Church — not to protect the church, but their various forms of indecency. Thank goodness for Justice Samuel Alito, the only dissenter. "In order to have a society in which public issues can be openly and vigorously debated," he wrote, "it is not necessary to allow the brutalization of innocent victims."[25]

For those of you who might think this section is calling politicians dumb, you need only to remember that *Touché Away* was the cry of a cartoon character Touché Turtle popular in the mid 60's. Dum Dum was his sidekick, his faithful dog.

"Code Blue — Code Blue"

Given the Supreme Court's rulings in more than a few cases, it would seem like, for all intents and purposes, the Constitution and the Bill of Rights are on life support. Far more important, it represents an extension of the most evil tendencies of Jacobin democratic theory that does not permit the survival of any peculiarities. Democratic equality, as the modern liberals understand it, is not the equality under the law: It is the destruction of all the human differences on which the social order rests. And by liberals I mean both the people called liberals who are really socialists and the old-fashioned liberals who are called libertarians or even so-called conservatives like John Roberts. As de Tocqueville says of similar French intellectuals before the French Revolution, "Not only did they loathe certain privileges, diversity as itself odious. They worshipped equality even if it meant servitude." And so we have Progressives and Liberals today who certainly agree with the French on that point. John Brown, St. Paul, Muhammad, Sun Myung Moon, they are all religious leaders, and their followers all have rights.[26]

The reasoning? Inexperienced individuals want to make impactful statements and do it with authority. They may not be an authority on the subject and what they say may not be true. Even so, why restrict them when someone objects? As long as something is not designed to harm someone, why should we be barred from speaking? Don't misunderstand my position; it is only courteous to season one's speech according to the circumstances of the moment, or to wait until another time to talk. We're not talking about shoehorning some point into a conversation no matter how much it may hurt the person listening. In this case it is simply a matter of sharing truth about America and rights of speech in the proper context of discussions.

But yet that is what we face today with liberals, who want to whip us all in shape by having us never say anything that is "uncomfortable" for some liberal to hear. Like saying to someone who chooses not to work in their life, that anyone who chooses not to work should be left to grovel at the feet of those who do choose to work. In the progressive world, this statement is wrong, unethical, and "illegal" because anyone they support with their resources they consider untouchable. How dare we make a member of a group which they support feel at all uncomfortable? That's their rules for not restricting free speech, unless of course they are speaking about Christians, conservatives, just someone who does not support the madness for one or more of their stances. If you don't support them, then you're considered an enemy and it is okay to make Christians, conservatives, et al, feel very uncomfortable. That sort of assault has been ongoing and growing by the decade, driven by the socialists and progressives over the last 50 years, I am hoping you can see the evidence for this now; they defend free speech for some groups and attack others with whom they disagree. It is becoming so noticeable, on the local or national news programs, etc. Be sure to check multiple news sources: foreign news sources for noteworthy events, since the network media is so far gone in their support for Marxist ideas and personalities. Hopefully you can see the growing trend of these assaults, even passive ones, and plan to prepare yourself for the coming days as we have finally arrived in the days of a degenerative and wicked populace and government.

In some ways, we only have ourselves to blame. After two generations of choking people away from moral truth and ethics in their "education process," we have succeeded in finally doing the unthinkable; raising well-educated individuals with no fixed moral code. Some can program software in C++ language, build a program for a fourth generation computer game, or dissect some cell trying to prove the ridiculous theory of Darwinism, but they have no benchmark in life, an ethic that is lacking, and a morality which teaches "do unto others, before they do unto you."

For the progressive wanna-be's, the conservatives, the zealots, and the timid, passive citizens, the founders put free speech in the position of our First Amendment in this Bill of Rights, because a society that is going to be free and vibrant needs to have challenging ideas spoken out loud, in many different forums, even to the emperor, even if he has no clothes. Suppression of speech does nothing for advancing a free-enterprise society; it only stalls it out and wraps it in chains to become like a Marxist dictatorship. Try telling any physicist or scientist in quantum mechanics that they cannot introduce new ideas (free speech). It does not work for the advancement of the discipline in which they work and live. And neither will it work in America today.

My favorite scientist of all time was a physicist named Richard Feynman. He had a formula for identifying and correcting the problems that caused the space shuttle tragedy of 1986. Through all the political correctness in Washington, he offered his own conclusion for the successful future of the space program, "For a successful technology, reality must take precedence over public relations for nature cannot be fooled." I also believe the same principles apply to the science of speech and especially the law of free speech. Freedom to speak to solve problems is essential in a growing, thriving culture. Our founders knew that, and so they passed to us what we have in the First Amendment of the United States Constitution.

While the 1st Amendment contains more than just adjudication on the right to free speech, the amendment has been used throughout the Twentieth Century in some far reaching and interesting ways.

Some History on the First

The First Amendment to the Constitution was adopted on December 15, 1791, as one of the ten amendments that comprise the Bill of Rights. The Bill of Rights was originally proposed as a measure to assuage Anti-Federalist opposition to Constitutional ratification. Initially, the First Amendment applied only to laws enacted by the Congress, and many of its provisions were interpreted more narrowly than they are today. Beginning with Gitlow v. New York (1925), the Supreme Court applied the First Amendment to states — a process known as incorporation— through the Due Process Clause of the Fourteenth Amendment.

In Everson v. Board of Education (1947), the Court drew on Founding Father Thomas Jefferson's correspondence to call for "a wall of separation between church and State", though the precise boundary of this separation remains in dispute. Speech rights were expanded significantly in a series of 20th and 21st-century court decisions which protected various forms of political speech, anonymous speech, financing of campaigns, pornography, and school speech; these rulings also defined a series of exceptions to First Amendment protections. The Supreme Court overturned English common law precedent to increase the burden of proof for defamation and libel suits, most notably in New York Times Co. v. Sullivan (1964). Commercial speech, however, is less protected by the First Amendment than political speech, and is therefore subject to greater regulation. The Free Press Clause protects publication of information and opinions, and applies to a wide variety of media.

In Near v. Minnesota (1931) and New York Times v. United States (1971), the Supreme Court ruled that the First Amendment protected against prior restraint—pre-publication censorship—in almost all cases. The Petition Clause protects the right to petition all branches and agencies of government for action. In addition to the right of assembly guaranteed by this clause, the Court has also ruled that the Amendment implicitly protects freedom of association.

In October 1947 the House Committee on Un-American Activities investigated the film industry, or Hollywood. When the "Hollywood Ten" as they were known, the defendants who were sought out and subpoenaed to testify in front of the Committee, each of them — Alvah Bessie, Herbert Biberman, Lester Cole, Edward Dmytryk, Ring Lardner, Jr., John Howard Lawson, Albert Maltrz, Samuel Ornitz, Adam Scott, and Dalton Trumbo — were asked by the Committee if they were or ever had been Communists, and all of them took the First Amendment; by doing so, some hoped to make a political statement declaring that the First Amendment forbade Congress to pass any law that could curtail the freedom of speech as opinion, and that therefore the government had no right to investigate a citizen's beliefs. (In that interpretation, the First guarantees the right to remain silent as well as the right to speak.) Interesting use of the First Amendment but the Committee found the Hollywood Ten guilty of Communist infiltration and they went to prison.[26] I suppose they were saying, "If you want to be quiet, do it in there."

Fast Forward to Today

Remember when America used to be a free country? Ah, the good old days when we could make fun of our President without fear of reprisal. We could speak out against his policies or join an opposition political movement without fear of being audited by the IRS. Remember February 2013 when Dr. Ben Carson spoke eloquently at the National Prayer Breakfast and how President Obama was the only one not clapping for Dr. Carson. Carson found himself being audited by the IRS, not once but twice — it appears because Obama took offense.

Chapter Seventeen — An Invitation to Sit Down and Shut Up!

I can even remember our presidents poking fun at themselves. Ronald Reagan, for example, saying, "I knew Thomas Jefferson." Books and movies about ways to kill George W. Bush were considered free speech, if not high art.

My, how things have changed in a few short years. Disagreeing with the President's policies can get you labeled a racist and excluded from polite society. Disagreeing repeatedly can trigger the audits, as Dr. Ben Carson discovered. So can calling people who enter our country illegally "illegal aliens." Such phraseology is now considered racist, offensive, unfair, derogatory and possibly "bullying". Don't EVEN get me started on this "bullying" left-wing, progressive, brain-numbing insanity.

There was a time when we actually made our own purchasing decisions without fear of government interference; let alone outright punishment. The IRS might have been feared at tax time, but there were no dossiers on individuals documenting their most intimate personal details from cholesterol levels to hemorrhoids and vasectomies. And there certainly were no death panels dictating how old you could be and still receive a pacemaker or hip replacement. You could actually pick your own doctor and keep the health insurance coverage of your choice. Remember when?[27]

Never dare call terrorism "terrorism." That is an emotionally charged term that's an indirect slur against Muslims and Islamic "freedom fighters." If you want to be invited to the right parties—and not attract unwanted attention from the government—you'll do well to refer to these incidents as "man-caused disasters" and "workplace violence." That way you're not casting aspersions at protected classes of citizens and particular minority groups.[28]

Actress Melissa Joan Hart reported death wishes and hateful insults because she tweeted her support of Mitt Romney in 2012. "I got called every name in the book. And told, they hope I die, and that they hope my children are gay which was, somehow, supposed to be some kind of punishment," Hart said. She also said there is a blacklist in Hollywood against conservatives. As if we didn't know.[29]

Above all, never ever use the "G" (God) word in public. That's the word that's recently been expunged from the U.S. Air Force cadet honor oath, which formerly concluded with "so help me G__." Thanks, Mikey Weinstein and the Military Religious Freedom Foundation for raising our consciousness level on that one.

"That is unpatriotic, it's un-American, it's inhuman, it's a crime, and in the military if it happens, it violates the oath that everyone in the military takes — not to the New Testament, or the Torah, or to the Koran, but to the United States Constitution," said Weinstein in an interview. "It should be punished vigorously, aggressively, and very visibly."

It reminds me of a song by Joanie Mitchell, "You don't know what you've got till it's gone." Free Speech in America? If you ask me, it's pretty near gone. I hope you are willing to fight for it. Speak UP! Speak OUT! Speak CLEARLY! Speak PASSIONATELY![30]

Be courageous as you speak however; there is an enemy at the gates. Several years ago, the Liberal Left took up "political correctness" as the weapon of choice; those assassins whose goal it is to silence any opposing beliefs and viewpoints. They carry an evil brand; threats of character destruction, termination of employment, boycotting a business, among other unpleasant consequences, are often enough to suppress one's inclination to speak up or speak out. But there is no room for political correctness in freedom of speech.

Freedom of speech carries with it the right to speak wisely, or the right to speak with foolishly, and even the right to speak reprehensibly. Consequences of speech accrue to the speaker, whatever the words and their tenor. The freedom to speak will always be judged by the hearers; they will assess the justification of the expressions and character of the speaker. In an address to the Institute of France on May 10, 1919, President Woodrow Wilson said that freedom of speech "was the greatest safety, because if a man is a fool, the best thing to do is to encourage him to advertise the fact by speaking. It cannot be so easily discovered if you allow him to remain silent and look wise, but if you let him speak, the secret is out and the world knows that he is a fool. The news media and corporations regularly sack those who express an honest opinion or offhandedly blurt a remark that is allegedly "offensive" to the fragile psyches of this or that ethnic, gender or special-interest group, even though this sort of speech rarely, if ever, involves a "clear and present danger" to society. Worse still are those who "demand" that those who break the imaginary laws of the "PC police" either resign, or be fired, or be boycotted, or, more subtly, be exiled away from polite company. Such reactions are childish, boorish, petty, and belittling. In fact, they reveal much more about the intellect as well as the frail and flimsy belief systems of those who claim victimhood than they do about those with the wherewithal to speak honestly and with the confidence of their convictions, or even about those who speak irrationally with no thought at all. "Political correctness" is nothing more than forced conformity by intimidation, and the "PC police" are nothing less than verbal thugs.

Witness the reaction against Chick-fil-A President Dan Cathy in the summer of 2013, when he expressed his opposition to same-sex marriage and his support for "the biblical definition" of marriage. You would have thought he was a cultural terrorist intent on rounding up homosexuals and burning them at the stake. The hue and cry only mildly succeeded in putting him on the defensive, as did the clarion call to boycott his restaurants. Thankfully, he stood his ground and Chick-fil-A continues to thrive.

Freedom of speech is allowed, sometimes tolerated, and even forgiven by God Himself, even when it is senseless and ridiculous. Still, we are warned in Scripture that "The tongue . . . is a fire, a world of evil . . . but no man can tame the tongue. It is a restless evil, full of deadly poison" (James 3: 6 & 8). Therefore, we shouldn't be shocked or appalled by nutty or odious speech to the same degree that we are edified and enlightened by wise or civilized speech. A. Whitney Griswold, former

Chapter Seventeen — An Invitation to Sit Down and Shut Up!

president of Yale, in a 1952 article, maintained that "In the long run of history, the censor and the inquisitor have always lost. The only sure weapon against bad ideas is better ideas. The source of better ideas is wisdom." The good news is that, in most cases, the knee-jerk threats against freedom of speech, thought and actions by the PC police result in most convictions being nullified by want of "better ideas," and certainly for the distinct lack of wisdom. Thomas Jefferson said it best: "Error can be tolerated, when truth is left free to combat it."

At this moment, we stand at an unimaginable crossroads. One of the most distressing aspects of America's current political and social climate is the spectacle of freedom of speech, thought and behavior being seriously threatened by the "PC police." With their attendant expectations and demands for rigorous accommodation to prevailing "politically correct" liberal dogma (homosexual rights, gay marriage, "women's rights," entitlements, etc.), it matters little that the freedom of thought, to voice an opinion, to speak one's mind, and to engage in activities that promote one's political, religious or social persuasions are the cornerstones of representative government, and of liberty itself. No less a personage than George Washington once warned, "For if men are to be precluded from offering their sentiments on a matter . . . the freedom of speech may be taken away, and, dumb and silent we may be led, like sheep, to the slaughter." What will you do? Which fork in the road will you take? Will you remain silent due to politically correctness pressure? Or will you firmly speak up while your country is being destroyed? So much more trouble is on the way . . . you cannot even believe what is about to happen.

"The Bible came with them. And it is not to be doubted, that to free and universal reading of the Bible, in that age, men were much indebted for right views of liberty. The Bible is a book of faith, and a book of doctrine, and a book of morals, and a book of religion, of special revelation from God; but it is also a book which teaches his own individual responsibility, his own dignity, and his equality with his fellow man."

~ Daniel Webster

Speech at Bunker Hill Monument, regarding the Founding Fathers' regard for the Bible, June 17, 1843

Appendix 1

Definitions (aka, Glossary of Terms)

To help you understand my use of terms in this volume, please refer to the following primer, or definitions;

Liberalism

There are two kinds of liberals in American history. Early on in American history, "classic liberals" were considered those who believed an individual could do and say what you wanted, without harm to another person. They desired a limited central government, low taxes, and a great many, or "liberal" individual freedoms. Classic liberalism was popular and predominant in America from the beginning of the nation through the 19th Century. Most of the Founding Fathers in America were classic liberals. John Locke and Adam Smith were perfect examples of classic liberals in the Colonial era of America. **Their key belief was securing the freedom of the individual by limiting the power of the government.** It is still popular today with many. The closest political party to hold their views in a platform today is the Libertarian Party.

"Modern liberals" (those described as opponents to freedom in this volume) are in direction opposition to classic liberals. They are focused very heavily on social and economic redistribution of power and wealth, usually done through heavier and heavier taxation. Modern scholars of liberalism will argue that no meaningful distinction between classical and modern liberalism exists. That is not only misleading. It is a lie! You cannot sell the idea of restricting personal freedom without promoting collectivism. (See Collectivism below) For example, conservatives will view taxation as a form of slavery; while liberals view it as their much preferred method of redistributing the nation's wealth. Modern liberals tend to live their lives within themselves. While they "believe" many of the same tenants of a Progressive, they differ from Progressives, who want to force liberalism on everyone else.

Socialism

Socialism is an economic concept that advocates public ownership of all resources. The production and distribution of resources with a society are then controlled by members of that society collectively or by the government that represents that society. Goods are produced and distributed based on need rather than on market forces such as profitability, price and consumers' purchasing power. In a socialist economy, workers contribute to society based on their ability and receive according to their needs, rather than being paid wages and using that money to purchase what they want. Private possessions are limited to personal-use items such as clothes, and there is no need or ability for individuals to accumulate wealth, so there is equality among the people. A Socialist believes in collectivism, and working toward eventual control of affairs by the government, which is communism.

Collectivism

The philosophy of viewing the whole rather than the individual unit. Translated for human activities and education, a student would be taught that individualism is wrong. The correct approach is viewed as seeing oneself as just a part of a mass of humanity. Politically, collectivism involves government ownership and run segments of an economy, such as manufacturing or agriculture. The theory of collectivism is prevalent is socialism, Marxism, Communism, and Progressivism. Case in point — A collectivist's Pledge of Allegiance would go something as follows: "I pledge allegiance to the Flag of the Divided States of America, and to the collective state to which we have evolved; one nation under secular humanism which has been divided into factions with level playing fields with justice for all — all those who are politically correct." This would be a more accurate pledge of our country in 2014. (While there are many cultural Americans today who love to say the true Pledge of Allegiance and wave the flag, they do not realize we have abandoned the principles our Founders gave us.)

Marxism

A Marxist Government is one which runs all business, manufacturing, and agriculture. There is no personal property. All income is equal and has an 80% tax paid to the government. This "theory" of economics and politics was taught by Karl Marx in the 19th Century, teaching elimination of private property. Government owns all property, manufacturing, and agriculture, a form of Communism. Marx taught that in following this system, all people would be equal in pay, in wealth, in outcomes.

Communism

Generally with small variations, another name for Marxism.

Progressivism

Simply stated to understand my use of the word, it means a "patient Communist," willing to wait long periods of time to see government intervention or collectivism, in every area of life. One of the major goals of a progressive is a one world government; such as was the goal of the U.S.S.R. leadership during the reign of the Soviet Union, and that takes time.

Historically in America, the progressive movement was a political reform movement, seen as starting generally between Reconstruction (The time after "The War between the States," aka, Civil War) and the beginning of World War I — or approximately between the 1880s and 1920. This time period is usually referred to as "The Progressive Era" for principally three reasons. 1) The concurrent growth of the industrial revolution; 2) people began lobbying for mass social changes, typically humanistic in nature, or as they called them, "progressive" in thought and design. Among the changes that occurred were renewed focus on the well-being of workers, especially factory workers, the women's suffrage movement, prohibition, and regulation on massive corporate businesses, and; 3) an "elitist" element for the era grew out of academia and major manufacturing. While both were centered in the Northeast at the time, academics put a heavy emphasis on science and reason, pushing for less reliance on religion and God, erroneously thinking a Christian faith would stand in opposition to true reason. Their reasoning? "Look at what we have been able to do on our own for the past 40 years!" Through this time period, all the seeds of secular humanism were sown. A key belief of the Progressive, the Liberal, the Socialist, and to a large degree the Fascist is in having a large, centralized government "leveling the playing field" to make outcomes equal — all by overseeing and regulating the affairs of citizens.

Fascism

Fascism is socialism in bed with bureaucratic 'crony' business, with the federal government picking winners and losers. A Fascist views society and the state through a totally different lens. The simple conventional virtues of commerce, that of producing, trading, and earning profit, working smart and hard, and moving on to the next day to repeat the process, are viewed with hatred and contempt when stacked next to the code of the warrior, which is what the fascist considers himself and what he truly respects. To the fascist, greatness comes not through these ordinary daily pursuits of the market, nor the conviction to perform the duties of your position description, or in the obedience to the duties of one's state in life, but it comes only through the struggle against other performers, who are viewed as ruthless and greedy, for which the fascist needs the watchful eye, the discipline and the help of the government "to level the playground." And therein the cry for social justice is born and raised.

Historically, Fascism is a form of government that was popular between 1919 and 1945, but became taboo after the Holocaust and the defeat of the Axis powers in 1945. Since 1945, few groups have applied the term to themselves, and the term has become a universal epithet for anything bad.

In 2005, scholar Richard Griffiths stated that the word is the most "misused, and over-used term of our times." In particular, fascism is frequently considered synonymous with white power, though many non-white and racially mixed countries have had fascist governments at one time or another, including Brazil, Mexico, Japan, and Zaire.

In contrast to Griffiths' statement and belief, today, fascism has reared its ugly head and is the predominant force within the United States Government.

<u>It is important to note that communism, socialism, progressivism, Marxism take away individual rights. Each of these systems see you no longer as a person but as part of a mass. As such, you are no longer in control of your own destiny. Rather government dictates the rules.</u>

Capitalism

Capitalism is a socio-economic system that allows private owners to profit from the goods and services they provide. One of the cornerstones of this system is the right of the individual to choose what to produce, how to produce it, and what price to sell it for. It is popular in nations that value the freedom of the individual over the stability of the society. Most modern nations use some form of capitalism, such as state, corporate, or social market.

How Capitalism Works

Also known as the free market system, capitalism requires unregulated supply and demand and little or no government interference in matters of trade. Each individual is free to produce what he or she wants and to sell it at whatever price the market will support. These decisions are typically made by the laws of supply and demand: if there is no demand for a particular product, the producer will not be able to make a profit, but if the demand is high, he or she can sell a lot of goods. Almost everyone benefits because producers create and produce what people want. Consumers will only pay what they think the desired product is worth. The more demand there is for a product, the more goods are produced, and, ideally, the more the price goes down because production is carried on by multiple producers. In this system, competition between businesses is good for consumers because it too drives prices down and usually the competition improves the quality of the products being sold.

Appendix 2

Hearl C. Smith, World War I

Notes

Introduction: How Did I Get Here?

1. Clair Kenamore, *From Vauquois Hills to Exermont* (St. Louis Guard Publishing Co., MO), 1919. See www.archieve.org for a complete electronic verson of the book, the history of the 35th Division of the U.S. Army. A full roster of Company F of the Missouri National Guard, within the 35th Division can be seen; a list of all the men and boys from my hometown, Willow Springs, Missouri who were in this company that served in World War I, p. 301-302.
2. See "U.S. Depart of Defense – Military Awards for Valor – Top 3," World War I, 1917-1918, *U.S. ARMY DISTINGUISHED SERVICE CROSS RECIPIENTS*, Hearl Smith, p. 153. May be viewed online at http://valor.defense.gov/Portals/24/Documents/ServiceCross/ArmyDSC-WWI.pdf
3. See Code of Federal Regulations, Title 32 – National Defense, Section 578.10 Distinguished Service Cross; See also Distinguished Service Cross (United States), Wikipedia.org
4. Tom Bethell, *The Noblest Triumph: Property and Prosperity through the Ages* (Martin's Press, NY), 1998, p. 32
5. Warren B. Billings, Editor, "George Percy's Account of the Voyage to Virginia and the Colony's First Days," in *The Old Dominion in the Seventeenth Century: A Documentary History of Virginia, 1606-1689* (University of North Carolina Press, Chapel Hill), 1975, p. 22-26; Cited in Bethell, *The Noblest Triumph*, p. 33
6. Ibid, p.28; See also Thomas J. DiLorenzo, *How Capitalism Saved America* (Crown Forum Publishing, NY), 2004, p. 53-54
7. Billings, George Percy's Account..., p. 28; Also see Di Lorenzo, *How Capitalism Saved America*, p. 54
8. Ibid, p. 55
9. Matthew Page Andrews, *Virginia, The Old Dominion*, Vol. 1 (Dietz Press, Richmond, VA), 1949, p. 59; See also DiLorenzo, p. 55-56
10. William Bradford, *Of Plymouth Plantation, 1620-1647*, with an introduction by Samuel Eliot Morison (Knopf, NY), 2002, p. 116; See also Di Lorenzo, p. 58-59
11. See Robert M. Calhoon, in *A Companion to the American Revolution*, Editors, Jack P. Greene and JR Pole (Wiley, MA), 2003, p. 235
12. Ibid
13. Robert Middlekauff, *The Glorious Cause: The American Revolution, 1763-1789* (Oxford University Press), 1989, p. 550
14. See R. M. Calhoon, in 'Loyalism and Neutrality, in *A Companion to the American Revolution*, p. 235
15. William Federer, *America's God and Country Encyclopedia of Quotations*, (Fame Publishing, TX), 1993, **See p. 482 regarding the Constitution of the State of North Carolina (1776)** which stated: Article XXXII That no person who shall deny the being of God, or the truth of the Protestant religion, or the divine authority of the Old or New Testaments, or who shall hold religious principles incompatible with the freedom and safety of the State, shall be capable of holding any office or place of trust or profit in the civil department within this State. (until 1876) In 1835 the word "Protestant" was changed to "Christian." **Also see p. 420-421 regarding the Constitution of the State of Maryland (August 14, 1776)** which stated: Article XXXV -That no other test or qualification ought to be required, on admission to any office of trust or profit, than such oath of support and fidelity to this State and such oath of office, as shall be directed by this Convention, or the Legislature of this State, and a declaration of a belief in the Christian religion. That, as it is the duty of every man to worship God is such a manner as he thinks most acceptable to him; all persons professing the Christian religion, are equally entitled to protection in their religious liberty; wherefore no person ought by any law to be molested... on account of his religious practice; unless, under the color [pretense] of religion, any man shall disturb the good order, peace

or safety of the State, or shall infringe the laws of morality... yet the Legislature may, in their discretion, lay a general and equal tax, for the support of the Christian religion. **Also see p. 429 regarding The Constitution of the State of Massachusetts (1780)** which stated: The Governor shall be chosen annually; and no person shall be eligible to this office, unless, at the time of his election... he shall declare himself to be of the Christian religion. *Chapter VI, Article I* [All persons elected to State office or to the Legislature must] make and subscribe the following declaration, viz. "I, _____, do declare, that I believe the Christian religion, and have firm persuasion of its truth." *Part I, Article III* - And every denomination of Christians, demeaning themselves peaceably, and as good subjects of the commonwealth, shall be equally under the protection of the law: and no subordination of any sect or denomination to another shall ever be established by law." **Also see p. 628 regarding The Constitution of the State of Vermont (1786)** which stated: Frame of Government, *Section 9*. And each member [of the Legislature], before he takes his seat, shall make and subscribe the following declaration, viz: "I do believe in one God, the Creator and Governor of the universe, the rewarder of the good and punisher of the wicked. And I do acknowledge the Scripture of the Old and New Testament to be given by divine inspiration, and own and profess the [Christian] religion. And no further or other religious test shall ever, hereafter, be required of any civil officer or magistrate in this State." **Also see p. 203 regarding The Constitution of the State of Delaware (until 1792)** which stated: *Article XXII* Every person who shall be chosen a member of either house, or appointed to any office or place of trust... shall... make and subscribe the following declaration, to wit: "I, _____, do profess faith in God the Father, and in Jesus Christ His only Son, and in the Holy Ghost, one God, blessed forevermore; I do acknowledge the holy scriptures of the Old and New Testament to be given by divine inspiration." **Also see p. 179 regarding The Constitution of the State of Connecticut (until 1818), contained the wording:** The People of this State... by the Providence of God... hath the sole and exclusive right of governing themselves as a free, sovereign, and independent State... and forasmuch as the free fruition of such liberties and privileges as humanity, civility, and Christianity call for, as is due to every man in his place and proportion... hath ever been, and will be the tranquility and stability of Churches and Commonwealth; and the denial thereof, the disturbances, if not the ruin of both. **See also p. 504 regarding The Constitution of the State of Pennsylvania that stated:** *Frame of Government, Section 10*. And each member [of the legislature], before he takes his seat, shall make and subscribe the following declaration, viz: "I do believe in one God, the Creator and Governour of the universe, the rewarder of the good and punisher of the wicked, and I do acknowledge the Scriptures of the Old and New Testament to be given by Divine inspiration." **Also see p,. 469 regarding The Constitution of the State of New Hampshire (1784, 1792)** requiring senators and representatives to be of the Protestant religion. **Also see p. 580-581 The Constitution of the State of Tennessee (1796), stating:** *Article VIII, Section II*. No person who denies the being of God, or a future state of rewards and punishments, shall hold any office in the civil department of this State. **See also p. 451 about The Constitution of the State of Mississippi (1817), stating:** No person who denies the being of God or a future state of rewards and punishments shall hold any office in the civil department of the State.

16 See David Barton, editor, My excerpts taken from Speech by John Quincy Adams, "Oration Delivered Before the Inhabitants of the Town of Newburyport at their request 'The Sixty-First Anniversary of the Declaration of Independence," July 4, 1837, See at Wallbuilders.com

17 See Juliet Walker, *The History of Black Business in America: Capitalism, Race, Entrepreneurship, Volume 1* (University of North Carolina Press, NC), 2009, p. 49.

Chapter 1: Lost in the Land of the Lost

1 John Dewey, *My Pedagogic Creed*, (School Journal, Volume 54), 1897, p. 77-80; Also seen in the reprint version, *My Pedagogic Creed* (Scholarly Publishing Office, University of Michigan, Ann Arbor), 2009

2 See Arthur M. Schlesinger, Jr., *The Politics of Upheaval, 1935-1936: The Age of Roosevelt* (Houghton Mifflin Co., NY), 1960

3 Rosalie M. Gordon, *What's Happened to our Schools* (America's Future, Inc.), 1956

4 See two volumes by George S. Counts, *The American Road to Culture; the Soviet Challenge to America*,

(The John Day Book Company, NY); See also, *Dare the School Build a New Social Order?*, (The John Day Book Company, NY), 1972

5   See Daniel J. Flynn, *Intellectual Morons, How Ideology Makes Smart People Fall For Stupid Ideas* (Three Rivers Press, NY), 2004
6   William Barclay, *Commentary on The Letters to Timothy, Titus, and Philemon*, p. 310
7   Joseph Farah, *Taking America Back*, (Thomas Nelson), 2003
8   See Jim Geraghty, *"The Infamous Reset Button: Stolen From a Hotel Pool or Jacuzzi,"* THE CAMPAIGN SPOT, National Review Online, March 3, 2014. See at: http://www.nationalreview.com/campaign-spot/372373/infamous-reset-button-stolen-hotel-pool-or-jacuzzi-jim-geraghty   See also Becket Adams article on the 2009 incident, *"Remember Hillary's Russian Reset Button? Guess Where She Got It?"* – The Blaze Network, March 3, 2014. See at: http://www.theblaze.com/stories/2014/03/03/remember-hillarys-russian-reset-button-guess-where-she-got-it/
9   See Reid J. Epstein, "Kerry: Russia behaving like it's the 19th Century," POLITICO NOW Instant News and Analysis, March 2, 2014. See at http://www.politico.com/blogs/politico-live/2014/03/kerry-russia-behaving-like-its-the-th-century-184280.html
10 Patrick J. Buchanan, *Churchill, Hitler, and the Unnecessary War*, Preface, (Crown Publishing, NY, NY), 2008, ISBN-978-0-307-40515-9d, p. xv-xvi
11 Russell Kirk, *America's British Culture* (New Brunswick, N.J.: Transaction, 1993), p. 7
12 My interpretive written account was based largely on research gleaned from Patrick J. Buchanan, *Churchill, Hitler*, p. xvi
13 See *Everyone's Mark Twain*, Compiled by Caroline Thomas Harnsberger (A. S. Barnes, NY), 1972, p.150.

Chapter 2: America's Secret War

1   J. Wallace Hamilton, *Horns and Haloes in Human Nature* (Fleming H. Revell), 1954, Lib. Of Con 54-9685, p. 36
2   See Benjamin Woods Labarce, *The Boston Tea Party* (Northeastern Classic Series Books, NY), 1979; See also Benjamin L. Carp, *Defiance of the Patriots: The Boston Tea Party and the Making of America* (Yale Press, New Haven, CT), 2010. My very brief account of the Boston Tea Party relies heavily on their scholarly research.
3   Judge Andrew P. Napolitano, *The Constitution in Exile* (Nelson Current, Nashville, TN), 2006, p. 1
4   See Popscreen for film of 1966 appearance of George Carlin on the Johnny Carson Show (Tonight Show), see at http://www.popscreen.com/v/5Xeb7/George-Carlin-on-the-Tonite-Show-with-Johnny-Carson-in-1966
5   See Rick Pearlstein, *Before the Storm; Barry Goldwater and the Unmaking of the American Consensus*, (Nation Books, NY), 2009; Also see Wikipedia
6   For background that led to this episode airing on the *Twilight Zone* in September 1961, Season 3, Episode 3, see Margot A. Henriksen, *Dr. Strangelove's America: Society and Culture in the Atomic Age* (University of California Press, Berkeley), 1997; Also Rick Perlstein, *Before the Storm: Barry Goldwater and the Unmaking of the American Consensus* (Nation Books, NY), 2009. Much of the description of the episode was taken from a Rod Serling Interview as seen on You Tube and from Wikipedia.
7   William J. Bennett, *The De-Valuing of America: The Fight for our Culture and Children* (Touchstone Publishing, NY), 1992, p. 33
8   Ibid, p. 33, See also Patrick J. Buchanan, p. xxi

Chapter 3: The Deception of Liberalism That Led to This Darkness

1   J. Wallace Hamilton, *Horns and Haloes in Human Nature* (Fleming H. Revell), 1954, p. 36
2   See The Revenue Act of 1913, Section II, C., 38 Stat. 114, 168.
3   Anne C. Heller, *Ayn Rand and the World She Made* (Doubleday, NY), 2009: ISBN 978-0-385-51399-9, p. xi
4   Kenneth C. Davis, *Don't Know Much About the American Presidents* (Hyperion, NY), 2012, p. 431
5   Ibid, p. 431
6   Ibid, p. 432
7   David S. Reynolds, *Waking Giant* (Harper Collins, NY), 2009, p. 370
8   Walter Thabit, *How East New York Became a Ghetto* (New York University Press, NY), 2003, ISBN

0-8147-8267-1, p. 42
9 Kenneth C. Davis, p.433
10 Ibid, p. 434
11 Allan M. Winkler, *Franklin D. Roosevelt and the Making of Modern America* (Pearson Longman, NY), 2005, p. 88
12 Ibid, p. 88
13 Ibid, p. 89
14 Kenneth S. Davis, *FDR: Into the Storm, 1937-1940: A History* (Random House, NY), 1993, P. 460-61; Joseph Alsop and Robert Kintner, *American White Paper: The Story of American Diplomacy and the Second World War* (London: Michael Joseph), 1940, p. 78
15 Allan M. Winkler, p.103
16 Patrick J. Buchanan, *Churchill, Hitler, and the Unnecessary War*, Preface, (Crown Publishing, NY, NY), 2008, ISBN-978-0-307-40515-9
17 Joseph Alsop and Robert Kintner, *American White Paper: The Story of American Diplomacy and the Second World War* (London: Michael Joseph), 1940, p. 78; Kenneth S. Davis, FDR, 460-61; John Gunther, *Roosevelt in Retrospect: A Profile in History* (London: Hamish Hamilton, 1950), 329-30. FDR's bedroom is described in Frances Perkins, *The Roosevelt I Knew* (London: Hammond & Hammond, 1948), 55-56; Life, January 20, 1941. FDR note, September 1, 1939, PPF 3737, FDRL
18 See US State Department, *The Neutrality Acts, 1930s*
19 Ibid
20 See Clarence Carson on Ideas on Liberty-The Americanist, "The Defamation of American Tradition," The Moral Liberal, April 2, 2014
21 Ibid
22 Ibid
23 Ibid
24 Ibid
25 Ibid
26 Ibid
27 Ibid
28 Ibid
29 Ibid
30 See Harold E. Stearns, *Civilization in the United States: An Inquiry by Thirty Americans*, article by Elsie Clews Parsons, (Harcourt, Brace and Company, NY), 1922, p. 309
31 Clarence Carson on Ideas on Liberty
32 Ibid
33 See Huffington Post Sports, "*Michael Sam Introduced By Rams: 'It's OK to be who you are'*", May 13, 2014
34 See Huffington Post Sports, "*Don Jones, Dolphins Player, Fined for Negative Tweet About Michael Sam,*" May 12, 2014
35 See CNN Entertainment, Lisa Respers France, "*Benham Brothers lose HGTV show after 'anti-gay' remarks,*" May 9, 2014
36 This is a reference to an AP story carried by Channel 5 News in Nashville. The story, "*Al Gore criticized for Mansion's Electricity Use,*" which aired in February, 2007.
37 This is taken from research done in the Washington Post. See "The Rich List" or "Forbes List of Richest in Washington," from 2012

Chapter 4: The Illusion of Government That's Captivated America

1 My brief account of the Boston Tea Party was gained partially from my research and written based on the comprehensive historical research and accounts of Benjamin Woods Labaree, *The Boston Tea Party* (Northeastern Classics, NY), 1964; and Benjamin L. Carp, *Defiance of the Patriots: The Boston Tea Party and the Making of America* (Yale University Press, CT), 2010. The historical account of the deeds and words of Joshua Wyeth are recorded in depth by Francis S. Drake, *Tea Leaves: Being a Collection of Letters and Documents* (Mass), 1884, pgs. lxxi - lxxii. Also my research included the account of Fremont-Barnes, Encyclopedia of the Age of Political Revolutions and New Ideologies (2007) 1:688
2 See Benjamin L. Carp, *Defiance*, p. 130

3   Francis S. Drake, *Tea Leaves*, p. lxxx
4   Ibid, p. lxviii
5   See Edmund S. and Helen M. Morgan, *The Stamp Act Crisis: Prologue to Revolution* (NC), 1953
6   See the global Organization for Economic Cooperation and Development (OECD), Tax Policy Analysis, Corporate and Capital Income Taxes, Table 11.1. There are four tables, 11.1-11.4 which show the corporate tax rates and the top tax burden on dividend income for the period 2000-2014. For the purposes of corporate tax, I have used data from Table 11.1. This data is available for viewing; http://www.oecd.org/tax/tax-policy/tax-database.htm#C_CorporateCaptial
7   See the UCLA HERI 2012 Survey, *Undergraduate Teaching Faculty: The 2011-2012 HERI Faculty Survey*, p. 36; see at http://www.heri.ucla.edu/monographs/HERI-FAC2011-Monograph.pdf
8   Matthey S. Edney (1996, rev.2009), "The Columbus Letter: The Diffusion of Columbus' Letter through Europe, 1493-1497," Columbus, in his letter of 1493 on his return to Europe from America, references the natives saying they had no religion and he thought favorably to facilitate "conversion to the holy religion of Christ, to which in truth, as far as I can perceive, they are very ready and favorably inclined." Also see Peter Marshall and David Manuel Jr., The Light and the Glory (1995), Introduction.
9   See Rick Scarborough, *Enough is Enough, A Call to Christian Involvement* (Whitaker House, PA), 1996, p. 35-36
10 See Charles Deane, Editor with notes, *History of Plymouth Plantation* (Harvard College Library, Mass), 1856 (A Google Ebook)
11 See Rick Scarborough, *Enough is Enough* (Frontline Publishing, FL), 1994
12 Gary DeMar, *America's Christian History, The Untold Story*, (Harper & Row, Philadelphia, Pa), p. 52
13 Gary DeMar, p. 58
14 Ibid, p. 58
15 Ibid, p. 59
16 Ibid, p. 60-61
17 Ibid, p. 73
18 Ibid, p. 73
19 William Federer, *America's God and Country*, (Amerisearch), 1994
20 See Derek Hunter, "We are the Problem," Townhall.com, April 3, 2014, see at; http://townhall.com/columnists/derekhunter/2014/04/03/we-are-the-problem-n1817968

Chapter 5: The Fifties – They Were Really Something

1   Lily Koppel, *The Astronaut Wives Club* (Grand Central Publishing, NY), 2013, p. 2-3
2   Frederick F. Siegel, *Troubled Journey: From Pearl Harbor to Ronald Reagan* (Hill & Wang, NY), 1984, p. 120
3   Andrew J. Bacevich, *The Short American Century* (Harvard University Press, Mass.), 2012, See chapter 1
4   Morris Janowitz, *The Last Half-Century: Societal Change and Politics in America* (University of Chicago Press, IL), 1978, p. 418-30
5   C. Wright Mills, *White Collar: The American Middle Classes* (Oxford University Press, NY), 1951, p. xv
6   George Lipsitz, "The Making of Disneyland," in William Graebner and Altina L. Waller, ed., *True Stories from the American Past* (Library of Congress, NY), 1993, p. 179-96
7   James T. Patterson, *Grand Expectations, The United States, 1945-1974* (Oxford University Press, NY), 1996, p. 346
8   Nora Sayre, *Running Time: Films of the Cold War* (Doubleday, NY), 1982, p. 198
9   Joseph C. Goulden, *The Best Years, 1945-1950* (Atheneum Press, NY), 1976, p. 175
10 Karel Ann Marling, *As Seen On TV: The Visual Culture of Everyday Life in the 1950s* (Harvard University Press, Mass.), 1996; Stephen J. Whitfield, *The Culture of the Cold War* (JHU Press, Baltimore), 1996, p. 153-54
11 James T. Patterson, *Grand Expectations, The United States, 1945-1974* (Oxford University Press, NY), 1996, p. 350
12 Ronald J. Oakley, *God's Country: America in the Fifties* (Barricade Books, NY), 1986, p. 428
13 William J. Bennett, *The De-valuing of America* (Simon & Schuster, NY), 1994

Chapter 6: Decades of Change in the U.S.

1. James T. Patterson, *Grand Expectations, The United States, 1945-1974* (Oxford University Press, NY), 1996, p. 82
2. Ibid, p. 179
3. Walter Goodman, *The Committee: The Extraordinary Career of the House Committee on Un-American Activities* (Farrar, Strauss & Giroux, NY), 1964
4. Richard M. Fried, *Nightmare in Red* (Oxford University Press, NY), 1990, p. 55-56
5. Gary Gerstle, *Working Class Americanism: The Politics of Labor in an Industrial City, 1914-1960* (Cambridge, England), 1989, p. 308-09
6. Arthur M. Schlesinger, *The Vital Center: The Politics of Freedom* (Houghton Mifflin, Boston), 1949, p. 130
7. Samuel Stouffer, *Communism, Conformity, and Civil Liberties: A Cross Section of the Nation Speaks Its Mind* (Garden City, NY), 1955, p. 87
8. Richard M. Fried, p. 166; Robert Griffith & Athan Theoharis, *Spectre: Original Essays on the Cold War and the Origins of McCarthyism*; See Mary McAullife, *The Politics of Civil Liberties: The American Civil Liberties Union During the McCarthy Years* (New Viewpoints, NY), 1974, p. 152-171
9. Diane Ravitch, *The Troubled Crusade: American Education, 1945-1980* (Basic Books, NY), 1984, p. 94ff
10. Richard H. Pells, *The Liberal Mind in a Conservative Age: American Intellectuals in the 1940s and 1950s* (University Press of New England, NH), 1985, p. 288
11. Diane Ravitch, *The Troubled Crusade*, p. 96; James T. Patterson, Grand Expectations, p. 186
12. William O'Neill, *American High: The Years of Confidence, 1945-1960* (NY), 1986, p. 168; James T Patterson, p. 186
13. Pells, *Liberal Mind*, p.288; John Diggins, *The Proud Decades: America in War and Peace, 1941-60* (NY), 1988, p. 166
14. Richard Powers, "Anti-Communist Lives," *American Quarterly*, (Dec., 1989), p. 714-23
15. Stephen J. Whitfield, *Culture of the Cold War* (JHU Press, NY), 1996, p. 50-51
16. David Halberstam, *The Fifties* (Random House, NY), 1993, p. 33
17. David Halberstam, p. 46
18. J. Ronald Oakley, *God's Country: America in the Fifties* (Barricade Books, NY), 1986, p. 45
19. Samuel Wells, "Sounding the Tocsin: NSC 68 and the Soviet Threat," *International Security*, 4 (Fall 1979), p. 129-30
20. Daniel Bell, *The Cultural Contradictions of Capitalism*, (Basic Books, NY), 1976, see p. 33-84; Daniel J. Boorstin, *The Americans: The Democratic Experience* (Vintage Books, NY), 1973, p. 525-55; James T. Patterson, p.343-44
21. David Kupelian, *How America morphed into 'Bizarro World'* from Worldnet Daily's Whistleblower Monthly, Kupelian, ed.
22. Marty Jezer, *The Dark Ages: Life in the United States, 1945-60* (Boston), 1982, p. 3; Arlene Skolnick, *Embattled Paradise: The American Family in the Age of Uncertainty* (NY), 1991, p. 98-99; William Braden, *Age of Aquarius: Technology and the Cultural Revolution* (Chicago), 1970, p. 6; James T. Patterson, p. 442
23. Daniel Bell, p. 81; William Braden, *Age of Aquarius: Technology and the Cultural Revolution* (Quadrangle Books, NY), 1970, p. 6; James T. Patterson, p. 443
24. Morris Dickstein, *Gates of Eden: American Culture in the Sixties* (Penguin Books, NY), 1977, p.250; Patterson, p. 443
25. Patterson, p. 443
26. In 1962, Eugene Burdick and Harvey Wheeler published *Fail-Safe*, a novel that became popular by leftists about a nuclear disaster caused by mechanical problems. It was made into a movie in 1964.
27. James T. Patterson, p. 443-44
28. James Miller, *"Democracy Is in the Streets;" From Port Huron to the Siege of Chicago* (NY), 1987; Kirkpatrick Sale, *SDS* (NY), 1973
29. Mark Day, *Cesar Chavez and the Farm Workers* (NY), 1971; Juan Gonzales, *Mexican and Mexican-American Farm Workers: The California Agricultural Industry* (NY), 1985; James T. Patterson, p. 444
30. Patterson, p.444
31. Engel v. Vitale, 370 U.S. 421, (1962); See also *Newsweek*, July 9, 1962, pp. 21-22, 43-45, for vocal public reaction.; Patterson, p 444-45
32. Jonathan Rieder, *Canarsie: The Jews and Italians of Brooklyn Against Liberalism* (Harvard University Press, Mass.), 1985, p. 134-36; James Davison Hunter, *Culture Wars: The Struggle to Define America*

(Basic Books, NY), 1991, p.67-106; James T. Patterson, p. 445
33   Maurice Immerman and Michael Kazin, "The Failure and Success of the New Radicalism," Steve Fraser and Gary Gerstle, eds., in The Rise and Fall of The New Deal Order, 1930-1980 (Princeton, NJ), 1989, p. 212-42; Patterson, p 445; George Lipitz, "Who'll Stop the Rain? Youth Culture, Rock' n' Roll, and Social Crises," David Farber, ed., in The Sixties: From Memory to History (Chapel Hill Press, NC), 1994, p. 206-34.
34   Smoking and Health: Report of the Advisory Committee to the Surgeon General of the Public Health Service (Education & Welfare US Dept. of Health, Washington D.C.), 1964
35   Patterson, p. 445; It should be noted, Americans cut back on smoking only temporarily; by 1966 consumption of adults per adult had risen to pre-report levels. See also, James T. Patterson, The Dread Disease: Cancer and Modern American Culture (Harvard Univ. Press, MA), 1987, p. 201-30.
36   W. J. Rorabaugh, Berkeley at War: The 1960s (Oxford University Press, NY), 1989; Kenneth Keniston, Youth and Dissent: The Rise of a New Opposition (Harvest Books, NY), 1971; Seymour Martin Lipset, Rebellion in the University (Univ. of Chicago Press, IL), 1971
37   Kenneth Cmeil, "The Politics of Civility" in The Sixties: From Memory to History, Farber, ed., (Chapel Hill Press, NC), 1994
38   W. J. Rorabaugh, Berkeley at War, see preface
39   James L. Baughman, The Republic of Mass Culture: Journalism, Filmmaking, and Broadcasting in America Since 1941 (Johns Hopkins University Press, Baltimore), 1992, p. 91
40   Named after the nearby town of Woodstock; Patterson, p. 447
41   Arlene S. Skolnick, Embattled Paradise: The American Family in Age of Uncertainty (Basic Books, NY), 1991, p. 92-93; Patterson, p. 447
42   Beth Bailey, "Sexual Revolution(s)," in Farber, ed., Sixties, p. 235-62
43   John C. Burnham, Bad Habits: Drinking, Smoking, Taking Drugs, Gambling, Sexual Misbehavior, and Swearing in American History (New York University Press, NY), 1993
44   Patterson, p. 448
45   John Burnham, preface
46   Patterson, p. 449
47   Steven Ruggles, "The Transformation of American Family Structure," American Historical Review, (Feb, 1964), p. 103-28
48   Diane Ravitch, The Troubled Crusade, p. 321-330
49   Alice Echols, "Women's Liberation and Sixties Radicalism," in Farber, ed., Sixties, p. 149-74; Skolnick, Embattled Paradise, p. 85-87; Patterson, p. 448
50   John D'Emilio and Estelle Freedman, Intimate Matters: A History of Sexuality in America (NY), 1988, p. 353
51   Two important histories of the 1960s point to the decentering of America after 1965; See Allen J. Matusow, The Unraveling of America: A History of Liberalism in the 1960s (HarperCollins, NY), 1984; and William L. O'Neill, Coming Apart: An Informal History of the 1960s (Ivan R. Dee, Chicago), 1971; Patterson, p. 448
52   O'Neill, Coming Apart, p. 269
53   Stephen Ruggles, "The Transformation of American Family Structure," American Historical Review, (Feb. 1964), 103-128
54   Diane Ravitch, The Troubled Crusade, p. 321-30
55   Michael Frisch, "Woodstock and Altamont," in William Graebner, ed., True Stories from the American Past (McGraw-Hill, NY), 1993, p. 217-39
56   Poll data supported this. See Daniel Yankelovich, The New Morality (McGraw-Hill, NY), 1974, p. xiii
57   Skolnick, Embattled Paradise, p. 181-91; Carl Degler, At Odds, Women and the Family in America from the Revolution to the Present (Oxford University Press, NY), 1989, p. 460-65; Patterson, p. 450
58   Richard A. Easterlin, Birth and Fortune (University of Chicago Press, IL), 1980, p. 60-61
59   James Q. Wilson, Thinking about Crime (Basic Books, 1975, p. 9-10
60   James T. Patterson, America's Struggle against Poverty, 1900-1994 (Harvard University Press, Mass.), 1995, p. 157-62
61   James T. Patterson, Grand Expectations
62   Ibid
63   Lionel Trilling, Liberal Imagination (Harcourt, NY), 1980

Notes

64 Allen J. Matusow, *The Unraveling of America*, p. x
65 Kenneth C. Davis, *Don't Know Much About the American Presidents* (Hyperion, NY), 2012, p. 490-91; Gerald Posner, *Case Closed*, p. 403
66 Kenneth C. Davis, p. 496
67 Frederick F. Siegel, *Troubled Journey, From Pearl Harbor to Ronald Reagan* (Hill and Wang, NY), 1984, p. 217-18
68 Frederick F. Siegel, p. 218
69 Henry Kissinger, *The White House Years* (Simon & Schuster, NY), 2011, p. 3
70 Frederick F. Siegel, p. 218
71 Frederick F. Siegel, p. 219
72 Frederick F. Siegel, p. 219-20
73 Jerry M. Lewis, Thomas R. Hensley, *The May 4 Shootings at Kent State University: The Search for Historical Accuracy* (Ohio Council for the Social Studies-Review 34, 1;9-21) 1998
74 See Frederick F. Siegel
75 Ibid
76 Ibid
77 Craig Shirley, *Rendezvous with Destiny, Ronald Reagan and the Campaign That Changed America* (ISI Books, Wilmington, DE), 2010, p. 2
78 Tom Fiedler & William J. Mitchell, "Bush Aims at Reagan in Florida after Tiny Massachusetts Victory," *Miami Herald*, March 6, 1980, A21; Craig Shirley, Rendezvous with Destiny, p. 188
79 Fiedler & Mitchell, "Bush Aims at Reagan in Florida"; Craig Shirley, p. 200
80 Bill Peterson & Lou Cannon, "Illinois: Bush Weary, Reagan Hopeful, Anderson Ecstatic," *Washington Post*, March 16, 1980, A4; Craig Shirley, p. 204
81 Craig Shirley, p. 204
82 David S. Broder & Bill Peterson, "Rivals Take Turns Ripping Anderson's Loyalty to GOP," *Washington Post*, March 14, 1980, A6.
83 Brit Hume, *World News Tonight*, ABC News Transcripts, March 14, 1980
84 Jules Whitcover, "Rivals Gang Up On Anderson in GOP Debate," *Washington Star*, March 14, 1980, A1; Craig Shirley, p. 206
85 David Hoffman, William Mitchell, and Remer Tyson, "Anderson's GOP Foes Join Forces; Attack His Loyalty to Party," *Miami Herald*, March 14, 1980, 31A.
86 Whitcover, "Rivals Gang up on Anderson"; Craig Shirley, p. 206
87 Adam Clymer, "Campaign Report," *New York Times*, March 17, 1980, A14
88 James Yuenger, "Anderson's Goal: Show GOP Loyalty," *Chicago Tribune*, March 15, 1980, 8; Merrill Hartson, "Anderson Says He's Tired of Having His GOP Loyalty Questioned," *Associated Press*, March 14, 1980,; Whitcover, "Rivals Gang Up on Anderson."
89 David S. Broder and Bill Peterson, "Rivals Take Turns Ripping Anderson's Loyalty to GOP," *Washington Post*, March 14, 1980, A6
90 Whitcover, "Rivals Gang up on Anderson
91 Martin Schram, "Carter Goes Into Debate with Lead in New Poll," *Washington Post*, October 27, 1980, A1
92 Robert J. Rosenthal, "He is a Man of Myth – And Mystique," *Philadelphia Enquirer*, April 16, 1980, 10A
93 Michael K. Deaver and Mickey Herskowitz, *Behind the Scenes: In Which the Author Talks About Ronald and Nancy Reagan...And Himself*, (William Morrow, NY), 1987, p. 87; Craig Shirley, p. 532
94 Craig Shirley, p. 532-33
95 Hamilton Jordan, *Crisis: The Last Year of the Carter Presidency*, (G. P. Putnam;s Sons, NY), 1982, p. 302; Jeff Greenfield, *The Real Campaign: How the Media Missed the Story of the 1980 Campaign* (Summit Books, NY), 1982, p. 181
96 Walter P. Mears, Associated Press, October 28, 1980: Craig Shirley, p. 533
97 "Transcript of the Presidential Debate Between Carter and Reagan in Cleveland," *New York Times*, October 29, 1980, A26
98 Ibid
99 Ibid
100 Craig Shirley, p. 534

101 See "Transcript of the Presidential Debate Between Carter and Reagan in Cleveland" Univ. of Texas Archives, http://www.reagan.utexas.edu/archives/reference/10.28.80debate.html
102 Robert A. Rosenblatt, "Carter, Reagan Agree, Oil Prices Must Increase," Los Angeles Times, October 27, 1980, B8
103 See "Transcript of the Presidential Debate Between Carter and Reagan in Cleveland"; Craig Shirley, p. 535
104 George H. W. Bush in discussion with Craig Shirley, February 16, 2007
105 See "Transcript of the Presidential Debate Between Carter and Reagan in Cleveland" University of Texas archives
106 Ibid
107 Ibid
108 Walter Issacson, Laurence I. Barrett, and Christopher Ogden, "Now a Few Words in Closing," Time, November 10, 1980
109 See "Transcript of the Presidential Debate Between Carter and Reagan in Cleveland"
110 Ibid
111 Ibid
112 Ibid
113 Ibid
114 Ibid
115 Ibid
116 Ibid
117 Craig Shirley, Rendezvous with Destiny, p. 538
118 "Transcript of the Presidential Debate Between Carter and Reagan in Cleveland"
119 Ibid
120 Ibid
121 Ibid
122 Ibid
123 Ibid
124 Ibid
125 Ibid
126 Ibid
127 Ibid
128 Ibid
129 Ibid
130 Ibid
131 Ibid
132 Ibid
133 Ibid
134 Ibid
135 Ibid
136 Ibid
137 Ibid
138 Craig Shirley, Rendezvous with Destiny, p. 542
139 Brad Knickerbocker, "A Governor's Report Card," Christian Science Monitor, October 1, 1980, 13
140 "Transcript of President's State of the Union Message to the Nation," New York Times, January 27, 1982, A16
141 "Transcript of the Presidential Debate Between Carter and Reagan"
142 Craig Shirley, Rendezvous with Destiny, see pages 531-544
143 Jimmy Carter, Keeping Faith: Memoirs of a President (Bantam Books, NY), 1987, p. 565
144 Memorandum from Gerald M. Rafshoon to the President, "1980 General Election Themes," July 3, 1980, Rafshoon Communications, Susan Clough Files, Box 5, Jimmy Carter Presidential Library, Atlanta, GA
145 "Both Sides Claim They Won the Debate," Los Angeles Times, October 29, 1980, B2
146 Jimmy Carter in discussion with Craig Shirley, July 11, 2006
147 Peter Goldman, James Doyle, Martin Kasindorf, Eleanor Clift, and Thomas M. DeFrank, "The

Notes

   Great Homestretch Debate," *Newsweek*, November 10, 1980, p. 34
148   Memorandum from Rafshoon to the President, "1980 General Election Themes," July 3, 1980
149   "Full Transcript of Debate Between Reagan and Carter," *Washington Post*, October 29, 1980, A4
150   Hans Christian Andersen, *The Emperor's New Clothes*, (Houghton, Mifflin, Harcourt, Boston, MA), 2004, p. 11
151   Jack W. Germond and Jules Witcover, "Debate Offers no Real 'Hook' for Undecided," *Washington Post*, October 29, 1980, A1
152   Robert G. Kaiser, "Looking for Old Ghosts," *Washington Post*, October 30, 1980, A1
153   David S. Broder, "Carter On Points, But No KO," *Washington Post*, October 29, 1980, A1
154   Tom Shales, "Live, from Cleveland....It's Debatable," *Washington Post Washington Post*, October 29, 1980, B1
155   Mary McGrory, "No Surprises, but Both Men Delivered Well," *Washington Star*, October 29, 1980, A4
156   Fred Barnes, in discussion with Craig Shirley, September 29, 2008
157   Bernard Weinraub, "Area Panel's Scorecard on the Debate: Reagan Won it by a Wide Margin," *New York Times*, October 30, 1980, B20
158   "Both Sides Claim They Won the Debate," *Los Angeles Times*
159   R. Emmett Tyrrell, Jr., "The Wise and the Wisenheimers," *Washington Post*, November 3, 1980, A21
160   Craig Shirley, *Rendezvous with Destiny*, p. 548
161   Ibid
162   "CBS Poll on the Carter-Reagan Debate," *Washington Star*, October 30, 1980, A4
163   United Press International, "Reagan Wins Dixville Notch," *Washington Star*, November 4, 1980, A5
164   Jerry Harkavy, "First Voters in New Hampshire Primary Cast Their Ballots," Associated Press, February 26, 1980
165   Craig Shirley, *Rendezvous with Destiny*, p. 568
166   Ibid, p. 568
167   Ibid, p. 569
168   D'Vera Cohn, "Election Fizzles as Cliff-Hanger," United Press International, November 5, 1980
169   Barbara Walters, *World News Tonight*, ABC News, November 4, 1980
170   James L. Perry and Albert R. Hunt, "Reagan Buries Carter in Roaring Landslide Throughout Country," *Wall Street Journal*, November 5, 1980, p. 1; Craig Shirley, Rendezvous with Destiny, p. 573
171   John Chancellor, *Decision '80*, NBC, November 4, 1980
172   "Transcript of Reagan's Remarks," *New York Times*, November 5, 1980, A22
173   George J. Church, Christopher Ogden, and Laurence I. Barrett, "Nation: Reagan: Coast-to-Coast," *Time*, November 17, 1980
174   "Transcript of Reagan's Remarks"
175   Craig Shirley, *Rendezvous with Destiny*, p.583
176   Ibid, p. 583
177   Peter B. Sperry, "The Real Reagan Economic Record: Responsible and Successful Economic Policy," *Heritage Foundation*, March 1, 2001; http //www.heritage.org/research/taxes/bg1414.cfm
178   Ronald Reagan, *A Time for Choosing: The Speeches of Ronald Reagan*, (Regnery Publications, Chicago), 1983, p. 186
179   Karl Vick, "U.S., Soviet Diplomatic License Plates Retain Cold War Symbolism," *St. Petersburg Times*, December 19, 1987, 8A
180   Christopher Andrew and Vasili Mitrokhin, *The Sword and the Shield: The Mitrokhin Archive and the Secret History of the KGB* (Basic Books, NY), 2000, p. 242
181   Craig Shirley, *Rendezvous with Destiny*, p. 586
182   R. Emmett Tyrrell Jr., "Mr. Can Do Versus Mr. Can't," *Washington Post*, September 15, 1980, A21
183   Ronald Reagan, *A Time for Choosing*, p. 189
184   Helene Van Damm, *At Reagan's Side: Twenty Years in the Political Mainstream* (Doubleday, NY), 1988, p. 119
185   Aleksandr Solzhenitsyn, "A Special Message," *National Review*, June 28, 2004, p. 26
186   Rick Scarborough, *Enough is Enough*, (Whitaker House, PA), 1986, p. 21
187   Samuel Blumenfeld, "We'd Better not Forget 1992," *World Net Daily*, December 26, 2000, http//

www.wnd.com/2000/12/7589
188 Kenneth C. Davis, *Don't Know Much About the American Presidents*, (Hyperion, NY), 2012, p. 580
189 Ibid, p. 581
190 Ibid, p. 582
191 Rick Scarborough, *Enough is Enough*, p. 22-23
192 Ibid, p 23
193 Saul Alinsky, *Rules for Radicals* (Random House, NY), 1971, p. xv
194 Rick Scarborough, p. 22-26
195 John F. Harris, *The Survivor: Bill Clinton in the White House* (Random House, NY), 2005, p. 432
196 Jeff Madrick, "What Bill Clinton Would Do," *New York Times*, December 9, 2011
197 National Commission on Terrorist Attacks Upon the United States, "Responses to al Qaeda's Initial Assaults," : http//www.9-11commission.gov/report/911report_Ch4.htm; Kenneth C. Davis, *Don't Know Much About the American Presidents*, p. 584
198 George Stephanopoulos, *All too Human: A Political Education* (Little Brown and Co., NY), 1999, p. 4
199 Ibid, p. 3-4
200 See *The Free Enterprise Institute*, Founder-Andrew J. Galambos; http//www.fei-ajg.com
201 Starr Parker, "Big Government Legacy: Leftism = Moral and Material Poverty," *World Net Daily*; http//www.wnd.com/2013/10/leftism-moral-and-material-poverty/
202 See Dr. Thomas Sowell, "Dismantling America," *Townhall.com*, August 17, 2010. See at, http://townhall.com/columnists/thomassowell/2010/08/17/dismantling_america

Chapter 7: Where's the Beef?

1   J. Wallace Hamilton, *Horns and Halos in Human Nature* (Fleming H Revell, NJ), 1954, p. 46
2   William Federer, *America's God and Country* (Amerisearch, Inc., St. Louis, MO), 2000, p. 26
3   Ibid, p. 101
4   Gary DeMar, *America's Christian History: The Untold Story* (American Vision, Inc., Atlanta, GA), 1993, p. 113
5   Anson Phelps Stokes and Leo Pfeffer, *Church and State in the United States* (Harper & Row, NY), 1964, p. 83
6   Ibid, p. 83; Gary DeMar, *America's Christian History*, p. 113-114
7   William Federer, *America's God and Country*, p. 248
8   Gary DeMar, p. 114
9   See Gary T. Amos, *Defending the Declaration: How the Bible and Christianity Influenced the Writing of the Declaration of Independence* (Wolgemuth and Hyatt, Brentwood, TN), 1989. See also "Is the Declaration of Independence 'Christian'?" *World*, December 9, 1989, p. 19-20
10 William Federer, *America's God and Country*, p. 411; Rick Scarborough, *Enough is Enough*, (Whitaker House, PA), 1996, p. 44-45
11 William Federer, *America's God and Country*, p. 273
12 Ibid, p. 274
13 Ibid, p. 274
14 Ibid, p. 318
15 Ibid, p. 669
16 Scarborough, *Enough is Enough*, p. 46-47
17 Ibid, p. 47-48; Federer, *America's God and Country*, p. 651-652
18 Ibid, p. 661; Scarborough, *Enough is Enough*, p. 48-49
19 Stokes and Pfeffer, *Church and State in the United States*, p. 83-84
20 Federer, *America's God and Country*, p. 785; Scarborough, p. 45
21 Federer, *America's God and Country*, p. 10-11; Scarborough, p. 45
22 Abraham Lincoln, "Proclamation Appointing a National Fast Day," April 30, 1863, *The Collected Works of Abraham Lincoln*, Roy P. Bassler, ed.,(Rutgers University Press, New Brunswick, NJ), 1953, 6:155-156; Also see DeMar, p.120-121
23 Stokes and Pfeffer, *Church and State in the United States*, p. 102-103
24 Ibid, p. 568
25 Ibid, p. 38ff
26 Ibid, p. 570

27 See the seventh edition of *The Capitol* (United States Government Printing Office, Washington, D.C.), 1979, p. 24-25
28 Ibid, p. 24; DeMar, p. 120
29 See the booklet, "The Prayer Room of the United States Capitol," published by the U.S. Printing Office, 1956
30 *The Capitol*, p. 25. The eighth edition of The Capitol (1981) has removed the material about the Congressional Prayer Room found in the seventh edition. While there is a picture of the Prayer room in the eighth edition (p. 22), a description of its religious features is absent.
31 David J. Brewer, *The United States: A Christian Nation* (The John C. Winston Co, Philadelphia, PA), 1905, p. 31
32 Peter J. Leithart and George Grant, *In Defense of Greatness: How Biblical Character Shapes a Nation's Destiny* (Coral Ridge Ministries, Ft. Lauderdale, FL), 1990, p. 4

Chapter 8: History Schmistory – Who Needs It?

1 See Peter Marshall, *The Light and the Glory*; Also see Gary DeMar, *America's Christian History* (American Vision, Atlanta, GA), 1993; p. 3 American Leadership Association, Brian Jacobs and Robert D Savage, Founders
2 See Peter Marshall, *The Light and the Glory*
3 Robert N. Bellah, *Habits of the Heart: Individualism and Commitment in American Life* (University of California Press, Berkeley, CA), 1985, p. viii
4 Alexis de Tocqueville, *Democracy in America, 2 Volumes* (Alfred A. Knopf, NY), 1945, See 1:303; Emphasis added
5 Jim Nelson Black, *When Nations Die: Ten Warning Signs of a Culture in Crisis* (Tyndale House, Wheaton, IL), 1994, p. 253
6 *U. S. News and World Report* (November 30, 1992), p. 21
7 See quotes by Robert Davis, ."Mississippi Governor's 'Christian Nation' Remarks Sparks Furor," *USA Today* (November 19,1992), 2A
8 John W. Whitehead, *Religious Apartheid: The Seperation of Religion from American Public Life* (Moody Press, Chicago, IL), 1994, p. 194; "Mississippi Governor Criticized for 'Christian Nation' Remark," *Dallas/Fort Worth Heritage* (January 1993), 14
9 "Mississippi Governor Criticized for 'Christian Nation' Remarks, p. 14
10 Terry Eastland, "In Defense of Religious America," *Commentary: A Monthly Publication of the American Jewish Committee* (June 1981), p. 39-41
11 Terry Witham, "'Christian Nation' Now Fighting Words," *Washington Times* (November 23, 1992), A1
12 Os Guinness, *The Gravedigger File: Papers on the Subversion of the Modern Church* (Inter-Varsity Press, Downers Grove, IL), 1983, p. 79
13 James W. Watkins, "A Try to Wrap Politics in Religion," *The Plain Dealer* (October 5, 1994, 11B; Michael Gartner, "Religion and Politics Just Don't Mix," *USA Today* (October 5, 1994), 11A
14 Gary DeMar, *America's Christian History* (American Vision, Atlanta, GA), 1993, p. 3
15 "Military Teaches Colonists Were Extremists," Bob Unruh, *World Net Daily* (August 23, 2013)
16 Ibid
17 *Art in the United States Capitol* (United States Government Printing Office, Washington, D.C.), 1978, p. 130
18 *Art in the United States Capitol*, p. 136
19 Gary DeMar, *America's Christian History*, p. 124
20 *Art in the United States Capitol*, p. 283, 287
21 Gary DeMar, *America's Christian History*, p. 124
22 Ibid, p. 125
23 Ibid, p. 126
24 *Art in the United States Capitol*, p. 349
25 Gary DeMar, *America's Christian History*, p. 127
26 See Ronald Reagan's National Speech, "A Time For Choosing," Broadcast live October 27, 1964; Also See Richard L. Burke, "Religion Issues Stirs Noise in G.O.P. Governors' 'Tent,'" *New York Times* (November 18, 1992), A13

27 "First Charter of Virginia" (April 10, 1606), *Documents of American History*, ed., Henry Steel Comanger, 6th Edition (Appleton-Century-Crofts, NY), 1958, p. 8
28 Charles Lemuel Thompson, *The Religious Foundations of America: A Study of National Origins* (Fleming H. Revell, NY), 1917, p. 81-82
29 Ibid, p. 83
30 Gary DeMar, *America's Christian Heritage*, p. 55
31 "The Mayflower Compact," *Annals of America: 1493-1754*, 18 Vols., ed., Mortimer J. Adler (Grosset & Dunlap, NY), 1968, Vol. 1, p. 64
32 Frank R. Donovan, *The Mayflower Compact* (Grosset & Dunlap, NY), 1968, p. 12
33 William Bradford, *Bradford's History of the Plymouth Settlement, 1608-1650*, placed into modern English by Harold Paget (American Heritage Ministries, Portland, OR), 1988, p. 21. Also a copy of Bradford's account of the Mayflower Compact, from his manuscript *Of Plymouth Plantation*, can be read in *Mourt's Relation: A Journal of the Pilgrims of Plymouth*, ed., Jordan D. Fiore (Plymouth Rock Foundation, Plymouth, MA), [1841, 1865], 1985, p. 10-11
34 George Bancroft, *History of the Colonization of the United States*, 10 vols., 4th edition (Charles C. Little and James Brown, Boston, MA), 1837, Vol. 1:403
35 Ibid, 1:404
36 "Fundamental Orders of Connecticut" (May 19, 1643), *Documents*, 23
37 Gary DeMar, *America's Christian History*, p. 58
38 "The New England Confederation" (May 19, 1643) *Documents*, 26
39 *Code of New Haven* (1656), p. 567; This is also a quote from Isaac A. Cornelison, *The Relation of Religion to Civil Government in the United States of America: A State Without a Church, but not Without a Religion* (Knickerbocker Press, NY), 1895, p. 59
40 *Code of New Haven*, p. 590; also a quote in Isaac A. Cornelison, p. 60
41 Gary DerMar, *America's Christian History*, p. 59
42 *Provincial Papers*, 1:363; Also see Isaac A. Cornelison, p. 41-42
43 Ibid, 1:363; Cornelison, P. 42
44 Gary DeMar, p. 60
45 B. F. Morris, *The Christian Life and Character of Civil Institutions of the United States* (George W. Childs, Philadelphia, PA), 1864, p. 88
46 Cornelison, p. 67
47 Herbert Schlossberg, *Idols for Destruction: Christian Faith and its Confrontation with American Society* (Crossway Books, Wheaton, IL), 1983, p. 209
48 Gary DeMar, *America's Christian History*, p. 97
49 John T. McNeill, *The History and Character of Calvinism* (Oxford University Press, NY), 1954, p. 196
50 Samuel Blumenfeld, *Is Public Education Necessary?* (Devin-Adair, Greenwich, CT), 1981, p. 10; Gary DeMar, p. 98
51 See "Funds for a College at Henrico, Virginia," in *Education in the United States: A Documentary History*, 5 vols., ed., Sol Cohen (Random House, NY), 1974, 1:336
52 Henry F. May, *The Enlightenment in America* (Oxford University Press, NY), 1976, p. 32-33
53 Gary DeMar, p. 99-100
54 Ibid, p. 100-101; George M. Marsden, *The Soul of the American University: From Protestant Establishment to Established Non-Belief* (Oxford University Press, NY), 1994, p. 322
55 William C. Ringenberg, *The Christian College: A History of Protestant Higher Education in America* (Eerdmans, Grand Rapids, MI), 1984, p. 38
56 Ibid, p. 42
57 Louis B. Wright, *The Cultural Life of the American Colonies* (General Publishing, Toronto, ON), 1962, revised 2002, p. 116
58 Gary DeMar, p. 101-102
59 Richard Hofstadter and Wilson Smith, editors, *American Higher Education: A Documentary History* (University of Chicago Press, Chicago IL), 1961, 1:9
60 Ari L. Goldman, *In Search of God at Harvard* (Random House, NY), 1991, p. 17
61 George M. Marsden, *The Soul of the American University*, p. 41; Peter Gay, *A Loss of Mastery: Puritan Historians in Colonial America* (University of California Press, Berkeley, CA), 1966, p. 23
62 Hofstadter and Smith, *American Higher Education*, "From the Beginnings to the Great Awakening," 1:1

63 H. G. Good, *A History of American Education* (Macmillan, NY), 1956, p. 61
64 William Ringenberg, *The Christian College*, p. 38
65 See "Yale Laws (1745)," in Sol Cohen, *Education in the United States*, 1:49
66 Hofstadter and Smith, *American Higher Education*, 1:49
67 See William F. Buckley, Jr., *God and Man at Yale: The Superstitions of "Academic Freedom"* (Henry Regenry Co., Chicago, IL), 1951; Gary DeMar, p. 105
68 Gary DeMar, p. 106; Dinesh D'Souza, *Illiberal Education: The Politics of Race and Sex on Campus* (The Free Press, NY), 1991, p. 214
69 Sol Cohen, *Education in the United States*, "Advertisement on the Opening of King's College," 2:675
70 Ibid, 2:675
71 Gabriel Sivan, *The Bible and Civilization* (Quadrangle/New York Times Book Co., NY), 1973, p. 273; Gary DeMar, p. 106-107
72 Archibald Alexander, *The Log College* (Banner of Truth Trust, London), 1968, pp. 14-22, [First published, 1851]
73 See Alexander Leitch, *A Princeton Companion* (Princeton University Press, NJ), 1978
74 Ibid
75 Ibid
76 B. F. Morris, *The Christian Life and Civil Institutions of the United States* (G. W. Childs, Philadelphia, PA), 1864, p. 94
77 Sol Cohen, *Education in the United States*, "Charter of William and Mary," 2:645
78 Will Herberg, "Religion and Education in America," *Religious Perspectives in American Culture*, eds., James Ward Smith and A. Leland Jamison (Princeton University Press, NJ), 1961, p. 12
79 Mark A. Noll, *A History of Christianity in the United States and Canada* (Eerdmans, Grand Rapids, MI), 1992, p. 365
80 Ibid, p. 366
81 Ibid, p. 366; Gary DeMar, see pp. 107-109
82 Ibid
83 Ibid
84 Romans 1:20 from the New International Version of the New Testament
85 My research shows this quote in Jim Nelson Black, *When Nations Die: Ten Warning Signs of a Culture in Crisis* (Tyndale, IL), 1994, p. 253

Chapter 9: Definitions in a Progressive Society

1 Joseph W. Bendersky, *A Concise History of Nazi Germany* (Rowan & Littlefield), 2007, p. 147
2 2 Kings
3 Matthew 6:1-5
4 J. C. Ryle, *Matthew, The Crossway Classic Commentaries*, eds., Alister McGrath and J. I Packer (Crossway Books, Wheaton, IL), 1993, p. 37
5 See Cornelius Tacitus, *Annals* (115 A.D.), Book XV, 44; Also see Robert E. Van Voorst, *Jesus Outside the New Testament: An Introduction to the Ancient Evidence* (Wm. B. Eerdmans, Grand Rapids, MI), 2000, pp. 39-53.
6 Tacitus, *Annals*, Book XV, 45; See also Suetonius, *The Lives of Twelve Caesars, Life of Nero*, 31
7 John F. MacArthur, *Nothing but the Truth* (Crossway Books, Wheaton, IL), 1999, p. 63
8 Ibid, p. 63

Chapter 10: Those "Robbin' Hoods" of 'Rotting'ham Forest

1 Aleksandr Isaevich Solshaneidsan, A World Split Apart: Commencement Address Delivered at Harvard University, June 8, 1978; Also see Ronald Berman, Editor, *Solzhenitsyn at Harvard: The Address, Twelve Early Responses, Six Later Reflections*
2 From my research, I have recorded an excerpt from the original quote from Barry Loudermilk reported in the "*VietNow National Magazine*," February 13, 2002.
3 Ibid. View at: http://web.archive.org/web/20020213210735/http://vietnow.com/artbar1.htm
4 Ann Coulter, *Godless, The Church of Liberalism* (Crown Forum, NY), 2006, p.1
5 Tim LaHaye, *The Battle for the Mind* (Fleming H. Revell, Grand Rapids, MI), 1980, p. 33
6 Ibid, p. 80-91

7 Ann Coulter, *Godless*, p. 1-2
8 Ibid, p. 2
9 Ibid, p.3
10 Saul Alinsky, *Rules for Radicals* (Random House, NY), p. 127-134
11 This is an excerpt from Steve Kroft's interview on the TV show "Sixty Minutes" with George Soros aired on December 20, 1998.
12 Ann Coulter, *Godless*, p. 3
13 See article, "Pope of the New World Order, beast, Anti-Christ, and false profit all in one bloodbag," *Time Magazine*, February 12, 2013
14 See Kyle-Anne Shiver, *"George Soros and the Alchemy of 'Regime Change,'"* American Thinker, February 27, 2008
15 See Jim ONeill editorial, "Soros: Public Enemy #1, Illegal Market Manipulation, Felony Insider Trading, Villain, Currency Collapses," *Canada Free Press*, September 15, 2009

Chapter 11: No Gods Allowed in Here

1 Ann Coulter, *Godless, The Church of Liberalism* (Crown Forum, NY), 2006, p. 203-04
2 Ann Coulter Godless, p. 200; Also see Michael Powell, "Doubting Rationalist," *Washington Post*, May 15, 2005; Michael Powell, "'Intelligent Design' Proponent Phillip Johnson, and How He Came to Be,'" *Washington Post*, May 15, 2005
3 Ann Coulter, *Godless*, p. 200; see also Ariel Hart, "Stickers Put in Evolution Text are the Subject of a Federal Trial," *New York Times*, November 4, 2004
4 Ibid, p. 200; Laurie Goldstein, "California Parents File Suit Over Origins of Life Course," *New York Times*, January 11, 2006
5 Laurie Goldstein, "Web of Faith: A Law and Science in Evolution Suit," *New York Times*, September 26, 2005
6 Ann Coulter, *Godless*, p. 200
7 Jay Tokasz, "Cheektowaga teacher sues over forced removal of religious items," *The Buffalo News*, January 10, 2013
8 Jay Tokasz, *The Buffalo News*, January 10, 2013; Also see Todd Starnes, "School Bans Bible Club Prayer Box, Reagan Quote," *Fox News*, January 14, 2013
9 See Jay Tokasz, *The Buffalo News*, January 10, 2013
10 Ibid,
11 Ibid,
12 Ann Coulter, *Godless*, p. 200
13 Tom Bethell Replies, *American Spectator*, February, 2001
14 Ann Coulter, *Godless*, p. 200-201
15 Quoted in *Scientific American* (July, 2000); Also see Lee Strobel, *The Case for a Creator* (Zondervan, Grand Rapids, MI), 2004, p. 31
16 See Larry Hatfield, "Education Against Darwin," *Science Digest* (Winter, 1979)
17 Lee Strobel, *The Case for a Creator*, p. 31-32; Also see "A Scientific Dissent From Darwinism," two-page advertisement, *The Weekly Standard* (October 1, 2001)
18 Art Toalston, "7-part PBS series on evolution challenged by 100 scientists," Intelligent Design and Evolution Awareness Center, (IDEA Center.org)
19 Ibid
20 Lee Strobel, p. 32
21 See Discovery Institute, *Getting the Facts Straight: A Viewer's Guide to PBS's Evolution* (Discovery Institute Press), 2001, p. 11
22 See Jonathan Wells, *Icons of Evolution* (Regnery Publishing, Washington, D.C.), 2000
23 See Jonathan Wells, *Charles Hodge's Critique of Darwinism: An Historical-Critical Analysis of Concepts Basic to the 19th Century Debate* (Edwin Mellen, Lewiston, NY), 1982
24 Lee Strobel, p.34
25 See Philip H. Abelson, "Chemical Events on the Primitive Earth," *Proceedings of the National Academy of Sciences USA* 55 (1966) p. 1365-1372
26 See Michael Florkin, "Ideas and Experiments in the Field of Prebiological Chemical Evolution," *Comprehensive Biochemistry* 29B (1975), p. 231-260

NOTES

27 Sidney W. Fox and Klaus Dose, *Molecular Evolution and the Origin of Life* (Marcel Dekker, NY), revised edition 1977, p. 43, 74-76
28 John Cohen, "Novel Center Seeks to Add Spark to Origins of Life," *Science* 270 (1995), p. 1925-1926
29 Lee Strobel, p. 35-41
30 Gregg Easterbrook, "The New Convergence,"
31 Douglas Futuyma, *Evolutionary Biology* (Sinauer, Sunderland, MA), 1986, p. 3
32 William E Dembski and James M. Kushiner, editors, *Signs of Intelligence* (Brazos Pub., Grand Rapids, MI), 2001, p. 44
33 Richard F. Carlson, editor, *Science and Christianity: Four Views*, p. 139; See Lee Strobel, p. 43
34 Lee Strobel, p. 43
35 Ibid, p. 46
36 Ibid, p. 46-47
37 Ibid, p.48 (Much of what Strobel shares came from an interview he had with Dr. Wells.)
38 Ibid, p. 56
39 R. Gore, "Dinosaurs," *National Geographic* (January, 1993)
40 Michael Denton, *Evolution: A Theory in Crisis* (Adler and Adler, Chevy Chase, MD), 1986, p. 162; Lee Strobel, p. 56
41 Michael Denton, *Evolution*, p. 172
42 Kathy A. Svitil, "Plucking Apart the Dino-Birds," *Discover* (February, 2003)
43 Ibid; See also Lee Strobel, p. 59;
44 Ibid, p. 60
45 See Charles Darwin, *The Origin of Species* (Gramercy Publishing, NY), 1995
46 "Ape Man: The Story of Human Evolution," Hosted by Walter Cronkite, seen on A & E Network, September 4, 1994, quoted in Hank Hanegraaff, *The Face that Demonstrates the Farce of Evolution* (W Publishing Group, Nashville, TN), 1998, p. 57; see also Lee Strobel, p. 60-61
47 See *World Book Encyclopedia*, Volume 10, p. 50; also see Lee Strobel, p. 61
48 Hank Hanigraff, *The Face That Demonstrates the Farce of Evolution*, p. 50; Lee Strobel, p. 61
49 See article, *"Piltdown Man – the greatest hoax in the history of science?"* Great Britain Natural History Museum. See at http://www.nhm.ac.uk/nature-online/science-of-natural-history/the-scientific-process/piltdown-man-hoax/
50 See Andrew Lamb, "'Southwest Colorado Man' and the year of the one-tooth wonders," *Creation Ministries International*, 2007
51 Robert H. Dierker, Jr., *The Tyranny of Tolerance*, (Crown Forum, NY), 2006, p. 159
52 Todd Starnes, "School Bans Bible Club Prayer Box, Reagan Quote,"
53 Ibid
54 Jay Tokasz, *Buffalo News*, Jan. 10, 2013
55 Robert H. Dierker, Jr., p. 159
56 Ibid, p. 159, the emphasis is mine
57 This is a brief excerpt from the opening narrative given by Ron Serling in "The Obsolete Man"; episode 65 of Season 2 of the Twilight Zone. This episode first aired on June 2, 1961.
58 See David Limbaugh, *Persecution: How Liberals Are Waging War against Christianity*, (Harper Collins, NY), 2003; also see Laura Ingraham, "IT'S THE WINTER SOLSTICE, CHARLIE BROWN!" World Net Daily, September 24, 2003
59 Ibid, see both Limbaugh and Ingraham
60 Ibid, see both Limbaugh and Ingraham
61 See Laura Ingraham article, "It's the winter solstice, Charlie Brown" World Net Daily, September 24, 2003; see at http://www.wnd.com/2003/09/20961/
62 Ibid
63 Ibid
64 See Michael Carl, "PERSECUTIONS OF CHRISTIANS ON RISE-IN U.S." World Net Daily, September 17, 2012
65 See Abigail Thernstrom article, "Courting Disorder in the Schools," The Manhattan Institute of Policy Research, Summer, 1999.
66 Ibid; See also Lino Graglia, "Our Constitution Faces Death by 'Due Process,'" *Wall Street Journal*, May 24, 2005, p. A12; see also See William Prosser, *Handbook of the Law of Torts* 167 (West), 1941

67 Ibid, also see William Prosser, Handbook of the Law of Torts 167 (West), 1941; also see 393 U.S. 503 (1969)
68 Abigail Thernstrom
69 Ibid; see also *Goss v. Lopez,* 419 U.S. 565 (1975)
70 Robert H. Dierker, Jr., p. 159-161; see also Abigail Thernstrom
71 See the legal case, *Board of Curators v. Horowitz,* 435 U.S. 78 (1978); see also Abigail Thernstrom
72 Ibid
73 Ibid; See Kay Hymowitz, "How the Courts Undermined School Discipline," *Wall Street Journal,* May 4, 1999
74 See the legal case, *Board of Curators v. Horowitz,* 435 U.S. 78 (1978)
75 Bill Smith, "Concord bans mom from praying at steps of school each morning," New Hampshire Union Leader, July 25, 2013
76 See article, *"Judge bans Bible from School; Appeal Filed,"* World Net Daily, June 28, 2008
77 See front page story, *"Gideons Chased from Maryland Schools,"* World Net Daily, July 2, 2008
78 See Laura Ingraham article, 9/24/2003; Also see News Report, "Federal Judge Rules Katy ISD Engaged In 'Viewpoint Discrimination' In Pattison Christmas Card Case," Instant News Katy. com
79 Laura Ingraham, 9/24/2003
80 Ibid
81 See front page story, "ACLU: Jail School Officials for Prayer," World Net Daily, April 9, 2005
82 See Exclusive Story, "Schoolbook Hunky-Dory with Islam, But Skunks Jesus?" World Net Daily, July 4, 2010
83 See David Horowitz and Jacob Laksin, *One-Party Classroom; How Radical Professors at America's Top Colleges Indoctrinate Students and Undermine Our Democracy,* (Crown Forum, NY), 2009, p. 239
84 Ibid, p. 244
85 Ibid, p. 262
86 Ibid, p. 265

Chapter 12: Honey, I Shrunk the Morals

1 Dietrich Bonhoeffer, *Letters and Papers from Prison* (McMillan Publishing, NY), 1976
2 See the Barna Research Group *2002 Survey on Morality,* at http://www.barna.org
3 William Lobdell, *"Pollster Prods Christian Conservatives,"* LA Times, September 14, 2002.
4 See Ben Johnson, Daily Caller, "If Pro-Lifers are Racists.....," March 5, 2014
5 Results of the Rand Research Study and Survey are in; Collins, Rebecca L., Marc N. Elliott, Sandra H. Berry, David E. Kanouse, Dale Kunkel, Sarah B. Hunter, and Angela Miu, *"Watching Sex on Television Predicts Adolescent Initiation of Sexual Behavior,"* Pediatrics, Vol. 114, No. 3, September 2004
6 See *"Poll-Most Americans see us lost per our Moral Compass," Washington Times,* May 22, 2013
7 Ibid
8 Laura Ingraham, *Shut up and Sing: How Elites from Hollywood, Politics and the UN are subverting America,* (Regnery, Washington, D.C.), 2003, p. 33
9 Ibid, p. 33-34
10 Ibid, p. 34
11 Ibid, p.34-35
12 See Phillip C. McGraw, Ph. D., *"Dr. Phil: The Love Survey,"* O: The Oprah Magazine, February 2004, page 34; See "Anatomy of an Affair," Men's Health: Best Life, Spring/Summer 2003, Laurence Roy Stains, page 78 — source: "Secret-Sex Stats," citing Anthony DeLorenzo, author of 28 Tell-Tale Signs of a Cheating Spouse and president of Infidelity.com; the study The Impact of Extramarital Relationships on the Continuation of Marriage; and the book Just Married.
13 NIV Translation of the Bible
14 See John Hawkins, "Five Horrific Examples of Cultural Decay in America," *Townhall.com,* January 25, 2014. See at, http://townhall.com/columnists/johnhawkins/2014/01/25/5-horrific-examples-of-cultural-decay-in-america-n1784484
15 Ibid
16 Ibid
17 Ibid

NOTES

18   Ibid
19   Ibid
20   Ibid
21   Ibid
22   Ibid
23   See Patrick Buchanan, "Is America Disintegrating?" *Townhall.com*, October 21, 2011
24   Ibid
25   Ibid
26   Ibid

Chapter 13: Who Moved the Hedge?

1   See *Jonathan Edwards, Basic Writings*, (New American Library, NY), 1966, p. xix. See the forward written by Ola Elizabeth Winslow. On this page she writes, "Characteristically also, he spoke quietly, using no gestures, holding the tiny sermon booklet in his left hand and occasionally speaking extemporaneously, by way of illustration or enlargement, as he read what he had written." Winslow writes in her biography of Edwards that there may have been something medically wrong with Edwards' throat.
2   See sermon from Jonathan Edwards at http://www.biblebb.com/files/edwards/je-sinners.htm
3   Ola Elizabeth Winslow, *Jonathan Edwards; 1703-1758, A Biography* (MacMillan Company, NY), 1966, p. 28
4   George M. Marsden, *Jonathan Edwards, A Life* (Yale University Press, CT), 2003, p. 110
5   Rick Scarborough, *Enough is Enough: A Call to Christian Involvement* (Whitaker House Publishing, PA), 1996,
6   See the Bill Clinton Draft Acknowledgement Letter, December 3, 1969. See at, http://www.pbs.org/wgbh/pages/frontline/shows/clinton/etc/draftletter.html
7   Rick Scarborough, p. 72-73
8   Joseph Farrah, WND Commentary, "When the Left Loved Guns," February 5, 2013; http://www.wnd.com/2013/02/when-the-left-liked-guns/
9   See OS Guinness, *A Free People's Suicide, Sustainable Freedom and the American Future* (IVP, Downers Grove, IL), 2012
10 My description came from research done primarily in Bob Gingrich, *Founding Fathers vs, History Revisionists*, (Author House Books), 2008
11 C. Everett Koop & Francis A. Schaeffer, *Whatever Happened to the Human Race* (Crossway Books, Wheaton, IL), 1979, p. 13
12 Ibid, p. 13-14

Chapter 14: There's Nothing Legal about Illegals

1   J. Wallace Hamilton, *Horns and Haloes in Human Nature* (Revell, NY), 1954
2   Ibid
3   See 2 King 18:11-12; See also Cam Rea, *The Assyrian Exile: Israel's Legacy in Captivity* (Wordclay), p. 47
4   See Matthias Schulz article, "Research Reveals Ancient Struggle over Holy Land Supremacy," Spiegel Online, April 13, 2012, see at http://www.sott.net/article/244124-Research-Reveals-Ancient-Struggle-over-Holy-Land-Supremacy
5   John Simkin, "The Roman Empire," *Spartacus International*
6   Tacitus, *Annals* 1.17 and XII.32; See also Ronald Boykin, "*Background on the City of Philippi*," Overview of the Letter to the Philippians
7   See Op Ed, "*A debate over 'official' English*," Cincinnati.com, June 8, 2008
8   See as an example Ezra Levant, "Multiculturalism Doesn't Work," *Toronto Sun*, May 25, 2013
9   Jennifer Gonzalez, "Reports Highlight Disparities in Graduation Rates Among White and Minority Students," *The Chronicle of Higher Education*, April, 13, 2014
10 See John Nolte, "Media Bigotry: Al Sharpton, Nancy Grace, and Alec Baldwin Still on TV," *Breitbart News*, July 23, 2013
11 See Michelle Malkin, This entire speech by Richard D. Lamm, which I adapted in part within this chapter. The reference to the Greeks is a direct quote from his speech, "I Have a Plan to Destroy America," Michelle Malkin, February 9, 2008

12 Timothy Egan, "A Widow's Wisdom," *New York Times*, February 14, 2012
13 See Francis Newton Thorpe, *The Constitutional History of the United States, 1765-1895* (Harper & Brothers), 1898
14 George Orwell, *1984* (Penguin Group, NY), 1948
15 See Agora Associates Heritage Project- http://www.baxtercountyrepublicans.com/reagan.html

Chapter 15: The Trouble with Islam

1 See Simon Reeve, *One Day in September* (Arcade Publishing, NY), 2000; See also Alexander B. Calahan, *Munich: The True Story of the Israeli Response to the 1972 Olympic Massacre*, (Ancient Wisdom Pub.), 2010, p. 10ff
2 See Ethan Allen, *Reason, The Only Oracle of Man*, (Cornhill, Boston), 1854; See Section IV- THE PROVIDENCE OF GOD DOES NOT INTERFERE WITH THE AGENCY OF MAN
3 Joseph Story, *Commentaries on the Constitution of the United States* (Boston: Hilliard, Gray and Company. Cambridge: Brown, Shattuck, and Co.), 1833, Volume III, page 728, §1871.
4 See David Miller, PhD, "Were the Founding Fathers Tolerant of Islam?" Apologetics Press. This article is the first installment of a two-part critique of an article written by James Hutson, Library of Congress Manuscript Division Chief, on the Founding Fathers' attitude toward Islam.
5 John Locke, *A Letter Concerning Toleration: Humbly Submitted* (Classic Books, NY), 2009, pps. 2-75
6 See the Belcher Foundation for full transcript of Ezra Stiles Sermon, "The United States Elevated to Glory and Honor," Editor's notes by John Wingate Thornton (1860), from: "The Pulpit of the American Revolution: Or, the Political Sermons of the Period of 1776." *With a Historical Introduction, Notes, and Illustrations*, edited by John Wingate Thornton (Boston: Gould and Lincoln/New York: Sheldon and Company, Cincinnati: George S. Blanchard, 1860), pp. 397-506
7 See John Quincy Adams, "Christianity—Islamism." "Unsigned essays dealing with the Russo-Turkish War, and on Greece," originally published in *The American Annual Register for 1827-1829* (New York, 1830), Chs. X-XIV, pps. 267-402.
8 Quote is taken from the Australian Islamic Monitor about excerpt from the book; General George S. Patton, *The War as I Knew it* (Houghton Mifflin, NY), 1974, p.49
9 Lewis, Bernard, *The Political Language of Islam*. (University of Chicago Press, IL),1988, p. 72; William M. Watt, "Islamic Conceptions of the Holy War". In Thomas P. Murphy, *The Holy War*, (Ohio State University Press, OH), 1976, p. 143.
10 See the Quran, Surah 9:5 - 9:29, also known as the "Sword verses"
11 See "Christian answers.net/Islam"

Chapter 16: The Right to Have and Bear Arms

1 This comment is taken from an article entitled "A Few Thoughts on the Colorado Shooting," Freedom's Fight Blog, July 23, 2012. Comment was made by Tom Clancey.
2 Helena Bachmann, "The Swiss Difference: A Gun Culture that Works," *TIME*, December 20, 2012
3 See John R. Lott, Jr., *More Guns, Less Crime* (University of Chicago Press, IL), 1998; See also the *Columbus Dispatch* article, "Research shows crime goes down with concealed-carry," May 3, 2014. Also see Philip Swarts, "Gun Advocates credit new concealed carry laws for sharp drop in Chicago Murder Rate," *The Washington Times*, April 5, 2014
4 See Susan Stamper Brown article, "Unholy trio: Gun control, the UN and Obama," *Standard Examiner*, November 23, 2012
5 Ibid
6 Ibid
7 Ibid
8 Ibid
9 See article by Leonard Blair, "Attorney General Eric Holder Condemns 'Stand Your Ground' Laws, Challenges Nation to Confront Stereotypes," *The Christian Post*, July 17, 2013
10 See Howard Zinn, *A People's History of the American Revolution*, (Metropolitan Books, NY), 2008
11 James Taranto, "Shot to the Heart: A how-to book about inciting a moral panic," *The Wall Street Journal*, August 8, 2013
12 Awr Hawkins, "ABC NEWS: One Child taken to Hospital with Gunshot Wounds every Hour," Breitbart, January 29, 2014

13 My research for the data on the mass shootings focused on statistics from The Roger Hedgecock Radio Show which aired January 17, 2013; See Eric Owens, "CALL TO ARMS: Texas A & M Law Prof says it's time to Repeal the 2nd Amendment," *The Daily Caller*, November 16, 2013
14 Ibid
15 See the complete Mary Sanchez editorial, *"Gun Lobby defends a cynical business model, not the Constitution"* February 22, 2013. See at; http://articles.courant.com/2013-02-22/news/hc-op-sanchez-gun-culture-in-decline-0224-20130222_1_gun-ownership-gun-lobby-guns-and-ammunition
16 Andrew Napolitano article, "Guns and Freedom," Reason.com, January 10, 2013
17 Ibid
18 Ibid
19 Ibid
20 Ibid
21 Ibid
22 Ibid
23 See Oren Dorrell, "Leaflet tells Jews to register in East Ukraine," *USA Today*, April 17, 2014

Chapter 17: An Invitation to Sit Down and Shut Up

1 The First Amendment of the United States Constitution
2 See Rich Tucker, "A Constitution for the 21st Century," *The Foundry*, June 18, 2013
3 Ibid
4 See David Azerrad, "Constitutionalism: Here Are a Few Things Richard Stengel Doesn't Know About," *The Heritage Foundation*, June 24, 2011
5 Ibid
6 Ibid
7 Ibid
8 Ibid
9 Ibid
10 Ibid
11 See Richard Stengel, "Cover Story: One Document under Siege," *Time Magazine*, June 23, 2011
12 David Azerrad
13 Ibid
14 Rich Tucker, "A Constitution for the 21st Century"
15 John Queally, "Snowden speaks on Obama Reforms as Supporters call for end of his Persecution," Common Dreams.com, March 26, 2014
16 Marc Pitzke, "War on Whistleblowers: Has Obama Scrapped the First Amendment?" Spiegel Online International
17 Ibid
18 Ibid
19 Refer to Al Cardenas, "Protecting privacy and free speech from an abusive, out-of-control government," Fox News, May 31, 2013
20 See Thomas Fleming article, "Free Speech or Federal Tyranny?" March 2, 2011
21 Ibid
22 Ibid
23 Ibid
24 Ibid
25 Ibid
26 I referred to Karl F. Cohen, *Forbidden Animation: Censored Cartoons and Blacklisted Animators in America* (McFarland, Jefferson, NC), 1997
27 See Jeff Mullen, "B-Bye! Will We Miss Free Speech When It's Finally Gone?" Clash Daily.com, January 28, 2014
28 Ibid
29 Ibid
30 Ibid

www.ingramcontent.com/pod-product-compliance
Lightning Source LLC
Chambersburg PA
CBHW031400290426
44110CB00011B/218